Techniques and Guidelines for Social Work Practice

FOURTH EDITION

Bradford W. Sheafor
Colorado State University

Charles R. Horejsi
The University of Montana

Gloria A. Horejsi
Community Medical Center
Missoula, Montana

ALLYN AND BACON
Boston London Toronto Sydney Tokyo Singapore

Managing Editor, Social Work: Judy Fifer
Vice President, Editor in Chief, Social Sciences: Karen Hanson
Editorial Assistant: Jennifer Jacobson
Executive Marketing Manager: Joyce Nilsen
Production Administrator: Annette Joseph
Production Coordinator: Holly Crawford
Editorial-Production Service: Lynda Griffiths, TKM Productions
Design and Electronic Composition: Denise Hoffman
Composition Buyer: Linda Cox
Manufacturing Buyer: Megan Cochran
Cover Administrator: Linda Knowles
Cover Designer: Susan Paradise

Copyright © 1997, 1994, 1991, 1988 by Allyn & Bacon
A Viacom Company
Needham Heights, MA 02194

Library of Congress Cataloging-in-Publication Data

Sheafor, Bradford W.
    Techniques and guidelines for social work practice / Bradford W.
Sheafor, Charles R. Horejsi, Gloria A. Horejsi. — 4th ed.
       p.   cm.
    Includes bibliographical references and index.
    ISBN 0-205-19177-0
    1. Social service—United States.   I. Horejsi, Charles R.
II. Horejsi, Gloria A.   III. Title.
HV91.S48 1996
361.3'2—dc20   96-1084
                                      CIP

Printed in the United States of America
10 9 8 7 6 5 4 3   01 00 99 98 97

To the next generation of social workers
who have chosen to devote their time and talents to
the service of others and the struggle for social justice

and

To our families
Nadine, Laura, Brandon, Perry, Christopher,
Angela, Martin, and Katherine
for their love and support

C O N T E N T S

CHAPTER 10
Personal and Professional Development   204

PART IV   Techniques and Guidelines for Phases of the Planned Change Process   263

CHAPTER 11
Intake and Engagement   265

Section A   Techniques and Guidelines for Direct Practice   265

CHAPTER 12
Data Collection and Assessment   319

PREFACE

An increasing number of people are significantly influenced, directly and indirectly, by the decisions and actions of social workers. Working in courts, clinics, hospitals, schools, businesses, private practice, and a myriad of social agencies, social workers deliver a wide variety of services directly to clients while they also work toward positive community and social changes. The whole society benefits from social workers' activities because improving the quality of life for an individual, a family, or the people of a community will ultimately impact the general society and elevate the health, happiness, safety, and productivity of all its members.

This book is about what social workers actually do when helping their clients solve problems and/or enhance functioning. Although many excellent books describe the general principles and theories used by social workers, *Techniques and Guidelines for Social Work Practice*, Fourth Edition, focuses on a more concrete level. It describes the basic techniques and guidelines that social workers use in everyday practice.

Recognizing that this emphasis on techniques and specific guidelines is unusual in a social work book, we offer the reader an explanation of why we believe this collection of practice tools is needed. It is our perception that most social workers have been exposed to a wide variety of practice theories and conceptual frameworks reported in the literature and taught in social work education programs.* Although that knowledge base is essential, practice is much more than a set of ideas. In reality, practice is a set of actions and behaviors by the social worker. Clients are not directly affected by theory; rather, they are influenced by what the worker actually does—by the specific actions taken by the social worker. In the Foreword to the first edition of this book (1988), Barbara Solomon clearly articulated this point and placed techniques and guidelines into perspective.

> It is the utilization of theory to determine practice that distinguishes the professional from the technician. However, our theoretical framework may provide insights as to how a problem develops and even in general terms what we ought to do to resolve it, but rarely will it specify our actions. An ecological systems frame of reference, for example, might dictate that a particular client should be referred to a community resource. It will not, however, specify *how* that referral should be made. Furthermore, no theoretical orientation goes so far as to point out the most effective ways for the social worker to utilize the telephone, testify in court, write a report, use supervision, or engage in many of the activities often considered essential to the social work change process and, therefore, included in this handbook. (p. xi)

---

* A short synopsis of many of these basic frameworks is included in Chapter 6, "Practice Frameworks for Social Work."

Our emphasis is not intended to suggest that attention to the techniques can or should replace attention to theoretical frameworks. Rather, techniques and specific guidelines complete the package of knowledge and skills that the social worker needs.

Plan and Structure

This book has four major parts. Parts I and II describe basic concepts and principles of practice that lay the foundation for understanding the over 160 specific techniques and guidelines found in Parts III and IV.

Part I, "Social Work and the Social Worker," reviews background knowledge and characteristics we believe a social worker must possess, including the following:

- A clear conception of the domain of social work and the competencies the social worker is expected to bring to the change process (Chapter 1)
- An understanding of the challenges a social worker faces in merging his or her personal life with professional roles and responsibilities (Chapter 2)
- The native talents or artistic abilities necessary for perceptively creating and entering into the interpersonal relations that are at the heart of practice (Chapter 3)
- A commitment to draw on and apply the science of social work, the profession's knowledge base, and its ethical principles (Chapter 3)

Part II, "The Building Blocks of Social Work Practice," stresses the need for the social worker to understand the roles, principles, theories, and change processes that are the central features of effective helping. To serve clients ranging from individuals to communities, a social worker must have:

- An understanding of the varied roles performed by social workers in delivering human services and the specific functions associated with these roles (Chapter 4)
- The ability to apply the fundamental practice principles of social work (Chapter 5)
- A basic knowledge of the various perspectives, theories, and models that have proven useful in practice (Chapter 6)
- Skill in guiding clients through the change process (Chapter 7)

From this point to the end of the book, we present specific techniques and guidelines. Each presentation follows the same format or structure. It begins with a technique or guideline *Number* and *Name* (e.g., 11.3: Making a Referral). In this example, 11.3 signifies the third technique or guideline in Chapter 11. This system of numbering is used to refer the reader to related information in other parts of the book. These numbers are also keys to using the *Cross-Reference Guide* as well as the new *Conversion Guide,* which has been included in this edition to help the reader locate material from the Third Edition.

Following each number and name is a one-sentence description of ***Purpose.*** This very brief statement is intended to help the reader quickly determine if the technique or guideline is relevant to his or her concern or interest.

Under the heading labeled ***Discussion,*** anywhere from a few to many paragraphs are used to describe the technique or guideline and its application. After the discussion is completed, we present a ***Selected Bibliography,*** which usually lists three to five books or articles that we consider particularly useful for obtaining additional information. We have made an effort to identify sources that are current and available in most university libraries.

In Part III of the book, "Techniques Common to All Social Work Practice," we have included techniques that strengthen the social worker's performance regardless of agency setting and independent of whether the client is an individual, family, group, organization, or community. Underlying our selection was the belief that the social worker must:

- Have the interpersonal competence to carry out effective communication and engage in a set of basic helping activities (Chapter 8)
- Be skilled at organizing the details of service delivery and effectively managing his or her own workload (Chapter 9)
- Be able to maintain a pattern of personal and professional growth and development that keeps him or her current, enriched, and energized (Chapter 10)

Part IV, "Techniques and Guidelines for Phases of the Planned Change Process," is a modification of the structure we followed in prior editions. We continue to list the techniques and guidelines in chapters organized around the five phases of the change process described in Chapter 7, but include both direct and indirect service techniques as sections of the chapters. Our rationale for this change is to encourage the generalist perspective in practice and to reinforce the importance of carefully working and moving through the phases of the change process. Although various authors use differing descriptions of the phases of the planned change process, we have elected to use the following:

- Intake and Engagement (Chapter 11)
- Data Collection and Assessment (Chapter 12)
- Planning and Contracting (Chapter 13)
- Intervention and Monitoring (Chapter 14)
- Evaluation and Termination (Chapter 15)

Because of this structure, the social worker dealing with a particular client and having unusual problems at one phase of the helping process can turn to the chapter relevant to that phase and examine a range of suggested techniques or guidelines that can move the helping process forward. These techniques and guidelines are not exhaustive but are of a sufficient range that one or more should either directly apply to the situation or suggest ideas that might help lead to other approaches. The worker should approach these techniques with the anticipation of both adopting and adapting them for practice.

Definition of Terms

Writing about social work practice inherently presents some language problems. One has to read only a few social work texts or articles to become at least a little confused with the terminology used to describe practice. Perhaps that is to be expected in a profession that focuses on complex and dynamic human and social interactions. This book cannot overcome these long-standing problems of terminology, nor can it present definitions that will be acceptable to every reader. Yet the ideas presented here will be more readily understood if we make the meanings of three terms more explicit.

The reader should be alert to the term *client.* Common usage implies a narrow view of an individual who is the consumer of services. As used in this book, the term has a broader connotation. The client of the social worker may be an individual, a family or another form of household, or even a small group, committee, organization, neighborhood, community, or larger social system. Throughout the book, the term *client* is occasionally expanded to mention *clientele, clients, client groups,* or *client systems,* reminding the reader that the narrow definition of client is not intended.

A *technique* is viewed as a circumscribed, goal-oriented behavior performed in a practice situation by the social worker. It is a planned action deliberately taken by the practitioner. The application of a simple technique (e.g., using an "I-message") may take only a few seconds, whereas more complex techniques (e.g., family sculpting) may require an hour or more.

Guidelines, by comparison, are a set of directions intended to influence the social worker's behavior and decisions. Guidelines are essentially lists of do's and don'ts. They might be used when working with a specific type of client (e.g., a child, a client with a mental illness) or when carrying out workload management tasks (e.g., recording or writing reports).

Acknowledgments

We would like to recognize a number of people who have contributed to the techniques and guidelines we present in this book, including current and former students and professional colleagues who have graciously given their time and expertise to offer constructive criticisms on various sections of this book. A special thank-you is extended to:

- Angeline Barretta-Herman, Ph.D. (staff meetings)
- Barbara Benjamin, M.S.W.; Bob Jackson, Ph.D.; Lowell Jenkins, M.S.W.; and Randy Wood, M.S.W. (practice frameworks)
- Jon Bertsche, M.S.W. (evaluation and informal resources)
- Mary Birch, M.S.W. (small groups)
- Charlotte Booth, M.S.W. (hard-to-reach clients)
- Vicky Buchan, Ph.D., and Charles Neidt, Ph.D. (understanding quantitative data)
- Robert Deaton, Ed.D. (suicide)
- Jerry Finn, Ph.D. (using electronic technology)
- Kathleen Gallacher, M.A. (child development)
- Cindy Garthwait, M.S.W. (working with the elderly)
- Sr. Anne Hogan, M.S.W.; Ryan Knee, M.S.W.; and Shaen McElravy, B.S.W. (merging person and profession)
- Mike Jakupcak, Ed.D. (mental retardation)
- Dan Morgan, M.S.W.; Cindy Bartling, M.S.W.; and Colleen Lippke, M.S.W. (children and adolescents)
- Jo Ann Blake, M.A.; Lance Eller, B.S.W.; and Lloyd Barron, B.S.W. (chemical dependency)
- Peter Pecora, Ph.D. (evaluation)
- Mona Schatz, D.S.W. (social work roles and functions)
- Barbara W. Shank, Ph.D. (sexual harassment)
- Michael Silverglat, M.D., and Mel Mason, M.S.W. (psychotropic medication and mental illness)
- John Spores, Ph.D.; Bonnie Heavy Runner Craig, J.D.; Rodney Brod, Ph.D.; Victor A. Baez, Ph.D.; and Janet Finn, Ph.D. (cross-cultural interaction)
- Elizabeth Tracy, Ph.D., and James Whittaker, Ph.D. (social support assessment)

We would also like to thank the reviewers of previous editions of this book:

- Larry Lister, University of Hawaii at Manoa
- Kay van Buskirk, Mankato State University

We also want to express our appreciation of the in-depth critique of this book we received from a focus group of students, practitioners, and educators who spent a full day examining and analyzing the materials we had planned to include in this new edition. We thank Barbara Benjamin, Lowell Jenkins, David Jones, Don Menne, Cath Stilwell, and Nadine Sheafor for making that session enjoyable and productive. Finally, thanks to Sue Polich (The University of Montana) who typed several portions of this book and to Joyce Takacs, Linda Tippett, Karen Scott, Dawn Carlson, and Karla Burleson (Colorado State University) who helped create a work environment that facilitated the completion of this manuscript.

Part I Social Work and the Social Worker

Social work is an indispensable profession in our increasingly complex and ever-changing society. But it is an often misunderstood profession, as well, in part because it cannot be easily described or explained. It is a profession characterized by diversity. Social workers engage in a broad range of activities within many types of settings and with many different people. Some work intensely with individuals and families, while others work with small groups, organizations, or whole communities. Some deal primarily with children, others with elderly persons. Some are counselors and psychotherapists, while others are supervisors, administrators, program planners, or fund-raisers. Some focus on family violence, others on how to provide housing or medical care to the poor. This variety is what makes social work so challenging and stimulating. But it is because of this diversity of both clients and activities that it is so difficult to answer the simple question: What is social work?

The problem of concisely defining *social work* in a manner that encompasses all of the activities in which social workers engage has plagued the profession throughout its first century of development. At a very fundamental level, *social work* is a profession devoted to helping people function as well as they can within their social environments and to changing their environments to make that possible. This theme of person-in-environment is clarified and illustrated throughout this book.

The authors' perspective of social work is made explicit in the following three-part definition of a social worker. A *social worker*

1. has recognized professional preparation (i.e., education in the requisite knowledge, ethics, and competencies);
2. is sanctioned by society to provide specific services targeted primarily at helping vulnerable populations (e.g., children, the aged, the poor, minorities, women, families) engage in efforts to change themselves, the people around them, or social institutions; and
3. has the purpose of helping others meet social needs or eliminate difficulties so that they might make maximum use of their abilities to lead full and satisfying lives and contribute fully to society.

Most of this book is devoted to a presentation of techniques and guidelines commonly used by social workers. Parts I and II, however, lay the groundwork for that presentation. In Part I, the essential mix of profession and person in social work practice is examined.

In order to be a responsible professional, the social worker must understand and function within the profession's domain. Chapter 1, "The Domain of the Social Work Profession," elaborates on the authors' definition of social work and presents its central mission as helping people change so they fit and function more comfortably within their environments, and also helping to modify those environments to be more supportive of the people. This help is provided through social programs that include making tangible social provisions available to people in need, offering intangible social services such as counseling or treatment, and engaging in organizational and community change activities.

The primary resource the social worker brings to the helping process is his or her own capacity to develop positive helping relationships and assist clients to take actions that will improve the quality of their lives. A social worker must have the ability to understand client issues, creatively select ways to address those issues (i.e., apply the appropriate techniques and guidelines), and assist clients in changing those factors that are negatively affecting their lives. To do this, the social worker must keep physically, intellectually, and emotionally "in shape" for this rigorous personal interaction with clients or client groups. At the same time, the social worker must avoid having one's personal life consumed by the events that arise in his or her work environment. Chapter 2, "Merging Person with Profession," identifies many of the factors a social worker should be prepared to address in keeping personally and professionally fit.

Throughout its history, social work has been portrayed as both an art and a science. Chapter 3, "Merging the Person's Art with the Profession's Science," builds on the material introduced in Chapters 1 and 2 and provides a more detailed description of the personal characteristics (i.e., the art) that contribute to effective practice. The chapter also identifies the knowledge base (i.e., the science) required of beginning-level social workers. During the last half century of the profession's growth and development, scant attention has been given to the unique artistic personal traits that are prerequisite to effective practice. Chapter 3 renews the consideration of these features of the social worker by recognizing the central place that such factors as compassion, empathy, genuineness, creativity, hopefulness, energy, values, and professional style play in the helping process. However, the chapter also reflects the view that the professional social worker is obligated to bring the best scientific knowledge to the helping process.

Part I, then, addresses the most fundamental elements of social work practice—the blending of the person and the profession—in order to most effectively assist individuals, families or other households, small groups, organizations, and communities as they work to prevent or resolve the complex social problems that arise in their daily lives.

The Domain of the Social Work Profession

When a person sets out to help others, especially those most vulnerable to social problems, he or she assumes a serious responsibility. The responsible professional must practice within his or her **professional domain** (i.e., the profession's area of competence or its "professional turf") if clients are to receive the services that the profession is sanctioned to provide. Indeed, professional helpers can harm clients if the helpers' activities extend beyond their professional boundaries because it is these boundaries that establish the content of the profession's formal education and training and identify the services its members are prepared to deliver.

This book is concerned with the profession of *social work* and how social workers assist people in addressing a variety of different issues that confront them. Social work is, indeed, a curious name for a profession. In times that emphasize image over substance, it is clearly a title that lacks pizzazz. In fact, the use of the word *work* makes it sound dreary. It is a title that many social workers have wished they could change, possibly without understanding where it came from in the first place.

The title is attributed to Jeffrey Brackett (1860–1949). Brackett, initially an influential volunteer in the Baltimore Charity Organization Society, served for nearly 30 years on the Massachusetts Board of Charities and later became the first director of what is now the Simmons College School of Social Work. In the early 1900s, Brackett argued that the word *social* should be part of this developing profession's title because it depicts the focus on people's interactions with important forces that shape their lives such as family members, friends, or a myriad of other factors including their relevant cultural or ethnic group, school, job, neighborhood, community, and so on. He added the word *work* to differentiate professional practice from what he considered to be the often misguided and self-serving philanthropic activity of wealthy volunteers. He believed including *work* in the profession's title emphasized that its activities were to be orderly, responsible, and disciplined—not something to be engaged in by the unprepared, curious, or whimsical.

Although Brackett did not select a name that generates a sense of deference or reverence, *social work* is an accurate title for a profession that applies helping techniques in a disciplined manner to address social problems. During the years since Brackett convinced early charity organization volunteers to accept this title, the domain of social work has expanded and its approach has been reshaped by the expanding knowledge generated by the social and behavioral sciences. It is understandably a dynamic profession.

The Social Work Domain

It is important for the social worker to examine periodically the ***domain*** of social work (i.e., to review its purpose, scope, and sanction). This is especially important for the student or new social worker because educational programs divide the study of social work into units, or courses, and this can lead to a familiarity with the parts without necessarily understanding the whole. Reexamination of the domain is also important for the experienced practitioner, especially one whose vision of the profession may have been constricted by years of practice in only one type of agency or possibly by the narrowing of vision that often follows the necessity to generate income from client fees. Taking time to stand back from one's daily routine to view the profession as a whole may help the practitioner truly appreciate the depth and breadth of the profession's concerns and the varied and creative approaches used by its practitioners.

A periodic examination of the social work domain is also important to guard against ***professional drift*** (i.e., the neglect of traditional social work purpose and functions in favor of activities associated with another profession or discipline). Shulman (1991, 10) alludes to the problem of professional drift when he observes that social workers who align themselves too closely with models and theories borrowed from medicine, psychology, and other disciplines that ignore social policy and social justice issues "can lead to social workers who adopt a view of themselves as therapists first and social workers second, or not even social workers at all." When this occurs, it is a disservice to both clients and one's employing agency for it results in a loss of the commitment, perspective, and competencies unique to social work.

Given the fact that all states now have laws regulating the practice of social work, the social worker must be familiar with how social work practice is defined legally and how this definition may overlap the legal definitions of related professions (e.g., clinical psychology, drug and alcohol counseling, marriage and family counseling, etc.). The social worker covered by a state law must conform his or her practice to that law.

By definition, the competencies of a professional person are learned during a prescribed course of study. Thus, the knowledge and skills included in a standardized course of study describe a profession's domain. In this sense, the Accreditation Standards and the Curriculum Policy Statement published by the Council on Social Work Education define the domain of social work and what is and is not social work practice. These documents serve as a baseline, or anchor, for establishing the boundaries of the profession's competence.

Social Work's Purpose

The *Social Work Dictionary* (Barker 1995, s.v. "social work") defines *social work* as the "professional activity of helping individuals, families, groups, or communities enhance or restore their capacity for social functioning and for creating societal conditions favorable to this goal." In other words, social workers are devoted to improving the social functioning of people by helping them as they strive to prevent and solve problems that are of a social, relational, or interactional nature.

In its Curriculum Policy Statement (CPS), the Council on Social Work Education (CSWE) expands on this definition of social work in a form that more clearly explicates the activities a practitioner would be expected to perform. The CPS (Council on Social Work Education 1994) indicates that professional social work practice serves the following four related *purposes.*

- The promotion, restoration, maintenance, and enhancement of the social functioning of individuals, families, groups, organizations, and communities by helping them to accomplish tasks, prevent and alleviate distress, and use resources.
- The planning, formulation, and implementation of social policies, services, resources, and programs needed to meet basic human needs and support the development of human capacities.
- The pursuit of policies, services, resources, and programs through organizational and administrative advocacy and social or political action, so as to empower groups at risk and promote social and economic justice.
- The development and testing of professional knowledge and skills related to these purposes. (pp. 97 and 135)

The first of these purposes is concerned with enhancing social functioning and preventing impediments to good social functioning. The final three relate to creating conditions that assure that clients receive appropriate human services when needed and, where possible, preventing social problems from occurring in the first place.

Social Functioning.   An understanding of social work begins with a deep appreciation for humans as social beings. People need other people. Human growth, development, and learning depend on the nurturance and protection people receive from others. One's sense of happiness and satisfaction is derived from the meanings he or she assigns to relations with others. An individual's concept of self—and even one's very survival, both physically and psychologically—is tied to the thoughts, decisions, and actions of other people. It is this interdependence and the need for interaction with family, friends, and community that underlie the need for competent professionals to help people improve those interactions (i.e., enhance their social functioning).

More than any other profession, social work focuses on the interactions or transactions among people, as well as among people and the multitude of social policies, agencies, and programs that comprise the social welfare system. These interactions include those of person to person, person to community, person to social agency, and agency to agency.

The concept of social functioning is pivotal to understanding the unique focus of social work and to distinguishing social work from the other helping professions. According to Longres (1995, 546) *social functioning* is "social well-being, especially with regard to the ability of an individual to meet the role expectations associated with a particular status or role." Karls and Wandrei (1988, 1) further define social functioning as "a client's ability to accomplish the activities necessary for daily living . . . and to fulfill major social roles as required by a particular subculture or community." In this definition, "activities necessary for daily living" refers to the decisions and behaviors required not only to meet basic human needs such as obtaining food, shelter, medical care, and transportation, but also for protecting self from harm, developing social supports, finding meaning and purpose in life, and so on.

The social roles to which Karls and Wandrei refer include those of parent, child, spouse, student, employee, friend, neighbor, citizen, and patient. A person's social roles change throughout the life cycle, and role expectations vary somewhat depending on the person's gender, ethnicity, culture, religion, occupation, and community. It is important to recognize that an individual responds to his or her social roles as a whole human being. Thus, the many interrelated dimensions of the human person (e.g., biological, emotional, intellectual, spiritual, social, etc.) are all elements of social functioning and are of concern to the social worker.

The concept of social functioning draws attention to the match, or fit, between the needs and capacities of the individual and the opportunities and demands of his or her social environment. Although social work is committed to improving the social functioning of everyone, it is especially concerned with addressing two broad categories of people: (1) those with few capacities and opportunities to function satisfactorily and (2) those whose actions seriously limit or interfere with the social functioning of others.

The first category of persons requires the social worker to engage in activities that broadly fit the concept of social caring. *Social care* includes actions and efforts designed to provide people in need with access to the basics of life (e.g., food, shelter, protection from harm) and opportunities to meet their psychosocial needs such as belonging, acceptance, and comfort in times of distress. Examples from this first category include people living in poverty, dependent persons such as children or people with serious physical or mental disabilities, and people who are devalued by others.

The second category of persons in need typically involves *social treatment* in which the social worker is engaged in actions and efforts designed to modify or correct dysfunctional or troublesome patterns of thought, feeling, or behavior. Examples of clients in this category include parents who abuse or neglect children, persons who commit crimes against others, those who restrict the opportunities or resources available to others, and persons who might harm themselves.

Prevention.   Social workers not only help people adjust to their reality but they also help to change the social realities people face. In short, social workers are both people changers and system changers. The third type of activity for a social worker, then, involves engaging in social change. *Social change* refers to the actions and efforts of the social worker intended to develop or modify those laws and social policies that affect the quality of peoples' lives. Examples of such change might include improving the social and economic conditions in which people live and expanding their opportunities to fully utilize their capacities.

Although improving the quality of life for any group of people has the indirect effect of improving conditions for others in this highly interdependent society, social work has historically been especially committed to social change efforts aimed at the members of society who are most vulnerable to social problems. Typically, these vulnerable populations have been victims of social injustices, discrimination, and oppression. Included in this category are children and youth, older people, people living in poverty, persons with physical limitations, persons with a mental or emotional illness, women, gays and lesbians, and people of minority ethnic, racial, and national backgrounds.

As society grows more complex, people must look to specialized organizations and social programs for the resources and opportunities they require. Social work is especially concerned about how people relate to and utilize resources provided by the organizations that make up the complex, legalistic, and highly bureaucratic social welfare system. Social change efforts to improve the social welfare system, for example, may range from attempting to create new services to correcting problems in agency service delivery that diminish the services to clients.

Focus on Person-in-Environment

Helping individuals, families, and communities improve their social functioning and prevent social problems from negatively affecting them requires that the social worker maintain a focus on how people interact with the relevant people and social systems in their lives. The social worker, then, must simultaneously address both person and environment—and the transactions between them.

Social workers must attend to the several interrelated dimensions of the person: biological, intellectual, emotional, social, familial, spiritual, economic, communal, and so on. This concern for the *whole person* contributes to the breadth of concern by the social work profession—for example, the individual's capacity to meet basic physical needs (food, housing, health care, etc.), the person's levels of knowledge and skills needed to cope with life's demands and to earn a living, the person's thoughts about others and his or her own life, the individual's goals and aspirations, and the like. It is important to note the person-in-environment construct uses the word *person*, not *personality*. Personality is but one component of the whole person. A focus only on personality would be incongruous with the domain of social work and slant it toward the domain of psychology.

The term *environment* refers to one's surroundings—that multitude of physical and social structures, forces, and processes that impact on humans and all other life forms. Of particular interest to social workers are those systems, structures, and other factors that most frequently and most directly affect a person's day-to-day social functioning (i.e., the person's *immediate environment*). One's immediate environment includes the person's family, close friends, neighborhood, workplace, and the services and programs he or she uses.

Based on their empirical analysis of social work practice tasks, Teare and Sheafor (1995) state that social workers devote a major part of their attention to clients' efforts to improve interactions with their immediate environment. Social workers focus to a lesser extent on the broader environment, possibly because the impact of problems in the more ***distant environment*** is less evident and more difficult to change. In order to grow, develop, and survive, humans need clean air, drinkable water, shelter, and good soil to produce food. And because biological well-being is a prerequisite to positive social functioning, social workers must also be concerned with problems such as prevention of disease and pollution. In addition, they seek to change damaging societal values, correct human rights violations, and address unjust political and economic structures that may affect the near environment of their clients. Concern over factors in both the immediate and distant environments is central to fulfilling social work's mission.

Social Work's Scope

A profession's *scope* can be thought of as the range of activities and involvements appropriate to its mission. Because the scope of social work is broad, social workers often have a difficult time giving a concise answer to the question: What do social workers do? Coming up with a simple answer is complicated by the fact that the social work client may be an individual or a whole social system including a family, group, organization, or community.

One useful way of describing social work practice involves classifying the intervention by the size of the client system being addressed (i.e., micro-, mezzo-, or macro-level practice). Social work practice at the ***micro level*** focuses on a person's most intimate interactions, such as exchanges between husband and wife, parent and child, close friends, and family members. The terms *interpersonal helping, direct practice*, and *clinical practice* are often used interchangeably with micro-level practice.

At the other extreme, ***macro-level*** practice may involve work with an organization, community, or even society as a whole. Obviously, macro-level practice also deals with interpersonal relations, but these are the interactions between people who represent organizations or who are members of a work group such as an agency committee or interagency task force. When engaged in macro-level practice, the social worker is frequently involved in activities such as administration, fund-raising, testifying on proposed legislation, policy analysis, class advocacy, and social resource development.

Between the micro and macro levels is ***mezzo-level*** practice. Practice at this level is concerned with interpersonal relations that are somewhat less intimate than those associated with family life but more personally meaningful than those that occur among organizational and institutional representatives. Included would be relationships among individuals in a self-help or therapy group, among peers at school or work, and among neighbors.

Some practice approaches are designed to address more than one intervention level. For example, social treatment, as defined by Whittaker and Tracy (1989), includes the micro and mezzo practice levels, and the generalist perspective (Schatz, Jenkins, and Sheafor 1990) requires the social worker to be capable of practice at the micro, mezzo, and macro levels.

Sources of Sanction
for Social Work

Sanction refers to the authorization, approval, or permission needed to perform certain professional tasks and activities. Sanction has the effect of defining the profession's domain. Four major sources of sanction for social work activities are (1) legal codes and government regulation, (2) legally incorporated human services agencies, (3) the collective body of social work professionals, and (4) the clients or consumers of social work services.

Federal, state, and city governments authorize the actions of social workers through legislation that creates social programs, through the allocation of funds for social work activities, through the licensing of organizations (e.g., licensed child-placing agencies) that employ social workers, and through the licensing and regulation of individual social work practitioners.

Many government and private human services organizations (both nonprofit and profit-making agencies) sanction social work by recruiting and hiring social workers to provide services or by purchasing services from those who are in private practice or employed by other agencies. Indirectly, then, the community sanctions and pays social workers to provide specific services. In return for this sanction to practice, social workers are obliged to provide high-quality services and to protect clients from possible abuse by the professional monopoly that the sanction creates.

The profession, acting through the National Association of Social Workers (NASW), sets standards for appropriate and ethical practice. By requiring adherence to its *Code of Ethics*, offering certification (e.g., the Academy of Certified Social Workers, Diplomat in Clinical Social Work, etc.), and providing education to its membership through publications and conferences, the NASW serves as a vehicle for protecting the public trust.

The true test of public sanction for practice, however, is the willingness of clients to seek out and use services offered by social workers. In order to win the trust of clients, social workers must demonstrate on a daily basis that they are capable of providing effective services and are committed to conducting their practice in a responsible and ethical manner.

An Overview of Social Work Practice

Figure 1.1 presents a model of the key factors that influence social work practice. It shows the client (or client system) and the social worker joining together in a process of change while both are being influenced by the social agency (e.g., its policies and programs) and by the wider social environment.

The reason clients and social workers come together is to engage in a ***planned change process.*** That process involves several phases of activity during which the client and social worker move from their decision to initiate a course of action, through the change activity, to an evaluation of its success and a decision to terminate the helping activity (see Chapter 7). Although the social worker is expected to guide this process, the client must ultimately make decisions about whether to make changes or utilize resources made available by the worker.

FIGURE 1.1   An Integrative View of Social Work Practice

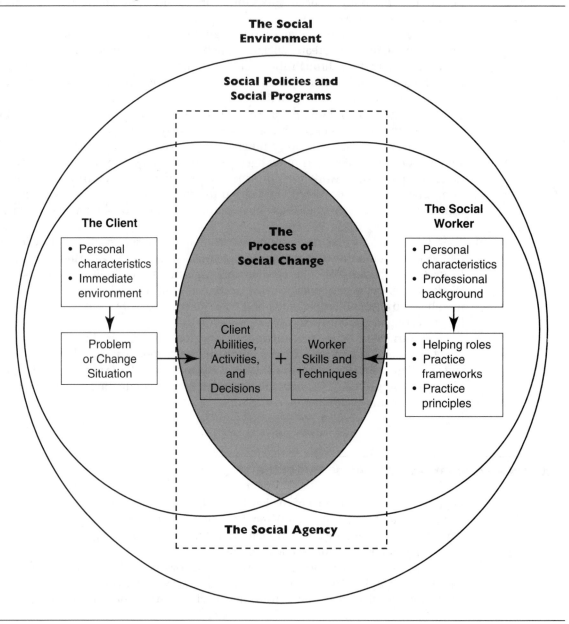

The Client side of Figure 1.1 indicates that the problem or situation the client seeks to change is the product of a combination of personal and environmental factors. Each client has *personal characteristics* that contributed to the situation being addressed and/or that might be used to help change that situation. Regardless of whether the client is an individual, family, or some larger system, every situation is unique due to the client's special needs, wants, capacities, knowledge, beliefs, physical characteristics, and life experiences.

Clients do not exist in isolation. They have an *immediate environment* that also influences the situation (sometimes called a *near environment*). This environment might include friends, family, school personnel, employers, natural helpers, neighborhood or community groups, or even other professional helpers, to mention just a few. Because environmental influences have contributed to the problem or concern creating a need for change, they must also be a part of the solution; people in the client's immediate environment must be kept in the foreground as possible targets and resources for the change activity.

The Social Worker side of Figure 1.1 suggests that the worker brings unique personal characteristics and a professional background to the change process. These are experienced by the client through what the social worker actually does with the client (i.e., the worker's activities and application of skills and techniques). What the worker does is a function of the specific professional role he or she has assumed and the conceptual frameworks selected to guide practice. The worker's *personal characteristics* encompass such factors as life experience and especially one's artistic talents or natural abilities in providing services. The social worker's unique perspectives on the human condition, as well as his or her particular values, are inevitably introduced into the change process. The worker's view on life and human problems is shaped by his or her racial or cultural background, socioeconomic status, gender, age, sexual orientation, and the like. All affect the social worker–client relationship.

At the same time, the practitioner brings the special contribution of a *professional background* to social work, which differentiates the social worker from the client's friends, family, natural helpers, and the professionals representing other disciplines who may also be working with the client or who attempted to help in the past. What is this professional background? First and foremost, the social worker brings the belief system, values, ethical principles, and focus on social functioning that are common to the domain of social work. Through education and experience, the social worker develops a practice wisdom and an ability to use his or her personal characteristics, special talents, and unique style to help clients. In addition, the social worker brings a knowledge base, much of it derived from the social and behavioral sciences. Chapter 3 presents an overview of the necessary artistic abilities, knowledge base, and value positions relevant to practice.

As social workers carry out their responsibilities, they perform various *helping roles*. As Chapter 4 describes more fully, social workers must be prepared to perform a wide variety of roles and functions, ranging from linking clients to appropriate resources, to assessing case situations and providing direct services, to planning and conducting social action.

An important element of professional background is that portion of the social worker's knowledge base consisting of various *practice frameworks* that guide practice (e.g., practice perspectives, theories, and models) and provide direction to the change process. The ways in which these frameworks might be selected and utilized are discussed in Chapter 6.

The profession has informally tested the applicability of its approach to providing human services, largely through trial and error. Some of these tried-and-true guidelines for practice have been reduced to *practice principles* that serve as the most fundamental directives to practice (see Chapter 5).

Finally, the social worker's *skills* and mastery of *techniques* are his or her most evident and tangible contribution to the change process. The skills or techniques selected by the social worker will depend, of course, on the nature of the client's problem or concern, the expectations of the practice setting, and the worker's own competence in using them. A wide variety of techniques and guidelines are described in Parts III and IV of this book.

Returning again to Figure 1.1, it is important to recognize that social work practice takes place within a **social environment** and, more specifically, usually within the context of a social agency. Typically, the agency has been shaped by local, state, and/or national social policies, and its programs are a reflection of society's values and beliefs. Commitment to the social welfare of its members varies among societies; within the United States, it even varies among regions, states, and communities. We know that having sound social programs supports quality living for all people—the more secure as well as the most vulnerable members of that society. Yet every social worker knows that our social policies and programs leave much to be desired. Moreover, U.S. society has demonstrated an ambivalent and transient commitment to people whose needs are not adequately met through their employment or help provided by family and friends. Therefore, social workers, who might be viewed as agents of the society, must frequently work with fewer than the desired tools for assisting their clients.

Through its legislative and other decision-making bodies, society creates **social programs** intended to help certain people. These programs take three forms. *Social provisions* involve giving tangible goods (e.g., money, food, clothing, and housing) to persons in need. *Social services* include intangible services (e.g., counseling, therapy, and learning experiences) intended to help people resolve and/or prevent problems. Finally, *social action* programs are concerned with changing aspects of the social environment to make it more responsive to people's needs and wants.

The particular philosophy on which social programs are built has a significant bearing on how they operate, how effective they are, and how they impact both the client and the social worker. The dominant social welfare philosophy in the United States contends that social programs should be of a residual nature; they should be a safety net that is available only to people who can demonstrate "real need." In other words, social programs should exist only to help people solve already serious problems and be available only to those who are deemed eligible. A second philosophy, the institutional conception, considers social programs to be first-line functions of society (similar to education and law enforcement). This approach places greater emphasis on prevention and avoids forcing the client to identify a problem or admit to some personal failure in order to benefit from human services (Wilensky and Lebeaux 1965, 138–140).

The benefits and services associated with a particular social program are typically offered through a *social agency.* Thus, for the most part, social work is an agency-based profession and most social workers are agency employees. A social agency might be a public welfare department, mental health center, school, hospital, neighborhood center, or any of a number of differing organizational structures. It may be a public agency supported by tax funds and governed by elected officials or a private agency operating under the auspices of a volunteer board and supported primarily by fees, voluntary donations, or purchase of service contracts. The basic functions of the agency are to administer social programs and to monitor the quality of the helping process. To perform these functions, the agency must secure money, staff, and other resources; determine which people in the community are eligible for its services; and maintain an administrative structure that will meet targeted social needs in an efficient and effective manner.

The most important ingredient of a social agency is its people. Receptionists, typists, custodians, administrators, and service providers all must work together to deliver successful programs. Often, several helping professions are employed by the same agency. In such interdisciplinary programs, each profession brings its own perspective on helping—as well as the special competencies appropriate to the domain of that profession.

Conclusion

Social work is one of several human services professions that have been sanctioned by U.S. society to help improve the quality of life for all people. Other such helping professions include clinical psychology, drug and alcohol counseling, marriage and family counseling, school psychology, medicine, rehabilitation counseling, nursing, and so on. The uniqueness of social work among these professions is its emphasis on helping people interact more effectively with their environments—both their near and distant environments. Social workers perform this role by assisting people to address issues in their social functioning and working to prevent social problems from emerging or, if they already exist, from getting worse.

Increasingly, conflict and competition arise among the various human services professions over issues of the domain (or turf) of each. These conflicts tend to center around competition for jobs, salary, status, and control, as well as disagreements over which profession is most qualified to perform certain tasks. To minimize the effect of these problems on clients, it is important for the members of these professions to engage in *interprofessional collaboration* as they provide their services. However, each discipline must avoid letting its practice activities drift into the areas of expertise of the other professions.

Social workers have historically claimed they represent the profession best prepared to help people resolve problems in social functioning and to guide social change efforts to prevent problems from occurring or becoming worse. It is important that social workers maintain their focus on these central features of their domain.

SELECTED BIBLIOGRAPHY

Barker, Robert L. *The Social Work Dictionary,* 3rd ed. Washington, D.C.: NASW Press, 1995.

Council on Social Work Education. *Handbook of Accreditation Standards and Procedures,* rev. ed. Alexandria, Va.: CSWE, 1994.

Karls, James, and Karin Wandrei. *Person in Environment: A System for Describing, Classifying and Coding Problems of Social Functioning.* Silver Spring, Md.: National Association of Social Workers, 1988.

Longres, John. *Human Behavior and the Social Environment,* 2nd ed. Itasca, Ill.: F. E. Peacock, 1995.

Schatz, Mona S., Lowell E. Jenkins, and Bradford W. Sheafor. "Milford Redefined: A Model of Initial and Advanced Generalist Social Work." *Journal of Social Work Education* 26 (Fall 1990): 217–231.

Shulman, Lawrence. *Interactional Social Work Practice.* Itasca, Ill.: F. E. Peacock, 1991.

Teare, Robert J., and Bradford W. Sheafor. *Practice-Sensitive Social Work Education: An Empirical Analysis of Social Work Practice and Practitioners.* Alexandria, Va.: Council on Social Work Education, 1995.

Whittaker, James, and Elizabeth Tracy. *Social Treatment,* 2nd ed. New York: Aldine, 1989.

Wilensky, Harold, and Charles N. Lebeaux. *Industrial Society and Social Welfare.* New York: Free Press, 1965.

2 Merging Person with Profession

Unlike people employed in many occupations, a social worker's job and his or her personal life are in constant interaction. Most social workers cannot simply go to work, do their job, and then psychologically or emotionally leave their thoughts and feelings about work at the office when returning home. They try to keep their professional concerns separate from their personal lives but the nature of the work makes this very difficult.

As explained in Chapter 1, the social work profession strives always to view the client as a *whole person,* with various dimensions such as the physical, spiritual, emotional, psychological, social, and intellectual. And, of course, the social worker is also a whole and fully human person who has no choice but to respond to professional responsibilities with his or her whole being. Consequently, the worker's own beliefs, values, physical and emotional well-being, spirituality, family life, financial situation, friendships, and other facets of living will both influence and be affected by the day-to-day experiences of social work practice.

The profession also strives always to view the client within an ecological context and to be cognizant of the client's many roles and responsibilities. The social worker, too, lives within and moves between several distinct environments and performs a number of roles, in addition to that of being a social worker. For example, he or she is frequently part of a family or household, often a spouse or partner, sometimes a parent, part of a friendship and social network, and a resident in a local community. Moreover, he or she may be a member of a particular ethnic group, affiliated with a religious denomination or faith community, a member of a special-interest group or political party, and a member of service and recreational groups. Given this multitude of roles and relationships, every social worker is challenged to resolve the inevitable conflicts that arise between personal and professional obligations.

This chapter examines the interplay between the person and his or her profession and job. It focuses on the two-thirds of each day spent away from work and examines some of the more personal concerns and dilemmas often mentioned by practicing social workers. Also, the chapter discusses how the realities of practice may impinge on the worker's private life, family, and friends. Hopefully, the observations presented here will assist social workers in striking a healthy balance between their personal needs and the demands of practice.

Selecting Social Work as a Career

The selection of any career or occupation has a far-reaching impact on one's life. Because choosing social work has some unique implications for self and family, those attracted to this profession must carefully consider (and periodically reconsider) if social work should be their life's work. It is of critical importance that there be a compatible match between the person and his or her profession and job. A mismatch can be destructive to one's health and emotional well-being. A person who feels trapped in a helping profession such as social work cannot bring the desired energy and commitment to the helping process, and consequently, clients will be poorly served.

Social Work as a Life Companion

Buscaglia (1978, 1) observes that "life is an immense journey and each of us has only one lifetime to travel it." As a social worker makes that one and only journey through life, it is important that he or she is truly comfortable with social work as a traveling companion. An individual considering a social work career must be satisfied with his or her answers to the following:

- Is being a social worker a meaningful and worthwhile way for me to live my life?
- Is there a good fit between my personal beliefs, values, and needs and the values and demands of the social work profession?
- Is the practice of social work an appropriate and satisfying use of my unique gifts, abilities, and skills?
- What impact will being a social worker have on my own physical and mental health, my intellectual development, my religious activity, and my economic situation?
- What impact, positive and negative, will a career in social work have on my family and friends?
- How will being a social worker affect where I live and work?

Each social worker needs to identify his or her core values and decide what is really important in life. The work and rewards that accrue from being a social worker should be consistent with those beliefs and goals.

The School-to-Job Transition

Many students do not fully realize that their program of social work education, including the practicum experience, takes place within a somewhat protected and controlled environment. Once they enter the world of full-time practice as a paid professional, they may experience reality shock. Many are surprised by the sheer difficulty of their jobs. For example, in describing her new job, a very capable recent graduate told one of the authors: "I simply had no idea that my clients would be so troubled, so difficult, and so frustrating and had no idea that my agency setting would be so complex."

Many of those beginning their first social work job are also surprised to discover that there is seldom enough time to do what needs to be done. Many are angered when they recognize that in far too many agencies, basic social work values and principles have taken a backseat to the forces of political pressure, administrative fiat, budget limitations, the fear of lawsuits, and the day-by-day struggle to cope with an overwhelming caseload. Many are disillusioned by the discovery that some fellow employees have lost their enthusiasm and are too fatigued and demoralized to be effective. Within such an environment, it can be a challenge to maintain one's professional ideals and standards.

Every new social worker is frustrated by the slowness of change, whether that be change by individual clients, the organizations in which they work, or their communities. They also discover that being able to "diagnose" a problem and identify what needs to change is relatively easy compared to actually achieving the change. Programs of social work education teach about the process of change and describe techniques for facilitating change, but they cannot teach the personal qualities of patience, perseverance, and tolerance so necessary to moving good ideas into reality.

Some new social workers who were high academic achievers in their programs of social work education face a special challenge when they move into an agency-based practice. Simply put, they are accustomed to doing grade A academic work and expect to do A-quality work on the job, but they discover that their workloads are excessive and that there is only enough time and resources to do average work. They now must learn how to be successful in an even more challenging and demanding role—that of a social work practitioner. Those unable to modify their expectations will surely experience much frustration on the job.

Some agencies provide a superb work environment—spacious, well maintained, and respectful of privacy. But far too many offer an environment that is noisy, crowded, unattractive, and sometimes even dangerous. Dissatisfaction with agency-based practice has led many skilled social workers to seek a practice setting that offers a more pleasant work environment and more control over what they do and how they do it. Specht and Courtney (1993) document a trend by social workers to set up private practices that cater to those clients who can pay for their services. Although a shift to private practice is an understandable response to frustrations often associated with agency-based practice, it has the effect of drawing social workers away from the profession's traditional commitment to the poor and oppressed. Throughout their careers, conscientious social workers will struggle to reconcile their desire for adequate income and a decent work environment with their concern for the poor and their commitment to social justice.

Indeed, social workers face many challenges as they move from the student role to that of a professional within our very human and imperfect service systems. But even frustrations and surprises have a positive side if people choose to see it. To a greater extent than occurs in other professions, the practice of social work will stretch one's abilities and self-image and force growth beyond the usual constraints of family and cultural conditioning. If it were not for the dilemmas, conflicts, and frustrations of life, people would not grow and might never get around to reexamining their assumptions, beliefs, and values concerning what is really important.

Earning a Living as a Social Worker

The social worker and his or her dependents are directly impacted by the worker's earning capacity. Social work has never been a high-paying profession. In contrast to some occupations, the earning power of social workers does not go up rapidly or continually as practitioners gain skill and experience. In general, social workers earn a modest income and have limited opportunity to reach the higher rungs of the economic ladder. However, the satisfaction of doing something truly worthwhile and making a difference in the lives of their clients is often viewed by social workers as an offsetting form of compensation.

Most entry-level jobs involve providing services directly to clients. After a few years in direct services, many social workers apply for higher-paying jobs in supervision and administration as a way of increasing their income and prestige. This may be a good change of job function for those genuinely attracted to management tasks such as budgeting, policy development, public relations, personnel selection, and staff training. It may be an unwise decision, however, for those whose job satisfaction comes primarily from direct contact with clients.

As an individual considers or plans a career in social work, he or she should answer the following:

- Given my current personal and family responsibilities, can I manage on a social worker's salary?
- Given probable changes in my personal and family life over the next 5, 10, and 20 years, will my salary keep up with my income requirements?
- How will my earning capacity impact on my family? How will it affect decisions concerning where I live and work?
- Will I be content and at peace with a modest income or will I become unhappy and dissatisfied?

Social workers, like people in most other occupations, should expect to change jobs from 5 to 10 times during their working years. Sometimes a job change is prompted by poor performance or an agency's staff reductions, but more often it is a matter of personal choice. Among the personal and professional reasons why social workers change jobs are the following:

- Desire for higher salary, better benefits, or more job security
- Desire to learn a new field of practice or test out one's ability to perform a new set of tasks and activities
- Desire to have more discretion and control over practice decisions than is permitted within a bureaucratic agency

- Desire to work in a setting that is more accepting of new ideas and new approaches to practice
- Desire to work with clients having a different set of problems, concerns, or situations
- Desire for a more pleasant or less stressful work environment
- Opportunity to receive better supervision and in-service training or the opportunity to learn new knowledge or skills
- Desire to remove self from conflicts with a supervisor or agency administrator
- Need to adjust work to changes in personal or family life (e.g., marriage, divorce, birth of child, illness, etc.)
- Desire to live and work in another city or state

Those preparing to enter social work are advised to identify their personal and career goals and formulate a tentative plan for reaching those goals. Examples of career goals include obtaining a particular type of job, having the opportunity to design an innovative program, becoming an administrator of a certain type of agency, becoming highly skilled in work with certain client populations, conducting research on a particular topic, and so on. The plan should cover the next 10, 20, and even 30 years. Needless to say, in these times of rapid change, it can be difficult to develop this plan and even more difficult to follow it. However, career planning provides a framework for making decisions about what work experiences to pursue and what special training to obtain. For social work students, a career plan provides guidance on which course electives to take and the type of practicum experience that would be most beneficial.

Establishing Oneself as a Social Worker

It is not enough for the new social worker to carry his or her credentials into a job and assume that everything is now in place for a satisfying and effective practice. The worker must first demonstrate to clients, other agency personnel, and other agencies in the community that he or she is a competent and trustworthy professional. The worker will be challenged to somehow reconcile his or her personal and professional standards with the everyday operations of an agency and human services systems that are very human and consequently far from being perfect. The new worker is beginning a life-long struggle to have some impact on large-scale social problems and promote social justice in a society that seeks simple answers to complex problems and is politically divided on how to respond deeply to human needs and growing levels of violence.

Acquiring a Reputation

Every social worker acquires a reputation within his or her agency, within the local human services network, and among the clients he or she serves. That reputation, whether good or bad, impacts his or her effectiveness with clients, interagency exchanges, and whether he or she is considered for a promotion or offered a job with another agency.

One need only sit in on a few support group meetings or spend just an hour in an agency waiting room to realize that many clients talk freely about the social workers, doctors, teachers, and other professionals they know. They tell friends, neighbors, and other clients about how they have been treated by social workers and agencies, and who does a good job and who to avoid. Clients are especially sensitive to whether social workers are willing to listen, available when needed, and fair in the decisions they make.

Within an agency, each social worker acquires a reputation as an employee. Over time, the other agency employees form an opinion about the worker's competence and whether he or she is dependable and carries a fair share of the workload. That reputation will affect the willingness of the other employees to offer their support, assistance, and cooperation.

One of the most painful situations social workers can experience is to find themselves employed by an agency or organization that does not respect clients nor value professional competence and ethical conduct. Such situations can arise when an organization's administration and policy-setting board is more concerned about politics, cost cutting, or profit than providing needed and appropriate services. All organizations develop a culture that consists of values and expectations through which its employees learn the group norms. Employees are rewarded when they accept this culture and ostracized when they do not. Once established, an organization's culture tends to perpetuate itself while exerting a pervasive effect on employees and their job performance. Social workers employed by organizations with destructive cultures may need to look for another job.

Reputation is also a determining factor in whether a private practice or fee-for-service program will succeed. If they have a choice, clients will avoid agencies and professionals who have a bad reputation. In addition, the professionals of a community who are in a position to refer clients to a social worker will do so only if the worker has a reputation for being competent and ethical.

Social workers and social work students should regularly review how their statements, actions, and associations, both private and professional, are shaping their reputations. Socrates observed that "the way to gain a good reputation is to endeavor to be what you desire to appear." A good reputation is difficult to build but easy for others to destroy. For this reason, many cultures consider slander and the spreading of gossip that could ruin a person's reputation to be among the most serious of moral transgressions.

Conflict over Agency Policy

Every social worker comes to the profession and to his or her agency setting with a set of personal beliefs, values, standards, and expectations. It is inevitable that he or she will, from time to time, disagree with agency decisions and methods of operation. There may also be times when the worker disagrees with official positions taken by the NASW or other professional organizations to which he or she belongs. How is a person to respond to such situations?

In the final analysis, the social worker must follow his or her conscience. However, the worker's decision about what to do must be based on a thoughtful examination of the principles and issues involved. One might begin this examination by seeking answers to the following:

- Why has my agency or professional organization taken this position at this particular time? What is the history and rationale behind this position? What are the arguments for and against this position? What data support this viewpoint? What political, economic, and social forces gave rise to this position? Was it prompted by political and administrative expediency or was it rooted in a concern for principles of social justice and efforts to allocate scarce resources in a fair and responsible manner? If it was driven by a lack of fiscal resources, what actions were taken to secure additional resources?
- Why do I disagree with my agency or professional organization? Specifically, which of my beliefs, values, or standards is being threatened or violated? Are my concerns based on identifiable values and principles or are my concerns possibly arising from personal bias or differences in personal, professional, and administrative style?
- Does the action or position in question recognize that every individual has worth and dignity, regardless of his or her strengths and limitations or successes and failings? Does it recognize that each person is unique and precious?
- Does the action or position recognize and respect the rights and responsibilities of each person? Does the position recognize that every mentally competent individual has a right to self-determination, as long as his or her actions do not cause harm to others? Does the position recognize that every competent person is responsible for his or her own actions and must accept the consequences for violating legitimate laws and rules?
- Does the action or position in question promote the common good? Does the position enhance and strengthen the functioning of individuals, families, and the community? Does the position recognize the obligation of individuals, communities, and society to expand social and economic opportunities and, where necessary, to provide direct assistance to persons who are at risk of harm, deeply troubled, affected by a physical or mental disability, or socially or economically oppressed?

Once the social worker understands why the agency or professional organization has taken the action or position in question and is also clear about why he or she disagrees, the worker must decide on a course of action. Each possible response needs to be examined in terms of its immediate and long-term consequences and in regard to what is to be gained and lost. As suggested earlier, the decision is ultimately a matter of following one's moral beliefs and conscience. The following guidelines, however, may prove useful.

- If the worker concludes that this is a significant and serious matter—one that demands a response—he or she might begin by seeking further advice and direction from trusted peers and/or the agency supervisor.

- If the worker is expected by his or her agency to take some action that would violate the worker's professional or moral standards, the worker should voice these concerns, document them in a letter to the administrator, and formally request to be excused from having to participate in the questionable activity.
- If the social worker objects to actions or positions taken by a professional organization to which he or she belongs, the worker should write to the organization's leaders and describe his or her concerns and objections. The worker might also volunteer to join the committee that recommended the position in hopes of having the issue and position reexamined in the future.
- In extreme cases and when there is no acceptable alternative, the worker will need to seek employment in a different agency. Similarly, in extreme cases, he or she may need to withdraw from a professional organization that has taken positions that are personally or professionally offensive.

When issues are complex, knowing what is right is never easy and doing what is right is always difficult.

Promoting Social Justice

Most individuals attracted to social work are somewhat idealistic. They want to make the world a better place. They possess a vision of a just and humane society. They believe that every individual has certain basic rights, such as those identified in the Declaration of Independence, the Bill of Rights, and the Universal Declaration of Human Rights issued by the United Nations. In short, they seek *social justice,* which Barker (1995, 354) describes as "an ideal condition in which all members of a society have the same rights, protection, opportunities, obligations and social benefits."

All considerations of social justice rest on a core belief: Every human being is intrinsically valuable. This worth is not something that must be earned or proven, nor is it a function of one's race, nationality, gender, IQ, income, social status, education, political affiliation, occupation, or other external characteristics or life circumstances. Simply by virtue of being human, every person has a right to be treated with fairness and respect, protected from abuse and exploitation, and granted opportunities to have a family, a basic education, meaningful work, and access to essential health care and social services. The Universal Declaration of Human Rights (United Nations 1948, 1) observes that the "recognition of the inherent dignity and of the equal and inalienable rights of all members of the human family is the foundation of freedom, justice and peace in the world."

Social justice is a complex ideal, and even among people of good will and compassion there will be different perspectives on what is fair and what specific actions will move us toward a more just and humane society. Social workers and others must work for social and economic justice and needed reforms in ways that recognize and consider legitimate differences of opinion. They must also maintain respect for those who may disagree with their ideas about how best to achieve a just society.

A multitude of complex and interrelated economic, political, historical, and social forces give rise to and perpetuate injustice. The term *social injustice* refers to various forms of exploitation, oppression, and discrimination that are embedded in community and societal attitudes and behaviors and reinforced by laws, organizational policies, and social norms. Because social injustice tends to be woven into prevailing belief systems and social structures, the existence and effects of injustice may go unnoticed by all but those directly harmed. This is in contrast to a crime, for example, where people can see a clear connection between the actions of the criminal and the harm caused to the victim.

Social workers must be especially sensitive to the insidious nature of social injustice and always open to the possibility that they may in some way unintentionally contribute to or perpetuate expressions of injustice. In many instances of social injustice, people are not conscious of having harmed others, and therefore they do not feel personally responsible. When an injustice is brought to their attention, they are likely to conclude that it is the fault of society and beyond their control. So often when people seriously examine a social injustice, they end up feeling helpless and conclude that they are too small a force to make any difference. Social injustice is a community or societal problem, but the responsibility to oppose injustice rests with the individual. Martin Luther King reminded us that "whoever accepts evil without protesting against it, is really cooperating with it."

In order to correct an injustice, people must become politically involved, speak out, and propose practical solutions. However, those who seek social reform must understand that they will often pay a price for challenging powerful individuals, organizations, or interest groups that stand to lose money, power, or position if the status quo is altered. Those who speak out may be ridiculed in public, lose their jobs, or, in extreme cases, be subjected to physical injury.

Political Involvement

Efforts to work for social justice and social reform require involvement in the political process. Some social workers are attracted to and fascinated by politics; others find it distasteful. How and to what degree one involves himself or herself in political activity is, of course, a matter of choice and a reflection of such factors as interest, available time, energy level, and personal style. Being an informed and conscientious voter is an essential first step, but more is required of social workers who wish to remain true to the "soul" of their profession.

Many social workers are in a position to identify responsible leaders and support their election—or to seek political office themselves. They are also able to observe the concrete impact of social policies and programs on the lives of people. These direct observations are rarely available to the politicians who consider legislation and the administrators who develop policy and design programs. Thus, the social worker has both the opportunity and an obligation to document and communicate the effects of social legislation and administrative decisions, as well as to offer ideas on how policies and programs can be made more humane, effective, and efficient. Social workers with special abilities to speak and write can make valuable contributions to the education of decision makers and the general public.

As social workers become involved in the political process, they must examine their beliefs and values and make difficult decisions about where they stand on complex issues. Politically speaking, most social workers tend to be on the liberal side of the conservative to liberal continuum. However, it is a mistake for social workers to assume that they must choose between being either a liberal or a conservative. They should be something of both. Everyone who is intellectually and spiritually alive is a liberal in the sense of being open to the truth, regardless of its source, and desirous of change and governmental action if those changes will improve the lives of people and their society. Similarly, every thoughtful and responsible person is a conservative in the sense of wanting to preserve traditional approaches that have been beneficial to people and because he or she knows that the newest idea is not necessarily the best one and that there is always a downside to legislative and governmental efforts to solve social problems. Thus, depending on the issue, a social worker might line up on either the liberal or conservative side of the debate. The merits and wisdom of a proposal, and not political ideology, should dictate one's stance on an issue.

Political involvement can be tiring and frustrating. Some social workers begin to lose heart and give up the fight when confronted with frequent setbacks and resistance. Some who are frustrated by the slowness of change become belligerent toward those who resist their ideas and actions. Such hostility can become an obstacle to real change. In order to continue working for desirable social and community change, year after year, social workers must strive to develop personal qualities of hopefulness, patience, perseverance, and tolerance.

The Interplay of One's Personal and Professional Lives

Being a social worker and having an opportunity to meet people who have overcome great obstacles and who care deeply about their families and communities can be a life-changing experience. When providing a service, social workers often receive intangible gifts from their clients. Social work jobs require a heavy commitment of time and energy. That, too, affects the social worker and sometimes the worker's family.

Being Changed by Clients

One cannot begin to really know a client without coming to understand how that individual thinks and feels about life. In many cases, the client's perspectives, beliefs, and values will be significantly different from those of the social worker. This difference, in itself, can challenge the worker to rethink his or her our own life experiences and values. Whenever one begins to understand things in a new way or look at the familiar from a different angle, one begins to change.

In every type of agency setting, social workers will meet clients who are truly remarkable in terms of their personal courage, wisdom, compassion, and generosity. Some have survived and overcome unbelievable hardships and trauma. Such encounters are memorable and uplifting. One of the great privileges of social work practice is the opportunity to meet these individuals and learn from them. Social workers and other professional helpers open themselves to learning when they set aside their desire to learn about their clients, and, instead, seek to learn from their clients. In a real sense, the professional relationship is an exchange of gifts, and both the social worker and client stand to be changed by what they give and receive.

The social worker may also be changed by clients who are critical of his or her work. Clients may accuse workers of being uncaring or claim that their decisions are unfair and arbitrary. The worker must always remain open to the possibility that the clients may be accurate in their assessments. And, if that is the case, the social worker must learn from those encounters and strive to modify the attitudes and behaviors that have offended the client.

The clients who cause the social worker great anguish and frustration are a particularly painful source of personal change. Not infrequently, the worker's skills and the available resources are insufficient to encourage or help clients make needed changes. Thus the worker must watch helplessly as clients make decisions that are likely to get them into trouble with the law, ruin their health, or cause further disruptions in their lives. These humbling experiences teach that even our best efforts and our most advanced knowledge and skills are often inadequate and that a social worker is but one small influence in a client's life.

Personal Responses to Clients in Need

Many of the clients served by social workers live in poverty or suffer other deprivations. They may, for example, experience constant stress because they cannot pay for even the basics such as food and shelter. By comparison, the social worker with only a modest income seems quite well off. This situation confronts the social worker with a very hard question of individual responsibility. Once a social worker has done all he or she can do as a professional and as an agency's representative, what, if anything, remains as a personal responsibility? Should a social worker use his or her own money to deal with a client's emergency? From time to time, every social worker struggles with these questions.

Some would answer that meeting basic needs is a community and governmental responsibility and that the employees who work in human services agencies should not attempt to make up for system deficiencies. To even try would be an unfair and unreasonable drain on the employees' fiscal and emotional resources. It might also make it too easy for the community to avoid its responsibility to correct system deficiencies.

Others might answer that even when our social welfare systems fail to meet basic needs, the individual social worker still has a moral and ethical responsibility to respond in certain individual cases. They might further argue that a social worker, because of his or her professional knowledge and values, has a unique obligation that is above and beyond that of the ordinary citizen.

The answer is ultimately a matter of conscience and a judgment call concerning what action would be helpful to the client and reasonable and proper for the social worker. The social worker might consider the following questions in formulating his or her response.

- When a client is without the basics, and after all other possible sources of assistance have been explored but are unable to address the client's needs, does the social worker, as an individual, have an obligation to do something more?
- What situations, if any, require some extraordinary and personal response? What if the situation involves a person who is especially vulnerable, such as a young child, a person who is sick, or a person at risk of being assaulted?
- Is a personal response realistic for a social worker who encounters truly desperate situations on a daily basis? If a personal response is not reasonable, is some type of political or community action required?
- Is it appropriate for a social worker to make a personal contribution to a client (e.g., purchase of food, pay for a night's lodging, pay cab fare, etc.)? If yes, under what conditions and how is this to be done? If one decides to make a personal contribution, should it be done in a way that keeps the donor's identity confidential so as to maintain a proper professional boundary between worker and client and so the client is not placed in a position of feeling obligated to a particular worker?
- What possible personal, ethical, and legal pitfalls await the social worker who makes an individual contribution to a client? What are the advantages and disadvantages of an agency having a policy on whether, when, and how a personal contribution is to occur? Is it appropriate for the workers of an agency to create and donate to a special, nonagency emergency fund?

The Social Worker's Family

Social workers, like everyone else, experience personal and family problems. Sometimes the problems are serious and they create much stress, anxiety, or depression. When worry associated with personal concerns is added to the stress of social work practice, the social worker may become overwhelmed. During these times, the individual needs the support and understanding of colleagues and friends and must be open to guidance provided by those able to see more objectively what is happening.

The social worker must protect his or her family relationships from interference by work-related responsibilities. The daily transitions between one's family relationships and the often harsh realities and tension-filled relationships encountered at work can be difficult. The norms and expectations of these two environments are quite different. Those social workers who provide direct services to seriously troubled and violent clients will observe behaviors and situations that are bizarre and cruel. Long-term exposure to deviant behavior can subtly distort one's moral compass and beliefs concerning what is socially acceptable. In an adult correctional setting, for example, the daily exposure to intimidation, violence, and manipulation can dull one's sensitivity and gradually increase one's tolerance for abuse and inhumane treatment. Skewed views on what is usual and normal, if brought home to one's family or into one's friendships, can strain those relationships.

In rare instances, an angry or distraught client will locate and approach a social worker's home and talk with the worker's family. Family members, especially children, must be instructed on how to handle this situation, should it occur. If a social worker is employed in a program that serves potentially violent clients, the worker's family needs to understand the safeguards in place to protect staff so worry by family members can be minimized.

It is very difficult to keep one's personal and family problems from affecting professional performance. And it is difficult to keep work-related concerns from adversely affecting one's personal life and family relationships. Nevertheless, social workers must strive to maintain a healthy separation.

A Fitness Program for the Whole Social Worker

To be of maximum assistance to clients, a social worker must be able to maintain a proper boundary in professional relationships. The worker's own need for meaningful relationships and friendships must be met outside of professional relationships with clients. In addition, effectiveness in practice requires that the worker be intellectually alert and physically, emotionally, and spiritually healthy.

Friendships and Community

Friendships meet some of the same needs as do family and kinship relationships. Good friends provide support and help each other examine assumptions, test reality, and maintain perspective. Also, good friends provide constructive criticism when one behaves inappropriately.

Because people tend to choose friends who are similar to themselves in age, interests, and socioeconomic status, many friendships develop in the workplace. All too often, social workers come to believe that no one, except another social worker, is capable of understanding their everyday concerns and frustrations. This role-centeredness in the selection of friends limits exposure to differing points of view and constricts opportunity for personal growth. In some cases, it leads to an "us against them" type of thinking. In addition to friendships with colleagues, the social worker needs to cultivate friendships with people who are from outside the work setting and the profession.

In addition to family and friends, people need a sense of belonging to a community. This spirit of community is increasingly missing in urban society because the fear of crime and violence breeds distrust and the search for privacy gives rise to social isolation. Many who deliberately seek this feeling of belonging are disappointed; too often they assumed that a lasting sense of community could be acquired during a weekend workshop or from a flurry of organizational activity. A genuine sense of community develops slowly. It begins to grow when the members of a group realize that they share the same concerns and that each member is making sacrifices of time, energy, or money to advance a common cause or reach a goal. Long-term associations, trust, mutual respect, and loyalty to the group are the building blocks of *community;* there are no shortcuts to achieving it.

Many social workers find a spirit of community in professional associations such as the National Association of Social Workers. This is fortuitous because it helps to advance the profession. However, social workers should also participate in neighborhood activities and local community projects so they meet people who have perspectives different from their own. Variety in one's life experiences is valuable to everyone.

Self-Worth and Self-Image

In U.S. society, social work is not among the most respected or esteemed professions. To a large extent, this is because social work is inherently controversial; it calls attention to problems and deplorable conditions that most other people want to ignore and deny. Many of those served by social workers (e.g., the poor, parents who abuse their children, persons who are mentally ill, persons addicted to drugs, the homeless, etc.) are devalued and avoided by the respected and powerful elements of society. In 1973, Richan and Mendelsohn described social work as the "unloved profession." Its status and image have improved since then, but not a lot.

Given the concerns they address, it is not surprising that social agencies and social workers are targeted for criticism from politicians and the media as well as from clients. These critics discount the profession, its purpose, its values, and its methods. Not infrequently, social workers are blamed for situations that are beyond the control and influence of any one person, profession, or agency. Even when the workers recognize that this criticism is unreasonable or misdirected, it is still painful. Social workers, like all people, want to be understood, valued, and respected.

The social worker must possess a sense of personal worth and dignity that will counter the discomfort of being devalued. That sense of worth can only arise from the worker's own firmly held beliefs concerning the value of the services provided by social work professionals. If the social worker doubts his or her own value or the importance of the profession, he or she is vulnerable to demoralization. No one needs to feel apologetic for being a social worker; the profession's mission, values, and history reflect that which is most noble about humankind.

Physical and Emotional Well-Being

When selecting a practice field and a specific job, a social worker needs to consider his or her physical limitations, disabilities, and health problems and also anticipate the normal developmental changes that will occur over the years of work. There must be a suitable match between the worker's physical abilities and the demands of the job. Physical abilities change over time. Generally speaking, as people grow older their level of energy decreases and they experience some degree of loss in vision and hearing. Even such ordinary changes can affect the performance of specific social work tasks. Family and group therapy, for example, require excellent hearing. Also, one's age can make it either easier or more difficult to build relationships with clients in certain age categories.

For the most part, social work is a sedentary occupation. Much of each day is spent sitting. Physical inactivity can place the worker at greater risk of heart disease and other health problems. In order to counter this risk, it is important for workers to adhere to a program of regular exercise.

One of the more challenging aspects of this professional role has to do with handling the stress and strong emotions (e.g., sadness, anger, fear) experienced during work with certain clients such as children who suffer great losses, those who inflict injury on other people, or those who verbally abuse or threaten the worker with physical harm. Other common sources of frustration on the job are the limitations of agency resources, the difficulty of adhering to complex agency policies, and the crazy quilt of state and federal laws, rules, and regulations. Because of these and other emotional and intellectual demands, along with the typically heavy workload, social work is a stressful occupation. (See Chapter 10, Item 10.7, for information on stress management.)

To be effective, social workers must genuinely care about their clients. Those providing direct services must care deeply, but this can be a painful experience. Key elements of practice such as empathy and compassion describe the worker's efforts to "be with" and "feel with" the client. In an attempt to cope with the pain and distress they experience when "feeling with" their clients, some workers suppress their own emotions. The frequent and long-term exposure to the pain and distress of others can have a numbing or dulling effect on the worker's own feelings. This is damaging, both professionally and personally.

Many clients are so overwhelmed by their problems that they come to feel completely helpless. They develop *learned helplessness*—a pervasive feeling of hopelessness and a belief that no matter what they do, the pain will return again and again. Social workers who meet these clients on a daily basis or who work in inflexible organizations are vulnerable to developing this same sense of helplessness. The gallows humor observed in some agency settings suggests that the workers are struggling to maintain perspective in the face of human problems that defy acceptance, but have neither the time nor the resources needed to respond in a truly humane manner.

A social worker must be able to endure the emotional pain and conflict of practice while keeping it from adversely affecting his or her own mental health and relationships with family and friends. Social workers who have not satisfactorily resolved issues in their own family relationships or who carry emotional "baggage" related to traumatic life experiences are prone to distort and mishandle a professional relationship when their clients are struggling with issues similar to their own. In extreme cases, vulnerable workers have been so knocked off balance emotionally that they could no longer function as professionals. It is critically important that social workers be willing and able to acknowledge their emotional weak spots and, if needed, obtain professional help. If that is not possible or successful, they should arrange for work assignments that help them avoid handling the types of cases that might threaten their emotional well-being. (See Item 10.11 on worker self-awareness.)

Intellectual Growth

Ideas are powerful. One's thoughts can bring joy and comfort and also cause fear and anguish. What people know about themselves and the world around them has a profound effect on the kind of people they become, on what they value, and how they behave toward others.

The United States, and the world as a whole, is changing at a fast pace. This is due, in part, to the explosion of new information. Social work practice and agency programs are also changing rapidly. Social workers are challenged to identify the information that is relevant to their practice and continue their learning while guarding against being exhausted from information overload.

Real and significant learning is often a difficult process. Learning begins with a question and an inner dissatisfaction with one's level of skill or understanding. It continues as the individual searches for answers, either alone or with others. Learning requires a willingness to give up old and comfortable ideas and experience the uncertainty of moving in new directions. In order to learn, people must allow themselves to feel unsure about what they "know" and open themselves to new and sometimes disturbing ideas.

It is hard to imagine a type of work that can evoke as many truly significant and challenging questions as does the practice of social work. The situations social workers encounter each day touch the very heart of questions about social justice; human rights and responsibilities; ethical behavior; the causes of individual, family, and organizational problems; and the nature of personal and social change. However, those who seek to become a social worker must recognize that social work is not a traditional academic discipline nor a pure science wherein the search for knowledge is driven by the excitement of ideas and the joy of discovery. Those who want most of all to acquire a theoretical understanding of behavior and social problems, are usually not content in the role of a social work practitioner. Social work is built on theory and knowledge, but it is mostly about human values and finding practical solutions to very common but serious human problems, dilemmas, and crises. It is an action-oriented profession.

Learning and intellectual growth should continue throughout one's life. Unfortunately, many people experience periods of stagnation. Some type of deliberate planning is often needed to maintain motivation and momentum. People can put themselves in touch with new ideas and clarify their thinking by engaging in serious reading, study, and writing; listening to presentations by experts; and participating in thoughtful discussions with family, friends, and colleagues. It is helpful to occasionally place oneself in situations that will generate pressure to study and think. Examples include teaching a class, making a presentation, or writing an article. (See Items 10.4 and 10.5.) Ideally, every new social worker will find a mentor within his or her agency or field of practice who will provide encouragement and direction as the worker seeks to learn a new job or develop his or her knowledge and skills.

It is important to strike a balance between personal and professional learning. Too much attention to professional interests can narrow one's vision. On the other hand, if attention is devoted mostly to topics of purely personal interest, one's professional knowledge will soon be outdated.

Religion and Spirituality

Throughout history, people have sought answers to such enduring questions as: What is the meaning and purpose of life? Why is there evil and suffering? How should I live my life? How am I to decide what is right and wrong? How am I to relate to God? Is there a God? These are not questions that the scientific method nor professional knowledge can answer. Rather, they are matters of religious faith, spirituality, and choice. The major religions of the world offer perspectives that have been meaningful and helpful to millions of people over thousands of years, but ultimately each individual must decide which beliefs make sense and provide direction and meaning.

Although the concepts of religion and spirituality are intertwined, it is helpful to make a somewhat arbitrary distinction. *Religion* can be defined as a set of beliefs, traditions, and practices that are passed from one generation to another and that nurture and support a particular approach to spiritual growth. Religion involves some form of institutional structure and observable practices such as community prayer, public worship, ceremony, and ritual. By contrast, *spirituality* is more a quality of the inner self or soul; it is personal, internal, and less visible. Both religion and spirituality involve a sense of the sacred and the recognition that there exists some power, life force, or divine being that transcends the material world and one's personal experiences and existence. For most individuals, religious practices and spirituality are interrelated and overlapping, but not always. For example, some individuals possess a deep spiritual life but engage in few religious practices. On the other hand, some participate in observable religious activities without possessing much in the way of an inner faith or spirituality.

Given that a social worker's clients come from diverse backgrounds in terms of culture, religion, and spirituality, a worker must understand and be accepting of how different individuals and groups formulate various answers to questions about the meaning and purpose of life and how best to live one's life. Just as importantly, the social worker must have grappled with these same questions. In other words, the social worker must be accepting of the beliefs and the spiritual paths chosen by others and also understand and be comfortable with his or her own beliefs and choices.

As people grow older and as they struggle to make sense of their experiences, especially those that bring great joy or cause great distress, they often gain new insights into the meaning of life. Thus, spirituality is dynamic and can be described as an ongoing journey. The deeply religious and spiritual people who have attempted to describe their own spiritual struggles and growth emphasize the importance of taking time for reflecting on life experiences, striving to achieve self-knowledge and self-discipline, providing service to others, developing a sense of humility, and having patience with themselves and compassion for others. They also identify common barriers to spiritual growth such as a desire for control, power, prestige, and possessions, and the fear of change.

Most approaches to spiritual development are built around the observation that people are shaped by their belief systems and values. What people pay attention to and think about influences how they perceive and respond to the challenges of living. Thus, by consciously choosing to cultivate, treasure, and ponder certain ways of thinking and understanding, people create a way of living or a spirituality that provides purpose and meaning. However, this is a slow process and one that requires much effort. Moore (1992) explains that one's

> spirituality does not arrive fully formed without our effort. Religions around the world demonstrate that spiritual life requires constant attention and a subtle, often beautiful technology by which spiritual principles and understandings are kept alive. For good reason we go to church, temple, or mosque regularly and at appointed times: it's easy for consciousness to become lodged in the material world and forget the spiritual. Sacred technology [e.g., prayer, meditation, ritual, study, fasting, etc.] is largely aimed at helping us remain conscious of spiritual ideals and values. (p. 204)

One's spirituality must be durable in the sense that it provides meaning and direction throughout the life cycle, during both good times and difficult times and especially as the person faces hardship, suffering, and impending death. A genuine and durable spirituality is difficult to develop outside of a supportive community made up of like-minded people who provide guidance and encouragement.

Philosophers and students of behavior have observed that, deep down, humans are a mystery to themselves. Throughout their lives they are trying to figure out who they are, why they do what they do, and what life is all about. People are a mystery to themselves because they come to realize that they are capable of great love and generosity but also unbelievable levels of hate and selfishness. One can easily find examples of the human capacity for good in the acts of caring and compassion observed every day within ordinary families, neighborhoods, and communities. And one need only to look at today's newspaper and its descriptions of war, corruption, and family violence for examples of the human capacity to hurt and destroy. An important task in one's spiritual journey is to recognize and come to terms with one's own potential to be cruel, dishonest, and destructive as well as one's capacity for self-deception. Kelsey (1981) describes this negative potential as our "inner murderer" and explains that

> I have come to trust only those people who are aware of their inner murderer. I have come to trust only those people who are aware of their inner rage, or the murderers within them capable of murdering me. Only those who know their capacity to destroy can keep it in check. . . . If we are to love others it appears that we must know and love ourselves, even the destructive and idiotic parts of us. (p. 18)

Social workers quickly learn to appreciate the complexity of human behavior, the uncertainties of life, and that life itself is extremely fragile. Every day social workers meet people who have been hurt by acts of injustice, discrimination, and violence. In order to cope with the pain and harshness encountered on a daily basis, the social worker must strive to develop a hopeful spirituality—one that views all people, including those that hurt others, as having inherent worth and dignity and being capable of positive change. In order to maintain a healthy and positive perspective, the social worker must seek opportunities to observe and to celebrate the goodness of people.

Artistic Expression

Another piece of the social worker's fitness program should be to develop and/or maintain his or her own capacities for artistic expression. There is evidence that creative people are effective social workers (see Chapter 3); it is not uncommon to meet social workers who are quite talented in various forms of artistic expression such as music, painting, acting, creative writing, sewing, photography, dance, woodworking, and so on.

At meetings of the Council of Social Work Education, for example, opportunities for participants to demonstrate their special creativity (i.e., in addition to their creative expression through teaching and practice activities) have become a regular part of annual conferences. In recent years, these programs have included a scene from a play acted by social workers that depicted social problems experienced by the aged, a social worker's photo exhibit that captures the essence of rural poverty, and music (see *Hull House Revival* 1992 and *Concerned in Concert* 1995) and dance performances that have not only entertained but also provided expressions of social concern.

It is important for social workers, and all people, to cultivate and share their artistic talents. Such activities can be a diversion from the stress of practice and a gift that enhances the quality of life of other people.

Having Fun in Social Work

Human beings need to play and have fun. Adults often satisfy this need by introducing various forms of humor (e.g., jokes, kidding, playful pranks, and silly antics) into their work environment. How is a social worker to reconcile his or her need for fun and humor with the serious business of social work? In many ways, the practice of social work is a rather grim and emotionally heavy endeavor. Clients are often in truly desperate and tragic situations and the helping resources at a social worker's disposal are woefully inadequate. Although human distress is not a laughing matter, humor can be a counterbalance to the frustrations and despair experienced in practice.

Humor is rarely mentioned in the social work literature. This probably reflects a concern that expressions of humor by a professional are easily misunderstood and misinterpreted as insensitivity. For example, Shulman (l991) observes that

> macabre humor is often noted in high stress situations. Workers can joke about events in a way that would shock the public. This humor is often a defense against the pain of the client's problems. It also provides a release for many stresses in the peer system. Unfortunately, when humor becomes a substitute for facing client pain and self-pain, . . . it can be a maladaptive form of coping. (p. 145)

Despite the risks associated with inappropriate expressions of humor, without an active sense of humor social work practice can be unbearable and social workers can be very boring. Social workers must take their work seriously but also acknowledge and appreciate those things that are genuinely funny about themselves, their jobs, the situations they encounter, and especially their social work professors.

Finding the humor in work requires that social workers not take themselves too seriously. Social workers need to feel secure enough about who they are and what they do so they can, on occasion, poke fun at themselves, their profession, and their agencies. Humor is most of all a willingness to accept life and ourselves with a certain lightheartedness. To cultivate this attitude, social workers must allow themselves to laugh at the absurdities of life and temporarily slip out from under societal demands for conformity and the many restrictions we place on ourselves. However, it is important to remember that real humor is an occasional and temporary state. Robinson (1991, 180) explains that "this release through humor . . . must be brief and our conventional view of life must be repeatedly re-established so that we can enjoy release from it again and again."

The use of humor with clients is always somewhat risky, but given proper precautions, it has a place in helping relationships. Often it is our clients who teach us the importance of finding the humor, irony, and absurdity in their situations. It is always wrong to laugh at clients and their problems, but it may be appropriate and even helpful to laugh with them as they describe the humorous aspects of their experiences. Humor is an essential coping mechanism that should be affirmed and supported. Many individuals who live with harsh realities come to deeply appreciate the value of humor. For example, Mahatma Gandhi once explained, "If I had no sense of humor, I would long ago have committed suicide." Similarly, Viktor Frankl (1963), a psychiatrist who survived three years in the Auschwitz and Dachau death camps, describes joking and laughable situations in the midst of unrelenting starvation, brutality, and murder. Frankl (1969) explains that both heroism and humor are forms of self-detachment.

> This unique capacity of man to detach himself from any situations he might have to face is manifested not only through heroism, as was the case in the concentration camps, but also through humor. Humor too is a uniquely human capacity. And we need not feel ashamed of this fact. Humor is said even to be a divine attribute. In three Psalms God is referred to as a "laughing" one. (p. 17)

Humor as an antidote to adversity, stress, and frustration is useful and necessary to maintaining one's ability to deal with difficulties. Social workers, who work with clients facing some of the most difficult issues people can experience, need to cultivate an appropriate use of humor in working with their clients and with their colleagues. (See Item 10.8 for more information on humor.)

Conclusion

Social work practice involves the blending or merging of a unique human being with a certain set of professional responsibilities. The social worker, like the client and all other people, has many dimensions such as the physical, emotional, intellectual, spiritual, and social. The social worker responds to his or her professional role and responsibilities as a whole person, and all these dimensions affect and are affected by the moment-by-moment activities of practice.

The social worker may be closely identified with his or her professional role but is not in that role 24 hours a day. He or she has a life, relationships, and responsibilities apart from those of being a social worker. Each worker must achieve a proper and healthy balance between his or her personal and professional lives.

SELECTED BIBLIOGRAPHY

Barker, Robert. *The Social Work Dictionary,* 3rd ed. Washington, D.C.: NASW Press, 1995.

Buscaglia, Leo. *Personhood.* New York: Holt, Rinehart and Winston, 1978.

Frankl, Viktor. *The Will to Meaning.* New York: World Publishing, 1969.

Frankl, Viktor. *Man's Search for Meaning.* Boston: Beacon Press, 1963.

Hart, Thomas. *Hidden Springs: The Spiritual Dimension of Therapy.* New York: Paulist Press, 1994.

Hull House Revival and *Concerned in Concert.* Compact disks and audiotapes of performances by social work educators. *Hull House Revival,* 1992, features Kathy Bentley, Fred Seidel, and Dean Santos. It is available from Local Folkel Records, P.O. Box 17196, Rochester, NY 14617. *Concerned in Concert,* 1995, features Phil Brown, Mari Ann Graham, Tom Lawson, Susan Martin Robbins, Dean Santos, and Fred Seidel. It is available from HRI Records, 2503 Cherokee Parkway, Louisville, KY 40204.

Kelly, Anthony, and Sandra Sewell. *With Head, Heart and Hand: Dimensions of Community Building,* 3rd ed. Brisbane, Australia: Boolarong Publications, 1988.

Kelsey, Morton. *Caring: How Can We Love One Another?* New York: Paulist Press, 1981.

Moore, Thomas. *Care of the Soul.* New York: Harper-Collins, 1992.

Reid, P. Nelson, and Philip Popple, eds. *The Moral Purposes of Social Work.* Chicago: Nelson-Hall, 1992.

Richan, Willard, and Allan Mendelsohn. *Social Work: The Unloved Profession.* New York: New Viewpoints, 1973.

Robinson, Vera. *Humor and the Health Professions.* Thorofare, N. J.: Slack Inc., 1991.

Shulman, Lawrence. *Interactional Social Work Practice.* Itasca, Ill.: F. E. Peacock, 1991.

Specht, Harry, and Mark Courtney. *Unfaithful Angels: How Social Work Has Abandoned Its Mission.* New York: Macmillan, 1993.

United Nations General Assembly. *Universal Declaration of Human Rights.* New York: United Nations, December 1948.

Whitmyer, Claude. *In the Company of Others: Making Community in the Modern World.* New York: Jeremy Tarcher/Perigee Books, 1993.

3 Merging the Person's Art with the Profession's Science

In addition to achieving a proper blending of one's personal and professional lives, the social worker must combine his or her personal qualities, creative abilities, and social concern with the profession's knowledge in order to help clients enhance their social functioning or prevent social problems from developing. Each person has unique personal qualities that represent the artistic component of social work practice. Professional education cannot teach these artistic features, although it can help the learner identify such strengths and develop the ability to focus and apply them in work with clients. Professional education can also assist the learner in developing a beginning understanding of the knowledge (or science) that is necessary for effective practice. This merging and blending of one's art and the profession's science is initiated in social work education programs, but it is a life-long activity, as social work knowledge is constantly expanding and the worker is being continually changed by life experiences.

The Social Worker as Artist

Art is defined as "a specific skill in adept performance, conceived as requiring the exercise of intuitive faculties that cannot be learned solely by study" (*American Heritage Dictionary* 1978, s.v. "art"). One need not look far to observe successful helpers who rely entirely on their artistic or intuitive abilities. For example, natural helpers, volunteers, and untrained human services providers demonstrate daily that even without formal education they can be helpful in many situations. Similarly, it is not uncommon to see well-educated and knowledgeable people fail in their efforts to serve clients because they lack artistic elements required for their practice.

What factors comprise the art of social work? The authors suggest there are numerous components: the compassion and courage to confront human suffering; the capacity to build a meaningful and productive helping relationship; the creativity to overcome barriers to change; the ability to infuse the change process with hopefulness and energy; the exercise of sound judgment; the appropriate personal values; and the formation of an effective professional style.

Compassion and Courage

A prerequisite to effective social work practice is the social worker's *compassion.* The word *compassion* means to suffer with others; it refers to a willingness to join with and enter into the pain of those who are distressed or troubled. Although most people see themselves as compassionate, it is important to recognize that a high level of compassion is not typical of most people. In fact, it is natural to want to avoid involvement in the pain of others. A social worker who lacks compassion is likely to distance himself or herself from client concerns.

Social work also demands personal *courage,* not in the sense of being bold or daring but rather in being able to confront on a daily basis human suffering and turmoil and, not infrequently, the negative and destructive behaviors of the human species. Aspects of human behavior that come to the social worker's attention are often ones that are unimaginable and unthinkable to most people in our society.

Day after day, case by case, the social worker must be able to respond constructively to people who are directly affected by disease, disability, violence, neglect, sexual abuse, addiction, criminal exploitation, poverty, bizarre and chaotic family life, separation from a loved one, loneliness, abandonment, and other types of human suffering. Moreover, the social worker must be able to respond constructively to people who have, by their acts of commission or omission, directly or indirectly inflicted suffering on others. They must be able to deal with sometimes appalling human problems without being distracted or immobilized by their emotional reactions.

Over time, an individual can develop this fortitude or courage but it is not something that can be learned from books or in a classroom. If it can be learned at all, it is learned from being with those who model an inner strength and a capacity to accept human suffering as part of the human condition and thereby avoid being consumed by anger or frustration. Those who have this courage are able to value and treat with dignity even those who have hurt others.

Professional Relationship

A bond of trust must usually exist before people are willing to risk that difficult human experience—change. Thus, the most fundamental tool of the trade is the use of a *professional relationship* to help people become open to the possibility of change and actively engage in the change process. A positive relationship is a precondition for effective work with individuals, families, or groups of clients, but it is also important in work with the people who make up organizations and communities.

The qualities of a helping relationship are elusive—almost mysterious. For example, what makes it possible for a social worker to somehow enter the life experience of a troubled individual and establish a bond that allows them to work together on making a needed change? Why are clients willing to reveal private information to a stranger? What is it about the presence of a social worker that enables a group of people to take action when they failed to mobilize their resources on previous tries?

The answers are that in all these situations the social worker was able to build and use the power of relationship.

In a critical analysis of casework practice, the question of whether an effective professional relationship is mostly a matter of personality or technique was addressed by Fischer (1978).

> One of the continuing debates in casework and related fields is between those schools of thought which believe that changes in the client are brought about by the professional's use of techniques and those which believe that . . . personality qualities of the worker . . . [are] responsible for the [change]. As research accumulates, it increasingly appears that "personality" and "techniques" both can have measurable, beneficial effects on other human beings. However, to date, only selected personality characteristics, or interpersonal skills of helping people, have been identified as related to successful outcome . . . [including] empathy, nonpossessive warmth, genuineness. (p. 191)

Within many Native American tribes there is a saying: "If you want to understand another person you must first walk a mile in his [or her] moccasins." In other words, one must get inside that person's thoughts, beliefs, and life experiences. But before that is possible, one must first set aside his or her own values, attitudes, and judgments. This ability to take on another's perspective is known as having *empathy.*

Although no one can ever fully appreciate the viewpoint of another person, the social worker needs to get as close as possible to that level of understanding. Empathy is needed, for example, to understand the fear and anger of a battered wife and her possible love and concern for the man who hurt her; to be sensitive to the anger and guilt of an abusive parent; to appreciate the difficulty of a teenager risking criticism by peers for speaking up in a group; or even to hear out the frustrations of an overworked staff member. A capacity for empathy is critical to all social workers—from caseworker to administrator.

Empathy requires an investment of energy; it is difficult to live vicariously—even temporarily—in another person's world. Moreover, it is easier to have empathy for some people than for others. For these reasons, a social worker cannot maintain the same level of empathy for all clients or for the same client at all times. Fatigue and stress, for example, can diminish one's capacity for empathy.

Nonpossessive warmth is a quality of relationship that communicates respect, acceptance, and interest in the well-being of others. But warmth is much more than just saying "I care," although at times, that is important. Warmth is transmitted in many forms of communication, from a reassuring smile to an offer of concrete and tangible assistance. Warmth is a highly individual quality that is expressed differently by each person, but inherent in all expressions of warmth is acceptance and a nonjudgmental attitude.

Linked to warmth and empathy is the quality of *genuineness.* Trite as it may sound, the social worker must behave like a "real" person and must truly like people and care about their well-being. The social worker may know the correct words to say or the proper action to recommend, but the client will assign them little value if the worker appears phony or does not seem to genuinely care.

Creativity

Creative thinking is characterized by the integration of diverse facts and information and the formation of original ideas. Parnes, Noller, and Biondi (1967, 14) describe *creative thinking* as "the association of thoughts, facts, ideas, etc., into a new and relevant configuration, one that has meaning beyond the sum of the parts." Creativity is important because each client's situation is unique and constantly changing. So-called textbook answers to human problems are always strained by this uniqueness. Overspecialization can result in a narrowing of vision and the loss of creativity. Heus and Pincus (1986, 10), for example, argue that "the creative generalist is better prepared [than the specialist] to confront the challenges facing social work."

A social worker with *imagination* can identify a variety of ways to approach and solve a problem, whereas the unimaginative one sees only one or two options—or perhaps none at all. For example, an agency board attempting to improve the accessibility of persons with physical disabilities to public facilities might think only of encouraging local merchants or the city parking control office to create more "handicapped parking" spaces. On the other hand, the imaginative social worker might help the board identify additional ways to address the problem. The number of existing spaces may be adequate; perhaps more effective enforcement of parking restrictions is a better solution. Still another option might be to deputize people with disabilities to ticket an auto illegally parked in a restricted parking space. The imaginative social worker might also encourage the board to examine the possibility of increased public information programs, or expanded public transportation, or any of a dozen other strategies.

Another area in which the social worker must be imaginative is in interpreting and implementing agency policies. Policies are created to serve the typical client, yet people are characterized by infinite variety. Although the social worker cannot ethically (or legally) ignore or subvert agency policy, he or she must find ways to adapt or bend a policy to meet unique client needs. The social worker who is bound by a literal interpretation of "The Manual" is simply not able to make the system work for many clients.

Flexibility is also a dimension of creativity. Helping others change requires an ability to understand the situation from the perspective of all those affected and to continually modify and adapt prior plans and decisions. The social worker making a foster home placement, for example, must have the flexibility to appreciate the often diverse perspectives of biological parents, foster parents, the child, the court, the agency, and even the neighborhood. To align oneself rigidly with any of the affected parties limits the social worker's ability to resolve problems and conflicts.

Practice requires that the social worker be flexible in how he or she relates to clients. At times, one needs to be supportive; at other times, it is necessary to challenge the client; and at still other times, the social worker must be hard nosed, be directive, or exercise legitimate legal or professional authority. The effective social worker must be able to shift from one approach to another and correctly decide when a shift is appropriate.

In addition, the creative social worker must possess the trait of *persistence* (Gelfand 1988)—the capacity to continue on a course of action, despite difficulties and setbacks. Self-discipline and goal directness are needed to translate creative ideas into action. The term *flexible persistence* was coined by McMullan (1976) to emphasize the need for both flexibility and persistence in the problem-solving process.

Hopefulness and Energy

The willingness and motivation of a client to work for change, when the prospect of change is often anxiety producing or painful, is often a reflection of the social worker's ability to communicate the perspective that together the two of them can improve the client's situation. Two characteristics of the social worker that are central to increasing client motivation are hopefulness and energy.

Hopefulness refers to a firm belief and a trust in the basic goodness of people, in their capacity to change in positive ways, and in their willingness to work cooperatively with others for the common good. Clients have typically been unsuccessful when attempting other avenues to address their issues or they would not be seeking professional help. Consequently, they often approach professional services with a carryover of skepticism and despair. Given the serious and intractable nature of many of the situations encountered in practice, the social worker, too, is vulnerable to feelings of discouragement. The worker's hopefulness makes it possible for him or her to approach each practice situation with a genuine sense that this helping effort can make a difference.

Energy may be defined as the capacity to move things along, get results, and bounce back from mistakes and failures. The social worker's energy is needed to activate the client or client group and counteract the client's hesitation. One need not assume the posture of an effervescent cheerleader to communicate energy nor should the worker offer a false sense of optimism. To simply reflect one's willingness to commit time and effort to the change process can encourage clients to also invest themselves in that activity.

Judgment

The nature of the helping process and the uniqueness of every client's situation require that social workers make difficult *judgments,* including assessing client situations, providing alternative solutions, helping plan and conduct change activities, and deciding when to terminate services. Helping also involves making judgments about when the services needed by the client are beyond the capacities of the social worker. Ultimately, professional judgments depend on clear and critical thinking by the social worker.

The qualifier *mature* is often used to describe the type of judgments expected of a social worker. Two definitions of maturity often become mixed in our thinking. One definition relates to having reached an advanced stage of growth. The second relates to the use of careful and wise consideration to arrive at judgments. Sometimes, we assume that chronologically mature people are better at making sound judgments. This is not so. Certainly, life experience presents ample opportunities to gain insight, and if one learns from those experiences, then age and wisdom are surely associated. However, some of us are apparently slow learners and the lessons of life have contributed little to our ability to make wise judgments.

Similarly, providing human services over many years affords opportunities to test and refine one's ability to make wise practice decisions. However, the repetition of an experience by itself does not assure that the social worker will gain insight. To grow in practice wisdom, the social worker must be analytical, reflective, and open to learning from successes as well as failures.

Personal Values

The reasons one might enter social work are varied, but the motive is almost always a concern for others and a desire to make the world a better place. No one should have to apologize for such a motive, since most would agree that living a life that makes a difference is what really matters. However, it is important to remember that when a person becomes an instrument for change, there is in that person's mind some notion about what constitutes a desirable and good life for people. In other words, social workers—like all people—possess ***personal values.*** *Values* are one's beliefs about how things ought to be and what is right and worthwhile.

The dilemma arises when there is a difference of opinion over what is "right." The social worker's view of the "right" outcome or the best course of action may be different from the client's, and both may differ from those who fund and sanction the agency that employs the social worker. Is it "right," for example, to encourage a single mother to find employment if having a job necessitates placing her children in day care? Is it "right" to refer a woman to an abortion clinic? Is it "right" to withhold further financial assistance from a client who has violated an agency rule by not reporting income from a part-time job? Is it "right" to force homeless people to reside in shelters against their will? Whose "right" is right? Whose values are to be followed?

Given that one person's values and conscience cannot serve as absolute guides for all others to follow, is it appropriate to expect the client to conform to what the social worker or his or her agency considers desirable or the right thing to do? Logic would answer no, but there is reason for believing that many clients feel pressured to go along with what they think the agency or social worker expects. If a social worker accepts the principle of maximizing clients' ***self-determination,*** he or she must allow clients to make the decisions and to move toward outcomes they believe are most desirable. And apart from those values codified in law and universally recognized moral principles, the social worker should hold his or her personal beliefs and values in abeyance in favor of client self-determination.

This is not to suggest that the social worker is always to remain neutral with regard to client behaviors or decisions that are socially irresponsible, self-destructive, or harmful to others. A social worker is of little help to a client if he or she sidesteps or avoids discussing moral and ethical issues directly related to a client's concerns. Laws, basic moral principles, and even the rules of civility do matter. They are an essential part of our social fabric and of life in a community and they are an important aspect of the client's social functioning. However, when such issues are discussed, it must be done in ways that are nonjudgmental and respectful of the client.

Prerequisite to developing a ***nonjudgmental attitude*** is a knowledge of one's own belief system. As new value conflicts arise, it is important for the social worker to consider what he or she believes about the situation and why. It is useful to discuss values and various moral dilemmas with family, friends, and colleagues to obtain alternate views that might contribute to refinements in one's thinking.

The social worker's personal values should be compatible with the values of the social work profession. If these two value systems are in conflict, one of two things is likely to happen: (1) the worker goes through the motions of being a professional social worker but because his or her heart is not in it, the lack of genuineness is apparent to both clients and colleagues, or (2) the worker rejects the profession's values and principles as a guiding force and responds to clients entirely on the basis of personal beliefs and values. In both instances, the client and the employing agency lose the benefit of the social work perspective.

What are the values that characterize professional social work? In what is perhaps the most thorough study of social work values, Abbott (1988) identifies four basic values inherent in the National Association of Social Worker's public social policy statements (NASW 1994), the NASW *Code of Ethics* (NASW 1993), and the Council on Social Work Education's "Curriculum Policy Statement" (CSWE 1992). These core values are:

- *Respect for basic rights.* All people should have equal access to resources and services that will help them accomplish their goals in life, prevent or alleviate problems, and realize their full potential as human beings.
- *A sense of social responsibility.* Social institutions such as the family, education, government, and social welfare should be humane and responsive to human needs.
- *Commitment to individual freedom.* Recognizing that there is great variation among people, society should minimize the social controls it imposes on its members.
- *Support for self-determination.* People should have the right to make their own choices; those who do not have freedom to make their own life choices must be empowered to do so whenever possible.

Abbott found that the values of social workers were similar to those of psychologists but different from teachers, physicians, and nurses and quite different from people employed in business and industry. Since social work practice involves the use of interventions and theoretical frameworks that have implicit value dimensions or are selected on the basis of value considerations, it behooves the social worker to examine frequently his or her own commitment to these four basic values.

Professional Style

In the final analysis, it is the social worker himself or herself who is the instrument of change and, as such, each social worker has an unique style of practice. According to Siporin (1993, 257), "The social worker's personality, craftsmanship, and artistry in the application of knowledge and skill are articulated through professional and personal styles." One's style can open up and facilitate the helping process or close it down.

Style is expressed in how social workers relate to clients—their energy, creativity, wisdom, and judgment, as well as their passion and commitment to particular social issues. In addition, their uniqueness is expressed in their clothing, hairstyle, posture, speech, and in a hundred other choices and behaviors that send out messages about who they are and what they believe about themselves and others.

One's professional style must be appropriate to the situation, the clients served, and the agency setting. For example, a social worker dressed in a three-piece suit will surely have difficulty establishing rapport with a group of street people, yet may be highly effective in persuading a city council to create needed services for people living on the street. Similarly, a worker might dress casually when working with children and families but should dress more formally when making a court appearance in their behalf.

Know thyself is an important admonition for the social worker. Continuing introspection helps the social worker monitor the impact of his or her style. Knowing oneself is never easy, however. It is helpful for the social worker to step back periodically and examine how others perceive his or her style. Clues from clients, family, friends, colleagues, and supervisors are helpful in making these assessments.

A social worker's practice style emerges as he or she balances individuality with the behaviors required for practice. Inherent in professional socialization is pressure to conform. The need to balance expectations of profession, agency, and clients with one's individuality is an issue for every social worker. The social worker must ask: How far am I willing to compromise my individuality and personal preferences in order to serve my clients and meet agency expectations? So long as clients are properly served and not alienated or harmed, one has considerable latitude. In fact, the profession is enriched by the varied styles of its members.

The Social Worker as Scientist

Social workers must use both heart and head when interacting with clients and providing services. With artistic abilities as a foundation, the social worker builds professional capacity by drawing on a knowledge base and learning to use a repertoire of techniques. Some of the knowledge is borrowed from other disciplines, especially the social and behavioral sciences, and some has developed out of the application of the scientific method to social work concerns. In addition, a form of knowledge called *practice wisdom* is derived from the collective experiences of several generations of social workers.

One dictionary (*American Heritage* 1979) defines **science** as "the observation, identification, description, experimental investigation and theoretical explanation of natural phenomena." McCain and Segal (1973, 11) explain that science is primarily an attitude toward problem solution; a scientist is distinguished not by what is believed but rather why he or she believes it. The beliefs of a scientifically minded social worker are tentative rather than dogmatic and are based on data, not on authority, faith, or personal preference.

A profession is considered scientific when it uses the scientific method in the development of its knowledge and practices. The *scientific method* is a particular approach to the study of phenomena and the building of knowledge. In its most rigorous applications, it involves carefully defining and isolating the problem under study, precisely defining all concepts and terminology used, formulating hypotheses to be tested, following appropriate sampling procedures and an established protocol for gathering data, using control and experimental groups for comparison, using valid and reliable tools of measurement, and, finally, submitting the research findings to scrutiny by professional peers so they can replicate the study and either confirm or repudiate the findings. Although the use of the scientific method is not the only source of knowledge, it is one that helps to minimize errors of judgment caused by bias and subjectivity.

The application of the scientific method is difficult within social work because many of the problems that concern social workers cannot be easily quantified, client confidentiality prohibits some studies, and identical client situations seldom exist for rigorous comparison and testing. Also, for ethical reasons, social workers and agencies cannot assign vulnerable, at-risk clients (e.g., an abused child) to a no-treatment or control group. Single-subject designs may be used or the relative effectiveness of two or more interventions may be studied, but seldom can the effectiveness of an intervention be directly compared to doing nothing at all. Further complicating the use of the scientific method is the fact that the various forms of intervention typically share several common characteristics (e.g., a worker-client relationship), and for that reason it is often difficult to determine the true impact of a single factor or variable.

Because so much of social work is based on values, the profession can never be a completely scientific discipline, nor should it. In addition to the focus on person-in-environment, it is the profession's values and philosophy that make its contribution among the helping professions unique. Nevertheless, the social worker must strive to be scientific in his or her thinking.

Social work is not a science to the same degree as, for example, physics, botany, or chemistry. However, social work makes use of scientific knowledge from other fields and increasingly uses the scientific method in developing its theoretical frameworks and evaluating its effectiveness. Social work can be said to be scientific in the following ways.

- It gathers, organizes, and analyzes data that describe the social functioning of people.
- It uses its observations, experiences, and formal studies to create new techniques, formulate new practice guidelines, and develop new programs and policies.
- It uses data as the basis for formulating propositions and conceptual frameworks that guide social work interventions.

- It objectively examines its interventions and their impact on the social functioning of people.
- It exchanges and critically evaluates the ideas, studies, and practices described by others in the profession.

Kadushin and Martin (1988) explain that, like many other professionals, the social worker is more of a technologist than a scientist. "The doctor, as technologist, uses the findings of the biologist, the engineer uses the findings of the physicist and the social worker uses the findings of the sociologist. . . . A social scientist seeks only to understand the world of the client. The social worker, as a technologist, seeks to change it" (p. 3).

In order to facilitate the process of change, the social worker draws on knowledge related to social conditions and problems, social policies and programs, social phenomena, the social work profession, and various practice theories.

Knowledge of Social Conditions and Social Problems

Social workers must understand the problems commonly brought to the attention of social agencies and how human problems cluster together and overlap. In discussing the problems of adolescent crime, school-age childrearing, school dropout, poverty, unemployment, drug abuse, family violence, and so on, Schorr (1989) states the following:

> Each can be studied separately, but in the real world they interact, reinforce one another, and often cluster together in the same individuals. Increasingly, the individuals also cluster [together in families] and the damage that begins in childhood and becomes so visible in adolescence reverberates throughout a neighborhood as part of an intergenerational cycle of social devastation. (p. 15)

The interrelatedness of human problems is an inescapable fact.

As background for dealing with social problems, the social worker should be familiar with factors that contribute to the overall quality of life on this planet. Some of these are clean air and water, a safe and sufficient supply of food and energy, opportunities for employment, worldwide political and economic conditions that support personal freedom and social justice, the wise use of technology to improve human welfare, success in controlling communicable illnesses and promoting wellness, and a world free of racial hatred and war. In short, the thoughtful social worker possesses a world view.

Social work practice and related social programs and services are particularly influenced by decisions at the national level. When practicing in the United States, for example, the social worker must understand the beliefs, values, and organization of U.S. society and its governmental, political, and economic systems.

Although some social conditions and problems are national and international in scope, others are a function of regional and state characteristics. For example, unemployment caused by fluctuating oil prices is most seriously experienced in the oil-producing states such as Oklahoma, Texas, Louisiana, and Alaska. The market success of Japanese automobiles affects most directly the economy of auto-producing states such as Michigan. Drought conditions or low prices for farm products directly affect people in the agricultural states of the midwest or Rocky Mountains.

Finally, some social conditions impact local communities but not whole states or regional areas. The well-publicized crime rate in Washington, D.C., and the high incidence of juvenile gang activity in Los Angeles have dramatically affected those cities, whereas towns a few miles away are relatively free of those problems. Rural areas may also experience locality-relevant social and economic problems caused by, for example, a decline in available timber in Montana and Oregon or the closing of a small town's single industry in Kansas.

Knowledge of Social Policies and Social Programs

When social conditions are perceived as either harmful to people or a threat to the community or the society, social policies may be formulated and social programs created to help those in need or to address the threatening problem. Essentially, a *social policy* is a set of principles, usually expressed in law and governmental regulation, that guides the assignment of specific benefits and opportunities or the regulation of behavior. Social policies and programs tend to develop around major problems. Thus, we have policy clusters related to areas such as health care, mental illness, crime, child welfare, education, disabilities, old age, poverty, unemployment, and so forth. Social workers must be familiar with the policies that most strongly influence the programs through which they work and understand their effect on the clients served by those programs.

Social programs reflect existing social policies, and the policies, in turn, reflect the values, beliefs, and judgments of those who establish policies. For example, beliefs regarding the worth of the individual, the responsibilities people have for each other, and the role of communities and governments to address human problems determine what, if any, social policies and programs are developed.

Social programs consist of three major elements: organizational structure, benefits or services, and providers. Social programs must be delivered through some form of *organization* or *agency*. No matter what service or benefit is provided, there must be an organizational and administrative structure that determines who is eligible, how it will be provided, who will provide it, and what costs are acceptable. Thus, social workers must be knowledgeable about the fiscal, administrative, and organizational aspects of service delivery.

The *benefits and services* provided by a social program can take the form of social provisions, social services, and/or social action (these terms were explained in Chapter 1). The social worker must understand the programs offered by his or her own agency and be familiar with those provided by the agencies to which clients might be referred.

Social programs require *providers,* people who are in direct contact with the client, or the consumers of the services and benefits. Providers may be volunteers, but most often they are paid professionals. Social work is only one of the professions that deliver services and benefits. Teachers, psychologists, physicians, nurses, occupational therapists, and others provide a wide array of human services. Each has its own focus but there are areas of overlap. Understanding the competencies of each profession, as well as the dynamics of teamwork and interprofessional cooperation, are important aspects of the social worker's knowledge base.

Knowledge of Social Phenomena

Given their focus on the social functioning of people as an outcome of person-in-environment interaction, social workers are especially concerned with interactions between and among people and interactions between people and the systems that deliver social programs. Therefore, they must understand social phenomena and the various levels of person-in-environment interaction. As described in Chapter 1, each level (i.e., micro, mezzo, and macro) varies in interpersonal intensity and closeness.

In addition to understanding the interrelatedness of the various system levels and the kind of situations being addressed in the social worker's practice, the worker must understand the individual person, for which a knowledge of physical and psychological development (including both normal and abnormal functioning) is essential. The social worker must also understand families and other households. The family has long been a dominant point of intervention for social workers, and knowledge of family dynamics is critically important. With the increase of nontraditional family structures, understanding alternate living and intimacy patterns has become especially important. Further, a considerable amount of practice takes place with small groups, including support groups, therapeutic groups, and committees. Thus, the social worker needs to understand small group behaviors and processes.

The social worker must also understand cultural and religious differences and personal and social issues related to ethnic identity, cross-cultural interaction, and the impact of racism and discrimination. Since people are influenced by the neighborhoods and communities in which they live, the social worker must be familiar with, for example, theories of decision making, intergroup conflict, and community change. In addition, he or she needs to understand prevailing community beliefs and attitudes related to ethnicity, race relations, gender roles, aging, sexual orientation, and disabling conditions.

Most social work practice takes place under the auspices of a formal organization such as a social agency, school, hospital, or correctional facility. The social worker must understand how clients and other members of the community view these organizations and how people are affected by the behavior of organizations. To work effectively within an agency or program, a social worker must understand organizational development, structure, methods of operation, and communication patterns. Indeed, the social worker is required to possess substantial knowledge regarding the people and organizations with which he or she works.

Knowledge of the
Social Work Profession

The social worker must understand the functions that a profession performs in society and the benefits, as well as the responsibilities, that accrue from this status. When society grants professions the authority to provide the specific services that fall within their domain, in essence, a monopoly is given to that profession to determine the qualifications of its members (e.g., educational and experiential prerequisites for membership). In return, the profession is charged with monitoring and policing its members to protect the public against abuses of that monopoly.

A profession is not so much an occupational activity as it is a means or a social mechanism for controlling an occupation. According to Hardcastle (1983)

> A profession exercises authority over an occupation, and the public recognizes the right of the profession to exercise that control. The rationale for this arrangement, instead of relying upon marketplace authority, stems from other attributes of a profession: a definable, systematic body of knowledge and specialized skills; a regulatory code of ethics; a professional culture or community; and most basically, a service ethic or commitment. This last attribute provides the justification for professional authority and peer regulation. (p. 826)

Social workers have been ambivalent about professionalizing their discipline. They have devoted considerable effort to identifying their knowledge base, creating professional organizations, staking out their domain, specifying criteria for identifying qualified social workers, and taking other steps to become a valued profession. At the same time, they have been uncomfortable about the inherent elitism that characterizes any profession, and have struggled with the conflict between assuring quality services to clients and keeping access to the profession open to as many people as possible.

Professional standards, as defined by the NASW, represent an important feature that has emerged from the professionalization of social work. These standards help both the consumers of social work practice (agencies and the general public) and prospective social workers by designating necessary preparation for various practice activities and specifying personnel standards for organizations that employ social workers. This classification system identifies the requisite educational and experiential preparation at four levels.

1. *Basic professional.* Requires a baccalaureate degree from a social work program accredited by the Council on Social Work Education (CSWE).
2. *Specialized professional.* Requires a master's degree from a social work program accredited by CSWE.
3. *Independent professional.* Requires an accredited MSW and at least two years of post-master's experience under appropriate professional supervision.
4. *Advanced professional.* Requires special theoretical, practice, administrative or policy proficiency or ability to conduct advanced research or studies in social welfare; usually demonstrated through a doctoral degree in social work or closely related social science discipline. (NASW 1981, 9)

In its complete form, this classification system elaborates the knowledge and skill the social worker at each level should possess, the kind of responsibilities that might appropriately be undertaken, and the variations in the difficulty of practice activities due to the complexity of the situation, vulnerability of the client, and potential consequences of the practice activity.

A second set of standards was developed by the NASW (1971) to guide social agencies in establishing ***personnel practices*** that support good social work practice. It includes such items as personnel selection, staff development, worker evaluation, promotion, fringe benefits, and termination of employment. An agency that does not follow these guidelines may be the subject of a complaint and, if found to be in violation after an investigation by the local NASW chapter and the National Committee on Inquiry, may be placed on the NASW's published list of agencies that have failed to operate in compliance with these standards. A study by the National Committee on Inquiry indicated that of those cases of violations of personnel standards that were substantiated through a review process between 1983 and 1993, more than half involved unfair performance evaluations, discharge without notice, or the worker being denied a grievance process (NASW 1995).

It is essential that the social worker possess a thorough understanding of a third set of professional standards—the ***ethical principles*** that guide practice. *Ethics* are concerned with what is morally right or, in a profession, what is the correct course of professional action. Perhaps no single document is more important to the practice of a social worker than the NASW *Code of Ethics* (1993).

When a social worker joins the NASW, he or she pledges to practice within the profession's ethical code (the *Code of Ethics* can be found in Chapter 10). The NASW uses the *Code* as a standard for determining if charges of unethical practice have a basis. If accusations are made that an individual worker has violated the *Code,* the local NASW chapter and NASW's National Committee on Inquiry may review the complaint and possibly apply negative sanctions to that social worker. The most typical violations of the *Code of Ethics* that were substantiated through this monitoring process involved exploitation of a worker's professional relationship with clients for personal gain, with sexual activity the leading violation (NASW 1995).

Knowledge for Social Work Practice

In a profession such as social work, it is not possible to separate theory from practice or concept from action. In fact, practice is the process of using knowledge and applying theory in order to bring about specific types of change. A practice uninformed by theory tends to become repetitive and sterile, whereas theory uninformed by the realities of practice tends to be merely interesting and usually irrelevant.

The many theories, models, and perspectives discussed in the social work literature can all be considered conceptual frameworks. A ***conceptual framework*** is composed of a coherent set of concepts, beliefs, values, propositions, assumptions, hypotheses, and principles. Such a framework can be thought of as an outline of ideas that help one to understand people, how people function, and how people change. These frameworks are important because they have utility. For example:

- They provide a structure for analyzing complex and often highly emotional human problems and situations.
- They organize information, beliefs, and assumptions into a meaningful whole.
- They provide a rationale for action and decision making.
- They promote a systematic, orderly, and predictable approach to work with people.
- They facilitate communication among professionals.

In their practice, social workers use a variety of theories, models, and perspectives. Although these terms have somewhat different meanings, they are often lumped together and simply termed *theory*. However, it is helpful to make some distinctions as to types and usage of terms used to describe these conceptual frameworks (see Figure 3.1). Howe (1987, 166) explains that, broadly speaking, there are theories of social work and theories for social work. The ***theories of social work*** focus on the profession and explain its purpose, domain, and character within a society. They explain what the profession is all about, who it is for, and why it functions as it does. By contrast, the ***theories for social work*** focus on clients and helping activities. They explain human behavior, the social environment, how change occurs, and how change can be facilitated by the social worker in order to benefit clients.

In their work with clients, social workers make use of orienting theories and practice frameworks. Mailick (1990) explains that ***orienting theories*** describe and explain behavior and how and why certain problems develop. They provide important background knowledge and are usually borrowed from other disciplines such as biology, psychology, sociology, economics, cultural anthropology, and the like. Examples include the various theories related to human development, personality, family systems, socialization, organizational functioning, and political power, as well as

**FIGURE 3.1
Types of
Conceptual
Frameworks**

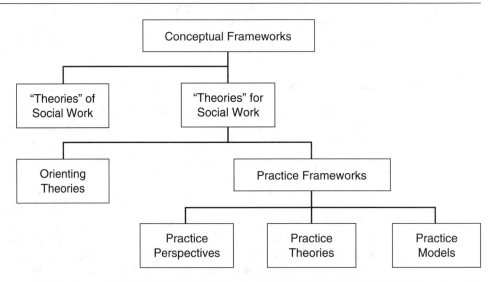

theories related to specific types of problems such as poverty, family violence, mental illness, teen pregnancy, crime, and racial discrimination. Orienting theories, by themselves, provide little guidance on how to bring about change. For such guidance one must look to a second category called *practice frameworks.* There are three types: practice perspectives, practice theories, and practice models.

The most overarching type of practice framework is a practice perspective. A *practice perspective* can be described as a conceptual lens through which one views human behavior and social structures and which, simultaneously, guide the selection of intervention strategies. Like a camera lens, a practice perspective serves to focus on or magnify a particular feature while placing other features in the background. Two perspectives, the general systems perspective and the ecosystems perspective, are commonly used in social work for assessing the relationships between people and their environment. Others, such as the generalist, feminist, and ethnic-sensitive practice perspectives, focus more on the philosophy and processes to be followed in working toward change.

A second type of framework is a *practice theory,* which offers both an explanation of certain behaviors or situations and broad guidelines about how those behaviors or situations can be changed. A practice theory serves as a road map for an intervention that will bring about a certain type of change. Most practice theories are rooted in one or more orienting theories. An example is the psychosocial approach that is based primarily on psychodynamic theory and ego psychology. Another is behavioral therapy that is based on theories of learning.

A distinction is made here between a practice theory and a practice model, the third type of practice framework. A *practice model* is a set of concepts and principles used to guide certain interventions. However, in contrast to a practice theory, a model is not tied to a particular explanation of behavior. For example, crisis intervention is viewed as a practice model rather than a practice theory because the action steps of this intervention are not tied to any one explanation of crisis situations. For the same reason, the task-centered approach is termed a model rather than a practice theory. Most often, a model develops out of actual experience or experimentation rather than evolving from a particular theory of behavior.

The term *model* is also used when referring to a conceptual framework that can be borrowed from one field and applied to another. For example, when someone refers to an approach to change based on the medical model, he or she is referring to activity that mirrors the approach used in scientific medicine—one that places emphasis on the practitioner as an expert and an authority figure, careful gathering and categorization of data (study), the use of a classification system to properly label the problem (diagnosis), and an intervention (treatment) dictated by the diagnosis. Similarly, social workers may refer to the legal model as a way of describing an approach to social action and client advocacy—one that emphasizes competition among adversaries and a conflict strategy. Many innovations in practice are spread from agency to agency by borrowing the key principles of a successful program. Thus, we hear such terms as the "Homebuilders Model," the self-help model, the grass-roots model, the 12-step model, the case-management model, and so on.

It is rare for a social worker to use a single orienting theory or a single practice framework. Rather, most social workers utilize a wide variety of orienting theories and a set of compatible and complementary perspectives, theories, and models. Such a combination can be termed one's *theoretical frame of reference* or *theoretical orientation to practice.*

This book presumes that social workers use many of the same techniques and guidelines, regardless of practice perspective, theory, or model. A *technique* is a set of actions directed at accomplishing a particular outcome. Although a worker's frame of reference might lead him or her to select particular techniques, they are, for the most part, independent of specific theories. *Guidelines,* on the other hand, are typically a mix of prescriptions (do this) and proscriptions (avoid this). (More precise definitions of these two terms appear in the Preface.)

Conclusion

In order to perform effectively, the social worker uses a combination of art and science. It is recognized that a worker brings certain intangibles to the practice situation that affect process and outcome—the art encompassed in building relationships, creative thinking, compassion and courage, hopefulness and energy, using sound judgment, and committing to appropriate values. At the same time, the social worker must combine his or her artistic abilities with the profession's knowledge and scientific base. Without art, the knowledge base is of little value. But without the knowledge, the art is of limited effectiveness.

The social worker merges his or her art and science into a practice framework. Chapter 6 provides descriptions of over two dozen selected practice perspectives, theories, and models that commonly are included in practice frameworks. The intent is not to provide a comprehensive description of any of these frameworks nor is it to provide a complete listing of all those available to the social worker. Rather, the chapter is intended to supply enough information to suggest how practice frameworks differ and what might be required for constructing one's own theoretical orientation to practice.

SELECTED BIBLIOGRAPHY

Abbott, Ann A. *Professional Choices: Values at Work.* Silver Spring, Md.: NASW, 1988.

American Heritage Dictionary of the English Language. New College Edition. Boston: Houghton Mifflin, 1978.

Council on Social Work Education. *Handbook of Accreditation Standards and Procedures,* rev. ed. Alexandria, Va.: CSWE, 1994.

Fischer, Joel. *Effective Casework Practice: An Eclectic Approach.* New York: McGraw-Hill, 1978.

Gelfand, Bernard. *The Creative Practitioner: Creative Theory and Method for the Helping Services.* New York: Haworth, 1988.

Hardcastle, David. "Certification, Licensure and Other Forms of Regulation." In *Handbook of Clinical Social Work,* edited by Aaron Rosenblatt and Diana Waldfogel. San Francisco: Jossey-Bass, 1983.

Heus, Michael, and Allen Pincus. *The Creative Generalist: A Guide to Social Work Practice.* Barneveld, Wis.: Micamar, 1986.

Howe, David. *An Introduction to Social Work Theory.* Aldershot, Honts, England: Wildwood House, 1987.

Kadushin, Alfred, and Judith Martin. *Child Welfare Services,* 4th ed. New York: Macmillan, 1988.

Loewenberg, Frank, and Ralph Dolgoff. *Ethical Decisions for Social Work Practice,* 4th ed. Itasca, Ill.: F. E. Peacock, 1992.

Mailick, Mildred. "Social Work Practice with Adolescents: Theoretical Saturation." In *Serious Play: Creativity and Innovation in Social Work,* edited by Harold Weissman. Silver Spring, Md.: NASW, 1990.

McCain, Garvin, and Erwin Segal. *The Game of Science.* Monterey, Calif.: Brooks/Cole, 1973.

McMullan, W. E. "Creative Individuals: Paradoxical Personages." *Journal of Creative Behavior* 10 (Fourth Quarter, 1976): 265–275.

National Association of Social Workers. *Overview of a Decade of Adjudication.* Washington, D.C.: NASW, 1995.

———. *Social Work Speaks: NASW Policy Statements,* 3rd ed. Washington, D.C.: NASW Press, 1994.

———. *NASW Code of Ethics,* rev. Washington, D.C.: NASW, 1993.

———. *NASW Standards for the Classification of Social Work Practice.* Washington, D.C.: NASW, 1981.

———. *NASW Standards for Social Work Personnel Policies,* Washington, D.C.: NASW, 1971.

Parnes, S. J., R. Noller, and A. Biondi. *A Guide to Creative Action.* New York: Charles Scribner's Sons, 1967.

Schorr, Lisbeth. *Within Our Reach: Breaking the Cycle of Disadvantage.* New York: Doubleday, 1989.

Siporin, Max. "The Social Worker's Style." *Clinical Social Work Journal,* 21 (Fall 1993): 257–270.

Part II The Building Blocks of Social Work Practice

Once the social worker is personally prepared to engage in practice, several other factors will shape the nature of that practice. These factors are (1) the roles and functions performed in an agency and with a specific client, (2) the basic principles that should guide each social worker's approach to practice activities, (3) the conceptual frameworks that direct the manner in which clients are served, and (4) the social worker's competence in leading clients through the various phases of the change process. An understanding of these four building blocks is prerequisite to the selection and application of the techniques and guidelines described in Parts III and IV of this book.

In Chapter 4, "The Roles and Functions Performed by Social Workers," attention is directed to 10 dominant roles typically performed by social workers. One can readily discern that social work differs from other helping professions simply by examining these roles. Although other disciplines perform some of these roles and associated functions, the collection of roles (e.g., broker, advocate, case manager, social change agent) reflects social work's breadth and its emphasis on helping people interact more effectively with their environments.

Chapter 5, "Guiding Principles for Social Workers," describes 21 fundamental principles that should guide the social worker's practice. These principles provide the "bottom line" for consistently offering appropriate and effective service to clients. To many social workers, the phrases used to communicate these principles have becomes clichés: "Begin where the client is," "Help the client help himself (or herself)," "Guide the process, not the client." The casual use of these phrases too often masks the wisdom of these principles.

A social worker selects and uses specific techniques that have been individualized to the needs and situation of the client or client group being served and to the resources that apply on the client's problem of concern. In helping the client formulate a plan, the worker draws on various conceptual frameworks that provide an overall strategy for the change process. Chapter 6, "Practice Frameworks for Social Work," identifies criteria one should consider in selecting practice frameworks. It also highlights the central features of nearly 25 perspectives, theories, or models that are commonly used in social work practice. Although no one social worker is expected to master all of these conceptual frameworks, each should be familiar with these possible approaches to practice in order to help clients connect with social workers who are competent to use the most appropriate frameworks for any specific practice situation.

Finally, practice research indicates that a key element in successful practice is the social worker's ability to systematically guide the change process. Assisting clients in becoming involved in and committed to addressing their issues, carefully assessing the factors that have created the need for social work service, planning a strategy to make that change, carrying out that plan, evaluating the success of that activity, and carefully terminating the service are all elements of a sound change process. Chapter 7, "The Change Process in Social Work Practice," outlines the essentials of the change process and makes the case for needing to appreciate the complexity of this process.

By examining these building blocks for social work practice, the foundation is established for the rest of the book. It is within this context that the social worker should select and apply the techniques and guidelines described in Chapters 8 through 15.

4 The Roles and Functions Performed by Social Workers

Every occupational category (e.g., engineer, teacher, farmer) is expected to perform a set of *occupational roles.* For example, when functioning as a physician, an individual is expected to conduct tests to diagnose a patient's condition, prescribe treatment, and monitor the results. Similarly, when functioning as a social worker, an individual is expected to think and behave in a manner consistent with the expectations of a social worker. It is important to note that these work-related expectations are determined by the position, not by the individual who happens to be occupying that position. Although there is individuality in how a person performs an occupational role, there are also boundaries that govern what can and cannot be done.

Associated with the roles are a number of *job functions* that can best be described as the tasks or activities one performs within a specific role. This chapter describes 10 roles and nearly 40 distinct functions expected of social workers. In the course of a day, most social workers engage in many practice roles. However, one's personal preferences, talents, or job duties may lead to specialized practice using a more limited number of these roles and functions. To fully appreciate social work, then, it is important to understand the roles typically performed by social workers and the job functions they are expected to perform.

Defining Professional Roles

The roles and job functions expected of the members of a given profession (e.g., physical therapy, nursing, social work, etc.) are defined by social norms and historical traditions, by the legal codes and administrative regulations that sanction the activity, and by agency policy and procedure. Professional roles, in effect, are the operationalization of a profession's domain (see Chapter 1).

Depending on the agency setting and work assignments, the social worker may perform only one of these roles but is more likely to engage in several. In any practice role, the performance of several distinct functions may be required. Similarly, a specific job function may be applied in the performance of more than one role. For

57

example, one might engage in an assessment of a client's situation in the role of a broker of human services, a counselor or clinician, and a case manager. In the following pages, however, each function is described only once.

I. The Social Worker as Broker

Purpose.   To link clients to appropriate human services and other resources.

Description.   Social work's particular emphasis among the helping professions is to assist people in relating to their social environment. That places the social worker in the position of being the professional person most likely to facilitate linkage between client and community resources (i.e., to bring together a person needing a service and a provider of that service). To carry out the **broker role,** the social worker identifies client needs, assesses their motivation and capacity to use various resources, and helps them gain access to the most appropriate resources.

As a broker of human services, the social worker must be knowledgeable about the various services and programs available, maintain an up-to-date assessment of each one's strengths and limitations, and understand the procedures for accessing those resources. These resources may include social provisions (e.g., money, food, clothing, and housing) and/or social services (e.g., counseling, therapy, group interaction experiences, and rehabilitative services).

Functions

Client Situation Assessment.   The first step in brokering is to understand thoroughly and accurately the needs and abilities of the client or clients. An effective broker should be skilled at assessing such factors as the clients' vulnerability, culture, resources, verbal ability, emotional stability, intelligence, and commitment to change.

Resource Assessment.   The social worker must assess the various resources available to meet client needs. For his or her own agency, as well as for other community agencies, the social worker must be familiar with what is offered, the quality of staff, the general eligibility requirements, and the costs of those services. Additionally, the social worker must know the best way to help clients gain access to those resources.

Referral.   The process of connecting the client to a resource involves preparing both sides for the initial meeting and monitoring the interaction. Referral requires that the social worker make a judgment regarding the motivation and ability of the clients to follow through and the likelihood that the resource will accept the client for service. Depending on these judgments, the social worker will be more or less active in the referral process. A proper referral entails a follow-up activity wherein the worker checks to assure the client-resource connection is working to meet the client's needs. If there has been a breakdown, further service may be warranted.

Service System Linkage.   Brokering requires that the social worker facilitate continuing interaction between various segments of the service delivery system. To strengthen the linkage among agencies, programs and professionals, the social worker may engage in networking to establish communication channels, negotiating resource sharing, and/or participating in interagency planning, information exchange, and coordination activities.

Information Giving.   Brokering often requires the transmittal of information to clients or community groups. As a repository of knowledge about the service delivery system, the social worker helps others by sharing this knowledge. Also, the social worker may make the general public aware of gaps between available services and needs.

2. The Social Worker as Advocate

Purpose.   To assist clients in upholding their rights to receive resources and services or to actively support causes intended to change programs and policies that have a negative effect on individual clients or client groups.

Description.   At the heart of social work is advocacy. This role is fundamental to social work's mission and is clearly embodied in the *Code of Ethics* (NASW 1993).

- VI.P.2. The social worker should act to ensure that all persons have access to the resources, services, and opportunities they require.
- VI.P.7. The social worker should advocate [for] changes in policy and legislation to improve social conditions and promote social justice.

Mickelson (1995) defines social work ***advocacy*** as "the act of directly representing, defending, intervening, supporting, or recommending a course of action on behalf of one or more individuals, groups, or communities with the goal of securing or retaining social justice" (p. 95). Social workers must balance their methods of advocacy with the principles of maximizing client self-determination and client participation in the change process (see Chapter 5). To the extent possible, advocacy should take the form of assisting clients to be their own advocates.

Functions

Client or Case Advocacy.   A common goal in this type of advocacy is to assure that the services or resources to which an individual client is entitled are, in fact, received. Such advocacy efforts may be directed toward one's own agency or to others in the human services network. Critical steps include gathering information and determining if the client is, in fact, entitled to the desired service. If so, negotiation, mediation, and, if necessary, more strident and confrontational tactics are used to secure the service. The client is helped to make use of available appeal procedures and, in some instances, to take legal action against the agency or service provider.

Needless to say, case advocacy is not usually popular within one's own agency or with the community service system. Nevertheless, advocacy is a necessary function performed by social workers. What is right is not always popular. The social worker should be prepared for negative responses to advocacy activities.

Class Advocacy.   The social worker must often serve as an advocate for groups of clients or a segment of the population that have a common problem or concern. Typically, class advocacy entails action intended to remove obstacles or barriers that restrict a class or category of people from realizing their civil rights or receiving entitlements or benefits due them. It usually requires efforts aimed at changing agency regulations, social policies, or laws. Consequently, class advocacy requires activity within the political and legislative arena and building coalitions with organizations that are concerned about the same issue.

3. The Social Worker as Teacher

Purpose.   To prepare clients with knowledge and skills necessary to prevent problems or enhance social functioning.

Description.   Much of social work practice involves teaching clients or client groups to deal with troublesome life situations or to anticipate and prevent crises. Some of the knowledge the social worker has gained through education and experience is shared with the client. This is empowering to clients. In the *Social Work Dictionary*, Barker (1995, s.v. "educator role") defines this *teaching role* as "the responsibility to teach clients necessary adaptive skills . . . by providing relevant information in a way that is understandable to the client, offering advice and suggestions, identifying alternatives and their probable consequences, modeling behaviors, teaching problem-solving techniques, and clarifying perceptions."

A fundamental purpose of social work practice is to help clients change dysfunctional behavior and learn effective patterns of social interaction. This may require teaching clients to adhere to the various rules or laws and norms of society, modify their immediate environment, develop social skills, learn role functioning, and gain insights into their own behavior. The teaching may occur informally during one-on-one interviews or in more structured educational activities such as presentations and workshops. The teaching method selected is based on an assessment of the readiness and ability of the clients to learn.

Functions
Teach Social and Daily Living Skills.   Teaching skills in conflict resolution, money management, use of public transportation, adjusting to new living arrangements, personal care and hygiene, and effective communication are examples of activities regularly engaged in by some social workers.

Facilitate Behavior Change.   The social worker may use intervention approaches such as role modeling, values clarification, and behavior modification in teaching clients more effective interpersonal behaviors. When dealing with larger social systems, the social worker may, for example, educate a board of directors about an emerging social issue or teach a client advocacy group how to redesign a change strategy that is failing.

Primary Prevention.   Throughout its history, the social work profession has been mostly concerned with addressing and modifying serious human problems and conditions. In recent years, social workers have given greater attention to primary prevention (i.e., preventing the development of problems). Many such prevention efforts place the social worker in the role of a teacher or even a public educator. Examples include such activities as providing premarital counseling, teaching parenting skills, offering information on family planning, and informing the public of ways to address a social problem or issue.

4. The Social Worker as Counselor/Clinician

Purpose.   To help clients improve their social functioning by helping them better understand their feelings, modify their behaviors, and learn to cope with problematic situations.

Description.   Perhaps the most visible and frequently performed social work role is that of counselor or clinician. According to the National Association of Social Workers (1991)

> *Clinical social work* shares with all social work practice the goal of enhancement and maintenance of psychosocial functioning of individuals, families, and small groups. Clinical social work practice is the professional application of social work theory and methods to the treatment and prevention of psychosocial dysfunction, disability, or impairment, including emotional and mental disorders. . . . Clinical social work encompasses interventions directed to interpersonal interactions, intrapsychic dynamics, and life-support and management issues. It is not limited to individual, marital, family, and group psychotherapy. (pp. 1–2, emphasis added)

In order to perform this role, the social worker needs a knowledge of human behavior and an understanding of how the social environment impacts on people, an ability to assess client needs and functioning and to make judgments about what interventions can help clients deal with these stresses, skill in applying intervention techniques, and the ability to guide clients through the change process.

Functions
Psychosocial Assessment and Diagnosis.   The clients' situations must be thoroughly understood and their motivation, capacities, and opportunities for change assessed. This involves selecting conceptual frameworks to organize the information in ways that promote an understanding of both the client and the social environment in order to produce a workable action plan. The labeling and categorizing process inherent in diagnosis is necessary in some settings for purposes of interprofessional communication, research, program planning and obtaining payment for services provided.

Ongoing Stabilizing Care.   The counselor/clinician role does not always involve efforts to change the client or social situation. Sometimes it consists of providing support or care on an extended basis. For example, counseling people who are severely disabled or terminally ill—or working with their families—may involve efforts to increase their choices and help them to more comfortably deal with difficult but unchangeable situations or conditions.

Social Treatment.   This function involves such activities as helping clients understand the relationships among relevant persons and social groups, supporting client efforts to modify social relationships, engaging clients in the problem-solving or interpersonal change efforts, and mediating differences or conflicts between individuals and/or between individuals and social institutions. Whittaker and Tracy (1989, 9) define *social treatment* as "interpersonal helping that utilizes direct and indirect strategies to aid individuals, families and small groups in improving social functioning and coping with social problems." Direct strategies might include face-to-face meetings with the client, whereas indirect strategies often involve helping the client negotiate the human services system by using such tools as advocacy, referral, and the provision of concrete services.

Practice Research.   Research at this direct-service level takes two forms. First, the social worker examines his or her own performance to assess the effectiveness of the interventions utilized. In this way the social worker can be accountable to clients, the employing agency, the general public, and the profession. Second, the social worker collects data to detect emerging social problems that might need to be addressed by new or revised services and public policies.

5. The Social Worker as Case Manager

Purpose.   To achieve continuity of service to individuals and families through the process of connecting clients to appropriate services and coordinating the utilization of those services.

Description.   The social work role of case manager is of critical importance for clients who must utilize multiple services provided by several different programs or agencies. This is especially true for vulnerable and highly dependent populations such as children, the seriously disabled, and the frail elderly.

The NASW *Guidelines for the Selection and Use of Social Workers* (1981a, 7) describes the *case manager role* as "the activity of developing, implementing, and monitoring a social service plan to meet the needs of an individual or family." Rothman (1991) explains how case management differs from the broker and clinician roles: "Community outreach through linkage with service agencies and informal resources is more pronounced; . . . information and referral role is more prominent, analytical, and time demanding; [and the worker] . . . helps the client to acquire skills for community living. Maintenance rather than cure is the objective" (p. 521).

There are two basic models of case management. One limits the activities of the case manager exclusively to coordination. In the other model, the case manager, in addition to the coordination function, also serves as the client's primary counselor or therapist. The coordination-focused model is common in fields such as child protection, whereas the coordinator-counselor model is common in mental health settings.

Effective case management requires a social worker who plans ahead and is goal oriented, proactive, and assertive. It requires a professional who can get things done.

According to Moxley (1989), activities common to case management include the following:

- Coordinating client-level goals, services, and information.
- Serving as a "fixed point of responsibility" for clients [and for service providers] so they have one specific professional (or team of professionals) to look to for assistance. . . .
- Obtaining access to services for clients who may "fall through the cracks" of a categorical service delivery system, or for clients who may not fit into existing categories because of multiple problems. (p. 16)

Modern case management practice strives to establish for the client *wrap-around services*—a package of services selected or created to address the client's unique situation and often paid for with funds drawn from several sources. This is in contrast to an expectation that the client's concerns and situation will fit a preexisting service or funding category. When funds are earmarked for only one type of service, the ability to creatively address the client's concerns is severely limited. A national movement to decategorize funding for public social services is intended to correct this problem.

Functions.   Drawing on the work of Rothman (1991, 1992), Rose (1992), and Moxley (1989), we can identify several core functions of case managers.

Client Identification and Orientation.   This involves directly identifying and selecting those individuals for whom service outcomes, quality of life, or the cost of care and service could be positively affected by case management.

Client Assessment.   This function refers to gathering information and formulating an assessment of the client's needs, life situation, and resources. It may also involve reaching out to potential clients who have not requested services.

Service/Treatment Planning.   In concert with the clients and other relevant actors, the social worker identifies the various services that can be accessed to meet client needs. Bertsche and Horejsi (1980, 96) describe these tasks as the work necessary to "assemble and guide group discussions and decision-making sessions among relevant professionals and program representatives, the client and his or her family, and significant others to formulate goals and design an integrated intervention plan."

Linkage and Service Coordination.   As in the broker role, the case manager must connect clients with the appropriate resources. The case manager role differs, however, in that the social worker remains an active participant in the delivery of services to the individual or family. The case manager places emphasis on coordinating the clients' use of resources by becoming a channel and a focal point for interagency communication.

Follow-Up and Monitoring Service Delivery.   The case manager makes regular and frequent follow-up contacts with both the client and the service provider to ensure that the needed services are actually received and properly utilized by the client. If not, action is taken to correct the situation or modify the service plan. Typically, it is the case manager that completes the necessary paperwork to document client progress, service delivery, and adherence to the plan.

Client Support.   During the time the services are being provided by the various resources, the case manager assists the client and his or her family as they confront the inevitable problems in obtaining the desired services. This activity includes resolving personality conflicts, counseling, providing information, giving emotional support, and, when appropriate, advocating on behalf of clients to assure that they receive the services to which they are entitled.

6. The Social Worker as Workload Manager

Purpose.   To manage one's workload to most efficiently provide client services and be responsible to the employing organization.

Description.   Social workers must simultaneously provide the services needed by clients and adhere to the ***workload management*** requirements of the employing social agency. In other words, they must balance their obligations to both clients and agency. Although the emphasis on accountability to funding sources has increased in recent years, social workers have always been responsible for maximizing the services provided within an environment of scarcity.

Functions

Work Planning.   Social workers must be able to assess their workloads, set priorities according to importance and urgency, and make plans that will accomplish work in the most efficient and effective way possible. They must be effective in managing the typically heavy workloads they carry.

Time Management.   If the social worker is to give each client proper attention, priorities for the use of one's time must be set and the working hours carefully allocated. Time management requires that the worker learn to use technology such as word processors and the agency's computer systems.

Quality Assurance Monitoring.   The social worker regularly evaluates the effectiveness of his or her own service provision and is also involved in the assessment of services provided by colleagues. These activities might include reviewing agency records, conducting job performance evaluations, and holding performance review conferences with colleagues or volunteers.

Information Processing. Social workers must collect data to document need and service provision, complete reports, maintain case records, and substantiate various expenditures. Further, information about agency regulations and procedures must be understood by all, which requires that workers be skilled at preparing and interpreting memoranda, participating in staff meetings, and engaging in other activities that facilitate communication.

7. The Social Worker as Staff Developer

Purpose. To facilitate the professional development of agency staff through training, supervision, consultation, and personnel management.

Description. Social workers often serve in middle-management positions. In that capacity, they devote a part of their energies to maintaining and improving staff performance. That might involve working with secretaries, receptionists, volunteers, and others, but most often the ***staff developer role*** centers on maximizing the effectiveness of professional helpers.

Staff development requires many of the skills used in the teacher role. In this case, however, the knowledge is transmitted to peers rather than clients or the general public. Staff development is predicated on an accurate assessment of the training needs, with the training taking the form of individualized instruction such as job coaching, supervision and consultation, and/or conducting or participating in training sessions and workshops.

Functions

Employee Orientation and Training. Orientation to the agency and training for specific job assignments are necessary for all new employees. Among the tasks required to perform this function are "specifying job expectations, orienting workers to the organizational policies and procedures, reviewing case records, and evaluating job performance" (Teare 1984).

Personnel Management. Personnel management activities may range from the selection of new employees to the termination of employment. Many of these middle-management activities affect the professional development of other workers. For example, the selection of case assignments not only involves judgments about the worker's capacities but also provides opportunity for new and challenging professional experiences. In addition, the staff development role may call for the social worker to allocate funds for attendance at workshops or conferences.

Supervision. This function involves overseeing and directing the activities of other staff members to enhance the quality of services they provide and making sure that agency rules and regulations are followed. It includes such tasks as making and monitoring work assignments, developing performance standards, and negotiating staffing changes to better address the needs of clients.

Consultation.   As compared to supervision, which is a part of the agency's administrative hierarchy, consultation is given on a peer level—from one professional to another. The consultee is free to use or not use the advice offered by the consultant. Typically, consultation focuses on how best to handle a particularly challenging practice situation.

8. The Social Worker as Administrator

Purpose.   To plan, develop, and implement policies, services, and programs in a human services organization.

Description.   In the administrator role, the social worker assumes responsibilities for implementing the agency policies and managing its programs. Skidmore (1983, 5–6) defines *social work administration* as "the action of staff members who utilize social processes to transform social policies of agencies into the delivery of social services . . . the basic processes most often used are planning, organizing, staffing, directing and controlling." When performing this role, the social worker might be the chief administrative officer, where administration is one's primary role, or the worker might engage in administrative tasks along with other practice roles.

In the role of administrator, the social worker is responsible for implementing policies, programs, or laws made by others. Agency boards or elected officials typically define agency purposes, establish administrative guidelines, and allocate the funds required to operate the agency. Normally, either the governing board of a volunteer agency or, in a public agency, a body designated by law appoints the chief administrative officer (or executive director) to administer the organization. Depending on the size and complexity of the organization, the agency administrator or a social worker occupying another position in the agency may perform all or some of the following functions.

Functions
Management.   The management function calls for the administrator to maintain operational oversight of a program, service unit, and/or the entire organization. It includes such responsibilities as facilitating the work of the agency board, recruiting and selecting staff, directing and coordinating staff activities, developing and setting priorities, analyzing the organizational structure, promoting professional standards within the organization, adjudicating employee conflicts, and obtaining the necessary resources to operate the organization. In addition, management involves budgeting, documenting the use of resources, and arranging for the acquisition and maintenance of buildings and equipment.

Internal and External Coordination.   A primary task of the administrator is to coordinate the work of the agency. Internally, this involves developing plans for implementing the agency's programs in an efficient and effective manner. Often this requires negotiating among several units or programs and working with staff to assure that new programs are understood and integrated into the agency's functioning. The administrator also serves as the primary representative of the agency to external constituencies. These external tasks include serving as a buffer to protect staff from external pressures, negotiating with consumers, and interpreting programs to the community in order to maintain viability. Thus, the administrator is engaged in external work not only with the governing board but is also a key figure in the agency's public relations and communication with consumers, other social agencies, and the general public.

Policy and Program Development. The effective administrator is proactive. Although considerable time and energy must be devoted to maintaining established programs, an administrator should regularly assess the need for new or different services by conducting a needs assessment, being knowledgeable about social trends, generating alternative policy goals for the governing body to consider, and translating new program or policy goals adopted by the governing board into services.

Program Evaluation. Finally, the administrator is responsible for quality control. When overseeing the functioning of an agency, the social worker must monitor and evaluate the agency's programs and collect data that will help document the adequacy of the services and/or suggest actions that might be taken to improve them. Program evaluation, then, is concerned with both program development and program compliance.

9. The Social Worker as Social Change Agent

Purpose. To participate in the identification of community problems and/or areas where the quality of life can be enhanced, and to mobilize interest groups to advocate for change or new resources.

Description. Social work's dual focus on both the person and environment requires that the social worker facilitate needed change in neighborhoods, communities, or larger social systems. The role of *social change agent* has been a part of social work since its beginnings in the late 1800s. Its inclusion in the social worker's repertoire of practice roles distinguishes social work from the many other helping professions.

When working directly with clients, social workers are in an excellent position to recognize conditions that are contributing to people's distress and the need for human services. The social worker must take responsibility for assuring that resources are available to meet those needs and/or stimulating action by others to address those problems. Social change typically does not occur rapidly or easily, and the authority to make the political decisions to achieve change is rarely held by social workers. Rather, change requires skill in stimulating action by influential groups and decision-making bodies that have the power to address the problems.

Functions

Social Problem or Policy Analysis.   A first requirement for social change is to understand the nature of the problem. Trends must be analyzed, data collected and synthesized, and findings reported in ways that are understandable to decision makers. Without this background work, change efforts have little chance of success. The *NASW Standards* (1981b, 16) identify the tasks involved in such analysis as (1) developing criteria for the analysis, (2) ascertaining the impact of the policy on clients and social problems, and (3) analyzing community values and beliefs that affect the issue.

Mobilization of Community Concern.   Translating one's understanding of problems into social change efforts requires mobilizing and energizing concerned individuals, groups, and organizations. This might involve encouraging clients, special-interest groups, human services organizations, and/or other citizen groups to address and speak out on the problem. Mobilization for action might involve assembling interested parties and presenting an analysis of the situation, helping expand their understanding of the issues and identify goals they could achieve, aiding in the selection of change strategies, identifying the decision makers who can effect the desired change, and planning and/or carrying out the activities necessary to induce change.

Social Resource Development.   The social change agent might also work toward the development of needed programs and services. The *NASW Guidelines* (1981a, 27) describe *resource development* as "the activity of creating new resources where they do not exist, extending or improving existing resources, [and the] planning and allocation of available resources in order to avoid unnecessary duplication of human services [and] . . . increase the effectiveness and efficiency of services offered by a unit, an agency, or a group of agencies." This may involve lobbying and providing expert testimony to legislative committees, or more informal communication with decision makers.

10. The Social Worker as Professional

Purpose.   To engage in competent and ethical social work practice and contribute to the development of the social work profession.

Description.   Basically, a *professional person* is one whose actions are thoughtful, purposeful, appropriate, responsible, and ethical. It is incumbent on the social worker to practice in a manner that reflects the highest professional standards. The social worker must constantly seek to develop his or her knowledge and skills and to examine and increase the quality of his or her practice.

As one who benefits from professional status, the social worker should actively engage in the enhancement and strengthening of the profession. Active participation in professional associations at the local, state, and national levels is an essential component of the professional role.

Functions

Self-Assessment.   The autonomy required for professional decision making carries with it the responsibility for ongoing self-assessment. In their national task analysis of social work practice, Teare and Sheafor (1995) state that social workers serving virtually every type of client, working in virtually every type of human services organization (including private practice), and working in virtually every social work role devote a substantial amount of effort to self-assessment and their own professional development based on that assessment.

Personal/Professional Development.   The corollary to self-assessment is further developing one's abilities and addressing any performance problems that have been identified. In his job-analysis study of social workers, Teare (1984) finds that they

> engage in activities designed to assess the effectiveness of [their own] functioning, keep informed, and improve . . . skills. Emphasis is placed on the development of insight into the adequacy of one's personal and professional performance. Tasks include reading journals and other professional literature, attending workshops, planning personal time, and having work-related discussions with colleagues and supervisors. (pages not numbered)

Enhancement of the Social Work Profession.   Social workers should contribute to the growth and development of the profession and the expansion of its knowledge base. Maintaining membership in the National Association of Social Workers and contributing time and energy to the efforts of NASW to strengthen the quality of professional practice, protect the domain of social work, and support legislative initiatives are obligations of each social worker. In addition, social workers should contribute knowledge gained from their practice or research to colleagues through presentations at conferences and by contributing to the professional literature.

Conclusion

The range of practice roles performed by the social worker is large and varied. The effective social worker must master at least the basic job functions associated with most of these roles. The specialist practitioner might develop more in-depth competence in fewer roles, but the generalist social worker, in particular, must seek to expand his or her competence in each.

SELECTED BIBLIOGRAPHY

Barker, Robert L. *The Social Work Dictionary*, 3rd ed. Washington, D.C.: NASW Press, 1995.

Bertsche, Anne Vandeberg, and Charles R. Horejsi. "Coordination of Client Services." *Social Work* 25 (March 1980): 94–98.

Hall, Glades Walton, Grace C. Clark, and Michael A Creedon. *Advocacy in America: Case Studies in Social Change.* Lanham, Md.: University Press of America, 1987.

Mickelson, James. "Advocacy." In *Encyclopedia of Social Work.* Vol. 1, 19th ed., edited by Richard L. Edwards. Washington, D.C.: NASW Press, 1995, pp. 95–100.

Moxley, David. *The Practice of Case Management.* Newbury Park, Calif.: Sage, 1989.

National Association of Social Workers. *NASW Code of Ethics,* rev. Washington, D.C.: NASW, 1993.

———. *Guidelines for the Selection and Use of Social Workers.* Silver Spring, Md.: NASW, 1981a.

———. *NASW Standards for the Classification of Social Work Practice.* Silver Spring, Md.: NASW, 1981b.

Rose, Stephen M. *Case Management and Social Work Practice.* New York: Longman, 1992.

Rothman, Jack. *Guidelines for Case Management.* Itasca, Ill.: F. E. Peacock, 1992.

———. "A Model of Case Management: Toward Empirically Based Practice." *Social Work* 35 (November 1991): 520–528.

Skidmore, Rex. *Social Work Administration.* Englewood Cliffs, N.J.: Prentice Hall, 1983.

Teare, Robert J. "Validation of the ACSW Examination: Status Report to the National Association of Social Workers." (Photocopy materials.) Tuscaloosa: University of Alabama School of Social Work, 1984, pages unnumbered.

Teare, Robert J., and Bradford W. Sheafor. *Practice-Sensitive Social Work Education: An Empirical Analysis of Social Work Practice and Practitioners.* Arlington, Va.: Council on Social Work Education, 1995.

Vourlekis, Betsy S., and Robert R. Green, eds. *Social Work Case Management.* New York: Aldine, 1992.

Weinbach, Robert W. *The Social Worker as Manager: Theory and Practice,* 2nd ed. Boston: Allyn and Bacon, 1994.

Whittaker, James, and Elizabeth Tracy. *Social Treatment,* 2nd ed. New York: Aldine, 1989.

Guiding Principles for Social Workers

Within each profession there exists a number of fundamental principles that guide practice decisions and actions. These principles apply in all practice situations, regardless of client characteristics, practice setting, or roles assumed by the professional. In addition, they are independent of any specific theories, models, and techniques selected in a specific practice situation. *Principles* are basic rules or guides to one's practice behavior, but they are not prescriptions that are to be applied without careful and thoughtful analysis.

Social work's practice principles are grounded in the profession's philosophy, values, ethical prescriptions, and practice wisdom. Most are not supported by empirical verification nor are they compiled in a single document. Yet, there are frequent references in social work literature to *the social work practice principles,* as if there is an agreed upon set of practice guidelines that all social workers follow. To the contrary, social work's practice principles are largely unwritten and typically are passed on informally from seasoned workers to those who are entering the profession. They are often expressed as clichés such as "start where the client is" or "accept the client as he or she is." Many of the principles seem so obvious and self-evident to the experienced worker that they often are not consciously taught in professional education programs or during new worker supervision. However, they are central to effective social work practice.

This chapter presents a synopsis of 21 fundamental principles that should guide social work practice. The first 5 focus on the social worker. The remainder are concerned with the social worker in interaction with a client or client group—whether it be an individual, family, small group, organization, neighborhood, community, or even larger social structure.

Principles Focused on the Social Worker as a Professional Person

I. The Social Worker Should Practice Social Work

This fundamental principle seems so obvious that it appears trite. We expect the teacher to teach, the physician to practice medicine, and the social worker to practice within the boundaries of the social work profession. Yet it is not uncommon to find these and other professionals extending their activities into the domain of another profession. This principle admonishes the social worker to do what he or she is sanctioned and trained to do.

As discussed in Chapter 1, social work is sanctioned to focus on social functioning and help improve the interaction between people and their environment—that is the social work domain. The requisite educational preparation equips the social worker with the knowledge, values, and skills to work at the interface of person and environment, and that, more than anything else, is the unique contribution of social work among the helping professions. The social worker is not sanctioned to be either a cut-rate psychiatrist, at one extreme, or a humanistic environmental planner at the other.

Due to areas of overlap, the "turf" problems among the disciplines are difficult enough when each practices within professional boundaries. Such problems are magnified when a member of one discipline strays into another discipline's area of operation. Ethical practice requires that the social worker function within his or her professional expertise. Although individual social workers may have special talents that exceed the profession's domain, they do not have license to offer services that exceed the sanction given to the social work profession. More importantly, the social worker who drifts from the profession's area of focus and expertise deprives clients of a critically important perspective on human problems and change.

2. The Social Worker Should Engage in Conscious Use of Self

The social worker's primary practice tool is the self (i.e., his or her motivation and capacity to communicate and interact with others in ways that facilitate change). The skilled worker is purposeful in making use of his or her unique manner and style of relating to others. One's ability to build and maintain positive helping relationships with clients is fundamental to social work practice.

In professional relationships, workers reveal—verbally or nonverbally, directly or indirectly—their values, life-styles, morals, attitudes, biases, and prejudices. Workers must be consciously aware of how their own beliefs, perceptions, and behaviors may impact on their professional relationships, as these personal attributes will surely affect the ability to be helpful to clients.

The social worker must also be comfortable with his or her unique personality and be at peace with whatever problems he or she has experienced in life. For most people, acquiring such self-knowledge and self-acceptance is a life-long journey that requires a willingness to take risks, for taking a close look at who we are can indeed be disquieting. (See Item 10.11 for more information on developing self-awareness.) But the worker must discover and build on his or her special strengths and minimize the impact of deficiencies, identify the types of clients and situations that respond positively to his or her practice style, and develop a pattern of regular, objective, and nondefensive examination of how one's professional self is functioning.

3. The Social Worker Should Maintain Professional Objectivity

By the time most clients come into contact with a professional helper, they have attempted to resolve their troublesome situation themselves—by either struggling alone or seeking assistance from family, friends, or other natural helpers. Often, these efforts are thwarted by high levels of emotion and the conflicting advice they receive. This may only add to the person's frustration and preclude clear understanding and response to the situation.

The professional adds a new dimension to the helping process by operating with a degree of personal distance and neutrality. Maintaining this neutrality without appearing unconcerned or uncaring is a delicate balancing act. The worker who becomes too involved and too identified with the client's concerns can lose perspective and objectivity. At the other extreme, the worker who is emotionally detached fails to energize clients or, even worse, discourages clients from investing the energy necessary to achieve change. The social worker can best maintain this balance through a controlled emotional involvement.

Further, this professional objectivity is important to the social worker's own mental health. A degree of emotional detachment is needed, allowing the worker to set aside the troubles of clients and society and separate the professional and personal aspects of one's life. Professional objectivity is, perhaps, the best antidote to worker burnout.

4. The Social Worker Should Respect Human Diversity

The practice of social work involves activity with and in behalf of people from virtually all walks of life, most racial and ethnic backgrounds, a variety of cultures and religions, a range of physical and intellectual abilities, both genders, as well as various sexual orientations and ages. Human diversity is expressed in the behavior of individuals, families, communities, and even societies.

The worker must understand and respect such differences and human uniqueness and recognize that what may appear to be deviance or unusual behavior from one perspective may be quite appropriate and normal given a different set of values and life experiences. To the social worker, diversity brings richness to the quality of life. Failure to accept and appreciate difference creates barriers to helping.

Respect for diversity requires sensitivity to the fact that various population groups have had differing experiences in U.S. society. In addition, individuals within a particular group or class may have had quite different experiences from other persons in that group. The social worker, then, must also appreciate the variations within any group and avoid making assumptions about any one person's cultural identity, beliefs, or values on the basis of that person's external characteristics or membership in a particular population or demographic group. Practitioners who respect diversity are careful to guard against jumping to conclusions or making decisions based on overgeneralizations and stereotypes.

5. The Social Worker Should Seek Personal and Professional Growth

Social work is a contemporary discipline. Its focus is on the here-and-now concerns of ever-changing people living in a dynamic environment. Helping people interact more effectively with their environments requires that the social worker be in tune with the world as it is experienced by others. One cannot be empathic and creative in working with a wide range of clients while holding a narrow and uninformed view of life. The social worker must continuously seek growth and development—both personally and professionally.

The rapid growth and change in the knowledge relevant to social work requires constant updating. New concepts, theories, and intervention techniques regularly appear in the literature or are presented at workshops or conferences. The social worker must be current with the professional information. However, the person who becomes immersed in social work to the exclusion of other activities and experiences actually limits his or her ability to be helpful. To appreciate the infinite variety of the human condition, one must understand life from various orientations. Ideas gathered from history, literature, science, the arts, travel, and interaction with a wide range of people are vital to the continuing development of the social worker.

Principles That Guide Practice Activities

In addition to the principles related to the social worker as an individual and a professional person, a number of other principles are concerned with the social worker's intervention with individual clients and client groups.

6. The Social Worker Should Do No Harm

Social work practice is about the facilitation of desired change. However, there is always an element of risk in any effort to bring about change, no matter how well intended and no matter how desireable the goal. Because planned change is a very human process, the responsible professional must assume that some mistakes will be made. The social worker must anticipate such possibilities and have a plan for dealing with the things that can go wrong in an intervention. In the effort to do good and enhance the social functioning of people, the social worker must be careful to do no harm.

A social worker's change goals and intervention activities should not damage appropriate and healthy levels of social functioning by an individual, family, neighborhood, or community. Professional actions and the programs social workers implement should in no way discourage or undermine responsible client behaviors nor erect barriers to appropriate social functioning. Furthermore, social workers engaged in efforts to change an unjust condition or unfair social policies must avoid using methods that inflict the type of harm or create conditions similar to those they seek to change. For example, social workers must fight oppression without oppressing others and should fight injustice with out being unjust or unfair to those they seek to influence.

7. The Social Worker Should Engage in Conscious Knowledge-Guided Practice

At the very core of society's trust in professions is the expectation that the professional will bring to the change effort the latest and most appropriate knowledge. A social worker cannot possibly stay abreast of all the knowledge that relates to the many dimensions of social work practice. However, the worker is obligated to be familiar with the most current knowledge that directly relates to his or her practice activities and should know how to retrieve needed knowledge in related areas.

A part of the knowledge of social workers is drawn from their own life experiences and, as they engage in social work practice over time, from practice wisdom. Through regular reading of professional journals and books, attendance at professional conferences, and participation in agency staff development programs, social workers can continuously update and expand the knowledge they bring into their practice.

It is also important that social workers are careful consumers of the knowledge presented in the social work literature and at social work conferences. After all, it is the clients that are most at risk if practice assessments and intervention decisions are based on faulty information. Each social worker should be prepared to engage in critical review of social work's theoretical and intervention knowledge before adopting that as a basis for his or her practice activities. (For assistance in critiquing research reports and studies of social work practice, see Items 10.13, 10.14, and 10.15.)

8. The Social Worker Should Engage in Conscious Value-Guided and Ethical Practice

It is critical that the social worker recognize and address key value and ethical issues as a part of social work practice. Values are at the center of many practice situations. For example, problems for which many clients seek help involve value differences between individuals or between individuals and relevant groups or organizations in their environment. The social worker must recognize that one's values are powerful forces in human behavior. Helping clients clarify and understand value issues in their lives can be a critical step in bringing about change. However, in many cases, if clients are to change themselves or their situations, they must take some action to adjust or adapt their values to be more congruent with those of others in their lives— or learn to help others adjust or adapt their values to be more congruent with those of the client. When working directly with clients, then, the social worker must be sensitive to the value issues that inevitably arise in the lives of their clients.

Organizations and communities also operate from values about who should be served, who should pay for the services, and how the services should be delivered. When engaged in practice activities that relate to the agencies that employ them, the social conditions that exist in the community, or the social programs that are created at the city, county, state, or federal level, the social worker should attempt to understand the values that have affected that situation. Societal problems are often a result of value differences, and an important step in finding solutions to those problems is to address the value issues.

Social workers must also be sensitive to their own values and beliefs and be prepared to suspend or set aside their own preferences and perspectives to avoid inappropriately imposing their beliefs on their clients. Social work practice, however, is not value free. At times, the social worker must take actions to protect the health and safety of others or achieve a broader social benefit than the interests of a single client. Making those practice decisions ethically requires careful consideration. (See Item 10.9 for guidelines that assist in sorting out ethical dilemmas that arise in social work practice.)

9. The Social Worker Should Be Concerned with the Whole Person

Most professions focus on a single dimension of the human person and human condition. Physicians are primarily interested in physical well-being, teachers focus on intellectual development, and psychologists are concerned with emotional and cognitive processes. Social work, however, is unique among the professions because of its concern for the whole person—biological, psychological, social, and spiritual. For the social worker, practice activities rarely relate to a single dimension of human life and living.

Concern for the whole person requires attention to the client's past, present, and future. It requires the social worker to look beyond the client's immediate or presenting problem and be alert to the possible existence of other issues, ranging from a lack of food and shelter to a lack of meaning and purpose in life. The social worker must focus attention on the client's problems as well as the client's strengths. He or she must attend to both the client's presenting problem or concern and to possible underlying causative factors (i.e., the symptoms as well as their causes). In keeping with the person-in-environment construct, the social worker must be concerned with the well-being of the client and also the many other people who may be affected by the client's behavior and by the worker's intervention. Finally, the social worker must be concerned with both the short-term and long-term implications of the change process for both the client and others.

10. The Social Worker Should Treat the Client with Dignity

Philosophically, the social worker must accept the proposition that each person or group deserves to be treated with dignity, respect, and understanding. The phrase "accept the client as he or she is" reminds and encourages the social worker to approach clients as people with dignity who deserve respect, regardless of behavior, appearances, or circumstances. Biestek (1957, 72) describes *acceptance* as occurring when the worker "perceives the client as he really is, including his strengths and weaknesses, his congenial and uncongenial qualities, his positive and negative feelings, his constructive and destructive attitudes and behavior, maintaining all the time a sense of the client's innate dignity and personal worth."

Communicating acceptance and respect requires that the social worker avoid making moral judgments concerning clients. The worker's nonjudgmental attitude helps clients overcome the common fear of being judged by others and frees up the helping relationship for positive action. Treating the client with dignity helps guard against the inappropriate intrusion of the social worker's biases into the client's life. Weick, Rapp, Sullivan, and Kisthardt (1989, 353) observe that the importance of acceptance and the nonjudgmental attitude in practice rests on the belief that people have "an inner wisdom about what they need and that ultimately, people make choices based on their own best sense of what will meet that need [and that] it is impossible for even the best trained professional to judge how another person should best live his or her life."

The need to treat each and every client with respect and acceptance does not imply approval of all behavior by a client. One can accept and care for the client as a person of worth and dignity without approving of, for example, illegal, harmful, or socially destructive behavior. The key to adhering to this principle is to remember that the purpose of social work is to help people make changes, and it has been amply demonstrated that acceptance of and respect for the person are prerequisite for change and that condemnation and judgmentalism erect barriers to change that are counterproductive.

11. The Social Worker Should Individualize the Client

"Starting where the client is" is frequently the first practice principle to which the social worker is exposed. From the first day in the first social work class, the social worker can expect to be taught that no two people are alike, and, therefore, the social worker must treat each as being unique. This means that the worker must be in tune with and pay attention to what the client is thinking and feeling and how he or she is behaving from moment to moment and from one session to another. In short, the worker must adapt his or her practice to the unique characteristics of each person, family, group, or community (i.e., individualize the client).

The principle of individualization requires that the social worker be sensitive to each client's unique history, characteristics, and situation. The social worker must also appreciate the differing ability and readiness of clients to participate in a particular intervention strategy. What works with one client may or may not work with others. Individualization asks social workers to be flexible in how they work with clients and what they expect from those with whom they work.

12. The Social Worker Should Lend Vision to the Client

A central feature of professional helping is to bring new ideas, new perspectives, and more effective change strategies to a problem situation. If an individual or group is to invest in the difficult process of changing, they must be convinced that the outcome will be worth the effort. The social worker must introduce and nurture a sense of hopefulness and offer a vision that change is possible and that there are new and better ways to deal with the situation.

Anderson (1981, 61) identifies four activities used to operationalize this principle: "(1) the revelation of faith in the individual's dignity and power to act on his or her own behalf; (2) the revelation of the worker's own investment in the transactions between people and their social systems; (3) the trust in the power of human relations for synergistic growth; and (4) the encouragement of synergistic growth in the individual's specific situation."

While offering new perspectives, encouragement, and support and techniques for change, the social worker must also be realistic and honest about limits and possibilities. Clients are not helped by raising false hopes or by projecting unrealistic outcomes for the helping process. A tempered infusion of energy and vision allows the client or client group to make real progress toward achievable outcomes.

13. The Social Worker Should Build on Client Strengths

All too often, social workers and other human services professionals become preoccupied with client problems and invest considerable effort in identifying all that is wrong with a situation and in describing the specific limitations or deficiencies of a client or client group. Such an essentially negative way of thinking about clients and their situations is reinforced by the diagnostic labels now required for statistical purposes within many service agencies or by insurance companies that pay for social work services. This preoccupation with the negative is so common that it is not unusual, for example, to observe an interdisciplinary staffing in which the client assessment reveals that, when the various disciplines combine their evaluations, the client is more than 100 percent disabled—and that none of the professionals addressed the client's abilities.

For the social worker, it is the clients' abilities and potentials that are most important in helping to bring about change (Saleebey 1992). Since a change in social functioning is largely under the control of the client, it is important to help clients recognize and utilize their strengths. The emphasis on maximizing and building on clients' strengths helps change the tone of the helping relationship from one of gloom over problems and pathology to one of optimism. Thus, the social worker should carefully assess and build on client strengths.

14. The Social Worker Should Maximize Client Participation

"Help your clients to help themselves" is a principle based on the belief that if meaningful and lasting change is to occur for an individual, group, community, or other client system, the people who will need to change must be active participants in the change process. It is the responsibility of the social worker in guiding the process to be sure that, as far as possible, all relevant persons participate in identifying the problem, formulating a plan of action, and implementing that plan.

In order to maximize client participation, the social worker should "do *with* the client and not *to* or *for* the client." For example, it does little good for the social worker to construct a sophisticated diagnosis of a client's situation if that client does not understand or accept those conclusions. Meaningful change will occur only when those who must change clearly understand the need for change and are willing and able to take action.

Similarly, an intervention plan is most likely to be followed when it is developed with active client participation. As opposed to the attorney, who single-handedly presents a case for the client, or the physician, who injects the patient with a chemical that can cure an illness with minimal patient involvement, the social worker must assume a very different posture. The social worker must view himself or herself as primarily a collaborator, facilitator, and catalyst. Although situations do arise in which a social worker must act in behalf of clients, the social worker should always seek to maximize client involvement.

15. The Social Worker Should Maximize Client Self-Determination

The instruction to "guide the helping process—not the client" captures another important principle. This principle maintains that those who must ultimately live with the outcomes of decisions should have the freedom to make those decisions. The job of the social worker is to help clients explore alternatives and the implications of various options but not to prescribe their final choices. Biestek and Gehrig (1978) summarize the major themes in this principle as it applies to working with individuals and families, although it is equally relevant when applied to other client systems, as follows:

1. The client has a right and a need to be free in making his [or her] own decisions and choices.
2. This right to freedom, however, is limited by the client's capacity, by law and authority, by written community standards, and by the function of the agency.
3. The social worker has a corresponding duty to respect this right, in theory and practice, by refraining from any direct interference with it, and by positively helping the client to exercise that right. (p. 75)

The principle of self-determination must be qualified in its application. It assumes that the client is capable and legally competent to make decisions in relation to self and others. Sometimes that is not a valid assumption. Some clients may not understand the consequences of an action or may lack the mental capacity to make sound judgments and might, therefore, make choices that are clearly harmful to themselves or others. At times, the social worker must take on a decision-making role for these clients (e.g., children, the person who is mentally ill, etc.). This may involve persuading them to take a particular action, using the authority or power that the social worker's position might command, securing a court order declaring mental incompetence, or, in the most extreme situations, calling for police assistance in order to prevent a tragedy.

The social worker should reluctantly assume the responsibility for making decisions in behalf of clients and then only after careful review of the situation, after consultation with others, and always with the intent of returning that responsibility to the client as soon as possible. In the final analysis, the social worker should attempt to maximize the client's ability to determine his or her own destiny.

16. The Social Worker Should Help the Client Learn Self-Directed Problem-Solving Skills

Most social workers are familiar with the idea of helping people help themselves. Perhaps this should be extended to "helping people help themselves *now and also in the future.*"

Many of us have had the experience of being pleased with our loss of weight only to discover a few months later that we had slipped back into old eating patterns and regained the lost pounds. Similarly, the changes in social functioning made by a client with the assistance of a professional helper can come unraveled unless the client is prepared to sustain that change over time. Ideally, a social work intervention helps prepare clients to cope successfully with future difficulties and to engage in self-directed problem solving when faced with another problem so they will not need to return to the social worker for additional assistance.

Hopefully, what the client learns during his or her interaction with the social worker can be applied to additional concerns in day-to-day living—in the present and in the future. The admonition "Don't do for clients what they can do for themselves" relates to this principle of helping clients learn the skills needed to be independent and self-reliant.

An important aspect of preparing clients for the future is to teach them how to identify and make use of resources and natural helpers that might be found in their immediate environment. Such resources may include family members, relatives, friends, service clubs, and church or synagogue groups.

17. The Social Worker Should Maximize Client Empowerment

Because social workers are committed to serving society's most vulnerable citizens, they regularly work with people who have been victims of various forms of discrimination and oppression. One especially helpful contribution social workers can make to their clients' social functioning is to help them gain increased power over their lives. While some of the principles described here have the effect of giving clients more control over some dimensions of their lives (e.g., maximizing participation, maximizing self-determination, or helping to develop problem-solving skills), a principle that should guide all of a social worker's practice activity is the goal of *empowerment.*

The goal of helping people, both individually and collectively, to gain power over their lives has been a part of social work's philosophy since its founding (Simon 1994). However, use of the term *empowerment* to capture this commitment to working collaboratively with people to attain their goals by increasing their personal and political power to influence their life situations has gained prominence in recent years.

A continuing challenge for social workers is to find ways to empower their clients. This is particularly difficult because many practice models are based on professionals using their expertise to make up for inadequacies experienced by their clients. To empower, a worker must creatively find ways to help individuals and families take control of their lives and assume responsibility for their actions.

18. The Social Worker Should Protect Client Confidentiality

Individuals and families seeking help from a social worker often discuss very private aspects of their lives. In groups, clients may reveal secrets and self-perceptions that could be embarrassing or damaging if made public. The community worker, too, encounters instances when information about individuals, agencies, and organizations must be protected. All social workers, therefore, must be capable of handling private and sensitive information in a confidential manner.

There are two basic forms of confidentiality: absolute and relative. *Absolute confidentiality* refers to a situation when information imparted by the client can never go beyond the social worker. That degree of confidentiality is rare in social work practice. It is only under the protection of some professional licensing statutes that a client can claim a legal right to privileged communication. Most social work practice involves *relative confidentiality,* meaning that the most the social worker can promise is to act responsibly within the profession's *Code of Ethics,* adhere to existing laws, and follow agency policy concerning the handling of client information.

The degree of confidentiality that can be provided will, of course, depend on the type of information communicated, the nature of the agency where the practice occurs, the state and federal laws and regulations that govern its operation, and the existence of other legal requirements such as the mandated reporting of child abuse. In correctional programs (e.g., prison, parole, probation), the client can expect little confidentiality. On the other hand, a client who receives social services within a hospital setting will have a much higher level of protection; but even here, a client's records might be reviewed by nonhospital personnel such as insurance companies, Medicaid or Medicare authorities, worker's compensation officials, hospital accreditation teams, and others who have authority to review patient records for purposes of quality control. When it may be an especially important issue for a client, he or she should be advised early in the helping process of the limits of confidentiality the social worker can guarantee.

The social worker must be prudent regarding what information is placed in agency files, and care must be taken in preparing clerical staff to respect the confidential nature of any materials they may type, file, or inadvertently overhear. To protect confidential information, social workers must carefully plan the location of interviews and cautiously select the information to be discussed during professional consultations and in case conferences. Further, clearly separating one's personal life and work life is important in protecting against breaches of confidentiality that might occur when discussing work experiences with family and friends.

19. The Social Worker Should Adhere to the Philosophy of Normalization

Many social work clients have significant mental and physical disabilities. Because of these limitations, they often experience discrimination and social isolation. The philosophy of normalization is a powerful force in efforts to integrate persons with disabilities into the life of the community and ensure that their lives resemble that of the so-called normal person as much as possible. This philosophy originated in the field of mental retardation but has spread to programs serving other groups such as the elderly, the physically disabled, and the seriously mentally ill.

The National Association for Retarded Citizens (NARC) (1973) defines *normalization* as follows:

> The concept of helping the developmentally disabled persons to obtain an existence as close to the normal as possible, making available to them patterns and conditions of everyday life that are as close as possible to the norms and patterns of the mainstream of society. Specifically, the use of means that are as culturally normative as possible to elicit and maintain behavior that is as culturally normative as possible. (p. 72)

The term *normative* in this definition can be equated with typical or conventional. This means, for example, that a person with mental retardation should, to the greatest extent possible, live in a typical or conventional home in an ordinary neighborhood. Also, his or her work, recreation, religious participation, clothing, transportation, and daily activities should be as conventional as possible. Likewise, the individual should be able to receive educational, medical, and social services in ways and in an environment that closely resembles how other citizens secure these formal resources.

Horejsi (1979) describes the behavioral rationale for seeking to normalize the life of persons with severe disabilities:

> The principle of normalization rests on the assumption that adaptive or socially acceptable behavior is learned and maintained because the individual has been given an opportunity to behave in conventional ways and that such behavior has been reinforced. Moreover, appropriate behavior is more likely to be emitted and reinforced in a normal environment. (p. 45)

The theoretical underpinnings of the normalization philosophy are rooted in learning theory, especially concepts of modeling and imitation. More importantly, it is a philosophy that recognizes the dignity and worth of all people, regardless of appearance or physical or mental limitation.

20. The Social Worker Should Continuously Evaluate the Progress of the Change Process

The practice of social work is far from an exact science. It involves working with ever-changing people and ever-changing situations. The objectives of helping activities, therefore, must be clearly delineated and regularly reviewed to be certain that they remain relevant to the client's needs. It is not enough to set the course of an intervention strategy and assume that the desired outcome will be achieved. Rather, a continuous monitoring and evaluation of the change process by both the social worker and the client is necessary.

Anderson (1981, 64) reinforces the need for regular evaluation of practice activities and comments that effective social work practice "requires mutual periodic reviews of the selected goals and targets, the method and skills used to achieve those goals, and the outcomes of the mutual work." To achieve this, both the worker and the client or client group must regularly collect and record data that are indicators of change and these data must be reviewed and carefully analyzed. If the desired change is not occurring, the worker is obligated to try another approach or redesign the intervention.

21. The Social Worker Should Be Accountable to Clients, Agency, Community, and the Social Work Profession

One factor that complicates practice is that the social worker must answer to a number of parties. Where practitioners in some disciplines might feel that they are accountable only to the client, the social worker—working at the interface of person and environment—faces multiple sources of accountability.

Social workers are obligated to give their best service to all clients at all times and, therefore, must be accountable to those individuals, families, and groups they directly serve. In addition, since virtually all social workers are employed in a social agency or are part of a private practice group, they are also responsible for carrying out the programs and procedures of that organization. Further, for the agency to be accountable to its public, the workers must be accountable to the organization since its reputation, funding, and success ultimately rest with the quality of services provided.

In addition, the existence of a professional monopoly demands that the members of the profession also be accountable to the community. For many social workers, this accountability is formalized through licensing. For others, the accountability is less structured but nevertheless expected.

As clearly stated in the NASW *Code of Ethics,* the social work profession expects accountability to clients, colleagues, employers, the profession, and society. At times, practice situations place the individual worker in a position that makes it impossible to be fully and equally accountable to all audiences. In those situations, the social worker should attempt to maximize the accountability to each.

Conclusion

The new social worker is often inundated with information that reveals, in bits and pieces, the knowledge and values that guide social work practice. Some of this information is formally taught in both baccalaureate and master's degree programs while other information, such as the principles described in this chapter, is typically transmitted in a more subtle and informal manner.

Practice principles reflect that combination of values and knowledge that should underlay all practice activities. If all else fails, the worker cannot go too far wrong if he or she is operating within these principles. They might be viewed as a fail-safe mechanism in social work practice. The 21 principles identified in this chapter represent the authors' efforts to ferret out such principles from the social work literature. With these principles firmly in mind, the social worker is prepared to engage the client in a change process and to identify and select appropriate techniques for addressing the problems or enhancement needs of the client.

SELECTED BIBLIOGRAPHY

Anderson, Joseph. *Social Work Methods and Processes.* Belmont, Calif.: Wadsworth, 1981.

Biestek, Felix P. *The Casework Relationship.* Chicago: Loyola University Press, 1957.

Biestek, Felix P., and Clyde C. Gehrig. *Client Self-Determination in Social Work: A Fifty-Year History.* Chicago: University of Chicago Press, 1978.

Cox, Enid, and Ruth J. Parsons. *Empowerment-Oriented Social Work Practice with the Elderly.* Pacific Grove, Calif.: Brooks/Cole, 1994.

Horejsi, Charles R. "Applications of the Normalization Principle in the Human Services: Implications for Social Work Education." *Journal of Education for Social Work* 15 (Winter 1979): 44–50.

Lee, Judith A. B. *The Empowerment Approach to Social Work Practice.* New York: Columbia University Press, 1994.

National Association for Retarded Citizens. *The Right to Choose.* Arlington, Tex.: National Association for Retarded Citizens, 1973.

Saleebey, Dennis. *The Strengths Perspective in Social Work Practice.* New York: Longman, 1992.

Simon, Barbara Levy. *The Empowerment Tradition in American Social Work: A History.* New York: Columbia University Press, 1994.

Weick, Ann, Charles Rapp, W. Patrick Sullivan, and Walter Kisthardt. "A Strengths Perspective for Social Work Practice." *Social Work* 35 (July 1989): 350–354.

6 Practice Frameworks for Social Work

It is said that there is nothing so practical as a good theory. Some social workers may question that notion when faced with the task of trying to understand and sort out the multitude of conceptual frameworks that are somehow supposed to help them become more knowledgeable, more effective, and more professional. For example, the *Encyclopedia of Social Work* (1995) and books by Turner (1986), Dorfman (1988), and Greene and Ephross (1991) describe dozens of the frameworks used in both direct and indirect practice. Given the complexity of these frameworks, it is understandable why one might get a bit confused. Nevertheless, these frameworks are important and their proper application does improve social work practice.

At the end of Chapter 3, under the heading "Knowledge for Social Work Practice," the topic of practice frameworks was introduced and the difference between a practice perspective, a practice theory, and a practice model was explained. The reader may want to review those pages before proceeding. Basically, a ***practice framework*** consists of a set of beliefs and assumptions about how and under what conditions people change and what a social worker can do to facilitate desirable change. Every framework is intended to accomplish some kind of change. Some focus mostly on individual change, whereas others focus on families, small groups, organizations, or communities. This chapter suggests criteria for selection, explains how different frameworks may be more or less useful depending on the phase of the helping process, and provides brief descriptions of commonly used practice perspectives, theories, and models. In each description, an effort has been made to identify the primary reasons social workers use the framework. Key concepts are noted, and a list of suggested readings about each framework is provided.[1]

Requirements of a Practice Framework

A practice framework should meet the following criteria.

- It should be consistent with the purpose, values, and ethics of the profession (i.e., the activities should be consistent with the profession's domain).

[1]*Note:* If a reference mentioned or cited does not appear under the relevant list of Suggested Readings, the full citation will be found in the Selected Bibliography at the end of the chapter.

- It should be capable of being communicated to others (i.e., its concepts, principles, and hypotheses should be clearly described and defined).
- It should make sense to laypersons (i.e., most clients and volunteers should be able to understand the framework's connection to their concerns and life experiences).
- It should help the worker analyze and understand highly complex and often chaotic situations.
- It should provide guidance and direction during the various phases of the change process.
- It should rest on an empirical foundation (i.e., it should be based on facts and observations).

Because of the wide variety of practice settings, types of clients, and situations addressed by social workers, it is not possible to identify a single social work practice framework that is superior to all others. However, a framework is most likely to yield successful practice outcomes if it encourages the social worker to do the following:

- Address both personal and environmental factors in the client situation and make use of both "hard" and "soft" services.
- Display a genuine sense of caring for clients.
- Recognize and build on client strengths and avoid focusing only on limitations, deviance, and psychopathology.
- Be proactive and reach out with offers of relevant and appropriate services.
- Permit the client to make final decisions on the methods to be used in the helping process.
- Offer services and use approaches that are congruent with the client's concerns, values, culture, and religion.
- Offer services for which the costs to the client in time and money are reasonable given the probable benefits or outcome.
- Achieve some immediate success so as to demonstrate the usefulness of intervention and maintain client motivation.
- Facilitate the acquisition of knowledge, skills, and power that will decrease client need for professional and formal resources.
- Encourage and facilitate the use of mutual support and self-help networks and groups in the client's community.

Guidelines for Selecting a Practice Framework

The choice of a practice framework can either enlarge or narrow the social worker's vision and options. Students and new workers especially must guard against becoming locked into a single practice framework and then assuming that it has universal applicability. Meyer (1987) warns that during their formal education, social workers often become committed to a single theory or modality and remain invested in that approach throughout their professional careers. Such a narrow, "have theory—will travel" mentality is both shortsighted and a disservice to clients.

Experienced professionals must also avoid falling into the habit of using practice frameworks in an uncritical manner. Wedenoja, Nurius, and Tripodi (1988, 427) warn practitioners against the "mindlessness [that often] . . . accompanies very familiar, habitual activities that have become so well-learned that underlying beliefs and assumptions are considered givens; judgments, decisions, and expectations are automatic, less conscious, and seldom open to question."

An additional caution is important. Within the human services, the term *theory* is loosely used. For example, some people apply the term to ideas that have no empirical basis or are so vague that they defy verification and testing. Sometimes, the ideas called a "theory" are little more than a description of someone's personal style. The social worker must be able to distinguish between practitioner style and a genuine conceptual framework for practice.

The utility of a given framework depends on the nature of the problems or issues receiving the worker's attention, the characteristics of the clients or consumers, the phase in the helping process, and the setting or organizational context of practice. A framework that is useful under one set of circumstances may be misleading in another. For example, a framework that is helpful in guiding work with voluntary clients may be of little use with involuntary, court-ordered clients. A framework that is useful with teenagers may not be useful with elderly persons, and one that is useful with persons of one ethnic group may prove ineffective when used with clients of another group. When selecting a framework, one must grapple with the question: With what types of clients, with what kinds of problems, in what practice settings, and under what circumstances will a particular conceptual framework provide guidance? In addition, the worker must always ask: Does the framework allow me to address the uniqueness of this particular client or client group? Social workers must beware of frameworks that are either so narrow or so abstract that they no longer describe life's realities as experienced by the clients.

In working with a specific client or client group, social workers may use several practice frameworks together or sequentially. They may shift from one to another as they move through the phases of the helping process (see Chapter 7). Frameworks have differing levels of utility during the various phases of helping and problem solving. For example, the general systems perspective and the ecosystems perspective are most helpful in the beginning phases (e.g., problem definition and assessment), but neither are prescriptive when it comes to the later phases of planning, implementing, or evaluating an intervention. On the other hand, a framework such as behavior modification provides detailed guidance on implementing behavior change, but presumes that a specific behavior has been identified as a problem and will be the focus of the intervention.

Several factors should be considered when selecting a practice framework. First, it should be consistent with social work's purpose and must never call for activities that are incompatible with social work's *Code of Ethics*. In addition, the activities required to utilize the framework must fall within the worker's competence.

Questions that a social worker might consider when selecting a practice framework include the following:

1. What is the unit of intervention? Does the framework focus on the individual? Couple? Family unit? Peer group? Organization? Community?

2. What type of client change is expected? For example, changes in values or attitudes? Changes in behavior? Expanded knowledge? Access to new resources? Acquisition of new skills?

3. Does the framework offer an explanation of how and why change occurs?

4. When applying the framework, what is the role of the social worker? For example, is the worker an advisor? Teacher? Counselor? Broker of services? Case manager? Administrator? Planner? Researcher? Advocate?

5. What are the implicit or explicit assumptions concerning the relationship between the professional and the client? For example, Lofquist (1989, 38–41) identifies three very different professional viewpoints toward clients:
   - *Clients as objects.* Professionals are experts and know what should happen and clients are encouraged or manipulated into doing what the professionals decide is "best" for them.
   - *Clients as recipients.* Professionals have concluded they have the services needed by the clients and the clients are expected to utilize the services in a cooperative and appreciative manner.
   - *Clients as resources.* Clients are viewed as having ideas and solutions to the problems they are experiencing and as being in the best position to know what they need and what will and will not work in their situations.

6. What power balance exists in the client-worker relationship? For example, is the worker to be viewed by the client as a friend? Expert? Authority figure? Advisor? Consultant? Companion? Colleague?

7. What is the primary medium of communication? Does the framework rely on verbal exchanges? Expression through art or games? Writing and reading? Precise and planned communication or unplanned and freewheeling exchanges?

8. Does the framework specify when its use is appropriate and effective, as well as when its use would be inappropiate? Are data used to support these beliefs?

9. Does the framework identify types of clients or situations for which use of this approach might be harmful?

10. Does the framework acknowledge the importance and impact of cultural or ethnic differences and religious values and beliefs? Do descriptions of the framework explain how it can be adapted to clients of various backgrounds?

11. Does the framework describe the setting or organizational context required for effective application? Agency-based practice? Private practice? Will the client be seen in an office? In the client's home?

12. Is the framework applicable when the client is involuntary or court ordered? When the client is not cooperative?

13. Does the framework offer an explanation of how it is similar to and different from other commonly used frameworks?

14. Does the framework require the application of a unique set of techniques or are the suggested techniques the same as those used with other frameworks?

15. Does the framework exclude certain clients or situations, either explicitly or implicitly? For example, what about the individual who does not understand the English language? The person who does not read? The individual who cannot or will not attend an office interview? The individual who cannot pay a fee? The individual whose primary concerns are a lack of food, shelter, health care, protection from harm, and so on? The individual with significant physical, sensory, or intellectual limitations?

16. Does the framework emphasize keeping the client within his or her family and social networks? Or does it emphasize removal of the client from the influence of family, peers, or others in the client's near environment?

It should be recognized that a worker's selection of a practice framework is never a completely objective process. Workers bring subjective factors to the selection process, such as the feeling that a particular approach fits best with the worker's practice style or that it works better than other approaches. However, subjective factors alone are not sufficient. By passing the various practice approaches through a screen of questions such as those just described, a greater degree of rationality can be added to the process.

Selected Practice Frameworks

Developing a *practice frame of reference* requires the thoughtful selection of the perspectives, theories, and models that will make up the social worker's repertoire. When first developing one's frame of reference, the worker may adopt only a limited number of frameworks. Gradually, the number can be expanded to fit the needs of one's employing agency and one's interests and abilities.

To aid in the selection process, a sampling of commonly used frameworks is described next. Each brief description highlights a few key concepts and assumptions that set the framework apart from others. Taken as a whole, these descriptions heighten one's awareness of how different professionals may view the problems of social functioning and how and why they might approach the change process in different ways. These descriptions begin with six perspectives (generalist, general systems, ecosystems, strengths, ethnic-sensitive, and feminist). A sampling of practice theories and models is also provided, beginning with those that are more individually oriented and progressively moving to families, small groups, organizations, and concluding with the identification of a few frameworks used in work with communities. The reader is reminded that no one approach is always best. Most social workers draw ideas and techniques from several theoretical frameworks and are, therefore, somewhat *eclectic* in their approaches.

Selected Practice Perspectives

One element of a social worker's practice framework is his or her practice perspective(s). As identified in Chapter 3, a practice perspective directs the worker to focus most attention on certain factors when approaching a practice situation. One or more of the following (or other) perspectives might be selected as part of the worker's frame of reference.

THE GENERALIST PERSPECTIVE

Purpose.   To ensure that the social worker will approach every client and situation in a manner open to the use of various models, theories, and techniques and will focus on several levels of intervention, from micro to macro.

Application.   This way of thinking about practice is most relevant and most needed during the beginning phases of the helping process, when the problem is being defined and assessed and when decisions are being made concerning what needs to be changed and what approaches might be used. This perspective directs the worker to identify and consider several possible points and levels of intervention and then select the one or ones that are most appropriate and feasible.

Description.   Social work practice has been described as inherently generalist (Landon 1995). According to the *American Heritage Dictionary*, a **generalist** is "a person with broad general knowledge and skills in several disciplines, fields, or areas." Thus, the terms *generalist practice* and *generalist social worker* refer to a social work practitioner who has a broad range of knowledge and skills, who draws on several practice theories and models, and who can move with minimal difficulty from one field of practice to another. The opposite of generalist practice is one characterized by specialization, either by type of client served, by method used, by level of intervention, or by primary role assumed by the social worker.

The social worker utilizing the generalist perspective is willing and able to focus on a variety of factors that may contribute to problems in social functioning. These include conflicts among values and beliefs; broken relationships; distortions of thinking; lack of knowledge and information; destructive individual and family patterns; alienation and loneliness; oppression, injustice, and racism; poverty and the lack of basic resources; misuse of power by those in authority; misguided or unworkable programs and policies; and so on.

The generalist social worker is prepared to work with a variety of client systems, such as the following:

- Face to face, one on one, with a single person
- A whole family
- A formal group such as a treatment or support group
- Committees or task groups
- A formal organization such as an agency or a network of agencies
- Legislators and policymakers

Given the wide range of activities, the generalist must be prepared to assume a variety of social work roles. These include, for example, the roles of advocate, case manager, counselor or therapist, group facilitator, broker of service, fund-raiser, program planner, policy analyst, and researcher.

The generalist expects to mold and fit his or her approach to the client's unique situation and concerns and to characteristics of the local community, rather than expect the client to conform to the professional's or agency's preferred method of responding to the client. Consequently, the generalist avoids selecting an intervention method or approach until after he or she and the client have worked together to complete a careful assessment of the client's concern or problem and considered the several ways in which the client's problem or concern can be defined and conceptualized.

Based on their study of the generalist conception of practice, Schatz, Jenkins, and Sheafor (1990, 223) identify four elements that most clearly characterize the generalist perspective.

1. *A multidimensional, theoretical orientation that emphasizes an interrelatedness of human problems, life situations, and social conditions.* At the heart of this perspective is the view that both the type and level of intervention should not be decided until after carefully considering the different ways in which the client's concern or problem might be defined and approached. This perspective is especially compatible with both the general systems and ecosystems perspectives as they too assist the social worker in assessing a situation by focusing on system interactions without predisposing that worker toward a specific intervention strategy.

2. *A knowledge, value, and skill base that is transferable between and among diverse contexts, locations, and problems.* The more specialized frameworks may, implicitly or explicitly, prescribe or limit the settings where a worker is prepared to practice or the type of client, problem, or concern the worker is prepared to address. However, the generalist perspective can be applied in any human services organization or geographic context and used with a wide variety of clients and concerns. That transferability has job mobility value to the worker, but is a trade-off for the more in-depth knowledge and skills that are required in specialized settings.

3. *An assessment unconstricted by any particular theoretical or interventive approach.* The generalist perspective requires that the social worker be *eclectic* (i.e., draw ideas and techniques from many sources). It requires that the worker be versatile enough to at least initiate practice activities in a variety of situations. That is not to say that the generalist is expected to be an expert in the application of all theories and models. Rather, the generalist should be knowledgeable enough to know when he or she can responsibly serve the client and when it is necessary to refer elsewhere for more specialized interventions.

   4. *Selection of strategies and worker roles are made primarily on the basis of the client's problem, goals, situation, and the size of the systems that are targeted for change.* The generalist perspective calls for the social worker to adapt his or her practice activities to the unique client situation. Sometimes that may require working directly with the client, with key persons in the client's immediate environment, and at other times working to change agency and community factors that affect the clients or the services.

   The flexibility offered by this perspective is particularly useful when the social worker's job description demands the performance of multiple roles (see Chapter 4). However, it is recognized that many agencies have missions, job descriptions, and policies that point practitioners in certain directions (e.g., individual change, group services, community development) that may not always make it appropriate to approach practice from a generalist perspective.

   Generalist is, perhaps, the most universally held perspective among social workers. The accreditation standards of the Council on Social Work Education (CSWE) require that all baccalaureate programs prepare graduates for generalist practice. Also, master's-level social work education programs are now required to build their more specialized programs on a generalist base and several schools have advanced generalist practice as the primary practice approach for which their graduates are prepared.

SUGGESTED READINGS

Heus, Michael, and Allen Pincus. *The Creative Generalist: A Guide to Social Work Practice.* Barneveld, Wis.: Micamar, 1986.

Kirst-Ashman, Karen, and Grafton Hull. *Understanding Generalist Practice.* Chicago: Nelson-Hall, 1993.

Landon, Pamela. "Generalist and Advanced Generalist Practice." In *Encyclopedia of Social Work.* Vol. 2, 19th ed., edited by Richard L. Edwards. Washington, D.C.: NASW, 1995, pp. 1101–1108.

Pincus, Allen, and Anne Minahan. *Social Work Practice: Model and Method.* Itasca, Ill.: F. E. Peacock, 1973.

Schatz, Mona S., Lowell E. Jenkins, and Bradford W. Sheafor. "Milford Redefined: A Model of Initial and Advanced Generalist Social Work." *Journal of Social Work Education* 26 (Fall 1990): 217–231.

THE GENERAL SYSTEMS PERSPECTIVE

Purpose.   To assist the social worker in maintaining a focus on the dynamic interplay of the many biological and social systems that affect client behavior and functioning.

Application. This way of thinking about clients and their situations is most useful in the beginning stages of the helping process, especially during assessment. Also, given the principle that every part of a system is affected by every other part, this perspective reminds the worker that usually there are several points of intervention and types of intervention that can help client systems to change.

Description. A *system* is an identifiable whole that consists of several interrelated and interdependent parts and processes. General systems theory seeks to describe the principles by which systems function, grow, develop, and interact with other systems. These principles are used to predict the behavior of biological and social systems and to formulate strategies for changing a system. Systems theory has been attractive to social workers because it provides terminology and metaphors for describing client systems (e.g., individuals, families, organizations) and the process of change.

As just indicated, a system consists of numerous parts. If, for example, a family is the primary system of attention—the *focal system*—it is possible to identify several subsystems: the spouse subsystem (husband-wife relationship), the parental subsystem (parent-child relationship), and the sibling subsystem (child-child relationships). Each system is also part of a larger *suprasystem*. The suprasystem for a social agency, for example, would be the community social welfare system.

A *symbiotic relationship* is assumed to exist among the parts of a system. Each component is, to some degree, affected by all other parts of the system. A change in one part will impact all other parts. Because of this, a social worker's assessment must anticipate how a given intervention will affect others in the client's immediate environment. For example, social workers usually want to work with both the husband and wife when focusing on a marriage problem, recognizing that a change by one will affect the other.

All systems have boundaries. It is a person's skin, for example, that defines the physical boundary of that individual. The boundary of a social system (e.g., family, organization, community) is less distinct. The *boundary* of a social system distinguishes between those individuals who "belong" and those who do not. That determination often requires a judgment call related to the situation being addressed. For instance, regarding a family's plans to purchase an automobile, an emancipated 30-year-old child would probably not be considered part of the system. However, if funeral plans for a grandparent were being made, that same adult-aged child might be an essential component of the family system. All biological and social systems are *open systems,* which means that the boundary is permeable and allows the exchange of matter, energy, and information across the boundary. However, systems vary in degree of openness.

Systems are constantly changing and are often more chaotic and unpredictable than it seems. However, systems tend to function in ways that preserve a dynamic equilibrium, or a *steady state,* but these times of relative stability are temporary at best. Although systems naturally seek a certain amount of growth and development, they resist radical change, attempting to maintain a safe degree of sameness. When significant change does occur, the system tends to move rather quickly to a more stable level of functioning, thereby establishing a new steady state. A pattern of ongoing change, therefore, tends to be one of plateaus rather than progress at a constant pace. It is useful for the social worker to recognize every system's inherent resistance to rapid or extensive change.

The concept of *entropy* refers to the tendency of systems to become disorganized, to disintegrate, or to run down and die. Without a minimum level of organization, a system loses its identity and ability to interact meaningfully with other systems. *Negative entropy* (or negentropy) refers to the forces that preserve the system's organization, promote its development, and keep it alive. All systems need matter (resources), energy, and/or information to counteract entropy and maintain organization. Social work practice often involves helping systems achieve a favorable steady state by preserving or increasing their negentropy.

System functioning includes four interrelated activities: (1) *input* (taking in needed energy, information, etc.); (2) *conversion operations* (activities that process the input and convert it into forms that can be used by the system to sustain functioning); (3) *output* (interactions with other systems); and (4) *feedback* (processes by which the system monitors its own functioning and makes needed adjustments in order to maintain a steady state). For a social worker to develop understanding of a client system, it is necessary to explore how each of these four major processes are operating.

Equifinality tells us that a particular effect may result from several causes. For example, the social worker who is providing services to the parent of a child with a severe disability should not assume that stress reported by the parent is necessarily caused by the child's disability. Although the child's disability may be one contributor, the concept of equifinality would suggest that the worker also look for other possible causes (i.e., many causes, same effect). The concept of *multifinality* helps us understand that a given action may produce several different outcomes. For example, a social worker may help an alcoholic husband stop drinking only to find that his new sober behavior is causing new forms of marital conflict (i.e., one cause, many effects). These two concepts speak to the inherent complexity and unpredictability of change processes.

The system concept of *interface* refers to the meeting or overlapping of two or more systems. One can visualize, for example, the interface of a family and a school or the interface of a patient and his or her family with a hospital. The social worker works at the interface of these systems (i.e., does "boundary work") in order to improve the interactions between the client system and other relevant systems in that client's environment.

SUGGESTED READINGS

Chess, William A., and Julia M. Norlin. *Human Behavior and the Social Environment: A Social Systems Model*, 2nd ed. Boston: Allyn and Bacon, 1991.

Greene, Roberta. "General Systems Theory." In *Human Behavior Theory and Social Work Practice*, edited by Roberta Greene and Paul Ephross. New York: Aldine, 1991, pp. 227–259.

Rodway, Margaret. "Systems Theory." In *Social Work Treatment*, edited by Francis Turner. New York: Free Press, 1986, pp. 514–539.

THE ECOSYSTEMS PERSPECTIVE

Purpose.   To maintain the social worker's focus on the person-in-environment context of a practice situation.

Application.   This conceptual lens adds to understanding of the various ways a client system may adapt to a changing environment in order to cope, survive, and compete for needed resources. It is most useful during the phases of assessment and planning because it conceptually places the client system within a situational and environmental context. For example, it reminds the social worker that families must function within and adapt to a certain neighborhood, community, and cultural environment and that the social agencies and social programs designed to serve families must operate and compete for resources within a particular economic and political context.

Description.   The ecological perspective draws selected concepts from the science of ecology and uses them as metaphors for describing social interactions and social change. *Ecology* focuses on the relationship between organisms and their biological and physical environment. Smith (1986, 344) defines an *ecosystem,* the unit of study in ecology, as "a partially or completely self-contained mass of organisms . . . [that engages in] energetic interactions and material cycling that link the organisms in a community with one another and their environment." It is this emphasis on describing and explaining interdependence, exchange, and interrelatedness that has attracted social workers to ecology.

Ecosystems are never static; each species in an ecosystem is slowly but constantly adapting to an ever-changing environment. If the environment changes too rapidly or if the species cannot change fast enough, the species may be overpowered by a competing and more adaptable species. *Competition* among the various species is the major process that shapes ecological communities. As long as commonly used resources are abundant, different species can share them, but since certain resources are usually limited, the species must compete in order to survive.

The concept of *symbiosis* refers to a close and frequent interaction between two species wherein one or both benefit from this interaction. There are three major types of symbiosis. In *mutualism,* both species benefit from the interaction (e.g., bees and flowers). In *commensalism,* one species benefits while the other is neither helped or harmed. However, in *parasitism,* the parasite benefits while its host is harmed. When assessing a case situation, the social worker can use these concepts to understand person-environment interactions and, when planning intervention activities, should attempt to maximize mutualism and commensalism.

In order to become more competitive and cope successfully with a changing environment, a species must be *adaptive.* One form of adaptation is *specialization.* When a species is specialized, it is at an advantage because its specialization has the effect of reducing competition. On the other hand, a highly specialized species is more vulnerable to the effects of a rapidly changing environment. As a general rule, specialization will increase a species' survivability in a relatively stable environment, but decreases survivability in a rapidly changing environment. These concepts, for example, are useful in helping clients make decisions concerning job-training opportunities or when considering whether an agency should change its mission.

The concept of *niche* refers to the composite of physical, chemical, and biological factors needed by a particular species to survive, remain healthy, and reproduce within its ecosystem. Niche can be thought of as the special place or environment (i.e., the "comfort zone") in which the species is most able to function effectively. Related to niche is the concept of *carrying capacity* (i.e., the maximum number of individuals of each species that can live in a particular ecosystem). If the population of a species exceeds the ecosystem's carrying capacity, disease, starvation, and predation will diminish the population. Most plant and animal species are limited to a narrow niche, but humans are quite adaptable and use tools and technology to alter their environment.

Concepts such as these provide new ways of thinking about the functioning of individuals and groups—and even about how social agencies might compete for funding. The ecological perspective reminds us that the environment in which we must function is constantly changing and that individuals, communities, and whole societies must adapt to these changes. Also, ecological thinking prevents social workers from defining only psychological processes or only the external environment as the cause of human distress. Germain and Gitterman (1987, 489) explain that, from an ecological perspective, "people's needs and predicaments are viewed as outcomes of people-environment exchanges, not as the products of personality or environment alone." Clearly, the ecosystems perspective has found its way into social work thinking and has proven useful in helping social workers view their concerns and clientele in new ways.

SUGGESTED READINGS

Germain, Carel B., and Alex Gitterman. "Ecosystems Perspective." In *Encyclopedia of Social Work*. Vol. 1, 18th ed., edited by Anne Minahan. Silver Spring, Md.: NASW, 1987, pp. 488–499.

Greif, Geoffrey, and Arthur Lynch. "The Eco-Systems Perspective." In *Clinical Social Work in the Eco-Systems Perspective*, edited by Carol Meyer. New York: Columbia University School of Social Work, 1983, pp. 35–71.

Meyer, Carol. "The Search for Coherence." In *Clinical Social Work in the Eco-Systems Perspective*, edited by Carol Meyer. New York: Columbia University School of Social Work, 1983, pp. 5–34.

THE STRENGTHS PERSPECTIVE

Purpose.   To ensure that the social worker is attentive to client strengths during assessment and intervention.

Application.   This perspective is necessary in work with all clients and during all phases of the helping process. It is an important counterbalance to the preoccupation with client problems, pathology, and deficits that is so pervasive in the service delivery system and inherent in many of the practice theories and models used by social workers.

Description. According to Saleebey (1992, 6), the *strengths perspective* asks the worker to be "guided first and foremost by a profound awareness of and respect for client's positive attributes and abilities, talents, and resources and aspirations." It is presumed that all individuals and groups have overlooked untapped reserves of capacity, energy, courage, fortitude, integrity, and other assets. If these strengths are recognized and used in the change process, they elevate the client's motivation and the potential for positive change.

Saleebey (1992, 7) also explains that a strengths assessment strives to understand how the client "has managed to survive, perhaps thrive, in an oppressive, even catastrophic environment." According to Weick, Rapp, Sullivan, and Kisthardt (1989),

> The fact that people have lacks is acknowledged, but the best strategy for supporting further gains is a conscious emphasis on gains already made. . . . The question is not what kind of life has one had, but what kind of life one wants, and then bringing to bear all the personal and social resources available to accomplish this goal. . . . Strengths are not thought to represent symptoms of underlying pathology. Therefore, there is no need for a clinical diagnosis. A client's expressed aspirations are accepted as sincere. Acceptance and validation replace skepticism about what clients can "realistically" achieve. (p. 353)

This approach also recognizes that in every environment, no matter how harsh, there are individuals and organizations that do care and have something positive to contribute. Because this perspective views clients as true experts on their situations, the professional's role is mostly that of facilitator or consultant (see Item 12.8).

SUGGESTED READINGS

Saleebey, Dennis, ed. *The Strengths Perspective in Social Work Practice*. New York: Longman, 1992.
Weick, Ann, Charles Rapp, Patrick Sullivan, and Walter Kisthardt. "A Strengths Perspective for Social Work Practice." *Social Work* 34 (July 1989): 350–354.

THE ETHNIC-SENSITIVE PERSPECTIVE

Purpose. To ensure that the social worker is attentive to ethnic, cultural, and religious diversity among clients and that the problem and effects of discrimination are addressed in practice.

Application. This perspective is needed whenever the practice involves a client who has a background different from the worker, and especially when there is reason to believe that social oppression and discrimination may be related to the client's problem or concern. It is relevant during all phases of the helping process.

Description. The ethnic-sensitive conceptual lens draws attention to the fact that many of the clients served by social agencies are members of an ethnic group and, therefore, social work practice and the service delivery system must be attuned to that reality. A client's social class, culture, ethnicity, and religious beliefs have a significant impact on help-seeking behavior and on whether a particular approach—or even a specific type of service—will be perceived as needed, relevant, and useful. It has a bearing on whether and how a client defines a particular situation as a problem, which possible solutions make sense, and, additionally, how the client expects to be treated by the service system and its service providers.

Norton (1978) observes that every person is simultaneously part of (1) a *sustaining subsystem,* which includes such powerful influences as those of our economic, political, legal, and educational systems; and (2) a *nurturing subsystem,* which consists of a person's more intimate relationships, such as those within one's family, support networks, and neighborhood. Conflict, tension, alienation, and deflated self-esteem can result if there is an incongruence between the values and beliefs represented by a person's nurturing system and those of the sustaining system. Such an incongruence is most likely to occur among minority populations and recent immigrants.

It is increasingly important for social workers to become culturally competent, which Green and Leigh (1989) describe as the ability

> to give aid or assistance to patients or clients in ways that are acceptable and useful to them because they are congruent with the [client's] cultural background and expectations. Ethnic competence also refers to the service provider's ability to learn about the cultural context of a presenting problem and to integrate that knowledge into a professional assessment, diagnosis, and intervention. (p. 8)

If a client's ethnic group is one that has been subjected to oppression and discrimination, the social worker must be alert to client fear and distrust based on prior experiences. (For more information on culture and ethnicity, see Items 8.8 and 12.2.)

SUGGESTED READINGS

Devore, Wynetta, and Elfride Schlesinger. *Ethnic Sensitive Social Work Practice,* 4th ed. Boston: Allyn and Bacon, 1996.

Ingelhart, Alfreda, and Rosina Becerra. *Social Services and the Ethnic Community.* Boston: Allyn and Bacon, 1995.

Lum, Doman. *Social Work Practice and People of Color,* 2nd ed. Pacific Grove, Calif.: Brooks/Cole, 1992.

Schlesinger, Elfriede, and Wynetta Devore. "Ethnic Sensitive Practice." In *Encyclopedia of Social Work.*Vol. 1, 19th ed., edited by Richard L. Edwards. Washington, D.C.: NASW, 1995, pp. 902–908.

THE FEMINIST PERSPECTIVE

Purpose.   To ensure that the effects of societal beliefs and stereotypes concerning gender and sex roles are addressed in social work practice.

Application.   This perspective is probably needed whenever the client is a female and always when there is reason to believe that gender discrimination or sex-role stereotyping is related to the concerns brought to the social worker's attention.

It is applicable throughout the phases of the helping process but is especially important during problem definition and assessment.

Description.   The feminist perspective emphasizes that societal beliefs concerning gender differences and sex roles affect how a client's problem is defined by a professional or agency, the nature of the relationship between helper and client, and the type of assistance actually provided to the female client. Central to this perspective is the assumption that the problems experienced by a female client and the problems of women, in general, always have a cultural and political dimension. Social workers need to be especially alert to the impact of societal values and ideologies that lead to the domination and exploitation of women by males or male-dominated organizations and institutions.

Among the other beliefs and principles that are important to this practice perspective are the following:

■ The client–social worker relationship is egalitarian. The helper is viewed as a partner or a colleague to the client, not as an expert or authority figure.
■ The client's concerns and problems are assessed within a sociopolitical context. Special attention is given to the assessment of power relationships in the client's life.
■ Helping is not limited to a clinical approach; rather, it also emphasizes advocacy and political action to modify societal institutions.
■ The helper is willing to share relevant personal experiences.
■ The helping process emphasizes empowerment and has a strong educational component, including teaching about sexism, sex-role stereotyping, gender discrimination, and social and historical factors that have affected attitudes toward women, including how women view themselves.
■ The client is expected to be an active participant in the helping process, and its focus is on client strengths rather than deficits or pathology.
■ An emphasis is placed on creating women's social networks and support groups.

The feminist perspective is intended primarily for practice with women but it has many characteristics—such as its emphasis on empowerment, social justice, and political action—that should be part of practice in all settings. This perspective might appropriately be a part of the practice frame of reference of both male and female social workers.

SUGGESTED READINGS

Bricker-Jenkins, Mary, Nancy Hooyman, and Naomi Gottlieb. *Feminist Social Work Practice in Clinical Settings.* Newbury Park, Calif.: Sage, 1991.
Bricker-Jenkins, Mary, and Patricia Lockett. "Women: Direct Practice." In *Encyclopedia of Social Work.* Vol. 3, 19th ed., edited by Richard Edwards. Washington: D.C., 1995 (pp. 2529–2539).
Hanmer, Jalna, and Daphne Statham. *Women and Social Work: Towards Woman-Centered Practice.* Chicago: Nelson Hall, 1989.
Van Den Bergh, Nan. *Feminist Practice in the 21st Century.* Washington, D.C.: NASW, 1995.

Selected Practice Theories and Models

A practice perspective does not stand alone; it is used in conjunction with various practice theories and models. For example, a social worker operating from the generalist perspective may elect to use behavioral techniques, small group theories, and/or theories of organizational change, depending on the roles being performed and the demands of the practice situation. More specialized practitioners may draw on a smaller number of theories or models, but apply them with more depth of knowledge and skill.

In addition to the reference books mentioned in the opening paragraph of this chapter and those listed as Suggested Readings, there exist a number of general reference books that provide one-chapter overviews of the common theoretical frameworks used in therapeutic work with individuals, families, and small groups. These include, for example, Corsini and Wedding (1995), Prochaska and Norcross (1994) and Vondracek and Corneal (1994).

PRACTICE BASED ON PSYCHODYNAMIC THEORY

Purpose.   To improve the social functioning of individuals by helping them to understand better their inner thoughts and conflicting feelings.

Application.   Prerequisite to the use of this approach is a client who is motivated, verbal, and willing and able to participate actively in a series of regularly scheduled sessions. This approach is seldom useful if the client has limited intellectual ability, is chemically dependent, or is overburdened by problems related to adverse social or economic conditions (e.g., poverty, inadequate housing).

Description.   This frame of reference is rooted in psychoanalytic theory and therapy. Psychodynamic explanations of behavior are built around the concept of unconscious motivation and the belief that much of our behavior serves some underlying and often hidden purpose. It recognizes the power of emotions (e.g., fear, anger, envy, revenge, sexual attraction) and the inner conflicts that arise in trying to cope with strong feelings in a socially acceptable manner. Largely unconscious *ego defense mechanisms* operate to manage our anxiety and intrapsychic conflict (see Item 12.9).

The concept of *ego* refers to various intrapersonal processes that mediate between primitive drives (e.g., fight-flight) and the demands of external reality and social norms. The ego is also the problem-solving part of personality. Thus, a term such as *ego supportive treatment* refers to interventions that maintain and enhance problem solving and adjustment. Many internal psychological conflicts and interpersonal problems are presumed to be rooted in early childhood experiences that disrupt or distort the normal stages of personality development. The concept of *object relations* (people relations) explains how current patterns of thinking, feelings, and behavior reflect, at an unconscious level, one's childhood relations with others, especially parent figures.

Change results from the cathartic expression of inner conflicts and emotion and from gaining insight (understanding) into how prior experiences gave rise to troublesome thoughts, feelings, and behavior. The change process requires a lengthy and in-depth therapeutic relationship wherein the client feels safe to explore and express private thoughts and feelings.

Social workers have adapted psychodynamically based therapeutic methods to the realities of agency-based practice and to the social work profession's emphasis on viewing the client within a situational and environmental context. Examples include those approaches that make heavy use of *ego psychology* (Goldstein 1995), *psychosocial therapy* (Woods and Hollis 1990; Turner 1988) and the *problem-solving approach* (Perlman 1957).

As a general rule, the practice frameworks based on psychodynamic concepts give relatively more attention to the client's inner thoughts and feelings than to the social and environmental factors that impact on client functioning. Recent contributions to this literature incorporate concepts from the cognitive behavioral approach and various theories of family treatment.

SUGGESTED READINGS

Goldstein, Eda. *Ego Psychology and Social Work Practice*, 2nd ed. New York: Free Press, 1995.
Polansky, Norman. *Integrated Ego Psychology*, 2nd ed. New York: Aldine, 1991.
Woods, Mary, and Florence Hollis. *Casework: A Psychosocial Therapy*, 4th ed. New York: McGraw-Hill, 1990.

PRACTICE BASED ON BEHAVIORAL THEORY

Purpose.   To improve the social functioning of individuals, couples, families, or organizations by helping them learn new behaviors and eliminate troublesome ways of behaving.

Application.   In order to use this approach successfully, it must be possible to specify and operationally define a behavior(s) that needs either to increase or decrease in frequency, duration, or intensity. Also, either the client or the professional must be able to control the consequences that follow the behavior targeted for change. This approach can be used with a nonvoluntary client if the professional has the ability to monitor the client's behavior closely and the authority to allocate reinforcement (rewards) to the client. It has less applicability when the client's concerns center primarily on covert mental processes such as decision making, value conflicts, and distorted thinking.

Description.   The key premise of behavioral theory is that people repeat behaviors that are rewarded and abandon behaviors that are not rewarded or for which they are punished. In other words, behavior is determined by its consequences. By manipulating and changing the availability of *reinforcement,* the worker can help clients eliminate dysfunctional behaviors and learn desirable patterns of functioning.

The change process requires modification of the client's immediate environment so that it elicits and rewards the desired behaviors and no longer reinforces dysfunctional ones. This approach, more than any other, emphasizes behavioral observation, data collection, and careful measurement before, during, and after the intervention. Decisions that guide the change process are made on the basis of data, not on the basis of assumptions about why people might behave as they do.

The behavioral approach has been attractive to professionals working in residential treatment and correctional settings where it is possible to observe the behavior of clients and exercise control over the rewards they receive. In many applications, the client is taught how to modify his or her own behavior through the self-administration of reinforcers. (See Item 14.4 for more explanation.)

SUGGESTED READINGS

Hudson, Barbara, and Geraldine MacDonald. *Behavioral Social Work.* Chicago: Dorsey Press, 1986.

Sundel, Sandra, and Martin Sundel. *Behavior Modification in the Human Services,* 3rd ed. Newbury Park, Calif.: Sage, 1993.

Thyer, Bruce, and Walter Hudson, eds. *Progress in Behavioral Social Work.* New York: Haworth, 1987.

Watson, David, and Ronald Tharp. *Self-Directed Behavior: Self-Modification for Personal Adjustment,* 6th ed. Pacific Grove, Calif.: Brooks/Cole, 1993.

PRACTICE BASED ON COGNITIVE-BEHAVIORAL THEORY

Purpose.   To improve social functioning by assisting the client to learn more realistic and positive ways of perceiving, thinking about, and interpreting their life experiences.

Application.   This approach requires that the client have the requisite intellectual capacity and be willing to invest the time needed to monitor and analyze his or her ways of thinking and to practice techniques designed to change long-standing habits of thought. Cognitive-behavioral theory is especially useful in work on problems of depression, low self-esteem, and self-defeating thoughts and behaviors. It can be used with children (age 10 and older), adolescents who are developing their patterns of thinking, and, of course, adults.

Description.   This framework integrates selected concepts from behavioral and learning theory and applied behavioral analysis with ones drawn from the study of cognitive processes (i.e., how people think and process information). It focuses on the interplay among cognitions (thoughts), emotions, and behavior.

How and what people think strongly influence their emotional reactions (feelings) and their behaviors. Problem behaviors and personal distress are often rooted in faulty, irrational, and rigid thinking and in unfounded and unrealistic beliefs about the way things ought to be. For example, if people operate on the belief that one must always keep others from getting upset, they face a lifetime of distress because this is an unrealistic expectation.

During a course of cognitive-behavioral therapy, the client is encouraged and helped to identify, monitor, reexamine, and correct patterns of thought and faulty assumptions that give rise to problems. The client is usually taught specific skills and procedures to recognize the content and impact of their cognitions, evaluate the validity of their perceptions and assumptions, and view events and situations with greater objectivity. A variety of techniques are used: cognitive restructuring, logical analysis, role modeling, behavioral rehearsal, paradoxical instruction, desensitization, covert extinction, cognitive flooding, and so on.

Within this general framework there are subdivisions, such as rational emotive therapy and cognitive therapy. Practitioners and theoreticians tend to differ on whether to emphasize the cognitive side or the behavioral side of the cognitive-behavioral construct and the degree to which they work to modify fundamental cognitive process such as perception, memory, information processing, judgment, and decision making (see Items 8.6, 14.8, and 14.12).

SUGGESTED READINGS

Beck, Aaron, Arthur Freeman, and Associates. *Cognitive Therapy of Personality Disorders.* New York: Guilford Press, 1990.

McMullin, Rian. *Handbook of Cognitive Therapy Techniques.* New York: W. W. Norton, 1986.

Schuyler, Dean. *A Practical Guide to Cognitive Therapy.* New York: W. W. Norton, 1991.

PRACTICE BASED ON PERSON-CENTERED THEORY

Purpose. To improve social functioning by increasing self-understanding and feelings of self-worth through a nondirective helping process that emphasizes intense listening and reflecting on the client's thoughts and feelings.

Application. This approach usually requires that the client be voluntary, highly motivated, articulate, thoughtful, and not overburdened by problems caused by external or environmental factors.

Description. With roots in humanistic and existential philosophic traditions, this approach emphasizes the uniqueness of every person, perceptions of self, and the meanings assigned to personal experience. It is built on a positive and optimistic view—people are fundamentally good, prosocial, striving for self-actualization, and in search of life's meaning.

Change occurs when self-imposed psychological barriers are identified and examined, thereby freeing the client's innate potential for positive personal growth. The social worker strives to demonstrate openness, empathy, warmth, and genuineness and makes frequent use of paraphrase, reflection, and other techniques of active listening (see Item 8.3). The practitioner must be deeply respectful and nonjudgmental, refrain from giving advice, and avoid diagnosing and labeling. The focus is on the here and now rather than on past experience.

SUGGESTED READINGS

Levant, R. F., and J. M. Shileim, eds. *Client-Centered Therapy and the Person-Centered Approach.* New York: Praeger, 1984.

Rowe, William. "Client Centered Theory." *In Social Work Treatment,* 3rd ed., edited by Francis Turner. New York: Free Press, 1986.

PRACTICE BASED ON REALITY THERAPY

Purpose.   To improve the social functioning of individuals or a group of individuals by focusing on the client's current realities, on taking responsibility for one's own behavior, and on respecting the needs and rights of others.

Application.   Reality therapy is one of the few approaches that presumes the client will be involuntary. Its use is popular among practitioners working in correctional settings and in substance abuse treatment programs.

Description.   This approach is associated with the writings of psychiatrist William Glasser. It recognizes that people always have choices and emphasizes the need for them to assume personal responsibility for their actions and to behave in ways that do not cause harm to self and others. The focus is on here-and-now problems and on recognizing and addressing the need to adapt to one's reality. An important aspect of reality therapy is attention to moral standards of right and wrong.

Generally speaking, Glasser rejects concepts of unconscious motivation and nonorganic mental illness because, he contends, they provide handy excuses for irresponsible behavior and result in much self-examination but little real change. Despite its seemingly no-nonsense and confrontive approach, Glasser emphasizes the need to treat clients with respect and dignity. Recent additions to the reality therapy literature suggest it is moving toward the cognitive-behavioral approach.

SUGGESTED READINGS

Glasser, William. *Reality Therapy: A New Approach to Psychiatry.* New York: Harper & Row, 1965.
Wubbolding, Robert. *Using Reality Therapy.* New York: Harper & Row, 1988.

THE INTERACTIONAL MODEL

Purpose.   To improve social functioning by mediating the interactions between people.

Application.   This model was developed by and for social workers and grew out of work with typical social work clients. It can be appropriately utilized in a wide variety of agency settings and is applicable to work with individuals, families, and small groups. It presumes that many clients are nonvoluntary.

Description.   This model of social work practice is associated with the research and writing of Lawrence Shulman. It focuses on four major elements: (1) people (i.e., clients); (2) the interactions among and between people; (3) the social systems and people with whom the client interacts; and (4) the element of time or the phases in the helping process. In addition to providing concepts for understanding interactions, this model describes nearly 30 specific skills or techniques that might be applied in the different phases of helping.

This highly process-oriented approach focuses on interaction as the client currently experiences it. It is presumed that both the client and those with whom the client interacts are striving toward deeper involvement and connectedness in interpersonal relationships, even though there is often conflict and ambivalence about these relationships.

Great emphasis is placed on social context. Neither the client's relationships with others nor the client's problem can be understood apart from their social and environmental contexts. And, of course, the social worker is part of that ever-changing context. The model calls on the worker to be very active, responsive, and human—a "third force" who functions as a mediator among people and between people and systems. Shulman (1992b) describes the helping process as a triangle.

> On the left is the client reaching out with all available strength, attempting to negotiate important systems while often simultaneously throwing up defenses that cut one off from the very systems one needs. On the right are the systems (family, school, hospital staff, etc.) reaching out to incorporate the client but often reaching ambivalently. In the center is the worker, whose sense of function and skills are mobilized in an effort to help client and system overcome the obstacles that block their engagement. (p. 21)

This model has also been applied to the process of staff supervision (Shulman 1993).

SUGGESTED READINGS

Shulman, Lawrence. *Interactional Supervision.* Washington, D.C.: NASW, 1993.
———. *Interactional Social Work Practice: Toward an Empirical Theory.* Itasca, Ill.: F. E. Peacock, 1992a.
———. *The Skills of Helping Individuals, Families and Groups,* 3rd ed. Itasca, Ill.: F. E. Peacock, 1992b.

THE STRUCTURAL MODEL

Purpose.   To ensure that a social work intervention gives adequate and appropriate attention to the client's social environment and to social change.

Application.   This model is intended for use in all social work interventions involving direct practice with individuals, couples, and families.

Description.   Given the social work profession's focus on the person-in-environment and the inherent difficulty of giving equal attention to both dimensions, social workers have tended to choose either a clinical orientation or a social change orientation. The structural approach addresses this tension by asking practitioners to consider, first, changing the client's environment. Whereas most other orientations to direct practice focus mostly on helping individuals adjust to their situations, the structural approach aims to modify the environment first so it better meets the needs of the individual. Goldberg and Middleman (1989) explain that this approach rests on two assumptions:

1) Problems are not viewed as individual pathology, but as a manifestation of inadequate social arrangements. Thus, clients . . . are not . . . seen as impaired or deficient individuals. . . . 2) Social change is the obligation of all social workers wherever they are in the bureaucratic hierarchy. In fact, [social change] begins with how the direct service practitioners conceptualize their response to a specific client. Social change is not . . . relegated to specialists within the social work profession (community organizers, planners, social policy-makers). Rather it is pursued at every level of assignment, every working day by all social workers, and especially by those who must face the clients directly. (p. 16)

The model identifies four social work roles (conferee, broker, mediator, and advocate) and assumes the worker will move from role to role, depending on the needs of the client. It is built on several fundamental principles: Be accountable and responsible to the client; take actions that identify and engage others who have concerns or problems similar to those of the client; maximize the supports that exist in the client's environment; proceed on the basis of "least contest" (e.g., assume the role of broker before mediator and mediator before advocate); and teach and reinforce behaviors and skills that will help the client take control of his or her life. For use with the structural model and other approaches, Middleman and Wood (1990) describe 63 specific interpersonal skills.

SUGGESTED READINGS

Goldberg, Gale, and Ruth Middleman. *The Structural Approach to Direct Practice in Social Work.* New York: Columbia University Press, 1989.
Middleman, Ruth, and Gale Goldberg Wood. *Skills for Direct Practice in Social Work.* New York: Columbia University Press, 1990.

THE CRISIS INTERVENTION MODEL

Purpose.   To address the special needs and concerns of a client in an acute, psychological crisis.

Application.   The crisis intervention model is applicable whenever the functioning of an individual or family has been suddenly and dramatically impacted by some personal loss or tragedy. It is to be used during a four- to six-week period following the event that precipitated the crisis.

Description.   This model emphasizes the importance of providing a focused and time-limited intervention to the person who is unable to function because of a personal crisis. Parad and Parad (1990) explain that crisis intervention is a process for

actively influencing psychosocial functioning during a period of disequilibrium in order to alleviate the immediate impact of disruptive stressful events and to help mobilize the . . . psychological capabilities and social resources of persons directly affected by the crisis . . . Interventive efforts have two principal aims: (1) to cushion the stressful event by immediate or emergency emotional and environmental first aid and (2) to strengthen the person in his or her coping . . . through immediate therapeutic clarification and guidance during the crisis period. (p. 4)

This approach differs from most others because it calls for (1) quick access to the client and rapid response by the helper; (2) use of time limits (e.g., five sessions over four-week period); (3) focused attention on the crisis configuration (i.e., on the nature of the precipitating event and its subjective meaning to client); (4) emphasis on helping the client make decisions and take action; and (5) mobilization of helping resources within the client's social network. Those using the model may draw on a variety of theories, techniques, and intervention procedures. (See Item 14.30 for more description.)

SUGGESTED READINGS

Greenstone, James, and Sharon Leviton. *Elements of Crisis Intervention*. Pacific Grove, Calif.: Brooks/Cole, 1993.

Hoff, Lee Ann. *People in Crisis*, 4th ed. San Francisco: Jossey-Bass, 1995.

Parad, Howard, and Libbie Parad, eds. *Crisis Intervention—Book 2*. Milwaukee, Wis.: Family Service Association of America, 1990.

THE TASK-CENTERED MODEL

Purpose.   To improve the social functioning of a client through the use of an intervention structure that emphasizes action steps by the client.

Application.   This approach can be used with individuals, couples, families, and small groups and can be adapted to work with the nonvoluntary client. Because of its emphasis on taking action and the completion of agreed upon tasks, it is especially useful with clients who are attempting to manage problems caused by insufficient resources such as a job, housing, day care, transportation, and so on.

Description.   After discussing their problem or situation, some clients know what they need to do but are unable to move ahead and take the actions necessary to significantly change their situation. The emphasis of this model is on helping the client take those actions. Specific actions are called *tasks*.

The tasks to be worked on can take many forms: making a decision within a certain time frame, securing a needed resource, learning a skill, expressing concerns to an employer, and so forth. Large tasks are broken down into several smaller ones so the client will experience success and sustain motivation. Priority setting is used to limit the number of tasks to only two or three per week. Such structuring and the time limits help the client stay focused and mobilize inner resources. The model is largely empirical, stressing the monitoring and measurement of task completion.

This model's emphasis on action and the completion of tasks should not be interpreted as a lack of concern about clients' inner thoughts and feelings. However, this approach rests on the belief that people are more likely to change as a result of taking action than as a result of simply discussing their thoughts and feelings. Task-centered practitioners draw on a variety of theories and techniques to help clients accomplish agreed upon tasks (see Items 13.1, 13.2, and 15.3).

SUGGESTED READINGS

Epstein, Laura. *Brief Treatment and a New Look at the Task-Centered Approach,* 3rd ed. New York: Macmillan, 1992.

Reid, William. *Task Strategies: An Empirical Approach to Clinical Social Work.* New York: Columbia University Press, 1992.

Tolson, Eleanor, William Reid, and Charles Garvin. *Generalist Practice: A Task-Centered Approach.* New York: Columbia University Press, 1994.

THE SOLUTION-FOCUSED MODEL

Purpose.   To improve social functioning and facilitate client change within 1 or not more than about 12 sessions.

Application.   This approach is used with both individuals and families. It is appropriate when the client and worker are limited in the number of times they can meet together. The model can be adapted for use with the nonvoluntary client.

Description.   A variety of influences, some of them economic, are forcing social workers and agencies to place great emphasis on efficiency and to limit the number of times they meet with a client. This has given birth to new models of brief and time-limited counseling and therapy. Solution-focused therapy is one of the better-developed approaches. It is built on several assumptions and principles.

- Rapid change and rapid resolution of problems are possible. (Research has not been able to demonstrate that long-term therapy is more effective that brief therapy.)
- All clients (individuals and families) have within them the ideas, strengths, and resources to begin resolving their problems; these must be identified, mobilized, and supported by the social worker.
- Clients do not resist changes that make sense and provide relief from distress. Problems do not serve a hidden purpose; clients are not invested in maintaining their problems for some unconscious motive.
- It is not necessary to understand the cause of a problem in order to resolve it. Because problems are social constructions, there are many ways of viewing and defining a situation and many ways of solving a problem. There is no one right way to deal with a troublesome situation.
- Because of the ripple effect, only small positive changes are needed because even small changes will, over time, have a positive impact on all other parts of the client system.

This model focuses on the nature of the client's solutions to a problem rather than on the nature of the problem. It emphasizes solution finding by the client rather than problem solving directed by the professional. The professional's task is to help the client identify and implement his or her own solutions. Various questioning techniques are used to help the client recognize that he or she already has some control over the problem and some workable ideas on how best to solve it.

SUGGESTED READINGS

Cooper, John. *A Primer of Brief Psychotherapy.* New York: W. W. Norton, 1995.

Fanger, Margot. "Brief Therapies." In *Encyclopedia of Social Work.* Vol. 1., 19th ed., edited by Richard L. Edwards. Washington, D.C.: NASW, 1995, pp. 232–334.

O'Hanlon, William, and Michele Weiner-Davis. *In Search of Solutions: A New Direction in Psychotherapy.* New York: Norton, 1989.

Walter, John, and Jane Peller. *Becoming Solution-Focused in Brief Treatment.* New York: Brunner/Mazel, 1992.

PRACTICE BASED ON THE FAMILY THERAPIES

Purpose. To improve the social functioning of families by working with the family as a system and changing the interactions among family members.

Application. Prerequisite to the use of the various family therapies are family members who have at least a minimum level of concern for each other and want to preserve or strengthen their families. At least some of the members should be voluntary clients, although it is expected that others will have been coerced into participation.

Description. Within this broad framework, there are numerous theories and models that have much in common: The family system is the unit of attention, all or most family members are engaged in the change process, focus is on the interaction of members within the family system, emphasis is on current behavior (here and now), and active techniques are employed (e.g., family sculpture, role-play, homework). The differences between the approaches are mostly a matter of emphasizing certain concepts and procedures over others. The practitioner of family therapy must be eclectic. In order to illustrate how work with families might differ from one practitioner to another, a few of the key assumptions associated with commonly used approaches are presented.

The *communications approach* (e.g., Satir, 1983, 1988) presumes that family problems are caused mostly by faulty communication. Change occurs when family members learn to really listen to each other and express themselves openly and honestly. The practitioner models forthright communication and uses various experiential exercises to help family members express themselves.

As suggested by its name, the *structural approach* (e.g., Minuchin and Nichols 1993) focuses primarily on a family's structures. Special attention is given to the delineation and interaction of the spousal, parental, and sibling subsystems and their interaction. Unhealthy alliances and splits among these subsystems and either overly rigid or overly flexible boundaries are major sources of family dysfunction. Change occurs when the roles and responsibilities of the family's members and the subsystems are clarified and agreed to by all.

The *family systems approach* (e.g., Papero 1990) focuses on the struggle of family members to simultaneously be a part of a family group and be individuals apart from the family system. Problems arise when an individual either suppresses the self and is overly involved (enmeshed) with his or her family or, at the other extreme, rejects his or her family connection. This approach also recognizes the tendency of a family to repeat patterns established in prior generations (i.e., the intergenerational transmission of dysfunction) and is sensitive to issues related to the family life cycle.

The *strategic family therapy* approach (e.g., Haley 1987) gives primary attention to family rules (the often unstated family beliefs about how family members should think and behave) and to the distribution and use of power. The word *strategic* connotes an active and directive role by the therapist in strategically selecting interventions that move the family toward a pattern of behavior deemed desirable by the therapist.

A model termed the *social learning approach* (e.g., Sanders and Dadds 1993) draws its concepts and techniques from behavior therapy and behavior modification. It presumes that family conflicts and problems arise because the members have not learned basic skills such as communication, relationship and conflict resolution, and/or that appropriate behavior is not reinforced within the family system. Thus, the practitioner places much emphasis on the teaching skills. *Functional family therapy* (Alexander and Parsons 1982) resembles the social learning approach but also examines the social context of family problems and the function served by problem behaviors. Problem behaviors are viewed as unsuccessful efforts by family members to cope with issues of dependence versus independence, freedom versus control, and intimacy versus distance.

The *narrative approach* (e.g., Gilligan and Price 1993) derives its name from its focus on personal stories and anecdotes and the stories of a community or culture (e.g., fables, movies, biographies, novels, etc.) that people use as frames of reference to describe their situations and create meaning and purpose. It recognizes the power of language and the patterns of thought embedded in our society to shape the way we think about ourselves, construct our "reality," and define our individual and family problems. Special questioning techniques are used to help family members reexamine the way they think and to construct alternative stories that lead to new patterns of behavior.

As is true of psychotherapy in general, most approaches to family therapy developed out of work with middle-class and upper-class families. They may not work as well with families that are economically poor or members of a minority group. Social workers are challenged to select approaches that can be adapted to agency-based practice and their profession's emphasis on social functioning and the person-in-environmental construct. To help them make that selection, Kilpatrick and Holland (1995) offer a practical *integrative model* that ties the use of various approaches or types of family interventions to four possible levels of family functioning. Consequently, the recommended approach for a family that is struggling with meeting basic needs (food, safety, etc.) is different from the approaches recommended for the economically stable family having problems around issues of unclear boundaries or a lack of intimacy in family relationships.

Other books of particular interest to social workers include those by Hartman and Laird (1983), Reid (1985), Ho (1987), Janzen and Harris (1996) and Carter and McGoldrick (1989). (For additional information on work with families, see Items 12.3, 12.7, 12.12, 12.13, 14.7, 14.13, and 14.14.)

SUGGESTED READINGS

Carter, Betty, and Monica McGoldrick, eds. *The Changing Family Life Cycle: A Framework for Family Therapy.* Boston: Allyn and Bacon, 1989.

Gurman, Alan, and David Kniskerm. eds. *Handbook of Family Therapy.* Vol. 11. New York: Brunner/Mazel, 1991.

Horn, Arthur, and J. Laurence Passmore. *Family Counseling and Therapy.* Itasca, Ill: F. E. Peacock, 1991.

Kilpatrick, Allie, and Thomas Holland. *Working with Families: An Integrative Model by Level of Functioning.* Boston: Allyn and Bacon, 1995.

Nichols, Michael, and Richard Schwartz. *Family Therapy,* 3rd ed. Boston: Allyn and Bacon, 1995.

PRACTICE BASED ON MODELS OF FAMILY PRESERVATION

Purpose.   To avoid having to place a child into foster care by focusing on those dysfunctions or circumstances that place the child at risk of placement.

Application.   This approach is appropriate whenever a child is at risk of placement and when there is reason to believe that an intense and focused intervention and frequent monitoring will sufficiently reduce the chances that the child will be abused or neglected.

Description.   There are several models of family-based or home-based services. All are designed to prevent out-of-home placements and all share a common set of beliefs about what works best with dysfunctional families in which children are at high risk of being removed and placed in foster care because of abuse, neglect, or the parent's inability to deal with a rebellious adolescent. Most of these programs share the following characteristics.

- A primary worker or case manager establishes and maintains a supportive, nurturing relationship with the family.
- One or more associates serve as team members or provide backup with the primary worker.
- Workers (or their backup person) are available 24 hours a day for crisis calls or emergencies.
- The home is the primary setting for service delivery (i.e., heavy to exclusive use of in-home interviews).
- A wide variety of helping options are used (e.g., both concrete and clinical services).
- Emphasis is place on identifying and building on family strengths.
- Keep the size of caseloads small (two to six families per worker).
- Employ maximum use of informal and natural helping resources, including the extended family, neighbors, churches, support groups, and so on.
- The parents remain in charge of and responsible for their family as primary caregivers.

- To prevent placement, the agency is willing to invest at least as much in a child's own family as society is willing to pay for the foster care of that child.
- Services are goal oriented and time limited, usually lasting from one to four months.

SUGGESTED READINGS

Berg, Insoo Kim. *Family-Based Services,* New York: W. W. Norton, 1994.

Kinney, Jill, David Haapla, and Charlotte Booth. *Keeping Families Together: The Homebuilders Model.* New York: Aldine, 1991.

Whittaker, James, Jill Kinney, Elizabeth Tracy, and Charlotte Booth. *Reaching High-Risk Families.* New York: Aldine, 1990.

PRACTICE BASED ON THE CLUBHOUSE MODEL

Purpose. To improve the social and vocational functioning of adults with serious mental illness by providing a supportive community based on mutual needs, interests, and shared work.

Application. Member and staff experiences in this model are structured and given meaning through work that benefits both the clubhouse and individual members of the community. Each member chooses the character and extent of his or her involvement in the activity of the clubhouse community at any given time. For many people with mental illness and their families, the clubhouse model is considered an especially helpful, noncoercive source of continuing support for adaptive community living.

Description. At the heart of the model is the opportunity for *membership,* through which participants are viewed as "members" of a clubhouse community rather than as clients or patients. Their days are ordered by shared work and by a focus on work roles instead of continuous receipt of treatment or rehabilitation services. Three additional themes characterize social work practice in clubhouses.

First, respect and equality among members and staff are emphasized. Both members and staff are full participants in the daily operation of the clubhouse. Typically, members and staff cook and serve meals, write and produce a regular newsletter, clean and maintain the club, reach out to isolated members in the community, and serve in other useful, contributing work roles. Members are involved in all aspects of program development, operation, and governance of the clubhouse. By design, member work is essential in the life of the club, yet is not coerced.

Second, attention is given to enhancing multiple related aspects of each member's life, including social relations, recreation, housing, transportation, medical care and medication management, and employment. The value of meaningful work and its regenerative potential is underlined in the "work-ordered day" of the clubhouse and in the array of competitive work opportunities found and developed by the clubhouse. Through competitive, *transitional employment* placements, members (as they become ready) choose the responsibilities of real jobs, as opposed to sheltered or "make-work" experiences often found in conventional treatment or rehabilitation programs.

Third, it is recognized that mental illness often produces complex, idiosyncratic, and disabling social and psychiatric symptoms and that most members utilize psychotropic medications to manage symptoms of illness. Nonetheless, clubhouses are based on the belief that illness should not define the person. Members are viewed as valued human beings with abilities to be discovered and applied. The focus is on developing strengths and competencies, providing a foundation for satisfying and successful social functioning. Members are not trained in daily living skills; rather, they use and develop such skills through the practical work of building, maintaining, and using the clubhouse "opportunity center" (Glickman 1992).

The central task of social work staff within the clubhouse model, then, is to lead the creation and maintenance of member roles within the club and the larger community. Members and staff collaborate to build and maintain a clubhouse, centered in work-ordered daily life (i.e., clubhouse work units, transitional employment placements, permanent placements). The staff assists members in developing and carrying out new roles and applying their skills and aptitudes in work, training, and/or education. Generalist practice skills are considered the most relevant preparation for work in this model (Dougherty 1994).

SUGGESTED READINGS

Beard, John H., Rudyard n. Propst, and Thomas J. Malamud. "The Fountain House Model of Psychiatric Rehabilitation." *Psychosocial Rehabilitation Journal* 5 (January 1982): 47–53.

Dougherty, S. J. "The Generalist Role in Clubhouse Organizations." *Psychosocial Rehabilitation Journal* 18 (July 1994): 95–108.

Glickman, Mark. "The Voluntary Nature of the Clubhouse." *Psychosocial Rehabilitation Journal* 16 (October 1992): 39–40.

Jackson, Robert L., Dorothy Purnell, Stephen B. Anderson, and Bradford W. Sheafor. "Emerging Opportunities for Social Work Education: The Clubhouse Model of Community Support for Adults with Mental Illness." *Journal of Social Work Education.* (Accepted for publication.)

Lamb, H. Richard. "A Century and a Half of Psychiatric Rehabilitation in the United States." *Hospital and Community Psychiatry* 45 (October 1994): 1015–1020.

Propst, Rudyard n. "Standards for Clubhouse Programs: Why and How They Were Developed." *Psychosocial Rehabilitation Journal* 11 (October 1987): 25–30.

PRACTICE BASED ON SMALL GROUP THEORIES

Purpose. To improve the social functioning of individuals or couples through participation in a small group experience under the guidance of a professional.

Application. The client must be willing to participate in discussions and small group activities and behave in ways that do not disrupt the group or harm other members. Group experiences can be designed for a number of purposes (e.g., training, therapy, mutual support, social action). A skillful group leader will be able to engage clients who are nonvoluntary participants.

Description. Work with groups occurs in a variety of settings for a multitude of purposes. Although there are some differences in approach, these differences are usually a matter of emphasis, rather than in terms of fundamental concepts and skills. The differences are related to the purpose of the group (e.g., a task group vs. a treatment group); the role assumed by the professional (e.g., group leader, therapist, teacher, mediator, facilitator); and whether attention is focused mostly on the behavior of the individuals that make up the group or mostly on the functioning of the group as a social system. Numerous small group-related orienting theories provide social workers with background knowledge on such dimensions as group leadership, goals, structure and norms, group cohesion, conflict, stages of group development, and intragroup communication. For purposes of illustration, it is useful to identify some of the ways in which work with groups may differ and a few of the frameworks that influence practice.

Task groups are common to practice in the indirect services. These goal-oriented groups tend to be quite structured and formal. Examples include agency boards, committees, staff meetings, and community planning groups. Such groups are characterized by the use of a written agenda, *Robert's Rules of Order,* and clear assignments of leadership roles and member responsibilities.

The *interactional model,* or mediating model, places the social worker in the role of a mediator between members of the group and between the group and its environment, including the agency that has sanctioned the group's formation. This approach places a high value on client self-determination.

The *group treatment approach* (remedial model) views the group as a therapeutic environment and a behavior-changing influence on its members. The focus is mostly on the members as individuals and on the problems they are having outside the group. However, a client's behavior within the group may be used as a way of assessing and illustrating his or her attitudes and behavioral patterns. In these groups, the social worker assumes the role of a therapist, expert, and group leader. In some groups, such as those used in the treatment of sex offenders and persons addicted to alcohol or drugs, there is heavy use of confrontation and members are required to complete assigned homework and strictly adhere to established rules. In such groups, self-determination is not a priority.

In many agency settings, groups are used to promote normal growth and development and the learning of ordinary skills for living rather than for the purpose of coping with serious problems or correcting dysfunctional behavior. Many of the groups that are part of the YMCA/YWCA programs, summer camps, after-school programs, and senior citizen programs are of this type. These groups make use of the *developmental approach.* The worker typically assumes the role of leader, planner, and arranger of group activities and makes heavy use of programming (see Item 14.23).

When groups are used for the purpose of *teaching and training,* they are goal oriented and the worker assumes the roles of leader and teacher. Depending on the topic being addressed (e.g., parent training, learning communications skills, learning job skills, learning about a medical condition, etc.) and the number of times the group will meet, there may or may not be a lot of emphasis on member interaction, building trust, and developing a sense of belonging to the group.

A number of theoretical influences from outside the social work profession have had an impact on how social workers approach their practice with groups and, of course, also with individuals and families. These include *Gestalt therapy, transactional analysis, encounter groups, psychodrama, behavior modification,* and *positive peer culture.* Descriptions of these can be found in the *Encyclopedia of Social Work* (1995), Fatout (1992), and Corsini and Wedding (1995). (For additional information on group work, see Items 12.29, 13.8, 14.23, and 14.41.)

SUGGESTED READINGS

Brown, Leonard. *Groups for Growth and Change.* New York: Longman, 1991.

Fatout, Marian. *Models for Change in Social Group Work.* New York: Aldine, 1992.

Reid, Kenneth. *Social Work Practice with Groups: A Clinical Perspective.* Englewood Cliffs, N. J.: Prentice Hall, 1992.

Toseland, Ronald, and Robert Rivas. *An Introduction to Group Work Practice,* 2nd ed. Boston: Allyn and Bacon, 1995.

PRACTICE BASED ON THE ADDICTION MODEL

Purpose.   To improve the social functioning of individuals by helping them overcome compulsive behavioral patterns.

Application.   This model has proven useful in explaining and changing behaviors that have certain common characteristics: They have a mood-altering quality, they have grown more frequent over time, and they are now out of control. Given the nature of addiction, this model presumes that most clients are nonvoluntary. Since a direct confrontation of the client's defenses is a first step in treatment, the structure and control provided by an institutional or hospital setting are often necessary during the beginning stages of the process.

Description.   The addiction model recognizes that many people are unable to discontinue patterns that cause them much misery. These patterns often take the form of alcohol, drug, and tobacco abuse; eating disorders; child molestation; dangerous risk taking; and compulsive sexual activities, spending, gambling, or physical exercise. Even the compulsive pursuit of money or power can be viewed as an addiction. It is believed that during the beginning phases of an addiction, the individual uses the substance or activity mostly as a means of feeling better and coping with distress caused by emotional pain or some unmet need. When it works to help the person feel better, usage is further reinforced and, subsequently, it is used again and again. Over time, the substance or activity consumes more and more of the individual's attention and resources and displaces other aspects of living. As the addiction spins out of control, the individual develops a system of denial, rationalizations, and behaviors that ensure access to the substance or activity.

Successful treatment requires the breakdown of the denial and helping the client learn more functional means of meeting his or her needs and coping with life's problems. The process of treatment and recovery from an addiction typically moves thorough six stages.

1. There is a breakdown of denial and defensiveness; the person recognizes that he or she has a problem.
2. The person with the addiction develops a sense of hope based on an awareness that other people with similar problems have made a successful recovery.

3. The person comes to understand how the addiction developed and why it has continued and gotten worse over time.
4. The person acquires the personal resolve, strength, and social support necessary to change the patterns of thought, behavior, and life-style that reinforce the addiction.
5. The person takes action, one step at a time and over an extended period of time, to abandon old patterns and practice healthy patterns.
6. The person continues to monitor and manage his or her life so as to stay free of the addictive substance or activity.

Both one-on-one counseling and small group experiences (e.g., 12-step programs) help the person move through these stages and achieve sobriety and a healthy life-style. Even after the individual is able to function without the addictive substance or activity, he or she must constantly work to avoid being drawn back into the addiction. (For further information, see Item 11.9 and the journal entitled *Addictive Behaviors.*)

SUGGESTED READINGS

Doweiko, Harold. *Concepts of Chemical Dependency,* 2nd ed. Pacific Grove, Calif.: Brooks/Cole, 1993.
Freeman, Edith. *The Addiction Process: Effective Social Work Approaches.* New York: Longman, 1992.
McNeece, C. Aaron, and Diana DiNitto. *Chemical Dependency: A Systems Approach.* Englewood Cliffs, N.J.: Prentice Hall, 1994.

PRACTICE BASED ON MODELS OF SELF-HELP

Purpose.   To improve social functioning through a group experience and discussions with others who have or have had similar concerns or problems.

Application.   In order for this approach to be effective, the client must be willing and able to attend a series of group meetings, listen to others, and share personal information and concerns. However, some self-help groups include nonvoluntary and even court-ordered participants.

Description.   This approach rests on the belief that an individual can be helped by those who have experienced similar problems and that, in the process of helping others, people learn to better cope with their own problems. Alcoholics Anonymous, Parents Without Partners, and Parents Anonymous are but a few of the many self-help groups.
     Self-help groups usually depend on leaders indigenous to the group. Some rotate the leadership role from one member to another. A few look to leadership by professionals or members who have received special training on how to conduct and facilitate meetings. Most self-help groups are designed around five basic assumptions and beliefs.

1. People have a need to tell their story and to be heard by others. They are especially receptive to suggestions from those who have similar concerns and life experiences.
2. All people have strengths that can be mobilized. People are helped as they help others. We all have much to learn from and to teach others.
3. People are attracted to and feel most comfortable in small groups that are informal, noncompetitive, nonbureaucratic, nonintellectual, and nonelitist.
4. People want and can use simple rules and principles that provide practical guidance on how to cope with day-to-day problems (e.g., live one day at a time, walk your talk, follow the 12 steps, etc.).
5. Helping and caring for others is a natural human activity and not a commodity to be bought and sold.

Social workers may relate to self-help groups in a number of ways: (1) refer clients to an appropriate group, (2) provide consultation when asked for assistance, (3) serve on the group's advisory board, (4) serve as a guest speaker when asked, and (5) help create and/or lead a needed self-help group.

SUGGESTED READINGS

Gitterman, Alex, and Lawrence Schulman. *Mutual Aid Groups, Vulnerable Populations and the Life Cycle,* 2nd ed. New York: Columbia University Press, 1994.
Powell, Thomas. *Understanding the Self-Help Organization.* Newbury Park, Calif.: Sage, 1994.
Powell, Thomas, ed. *Working with Self-Help.* Silver Spring, Md.: NASW, 1990.

MODELS FOR CHANGING ORGANIZATIONS

Purpose.   To change the functioning of a human services agency in order to increase its ability to address the needs and concerns of its staff and clients or consumers.

Application.   The various models of organizational development and change can be used with both private and public agencies. However, their application presumes that the social worker has been given sanction by the agency's governing board or administration to plan and facilitate a change process.

Description.   The complexity of organizational change becomes evident when one recognizes that organizations are made up of numerous individuals, each with a unique personality and each with numerous roles, functions, and tasks to perform; a set of formal and informal structures, processes, and norms; and a system of power and authority relationships. Moreover, an organization is a legal entity whose functions are tied directly to its bylaws or charter and conditioned by its financial resources. Working with organizations is complicated by the fact that they are dynamic systems that must function within an ever-changing social, political, and economic environment.

Every social worker employed by an agency, regardless of position, must give some attention to agency functioning. The agency must operate in an effective and efficient manner if it is to provide appropriate client services and receive the funding it needs to achieve that objective. As one moves from line worker to supervisor or middle manager, or to agency administrator, the responsibility to engage in organizational maintenance and change activities increases. The activities at any level, however, may include informing upper-level administrators and/or board members of staff concerns and client needs, proposing specific changes in agency policies and procedures, arranging input from consultants or persons providing training programs, participating on committees to study specific aspects of the organization's performance, designing program evaluation tools, and so on.

Kettner, Daley, and Nicols (1985) identify three approaches to planned change in a human services organization. The *policy approach* achieves change by developing and adopting new policies that will guide the organization and its operation. Those working for change direct their efforts toward the groups and individuals who are authorized to make policy and allocate resources at either the local, state, or national level. They provide these decision makers with data and new insights concerning a specific condition, problem, need, or issue and advocate for a specific type of policy change.

The *program approach* seeks to change the organization by designing and introducing new or additional programs and services to better express and implement existing policy. Change efforts are directed primarily at persons in administrative and managerial positions (i.e., those who have authority to modify programs and alter the procedures and technology used to carry out the work of the organization).

The *project approach* introduces change at the interface between line staff and the clients or consumers of the organization's services. Small-scale projects are used to try out or demonstrate new ways of working with agency clients. Policies and programs remain the same but staff skills and performance are enhanced. Change efforts often take the form of in-service training and increasing sensitivity to clients' needs and behavior.

Rapp and Poertner (1992) add a supplementary approach to this list—the *client-centered management approach*—which focuses attention on the relationship between managerial behaviors and client outcomes. It is predicated on the belief that an excessive emphasis on powerful decision makers, funding bodies, interagency communication, and personnel issues has diverted the attention of administrators from their primary purpose—assuring that the social agency provides high-quality services that truly respond to client needs. This approach strives to secure client input into agency decision making and planning.

One additional approach to organizational change, *the teamwork model,* is primarily concerned with the manner in which workers interact to implement agency programs. It is based on two premises. First, it recognizes that the typical bureaucratic organization places excessive control in the hands of administrators, which, in turn, reduces innovation and consensus among workers about how best to provide services (Shuster 1990). Second, it recognizes that given the explosion of knowledge and technology, specialization is increasingly required in almost every occupation. But with specialization comes the need for better coordination. The providers of human services must be especially able to coordinate practice activities since services to clients are often provided simultaneously by several disciplines and several different agencies. Unfortunately, the usual ways of structuring an organization may erect barriers to coordination. Garner (1988), for example, notes that within the typical agency departmental structure,

> employees are grouped together according to role, function, and title for the purposes of program implementation and staff supervision. Social workers, teachers, child care workers, nurses, psychologists, and psychiatrists are assigned to separate departments or to distinct sections of a large, all-encompassing administrative unit. These staff groupings . . . allow staff members with similar training and job responsibilities to work together in setting goals, developing program ideas, implementing therapeutic interventions, and evaluating results. And yet, this reasonable and logical form of organization results ultimately in more disconnection and less therapy. (p. 7)

The teamwork approach has proven especially useful as a means of retaining the specialized knowledge and competencies of the several helping professions, and at the same time coordinating their practice activities. To make multidisciplinary teams viable working units, they are given the authority to plan and implement programs and to make decisions about the personnel and resources necessary to carry out their assignments. In this process, the teams become powerful forces for innovation and policy and program change.

The selection of an approach to organizational change depends, of course, on one's assessment of the organization's functioning and internal dynamics. A pivotal issue in that assessment is how and why the organization behaves as it does. Gummer (1987) identifies three models for examining that question: the rational model, the natural-system model, and the power-politics model.

The *rational model* of organizational functioning assumes that the people making decisions are in agreement about the organization's goals and are committed to those goals. Thus, they view their organization simply as an instrument or a way of structuring the work that needs to occur in order to reach a goal. Given that view, proposed changes (e.g., restructuring, personal assignments, adoption of new technologies, reallocation of resources, etc.) will be accepted if it becomes apparent that they would improve the organization's capacity to achieve its goals. Change, therefore, results from such activities as self-study, obtaining the advice of consultants, examining the complaints or suggestions made by clients or consumers, in-service training on new technologies, and so forth.

The *natural-system model* views an organization as a system made up of a multitude of individuals, roles, subsystems, and formal and informal processes striving to function and survive in a wider social environment. It recognizes that the personnel and the many subdivisions of an organization can be easily distracted from the organization's official mission by such things as job stress, unclear work assignments, and disagreements over duties and responsibilities. This model views an organization as needing to balance its goal achievement with maintenance functions. Change efforts emphasize the clarification of goals and objectives, improving communication, recognizing and addressing the social and emotional needs of personnel, morale building, and the like.

If one approaches an organization from the *power-politics model,* the organization is viewed as essentially a political arena in which various individuals, departments, units, and other subsystems compete for power, resources, and personal advantage (Gummer 1990). The achievement of the organization's official or stated goals may take a backseat to other agendas. To change such an organization, one needs access to persons in positions of influence over the organization and must be able to persuade those within the organization that a specific change is in their self-interest. External forces such as media exposure, investigations by citizen groups, legislative oversight, and lawsuits might be necessary for modifying organizations.

SUGGESTED READINGS

Gummer, Burton. *The Politics of Social Administration: Managing Organizational Politics in Social Agencies.* Englewood Cliffs, N.J.: Prentice Hall, 1990.

Kettner, Peter, John Daley, and Ann Nicols. *Initiating Change in Organizations and Communities.* Monterey, Calif.: Brooks/Cole, 1985.

Rapp, Charles A., and John Poertner. *Social Administration: A Client-Centered Approach.* White Plains, N.Y.: Longman, 1992.

Shuster, H. David. *Teaming for Quality Improvement: A Process for Innovation and Consensus.* Englewood Cliffs, N.J.: Prentice Hall, 1990.

MODELS FOR CHANGING COMMUNITIES

Purpose.   To improve the functioning of a community and increase its capacity to address the social needs and concerns of its members.

Application.   The selection of a particular approach to community change must be based on an assessment of the problem or concern targeted for change and, to a large extent, on political factors. Unless the social worker has the authority, responsibility, and/or support of others to work toward a specific community change, his or her efforts are unlikely to succeed, no matter how noble the cause or how much the change is needed.

Description.   Rothman (1995) identifies three models of community organization and planning. Each rests on a different set of assumptions concerning how *community* is defined, the change process, and the role of the professional. The three models are locality development, social planning, and social action.

The *locality development model* (or community development) presupposes that the community consists of people who share a sense of belonging to their locality and can, therefore, reach a consensus on the nature of community problems and what should be done about them. It emphasizes broad citizen participation, sharing of ideas, democratic decision making, cooperative problem solving, and self-help. In the process of working on problems, people learn the practical and leadership skills needed to tackle other concerns of the community. Brilliant (1986) concludes that in performing most community-level social work practice (including activities connected to federated fund-raising, coalitions of human services organizations, ad hoc task forces, and neighborhood organizations), the professional assumes the roles of enabler, facilitator, coordinator, and teacher.

The model known as *social planning* focuses on specific social problems (i.e., crime, inadequate housing, lack of health care, etc.) and the response of the human services delivery system to these problems. It recognizes the complex legal, economic, and political factors that must be addressed in solving a major community problem. Although involvement by ordinary citizens is welcome, the key to community problem solving and change is involvement by influential persons, government officials, and organizations that have authority, power, and influence. This approach also recognizes the vertical dimension in community dynamics and, therefore, the need to involve influential persons and organizations from outside the immediate locality such as city, county, state, and federal government agencies, as well as major national corporations that do business in the community. The social worker using this model gives much attention to fact gathering, data analysis, policy analysis, sharing technical information, and program planning.

The third model, ***social action,*** is usually associated with efforts to correct a social injustice or achieve a needed change for a devalued or disadvantaged group (e.g., those living in poverty, those who suffer discrimination, etc.). It views a community as consisting of diverse groups and special interests that are competing for power and limited resources. Thus, in order to bring about a change in human services programs, there must be a shift in the decisions of those who exercise power and influence—or new decision makers must be given authority to take action. Since it is assumed that those in control will not easily relinquish their power, change requires confrontation with those who have power. The roles of the professional within this model include those of organizer, activist, advocate, and negotiator.

SUGGESTED READINGS

Homan, Mark. *Promoting Community Change.* Pacific Grove, Calif.: Brooks/Cole, 1994.
Rothman, Jack. "Approaches to Community Intervention." in *Strategies of Community Intervention,* 5th ed., edited by Jack Rothman, John Erlich, and John Tropman. Itasca, Ill.: F. E. Peacock, 1995, pp. 26–63.
Rubin, Herbert, and Irene Rubin. *Community Organizing and Development,* 2nd ed. New York: Macmillan, 1992.

Conclusion

As suggested by this survey of conceptual frameworks, the intervention approaches used by social workers have similarities but may differ in what they emphasize. Some differ in terms of basic assumptions about how and why change occurs (see Chapter 7 for additional ideas about the nature of change) and others differ in the characteristics of the clients they are intended to serve. A lifelong activity of the social worker is to carefully select a configuration of perspectives, theories, and models that matches his or her practice style and best meets the needs of his or her clients.

The reader is reminded that no one approach is always superior to others and that a social worker needs to have a basic understanding of several. One's practice framework might include multiple perspectives and an ever-growing repertoire of practice theories and models. Since all frameworks are concerned with helping people change, the worker must always be cognizant of the whole person—humans are thinking, feeling, and behaving biological beings whose survival, growth, and development depend on constant interaction with others and their environment.

SELECTED BIBLIOGRAPHY

Alexander, James, and Bruce Parsons. *Functional Family Therapy*. Monterey, Calif.: Brooks/Cole, 1982.

Brilliant, Eleanor L. "Community Planning and Community Problem Solving: Past, Present, and Future." *Social Service Review* 60 (December 1986): 568–589.

Corsini, Raymond, and Danny Wedding. *Current Psychotherapies*, 5th ed. Itasca, Ill.: F. E. Peacock, 1995.

Dorfman, Rachelle, ed. *Paradigms of Clinical Social Work*. New York: Brunner/Mazel, 1988.

Dryden, Windy, and Ramond DiGiuseppe. *A Primer on Rational Emotive Therapy*. Champaign, Ill.: Research Press, 1990.

Encyclopedia of Social Work, 19th ed., edited by Richard L. Edwards. Washington, D.C.: NASW, 1995.

Fatout, Marian, and Steven Rose. *Task Groups in Social Services*. Newbury Park, Calif.: Sage, 1995.

Gambrill, Eileen. *Critical Thinking in Clinical Practice*. San Francisco: Jossey-Bass, 1990.

Garner, Howard Glenn. *Helping Others Through Teamwork: A Handbook for Professionals*. Washington, D.C.: Child Welfare League of America, 1988.

Gilligan, Stephen, and Reese Price, eds. *Therapeutic Conversations*. New York: W. W. Norton, 1993.

Green, James, and James Leigh. "Teaching Ethnographic Methods to Social Service Workers." *Practicing Anthropology* 11 (1989): 8–9.

Greene, Roberta, and Paul Ephross, eds. *Human Behavior Theory and Social Work Practice*. New York: Aldine, 1991.

Gummer, Burton. *The Politics of Social Administration: Managing Organizational Politics in Social Agencies*. Englewood Cliffs, N.J.: Prentice Hall, 1990.

———. "Organizational Theory for Social Administration." In *Strategies for Community Organization*, 4th ed., edited by Fred Cox, John Erlich, Jack Rothman, and John Tropman. Itasca, Ill.: F. E. Peacock, 1987, pp. 427–440.

Haley, Jay. *Problem-Solving Therapy*, 2nd ed. San Francisco: Jossey-Bass, 1987.

Hartman, Ann, and Joan Laird. *Family Centered Social Work Practice*. New York: Free Press, 1983.

Ho, Man Keung. *Family Therapy with Ethnic Minorities*. Newbury Park, Calif.: Sage, 1987.

Janzen, Curtis, and Oliver Harris. *Family Treatment in Social Work Practice*, 3rd ed. Itasca, Ill.: F. E. Peacock, 1996.

Lofquist, William. *The Technology of Prevention Workbook*. Tucson, Ariz.: Associates for Youth Development, Inc., 1989.

Meyer, Carol H. "Direct Practice in Social Work: Overview." In *Encyclopedia of Social Work*, 18th ed., Vol. 1, edited by Anne Minahan. Silver Spring, Md.: NASW, 1987, pp. 409–422.

Minuchin, Salvador, and Michael Nichols. *Family Healing*. New York: Free Press, 1993.

Norton, Dolores. *The Dual Perspective*. New York: Council on Social Work Education, 1978.

Papero, Daniel. *Bowen Family Systems Theory*. Boston: Allyn and Bacon, 1990.

Perlman, Helen. *Social Casework: A Problem Solving Process*. Chicago: University of Chicago Press, 1957.

Prochaska, James, and John Norcross. *Systems of Psychotherapy*, 3rd. ed. Pacific Grove, Calif.: Brooks/Cole, 1994.

Reid, William. *Family Problem Solving*. New York: Columbia University Press, 1985.

Roberts, R. W., and Helen Northern, eds. *Theories of Social Work with Groups*. New York: Columbia University Press, 1976.

Sanders, Matthew, and Mark Dadds. *Behavioral Family Intervention*. Boston: Allyn and Bacon, 1993.

Satir, Virginia. *The New Peoplemaking*. Mountain View, Calif.: Science and Behavioral Books, 1988.

———. *Conjoint Family Therapy*, 3rd ed. Palo Alto, Calif.: Science and Behavior Books, 1983.

Smith, Robert. *Elements of Ecology*. New York: Harper & Row, 1986.

Turner, Francis. "Psychosocial Therapy" in *Paradigms of Clinical Social Work*, edited by Rashelle Dorfman. New York: Brunner/Mazel, 1988.

———, ed. *Social Work Treatment: Interlocking Theoretical Approaches*, 3rd ed. New York: Free Press, 1986.

Vondracek, Fred, and Sherry Corneal. *Strategies for Resolving Individual and Family Problems*. Pacific Grove, Calif.: Brooks/Cole, 1994.

Wedenoja, Marilyn, Paula Nurius, and Tony Tripodi. "Enhancing Mindfulness in Practice Prescriptive Thinking." *Social Casework* 69 (September 1988): 427–433.

7 The Change Process in Social Work Practice

In previous chapters, social work has been described as a profession devoted to helping people make changes in their own behaviors and in their relationships with social systems such as families, groups, organizations, and communities. Although much social work activity is concerned with bringing about change that will ameliorate or solve an already existing problem, the profession is also concerned with changes that will prevent problems from developing. Change is at the core of practice. In this chapter, the nature of change and the change process are examined.

The Concepts of Change and the Change Process

Humans and all of the social systems created by humans share a common characteristic: They are dynamic; that is, they are in a state of constant change. Some change slowly and some rapidly but they are always changing as they adapt and adjust to the ever-changing environment.

Most of the changes we experience in life occur as a result of biological processes (e.g. growth, development, aging) or choices such as marriage, divorce, becoming a parent, making a job change, and so on. We also experience change forced on us by illness, accidents, injury, and natural disasters (e.g., flood, earthquake, house fire, etc.). Changes in our lives are also tied to large-scale dislocations such as those related to the condition of the economy, drought and famine, and world events such as wars, revolutions, or the collapse of a government. We have a degree of control over some changes but many are beyond the control of individuals and even governments.

Although much of the change we experience just happens, some changes can be chosen, planned, and achieved through individual or group effort. Thus, it is possible to classify changes as either planned or unplanned. A *planned change,* also termed an *intervention* when related to social work practice, is a deliberate action intended to alter a situation or interfere with an expected or usual course of events. Making a planned change happen is far from an exact science. Moreover, an intervention usually has both expected and unexpected consequences that may be either positive, negative, or a mix. Because it is seldom possible to accurately anticipate the future, it is fair to say that trying to make a deliberate change always involves risk taking. For instance, after deliberately moving from *A* to *B*, we may discover that *B* is not quite what we had hoped for or perhaps *B* has an unanticipated adverse effect on ourselves or others.

The term *process* refers to the path or manner of getting from *A* to *B*. In order to facilitate change, the social worker must know how to nurture the process. When one attends to process, one focuses less on what is happening than on how and why it is happening. It is the awareness of and attention to process that usually separates the professional from the well-intentioned but often ineffective layperson. Trying to rush the process is a major reason that change efforts fail.

A planned change does not occur in a quick and steady manner, even when the client is eager for the change. Rather, change occurs in a sequence of several *phases,* or stages, with each phase building on the preceding ones. At each phase, primary attention is given to one set of decisions or actions, but secondary attention may include attention to work to be done in subsequent phases. For example, the primary focus in the first phase of the change process is determining if the client is eligible for service (i.e., an intake decision) offered at the worker's agency. In the course of making that determination, the social worker is also collecting part of the data that will be used for the comprehensive assessment of the client's situation that will later lead to the intervention plan. If lasting change is to occur, certain activities must happen at each phase and they should not be hurried or skipped. The social worker must be alert to what tasks need to be accomplished during a particular phase in order to guide the flow of the change process.

The work of real change is usually difficult and frustrating. Consequently, some degree of *conflict* accompanied by expressions of strong emotions are to be expected during the change process. The social worker must not seek to avoid dealing with such conflict. Rather, he or she must be able to directly address and discuss these conflicts and must be comfortable with the client's expressions of strong feelings.

Resistance to change is a characteristic of all humans and social systems. Systems naturally tend toward preserving the status quo and, therefore, resist or oppose change—particularly if it is rapid, is extensive, or involves significant conflict. Thus, whenever working toward change, attention must be given to the forces of resistance. Resistance can be expected even when the client has demonstrated a strong desire to change.

Closely related to resistance is *ambivalence,* which is a situation of both wanting and not wanting change to occur. For example, an abused spouse may want to leave the abusing partner, but at the same time not want to risk the loss of income and housing. Thus, the client is pulled in opposing directions. Ambivalence can result in the client becoming stuck at a particular phase in the change process. The social worker must be alert to the forces of ambivalence and, when necessary, assist the client in working through this blockage.

The willingness of a client to work actively toward a particular change depends, in large part, on his or her perceptions of the *risks and rewards* associated with the change. If the potential rewards far outweigh the risks, most clients will want to attempt the change. On the other hand, if the change involves high risk, but promises few or uncertain rewards, most clients will be reluctant to engage in the change process. The balance between risks and rewards must be carefully assessed in all change efforts in social work practice.

Actors in Planned Change

Change efforts involve numerous individuals, groups, and organizations. In order to help the social worker clarify his or her professional purpose and relationships with these many people, Pincus and Minahan (1973) suggest the following terminology.

1. *Change agent system:* The change agent [e.g., social worker] and the people who are part of [the change agent's] agency or employing organization.
2. *Client system:* People who sanction or ask for the change agent's services, who are the expected beneficiaries of service, and who have a working agreement or contract with the change agent.
3. *Target system:* People who need to be changed to accomplish the goals of the change agent.
4. *Action system:* The change agent and the people he [or she] works with and through to accomplish [the] goals and influence the target system. (p. 63)

This terminology is especially helpful when planning change at the organizational and community levels, but it also helps describe many situations of individual, family, and group change. It should be noted that in the case of individual counseling or therapeutic intervention, the client, target, and action systems maybe one and the same.

It is useful to remember that when social workers use a term such as *organizational change* or *system change,* they are really talking about how people change—how they change their behaviors, beliefs, values, attitudes, priorities, and so forth. Pincus and Minahan (1973) further explain that social workers seek to change people, not abstractions such as the community, the organization, or the system.

> When we say that communities or organizations or families or groups are client or target or change agent systems, we are referring to the people who make up these systems. If the goal of the change agent is to change the structure of a system—the web of patterned relationships between people—he [or she] does this by influencing people in the system to change the ways they interact with one another. (p. 63)

The Situation as an Arena of Change

Basic to the social work approach to change is giving simultaneous attention to both the person and the environmental context of the practice situation. In a particular episode of practice it is usually not feasible for either the client or the social worker to maintain a focus on all aspects of the person and the total environment. Instead, one must focus on the portion of the total person-in-environment interaction that is of particular concern to the client or the social agency. The selected segment must, of course, be one over which the social worker and/or client have some control or influence. We call that unit of attention the client's situation. We can further describe the ***client situation*** as those aspects of living that the client can experience, comprehend and interpret, and influence at a given time.

Both subjective and objective elements make up the client's situation. For purposes of explanation, these are labeled the actual situation and the perceived situation. The *actual situation* has an objective quality and is defined by such variables as physical characteristics, (e.g., age, sex, size), place (e.g., classroom, house, office), sociocultural factors (e.g., laws, norms, rules, roles), and overt behavior. It can be observed and validated by others. The *perceived situation,* by contrast, is the situation as it is subjectively perceived, interpreted, and constructed in the mind of the individual. Human behavior cannot be understood apart from both its actual and perceived situational contexts.

The concept of client situation becomes even more complex when we recognize that humans respond not only to their perceptions of environment but also to their inner thoughts and feelings. We assume humans are unique among living creatures in that they alone have consciousness—an awareness of self. Only humans form a self-conscious identity, think about themselves, and then interpret, judge, and react to these evaluations of self. People, then, are not passive recipients of environmental forces. Rather, they selectively experience their environment, responding to some parts while ignoring others.

The importance of the perceived or subjective situation is recognized in the social work axiom of "Start where the client is." The social worker must always begin with an exploration and examination of the client's perceptions and interpretations (i.e., individualize the client in order to understand his or her perceived situation). The worker should never assume that because he or she has observed the client's actual situation that the worker also understands the client's perceptions of that situation. It is the subjectiveness of human experience that makes it so difficult to predict how people will respond to a given intervention.

Attention to the person-in-environment and person-in-situation constructs yields some very fundamental ***guidelines for planned change.***

- The social worker must give primary attention to the client's problem or concern as it is defined, perceived, and experienced by the client.
- The worker must focus primarily on those aspects of the situation and the client's environment that most immediately and directly impact on the client.
- The intervention must address those aspects of the situation over which the client and/or the worker have some control and influence.
- The social worker must recognize the multitude of forces pushing and pulling on the client but understand that the actual impact of those forces is at least partially dependent on the client's subjective interpretation.
- The worker must be prepared to intervene at one or more levels (e.g., individual, family, organizational, community, etc.), depending on the nature of the client's concern, the client's interpretations, and what the client wants to do about it and can do about it.
- The worker must be prepared to use a variety of techniques, approaches, and services since whatever is done must make sense to the client, given his or her perceptions and interpretations of reality.

Reasons Why Change Occurs

To be effective in achieving a planned change, social workers must understand the reasons behind unplanned change. Similar forces are at work during both planned and unplanned changes. In fact, most of the approaches used to achieve a planned change are essentially a redirection or a manipulation of the forces also at work in unplanned change. If one can figure out how people change in a natural or an unplanned fashion, one can often bring about a planned change by redirecting these same forces. This point may become more clear by reflecting on some of the reasons why people and systems change—even when no agent promoting change is present.

Individual Change.   Some of the reasons individuals change include the following:

- Response to a crisis (old patterns no longer work and the individual is forced by circumstances to try a new way)
- Making rational, deliberate decisions and actions to secure something of value or create a desired state of affairs
- Avoidance of physical or emotional pain and discomfort
- Adjustments to changes that have occurred in other people or systems such as family, peer group, work environment, and so on
- Spiritual or religious awakening (i.e., finding new meaning and purpose in life, arriving at a different view of what is right or wrong)
- Discovery of a dramatically new way of conceptualizing and thinking about some area of concern (i.e., a paradigm shift)
- Observing others and choosing to imitate their behavior
- Discovery of heretofore unknown possibilities and opportunities
- Learning new and more effective ways of behaving and coping with responsibilities and problems
- Taking actions necessary to resolve an intolerable dissonance between one's values or beliefs and one's behavior
- Conforming to the wishes of a valued and respected person
- Alterations in neurochemistry and brain functioning

Family and Group Change.   Family and small group systems change for many of the reasons listed above. Other reasons include the following:

- Addition or loss of members, which alters the patterns of communication, leadership, daily routines, and so on.
- Adjustment or response to a change made by an individual or a subgroup within the system
- Adaptations to external forces such as large-scale economic and social realities (e.g., availability of housing and jobs, cost of transportation, fear of crime, etc.)

Organizational Change.   Broadly speaking, organizational change involves a change in one or more of four elements: (1) organizational goals and objectives, (2) structure or patterns of relationships, (3) technology, or (4) the individuals occupying specific positions. Both internal and external factors can modify the functioning of an organization. For example:

- Realization that the organization's accomplishments are not in keeping with its mission and goals
- Availability of new technology (i.e., new ways of doing the work are discovered)
- Redistribution of power, authority, and responsibility
- Responses to changes in personnel and interactional style, especially by persons in positions of leadership
- Alterations in organizational structure causing shifts in information flow, interpersonal and interdisciplinary interaction, lines of authority, and so on
- Responses to changes in fiscal resources (i.e., additions or losses in funding)
- Responses to public opinion (e.g., reactions to negative exposure in the media)
- Responses to powerful external regulators (e.g., adaptations to new laws, government regulations, accreditation standards, etc.)

Community Change.   Warren (1978) describes a *community* as a locality-relevant combination of social units and systems that perform the functions of production, distribution, consumption, socialization, social control, social participation, and mutual support. Changes in the relationships among the people and organizations in a community are usually a response to changes in leadership or to economic and demographic shifts. These include such factors as the following:

- Additions or losses of industries that are major employers (e.g., changes in type of jobs available)
- Alterations in age distribution or family structure (e.g., aging of a population, increase in single-parent households, etc.)
- Shifts in values and belief structure, often related to the addition or loss of certain ethnic or religious groups
- Shifts in political and governmental leadership, tax base, form of government, and so forth
- Shifts in interactional and travel patterns caused by actions such as relocation of highways, building dams, zoning changes, new housing developments or industrial tracts, and so on
- Shifts or redistribution of economic and political power
- Events that increase or decrease a sense of belonging and cohesion (e.g., flood, riot, pride in a baseball team, etc.)

Elements of Change

Success in making change largely depends on people's motivation to change, their capacity for change, and their opportunity to change. *Motivation* can be viewed as a state of readiness or eagerness to take some specific action. One can be highly motivated toward one action yet have no motivation toward another. One's level of motivation is not static; it varies from one time to another and from one situation to another.

Motivation also consists of the *pull of hope* and the *push of discomfort.* Clients will work and struggle toward a desired change if they truly believe that change is possible (i.e., the pull of hope) and if they are also dissatisfied or uncomfortable with their current situation (i.e., the push of discomfort). Change requires a balance between these two forces. If people have hope but no discomfort, they tend to give up when they encounter the stress and conflict associated with making real change. On the other hand, if they feel discomfort but have no hope, they see little reason to engage in a fruitless attempt to change something that seems unchangeable.

Change also requires capacity. ***Capacities*** can be thought of as the abilities and resources that people or clients bring to the change process. These might include time, energy, money, communication skills, knowledge, problem-solving skills, self-discipline, encouragement from others, political power, and so on. Different types of change require different types of capacity. For example, the capacities needed to obtain a job may be different from those required to improve family relationships or those necessary to adapt to a chronic illness. Also, different types of capacity are required depending on whether the practice activity is concerned with individual, family, or organizational change.

Change further requires opportunity. As used here, ***opportunity*** refers to conditions of the environment that invite and support change. For example, consider the situation of a young man on probation who wants to find a job and stay out of trouble. His social environment consists of his family, peer group, neighborhood, law-enforcement agencies, and so on, that will influence his ability to bring about change. His opportunity for change may also be impacted by community attitudes, available jobs, discrimination, and other social forces. Some aspects of his environment may support change (e.g., an encouraging family), whereas other factors may inhibit change (e.g., lack of available jobs). The types of opportunities necessary for organizational and community change are usually of a fiscal, political, and attitudinal nature.

When a social worker becomes involved in the change process, he or she brings a fourth element—***professional actions and services***—to the motivation, capacity, and opportunity brought by the client. The role of the social worker in helping people to make change can be conceptualized as taking action designed to increase motivation, expand capacity, and create or uncover opportunity.

The relationship among these factors—motivation, capacity, and opportunity—and their affect on social functioning can be presented as a formula (Horejsi 1976).

$$F = \frac{(M \times C \times O)\, S}{P}$$

In this formula, *F* refers to level of functioning or an outcome of planned changed, *M* refers to motivation, *C* to capacity, and *O* to opportunities for change. *S* represents the services or actions provided by the social worker. Finally, *P* refers to the problem or situation that the client and worker are addressing.

An examination of this formula shows a number of important interrelationships. For example, as the client's problem (*P*) grows larger, the need for outside assistance, or services (*S*), becomes more critical. Also, note that high motivation can compensate for low capacity. No amount of motivation can make up for a complete lack of opportunity or capacity, however. Likewise, no amount of opportunity or service can compensate for an absence of motivation or capacity.

An Overview of the Change Process

Descriptions of the change process have been a part of the social work literature throughout the development of this profession. In her classic book, *Social Diagnosis* (1917), Mary Richmond described steps necessary in helping people. Forty years later, the work of Helen Perlman (1957) echoed the same theme when describing helping as a problem-solving process that involved three major phases: (1) beginning with *study* that would ascertain and clarify the facts of the problem, followed by (2) *diagnosis,* where the facts would be analyzed, and concluding with (3) *treatment* that involves making choices and taking actions to resolve the problem. In subsequent years, various authors divided these phases into more discrete units, described them in more detail, and demonstrated their application in a range of helping approaches. Although different authors use varied terminology and differentially emphasize activities to be accomplished at each phase of the change process, the fundamental concepts are similar, whether the social worker is engaged in direct practice, community or organizational change, or research.

Planned change—because it is usually an effort to address some problem—typically requires that the worker, in collaboration with the client, do the following:

- Identify and define the client's problem, troublesome situation, or concern.
- Collect data and study the problem or situation.
- Assess the problem (i.e., decide what needs to change, what can be changed, and how it might be changed).
- Establish goals and objectives for change.
- Formulate a plan on how to proceed.
- Take action based on the plan (i.e., intervention).
- Monitor progress and determine if the intervention is achieving the desired goals and objectives and, if necessary, modify the plan and try again.
- Once goals and objectives have been reached, terminate the intervention and evaluate the process to learn for future practice activities.

The logical progression of these activities makes the change process appear to be a linear, step-by-step set of activities. In reality, it is more of a spiral (see Figure 7.1), with frequent returns to prior phases for a recycling or reworking of tasks and activities. Because change involves people—those who are trying to effect a change and those who are expecting or expected to change—change efforts are characterized by false starts, errors in judgment, miscalculations, and surprises. Change rarely proceeds in an orderly fashion.

FIGURE 7.1   Phases of the Planned Change Process

Intake and Engagement	Data Collection and Assessment	Planning and Contracting	Intervention and Monitoring	Final Evaluation and Termination
Begin relationship; identify and define client's concern or problem; determine eligibility for service.	Gather information and "study" problem or situation; decide what needs to change, what can be changed, and how it can be changed.	Formulate objectives; evaluate possible strategies; agree on an intervention plan; determine who shall do what and when it shall be done.	Carry out plan; monitor progress; revise plan if not getting results.	Evaluate overall progress; bring relationship to an end; give feed back results to agency.

In this book, the change process is segmented into five phases, each with two central tasks.

Phase I   Intake and Engagement

Phase II   Data Collection and Assessment

Phase III   Planning and Contracting

Phase IV   Intervention and Monitoring

Phase V   Termination and Evaluation

At any time, the primary focus of the social worker's activity with clients will depend at least partially on the phase of the process. The worker will need to draw on somewhat different techniques to accomplish the tasks and activities of each phase. What might be helpful in one phase might be ineffective or even counterproductive in another. For example, it would be an error for a worker to discuss with an abusive mother her possible participation in an anger-management group (i.e., planning and contracting) when the client has not yet fully explored the view that there is something inappropriate about the manner in which she disciplines her children (i.e., problem definition).

The techniques and guidelines presented in Part IV of this book are organized to reflect this five-phase model. By selecting the chapter corresponding to where in the change process a particular case situation might be, the reader can find a collection of potentially useful tools for practice.

Phase I: Intake and Engagement

The manner in which the helping process begins is critically important. First experiences and impressions affect all that follows. Clients are often ambivalent, fearful, or hesitant about meeting with a social worker. Clients may wonder, for example: Will I be treated with respect? Will she be able to help? Does he really care? What if I don't like her? Will he really listen to what I have to say? Will I be treated like just another "case"? How can I get this over with as quickly as possible?

Preintake Considerations.   Typically, the direct-service client has a history of prior efforts to secure assistance from family, friends, or other professionals. People do not easily go to a social agency; usually they go because they are pushed by inner turmoil or pressure from others. By the time they finally reach the social worker, they are often discouraged and their problems have grown even more serious and complex and, if they have been forced to see a social worker, they are probably angry and resentful.

The first meeting may occur in a variety of places depending on the type of agency and client circumstances. Many meetings are in an agency office. Another fairly common site is the client's own home. Sometimes the worker meets the client in a building apart from the social worker's own agency. For example, a child welfare social worker might meet a client at a hospital, jail, group home, or neighborhood center. Wherever they meet, the social worker must attend to such concerns as comfort, privacy, and accommodation to special requirements (e.g., client using a wheelchair).

The behavior of other employees and the agency's physical features also have an impact on the client. For example, how the telephone is answered, how the receptionist greets the client, and the comfort of the reception area can all make a difference. Although the creation of a favorable environment is the primary responsibility of administrators, it must be monitored by direct-service workers.

The social worker's preparation for the first meeting is also important. Factors such as the social worker's clothing and being on time for an appointment also help to set the tone for the first meeting. Preparing a comfortable and private meeting room, and having studied available information concerning the client are preintake activities that influence the client's readiness to begin the change process.

Engagement.   Many of the barriers to establishing a productive working relationship are removed when the client is voluntary (i.e., has chosen to seek help). In these situations, the client has identified some concern and demonstrated, at least implicitly, a desire to take action and make a change. However, a large percentage of clients served by social workers are nonvoluntary; they prefer not to see a social worker but have been pressured to do so by a spouse, friends, the court, or other agencies to seek service either to avoid punishment or receive some service or benefit, possibly one they need but are reluctant to accept. Dealing with resistance, ambivalence, and hostility from the nonvoluntary client is a significant test of the social worker's skill (see Item 11.7).

During engagement, the artistic aspects of social work practice are of foremost importance. The ability to establish a relationship that reflects empathy, warmth, and genuineness; the ability to infuse the activity with energy and hopefulness; and the demonstration of sound judgment helps reduce the client's fear and anger and builds confidence in the helping process.

Formal Intake.   The process of engagement is concerned with the interpersonal exchanges between the client and the social worker, whereas intake involves discrete actions and official decisions by the worker. First, the client and social worker must come to an understanding of why the client is seeking help and discuss generally the client's expectations of the agency and the helping process. Second, the client's situation must be appraised, if only initially, and the worker and client must arrive at a tentative agreement on what concerns or issues need be addressed (i.e., problem identification). Third, the match between the client and the agency must be assessed, which involves a review of the fit of the client's concerns with the agency's purpose, eligibility requirements, and resources. At this point, a decision must be made. Either the client is referred elsewhere for service or the relationship moves to the next phase of the helping process.

As identified by Epstein (1988, 87–88), *referral* might be made because the agency does not have sufficient staff, the current staff lacks the necessary skills, the client's concerns do not fit the agency's mission, another agency possesses clear superiority in being able to address the client's concerns, or another agency has an exclusive or primary responsibility for the concerns described by the client. The social worker has a special responsibility to help clients gain access to needed services, whether offered by the worker's own agency or elsewhere in the community.

A decision to discontinue service at the point of intake may be appropriate if the client cannot or chooses not to invest the time, energy, or resources required by the helping process. In such a case, it is important that the social worker leave the door open for the client to return should circumstances change.

If the decision is to continue service, the process of *role induction* is begun. This term refers to preparing a client to use the social worker as a helper or to make effective use of a specific program. These initial efforts to provide information and guidance to the client are of critical importance because they set the stage for all subsequent communication, interaction, and negotiation.

Phase II: Data Collection and Assessment

This phase is concerned with fact gathering and the study of those facts. Its purpose is to establish a solid factual basis for understanding the client's problem and situation, goals and motivation, and capacity and opportunity for making change. It is during this phase that the resources that might be needed are identified and mobilized. Decisions on what can be done and how best to proceed must be based on sufficient and accurate data. Although data gathering and assessment are interrelated, it is helpful to examine them separately.

Data Collection.   The types of data required and their sources will vary according to the situation being addressed and the client system involved (i.e., whether individual, family, group, organization, or community). It is essential that the client and his or her problem or situation be individualized, while at the same time recognizing how it might be similar to that of other clients served by the agency. The client or client system is expected to actively participate in gathering the data but the worker will usually need to identify the type of information needed and provide guidance on how it is to be gathered and organized.

The social worker must be resourceful in selecting techniques for gathering data. These techniques might involve questioning, observation, testing procedures, use of existing written materials, and various other methods or information gathering. It is important that distinctions are made between what is fact and what is opinion. When impressionistic data are used, they should be recognized as such.

Due to the complexities of matters addressed, the fear of making a mistake can cause a social worker to gather excessive information. Indeed, insufficient data can lead to erroneous conclusions and possible harm to the client. But almost as problematic is having more data than one can analyze or comprehend. The data-collection process must be limited to information that is essential and relevant. The worker's practice framework and the agency's purpose help to set limits on the type and amount of information needed.

Assessment.   *Assessment* can be described as the thinking process by which one reasons from the facts to tentative conclusions regarding their meaning. The available data and information are organized and studied to make sense of the client's situation. Assessment answers the question: Given what we know about the client's problem or concern, what needs to change and how can it be changed?

As with all phases of the change process, the client is expected to be an active participant in the assessment. After all, it is the client who must act on the conclusions and live with the outcomes. If the client does not understand or take ownership of these conclusions, it is unlikely that he or she will want to proceed further.

Because assessment is an intellectual activity, both the client and the social worker must guard against endless speculation and theorizing as to the meaning of the data and the cause of the problem. Social workers must also guard against trying to make the client's problem fit a particular theory or diagnostic category. The worth of an assessment is measured not by the intellectual stimulation it provides but rather by the success of the action plan derived from the assessment.

Particular attention needs to be given to client strengths. Too often, both the client and the social worker become preoccupied with the presenting problem and all that is wrong. This can generate a sense of pessimism and yield an incomplete or distorted intervention plan. A focus on strengths builds hopefulness and uncovers possibilities for dealing with the problem.

Value choices and preferences are inherent in assessment. Both the client and the social worker have beliefs about the way things ought to be. These beliefs determine whether a particular condition is defined as a problem and affect the conclusions concerning what can and should be done about it. To the extent possible, these values and beliefs should be made explicit during assessment.

The assessment should be creative and multidimensional in the sense of examining data drawn from numerous sources that reflect various perspectives and yield alternative interpretations. From these interpretations, options are identified and the client and worker select the one that is most promising as a basis for planning an intervention. As differing explanations are compared, more data may be required, or perhaps it will become evident that the initial definition of the problem was in error or incomplete.

The conclusions reached are tentative and should be thought of as working hypotheses. As the client and worker move through the change process, and as more information is accumulated, it is likely that the initial hypothesis will be reworked. The remaining phases of the helping process involve confirming or disproving the hypothesis derived from assessment.

During assessment (but hopefully earlier) there must be clarity as to who is the client and who will become the target system. In other words, who is asking for the social worker's services (the *client system*) and who is expected to change (the *target system*). They are not always the same. For example, when a mother requests counseling for a rebellious daughter who is forced to attend the sessions, who is the client? We would probably conclude that the mother is the client and the daughter is the target of the intervention. Another example might be a group of parents who seek the assistance of a social worker in creating an organization aimed at clearing the neighborhood of drug dealers. Obviously, those who have sought and sanctioned the intervention are different from those identified as the target.

Phase III: Planning and Contracting

Once the client and social worker have reached agreement as to assessment, they move on to the next step of formulating an action plan and also a formal or informal contract concerning how they will work together to implement the plan. During this phase, the *action system* must be identified. Who are the people and organizations that the social worker and client must work with and through in order to achieve the goals? This question must be answered in order to construct a feasible plan.

Planning. A *plan of action* is the bridge between the assessment and intervention. Clients, and sometimes inexperienced workers, may want to shortcut this planning activity. However, action without a clear plan is a sure recipe for failure.

Planning begins with specifying exactly what the client hopes to change or achieve. Clarification of the desired outcome at this point helps the worker and client remain focused on the goal and avoid being sidetracked onto irrelevant tasks or unrelated issues. In addition to goals, objectives are needed. The objectives must be concrete, attainable, and measurable.

Once goals and objectives have been established, the client and social worker can consider various strategies for reaching these ends. This places a special demand on the creativity of the social worker and the willingness of the client to consider alternative courses of action. The range of possibilities is limited only by the creativity of the client and social worker. Each possible option and plan must be evaluated. For example: What can be predicted about its helpful and harmful impact on the client and others? What resources are required? What will it require of the client, worker, and agency? Can it be carried out in a realistic time frame?

A wide variety of practice frameworks—perspectives, theories, and models—may be used to plan and guide the change process. Each rests on a set of assumptions about how and why change occurs and, given those assumptions, what the social worker can do to facilitate change.

The social work *Code of Ethics* serves as a screen or filter in relation to the practice activities used to bring about change. Some methods of securing change are effective but unethical. For example, it may be possible to achieve change by using violence but social work's ethical code rejects that approach. The *Code* provides general guidance on selecting the means to achieve the desired ends.

After an examination of the various strategies for change, the worker and client must select and develop in detail the plan they will follow. Each action to be taken must be identified and the reasons for that action understood. It is helpful to design the plan so that some success can be achieved early in the process and the client can be quickly rewarded with a sense of accomplishment.

Contracting.   Barker (1995, 79) defines a *social work contract* as "a written, oral, or implied agreement between the client and the social worker as to the goals, methods, timetables, and mutual obligations to be fulfilled during the intervention process." Its purpose is to clarify the roles and responsibilities of the worker and client and to prevent misunderstandings.

In some cases, the use of a written contract has advantages. Its explicitness identifies points of agreement and disagreement between worker and client; it serves as a basis for providing accountability to the client and agency; and it can be an effective tool in facilitating the transfer of cases to another social worker, should that become necessary.

Even though the language and format may vary, the basic elements of a contract are similar, whether working at the individual, family, group, organization, or community level. Although discussing only direct practice, Epstein (1988, 149) delineates the elements to be specified in a contract: problems to be addressed; specific goals; activities the client will undertake; the social worker's tasks; duration of the intervention; scheduling of interviews or other contacts, as well as where the meetings will occur; and identification of persons who will participate.

Even the most detailed and carefully developed plan may prove inadequate once implementation is attempted. Thus, the worker and client must be open to revising the plan and renegotiating the contract in light of changing circumstances.

Phase IV: Intervention and Monitoring

The intervention and monitoring phase is the transformation of the prior work on assessment, planning, and contracting into action. At this point, the social worker is responsible for carrying out his or her part of the plan, helping the client perform agreed upon tasks, bringing necessary resources to bear on the situation, monitoring progress, and helping to stabilize the positive changes that occur.

Intervention. The fundamental role of the social worker is to help the client achieve change. Siporin (1975, 293) indicates that "the basic intervention in helping people is to influence them, arouse their wills, and move them to choose and to act so as to accomplish change in their behavior, in their life situations, and in their relationships with their environment." The social worker acts to encourage and facilitate change, but, with few exceptions, it is the client who must take ultimate responsibility for making change.

The role assumed by the social worker and the techniques and procedures utilized will depend on the concerns being addressed and the agency context. If the agency's purpose is primarily that of administering social provisions or so-called hard services (e.g., financial assistance, child care, shelter, etc.), the worker's actions will be primarily those necessary to enroll the client in the program, monitor the client's use of the program benefit, and possibly engage in case advocacy. On the other hand, if the worker's agency provides social services (i.e., soft services), such as teaching needed skills, furnishing social support, or providing counseling or therapy, the practitioner's actions will be of a more clinical nature requiring an emphasis on relationship building; examination of client thoughts, feelings, and behaviors; decision making; and helping the client learn new ways to cope, solve problems, and so forth. And finally, if the social worker's agency is concerned primarily with social action and community change, practitioner actions will be related to, for example, social research, interagency communication and coordination, policy analysis, program evaluation, fund-raising, and class advocacy.

Monitoring. As the interventive activities unfold, the social worker is responsible for keeping track of what is happening and continuously evaluating the success of the intervention. This ongoing evaluation focuses on the appropriateness and efficacy of the services provided. Depending on how well the intervention is progressing, the intervention might be continued or modified, or the plan and contract could be aborted and new ones negotiated.

Stabilizing. Whenever change occurs, various systems are in a state of disequilibrium and there exists the possibility of reversal or deterioration. The social worker must ensure that the change is more than a temporary accommodation to the interventive activities and that the desired change becomes firmly established as part of the ongoing functioning for the client and/or the relevant environment.

Phase V: Evaluation and Termination

The final phase of the change process is concerned with the termination of service to the client and the final evaluation of the intervention. Evaluation has implications for both future administrative decisions within the agency and for upgrading the quality of the social worker's own practice.

Termination. Every helping relationship must end. Counseling must be concluded and groups or committees must eventually be disbanded. The attention given to this ending phase by the worker and client is important to the success of the change process. It is a particularly important consideration when providing direct services where an abrupt termination could be upsetting for the client. Even in work with community groups and organizations, termination should occur in a manner that will maintain the interest and commitment of those who may later become involved in related community activities.

There are two points of view regarding the significance of termination to individual clients. One holds that when client and worker engage in change activity, meaningful relationships are formed and emotional bonds develop. Thus, when the helping relationship ends, the client experiences a sense of loss and feelings of anger and rejection that may contribute to regression from the progress achieved.

A second viewpoint is that social workers and other helping professionals tend to overdramatize their impact on clients and that, for most clients, termination is no big deal. For example, Epstein (1988, 215) notes, "It is a rare client indeed who truly becomes unhappy or is set adrift when termination occurs. The rewards of termination to a client are great: more money in the pocket (if the client is paying a fee), more time, freedom from the practitioner's influence and surveillance, and greater independence."

Both perspectives have merit. In either case, the worker must be sensitive to how and when the termination occurs. It should be anticipated from the beginning of the professional relationship and treated matter of factly. Given ample opportunity to anticipate the end, the client will usually appropriately disengage from the relationship. A gradual reduction of activity toward the end helps avoid feelings of abandonment.

Occasionally, service will terminate unexpectedly, at a time other than that planned by the worker and client. For example, external factors may make it necessary: The worker may accept employment elsewhere, the work may be blocked by a problem in the worker-client relationship and a transfer of the case may be best for the client, or specialized services may be needed from another social worker, professional, or agency. In these cases, it is important that the worker clearly explain what is happening and why.

Evaluation.   As compared to the ongoing monitoring that occurs throughout the helping process, a final evaluation occurs at or after termination. The final evaluation answers the questions: Did the intervention achieve its purpose? Was it effective? Were there problems in service delivery that might be corrected? Needless to say, evaluation is not possible unless the purpose and objectives of the intervention were clearly identified from the beginning.

From the perspective of the agency, evaluation is part of the obligation to be accountable to clients and the public. The agency must be concerned with whether its services are effective and how well its staff performs. This information is useful in conducting personnel evaluations and in planning in-service training aimed at correcting performance shortcomings. Also, the ability of the agency to assess how its services affected clients is essential if its financial support is to be maintained.

The social worker, too, is ethically obliged to be accountable to clients. It is important to engage clients in a final review of the change process, encouraging them to judge the success and usefulness of the experience from their vantage point and to help the social worker assess his or her own performance. From this information, the worker can make a self-evaluation and, if necessary, seek consultation or training that will improve performance. The social worker's openness to this evaluation is a key to professional development.

Conclusion

The belief that change can resolve problems or create better conditions is common to Western culture and especially in U.S. society. Social workers perform an important function in that society by assisting clients as they solve problems by changing themselves or engaging in effort to change their environment. Faith in the potential to change social conditions is at the very heart of social work practice and a prerequisite characteristic of the effective worker.

The social worker's primary task in helping clients is to guide them through the several phases of the planned change process. The social worker should know this process so thoroughly that it becomes second nature. For the new social worker, it is useful to periodically review the phases of planned change to be certain that he or she is not neglecting important aspects. Even the experienced worker should examine his or her practice to determine if sufficient attention is being given to all phases of this important activity.

SELECTED BIBLIOGRAPHY

Barker, Robert. *The Social Work Dictionary*, 3rd ed. Washington, D.C.: NASW Press, 1995.

Epstein, Laura. *Helping People: The Task Centered Approach*, 2nd ed. Columbus, Ohio: Merrill, 1988.

Gallagher, Thomas J. *Problem Solving with People: The Cycle Process*. Lanham, Md.: University Press of America, 1988.

Horejsi, Charles. "A Mathematical Presentation of the Motivation, Capacity and Opportunity Construct." *Journal of Social Welfare* 3 (Winter 1976): 17–25.

Miller, William, and Stephen Rollnick. *Motivational Interviewing: Preparing People to Change Addictive Behavior*. New York: Guilford Press, 1991.

Perlman, Helen Harris. *Social Casework: A Problem-Solving Process*. Chicago: University of Chicago Press, 1957.

Pincus, Allen, and Anne Minahan. *Social Work Practice: Model and Method*. Itasca, Ill.: F. E. Peacock, 1973.

Richmond, Mary E. *Social Diagnosis*. New York: Russell Sage Foundation, 1917.

Siporin, Max. *Introduction to Social Work Practice*. New York: Macmillan, 1975.

Warren, Roland. *The Community in America*, 3rd ed. Chicago: Rand McNally, 1978.

Part III Techniques Common to All Social Work Practice

The three chapters in Part III focus on techniques and guidelines basic to social work practice, regardless of agency setting or type of client served. In every practice setting, the social worker must be a skillful communicator, be able to develop relationships, know how to manage a workload, cope with job-related pressures, and continue to learn and grow as a professional person.

Chapter 8, "Basic Communication and Helping Skills," presents information on effective communication and relationship building. The chapter lays a foundation for understanding and applying the more specialized practice techniques and guidelines discussed in Part IV. Although many of the examples used to illustrate these skills are drawn from direct service, most can and are applied in administrative, community organization, and social planning activities. It is assumed that those using this book have been exposed to the ideas in this chapter; however, the authors' experiences suggest that readers will appreciate this concise review.

Chapter 9, "Workload and Caseload Management," is especially important to the worker who is going into a social agency for the first time. Few new workers are adequately prepared to cope with the time pressures and paperwork they encounter. This chapter provides practical guidance on such things as time management, how to write reports, and how to maintain records. The worker's ability to master these tasks often determines whether an individual can make it in social work.

Chapter 10, "Personal and Professional Development," recognizes the importance of the social worker being able to handle job-related pressures and dilemmas while continuing to acquire new knowledge and professional skills. The day-to-day struggles of the practicing social worker are frequently overlooked by agency administrators, program planners, and sometimes even supervisors. Consequently, many workers get little or no guidance on how to survive and grow as professional people.

8 Basic Communication and Helping Skills

INTRODUCTION

This chapter presents what might be called "the basics" of social work communication and relationship. The focus is on generic communication and helping skills—namely, those used with all clients, whether the client is an individual, a family, a small group, an organization, or a community.

The specific purpose of a professional interaction will determine the type of relationship the worker attempts to develop and the messages communicated to the client. In general, the social worker providing direct services attempts to develop a relationship that has attributes known to positively affect the outcome of the helping process. These include empathy, warmth, and genuineness. The worker in the indirect-service area places more emphasis on precision, clarity, and goal directness. This is not to say, however, that the factors of empathy, warmth, and genuineness are not important in the relationships of the indirect-service worker. Rather, it is a matter of emphasis.

Essentially, *communication* is a process where one individual conveys information—either intentionally or unintentionally—to another person. It occurs when one person attaches meaning to the verbal or nonverbal behavior of another. Communication is a form of behavior, but not all behavior is communication; it all depends on whether a person perceives a message in the words or behavior of another. Communication is primarily a receiver phenomenon; regardless of what one says in words or intends to communicate, it is the person on the receiving end that assigns meaning to those words and body movements.

It is important to be constantly aware of the complexity and limitations inherent in human communication. Because each individual is a unique personality and has had a unique set of life experiences, each person has developed various perceptual filters and patterns of thought that affect how messages are sent and received. Thus, one individual may notice things that others overlook and messages that are very important to one person may seem inconsequential to another.

A word is but a symbol and it may have somewhat different meanings to different people depending on a person's familiarity with the language, ethnicity, belief system, and capacity for abstract thinking. The words and other symbols used in communication have both denotive and connotative aspects. Thus, the meaning of a word or a gesture may change depending on who says it, and when, where, and how it is said.

Communication depends on the proper functioning of the senses (e.g., vision, hearing, touch, etc.) and the cognitive activities of the brain, which include: ***attention*** (focusing on certain stimuli while disregarding others); ***perception*** (using attention, pattern recognition, and sensory memory to interpret stimuli picked up by our senses); ***memory*** (retaining information over time); ***language*** (interpreting, expressing, and remembering verbal and written words and symbols); ***conceptualization*** (organizing information and ideas into categories); ***reasoning*** (drawing conclusions from information); and ***decision making*** (making choices based on an anticipation of future events). These cognitive processes are interrelated and overlapping. If the senses are impaired or if the brain has been damaged, the ability to communicate will be limited to some degree. Common causes of brain damage are strokes, trauma, chemical intoxication, tumors, and dementia-type illnesses such as Alzheimer's disease.

The capacity to send and receive messages accurately can also be distorted by one's emotional state and expectations. In general, we tend to hear what we want to hear, hear what we have learned to expect, and hear what serves our self-interests at the moment. In other words, we often distort messages in order to avoid discomfort and to meet our emotional needs. For example, often we do not really hear bad news. Also, individuals with certain personality disorders characteristically distort messages in a self-serving fashion. Situational and social-interactional factors also have a powerful influence on how words and gestures are interpreted. How, when, and where a message is sent are usually as important as the literal meaning of the words used.

The lack of clear communication is a common cause of problems within families, organizations, and other social systems. In general, communication problems develop when:

- We speak for others rather than let them speak for themselves.
- We let our prejudices and stereotypes affect what we hear and say.
- We do not take the time to listen to and to understand what the other person is trying to say.
- We keep things to ourselves because we think others will disapprove of what we believe and feel.
- We make no attempt to communicate because we assume others already know how we feel and what we think.
- We are afraid to take the risks that are necessary to communicate honestly and openly with others.
- We discourage or suppress communication by ordering, threatening, preaching, judging, blaming, or humoring.
- Negative feelings about ourselves (low self-esteem) cause us to conclude that we have nothing to say and that no one wants to listen to us.

Cross-cultural communication and helping present a special challenge. Factors such as a person's ethnicity, gender, religion, and socioeconomic class can have a significant impact, not only on communication but also on help-seeking activity, how problems are defined, and what is expected of a professional relationship.

8.2	**Basic Communication Skills**

PURPOSE: To improve verbal communication with other professionals and agencies.

DISCUSSION: Communication, especially verbal communication, is at the heart of social work practice. Social workers make frequent use of two broad categories of communication skills: (1) those intended to facilitate interpersonal helping and (2) those intended to facilitate the exchanges of information within an agency, between agencies, and among professionals. The communication skills used in direct practice activities (e.g., face-to-face work with individual clients, families, therapeutic groups) are described in Item 8.3. The other category, basic communication skills, is used frequently when the social worker is communicating with another social worker, another professional (e.g., physician, lawyer, judge), an agency supervisor or administrator, and with members of a committee or other task group. A description of those skills is presented here.

Among the attitudes that lay a foundation for good communication are the following:

- Understanding that every human being is unique; consequently, each person experiences and perceives events and interpersonal exchanges in a unique manner. Thus, you should anticipate some degree of misunderstanding and plan to take steps to minimize problems of miscommunication.
- A willingness to organize your thoughts and present your message in ways that make it easy for others to understand.
- A willingness to lower your defenses so you can hear what others have to say.
- A willingness to listen carefully to the person who is speaking.
- A willingness to take responsibility for your own thoughts, feelings, and behaviors.
- A willingness to take the time needed to communicate; to understand and to be understood.

Communication involves both a message sender and a message receiver. The sender has a responsibility to convey his or her message in a way that is easily received and not likely to be misunderstood. The receiver has a responsibility to make sure that he or she has accurately received the intended message and has not, in some way, distorted or misunderstood the sender's message.

When in the position of listening to or *receiving a message,* remember these rules:

- Stop talking. You cannot listen when you are talking.
- Put the message sender at ease. Do what you can to lessen his or her anxiety. Remove distractions (e.g., close the door).
- Demonstrate, verbally and nonverbally, that you want to listen. Really pay attention.
- Be patient with the message sender. Do not interrupt.

- Ask questions if it will help you understand or help the sender to clarify his or her message.
- Control your emotions. Do not criticize or argue, for that will erect a barrier to further communication.

When *sending a message,* follow these rules:

- Use clear, simple language. Speak distinctly and not too fast.
- Pay attention to your body language; make sure it is congruent with your message. Maintain appropriate eye contact and utilize gestures.
- Do not overwhelm or overload the receiver with information. Break up a lengthy or complex message into several parts so it can be more easily followed and understood.
- Ask for comments, questions, or feedback so you will know whether you are being understood.

A number of specific skills can help the social worker communicate more effectively. The skill of *planning a message* refers to the worker thinking about an upcoming episode of communication and planning the message around the answers to several questions or concerns, such as the following:

- How much time is available for this exchange?
- What are the essential points of my message?
- What aspects of my message are most likely to be misunderstood or possibly confusing?
- How can I organize or frame my message so it will be easily understood and accepted by the receiver?
- When and where am I most likely to have the full attention of the person who is to receive my message?
- Do I have the credibility, position, and status to deliver this message or should it be sent by someone else?

It is the middle portion of a message that is most likely to be distorted by the receiver. Thus, the most important points should placed at the beginning and the end of your message.

The skill of *identifying self* is an important first step in meaningful communication. It requires a concise description of who you are and how your role and responsibilities relate to the intended message or exchange of information. For example:

You may remember me from a previous meeting, but let me begin by introducing myself. My name is Mary Jones. I am a social worker with the Evergreen Family Services Center. A client of mine has asked me to speak with you to find out if . . . .

The skill of *explaining the purpose of the communication* refers to the sender's statements that explain the reason behind the message. This helps the receiver place the message in a proper context. For example, a child welfare social worker speaking to a prosecuting attorney might say:

> As you know, my agency has Jimmy Johnson in one of our foster homes. I need to talk with you and get a clear idea about when you plan to have Jimmy testify in court. This information is important to us because we have to inform his school of a planned absence and also work out his transportation to the courthouse.

Sometimes it is important to respond to a receiver's nonverbal communication if it suggests confusion or disagreement with the message. The skill of *following up on nonverbal communication* refers to such efforts. For example:

> John, I noticed that you looked a little confused when I was explaining the new agency procedure. If you have any questions, please feel free to ask me at this time.

Similar follow-up efforts are important when the receiver's nonverbal communication suggests that he or she disagrees with the message. For example:

> When I was explaining the proposed policy change, I could not help but notice that several of you were looking rather distressed. It is important for me to know how you feel about the proposal. I really want to know what you are thinking. Bob, Mary, and Judy—please react to the proposed policy change.

The skill of *checking for message reception* refers to various questions and probes intended to verify that your message was completely and accurately received by the other party. For example:

> I am aware that what I have described as needed modifications in the agenda for our meeting might be confusing. I want to make sure you understand. Would you please repeat to me what you heard me say?

When on the receiving end of a message, it is desirable to use the skill of *checking one's receipt of a message.* This refers to various probes and questions intended to verify that you have, in fact, received the message and did not misunderstand what was intended by the sender. For example:

> Before we end this conversation, I want to make sure I understand completely what you have said. Let me take a minute and repeat what I heard you say. If it sounds as if I have misunderstood, please correct me.

It is surprisingly difficult to ask questions so that they can be answered in a clear and concise manner. All too often we attach unnecessary words and extraneous topics to our questions that can confuse the point of our query. In order to receive a clear answer, your question needs to be very focused and precise. This calls for the skill termed *asking a focused question.* Consider this example of a confusing question directed to an agency administrator:

I am confused about these new agency policies, especially the ones about foster care and, in some ways, about a lot of the policies. This manual is organized in an unusual way. What is really expected of us? I mean, what are we supposed to do with new cases and how do we handle the court-ordered evaluations?

It would be difficult for the administrator to give a clear answer to this communication because many different questions are being asked at the same time and all of them are rather vague. A much more focused question would be:

I have a question about policy number 8.6 on page 99 of our agency manual. In order to secure a psychological evaluation on a foster child, do I need my supervisor's written approval?

The skill of *answering a question* refers to statements that respond directly to the question asked and answering it in a complete manner. This seems simple; however, people often fail to really listen to the question. In the following example, a supervisor makes this error but then makes a correct response:

Worker: I need some direction on where to send this report. Do I send it to the County Attorney or directly to Judge Smith?

Supervisor: Just remember that Judge Smith is a real stickler for details. Also, he wants the report as concise as possible.

Worker: Well, yes, I know that but what I want to know is where to send the report.

Supervisor: Oh, I'm sorry. I didn't answer your question. Send it directly to Judge Smith.

When responding to a question, do not make assumptions or engage in "mind reading" about what the person meant to ask or should have asked. Listen carefully to the question and answer it without adding extraneous details.

Many communication problems arise because people use words or phrases in different ways. The skill of *checking for word meaning* refers to inquiries intended to make sure that all parties in an exchange agree on the meaning of key words. Consider the following example:

Chair of Planning Group: I think we need to shift about 20 percent of our budget into child abuse prevention programs.

Committee Member (checking for meaning of words):   Well, I may or may not agree, depending on what you mean by prevention. What level of prevention are you talking about? Primary or secondary?

SELECTED BIBLIOGRAPHY

Burley-Allen, Madelyn. *Listening: The Forgotten Skill.* New York: John Wiley and Sons, 1995.

Gordon, Raymond. *Basic Interviewing Skills.* Itasca, Ill.: F. E. Peacock, 1992.

Nunnally, Elan, and Caryl Moy. *Communication Basics for Human Service Professionals.* Newbury Park, Calif.: Sage, 1989.

8.2   Creating an Effective Helping Relationship

PURPOSE: To develop a helping relationship with a client.

DISCUSSION: At the very heart of an effective helping relationship is human caring. A social worker must genuinely care about his or her clients. Clients want a social worker to be knowledgeable but they do not pay attention to how much the worker knows until they know how much he or she cares.

Studies of helping and therapeutic relationships conclude that a positive relationship between the helper and client is necessary but not sufficient for client change to occur. The application of appropriate techniques and procedures is also necessary. Without a positive relationship, change is not likely. With a positive relationship, the techniques and procedures designed to promote change are likely to have their intended effect.

Some type of relationship will develop whenever a social worker and client interact. However, this relationship may be either a positive or negative one, depending on the worker's behavior and the client's perception or interpretation of that behavior. Thus, the social worker cannot *make* a positive relationship happen. At most, he or she can strive to be the type of person that most clients find helpful and to do those things that increase the chances that a therapeutic relationship will develop.

The content and character of a specific relationship will be shaped by such influences as the treatment plan, the social worker's practice framework, and the agency's purpose and procedures. But fundamentally, a professional relationship is a very human struggle for meaningful communication and interaction. It is important to recognize that a helping relationship is not necessarily pleasant and free of conflict. In fact, a genuinely helpful, positive, and therapeutic relationship can be an emotionally painful experience for both the client and the social worker.

Extensive research has identified the core conditions or key characteristics of a helpful relationship. These are empathy, positive regard, personal warmth, and genuineness. *Empathy* refers to the worker's capacity to perceive accurately a client's feelings and subjective experiences and to grasp the meanings they have for the client. Empathy is sometimes described as stepping into the client's shoes and feeling and seeing things as the client does. The truly empathetic social worker is able to sense the meaning of a client's experiences even when the worker has not had a similar life experience. Empathy is conveyed primarily by giving the client one's undivided attention and by a sensitivity and responsiveness to nonverbal cues. Fischer (1978, 192) explains that "this active process not only provides the framework for the moment-to-moment contact necessary for accurate empathy, but ensures the errors in the worker's perception or understanding of what the client has communicated will be quickly recognized." It should be noted that the techniques of active listening such as paraphrasing and reflection are critical to the worker's display of empathy (see Item 8.3).

Essentially, *positive regard* means believing that all clients are persons of value and treating them with dignity regardless of appearance, behavior, or life circumstances. This does not mean that the social worker must accept or approve of destructive behaviors but rather that the client is seen as a person of inherent worth. Our tendency to judge others is a major barrier to effective communication; it is strongest when our feelings and emotions are stirred. When we judge, we are usually looking at a situation from our point of view rather than the client's. Communication can be improved by maintaining a *nonjudgmental attitude,* which Cormier and Cormier (1991, 29) define as the "capacity to suspend judgment of the client's actions or motives and to avoid condemning or condoning the client's thoughts, feelings or actions."

The core condition of ***personal warmth*** exists when the social worker responds to clients in ways that make them feel safe, accepted, and understood. Without the quality of warmth, the worker's words will sound hollow and insincere and will have no therapeutic impact. Warmth is mostly nonverbal communication and is expressed in a smile, a soft and soothing voice, a relaxed but interested posture, eye contact, and gestures that convey acceptance and openness.

Genuineness means being one's self, being real, and "speaking from the heart." Fisher (1978) explains:

> Genuineness may be best understood as the absence of phoniness, as nondefensiveness, as congruence, and as spontaneity. In fact, it would be difficult to conceive of the meaningful communication of empathy and warmth by someone who was not at least minimally "real." . . .
>
> Genuineness is not synonymous with being totally honest. Workers need not disclose their total selves; but whatever they do reveal should be a real aspect of themselves, not a response growing out of defensiveness or a merely "professional" response that has been learned and repeated. . . . This, again, does not mean that workers cannot 'have' negative or defensive responses. Rather, and this is crucial to the concept of genuineness, if workers do have such responses, they do not employ them in ways that will be destructive to their clients. (p. 199)

Those who are new to social work sometimes worry that they cannot simultaneously step into a professional role and be truly genuine in their relationships with clients. Being professional has nothing to do with "playing the role" or trying to imitate some idealized or stereotyped image of a professional person. A true professional is knowledgeable, self-disciplined, responsible, ethical, and, most of all, effective. There is no conflict between those qualities and being genuine.

Much of the research on helping relationships has been conducted outside the field of social work, but those research findings are consistent with ones that have emerged from social work research. Fischer (1981, 204) concludes that the core conditions of empathy, positive regard, warmth, and genuineness are clearly relevant to social work: "They constitute the essential skills involving relationships and therapeutic interviewing that are the heart of practice." Maluccio (1979) used in-depth interviewing to secure clients' opinions about social workers and his data also underscore the importance of these core conditions. However, three additional worker qualities emerged from his study: *concreteness* (ability to communicate thoughts and ideas clearly and specifically), *competence* (proficiency in carrying out professional tasks and activities), and *objectivity* (being unbiased and able to appreciate differing points of view).

Maluccio (1979, 125) states that, from the client's perspective, an ideal social worker is "warm, accepting, understanding, involved, natural, genuine, competent, objective and able to share of himself or herself with the client." Fischer (1978) concludes that the effective social worker is

> deeply involved, deeply personal, deeply caring. Effective caseworkers are *real* people, unafraid of their own experiences, trusting those experiences, knowing who they are, and offering every client all they are. Effective caseworkers are not afraid of emotions, their own or their client's; they are not afraid to *feel* or express those feelings. And when they express feelings, they do so in a way that is constructive for others. Effective caseworkers are both secure and competent enough to recognize that one can be deeply involved with the problems of others, yet retain the objectivity necessary for appropriate selection and use procedures that will be facilitative for clients. (p. 213)

The term *structuring* refers to the use of various interpersonal arrangements (e.g., worker-client matching) and symbols (e.g., worker dress and office environment) to enhance relationship building. For example, a client is most likely to be influenced by someone to whom he or she is attracted. People are usually attracted to and feel most comfortable with those who have beliefs, backgrounds, and a life-style similar to their own. It follows, therefore, that a social worker who wants to increase his or her attractiveness to a client and decrease a client's uncomfortableness should look for similarities and mention them to the client. For example, the worker might point out that he or she and the client both have children of about the same age or that both grew up on a farm. It should be noted, however, that some studies have found that client-worker matching by age, race, sex, marital status, parenthood, and socioeconomic status had little or no effect on intervention outcome.

Whether particular differences between the client and the worker have a significant impact on the helping relationship is mostly a function of the client's expectations and perceptions. Davis and Proctor (1989) suggest that a client who is different from the social worker in terms of race, gender, or socioeconomic status is likely to have three major concerns.

1. Is the helper a person of goodwill? That is, does this person have my best interests at heart? Does he or she dislike . . . people like me? The client's answer to this question determines the extent to which the client will initially trust the helper.
2. Does the worker have professional expertise or mastery of skills that can resolve my problems? That is, is this person adequately skilled or trained? The answer to this question will also affect the client's trust in the worker. The central issue, however, is the worker's competence, or capacity to be helpful.
3. Does the worker have sufficient understanding of my social reality or my world view? That is, is this person sufficiently familiar with people like me? Will this person understand my life experiences? The answer to this question will determine the extent to which the worker is seen as credible, and the extent to which advice and suggestions can be accepted as valid and meaningful. (p. ix)

How the client answers such questions will obviously have an impact on whether and how the client uses the services of the social worker.

One's waiting room and office can also have a significant impact on clients, either positive or negative. For example, if a client must talk with the social worker in a space that lacks privacy and comfort, respect for the worker is greatly diminished. It is important to make offices and meeting rooms as comfortable and respectful as possible.

Research findings tell us that *expertness*—or at least the appearance of expertness—can have a positive impact on the initial phases of the helping process. According to Cormier and Cormier (1991), such things as certificates and diplomas on the wall, type of agency setting, office size, proper use of language, and clothing style can increase the client's respect for the helper and result in the client being more open to influence. Clearly, one must be alert to the importance of such factors, but the social worker should remember that clients, like all people, make deliberate decisions about whose influence they accept and whose they reject. Moreover, one's "expertness" is often measured in ways other than counting college degrees and credentials.

SELECTED BIBLIOGRAPHY

Cormier, William, and L. Sherilyn Cormier. *Interviewing Strategies for Helpers,* 3rd ed. Monterey, Calif.: Brooks/Cole, 1991.

Davis, Larry, and Enola Proctor. *Race, Gender and Class: Guidelines for Practice with Individuals, Families and Groups.* Englewood Cliffs, N.J.: Prentice Hall, 1989.

Fischer, Joel. "The Social Work Revolution." *Social Work* 26 (May 1981): 199–207.

———. *Effective Casework Practice: An Eclectic Approach.* New York: McGraw-Hill, 1978.

Maluccio, Anthony. *Learning from Clients: Interpersonal Helping as Viewed by Clients and Social Workers.* New York: Free Press, 1979.

8.3 Basic Helping Skills

PURPOSE: To use verbal messages that can assist and encourage a client during the intervention process.

DISCUSSION: As used here, the term *helping skill* refers to a message that the practitioner conveys to the client because the worker believes it will have a beneficial effect on the client's thinking, feelings, or behavior. The moment-to-moment decisions concerning what message to send should be guided by the purpose of the interview and based on what the social worker knows about the client and his or her situation, and his or her working hypothesis about how the client will respond to the message. Moreover, it must be recognized that a specific skill or message will be more or less useful depending on the phase of the change process (i.e., intake, assessment, planning and contracting, intervention, and termination). The appropriateness of a message also depends on whether it is offered during the beginning, middle, or ending phase of an interview or meeting. Needless to say, all communication has a significant nonverbal component, including the use of eye contact, gestures, and other movements, to help convey the message; information on nonverbal communication appears in Item 8.4.

Writers in the fields of social work, clinical psychology, and counseling have described dozens of helping skills. There is no agreed upon terminology and various authors use different names for what are essentially the same skills. Possible exceptions are the terms associated with the skills of active listening (e.g., paraphrase, reflection, summarization). These are used fairly consistently by most writers. On the following pages brief descriptions of commonly used helping skills are offered. In several instances, terminology is borrowed from Shulman (1981, 1992). The examples that illustrate how a particular skill might be used are drawn from one-on-one interviews, but these same skills can be adapted for use in work with families and therapeutic groups. Many of the more specialized techniques presented in Part IV of this book can be viewed as elaborations and special applications of the basic skills described here.

Getting Ready

In a sense, the social worker's helping actions begin *before* the first face-to-face meeting with the client. Prior to the meeting, the worker should imagine what the client might be thinking and feeling as he or she enters the agency or office expecting to discuss personal matters with a stranger. By trying to anticipate how the client might feel, the worker begins to develop empathy for the client and mentally prepares to address the client's initial feelings (e.g., anger, fear, confusion) and to identify ways to ease the client into the helping relationship. Shulman (1992, 56) has termed this the *tuning-in phase* of the helping process. (See Items 11.1, 11.2, and 14.1 for more information on how to prepare for an interview.)

Getting Started

During the intake and engagement phase of the change process and also at the beginning of each session with a client, the social worker must give special attention to clarifying the purpose of the meeting and the worker's role. The helping skill of *explaining purpose* refers to a simple, nonjargonized statement by the worker about the general purpose of the meeting. It serves to define expectations and reduce client confusion and anxiety. For example:

> *Worker:*   I am pleased that you were able to meet with me today. As you know, your wife first came to this agency about three weeks ago. She expressed concern about your marriage. I would like to hear your thoughts and find out if you also believe there are problems in the marriage, and, if so, what you think they are.

When the first contact is initiated by the client, the worker should encourage the client to begin by describing the reason for requesting the interview. If the client has a hard time explaining his or her purpose, the worker might ask some general questions about the circumstances that led up to the request for an interview and what the client hopes will come from the meeting.

When the social worker initiates the first contact, he or she should begin by explaining the purpose. The explanation should be clear and to the point.

Good Explanation: I need to talk with you about your son, John. He has missed 14 out of the last 20 school days. This is a serious problem.

Poor Explanation: Hi there. I know your son, John. I was in the neighborhood so I decided to stop by to chat. How are things going?

The skill of *encouraging the client's feedback on purpose* (Shulman 1981) refers to statements that encourage the client to respond to the worker's explanation. This gives the client an opportunity to ask questions or perhaps voice disagreement. Consider these two examples:

Worker: What are your reactions to what I have said about the purpose of this meeting? Do you see things differently?

or

Worker: It's quite possible you and I have different thoughts about why we are talking today. I want to know if you were expecting something else.

The skill of *describing the worker's role and method* refers to statements intended to give the client a beginning idea of how the worker might be able to help and the approaches or methods to be used. For example:

Worker: As you get ready to leave this hospital, it is important to anticipate the problems you may face and to figure out how to deal with them. Basically, that is why I want to meet with you two or three times before you leave. I will ask for your ideas and I will share my ideas, as well. Between the two of us, I hope we can come up with a plan that will minimize the difficulties you will have when you are at home.

Each session with a client has three time phases: (1) getting started, (2) the central work of the session, and (3) drawing the session to a close. At the beginning of each session, the social worker should provide an opportunity for what Shulman (1981, 12) terms *sessional contracting.* Even when there has been a prior agreement on how the session's time will be used, it is important to check once again for consensus. Quite possibly, some change in the client's situation has altered the client's sense of priorities. The skill of *reaching for between-session data* (Shulman 1981) is used to initiate sessional contracting. This form of "checking in" involves asking the client to bring the worker up to date and to identify the key topics to be discussed, even if they are different from what was planned during the previous meeting. This can be viewed as an attempt to adhere to the principle of *starting where the client is.* For example:

Worker: You will recall that during last week's session we agreed to spend today's session talking about your reluctance to visit your children in foster care. Do you still think that is how we should spend our time today, or do you now have a more pressing concern?

Asking Questions

A social worker uses various types of questions to obtain needed information and assist the client in expressing his or her thoughts and feelings. A question such as "What are the names of your children?" is termed a ***closed-ended question;*** it limits how the client can respond. By contrast, a question such as "Tell me about your children" is called an ***open-ended question*** because it gives the client an opportunity to say whatever he or she thinks is important. However, open-ended questions can vary in the amount of freedom they allow. The three questions below are all open ended, but some are more open than others.

> "Tell me about your job."
>
> "What do you like and what do you dislike about your job?"
>
> "I don't understand the nature of your job. What are some examples of the tasks and responsibilities that are part of your job?"

During counseling sessions, the worker will use mostly open-ended questions. Close-ended questions are appropriate when the worker needs specific information or when the client is so confused or overwhelmed that structure is needed to maintain focus and direction.

The skill of ***narrowing the focus*** (or *funneling*) refers to a series of questions intended to assist the client in describing his or her concerns or situation with more specificity. For example:

> *Client:*   Things are really a mess at home.
>
> *Worker:*   I'm not sure what you mean by "a mess." What happened?
>
> *Client:*   We were eating when Dad came home from work. He was drunk and ended up hitting Mom.
>
> *Worker:*   What did you do when all this was happening?
>
> *Client:*   First I ran out of the room. Then I came back and yelled at my dad to stop it or I would call the cops.
>
> *Worker:*   What were you thinking and feeling at that time you threatened to call the police?

Common errors in questioning technique include the overuse of close-ended questions, stacking questions, asking leading questions, and asking too many "why" questions. *Stacking questions* refers to the undesirable practice of asking several questions all at once. Consider this example:

> *Worker:*   So, you are interested in adoption. How long have you been thinking about adoption? Have you known others who have adopted? Are you thinking about an infant? Have you thought much about an older child or one who has a disability?

Stacked questions are confusing to clients. It is best to ask questions one at a time.

Leading questions are those that push or pull the client toward a certain response; for example, "Didn't you think that was wrong?" or "I assume that you explained to your boss why you missed work?" or "Isn't it true that you were hoping for a fight?" Leading questions are intimidating and insulting to clients. A leading question may prompt the client to lie rather than suffer embarrassment or openly disagree with the worker.

Another common error is to ask *"why" questions;* for example, "Why do you get so angry when Johnny spills food?" Essentially, "why" questions ask the client to justify his or her behavior, and this tends to produce defensiveness. Moreover, most people do not know the "whys" of their behavior, so, when asked, they simply guess or give socially acceptable answers. Instead of asking why, use questions that focus on the what, where, when, and how of the client's behavior and situation.

Active Listening

In active listening, the worker attends to both the client's verbal and nonverbal messages. The worker also reflects back to the client what has been heard so that the client will know that his or her message has been accurately understood. When engaged in active listening, the social worker should remember the following:

- Pay attention to the client's underlying feelings rather than to only the literal meaning of the client's words.
- Use a clear, calm, and interested tone of voice.
- Use body language that communicates attentiveness and demonstrates openness and concern.
- Ask questions that clarify what is being said by the client.
- Speak in order to better understand the client, and not primarily to make a point or offer an opinion.

The specific skills of active listening are those of clarification, paraphrase, reflection, summarization, and exploring silence.

Clarification refers to asking a question designed to encourage a client to become more explicit or to verify the worker's understanding of what the client has said. Such questions might begin with "Are you saying that . . . " or "Do you mean that . . ." and end with a rephrasing of the client's words. For example:

> *Client:* My life is a disaster. I thought I could get things squared away, but it doesn't look like that will be possible.
> *Worker:* I am not sure I am following you. Are you saying that things are changing more slowly than you expected or that your situation is now worse than before?

Another example:

> *Worker:* I am not sure what you mean when you say that you and your wife had a fight. Did this involve hitting?

When a worker becomes confused by what a client is saying, it is best to acknowledge the confusion and seek clarification. Here are a couple of examples:

> *Worker:*   You have been talking very fast. I cannot keep up and I am getting confused. Please start over, one point at a time. Also, try to slow down so I will not miss anything that you have to say.
>
> *Worker:*   I am sorry, but I didn't follow that. Please tell me once more.

A skilled social worker focuses on both the literal meaning of the client's words and on the affective component associated with those words. To do this effectively, he or she will make frequent use of the paraphrase and reflection. The skill known as *paraphrase* is a rephrasing of the literal meaning of the client's statement, whereas the skill termed *reflection of feeling* is an expression of the feeling or emotional component of the message. Examples of paraphrase and reflection are as follows:

> *Client:*   That guy down at the employment office is a real jerk. How does he get away with treating people like that? I feel three inches tall when I go down there.
>
> *Worker:*   I hear you saying that when you go to that office you are treated badly. (paraphrase)

or

> *Worker:*   It sounds like you feel embarrassed and humiliated at the employment office. (reflection of feeling)

The skill of *summarization* refers to pulling together the content and affective components of several messages. For example, a worker might use summarization to draw together the key affective and content elements of what was discussed during the previous five minutes. Here is an example of summarization:

> *Worker:*   From what you have been saying, I am hearing a number of things. You are desperate for a job and feel a mix of anger and depression because you haven't found one. You have been going to the employment office but that adds to your feelings of frustration and humiliation. On top of that, you have begun to feel deep regret for having dropped out of high school. Is that an accurate summary of what you have been saying?

Active listening also requires careful attention to times when the client is silent. Silence is a behavior that has meaning, and sometimes it is important to discover that meaning. The skill of *exploring the client's silence* refers to efforts to gently probe the silence. For example:

> *Client:*   (thoughtful silence)
>
> *Worker:*   You appear to be puzzling over something. Can you tell me what you are thinking about?

or

> *Client:*   (thoughtful silence)
>
> *Worker:*   Our discussion about your mother's illness seems to be pretty hard on you. Am I asking you to talk about something that is too painful to discuss?

An error commonly made by beginning social workers is to respond to silence with a change of topics. This happens because the worker becomes uncomfortable when the client is quiet. A brief silence is best responded to with polite quietness. If the silence is a long one, the worker should attempt to explore the silence.

Displaying Empathy, Genuineness, and Warmth

Item 8.2 of this chapter described the importance of the social worker's capacity for empathy, genuineness, and personal warmth in a helping relationship. A number of skills or techniques are used to display these qualities to the client. The skill of *displaying understanding* refers to verbal and nonverbal communication intended to demonstrate that the social worker comprehends and can identify with the client's thoughts and feelings. For example:

> *Client:* Having to place Mary in foster care is one of the most difficult decisions I have ever made.
>
> *Worker:* It must be hard to make a decision that is going to be very upsetting to Mary. It seems like this decision is tearing you apart inside.

It is especially important to acknowledge and display an understanding of a client's negative feelings such as anger and resentment. For example:

> *Client:* I am sick of this place. I don't need to be in a treatment program. I feel like punching the next person who asks me about my drinking.
>
> *Worker:* Well, I am part of this treatment program and you know that I will ask about your drinking. I guess that means you want to hit me. I am not sure how to respond to your threat. What are you expecting me to do?

The skill of *putting the client's feelings into words* refers to the articulation of what the client is feeling but has stopped just short of expressing in words. For example:

> *Worker:* How did the visit with your mother go?
>
> *Client:* OK, I guess, but I don't know if I can take this much longer.
>
> *Worker:* Watching your mother die is putting you under a lot of stress. It sounds like you hope death will come soon, but I assume that such a thought makes you feel guilty. Is that the way you are feeling?

This helping skill gives the client a supportive invitation to express what he or she is feeling but is reluctant to say aloud. Here is another example:

> *Worker:* Do you have any other questions about adoption or the agency's adoption program?
>
> *Client:* No, I don't think so. You explained it pretty well. I guess it's just a lot different from what I expected.
>
> *Worker:* I have the impression you were disappointed with what I had to say. You looked quite sad. Can you tell me how you are feeling about what I have told you?

It is important to recognize that encouraging a client to express feelings is appropriate only when those feelings are directly related to the overall goals of the professional relationship and intervention.

The helping skill of *self-disclosure* refers to a worker's statements that reveal some of his or her own thoughts, feelings, or life experiences. When properly used, self-disclosure has the effect of making it easier for the client to talk about a sensitive topic and to feel more at ease with the worker. On the other hand, the improper use of self-disclosure can cause the client to question the worker's emotional stability and professional competence and even cause the client to feel manipulated.

In some instances of self-disclosure, a social worker may elect to reveal feelings. These may be either positive or negative, as shown in these examples:

> *Worker:*   I feel disappointed and angry when I think about all the time we spent looking for your job and now, after just one week, you are talking about quitting.

or

> *Worker:*   I really feel good about what you have done. When we first met, I was worried about your financial situation. I feel proud and happy that our agency's training program helped you find that job.

At other times, a social worker may elect to share information about some life experience. For example:

> *Worker:*   I am sorry about how I reacted on the phone. I guess you noticed that I become sad when we talk about your mother's death. That touches me deeply. I had a real hard time adjusting after my mother died of cancer two years ago.

As a general rule, the use of self-disclosure should be avoided in the early stages of relationship building and used sparingly at other times. The information revealed by the worker should always have a clear connection to the client's concern. It is inappropriate for the worker to talk about personal experiences that are unrelated to the purpose of the interview.

Sustaining Client Motivation

In Chapter 7, motivation was described as a type of hope-discomfort balance. In order for people to make a change, they must feel hopeful about the possibility of change and must also feel some discomfort or dissatisfaction with their current behavior or situation. Several skills can be used to increase or sustain a client's motivation for change.

Displaying a belief in the potential of work (Shulman 1981) refers to statements intended to convey the worker's belief that professional intervention can be helpful. It is an offer of realistic hope to the client. For example:

> *Worker:*   The problems you have described are serious. I can understand why you feel overwhelmed. But I think you can successfully deal with these

problems if we work together and start chipping away at the problems, one at a time. It won't be easy, but I think we can make some progress over the next few weeks.

The skill of *recognizing client strengths* refers to expressions of confidence in the client's ability to accomplish some specific tasks or to cope with a difficult situation. Here are two examples:

> *Worker:* I know it is going to be difficult and painful for you to visit your kids in their foster home, but your visits are important to them, and I think you can handle it because you have been through this experience once before.

or

> *Worker:* You faced this problem in the past, and somehow you weathered the storm. I know you just want to run away from the whole thing, but you are an intelligent person and I really believe that you can figure out a solution.

(See Item 12.8 for more information on client strengths.)

The skill of *pointing out negative consequences* refers to statements that remind the client that change is needed in order to avoid undesirable consequences. For example:

> *Worker:* When you talk about wanting to drop out of the sex offender treatment program, I feel that I must warn you of the consequences. If you do not work on your problems and demonstrate a capacity to control your attraction to children, the judge will revoke your probation and you will go to prison.

Another example:

> *Worker:* When we first met, you were frantic because you owed so much money on your credit cards. Over the past months, you have made some real progress on controlling your spending. Now, you are talking about a very expensive vacation. I am concerned that you might slip back into your old habits.

Maintaining Progress Toward Change

Effective helping involves much more than understanding the client's problem or situation. The client needs to be helped and encouraged to make decisions and take action. Realistic, gentle, and supportive demands for change are necessary. Change usually involves having to reexamine one's assumptions and reevaluate past behavior; this can be painful and embarrassing. Change also involves trying out new behaviors and completing unfamiliar tasks; this can be frightening because it requires risk taking. It is important to recognize that a degree of fear, ambivalence, and resistance is a normal part of change. In fact, a lack of ambivalence and resistance may indicate that what looks like an effort to change is, in reality, only an illusion. Shulman (1981) explains that

> the worker must make a consistent ***demand for work***. The demand may be expressed in many ways, but it is generally experienced by the client as the worker saying "I mean business." It is a critical skill because it conveys to the client the worker's belief in the client's strength and the worker's willingness to deal with even the toughest problems and feelings faced by the client. It is precisely this additional pull that clients need at that moment to mobilize their strength and to take their next steps. . . .
>
>   The demand for work needs to be linked closely to the empathic skills. . . . A worker who is demanding, but not empathic, will be seen by the client as rejecting. On the other hand, the worker who is empathic, but makes no demands, will appear to the client as easy to put off. It is a critical synthesis of these two behaviors that will lead to effective work. (p. 20)

Several skills are helpful in maintaining momentum in the change process. One of these, ***partialization***, refers to breaking down a seemingly insolvable problem into smaller, more manageable components. Clients often feel overwhelmed or helpless when faced with large, complex problems. When a problem is broken down into several smaller concerns, it seems less frightening, and the client is better able to focus on a solution. For example:

Client: I cannot believe what is happening. Jimmy cut his head and I took him to the hospital. That crazy doctor notified child protective services and accused me of abusing Jimmy. Then my oldest son got into a fight with the landlord, and now the landlord has asked me to find another apartment. I cannot afford a lawyer, my child support check is late, and, on top of everything else, our car won't start. Things are so screwed up I cannot even think straight. All of a sudden the whole world has fallen in on me.

Worker: I think we better talk about your concerns one at a time. Otherwise, we will get confused and feel even more frustrated. Let's first focus on the child abuse report. We will return to the other problems later. First, tell me more about Jimmy's injury and the abuse report. For now, let's talk only about that problem, OK?

The skill of ***staying on track*** involves worker statements intended to keep the client's attention focused on a specific concern or objective. This is especially important if the client tends to ramble or wants to avoid work on a relevant concern. For example:

Worker: Because your boss has threatened to fire you, I think we better focus on that problem.

Client: Yeah. I guess so. I really wish I could get a transfer. But the company has such old-fashioned policies on things like that. I'm surprised they make any money at all. With the economy the way it is, you would think they would change the whole operation. They are not prepared for competition from Japanese industry. I recently read an article on new styles of management and . . . .

Worker: I think we better come back to the conflict between you and your supervisor. You have lost other jobs because of conflict. I know you need this job, so I think we better figure out a way of dealing with the problem between you and your supervisor.

The skill of ***building a communication link*** refers to efforts by the worker to establish a connection between the client and those with whom he or she needs to communicate. For example:

Worker: This is the third time you have told me that you haven't been able to tell your doctor about your concerns. What do you think about me giving her a call and explaining that I know you have something to talk to her about? I think that might cause her to spend more time with you when she visits you in the hospital tomorrow. Is that OK with you?

Sometimes a client will outwardly agree to take a certain course of action but inwardly have no real commitment to that plan. It is also fairly common for a client to decide on an action without being fully aware of the difficulties he or she will encounter. The skill of ***checking for acquiescence*** refers to efforts aimed at flushing out a client's resistance to or ambivalence regarding a certain decision or action. For example:

Worker: I certainly agree that you should talk to your math teacher about your failing grade. That needs to be done and I am pleased to hear that you intend to do it. But I also know that you often feel intimidated by that teacher. Don't you think this is going to be a difficult step for you?

Because genuine personal change is often an emotional struggle, the helping process and the content of the client-worker communications are usually emotionally charged. If, over a period of several sessions, there is little or no affectively charged discussion and no significant change in the client's behavior or situation, it is likely that the client is not really engaged in the change process. This needs to be discussed with the client. The skill of ***challenging the client's avoidance of change*** is a type of confrontation aimed at pointing out the client's resistance. The next example illustrates the use of this challenge during a marriage counseling session:

Worker: There is something that concerns me. When you two first came to the agency a few weeks ago, you requested help with your marriage. We have met three times. However, both of you have spent most of our time talking about your jobs, your kids, and your wish for a new house. You have said that there have been times when you were close to a divorce. Yet you seem to be avoiding any discussion of your marriage relationship. Unless we focus on your interaction, we are not going to make any progress.

(See Item 14.11 for additional information on challenge and confrontation.)

Sometimes a client's movement toward change is blocked because he or she does not want to grapple with painful feelings. The skill of *identifying emotional blocks* refers to messages aimed at increasing the client's awareness of how these feelings are getting in the way of progress. For example:

> *Client:*   I know I said I wanted to visit my kids more often, but I have been too busy at work to get away for a visit.
>
> *Worker:*   You are a hard worker and your job demands much of your time, but I suspect the anger and guilt you feel about your divorce is also caus-ing you to avoid visiting your kids. Perhaps you need to come to terms with those feelings.

A second example:

> *Worker:*   I have noticed something, and I think we need to talk about it. We started meeting together because you wanted help in learning how to handle your children. Yet each time I ask about Jimmy, you become tense and start talking about the other children. What is it about your relation-ship with Jimmy that makes you so uncomfortable?

In some cases, the change process is blocked when a client has unusual diffi-culty talking about an important but embarrassing topic such as sexual behavior, spending habits, or irresponsible behavior. The skill of *supporting the clients in taboo areas* (Shulman 1981) refers to communication intended to assist the client in discussing sensitive topics. For example:

> *Client:*   I always feel nervous when I get to the topic of sex. It's hard for me to talk about it because of the way I was raised.
>
> *Worker:*   You are not alone. Many of us were raised the same way. But I want you to try. You and your husband need to discuss your sexual relation-ship. That area in your marriage is causing you some real problems. It's difficult to discuss, but let's keep at it.

Some clients have had difficulties with authority figures (e.g., parents, employ-ers, police, etc.) and view the social worker as one more authority wanting to control their life. It is important to invite the client to talk about this concern. The skill of *ad-dressing the authority issue* refers to worker communication that invites the client to express concerns or complaints about the worker or the helping process. Consider this illustration:

> *Client:*   I think things are a lot better now at home. I don't think we need to set up another meeting.
>
> *Worker:*   I hope things are better, but I think something else is going on here. I have the impression that you think my job is like that of a parole officer and that I am trying to catch you doing something wrong. How about that? Are you scared of me and the trouble I might cause you?

(See Item 11.7 for more information on authority and the helping process.)

Bringing Things to a Close

Not infrequently, clients will wait until the last few minutes of a session before bringing up an important issue. There are several possible motives behind this *doorknob communication,* such as fear of the topic, wanting to inform the worker of a concern but not wanting to discuss it, and so on. The skills of **setting time limits** and **giving a 10-minute warning** are ways of encouraging the client to bring up difficult topics and to stay focused on high-priority topics. Here are a couple of examples:

> *Worker:* Before we begin, I want to remind you that we can talk until 4:00 PM. I say that because I want to make sure that we use our time to discuss issues that are of greatest importance to you.

> *or*

> *Worker:* I just noticed that we have to end this session in 10 minutes. Have we gotten to all the topics you wanted to discuss or is there something else that you wanted to talk about today?

The skill of **looking ahead to the end** is designed to remind the client of a planned ending for the intervention so the best possible use can be made of the remaining sessions. For example:

> *Worker:* When we began meeting a month ago, we agreed to meet for a total of eight times. We have three sessions left. Let's discuss what remains to be done so we can use those three sessions to focus on your high-priority concerns.

The client–social worker relationship may end either because their work together is finished or because the social worker must transfer the client to another worker. If the relationship has been a meaningful one, the ending can be difficult. Because so many clients have experienced losses during their lives, the ending may be painful because it reactivates feelings attached to prior losses. These feelings must be addressed directly by the worker. Shulman (1981) explains that

> because of the general reluctance to face endings, both on the part of the worker and the client, endings often are handled too quickly, without an opportunity for the client and worker to deal with the complex feelings involved. . . . Since the client needs time to deal with the ending, encompass it, and not experience it as a sharp rejection by the worker, it is important for the worker to point out the ending well in advance in order to allow the process to become established. . . . It is only when workers can come to grips with their own feelings that they can begin to help the client in this important phase. (pp. 26–27)

The worker can help the client deal with the emotional aspects of separation by voicing feelings about termination. This is termed **sharing ending feelings** (Shulman 1981). For example:

> *Worker:* I have been thinking about our relationship. Since you came to this hospital in September, we have gotten to know each other very well. I am glad you are finally able to go home, but I want you to know that I will miss our discussions.

The review of what the client and worker have done to address the client's concerns is an important element in termination. This skill is referred to as *reviewing progress*. Here is an example:

> *Worker:*   Altogether, we have been meeting for about four months. A lot has happened since you were reported for child abuse. You have made some positive changes in how you deal with your son, Michael. What have you learned from this whole experience?

It is important to encourage the client to express his or her feelings about termination. These feelings may be positive or negative or a mix of both. The skill of *reaching for ending feelings* (Shulman 1981) refers to worker communication that helps the client articulate his or her feelings. For example:

> *Worker:*   I know you are pleased about getting off probation. You are no longer required to see me. But I also sense that you have mixed feelings about our weekly meetings coming to an end. I wonder if it will be difficult for you to say good-bye. How about that?

(See Item 15.8 for more information on termination.)

SELECTED BIBLIOGRAPHY

Egan, Gerald. *The Skilled Helper*, 5th ed. Pacific Grove, Calif.: Brooks/Cole, 1994.
Kadushin, Alfred. *The Social Work Interview*, 3rd ed. New York: Columbia University Press, 1990.
Nelson-Jones, Richard. *Life Skills Helping*. Pacific Grove, Calif.: Brooks/Cole, 1993.
Shulman, Lawrence. *The Skills of Helping: Individuals, Families and Groups,* 3rd ed. Itasca, Ill.: F. E. Peacock, 1992.
———. *Identifying, Measuring and Teaching Helping Skills*. New York: CSWE, 1981.
Sommers-Flanagan, John, and Rita Sommers-Flanagan. *Foundations of Therapeutic Interviewing*. Boston: Allyn and Bacon, 1993.

8.4   Nonverbal Communication

PURPOSE: To understand and use nonverbal messages.

DISCUSSION: About 90 percent of face-to-face communication is nonverbal. Some researchers suggest that about 50 percent of every message is sent by facial expression alone, especially through the eyes, and about 30 percent is expressed by voice tone, pitch, and resonance. By paying attention to the client's nonverbal communication, the social worker can determine how he or she is being perceived by the client. Observing nonverbal behavior also tells the worker if what the client is saying in words reflects his or her thoughts and feelings.

Eye contact is a powerful means of communication. Eyes reveal much about our emotional state and have been called the "windows of the heart." Eye contact usually indicates a willingness to engage in communication and is an indicator of sensitivity and understanding. A lack of eye contact is often interpreted as a lack of interest or lack of sincerity. It is important to maintain eye contact with the client; however, glaring and staring are taken as rudeness and anger. Also remember that intense eye contact is not acceptable within some ethnic groups.

Tone of voice reveals feelings. A loud, forceful tone suggests aggressiveness, control, and strength. A meek, scarcely audible tone suggests withdrawal, fear, and weakness. A monotonous or flat voice suggests a lack of interest.

Facial expressions—such as smiles, frowning, nodding the head, shaking the head, lip quivering, and blushing—send messages to the observer. Quite often, facial expressions reveal that the person is saying one thing but thinking or feeling another. And it is often facial expressions that reveal a worker's disapproval of a client, even when the worker is trying hard to be nonjudgmental.

Arm and hand movements frequently communicate strong but unexpressed emotions. Crossed legs, arms folded across the chest, and body rigidity usually suggest defensiveness, whereas arms and hands at the body's side or in an outreached position suggest openness to others. Clenched fists indicate anger or anxiety. Fidgety movements, toe and finger tapping, leg bouncing, and similar movements suggest impatience, nervousness, or preoccupation.

Body positioning conveys various attitudes and intentions. It is best to face the client at a 90-degree angle, since this suggests both safety and openness. Facing the client directly may communicate aggressiveness. A desk separating the client and worker inhibits closeness and openness and also suggests the worker is in a superior position. Leaning slightly toward the client communicates interest and acceptance. Physical closeness invites trust and involvement, but being too close is threatening. Each client has his or her own sense of personal space. The worker can avoid invading this space by reading the client's body movements and adjusting his or her chair to accommodate the client's preferences.

Dress and appearance are important forms of nonverbal communication. The worker must give special attention to his or her own clothing and hairstyle. Dress that would be appropriate in an agency serving children may be inappropriate in a hospital or court setting. Likewise, dress that is acceptable to adolescent clients may be offensive to elderly clients. Some agencies have established dress codes. The new worker should consult his or her supervisor for guidance on selecting appropriate dress.

SELECTED BIBLIOGRAPHY

Morris, Desmond. *Body Talk: The Meaning of Human Gesters.* New York: Crown Trade Paperback, 1994.

Leathers, Dale. *Successful Nonverbal Communication.* New York: Macmillan, 1992.

8.5   The "I-Message"

PURPOSE: To send a clear and direct message.

DISCUSSION: The term *"I-message"* refers to a type of message structure that increases the effectiveness of communication. This structure makes it possible to send a clear, direct message and reduce the chance that the person receiving the message will be put on the defensive. It is especially useful in situations of confrontation and conflict because it allows the sender to express disappointment, anger, or frustration while minimizing the chance that the discussion will turn into a fruitless argument.

All too often, the messages we send are "You-messages"; for example, "You should clean up your room," "You need to have more confidence in yourself," or "You are driving me crazy." Such messages, even when well intended, cause the person on the receiving end to feel put down. The intention of a You-message may be to bring about a needed change in the behavior of another, but it usually ends up creating added resistance to change. Other forms of the You-message are orders and commands (e.g., "Stop doing that!"), blaming or name-calling statements (e.g., "You are acting like a baby"), and statements that give solutions (e.g., "You better forget that idea and take my advice"). Perhaps the most disturbing form of the You-message is the "if-then threat" (e.g., "If you don't . . . , then I will . . . .").

In contrast to the You-message, which usually blocks communication, the I-message allows the person bothered by the behavior of another to describe, in a noncritical or nonaccusatory manner, the impact the behavior is having, while leaving the responsibility for modifying the behavior with the person exhibiting the troublesome behavior. In effect, the I-message says, "This is my concern, this is how it bothers me, this is how I feel." The I-message does not accuse or blame; instead, it says implicitly, "I trust you to decide what change in your behavior is necessary." An I-message consists of three parts.

1. A brief, clear description of a *specific behavior*
2. The *resulting feeling* experienced because of that specific behavior
3. A description of the *tangible impact* the behavior has had

For example, a social worker using an I-message might say to a client:

> *Worker:*   When you did not show up for our scheduled appointment (specific behavior), I felt upset and put down (feeling) because I don't like having to wait around and because it disrupts my work schedule (tangible impact).

The I-message is a basic communication technique that has wide applicability. The typical social worker will use it many times each day with clients and other professionals. Also, it can be taught to clients as a method of helping them deal with common interpersonal problems, such as those that occur between parent and child, husband and wife, and so on.

SELECTED BIBLIOGRAPHY

Gordon, Thomas. *Parent Effectiveness Training.* New York: Peter Wyden, 1973.
Stayhorn, Joseph. *Talking It Out.* Champaign, Ill.: Research Press, 1977.
Zastrow, Charles. *The Practice of Social Work,* 5th ed. Pacific Grove, Calif.: Brooks/Cole, 1995.

8.6   Understanding Emotions and Feelings

PURPOSE: To assist the client in understanding and appropriately expressing his or her feelings.

DISCUSSION: A social worker's capacity to understand and communicate with others depends on his or her ability to accurately "read" and "tune in" to human emotions and feelings. Many of the clients served by social workers are confused, frightened, or overwhelmed by their emotions and many have not learned to express their feelings in a healthy manner. A social worker must be able to explain the nature of emotion in ways that clients can understand and also help clients learn ways of gaining greater control over troublesome feelings.

Emotions are complex, physical, biochemical, and psychological responses to conscious and unconscious interpretations of an event or experience. Neuroscience is just beginning to understand how emotions arise within us and how normal emotions can go awry, as when, for example, fear grows into a phobia or sadness turns into a disabling depression.

The word *emotion* means "to move." Our emotions move or motivate us to take action that has, at that moment, an adaptive or survival value. For example, the emotion of fear moves us to withdraw from a dangerous situation, whereas anger moves us to attack those who cause us harm. The emotion of anticipation moves us to persist in efforts to reach a goal, and the emotion of sadness attracts the attention and caring of other people. Thus, our emotions are a type of innate survival wisdom that is programmed into our very being. Emotions warn us of danger and push us or pull us toward activities that are likely to protect us from harm or meet our basic needs. Also, emotion is a type of communication that signals our intentions and reactions to others. The facial representations of certain emotions, such as sadness, fear, anger, disgust, joy, and others, are recognizable around the world, regardless of culture.

Still lacking is an agreed upon taxonomy of emotion. An interesting classification effort by Plutchik (1980) identifies eight primary emotions (joy, acceptance, fear, surprise, sadness, disgust, anger, and anticipation). Various combinations of these primary emotions yield others. For example:

joy + acceptance	=	love
acceptance + fear	=	submission
fear + surprise	=	awe
surprise + sadness	=	disappointment
sadness + disgust	=	remorse

disgust + anger   = contempt
anger + anticipation = aggressiveness
anticipation + joy   = optimism

Each emotion can vary in intensity. For example, joy can range from serenity to ecstasy, fear can range from apprehension to terror, and anger from annoyance to rage. While all emotions involve some level of physiological change, the bodily reactions that accompany the primitive fight-flight emotions such as fear, anger, panic, and terror are the most intense of all. Strong emotional reactions can overpower one's capacity to reason and maintain self-control; they can interfere with the ability to concentrate, remember, and learn.

Although the words *emotion* and *feeling* are often used interchangeably, it is useful to define an *emotion* as a particular physiological and psychological response and a **feeling** as one's subjective awareness of that emotion. As explained earlier, emotions motivate us to take action when our physical or psychological survival or our well-being is perceived by us to be threatened or when the satisfaction of our needs is perceived to be blocked. It is critically important to understand that our emotions are a response to our perceptions of what is happening at a particular time and that these perceptions may or may not be an accurate interpretation of reality.

The usual sequence between perception and thought and emotional and behavioral responses is as follows:

1. An event or situation occurs.
2. We notice, interpret, and think about the event.
3. Depending on our interpretations and thoughts, we experience a certain emotion.
4. The emotion moves us to engage in a certain behavior.

Some emotional reactions are immediate and do not involve thinking or cognition at a conscious level. For example, no real thought or analysis is necessary to interpret the danger of an attacking dog, elicit the emotion of fear, and move us to escape. Also, because of past "conditioning" (learning), we may interpret certain experiences in a habitual and almost automatic (unconscious) manner that involves little or no conscious thought. Thus, learning associated with prior painful life experiences may cause us to "misread" a situation or event and thereby elicit emotions and behaviors that are seen as inappropriate by others. An example would be a woman who feels fearful around all men because during childhood she was sexually abused by one man.

It is important to recognize that we respond emotionally not only to our interpretations of events and situations but also to our own feelings and behavior. For example, as we experience an emotion, we often think about whether it is "right" or "wrong" to be feeling as we do, and these thoughts may, in turn, elicit still other emotions. Similarly, we frequently pass judgment on our own behavior, and these judgments may give rise to still other emotions and behaviors or perhaps prompt us to reinterpret the situation in a different light. Thus, our thoughts, emotions, and behaviors are interrelated and interactive.

Because of the interplay between thought and emotion, we can, to a degree, alter and control our emotions and feelings by striving to change the usual ways we think about and interpret events and experiences. Several steps are involved in this learning process.

1. *Noticing our feelings.* People who are aware of their feelings are, by definition, in touch with their bodies, since all emotions have physiological correlates. Certain bodily sensations inform us that an emotional response is occurring. However, many of us tend to ignore or deny these sensations. Consequently, we may need help in learning to recognize the bodily reactions associated with emotion. One approach is to stop periodically throughout the day and reflect on our body's reactions and ask, for example, "What part of my body is experiencing emotion?" "Does some part of my body feel tense or strange?" "Is my body trying to get my attention?" "Why?" "What thoughts and interpretations are giving rise to these emotions?" Our bodily reactions during difficult interpersonal encounters or during times of stress are important windows to our underlying assumptions about self and others and our habitual ways of interpreting experiences.

2. *Naming our feelings.* Assigning a name to emotions and feelings helps us to accept them as real and provides a beginning sense of control. But attaching a label to something as subjective and nebulous as feelings is more difficult than it sounds. Many people lack a vocabulary for feelings. A list of feeling words may be of assistance in this naming process (see Item 14.25). If we learn to reflect on an emotion, locate it in our body, and give it a name, it becomes more familiar and is less upsetting.

3. *Owning our feelings.* Before we can really examine an emotion or feeling, we need to claim it as ours. Taking ownership of a feeling can be difficult if we are in the habit of denying and ignoring our feelings. Owning and accepting a feeling can be made easier if its name is spoken aloud, possibly to another person (e.g., "I am afraid" or "I am feeling sad"). Many people are surprised to discover that this simple verbalization helps them cope with troublesome feelings.

4. *Examining our habits of thought.* Our ways of interpreting and thinking about events and situations are often habitual. To a large degree, those patterns are learned during our childhood and carried into adulthood. Thus, in order to understand and modify troublesome thoughts and feelings, it may be necessary to reevaluate what we were taught during our childhood—a time when we uncritically form beliefs about ourselves and others. We must then decide if what we came to believe years ago as a child is still valid.

5. *Looking under and behind our emotions.* It is useful to think of our emotions as windows through which we can view the underlying and often unconscious interpretations that give rise to particular emotions. For example, when feeling anxious or fearful, we might ask ourselves, "Why does this situation seem frightening or threatening?" "Is it really so or am I interpreting it this way out of habit or because of a prior painful experience?" "Are there alternative ways of interpreting this situation or experience?" By looking at things from a different angle or coming up with other interpretations, we can often gain some control over the direction and intensity of our emotions and feelings.

6. *Choosing a course of action.* Even when we cannot significantly change our emotional reaction to a particular situation or event, it is still possible to make choices about how to behave. We begin to gain control over our behavior by asking ourselves, "When I feel this way, what choices do I have?" "Is my instinctive response (e.g., running if I am afraid, attacking if I am angry) an appropriate one under the circumstances?" "What destructive responses must I avoid?" "What responses would hurt me or others?" "Which response would be most positive for me and others?"

SELECTED BIBLIOGRAPHY

Ekman, Paul, and Richard Davidson, eds. *The Nature of Emotion: Fundamental Questions.* New York: Oxford University Press, 1994.
Lewis, Michael, and Jeanette Haviland, eds. *Handbook of Emotions.* New York: Guilford Press, 1993.
Plutchik, Robert. *Emotion: A Psychoevolutionary Synthesis.* New York: Harper and Row, 1980.

8.7 Responding to Defensive Communication

PURPOSE: To reduce the client's defensiveness.

DISCUSSION: The social worker must be skilled in reducing a client's need to be defensive and guarded. Schlosberg and Kagan (1988, 7) identify a number of common defensive maneuvers used by clients: "We do not have a problem" (denial); "It's all John's fault" (blaming); "She can't help it, she's retarded" (labeling); "If I get one more pressure, I'll go crazy" (being fragile); "My husband couldn't come today!" (avoidance); "Johnny was in another fight and I must talk about it!" (using crisis or distraction); and "What's the use, nothing will ever change" (helplessness). In addition, some clients use their physical environment (e.g., drawn shades, vicious dogs, terrible smells) and even their style of dress as a means of intimidation and keeping people at a distance. Still others use cursing, aggression, and threats.

Often the client is defensive before he or she even meets the social worker, but sometimes the worker's behavior or style can add to the problem. Behaviors that increase client defensiveness include appearing rushed, being brusque or insensitive to a client's feelings, making judgmental statements, using jargon or quoting agency rules and policy without explanation, failing to identify yourself and your role clearly, calling an adult by his or her first name without permission, being authoritarian, and creating long waits and delays. By following several guidelines, the social worker can reduce a client's defensiveness.

1. Remember that defensiveness is an attempt to protect oneself from real or imagined danger. Within a context of social service delivery, the dangers or threats perceived by clients are those of embarrassment, humiliation, loss of control over

one's life, loss of privacy, or failure to receive a desired social provision. Thus, do not respond to the defensive behavior as such but rather focus on what might be the client's underlying fear. Determine what is causing your client to feel threatened and try to remove that cause. Acknowledge those aspects of the situation that may cause your client to feel awkward, threatened, or humiliated (e.g., "I know it can be embarrassing to have to ask for financial assistance"). Use a generous amount of active listening (see Item 8.3) and make it as easy as possible for your client to verbalize feelings, but do not pressure him or her to do so.

2. Expand your tolerance of defensive behavior by understanding that it may have served a purpose in the past. If the client's defensiveness is a long-term pattern rather than situational behavior, hypothesize how it may have protected the client from pain associated with some fundamental disruption (e.g., rejection by a parent, breakup of one's family, or separation from loved ones) or a frightening event (e.g., major personal problem, family violence, or a life-threatening illness). Patterns of defensiveness often develop in response to such fear and pain. Your gut reactions to the client will often provide clues as to the function served by the defensiveness. For example, if you feel a strong desire to walk away from the client, the client's defensiveness may serve as protection against interference by outsiders. If the client's sad and helpless behavior makes you feel sorry and want to protect the client, this defensive pattern may help the client avoid a frightening responsibility.

3. If your client exhibits a positive or nondefensive behavior, respond with reinforcement and use the technique of ***mirroring.*** This technique is similar to *pacing,* which Cormier and Cormier (1991, 23) describe as "simply moving as the client moves or matching the client's non-verbal behavior without mimicking the client or doing it so deliberately that the client becomes aware of it." In other words, follow a nondefensive conversational exchange with a vocal tone and cadence, posture, and nonverbal behavior that mirrors or imitates the client's verbal and nonverbal behavior. On the other hand, if your client assumes a defensive posture or tone of voice, respond with exactly the opposite (e.g., an open, nondefensive posture and a soft comforting tone of voice). If your client's conversation speeds up as a result of anxiety or anger, respond with a slow and nurturing manner; this usually has a calming effect on the client.

4. To the extent possible, use words and phrases that match your client's dominant mode of receiving information. The three basic modes are visual, auditory, and touch. A client reveals his or her dominant mode in the frequent use of certain predicates in phrases such as "I see what you mean" (visual), "I hear what you are saying" (auditory), or "That idea is beyond my reach" (touch). If you can identify your client's dominant mode, try to match your phrases to his or her mode—for example, "Do you have a clear picture of what I am suggesting?" (visual), "Does this plan sound OK to you?" (auditory), or "I don't think this plan is going to hurt you—do you feel the same way?" (touch).

5. Whenever possible, give your client opportunities to make choices and remain in control of what is happening in his or her life. Use words such as *we, us, together,* and *it will be your decision;* these imply cooperation, respect, and choice.

6. Consider using the technique of *joining the resistance* by aligning yourself with the client's feelings—for example, "After such a long wait, you deserve to be angry. I would be angry also." Such an alignment with the client's hurt feelings reduces resistance by removing the client's need to keep defenses up and it gives the client permission to vent feelings.

7. Do not label or categorize your client (e.g., "All Medicaid recipients have to fill out this form"). People become defensive when they experience a loss of individuality. Also, do not embarrass or back your client into a corner, either physically or psychologically. Arrange your office and your own seating position so your client does not feel trapped. Allow your client to save face in embarrassing situations.

8. A defensive or resistant individual may attempt a number of maneuvers to block a worker's engagement efforts. In situations where it is critically important to engage the resistant client (e.g., in cases of child abuse), you will need to be assertive and deal directly with the issue. For example, if your client is silent, you might say something like, "I can see you do not want to talk to me about how your child was injured, but I am going to stay here until we have discussed it." If your client appears overly agreeable to what you have said, you could say, "I certainly hope you will take the actions you have promised, but how will I know that you have followed through on those plans?" Some defensive clients attempt to divert attention away from the real issue. When that happens, you might say, "I can sense you do not want to focus on the child abuse report, but that is why I am here and we have to get back to that topic." If your client attempts to avoid the central issue by talking about secondary concerns, you may need to take control by saying something like, "You have mentioned at least five other problems and I can understand that they are of concern to you, but we have to come back to the question of how Jimmy got those bruises—that must be the primary focus of this interview." Sometimes clients defend themselves by trying to make the worker feel guilty. When that happens, you may need to say, "I know you are upset and I don't like to see people cry, but your child has been seriously injured and it is my job to find out what happened. Take a few minutes to compose yourself and then we must get to the bottom of this. If you cannot talk to me I will ask someone from the prosecutor's office to speak with you." If your client verbally or physically threatens you, you will need to say something like, "I have no intention of harming you. I will not argue with you and I cannot continue the interview under these conditions. If you are too angry to talk now, I will come back this afternoon with a police officer. Do you prefer to talk now or later?" (See Items 11.7, 11.10, and 11.11.)

9. If your client uses obscene or abusive language, remain calm and do not respond in ways that might reinforce the behavior (e.g., shock, attention, etc.). Respond immediately with verbal and nonverbal attention and reinforcement to any part of the client's communication that is appropriate and constructive.

10. If the client persists in verbal attacks, consider using the technique termed *fogging.* This name comes from the notion that rocks thrown into a fog bank have no effect. If the person under verbal attack can mentally and emotionally behave like the fog, the verbal "rocks" have no impact and, hopefully, the attacker will soon abandon his or her efforts to cause discomfort. This technique works because the person under attack offers no resistance and avoids responding with either anger or defensiveness and because it calmly acknowledges that the angry person may have a point and is possibly accurate in his or her criticism and judgments. For example:

Angry Client: All you ever do is talk!

Worker: You're right. I do talk a lot.

Angry Client: If you would pay attention to what I have been saying, you wouldn't have to ask these dumb questions!

Worker: That may be true. I could be more attentive to what you say.

Angry Client: You are just like all the other lazy government employees and state social workers! You are always telling people what to do and butting into things that are none of your damn business.

Worker: I am a state employee. It does make sense that all state employees would do their job in similar ways.

SELECTED BIBLIOGRAPHY

Cormier, William, and Sherilyn Cormier. *Interviewing Strategies for Helpers,* 3rd ed. Monterey, Calif.: Brooks/Cole, 1991.

Rooney, Ronald. *Strategies for Work with Involuntary Clients.* New York: Columbia University Press, 1992.

Schlosberg, Shirley, and Richard Kagan. "Practice Strategies for Engaging Chronic Multi-problem Families." *Social Casework* 69, No. 1 (January 1988): 3–9.

8.8   Cross-Cultural Helping

PURPOSE: To become sensitive to the importance of cultural differences and minority group status in the helping process.

DISCUSSION: Social workers interact with many individuals and families who have cultural, ethnic, religious, and socioeconomic backgrounds different from their own. In doing so they must guard against being *ethnocentric,* which is the tendency of people to assume that their own way of life is superior to all others and always an appropriate standard for judging the beliefs and behavior of other people. Social workers must appreciate the many ways in which people might define themselves or feel different from others. If people believe and feel that differences exist, those differences are important and they will affect communication, interactions, and professional relationships.

Culture refers to the learned patterns of thought and behavior that are passed from generation to generation. Fundamentally, all cultures are particular patterns of meeting human needs and coping with the ordinary problems of living. The culture of a people is an expression of their definitions of meaning and their negotiations of power relationships both within and outside their own group.

The differences between cultures are expressed in many ways: language, religion and spirituality, world view, values, art, custom, rhythms of everyday life, preferred foods and leisure activities, clothing and body decoration, facial expressions and gestures during communication, manner of emotional expression, and so forth. Cultures are always changing; some change slowly and others change rapidly. Cultural change always occurs within a political and historical context. Something new (e.g., TV, computers, drug use) cannot be added to a culture without displacing or distorting other aspects of that culture.

Related to the concept of culture is ethnicity. An *ethnic group* is a segment of a larger population that defines itself and is regarded by others as a distinct people because they share a common culture, language, religion, ancestry, physical appearance, or some combination of such characteristics. The group's sense of identity is valued and passed from generation to generation. Green (1995, 19) explains that ethnicity is primarily about "perceptions of boundaries, with how . . . [perceived differences] are manipulated, managed, denied, asserted, and proclaimed."

The word *race* refers to our physical characteristics (e.g., skin color, facial features), whereas *culture* and *ethnicity* have to do with how people think and behave. Although the notion of race has no scientific standing as a biological concept for classifying people, the widely held assumption that there are distinct biological types of people has a profound negative effect on intergroup relations. The term *racism* refers to the judgment of others solely on the basis of superficial physical or social characteristics (e.g., skin color, facial features, language patterns) common to a people. Like many societies around the world, our society is racist in its prevailing attitudes. We still fall far short of Martin Luther King's dream of a society where people "would not be judged by the color of their skin, but by the content of their character."

Some ethnic and racial groups are also a *minority group,* which Schaefer (1993, 5) defines as a "subordinate group whose members have significantly less control or power over their own lives than that held by the members of the dominant or majority group." Minority group status is often tied to skin color, ethnicity, religion, gender, and physical or mental abilities. Schaefer (1993, 6) further explains that the members of a minority group typically have five things in common.

- Physical or cultural characteristics distinguish them from the dominant group.
- They experience prejudice and discrimination.
- Membership in the minority group is not voluntary.
- Minority group members experience a strong sense of solidarity with others of the group.
- Members usually marry those from the same group.

Minority group status has a very powerful impact on individual behavior and on a person's opportunity for socioeconomic advancement.

It is helpful to distinguish between prejudice and discrimination. *Prejudice* (i.e., to prejudge) refers to a person's unfavorable beliefs and attitudes toward a particular group or category. *Discrimination* refers to behavior and actions that are unfavorable toward a group and that deprive them of certain basic rights and opportunities. Given this distinction between beliefs (prejudice) and behavior (discrimination), one sees that being prejudiced does not always lead to discrimination. Also, it is possible to engage in discriminatory behavior without being prejudiced, such as when a person acts out of ignorance or when one's behavior is directed by an insensitive organizational policy or procedure. Thus, discrimination can be of two broad types: personal and institutional. In *personal discrimination,* an individual acts out his or her negative views toward members of a group. In *institutional discrimination,* the negative behavior is primarily a reflection of values, norms, and assumptions rooted in the laws, systems, and structures of a society. As such, institutional discrimination is more complex, subtle, and less visible.

Prejudice and discrimination may also exist within an ethnic or cultural group. For example, some members of the group may be predjudiced or discriminate against others of the group on the basis of differences of gender, education level, religion, and socioeconomic status. These intragroup dynamics may have a significant impact on how a member of the group views himself or herself in relation to other members of the group.

It is difficult to completely rid ourselves of the prejudices we all acquire during our upbringing. However, it is possible and necessary for social workers to become aware of their prejudices and refrain from acts of discrimination. Certain behaviors are characteristic of professional helpers who are racist and prejudiced in their thinking.

- Stereotyped explanations are given for the behavior of persons of a specific ethnic or minority group.
- The same helping strategies are used for all clients who are members of a particular ethnic or population group.
- The importance of cultural and ethnicity in a person's life are easily dismissed or, on the other extreme, they are used to explain nearly all behavior.
- Discussions of race and culture are avoided or are talked about continuously.

Social workers must strive to learn about their clients' cultures and ethnicities, but also must recognize that one can seldom acquire more than a superficial knowledge of another culture. It is very difficult to understand another culture, especially when differences of language are involved. In fact, most of us have little awareness of our own culture until we travel in a foreign country and have an opportunity to examine our way of life from a distance and with some objectivity. Every attempt to describe a group of people requires the use of generalizations. Even when a member of a particular group attempts to describe the beliefs, values, and behaviors common to his or her own culture or ethnic group, he or she is forced to make generalizations. Of course, all general statements about a group—whether it be people of the white middle class, people who are blind, people who are African Americans, or people who are Democrats—give rise to the dangers of stereotyping and overgeneralization. Among the people of a particular group, there are always significant individual differences.

Social workers and administrators must be alert to the possibility that their agency's policies and programs might, in some way, discriminate against an ethnic or minority group. An openness to this possibility, ongoing self-studies, and reviews by persons from outside the agency who are members of various ethnic and minority groups are of critical importance in identifying and eliminating discrimination.

Because most social agencies and social programs are created by decision makers representing the majority groups in society, the social workers employed by these programs may be viewed with fear or suspicion by clients who are members of a minority group. Whittaker and Tracy (1989, 158) explain that a major obstacle in working with a member of an ethnic minority is the "differing expectations as to what constitutes 'help,' making it extremely difficult to select appropriate and effective intervention methods." Whittaker and Tracy also warn that some of the most popular and commonly used techniques may not be effective when working cross-culturally. For example:

- Self-disclosure may be particularly difficult between dominant-culture workers and discriminated minority groups, since it presumes a degree of trust which may not exist initially.
- Short-term, task-oriented styles of social work may be ineffectual with clients who feel that extended periods of time "just talking" is an appropriate way to enter a relationship. . . .
- Reflection, reaching for feeling, or asking for insights may appear inappropriate or intrusive.
- Some ethnic groups, for example Asian-Pacific Americans, may view help-seeking as a shame-inducing process and will be extremely reticent to disclose personal problems. . . .
- Many ethnic minority groups (e.g., Puerto Rican, Hispanic) expect a more active helping relationship with the worker offering advice and tangible assistance.
- Techniques that rely on intrapersonal solutions versus social resolutions may be less appealing.
- Cognitive behavioral or rational emotive techniques . . . [e.g., managing self-talk, imagery, challenging irrational beliefs, etc.] may run counter to important cultural values and beliefs. (pp. 158–159)

Closely related to ethnic sensitivity is the need to adapt practice to the client's religious beliefs and spirituality. In fact, one's ethnicity, culture, and religion are usually interwoven. The social worker should be aware that the lives and decisions of a large portion of the clients they serve are influenced by particular religious and moral beliefs. Practice that neglects the client's religion may miss opportunities to be helpful to the client. Loewenberg (1988), for example, observes that

avoiding one segment of a person's life, such as religion, will handicap the interaction, even if it is a professional relationship between a social worker and client. One may wonder whether a social worker can really have a meaningful or helpful relationship with clients who have a strong religious commitment when such a social worker avoids the religious aspects of their lives. (p. 86)

In work with all clients, but especially with clients of a different cultural or ethnic background, the social worker is advised to individualize the client. The social worker must be alert to human diversity and never assume that a client's physical features or ethnic identity will predict the client's values, beliefs or patterns of behavior.

Other guidelines that a social worker should keep in mind are the following:

1. Appreciate the subjectiveness involved in how people see themselves and others. Remember that human differences are whatever people define them to be and their relevance is whatever people believe them to be.

2. Self-awareness is of critical importance. Green (1995, 10) observes that

> social workers often emphasize . . . the value of knowing "where the client is coming from." But it is equally important that professionals know where they themselves are "coming from." Their biases and assumptions should be explicit, at least to themselves. Assumptions, even assumptions that attain the status of scientifically validated theories, are usually culture-bound and expressive of some set of values and interests. (p. 10)

Constantly examine your attitudes and behavior and be alert to the possibility that you are making judgments based on racism, prejudice, and stereotypes, or perhaps behaving in a discriminatory manner. Frequently ask yourself, "What is my attitude toward people of different cultural backgrounds?" "How do I feel about people who have a different skin color or speak a different language?" "How do I feel about people who have religious beliefs different from my own?"

3. Very early in the relationship with a client, you should acknowledge the existence of differences of ethnicity or race as a way of giving the client permission to talk about these matters and perhaps express concerns about not being accepted or understood by you. Encourage the client to identify and define perceived differences and to explain how these differences might be addressed in the professional relationship and service delivery.

4. Show a special interest in your client's name, place of birth, and home community, for these topics are good icebreakers and lead naturally to a discussion of the client's cultural background and ethnic identity. A client who might experience difficulty with the English language should be asked if an interpreter is needed.

5. Realize that overlooking client strengths, misreading nonverbal communication, and misunderstanding family dynamics are among the most common errors made in cross-cultural helping. Behaviors motivated by religion and spirituality, family obligation, and sex roles are often misunderstood. Because of the difficulty in reading nonverbal cues cross-culturally, the worker should move slowly when reaching for feelings and putting the client's feelings into words. Overlooking strengths results when the worker does not fully appreciate the situation—especially the contextual and systemic aspects—with which the client must cope.

6. Be alert to the fact that in many ethnic families, certain members are the key decision makers and other family members will not make an important decision without consulting that member. For example, in many Hispanic families, the husband and father typically has considerable authority and his wife and even his adult children may feel obligated to obtain his approval before taking a course of action. Also, within the extended families common to the American Indian tribal cultures, certain individuals perform the role of advisor and other family members will delay making a decision until they have obtained his or her advice on the matter. Thus, it is always a good idea to ask the client if he or she wants to invite others to the interview or somehow involve them in decision making. Not infrequently, clients will simply bring these respected individuals to important meetings.

7. Be alert to the subtleties and the limitations inherent in the use of language. Recognize the influence of language on how one thinks or is able to think about certain matters. Whenever we use a word, we call up in our minds a concept or "picture" of what that word means. A given word may call forth somewhat different thoughts and ideas, depending on one's culture. Clearly, it is in our use of language that we encounter differences in how people think and interpret experiences.

8. Because members of many ethnic minority groups have suffered from discrimination, it is to be expected that they will be somewhat distrustful of professionals and agencies that represent and reflect the dominant groups in society. They will enter a helping relationship with caution as they size up the social worker. Lum (1992, 103) explains, "At first, . . . [the client] may be aloof, reserved or superficially pleasant. . . . Then the client checks out the helper by asking about his or her personal life, background, opinions and values. These probes are intended not only to evaluate the worker but also become acquainted and to establish a personal relationship." The worker needs to respond to these probes with honest, nonevasive answers. Because visiting people in their own home is usually seen as an indication of caring and respect, the home visit may help the worker build trust.

9. Ask your clients to explain their beliefs and culture and ask for their advice in how you might adapt your helping methods to their values, traditions, and customs. Do not be afraid to say that you do not understand. If you genuinely care for the clients and demonstrate concern for their situation, most will explain what you need to understand and know about their way of life. It often helps to use a bit of self-effacing humor (i.e., laughing at your own ignorance) when asking questions about things you do not understand. This display of humility makes you less threatening.

10. When you need to better understand certain cultural or ethnic factors, seek appropriate consultation. Also, contact leaders in the ethnic community and express your desire to learn about their values, beliefs, and way of life. They will usually offer their assistance if they perceive your interest to be genuine. Also, attend celebrations, ceremonies, and other cultural and religious events sponsored by the group.

11. Be alert to the fact that societal or systemic problems (poverty, unemployment, poor housing, lack of access to health care, etc.) bring ethnic minorities to agencies more often than do psychological problems. Thus, the provision of concrete services and the practitioner roles of broker and advocate are of special importance.

SELECTED BIBLIOGRAPHY

Davis, Larry, and Enola Proctor. *Race, Gender and Class: Guidelines for Practice with Individuals, Families and Groups.* Englewood Cliffs, N.J.: Prentice Hall, 1989.

Devore, Wynetta, and Elfriede Schlesinger. *Ethnic Sensitive Social Work Practice,* 4th ed. Boston: Allyn and Bacon, 1996.

Green, James. *Cultural Awareness in the Human Service,* 2nd ed. Boston: Allyn and Bacon, 1995.

Horejsi, Charles, Bonnie Heavy Runner Craig, and Joe Pablo. "Reactions of Native American Parents to Child Protection Agencies." *Child Welfare* 71 (July–August 1992): 329–342.

Iglehart, Alfreda, and Rosina Becerra. *Social Services and the Ethnic Community.* Boston: Allyn and Bacon, 1995.

Loewenberg, Frank. *Religion and Social Work Practice in Contemporary American Society.* New York: Columbia University Press, 1988.

Lum, Doman. *Social Work Practice and People of Color: A Process-State Approach.* Monterey, Calif.: Brooks/Cole, 1992.

Ponterotto, Joseph, J. Manuel Casas, Lisa Suzuki, and Charlene Alexander, eds. *Handbook of Multicultural Counseling.* Newbury, Calif.: Sage, 1995.

Schaefer, Richard. *Racial and Ethnic Groups,* 5th ed. New York: Harper/Collins, 1993.

Whittaker, James, and Elizabeth Tracy. *Social Treatment,* 2nd ed. New York: Aldine de Gruyter, 1989.

9 Workload and Caseload Management

INTRODUCTION

The new social worker learns quickly that there is not enough time to do all that needs to be done. Faced with that reality, the worker must make the best possible use of limited time and focus on matters of highest priority. Time and workload management skills are essential.

Paperwork and recordkeeping consume much of a social worker's time. Most workers dislike these tasks, but they are an essential component of service provision. Professional records must be complete, concise, legible, and accurate. Ideally, an agency's recordkeeping system will create documentation useful for the following purposes: (1) provide an accurate and standardized account of services provided; (2) provide data that can be used to plan and justify needed changes in policy, service delivery, and staff deployment; (3) provide data for retrospective and prospective research; (4) provide data that reveal the judgments behind key decisions and are therefore useful in staff development and professional education; (5) provide data needed to meet relevant legal and policy requirements; and (6) provide information that is understandable to and will withstand scrutiny by external reviewers (e.g., accreditation bodies, ombudsmen, lawyers, insurance companies, quality control personnel, etc.).

In our litigious society, social workers are increasingly named in lawsuits alleging professional negligence or misconduct. Proper documentation is of critical importance in defending oneself against such suits. From a legal perspective, "If it is not documented in the record, it was not done." In other words, in the absence of documentation, there is no evidence that a particular action was completed or that a decision was appropriate and justified.

This chapter discusses report and letter writing and recordkeeping. Also included are guidelines and techniques that can help workers increase their efficiency on the job: time management, using a telephone and dictation machine, incorporating information technology, and refusing and accepting added workload. The chapter ends with a section on testifying in court. With increasing frequency, social workers in all fields are called to be witnesses in court proceedings. The new worker, and even the practicum student, need to prepare for this inevitable experience.

The social worker must strive to be efficient. Efficiency can best be improved through using better tools of workload mangement, such as computers, and improving the paper flow in an agency. Social workers should be cautious, however, about actions in the name of efficiency that would compromise the requirements of the helping process. If workers attempt to hurry people along or rush the helping process, they lose their capacity to be helpful and effective.

9.1   Managing Time at Work

PURPOSE: To make the best possible use of limited time.

DISCUSSION: Nearly every social worker is faced with the problem of having too much work and too little time. Thus, the worker must use time-management skills as a way of increasing efficiency on the job. Consider these guidelines:

1. Come to terms with your resistance to using time-management principles. Do not hide behind the claim that you are too busy to get organized. Some people appear busy because they are always in motion, but activity does not always mean that something is being accomplished. Make sure your activity is productive.

2. Understand your agency's mission and your job description. Unless you are clear about what needs to be done, you cannot figure out ways to do it effectively and efficiently. If your assignments and responsibilities are not clear, discuss them with your supervisor or administrative superiors. Find out what tasks and assignments are of highest priority within the agency.

3. Recognize that in order to be effective and efficient, your job must be consistent with your personal and professional values, goals, and style. A mismatch between what your agency expects and what you can do or want to do is a recipe for frustration for both you and your colleagues at work.

4. Be proactive, not reactive. Anticipate tasks that need to be accomplished and the problems that may arise in completing those tasks and then take action. Do not procrastinate.

5. Use "to-do" lists. Good managers of time use a *"things-to-do" checklist* that they always carry with them. The list should include an estimate of how long it will take to complete each task on the list, so adequate time can be budgeted. Anticipate deadlines and begin tasks early enough to meet them. It is usually best to tackle lengthy tasks before those that can be completed in a short time. It is also best to work on the most difficult tasks when your energy level is highest (e.g., first thing in the morning). Save some time at the end of each day for clearing your desk, taking care of last-minute activities, and starting your "things-to-do" list for the next day.

6. Plan your work and set priorities. Every hour spent in planning can save three or four hours in the execution of a major activity. Develop both daily and weekly plans. At the end of each day, as well as at the end of each week, write down what

you plan to accomplish the next day and the next week. Prioritize this list of tasks by using, for example, the ABC Priority System (Laken 1973). Write an *A* next to those tasks that are most important and have highest priority. Write a *C* next to tasks that are of least importance and a *B* next to tasks in the middle range. Next, prioritize each *A* task in order of importance, labeling them *A–1, A–2, A–3,* and so on. The *B* tasks can be labeled in the same way: *B–1, B–2,* and so on. At the beginning of the working day, start at once on task *A–1* and stay with it until it is completed. Then move to *A–2* and on down the list.

A less complex approach is to classify all tasks into three categories: (1) tasks that must be completed today, (2) tasks that should be started today, and (3) tasks that can wait a few days. Realize that priorities may change over the course of a day or week. Thus, it is necessary to continually review your "to-do" list. Also, cultivate equanimity about priority setting. If a task you thought was a low priority suddenly becomes a pressing high-priority task, do not chastise yourself for poor planning. Accept such shifts as inevitable.

7. Plan for the unexpected. Allow time in your schedule for emergencies. Remember Murphy's Laws: "Nothing is as simple as it seems," "Everything will take longer than you think," and "If anything can go wrong, it will." Try to schedule at least one hour each day to deal with unanticipated tasks.

8. Reduce interruptions to a minimum. When you are interrupted, maintain control of the situation by giving the interruption full attention, avoiding irritation, and, where appropriate, setting a time limit on the interruption. Drop-in clients are often less of a problem than staff who interrupt other workers. Being able to say no to the question, Do you have a minute? is an important time-management skill. Closing your office door or standing up to converse with someone who just stopped by can help control unnecessary interruptions.

9. Make decisions in a timely manner. Setting a limit on the time to be spent on deliberation can reduce procrastination. Some workers are too afraid of making mistakes; as a result, they delay making decisions. Some workers avoid making decisions because they cannot arrive at a perfect solution. There are few, if any, perfect solutions in the real world of social work practice. One must strive for excellence, but striving for perfection will result only in frustration. Everyone makes mistakes. When you make a mistake, learn from it; do not waste time brooding over it. A "good" mistake is one from which you learn and do not repeat. A "bad" mistake is one you will repeat again.

10. Keep your agency's policy and procedure manual up to date. As changes occur, insert the new information and discard the old. Much time can be lost in fervid search for misplaced information or when you erroneously follow an outdated procedure.

11. Develop a *tickler file* to keep track of deadlines for submitting monthly reports and other tasks that must be completed according to a schedule. A tickler file can be as simple as notations on a calendar or a complex system, such as a desktop file or computerized calendar.

12. Develop a desktop system for the rapid retrieval of frequently used information such as telephone numbers and addresses (e.g., a Rolodex). As you learn about new programs and meet human services personnel, place their names, phone numbers, and other relevant data in the file for future reference.

13. When appropriate, delegate a task to staff at the next lowest level within the organization (e.g., a secretary, case aide, or paraprofessional). However, be careful not to overburden others or make assignments they are not prepared to carry out.

14. Limit the time spent in meetings. The following suggestions are helpful:
- Consider alternatives to a meeting (e.g., conference phone calls, exchange by e-mail).
- Define the purpose clearly before scheduling the meeting so all participants understand why they are attending and can properly prepare.
- Choose a convenient time and location for the meeting.
- Attend only for the time needed to make your contribution.
- Prepare an agenda and follow it. Start on time and end on time. Control interruptions. Stay on task; accomplish the purpose of the meeting.
- Evaluate the success of the meeting and agree on necessary changes in future meetings.

(See Item 14.39 for additional guidelines on meetings.)

15. To the extent possible, structure your day by using scheduled appointments for interviews, collateral contacts (contacts with other service providers), and the like. Reduce travel time by scheduling all meetings in a given locality for the same day.

16. Organize your desk and eliminate clutter in your workspace. Keep those things you are working on in front of you, but clear your desk of other materials. This will help keep your attention on the task at hand. Focus on one thing at a time until you either complete the task or reach a present time limit for that activity. Avoid jumping from task to task.

17. An important rule in managing paperwork is to handle each paper only once. If you pick up a letter, report, or request, take the action required or discard it if no action is necessary. Do not set it aside; do not let papers pile up on your desk.

18. Learn to use a word processor to prepare letters and reports. Also learn to use e-mail, the agency's computer, the fax, and other office machines that can speed communications (see Item 9.4).

19. Secure needed training. If lack of skill or knowledge is slowing you down or causing you to make mistakes, request training or consultation.

20. Develop a workable recording and notetaking system. Ask experienced workers to help you develop an efficient system of keeping notes and records (see Items 9.7 and 9.8).

21. Practice clear communication. Much time is wasted trying to deal with problems caused by poor communication. Learn to use the telephone effectively and efficiently. Poor telephone communication technique causes confusion and wastes time (see Items 8.1 and 9.5).

22. Avoid being drawn into doing someone else's work. Nothing reduces your energy or motivation more quickly than trying to compensate for someone's incompetence. This does not preclude helping others on occasion but do not make a habit of rescuing others.

23. Keep track of how you spend each day and week. Once you have this information, analyze it and identify those areas that need special attention and those areas in which you can make time-saving changes.

SELECTED BIBLIOGRAPHY

Culp, Stephanie. *Conquering the Paper Pile Up*. Cincinnati: Writer's Digest Books, 1990.
Glesson, Kerry. *The Personal Efficiency Program*. New York: John Wiley and Sons, 1994.
Laken, Alan. *How to Get Control of Your Time and Your Life*. New York: New American Library, 1973. (Signet Book)
Winston, Stephanie. *Best Organizing Tips*. New York: Simon and Schuster, 1995.

9.2   Report Writing

PURPOSE: To prepare a clear and useful professional report.

DISCUSSION: A social worker must write many reports. Reports that are inaccurate, incomplete, or unclear create misunderstanding, antagonism, and costly errors. A number of guidelines can improve the quality of reports.

1. A report is always addressed to someone; thus, it is important to analyze the report's audience and determine what information they really need. Also determine whether the report may be passed on to other organizations and possibly clients. Keep these readers in mind as you write. Always think about how the readers will interpret your words or perhaps misinterpret what you have written.

2. Decide whether a formal report or just a memo is required. A formal report usually follows the format prescribed by the agency. A copy of a report—one judged by others in the agency as a good model—can be used as your guide. A memo may contain abbreviations, first names, and jargon, but such shorthand should be avoided in a formal report.

3. Before you begin to write, organize the information to be presented in a logical structure. Construct an outline. If you present your ideas in an orderly way, the reader will be more likely to understand.

4. Two or three drafts or revisions may be needed before the final version is produced. Ask peers to review your drafts. If they are not sure of what you are trying to say, you can be certain that the intended reader will not understand either. Also read the drafts aloud; if one does not sound right, revise it.

5. Use language that is simple and clear. Select your words carefully, using only those your reader will understand. Avoid words that have different meaning in different contexts. Also avoid using slang or phrases that might offend the reader. For example, consider the following series of words: *inebriated, intoxicated, drunk, stoned; portly, stout, obese, fat; firm, obstinate, stubborn, pig-headed.* Each of the words in a given series has the same basic meaning, but each strikes the reader in a different way. Thus, word connotation—the emotion or attitude the word implies—must be considered.

6. Do not use "weasel words"—words or phrases that let the writer avoid responsibility for his or her statements. The weasel words *feel* and *seems* appear frequently in social work reports. Instead of saying, "I feel placement is necessary," it would be better to say, "I believe placement is necessary." Also avoid language such as, "It would appear that . . . ," "There may be a tendency toward . . . ," "It seems as though . . . ," "There is some reason for believing that . . . ," or "I feel there might be. . . ." Such wishy-washy language gives the reader the impression that the report writer is unsure of what he or she is talking about. This causes the reader to doubt the validity of the report and question the worker's competence. Be direct in both writing and speech.

7. Avoid hackneyed expressions such as, "It certainly merits study . . . ," "The matter is receiving our closest attention . . . ," "We will explore every avenue . . . ," or "Naturally, the child's interest is our concern. . . ." Such trite phrases suggest that the writer is insincere or responding as a mere formality. Be specific about what action will be taken.

8. Use the number of words necessary but no more. Wordiness lessens the force of expression and distracts the reader from the point you want to make. Also avoid redundant phrases such as, "first beginnings," "the present time," "join together," and "point in time."

9. Keep your sentences short, usually 20 words or less. Most often, the straightforward subject-verb-object sentence is the best arrangement because it can be read quickly and is seldom misunderstood. Consider these two sentences:
- After much discussion, not all of which was productive, a foster home placement—the agreed upon arrangement—was made for the child.
- The child was placed in a foster home.

Although both sentences say essentially the same thing, the second sentence is easier to read and understand; it is short and it follows the subject-verb-object structure.

10. Use active verbs whenever possible. The passive voice adds unnecessary words, weakens the statement, and makes the meaning less clear. For example, "Don hit John" has a clearer, stronger impact than "John was hit by Don."

11. Give special attention to paragraph construction. Each paragraph should focus on a single idea. The outline for a good paragraph is as follows:

- In the first sentence, state the central point of the paragraph.
- If necessary, restate the central point in other words or provide additional clarification.
- Present evidence or background supporting the central point, including examples, where appropriate. Draw conclusions.
- Finally, draw the paragraph to a close, summarizing the key point in a single sentence.

By reading only the first and last sentence of a paragraph, the reader should be able to pick up much of what you are trying to communicate. In general, a page of double-spaced typewritten copy should contain two or three paragraphs. If there is only one paragraph per page, it is likely that too many ideas have been crammed into a single paragraph.

12. Use the dictionary to determine the exact meaning of a word, the correct spelling, whether or not a word should be capitalized, correct word forms for different parts of speech, how a word should be divided at the end of a line, correct punctuation (i.e., hyphens, apostrophes, accents), and whether a hyphen should be used in a compound word. Most dictionaries contain a section that lists the basic rules of pronunciation, capitalization, and spelling; some contain information on grammar. A thesaurus, which contains synonyms and antonyms, will help the writer add variety and freshness in word selection.

13. The word processor has dramatically changed the tasks of writing and editing. Computer programs now include a thesaurus, spelling checks, and grammar checks. Because writing is so much a part of social work practice, all social workers must learn to use a word processor.

SELECTED BIBLIOGRAPHY

Hairston, Maxine, and John Ruszkiewicz. *The Scott Foresman Handbook for Writers,* 3rd ed. New York: Harper/Collins, 1993.
Houp, Kenneth, and Thomas Pearsall. *Reporting Technical Information,* 8th ed. New York: Macmillan, 1994.

9.3 Letter Writing

PURPOSE: To communicate ideas and information clearly and concisely in letters.

DISCUSSION: Most of the principles that guide report writing (see Item 9.2) also apply to letter writing. In addition, the following guidelines will improve correspondence.

1. Plan carefully before you write even the shortest letter. If it is worth doing, it should be done well. Your image as a professional person is shaped by the appearance of your letter.

2. Revise and polish all drafts of letters and proofread the final version. All letters to other agencies and professionals should be typed on letterhead stationery. Ordinarily, letters to a client should also be typed. If you know the client well, short notes may be handwritten.

3. A copy of all letters and notes should be retained for agency files. Use certified or registered mail when necessary to document that a letter was delivered.

4. Always use proper titles, such as "Mr.," "Mrs.," "Miss," "Ms.," "Dr.," "Rev.," and so on. The use of "Ms." is appropriate when a woman's marital status is unknown. First names should be used only when addressing children or persons with whom you have a close relationship.

5. Develop several model or sample letters based on situations commonly encountered in your agency. Use these as a starting point when preparing new letters.

6. Remember that a professional letter will have at least the following parts: letterhead, date, inside address, reference line or subject line, salutation, body, complimentary close, typed signature, and written signature. When appropriate, there should also be an enclosure notation ("enc.") and a copy notation ("pc") that names others receiving the letter.

7. In some letters, you will be complaining or making demands. You can usually make your point clearly and emphatically without being too aggressive. On the other hand, do not go to the opposite extreme by humbling yourself or avoiding an important issue. Write with directness, clarity, and authority.

8. Humanize and personalize your letters, especially those to clients. The recipient of your letter should feel that he or she is dealing with a real person, not an impersonal representative of an organization.

9. When writing to people in important positions, avoid sounding too friendly. Use a businesslike tone. Be pleasant but not folksy.

10. Be cautious about using the "I" point of view. This occurs when the writer constantly refers to himself or herself, especially by beginning sentences with the word *I*. Employing an *I* two or three times in an ordinary letter will not hurt; even starting an occasional sentence with it is all right, but do not overdo it.

11. Do not include material that would violate confidentiality or prove embarrassing if read by persons other than the intended recipient of the letter. Be alert to the fact that an agency's name and address on an envelope may reveal the client's involvement with an agency.

SELECTED BIBLIOGRAPHY

Berger, Arthur Asa. *Improving Writing Skills: Memos, Letters, Reports, and Proposals.* Newbury Park, Calif.: Sage, 1993.
Davidson, Wilma. *Business Writing.* New York: St Martin's Press, 1994.

9.4   Using Information Technology

PURPOSE: To employ various forms of information technology for increasing practice effectiveness and workload efficiency.

DISCUSSION: As computers have become smaller, more powerful, less expensive, and more user-friendly, social workers have increasingly incorporated information technology into their practice. An increasing array of software that support both the administrative functioning of human services agencies and private practice, as well as providing tools for practice assessments and efficient communication, have opened electronic technology to social workers. Although highly technical skills are required to create computer equipment and software programs, to make use of existing technology the social worker needs only a "functional computer literacy." Familiarity with three aspects of information technology (i.e., the hardware, software applications, and on-line resources) provides the base for becoming computer literate.

Hardware refers to the physical or machine components of information technology. The hardware serves three distinct purposes: the input of data, its processing (or throughput), and the final product (output). *Input* is accomplished through a keyboard, mouse, touch screen, computer disk or tape, scanner, CD-ROM, or other data entry forms. *Throughput* is accomplished by the "brains" of the computer, the central processing unit (CPU), which receives instruction and data from the input devices, performs arithmetic and logical operations, and stores the results in its memory. It is the speed with which the CPU can process large amounts of information that makes information technology a valuable asset to the social worker. *Output* takes several forms, including images appearing on a monitor, hard copy from a printer, or storage on a disk or magnetic tape.

Computers vary greatly in their size and capacity. *Mainframe computers* with multiple terminals often are used by statewide human services agencies to collect large amounts of standardized data for reports of agency activity. *Microcomputers* (i.e., desktop computers) are used by midsized and small agencies. By using a local area network (LAN), these agencies can link workers to the agency's central data base to aid interagency communication and collect data for program evaluation. They can also be linked to resources throughout the world over telephone lines and through electronic mail (e-mail) programs.

The term *software* refers to the programs that can be purchased or developed to provide the instructions to the computer. Typically, the program for each *application* (e.g., word processing, spreadsheet, etc.) is stored on the computer's hard disk to be called up by the operator when needed. The social worker needs only to know which programs to use for the intended purpose and how to access those programs.

The most frequent use of information technology by social workers is *word processing.* Word processing is used for composing and editing case summaries, correspondence with clients and other agencies, agency information sheets, news releases, letters to legislators, and so on. A specialized form of word processing is *desktop publishing* software, which provides templates that facilitate the creation of newsletters, flyers, and brochures. Similarly, *presentation packages* assist in the creation of text and graphics for preparing professional-looking overheads and slide shows that can be used in making presentations at professional meetings (see Item 10.4) or in interpreting agency services.

Spreadsheets (and accounting application programs based on spreadsheets) allow users to work with mathematical and accounting data. The primary advantage of spreadsheets is their ability to use formulas so that when one value is changed, all other numbers based on that value change accordingly. For example, in developing an agency budget it is possible to quickly see the effects of an across-the-board 3 percent reduction or increase in funds. Most spreadsheet programs incorporate presentation graphics allowing the data to be viewed as charts or graphs.

Database programs are recordkeeping systems—the electronic equivalent of the filing cabinet and file folders. For a social worker, a database will typically contain client demographic characteristics, social histories, intake information, treatment plans, and progress notes. These data can be readily accessible to the social worker to track the progress of an individual client, review report data, schedule appointments, identify items due and pending, and reduce paperwork. For the agency, a database can provide aggregate data for planning and accountability purposes, forecast demand for services, monitor the impact of services on clients, and compare anticipated outcomes with those actually achieved. Another form of database is *The Social Work Reference Library* (NASW 1995) on a CD-ROM that combines the entire social work encyclopedia, social work dictionary, and social work almanac into a single database that can search for information about social work and social work practice.

Decision support systems utilize the data in an agency information system along with computer modeling capabilities to assist professionals in making decisions. A decision support system, for example, might prompt a worker to obtain additional client information regarding a specific problem. It would then provide the worker with a description of similar cases and how they were resolved, offer suggestions for use of further diagnostic tests, provide a list of actions followed in similar cases that were successfully resolved, or give a list of abstracts of studies or articles related to the client's problem or culture.

Expert systems are databases with aspects of artificial intelligence that combine a "knowledge base" with rules for reasoning about the contents of that information. Expert systems are used to provide the worker with an electronic form of consultation about a practice situation. Due to the complexity of developing them, expert systems are still rare in human services agencies.

Computerized assessment instruments facilitate assessment of individual and family case situations and assist in ongoing monitoring of cases. A variety of intake, social history, and problem assessment inventories are available, as well as scales to assess such factors as depression, eating disorders, grief, anxiety, marital satisfaction, spouse abuse, suicidal ideation, and others. (See Item 12.18 for examples of some assessment instruments.) Recent research suggests that having tests available on computer has resulted in more use of assessment tests, better professional performance, and higher client satisfaction (Nurius and Hudson 1993).

Research-related software also serves an important function in social work. Such software can be used to select a sample size, construct data-entry forms, calculate the margin of error for given return rates, suggest and perform appropriate statistical tests, analyze qualitative data, and present the results in graphic format. Research-related software can also assist in practice activities ranging from testing hypotheses about the relationship between various client variables and practice outcomes to conducting agency program evaluations and community needs assessments.

Software programs have also been developed for worker *education and training.* Computer-based education and training activities range from relatively simple text-based programs to multimedia programs that incorporate text, graphics, sound, and video. In addition to self-paced programs for agency staff regarding client assessment, policy interpretation, and so on, computer-based training has been designed to provide clients with parent education, relaxation training, and sex education. Similarly, *computer games* have been used with children, adolescents, and the elderly to enhance self-concept and feelings of success, to provide art therapy, and to stimulate social interaction.

Social workers use *on-line resources* as a communication tool for networking, information sharing, consultation, and social support among geographically dispersed human services professionals, agencies, and client self-help groups. Through on-line resources, workers can access e-mail, search for government and library documents and have them delivered, and examine databases of local and national information through bulletin board systems (BBS). Private companies such as America Online, Compuserv, and Prodigy, and the vast resources of the Internet link thousands of computers in universities, human services agencies, government, and other sources in a worldwide network.

Several on-line resources are particularly useful for social workers. *Electronic mail,* for example, provides each worker with an "electronic mailbox" to which messages can be sent and stored. It is especially helpful for busy workers who must coordinate the activities of many people in order to serve their clients. The same message can be sent to several people at once, time and energy are not lost in "telephone tag," messages can be read and answered at one's convenience, and the messages can be printed and saved for case records. It is an effective, fast, and inexpensive way of communicating information among staff members that can be accessed from home or office.

E-mail–based discussion groups (also known as e-mail groups, special-interest groups [SIGS], newsgroups, USENET groups, or LISTSERVs) permit people to discuss specific topics with experts from around the world. Such groups relate to various topics as welfare reform, gay rights, AIDS, Alzheimer's disease, adoption, community revitalization, gangs, and child maltreatment. Some e-mail (LISTSERVs) groups specifically for social workers can be accessed on the Internet, such as:

SOCWORK@UAFSYSB.UARK.EDU	General social work issues
CUSSNET@STAT.COM	Computer users in social work
SWMGLST@STAT.COM	Social work evaluation and research
FEMS-L@MOOSE.UVM.EDU	Feminist social work issues
INTSOCWORK@NISW.ORG.UK	International social work
CWKGROUP@UMASSD.EDU	Computerization of client records

Another resource for social workers is *the computer-based self-help/mutual aid groups.* These groups provide support to thousands of people with a variety of concerns including, for example, physical and sexual abuse, addictions, AIDS, disabilities, catastrophic illness, mental illness, and care giving. These groups are especially useful for persons who wish to participate in a self-help group anonymously, who have limited verbal communication skills, who are homebound due to disability or caregiver responsibilities, and those in rural areas or other places where local groups are not available (Finn 1993; Finn and Lavitt 1994).

The Internet also makes it possible to access *files and databases of social work information* without leaving one's home or office. Using *FTP* (File Transfer Protocol) software allows transfer of files from a remote computer site, whereas *Telnet* allows a worker to search over 700 professional journals on the Educational Resources Information Center (ERIC) and have articles faxed (for a fee). Some computers, known as *Gopher* sites, contain information that can be accessed to support one's practice, such as funding and grant information, the latest research on a specific topic, evaluation studies of innovative human services programs, and assistive technology devises or summer camps for people who are disabled. For example, the Internet gopher address GOPHER://MUDHONEY.MICRO.UMN.EDU:7000/11/LEGISLATION/103/ALPHA contains information about all bills before Congress, arranged by subject category.

Finally, the *World Wide Web* (WWW) links Internet information through hypertext documents called Web pages. A human services agency, for example, may create a Web page with its eligibility requirements, fee scale, service descriptions, and staff expertise that others can readily access using a Uniform Resource Locator (URL) address (e.g., the U.S. Department of Health and Human Services can be found at URL:HTTP://WWW.OS.DHHS.GOV).

As information technology increasingly becomes part of social work practice, practitioners at all levels within the service organization must participate in shaping the technology of human services computing rather than permitting the technology to shape and drive practice (Nurius and Hudson 1993). Social workers should understand both the potential benefits and dangers in these changes. They must also address the associated *ethical issues* such as making sure disenfranchised groups will have access to information technology and protecting the accuracy, security, and confidentiality of social work records when agencies share records via telecommunications (Finn 1990). In the end, however, social workers must recognize that electronic technology only provides tools to assist practice; it is the workers themselves who must ultimately decide how to use this technology in an appropiate and responsible manner.

SELECTED BIBLIOGRAPHY

Finn, Jerry. "An Exploration of Computer-Based Self-Help/Mutual Aid Groups. In *Human Welfare and Technology,* edited by Bryan Glastonbury. The Netherlands: Van Gorcum, 1993.

———. "Security, Privacy, and Confidentiality in Agency Microcomputer Use." *Families in Society* (formerly *Social Casework*) 71 (May 1990): 283–290.

Finn, Jerry, and Melissa Lavitt. "Computer-Based Self-Help/Mutual Aid Groups for Sexual Abuse Survivors." *Social Work with Groups* 17, 1/2 (1994): 21–46.

Geiss, Gunther R., and Narayan Viswanathan, eds. *The Human Edge: Information Technology and Helping People.* New York: Haworth Press, 1986.

National Association of Social Workers. *The Social Work Reference Library* (CD-ROM). Washington, D.C.: NASW Press, 1995.

Nurius, Paula S., and Walter W. Hudson. *Human Services Practice, Evaluation, and Computers: A Practical Guide for Today and Beyond.* Pacific Grove, Calif.: Brooks/Cole, 1993.

Schoech, Dick. *Human Service Computing.* New York: Haworth Press, 1990.

9.5 Effective Telephone Communications

PURPOSE: To communicate clearly and concisely when using the telephone.

DISCUSSION: Many social work transactions occur over the telephone, making this a frequently used tool in social work practice. However, the telephone is not always the most effective method of communication.

The telephone should be used when a quick response is needed and the matter under discussion is relatively uncomplicated. It is important to remember that a phone call does not establish a permanent record of the transaction. A letter or memo may be preferred when time is not critical, when a record must be established, or when the message involves many details.

The following guidelines will help improve telephone use.

1. The task of communicating over the telephone has to be accomplished by your voice. The person to whom you are speaking does not have the advantage of being able to observe your body language. Take care to enunciate distinctly. Use a normal speaking voice.

2. When making and receiving calls, always fully identify yourself by name, organization, and department.

3. Jot down the major points you wish to cover before placing the call. Take notes while on the phone. Before saying goodbye, it may be appropriate to summarize the information you intended to convey and the information you received.

4. If the person on the other end is talking at some length, interject a brief comment at intervals: "Yes, I see" or "I understand." This lets the other person know that you are still listening. If your caller gets sidetracked, steer him or her back to the main point of the call.

5. Whenever possible, answer the telephone on the first or second ring—and immediately respond to the caller. Do not just pick up the receiver and hold it while you finish a conversation with another person.

6. If you must leave a message for a person you did not reach by phone, keep the message short (e.g., your name, phone number, and reason for calling) and assume

there is a good chance that the message will get garbled. If you must leave a long message or suspect that your message was misunderstood, ask the person taking your message to repeat it back to you. Suggest a specific time for the person to return your call, or find out what time you can call again. You will probably save time by calling back yourself rather than waiting for your call to be returned.

7. When you leave your office, always tell the office secretary where you can be reached or when you will be back. If needed, establish a regular time of day to receive telephone calls.

8. Master the skills of using your agency's phone system such as transferring calls, using voice mail, and so on. When transferring calls to other lines, let callers know what you are doing: Tell them the name and title of the person to whom they will be speaking and why you are transferring their call. When you must leave the phone, explain why: "Please hold on for a few seconds while I get that file." Unless you are sure you will be away for only a few moments, tell your caller that you will call back. If you have left the phone, alert your caller to your return before resuming the conversation: "Hello" or "Thanks for waiting" or "I have that file now."

9. Realize that the voice mail systems used in many agencies can be confusing and frustrating to callers. Appreciate the fact that the caller may be upset after having to carefully listen to a recorded voice and perform numerous dialing maneuvers. Instruct your clients and other frequent callers how to use the system.

SELECTED BIBLIOGRAPHY

Guffey, Mary. *Business Communication.* Belmont, Calif.: Wadsworth, 1994.

9.6 Controlling Workload

PURPOSE: To manage workload by refusing and accepting additional work assignments.

DISCUSSION: Given the demands placed on a social worker, the worker must view his or her time as a limited resource. If the worker does not control workload, he or she will be spread too thin and effectiveness will diminish. There are only a couple ways to control an ever-growing workload—you can either say no to additional work assignments or you can ask other staff for their assistance.

Saying no is difficult for many people. When someone asks you to take on additional work, it may seem easier to say yes in order to avoid conflict or feeling guilty. Nevertheless, you must take responsibility for managing your workload and this requires saying no to some requests. Follow these guidelines:

1. Decide if the proposed assignment or request for your time is reasonable, given your job description and current workload. Ask yourself: Is this a matter of high priority? Am I responsible for this matter or is someone else? If I say yes, will I soon regret it and feel angry and put upon? Am I tempted to say yes mainly because I want to avoid a conflict or the appearance of selfishness?

2. When unsure if the request is reasonable, obtain more information before saying yes or no. If still in doubt, ask for time to think about the request and set a deadline for making the decision (e.g., "I'll let you know in a half hour").

3. If you must refuse, say no firmly and calmly. It may be appropriate to give a straightforward explanation of why you must say no. But say no without saying "I'm sorry" or offering excuses and rationalizations. If you have a good reason for refusing, there is no need to apologize.

Whenever you ask others for assistance, explain why you think it is an important and reasonable request and why you are asking them to take on the task. If your request is refused, adhere to three guidelines.

1. Accept the answer graciously. Do not put pressure on the person and do not make the individual feel guilty for having refused.
2. Be pleasant and appreciative. Respond with something like, "I understand; thank you for your consideration."
3. If appropriate, ask if your request might be acceptable under other circumstances, such as at a later time or date.

It is important to note that this brief discussion of refusing and accepting additional assignments presumes a situation in which there is room to negotiate. Such a situation does not always exist. Within an agency, a supervisor or administrator has the legitimate authority to assign additional tasks, even when he or she knows you are already overloaded. In other words, a worker does not always have the freedom to refuse.

SELECTED BIBLIOGRAPHY

Alberti, Robert, and Michael Emmons. *Your Perfect Right,* 6th ed. San Luis Obispo, Calif.: Impact, 1990.
Jakubowski, Patricia, and Arthur Lange. *The Assertive Option.* Champaign, Ill.: Research Press, 1978.

9.7 Maintaining Casenotes for Narrative Recording

PURPOSE: To improve efficiency in creating narrative case recordings.

DISCUSSION: Each social agency develops its own procedures for recordkeeping. What is recorded and the format used will depend on factors such as the agency's mission, relevant state and federal laws and regulations, type of service provided, and who has access to the records.

Narrative recording is still a common format in direct-service agencies, even though many are moving toward using brief progress notes, computer-assisted systems, problem-oriented recording, and other structured formats. The narrative record remains popular because it is flexible—anything deemed important can be written into the record. The major disadvantage is that it is a time-consuming method. Another disadvantage is that the narrative does not lend itself to the easy retrieval of information; individuals looking for specific information may have to read many pages before they find what they are looking for. Also, because narrative records tend to grow so large, storage is a problem. Kagle (1991) observes that

> these problems have led some agencies to eliminate the use of narrative records entirely. Many agencies, though, cannot or do not wish to take such a step. Their goal should be to maximize the assets of narrative records while minimizing their limitations. Agencies can achieve this goal by
>
> ■ Limiting the use of narrative records to complex, individualized services; using structured forms for short-term or routine services.
> ■ Limiting narrative recording to those elements of the record which focus upon individualization; using forms, lists, or outlines for systematic or typical information.
> ■ Establishing guidelines for what to include in the narrative; these guidelines might suggest relevant topics for records of different client groups, service programs, and practice modalities.
> ■ Establishing guidelines for what to exclude from the narrative, especially: content that is documented elsewhere, content that needs to be readily accessible, and content that could be sufficiently documented using a more efficient style. (p. 91)

Two steps are involved in the preparation of a narrative record: the worker creates many handwritten notes and then, at a later date (sometimes weeks or even months later), the worker reviews these notes and prepares a summary of his or her work with the client. The handwritten notes record the day-to-day actions and activities related to a specific case (e.g., "Mr. Smith, Johnny B's teacher, called to say . . ."). Notes help the worker keep track of what is happening. Some of these notes are merely reminders that a specific task should be undertaken (e.g., "Contact Mrs. Jones's attorney and request . . .").

In order for the worker to do the summary efficiently, he or she must develop a system of notetaking that (1) keeps all casenotes in one place so this information is always at hand, (2) maintains a chronological record of activities, and (3) facilitates summarization. One such method is to utilize a loose-leaf notebook filled with sheets specifically designed for brief handwritten and chronological entries. The sheets can be constructed to facilitate the recording of statistics kept by the agency (e.g., number of office interviews). Figure 9.1 is a sample with several typical entries. All of the notesheets are kept in one place and used as a basis for the periodic (e.g., once a month or bimonthly) dictation of a summary entry into the agency record.

FIGURE 9.1   Sample Recording of Casenotes

| Client | _Jimmy Jones_ | Case Number | _321_ | Cross Reference | _L. Smith Foster home_ |

Client (child)	Client (adult)	Foster parent	Collateral	Other	Office	Out-of-Office	Telephone	Letter	Other	Date	Time spent	To Do	Notes
	✓						✓			Jan 27			Mrs Smith called to say Jimmy ran away. He did not come home from school. She will call his friends and will inform Jimmy's probation officer. (Leland Green)
	✓						✓			1/28			I called Mrs. S. Still no word on Jimmy. Police have been informed.
			✓				✓			•••			Learned from L. Green that Jimmy was picked up. No charges.
✓	✓						✓			•••			Jimmy returned to Smith home. Jimmy having trouble in school. Failing math. Picked on by other kids. Wants to quit school.
												✓	(set up meeting with math teacher + school counselor. Is tutor possible?)
	✓						✓			1/29			Mr. + Mrs Smith and I will meet at school for conference, 4 pm today. Room 104
✓							✓			1/29			Spent hr with Jimmy. He is angry with math teacher. Feels he is not treated fairly because he is "foster kid." Also upset because mother forgot his birthday. "She is probably drunk again." He cried as he talked about mother. He cares for her and worries about her but "hates her when she drinks." He wants to visit older sister, Mary. "Mary helps me understand Mother."
												✓	(arrange meeting between Jimmy and Mary.)

SELECTED BIBLIOGRAPHY

Kagle, Jill. *Social Work Records,* 2nd ed. Belmont, Calif.: Wadsworth, 1991.
Wilson, Suanna. *Recording: Guidelines for Social Workers.* New York: Free Press, 1980.

9.8   Problem-Oriented Recording (POR) and the SOAP Format

PURPOSE: To facilitate concise recordkeeping that focuses on the client's problem and the professional interventions to deal with that problem.

DISCUSSION: *POR,* Problem-Oriented Recording, is a method of recordkeeping often used in hospitals and medical programs. Its use has spread to many social agencies. POR has a number of advantages, such as the following:

- It permits the worker, agency supervisor, outside consultants, or researchers to review the way in which a particular problem was approached by the worker or agency.
- It displays the multiplicity and interrelatedness of problems experienced by a client, yet it permits focused attention on each specific problem.
- It promotes case coordination and teamwork because it facilitates interprofessional communication and clarity of direction.
- It provides continuity of professional attention on specific problems, even when there is personnel turnover in the agency.
- It provides a mechanism for follow-up and the monitoring of progress toward problem resolution. A review of a problem-oriented record will quickly reveal inaction or actions unrelated to the client's problem.
- It encourages concise recording. Because specific problems are kept in focus, irrelevant information is kept out of the record.

POR consists of four components, which are related to the basic steps of the problem-solving process: (1) establishment of a database; (2) listing of specific problems, each of which is assigned an identifying number; (3) development of an action plan to address each problem; and (4) implementation of the plan.

The database consists primarily of the information collected during the intake phase and includes a description of the problem that brought the client to the agency. Much of the data appears on the record facesheet. These data should be systematically collected, organized, or recorded, for they provide a foundation for identifying and conceptualizing the client's problems and yield a preliminary problem list.

A problem can be anything of concern to the client, the social worker, or both. All problems become part of the problem list. Each problem is assigned a number and described in behavioral language. Diagnostic labels are avoided, if possible. The problem list serves to focus case planning and intervention. What the social worker does should be logically related to a specific problem in the list. As problems are resolved, they are removed from the list. However, the resolved problem's number is not reassigned; each number is used only once. Thus, the intervention and progress on a specific problem can be traced throughout the case record. In a sense, the numbering system serves as a audit trail. It is important that the problem list be on a separate page in the case record; this makes it easy for the user to find the list and provides a ready reference point for a review of progress and planning.

Figure 9.2 is a sample problem list for Mrs. Brown, a mother of three, who was reported to a protective services agency for child neglect. Note that each numbered problem is dated according to when the problem was first identified. If additional problems were identified in the Brown case, they would be added to the list. Problems 2 and 3 have been resolved, but problems 1 and 4 continue to receive the worker's attention.

Some agencies have adopted the concept of a master problem list, which utilizes a standard nomenclature and numbering system. For example, the number 15 might be assigned to the problem of unsafe housing. This uniformity of problem numbering facilitates research on the type of problems brought to an agency.

FIGURE 9.2   **Problem List for the Brown Family**

Problem Number	Problem	Date	Inactive or Resolved	Date Resolved
1.	Crowded housing	4/10		
2.	Short of food money	4/10	Client enrolled in food stamp program	4/20
3.	Johnny (age 8) needs glasses	4/15	New prescription issued by Dr. Green at Clinic	4/25
4.	Ann (age 10) failing in school	4/28		

POR requires some type of action or response to each item on a client's problem list. Basically, three actions are possible: (1) intervention, (2) secure additional information in order to more fully understand the problem, or (3) do nothing except monitor the situation and wait for further developments. The social worker records his or her action in the main body of the case record and is careful to utilize the problem number to reference the action to a specific problem.

When intervention is required, it is helpful to use the SOAP format to describe this action. The acronym *SOAP* can be explained as follows:

S: *Subjective information* describes how the client feels about or perceives the situation. It is derived from client self-report. By definition, subjective information does not lend itself to independent or external validation.

O: *Objective information* is that which has been obtained by way of direct observation by professionals, clinical examinations, systematic data collection, and the like. As compared to subjective information, this category of information can be independently verified.

A: *Assessment* refers to the professional's conceptualization or conclusions derived from reviewing the subjective and objective information.

P: The *Plan* spells out how the professional intends to address or resolve the specific problem.

The POR requires the use of the SOAP format; however, the SOAP format can be used apart from the POR system.

Figure 9.3 is a SOAP entry related to problem 2 (lack of money for food) in the Brown case (Figure 9.2). Note the deadline set for making the application. It is important to set a deadline for accomplishing a particular task; this encourages implementation and action.

**FIGURE 9.3
Sample SOAP
Entry**

Subjective: Mrs. Brown states she worries about children's diet. The children complain of being hungry and to her embarrassment they have asked neighbors for food. Since Mrs. B grew up on welfare, she has vowed "never to go on the dole." She says she is in a "panic" about the thought of losing her children.

Objective: Her part-time job earns $150 take-home pay per week. Rent is $350 per month. It is hard to follow Mrs. Brown in conversation; she jumps from topic to topic. Agency records indicate that she was herself neglected as a child and placed in foster care for two years.

Assessment: Family clearly does not have enough money for food. Mrs. Brown is probably eligible for food stamps. Much of her disorganization is due to her anxiety about losing children to foster care, which is, in turn, related to her own experience is foster care. She fears that accepting welfare will label her as a "bad parent."

Plan: (Problem #2) Need to support Mrs. Brown's application for food stamps and show her that application is a way to be a "good mother" under these very trying circumstances. Need to assure her that agency has no plans to place her children. Begin long-term effort to help Mrs. B find higher-paying job. Complete food stamp application by 5/25.

Once the plan has been formulated, intervention follows. Clients are only helped by *action,* not by *plans,* no matter how logical or well written.

SELECTED BIBLIOGRAPHY

Burrill, George. "The Problem-Oriented Log in Social Casework." *Social Work* 21 (January 1976): 67.

Hartman, Barbara L., and Jane M. Wickey. "The Person-Oriented Record in Treatment." *Social Work* 23 (July 1978): 296–299.

Schmitt, Barton. "The Problem-Oriented Record and Team Reports." In *Child Protection Team Handbook,* edited by B. Schmitt. New York: Garland STPM Press, 1978, pp. 175–185.

9.9   Process Recording

PURPOSE: To establish a record of the social worker's practice so the process of helping and client-worker interaction can be studied.

DISCUSSION: Process recording is a detailed form of case recording often used to assist students and new workers in learning basic skills. It is also used when a worker is having unusual problems with a client and wants to create a record that can be examined by his or her peers, supervisor, or consultant as a basis for making suggestions on how the worker might overcome the problems.

A social work student's process recording might include the following components.

1. Names of those in attendance at interview or meeting
2. Date, location, and length of session
3. Purpose of session (i.e., why client and student were meeting and how this session fits within goal of intervention)
4. Student's plan for session (i.e., what student hoped to accomplish and how)
5. Description of interaction and content—for example:
   - how session began
   - significant exchanges during session (e.g., what client said and how student responded; what student said and how client responded)
   - specific topics discussed, decisions reached, plans made
   - new facts and information obtained by student
   - mood and feeling tone of session
   - plans made for next session
   - how session or meeting ended
6. Student's role and activities (e.g., techniques and skills used during session; roles and responsibilities taken on by student during session)
7. Student's assessment of client's concern, situation, or problem and client's current response and reactions to student social worker and to helping process
8. Student's assessment of his or her own performance during the session (e.g., problems encountered, strengths, limitations)
9. Student's plan for next interview or meeting with client

A process recording is an excellent teaching tool because it encourages the worker to analyze his or her practice behavior and decisions. A major disadvantage is that it requires a great deal of time to prepare. Many experienced social workers recommend the process recording of at least one case in a worker's caseload. A careful and detailed study of even one case can provide valuable feedback for skill development and increase self-awareness.

Audio- or videotape recordings are, in many respects, superior to process recording as a teaching tool. However, many agencies do not have video equipment; even if they do, it often requires that the interview take place in a studio atmosphere in order to escape background noise. Compact camcorders may expand opportunities for students and workers to study their own performance. Although the video- or audiotaping of an interview can be useful, listening to a tape is often tedious.

SELECTED BIBLIOGRAPHY

Kagle, Jill. *Social Work Records,* 2nd ed. Belmont, Calif.: Wadsworth, 1991.
Urbanowski, Martha, and Margaret Dwyer. *Learning Through Field Instruction.* Milwaukee: Family Service America, 1988.

9.10 Testifying in Court

PURPOSE: To prepare for a court appearance as a witness.

DISCUSSION: Social workers employed in child protective services, probation, and parole settings make frequent appearances in court. Sooner or later, nearly every social worker—regardless of agency setting—will serve as a witness. A number of guidelines can help the worker perform effectively on the witness stand.

1. Prepare for the court appearance. Consult with the attorney who will call you as a witness and learn about the questions he or she will ask, as well as the questions you are likely to be asked by the attorney who will cross-examine you.

2. Inform the attorney representing the side for which you are testifying of any weaknesses in your testimony. He or she should know of these problems before you get on the witness stand.

3. Tell the truth, regardless of how you think it will affect the case. Remember that you will be under oath. Any exaggeration or departure from facts will be uncovered and your credibility as a witness will suffer.

4. Appearance and demeanor are critical. You should be properly dressed and well groomed to reflect the solemnity of the courtroom. When seated in the witness chair, you should be attentive and courteous.

5. Your testimony will probably fall into one or more of three categories:
   a. *Personal observations.* Prepare to testify with little, if any, reference to your notes. If your observations occurred over a long period of time, you can prepare a chronology or list of events, to refresh your memory and keep your recollections organized. The opposing counsel and judge will probably look at your list, but it will not usually be introduced as evidence unless it differs from your oral testimony. Memorize the facts, but avoid sounding as though you are giving a recitation.
   b. *Reading reports.* Portions of your case record may be admitted into evidence. If so, you may be asked to read aloud segments of the record. Prepare by being thoroughly familiar with the content and organization of the record. Make sure you can read any handwritten parts. You should be able to explain the method for producing, transcribing, and storing a case file in your office.
   c. *Expert conclusions.* An individual who is designated by the judge as an expert witness is permitted to offer opinions as to the meaning of facts and observations. All other witnesses must confine their testimony to facts and observations. Opposing attorneys often argue over whether a person should be qualified as an expert. If an attorney plans to qualify you as an expert witness, be prepared to explain:

- your professional qualifications (e.g., degree, experience, special training, publications, memberships in professional associations, etc.)
- the theories and principles you used in forming an opinion
- your mode of practice and how it is similar to or different from that of other social workers or professionals in your field
- the opinions you formed and why (the major portion of your testimony as an expert)

6. Speak clearly and avoid using slang and jargon. Much of the jargon used by social workers is incomprehensible to judges, attorneys, and juries.

7. Listen carefully to the questions you are asked. If you do not understand a question, ask that it be rephrased or explained. If you do not know the answer, say so. Never speculate or guess. Answer only the question that is asked. Answer questions in a confident manner. Phrases such as "I feel" or "I guess" weaken the impact of your testimony.

8. If an objection is made during the course of your testimony, stop speaking immediately. If the judge overrules the objection, you will be told to answer the question. If the objection is sustained, you will not be permitted to answer and a new question will be asked.

9. When being cross-examined by the opposing attorney, keep in mind that he or she is not your friend. Even a friendly cross-examiner is looking for ways to trip you up and discredit your testimony. Do not volunteer information that is not asked for. Do not explain why you know something unless you are asked. And finally, remember that the attorney offering your testimony has a chance to follow up and ask additional questions after the other attorney's cross-examination. This may help clear up any problems in your testimony.

10. Many times, cross-examiners ask compound questions. When responding to a compound question, divide it into sections and then answer each part. Do not agree or disagree with a partially untrue statement, because the attorney may cut you short and not allow you to complete your response, thus giving an erroneous impression of your actions or beliefs.

11. When being cross-examined, do not lose your temper at questions you consider impertinent or offensive. Exercise absolute self-control. If you maintain your composure, you will be less likely to become confused and inconsistent. If the questioning is truly improper, your attorney will object. Pause before answering a provocative question to allow the objection to be made, but not so long that you appear hesitant or unsure. All questions should be handled with tact and truth. Fortunately, judges are familiar with the histrionics of some trial attorneys and are rarely impressed by them.

12. Do not get caught in the "yes-or-no" trap. If, on cross-examination, the attorney asks a question and ends it with "Answer yes or no," don't feel obliged to do so if you believe such an answer will be misleading. Instead, begin your answer with "Well, that needs explaining." The attorney may again push you to answer yes or no and the judge may require you to give a yes or no answer, but the jury will understand your position and look forward to your explanation when your attorney clarifies the situation on redirect examination.

13. Often, a witness will be asked a question regarding sympathy for one side or the other in the case. If asked, admit your beliefs or sympathies honestly. It is absurd to deny an obvious sympathy, and an honest admission of favoritism will not discredit a witness.

SELECTED BIBLIOGRAPHY

Barker, Robert, and Douglas Branson. *Forensic Social Work.* New York: Haworth Press, 1993.

Haralambi, Ann, and Donna Rosenberg. "The Expert Witness: Social Work, Medical, Psychiatric." In *The New Child Protection Team Handbook,* edited by Donald Bross et al. New York: Garland, 1988, pp. 396–413.

Saltzman, Andrea, and Kathleen Proch. *Law in Social Work Practice.* Chicago: Nelson-Hall, 1990.

10 Personal and Professional Development

INTRODUCTION

Social work is a difficult and demanding profession but also a rewarding one. However, the rewards are mostly intrinsic. By selecting social work as a career, one is virtually assured of never attaining wealth or prestige. Social work is about caring, sharing, and social responsibility; these are not the values rewarded by our economic system. Gordon Allport, a respected social psychologist, once observed that the low status given to social work in the United States may be due to the emphasis social workers place on compassion, cooperation, and mutual respect within a society that places high value on competition and individualism.

From its beginnings, the social work profession has demonstrated special concern for those who are powerless, stigmatized, and devalued—the people who others tend to avoid or ignore. Because social workers are in a position to see so many people in need and see the inadequacy of our professional, agency, and societal resources, they frequently suffer the anguish of knowing that no matter how hard they work, efforts will fall short of the mark. This is a frustration with which the social worker must learn to live.

Because many clients are economically poor, few are in a position to pay directly for services. For this reason, most social workers are employed by governmental or nonprofit agencies. This means that most workers find themselves in resource-poor organizations—ones with few perks and with limited opportunities for continuing education and in-service training.

This chapter provides social workers with guidance aimed at helping them develop their skills and cope with work-related frustrations. More specifically, it offers guidance on using supervision, making a presentation, writing an article, coping with bureaucracy, managing job-related stress, developing self-awareness, making ethical decisions, avoiding malpractice suits, dealing with sexual harassment, and analyzing and interpreting research reports and statistical data.

10.1 Getting a Social Work Job

PURPOSE: To secure employment as a social worker in a human services organization.

DISCUSSION: Once a social worker has completed professional education, the next task is to secure employment in the capacity of a social worker. That usually takes time and effort, as agencies are necessarily careful in their selection of staff to serve their clientele. (To examine this process from the viewpoint of the agency, see Item 11.13.) It is important, therefore, for the social worker who is seeking a job to present himself or herself in a manner that ensures the best chance of being hired.

The first step in finding employment is to discover the *job openings.* In most communities several sources of information might be examined. Agencies with good affirmative action plans will advertise their positions. The classified advertisements in the local newspaper and/or the *NASW News* should be read on a regular basis. The personnel departments of city, county, or state agencies will post all job openings on agency bulletin boards. Those should be checked periodically. The local United Way staff will frequently be aware of current and future job openings in its member agencies. Finally, informal networks among professionals are an excellent source of information. Attending local NASW meetings is a good way to tap into the professional network in most communities.

Once an open position is located, an application must be prepared. The application typically has two parts: a cover letter and a professional resumé. The *cover letter* should focus on the particular job being applied for and should stress the applicant's qualifications for that position. It should be approximately one page in length and must be carefully written with no spelling, punctuation, or grammatical errors. The letter should clearly indicate that it and the resumé represent an application for the position, describe why the applicant is interested in that job, and discuss qualifications for the position. The cover letter is not the place to discuss salary expectations or reasons for leaving past jobs. Indicate that a list of references will be provided on request (unless the job announcement asks that references be supplied as part of the application). Be sure to obtain advance permission from the people named as references. The letter should be upbeat and positive about the position for which one is applying.

The professional *resumé* is more generic than an application letter and might be used when applying for several positions. It is an organized summary of one's professional qualifications. Its purpose is to present the applicant's background in a manner that will convince the employer to invite him or her for an interview. There is no prescribed format or style for a resumé. Rather, use a creative approach to attract the attention of members of a screening committee who may be selecting a few finalists from a large number of applications. However, avoid being cute or clever. Often photocopy shops provide layout consultation, have laser printers available, and can recommend good quality paper, making it relatively inexpensive to prepare an attractive resumé. In addition, many colleges or universities have an office that provides workshops and consultation to students in preparing job applications.

At a minimum, the following information should be included in a resumé. Other items may be added at one's discretion.

■ *Personal data.* Include your name, address, and phone number. If you have a number where you can be reached during working hours, be sure to include it to facilitate scheduling an interview.

- *Education.* Give the name of your degree(s), your major, the colleges or universities you attended, and graduation dates. List all schools you have attended (listing in reverse order) and possibly add grade-point average, honors, special projects, or any special skills or training that might be relevant to a social work job (e.g., computer, foreign language).
- *Experience.* List employment in reverse order (i.e., beginning with your current or most recent job), giving the job title, name of organization, dates of employment, and job duties. It is also helpful to list any volunteer experience that might have contributed to your social work competencies.
- *Activities and interests.* Identify your professional interests as well as those that extend beyond social work. Note membership in professional organizations, your participation in various clubs or organizations and any offices held, and any hobbies or special interests.
- *References.* A statement such as "References Available On Request" is usually best to place on a resumé. If a job announcement calls for references, they should be listed in the cover letter. This flexibility allows for selecting the most appropriate references for each position. In general, the persons selected as references should be able to comment on your skills and might include a faculty member, a field instructor, and/or job supervisors or persons who supervised volunteer experiences. In many instances, an agency will contact the references by telephone rather than by letter, so give telephone numbers.
- *Other information.* It may be desirable to add other information such as publications, travel experiences, and unique experiences that may enhance your competence as a social worker.

If the application is successful, the applicant will be invited to an **interview.** Typically, the interview process will involve appearing before a panel of interviewers, although there will usually be some one-to-one discussions as well. Many review panels will present the applicant with hypothetical situations or case vignettes and ask how he or she would handle the situation. The interviewing procedures used by government agencies are usually highly structured and many require a written exam in addition to oral interviews.

Preparation is essential. First, research the agency thoroughly. Know the services it offers, its target clientele, and something about its structure and goals. This information might be obtained by stopping by the agency in advance to pick up informational materials, by talking with the receptionist about the agency, or by discussing the agency with clients and/or other social workers in the community. Second, dress professionally and be as relaxed as possible during the interview process. Third, be prepared for questions about your personal and professional interests, as well as your preparation for the specific job duties. Grobman (1994, 16) identified seven questions that are commonly asked in an interview:

- What are your qualifications for this job?
- What are your strengths?
- What are your weaknesses?
- Why do you want this job?
- What are your career goals?

- What would you do in the following situation? (For example, a client tells you he wants to hurt himself. What is your response?)
- Why should I hire you?

Finally, be prepared with your own questions about the agency and the job. Remember that an interview is a two-way street—both the applicant and the agency are deciding if there is a good match between one's skills and interests and the requirements of the job.

If offered the position, be sure to know what will be expected of you on the job, and negotiate the salary or other benefits with the employer. NASW (1995, 16) recommends that before accepting a new position, (1) you should obtain a letter of appointment that states the starting salary, duties, and other pertinent information; and (2) you should review the agency's personnel manual to be sure the provisions are understood. Clarifying these matters before employment can prevent subsequent misunderstandings.

SELECTED BIBLIOGRAPHY

Grobman, Linda May. "Job Recruiters: What Do They Really Want?" *The New Social Worker* 1 (Spring 1994): 16–21.

National Association of Social Workers. "NASW Advertising Policies." *NASW News* 40 (July 1995): 16.

10.2 Elements of Professional Behavior

PURPOSE: To clarify the nature of professional behavior.

DISCUSSION: It has been said that a professional is "someone who can be counted on to do what needs to be done, even when he or she does not feel like doing it." There is much wisdom in that description. It suggests that a professional knows what should be done, can be trusted to do it, and does not let matters of personal convenience or personal feelings interfere with his or her performance.

It is important for social workers to continually examine their performance and make sure their behavior is of a professional nature. Consider the following comparison of professional and nonprofessional behavior:

Professional Behavior	*Nonprofessional Behavior*
Decisions and actions are based primarily on a body of knowledge learned through a process of formal education and training.	Decisions and actions are based primarily on personal opinions and personal preferences.
Principles of good practice are followed, regardless of other pressures.	Political and fiscal pressure and other forces are allowed to dictate decisions and actions.

Professional Behavior	*Nonprofessional Behavior*
Objectivity is employed and decisions are based on the facts of the situation.	Subjectivity rules and decisions are based mostly on personal bias and personal convenience.
The profession's values, principles, and *Code of Ethics* are used to identify and resolve ethical issues.	Only personal moral judgments are used to resolve ethical questions; many ethical issues go unrecognized or are ignored.
Knowledge and skills are continually developed so that services to clients can be improved.	Only what is required to keep the job is learned.
The relationship with the client is purposeful, goal oriented, and time limited.	The relationship with the client resembles a friendship.
The well-being and needs of the client are of primary concern; worker's personal needs are not expected to be met within work-related relationships.	The well-being and needs of the worker are of primary concern; worker expects to have personal needs met through contact with the client and within work-related relationships.
Review of performance by peers is expected and invited.	Peer review is threatening and is avoided.
Self-discipline in decision making and action is excercised; when with an angry or frustrated client, emotional reactions are under control; personal emotions are expressed in a helpful and purposeful manner.	Personal feelings shape decisions and actions; when with an angry or frustrated client, reacts with anger and frustration; emotions may be expressed in a thoughtless and hurtful manner.
The client's expressions of negative emotion are not taken personally; worker seeks to understand the reasons behind the client's frustration and anger.	The client's frustrations and anger are taken personally.
Accurate and complete records of decisions and actions are kept.	Recordkeeping is avoided; records are incomplete or inaccurate.
Responsibility is taken for seeking new knowledge and information and for sharing it with peers.	The worker does not see self as responsible for the development of new knowledge or for teaching peers.
Personal responsibility is assumed for examining the quality of services delivered and for working to make the agency, program, or policy changes that would improve services to the client.	The worker is concerned only about doing the job as assigned or described by others; worker does not see self as responsible for agency, policy, or program changes.
Social work is regarded as a lifelong commitment; the occupation and work are seen as a "calling."	Social work is seen as a job that can be easily abandoned if something better comes along; Another occupation or type of work could easily be sought.

SELECTED BIBLIOGRAPHY

Lauffer, Armand. *Working in Social Work.* Newbury Park, Calif.: Sage, 1987.
Morales, Armando, and Bradford W. Sheafor. *Social Work: A Profession of Many Faces,* 7th ed. Boston: Allyn and Bacon, 1995.
Reid, P. Nelson, and Philip Popple. *The Moral Purpose of Social Work.* Chicago: Nelson-Hall, 1992.

10.3 Using Agency Supervision

PURPOSE: To obtain knowledge and learn skills through guidance provided by an agency supervisor.

DISCUSSION: In order for a social worker to learn job-related tasks and procedures and to develop as a skilled professional, he or she must make effective use of supervision. The term *supervision* is rooted in a Latin word that means to "look over." However, modern supervisory practice places less emphasis on viewing the supervisor as an overseer or inspector and more emphasis on the supervisor as being a master of the work to be done, a leader, and a teacher.

An agency and its line workers, supervisors, and administrators exist for the purpose of providing quality services to its clients or consumers. All agency and staff activities must be viewed as the means to that end. Supervision is also a means or a method of serving clients. Thus, the fundamental purpose of supervision is to ensure that the agency's services and programs are provided in an efficient and effective manner. According to Kadushin (1992), there are three interrelated and overlapping components in supervision: (1) administration, (2) staff support, and (3) staff education.

Within an agency's organizational structure, it is the supervisor and the function of **administrative supervision** that links the line worker to the agency's upper-level administrative and management personnel. As a midlevel administrator, the supervisor must attend to such tasks as recruiting, selecting, and orienting new staff; planning, delegating, and coordinating work activities; monitoring and evaluating worker performance; ensuring compliance to agency policy and procedure; serving as a channel of communication between line workers and the administration; protecting workers from organizational forces that would distract them from their primary responsibilities or interfere with their work; serving as an advocate for workers; and representing the agency in community affairs and interagency coordination.

The term **supportive supervision** refers to supervisory activities that address issues and concerns related to staff morale; work-related anxiety and worry; job satisfaction; commitment to the agency's mission and policies; worker self-confidence and self-esteem; and emotional well-being. This aspect of supervision is extremely important in human services agencies where high levels or stress and worker burnout are serious personnel problems.

Kadushin (1992, 135) explains that **educational supervision** "is concerned with teaching the worker what he needs to know in order to do his job and helping him to learn it. Every job description of the supervisor's position includes a listing of this function: 'instruct workers in acceptable social work techniques;' 'develop competence through individual and group conferences;' 'train and instruct staff in job performance." The educational component relates to the transmission of knowledge, skills, attitudes, and values.

Several guidelines can help the social worker make appropriate and effective use of supervision.

1. Realize that your supervisor will expect you to:
   - Be effective and get results consistent with the agency's mission, program, goals, and your job description.
   - Follow agency policy, procedure, and specific instruction.
   - Consult with your supervisor when you are unsure about how to proceed or when a course of action is raising unforseen issues or encountering unexpected problems.
   - Immediately inform your supervisor when you become aware of an ethical, legal, or procedural violation that could give rise to a formal complaint or in some way harm the agency or its clients.
   - Demonstrate an eagerness to learn the details of your job, to become more efficient and effective, and to accept constructive criticism and suggestions on how you could improve the quality of your work.
   - Take initiative and assume responsibility for work that needs to be done.
   - Work cooperatively with and be respectful of colleagues and engage in behaviors that improve staff morale.
   - Maintain accurate and up-to-date records of your work with clients.

2. Expect your supervisors to:
   - Provide needed on-the-job training.
   - Keep you informed of changes in agency policy or procedure and any changes in your responsibilities.
   - Explain the reasons behind agency policy and procedure.
   - Provide encouragement and support when your work is particularly difficult.
   - Evaluate your performance on a regular basis and offer specific suggestions on how it can be improved.
   - Give you a clear warning when your performance falls below standards.

3. Establish a regularly scheduled time to meet with your supervisor. This should be at least once a week. Having adequate time to discuss work and job-related concerns is of critical importance.

4. Seek your supervisor's assistance in formulating an individualized training plan that will build on your personal and professional strengths and address limitations in your performance. Such a plan should be in writing. Identify specific tasks and objectives to be accomplished over the next 6 and 12 months, and list specific learning activities (reading, study, conferences, workshops).

5. The newly hired social worker and the student beginning a practicum must recognize that agency staff often adopt a "wait and see" attitude toward newcomers. The staff may be offended and angered if the newcomer criticizes the agency's programs or makes suggestions for "improvement" without appreciating or understanding how and why the agency operates as it does. The newcomer will quickly lose respect if he or she attempts to display his or her knowledge. Shulman (1993, 72) observes that if recent graduates of a school of social work "articulate highly theoretical positions or arguments that tend to denigrate the services of the agency, they put the supervisor on the defensive and this often leads to an initial battle of wills." New employees and students are advised to see themselves as learners and to withhold making judgments until they have at least six months of experience on the job.

6. Recognize that the recommendations of experienced and respected supervisors are usually pivotal to your effort to secure a promotion or career advancement. When making such a recommendation, a supervisor will be especially attentive to the quality and quantity of your work, your understanding of the agency and the work to be done, your ability to formulate a feasible plan and carry it out, your leadership skills and the ability to win the respect of others, your time-management skills, your capacity to learn and adapt to change, your initiative and willingness to assume responsibility, and your emotional stability and dependability.

7. Judah (1982, 156–157) notes that the social work student has a special set of responsibilities to his or her practicum agency and school. Among the student's responsibilities to the practicum agency or field setting are the following:

- Provide agency service and carry out other field-related activities in compliance with agency policy and procedure.
- Help the field instructor to maintain an educational focus, if this is needed.
- Complete all required reports on time and use prescribed format.
- Devote to the practicum the full amount of time expected by the agency and keep the agreed upon schedule.
- Enhance agency programs and efforts, when possible, through extra service to clients, development of new resources, research projects, public relations contacts, sharing new learning, and so on.

Among the student's responsibilities to the school are the following:

- Maintain clear and open communication with the coordinator of field education and others concerned with the practicum experience.
- Fulfill all educational requirements, including spending the full number of hours expected of the field experience.
- Work diligently to solve problems arising out of inadequacies or misunderstanding in the field instruction system, including evaluation of the system as well as its functioning and its objectives.
- Work to improve ways in which the school functions with respect to field instruction through channels provided, such as committees, evaluations, communications with the coordination of field education, and so on.
- Responsibly budget time to allow for adequate attention to class, field, and other responsibilities.

8. Always remember that what you get out of a job or learning experience reflects what you put into it. Most often, a satisfying work situation or a good learning experience happens because you make it happen. Take responsibility for the quality of your work and learning.

SELECTED BIBLIOGRAPHY

Holloway, Stephen, and George Brager. *Supervising in the Human Services: The Politics of Practice.* New York: Free Press, 1989.

Judah, Eleanor. "Responsibility of the Students in Field Instruction." In *Quality Field Instruction in Social Work*, edited by Bradford W. Sheafor and Lowell E. Jenkins. New York: Longman, 1982.

Kadushin, Alfred. *Supervision in Social Work*, 3rd ed. New York: Columbia University Press, 1992.

Munson, Carlton. *Clinical Social Work Supervision*, 2nd ed. New York: Haworth Press, 1993.

Shulman, Lawrence. *Interactional Supervision.* Washington D.C.: NASW Press, 1993.

10.4   Presenting to a Professional Audience

PURPOSE: To organize and plan a speech or other oral presentation to communicate professional information.

DISCUSSION: Because social workers make numerous presentations to decision makers and professional colleagues, it is important that they develop the skills of public speaking. Making a good presentation can be an effective way of improving services to clients. For example, a single speech to a group of community or political leaders can have far-reaching effects if that speech moves the group to modify a policy or create a needed program. Similarly, throughout their careers, social workers will be expected to make presentations at workshops or conferences in which they exchange information and describe new insights or developments in practice in order to improve the quality of services provided to clients. To make these presentations as effective as possible is an important responsibility of the professional social worker.

Speeches can vary considerably in structure. At one extreme is an "off-the-cuff" presentation; at the other extreme is reading from a prepared paper. Neither is usually effective. The former is likely to be difficult to follow and the latter can easily lull the audience to sleep. Somewhere between the two extremes is the recipe for a effective oral presentation.

Considerable planning is required for an effective oral presentation. The presenter must keep in mind the fact that the audience must grasp the material when it is presented. As opposed to reading a book or article, members of the audience do not have the luxury of skimming the outline to understand where the author is headed, skipping over sections of material that are not of interest, or rereading to be sure material is understood. The presenter, then, must carefully plan the speech to be sure the communication is accurately received.

The first step in preparing for a presentation is to know the content and be familiar with the audience. Second, one must select and adapt the content to be presented to the interests of the audience being addressed. For example, a presentation on the tasks performed by social workers would be quite different at a junior high school career day than when presenting to a state personnel board. Third, it is essential to carefully organize the flow of information. In broad terms, the speech should include three major components: a preview of the topic, the main body of the speech, and a summary pointing out the conclusions reached about the topic. Last, the presenter should consider creative ways to make the presentation interesting and understandable to the audience.

Careful preparation and a relatively relaxed presenter are the two essential conditions for successful speeches. The following guidelines can be helpful in achieving these conditions.

1. *Be clear about the purpose of the speech.* For example, is it to inform or persuade? If the purpose is to *persuade,* the presentation should be planned to (a) identify the nature and extent of the problem using facts or case examples, (b) identify the consequences of not changing the situation for the individuals affected and the society (including the members of the audience) in general, (c) suggest solutions, and (d) propose actions the audience can take to help. If the purpose is to *inform* (e.g., a professional presentation), the presenter should (a) identify the relevance of the information to be presented, (b) explain the status of the current knowledge about the subject based on a review of the literature, (c) give a summary of the manner in which the data or concepts to be presented were developed, and (d) provide an analysis of the practice implications or conclusions drawn from the information.

2. *Carefully analyze the audience—both when preparing the presentation and just before presenting.* When planning what to present and how to present it, it is desirable to have a clear picture of the people who will be in the audience. It is often useful to visualize a particular person who is expected to be in attendance and prepare a presentation that will interest that person. A practice run-through and critique by a colleague can help to identify areas that need reworking. To reduce anxiety and provide information to help fine-tune the presentation about to be delivered, it is often helpful for the presenter to mingle with the audience before the session begins. By introducing oneself to audience members who arrive early, asking what they hope to get from the session, and simply cultivating a few familiar and responsive faces in the audience can increase the comfort level of the presenter considerably.

3. *Be enthusiastic about the topic.* If the audience can feel that the presenter is excited and interested in the material being presented, they too will look at the material in a positive light. A little of the "salesperson" in each of us should be used to capture the attention of the audience.

4. *Be responsive to the ability of the audience to absorb the content.* The time of day, length of available time for both presentation and discussion, size of audience, atmosphere of the room, and other factors all can affect audience attention. In general, it is best to be as brief as possible. After all, the mind can absorb only what the seat can endure. A good rule is to cover the content as efficiently as possible in the presentation and to reserve time for the audience to explore the material that is of most interest to them in a question-and-answer period.

5. *Use 5 × 7 notecards to help maintain the planned organization of the presentation.* The notecards should be numbered in case they get out of order and should be prepared in large and legible print.

6. *Use language and visual aids that will help the audience follow the organization of your presentation and comprehend the data that are presented.* One way to help the audience remember the key points is to put together key words that spell something (acronyms). Visual aids may take the form of handing out hardcopy materials, presenting information with an overhead projector, or using videotaped materials. Given the availability of portable overhead projectors and the ease of preparing charts, figures, and tables on home computers, the well-prepared presenter can readily present considerable information while holding the attention of his or her audience.

7. *Examine your mannerisms while speaking.* Words and phrases such as "you know" and "uh" are annoying and distracting, as are physical mannerisms such as elaborate hand movements or pacing while presenting. Practice delivering the speech before a mirror to get a sense of the time required (although the time it takes to deliver a speech is often underestimated), and then try not to depend too heavily on notes when actually presenting. An audiotape or videotape of a practice run or the honest critique of a colleague can help to minimize distracting behaviors. Also, be sure to dress appropriately for the nature of the meeting, as attire that is out of place can be distracting to the audience.

8. *Present with an aura of confidence.* If the presenter knows the material, is well organized and enthusiastic, and responds effectively to the discussion with the audience, most errors will be forgiven. It is the message, not the messenger, that is most important.

SELECTED BIBLIOGRAPHY

Cook, Jeff. *The Elements of Speech Writing and Public Speaking.* New York: Collier Books, 1989.
Ehrlich, Henry. *Writing Effective Speeches.* New York: Paragon House, 1992.
Osborn, Michael, and Suzanne Osborn. *Public Speaking,* 2nd ed. Boston: Houghton Mifflin, 1991.

10.5   Writing to a Professional Audience

PURPOSE: To share one's knowledge in written form with colleagues in order to strengthen the quality and effectiveness of social work practice.

DISCUSSION: When a social worker develops or discovers some new knowledge that will enhance the practice of social workers, he or she is obligated to share that knowledge. The *Code of Ethics* (NASW 1993) is clear about this expectation: "The social worker should contribute to the knowledge base of social work and share research knowledge and practice wisdom with colleagues" (National Association of Social Workers, 1993, Sec. V.0.3). This knowledge might be shared through a conference presentation (see Item 10.4) or through preparing an article for publication in a professional journal.

Oral presentations have the advantage of allowing the presenter to tailor the presentation to a specific audience and to have the benefit of feedback from that audience. However, the number who can benefit from such a presentation is limited to those who are able to attend the meeting. Written presentations are less dynamic and flexible than speeches but can reach large audiences. Each issue of *Social Work*, for example, is mailed to the more than 155,000 members of NASW and is maintained for many years in hundreds of libraries. A single social worker can have a substantial effect on practice through the preparation of journal articles and other written materials.

When preparing a journal article, it is important to remember that the reader ultimately decides if the material will be read at all and, if so, how it will be approached. Some readers will begin with the first paragraph and read each word as the author has presented the material. Some will skim and return to read carefully the parts that most interest them. Others may read the introduction and conclusion and, if their interest is not captured, move on to other materials. The author, then, must write to help the reader determine if it will be worth the time to read the material and to keep the interest of those who decide to read the article carefully. The following guidelines are useful when preparing written materials.

1. *Have a clear and important message.* Although some articles are built on original ideas and data, most update and expand existing information, synthesize or combine available knowledge in a unique way, or simply express something already known in a form that makes it more understandable. The author must help the reader understand how this message relates to what is already known and why reading this article could enhance the social worker's practice. Since articles are limited in length, the scope of the article cannot be too broad nor the content too complex. A good test of scope is to see if the key ideas can be stated in a single paragraph. If it is not possible to be this succinct, the topic is probably too broad and may need to be broken into subparts and presented in more than one article.

2. *Select an appropriate journal.* A large number of journals address matters of interest to social workers. Some publish articles on a wide range of topics (see "generic" journals below), but most specialize. The NASW guide to authors (Mendelsohn 1992) contains information about publishing requirements for 130 different journals. Each has its own focus and will attract a specific readership. Some journals in which social workers frequently publish are the following:

Generic Topics

Journal of Baccalaureate Social Work
Journal of Sociology and Social Welfare
*Journal of the National Association of
    Black Social Workers*
*New England Journal of Human
    Services*
New Social Worker, The
Smith College Studies in Social Work
Social Service Review
Social Work

**Specialized Fields, Methods,
and Settings**

*AFFILIA: Journal of Women and Social
    Work*
*Child and Adolescent Social Work
    Journal*
Child Welfare
Clinical Social Work Journal
Families and Society (formerly *Social
    Casework*)
Health and Social Work
Human Services in a Rural Environment
Journal of Community Practice
Journal of Family Social Work
*Journal of Gay and Lesbian Social
    Services*
Journal of Gerontological Social Work
Journal of Independent Social Work
Journal of Law and Social Work
Journal of Multicultural Social Work
Journal of Specialists in Group Work
Pediatric Social Work
Public Welfare

School Social Work Journal
*Social Thought: The Journal of Religion
    and Social Work*
Social Work in Education
*Social Work with Groups: A Journal of
    Community and Clinical Practice*
Social Work in Health Care

Research

Computers in Human Services
Journal of Social Service Research
Research on Social Work Practice
Social Work Research

Administration and Supervision

Administration in Social Work
Clinical Supervisor, The
Journal of Social Work Supervision

Social Work Education

*Journal of Continuing Social Work
    Education*
Journal of Social Work Education
Journal of Teaching in Social Work

International and Foreign

British Journal of Social Work
Canadian Welfare
Indian Journal of Social Work
International Child Welfare
International Social Work
*Journal of International and
    Comparative Social Welfare*
Social Work Today
Social Worker-Travailleur Social

Before beginning to write, examine several issues of the journal most appropriate for the content and make an assessment of the probable readership, type of articles accepted for publication, and typical format of the articles (e.g., research based, theoretical, case applications). Each journal will periodically include a statement of its publishing requirements and provide information on preferred topics, length, style, and procedures for submitting articles. Increasingly, journals are using the APA style (American Psychological Association 1994) and typically have a maximum length of 12 to 15 double-spaced pages.

3. *Picture the audience.* It is helpful to write to an individual rather than an unknown audience. Select someone who would be likely to read the article, and write to that person. Use language that communicates your ideas clearly to him or her, and use concepts familiar to that person.

4. *Prepare an abstract.* Most journals require a 75- to 100-word abstract to accompany the article. Although it is often easier to write an abstract after the article is completed, preparing a first draft before writing the article can help focus attention on the most important points. The abstract should be clear, concise, and factual, as it may ultimately appear in *Social Work Abstracts,* on *Social Work Abstracts Plus* (CD-ROM), or on other databases that will assist students or other potential readers to locate this information.

5. *Develop an outline.* How well the readers will be able to comprehend and consume the information is influenced by the organization of the article. Think through the logical connections between elements to be included. Preparing an outline will help achieve smooth and understandable transitions between the various parts of the article.

6. *Write the introduction.* The opening two or three paragraphs should tell what the article is about, explain why it is important, and suggest which social workers might be especially interested in this material. A good introduction maintains the reader's attention and stimulates continued reading. Tying the subject to a current issue or including a short case example related to the topic may help the reader see the benefit in reading the entire article.

For many writers, getting started is the most difficult part of writing. Do not let frustration over the introduction block the process. Some writers find it helpful to write a rough introduction with the intent of completely rewriting it later.

7. *Set the context or background.* It is important to let the reader know where this material fits in social work (e.g., practice theory, practice techniques, social welfare policy issues). The reader also needs to know the theoretical context in which this material is placed. A literature review or even clarification of its relationship to a particular concept or school of thought helps provide this background information. However, this contextual material cannot be extensive and must be focused clearly on the topic of the article.

8. *Prepare the body of the article.* Concisely report the facts and observations that are the heart of the article. Recognizing that readers learn differently, it is helpful to supplement narrative material with alternative means of presenting the information (e.g., charts, figures, tables, and lists). If case examples are used, be sure that they are presented in a way that helps the reader generalize from that example to other case situations.

Make frequent use of headings and subheadings so the reader can easily follow the flow of ideas and information. Articles are most readable when they contain short paragraphs with clearly focused content.

Write simply and clearly and avoid social work jargon. Omit gender-specific language and any terms that might reflect bias or stereotyping based on race, ethnicity, gender, age, handicapping conditions, or sexual orientation.

9. *Prepare a summary and/or conclusion.* End the article with a short statement that pulls together the key points and presents conclusions that can be drawn from this material. If relevant, point out additional research that is needed to further develop the subject.

10. *Collect and format references.* Using the format appropriate for the selected journal, list the references that support the ideas and information presented. Endnotes or some type of reference list are most often used.

11. *Choose a good title.* The title will be the first clue the reader will have about the article, so be sure it clearly identifies the subject. A creative or provocative title can attract reader interest.

12. *Rewrite, rewrite, rewrite.* Expect to revise and rewrite a number of times before concluding that the article is completed. Polishing the structure, content, and language time and time again is an essential part of good written communication.

13. *Let it cool.* Avoid sending an article to a journal as soon as it comes out of the word processor. A week or two away from the material provides a fresh perspective and may yield alternative ideas for presenting the material or strengthening the way ideas are expressed. It may be helpful to use this time to get colleagues to review the work and offer comments. Remember, however, that it is your article, and you must own the final result. Do not feel obligated to incorporate all suggested changes. Also, do not allow this "cooling" period to become an excuse for procrastination. You may never be completely satisfied with your writing, but one simply must stop refining it at some point.

14. *Mail the manuscript and wait.* Send the required number of copies to the selected journal. Typically, the publisher will acknowledge receipt of the manuscript and send it on to two or three reviewers. The review process may take several months.

15. *Dealing with acceptance or rejection.* Reviewers will usually offer comments on the strengths and limitations of the article and how it does or does not meet the focus of that journal. Reviewers will typically conclude with a recommendation to (a) reject, (b) accept if revised in specific ways, or (c) accept the article for publication. Some journals will, on request, provide the reviewers' comments if the article is rejected. If that occurs, seriously consider those comments and either revise and resubmit the article, send it to another journal, or drop the plan to publish this material.

If the article is accepted, you will work with the professional editors who will offer suggestions for strengthening the presentation. You will have the opportunity to be sure that their editing does not misrepresent the content. Depending on the backlog, it may take as much as a year for the article to appear in print. When it is printed, most journals will send the author several copies of the issue in which the article appears or provide reprints of the article.

When an article is accepted, the author will be required to assign the legal rights to this material to the publisher. It will then be necessary for the publisher to approve any subsequent reprinting or extensive quoting of the article in other books or articles, including your own.

SELECTED BIBLIOGRAPHY

American Psychological Association. *Publication Manual of the American Psychological Association,* 4th ed. Washington, D.C.: APA, 1994.

Beebe, Linda, ed. *Professional Writing for the Human Services.* Washington, D.C.: NASW, 1993.

Henson, Kenneth T. *The Art of Writing for Publication.* Boston: Allyn and Bacon, 1994.

Mendelsohn, Henry N. *Author's Guide to Social Work Journals.* Washington, D.C.: NASW, 1992.

National Association of Social Workers. *Code of Ethics.* Washington, D.C.: NASW, 1993.

10.6 Coping with Bureaucracy

PURPOSE: To function effectively within a large, complex organization.

DISCUSSION: Every day, many social workers go home from their jobs feeling frustrated. Their complaints are usually not about their contact with clients but rather about the bureaucratic aspects of the agencies and service systems in which they work. Some complain that a myriad of laws, agency rules, regulations, and policies stifle their creativity and keep them from practicing good social work. Others complain that political manipulations, self-serving superiors, and power struggles between departments and divisions interfere with the delivery of service to clients.

Being part of a bureaucracy is unavoidable for most social workers because most social work jobs exist within large organizations. To find satisfaction in their work, social workers must develop the attitudes and skills needed to function and get things done within a large organization. Here are several suggestions.

1. Large agencies are by nature bureaucratic and political. This is a reality. It is important that you learn to maneuver and negotiate within this political and organizational arena. Develop the fine art of reframing the agency context of practice in ways that turn a negative into a positive. For example, do not view policies, rules, and regulations as barriers and constraints. Rather, view them as guidelines to be managed and as opportunities to be exploited in order to achieve important goals and objectives.

2. Study your agency. An in-depth knowledge of one's work setting is a form of organizational power. If you understand your agency's history, mission, goals, structure, culture, budget, policies, and procedures, you are better able to address problems and bring about needed changes (see Item 11.12).

3. It is important to view yourself as a partner with your agency and not just an employee. Carefully examine your own values, beliefs, and professional goals. They must be compatible with the mission and the goals of your agency. In order to be effective within your agency, you must believe in the agency's purpose and feel a proper fit with the agency.

4. Identify your personal and professional strengths and seek a niche within the organization where those strengths can be utilized and rewarded and where you can

obtain a sense of job satisfaction. Think seriously before accepting a promotion or a transfer that would take you away from the type of work you really enjoy. Maintain direct contact with agency clients even as you rise to a supervisory or administrative level, for this provides you with a constant reminder of the agency's mission and what needs to be changed to improve service to clients.

5. Acquire the skills needed and valued by your agency. Examine your agency's programs and operations and then strive to develop your knowledge or skills in an area that is especially valued by the agency (e.g. computer operations, report writing, public speaking, work with a special client group, etc.). Having a special competency not only contributes to job satisfaction but it also increases your power and influence within the agency.

6. Respect the chain of command. Your superiors will want to be informed about any situation that could have an impact on the unit for which they are responsible. They will need to decide when and how their own superiors are to be informed. Thus, any attempt to go around or over the head of your immediate superior is a risky move. Violating the chain of command is likely to have negative repercussions.

7. When frustrated by a specific rule or procedure, seek answers to the question of why it exists. Many rules, procedures, and policies come into existence as a reaction to some problem and remain in force even when no longer necessary. Knowing the history behind a certain rule will at least make it seem more sensible, and if you should discover that it has outlived its usefulness, you have taken the first step toward eliminating unnecessary requirements.

8. Although a bureaucracy can be changed, the rate of change is slow. Many months—even years—of effort may be needed to achieve a significant change. Only frustration results when you expect to see rapid change. Focus your limited time and energy on only one or two issues at a time. Do not try to change things that are clearly outside your scope of activity or responsibility. Do not waste time on insignificant or petty concerns or on matters that are beyond your influence. Work for changes that are realistic and feasible. And always work as part of a group; a group has more influence and more knowledge than an individual.

9. When working toward change, select your tactics with great care. Be very attentive to the question of who has power within the organization and who stands to gain or lose from a particular change in structure, policy, or procedure. Always assess the risks associated with a proposed change. Those who challenge well-entrenched power groups and those who acquire a reputation within the organization for being troublemakers are likely to be stripped of their power or squeezed out of the organization. Be a diplomat rather than a combat soldier. Aggressive tactics seldom work.

10. As an agency employee, you have no choice but to work cooperatively and respectfully with other agency employees, committees, and departments, even when you disagree with their approaches and even when you do not personally like the people with whom you must work. Employment within a large agency requires that you make accommodations and adapt to administrative and organizational requirements. If you lack this personal flexibility and are unable or unwilling to make concessions, you will always be dissatisfied with your job and become a source of conflict within the agency.

11. Maintain a proper perspective and a sense of humor about your job and place within your organization. Work hard and be a responsible employee but do not take yourself or your agency too seriously. Realize that the modern bureaucracy is incapable of providing a sense of meaning in life or of meeting other emotional or spiritual needs. Look elsewhere for the activities and relationships that can meet those needs.

SELECTED BIBLIOGRAPHY

Lauffer, Armand. *Working in Social Work.* Newbury Park, Calif.: Sage, 1987.
Pruger, Robert. "The Good Bureaucrat." *Social Work* 18 (July 1973): 26–32.
Russo, Robert. *Serving and Surviving as a Human-Service Worker.* Prospect Heights, Ill.: Waveland Press, 1993.

10.7 Stress Management

PURPOSE: To cope effectively with the stress common to social work practice.

DISCUSSION: Social work is a demanding and stressful profession. Basically, job-related stress can have three sources. First, there is the stress that is simply a part of a particular job. Everyone placed in a high-stress job will feel stressed—it comes with the territory. Second, there is stress caused by a lack of skills necessary to do the job. For example, a particular job may not be highly stressful for most people but will be for the individual who is poorly prepared. Third, some individuals create their own stress. For example, an individual may feel stressed because he or she has unrealistically high expectations or takes on an excessive number of responsibilities.

Every social worker responds to the demands of the profession in a unique manner; some thrive while others become emotionally drained. The term **burnout** refers to a state of physical, mental, and emotional exhaustion caused by an inability to cope with work-related stress. Burnout is not inevitable; it can be prevented if the professional is committed to taking care of himself or herself and develops a strategy for stress management. The following guidelines suggest ways to handle stress.

1. The key to preventing negative stress reactions is to find your proper niche in the world of work. There must be a good fit or match between you as a person and the demands of your job. As a social worker, you must feel positive about your chosen profession and feel that you are effective in what you do. If not, you will experience much distress and dissatisfaction. A century before stress reactions were studied in the laboratory, an unknown author wisely stated, "In order that people may be happy in their work, these three things are needed: they must be fit for it, they must not do too much of it, and they must have a sense of success in it."

2. Make an honest attempt to recognize stress in your own life. Listen to those who care about you for clues that you may be under more stress than you think (e.g., "You're so crabby when you get home," "You're not as much fun as you used to be," "You never go anywhere with us anymore," and "You've looked so tired lately"). Other signs of dangerous stress levels include low-level and persistent soreness in the muscles, joints, and tendons; frequent mild colds and sore throats; swelling and aching in the lymph glands, particularly in the neck, underarm, and groin areas; skin eruptions among nonadolascents; excessive nervousness, depression, and irritability; headaches; inability to relax or sleep; fatigue and sluggishness that lingers from day to day; aching stomach, often accompanied by loss of weight; diarrhea or constipation; unexplained drop in performance levels; and disinterest in normally interesting and exciting activities.

3. Examine the fit between your work and your values. Are you spending your time and energy on activities you consider important? For example, if you value family and friends, are you making choices that enable you to be with them? On the other hand, if you find that life on the job is more exciting than your personal or family life, that, too, must be faced with honesty. As a general rule, people find time for what they really want to do and for that which they truly value. Part of stress management is to become clear about what you value.

4. Take time to recognize and enjoy the positives in both your personal and professional lives. Avoid dwelling on the negatives and on what is lacking in your work. Cultivate a sense of humor. Take your work seriously and do the best job you can, but do not take yourself too seriously.

5. Develop hobbies and outside interests that lead you into activities that are very different from what you do at work. Doing something different can be like a minivacation. And do not underestimate the genuine pleasure that can come from the simple everyday things in life.

6. Exercise, good nutrition, and adequate sleep build natural defenses against the harmful effects of stress. Reduce or eliminate the use of alcohol, nicotine, caffeine, and other drugs. Obtain regular medical checkups and take action concerning the treatable conditions that you may have, such as hypertension, obesity, and depression. In our sophisticated but fragmented health care system, assuming responsibility for one's own health is essential.

7. Take several breaks during your workday. Keep the break simple but enjoyable. For example, take a walk at lunch and notice the changing seasons, read something that makes you laugh, or watch children at play. Take brief physical exercise breaks while doing paperwork; try isometric exercises or climb a few flights of stairs.

8. Learn to manage your time. Time management is, in effect, stress management. When we properly manage our time, we accomplish more and are more effective. This contributes to a feeling of satisfaction at work (see Item 9.1).

9. The feeling of not being in control is a major source of stress. If you are unable to gain some sense of control at work, consult with an experienced worker who seems to enjoy what he or she does. What is he or she doing that you might try? Unless you start making changes, the problem will only get worse. Setting priorities is the first step; the next step is making your time and energy fit your priorities.

10. Build a support group of friends or colleagues with whom you feel comfortable and are able to share your frustrations. Find enjoyable ways to spend time together—eat out, see a movie, take a walk, or travel together. Talk a co-worker into trying a new physical activity with you so you can encourage each other, but do not get competitive.

11. Recognize that perfection is not required in most work-related tasks. Realize that you and all others have made mistakes and will continue to make them. Help yourself recover from a setback or mistake by thinking of prior accomplishments.

12. Like a long-distance runner, set your pace at a rate you can maintain without wearing down. For most people, it is better to do a few things well than to do many things poorly. Arrange work activity so you accomplish at least one important thing each day; this can produce a surprising amount of satisfaction.

13. If you are having personal problems, seek help from trusted friends or professionals. The longer you avoid getting needed help, the more areas of your life will be negatively impacted.

14. Listen for thoughts or sayings that have special meaning for you or that soothe or lift your spirit. For example, from *The Desiderata:* "Nurture strength of spirit to shield you in sudden misfortune. But do not distress yourself with dark imaginings. Many fears are born of fatigue and loneliness. Beyond wholesome discipline, be gentle with yourself."

15. Learn stress-management techniques and begin making needed changes. Do not try to make large changes too quickly, however. Small steps in the right direction will add up. Apply to yourself the techniques you use with clients. For example, when faced with a stressful interpersonal task, use techniques of role-playing or behavioral rehearsal to reduce anxiety and build confidence (see Items 14.5 and 14.7).

16. As a technique for handling your fears, try exaggerating them out of proportion. For example, if you fear being embarrassed, visualize yourself blushing to the point of turning beet red, sweating profusely, and shaking so hard your watch vibrates off your wrist. Exaggerating your fears to the point of being ludicrous may help you laugh at yourself and put your fear into perspective.

17. Apply problem-solving and organizational change techniques to the stressors common to most work settings: poor working conditions, unreasonable deadlines, heavy workloads, interruptions, and problems with co-workers and supervisors. Serious problems require careful analysis and intervention. They will not go away without intervention. Do something about them!

18. Visitors to the United States often observe that our life-style is characterized by a fast pace, complexity, materialism, and a "coolness" in our human interactions. These characteristics contribute to the stress we experience but often we are not even aware of their influence. Look for ways to simplify your life and slow its pace by reducing the number of decisions you must make each day. For example, simplify your wardrobe and your meals so you have fewer decisions to make about what to wear and what and where to eat. Give up nonessential possessions and activities that demand your attention and consume your time and money but provide little in the way of joy and relaxation. Replace the "things" in your life with meaningful relationships with family and friends.

SELECTED BIBLIOGRAPHY

Davis, Martha, Elizabeth Eshelman, and Matthew McKay. *The Relaxation and Stress Reduction Workbook,* 4th ed. Oakland, Calif.: New Harbinger Publications, 1995.

Edelwich, Jerry, and Archie Brodsky. *Burn-Out.* New York: Human Services Press, 1980.

Ehrmann, Max. *The Desiderata of Happiness.* Boulder, Colo.: Blue Mountain Press, 1948.

10.8 Using Humor in Social Work

PURPOSE: To make use of humor as a counterbalance to the grimness and frustration often experienced in professional practice.

DISCUSSION: In recent years, humor has been recognized increasingly as an appropriate tool for use within professional helping relationships. Hageseth (1988, 18) notes that positive humor (i.e., that which is loving and healing) can "help you deal with grief, interpersonal strife, marital conflict, workplace stress, life threatening illness, baldness, excess adipose, and teenage children." However, one must be alert to the negative use of humor that is frequently used to hurt or denigrate others. In social work practice, one often sees negative humor used in family and small group interaction, as well as in agency staff and interagency exchanges.

Robinson (1991) and Fry and Salameh (1987) have formulated guidelines for the use of humor in the helping process. Basically, they recommend that professionals view the use of humor as one would any other technique and realize that what may be helpful, appropriate, and effective with one client may be offensive to another. Factors such as a client's age, culture, ethnicity, education, or gender may determine whether a particular use of humor is perceived as funny or offensive. It is recommended that the professional helper conduct a "humor assessment" before attempting to use humor in a practice situation. Such an assessment might include questions such as the following:

- Tell me about the last time you had a good laugh.
- Can you recall something funny that happened in recent weeks?
- Would you tell me your favorite joke?

The client's response to such questions will indicate his or her receptivity to humor and capacity to perceive humor in a practice situation.

It is also important for social workers to allow humor to become part of the office atmosphere. A number of activities can encourage humor in the workplace. Consider the following:

- Devote the first five minutes of each agency staff meeting to sharing jokes or to describing "this week's most embarrassing moment."
- Create a humor bulletin board on which staff can tack jokes, cartoons, comic strips, and so on. Create a second board and invite clients to post humorous items.
- Design a staff training session on how to use humor to handle stressful situations or the effective use of humor in work with clients.
- Develop a lending library of humorous books, articles, and tapes.
- Keep a file of jokes, anecdotes, and humorous agency stories from which ones can be selected and shared with staff at times when comic relief is especially needed.

Poking fun at our professional shibboleths and sacred cows is a first step toward developing a social work humor. For example, one might ask:

How many social workers does it take to change a lightbulb?

Responses might include the following:

"I hear you saying that you are concerned about the lightbulb. Tell me more about that."

"Is the lightbulb the thing you most want to change about your situation?"

"Only one—but the social worker will need a M.S.W. degree and two years' experience."

"I am sorry but I cannot answer that question; it is confidential."

"We will let you know as soon as our agency's study committee finishes its report."

An irreverent look at our professional jargon will also uncover some humor. For example, Brown (1976) offers the following definitions:

Crisis Intervention: Technique for rapid transfer of anxiety from client to social worker.

Unmotivated: Frequently stated reason for termination of services. What is not clear, however, is who is being described—the client or the social worker?

Intake: The process by which clients are screened out or screened in—depending on what is needed for the agency's annual report.

Here is another example of poking fun at our profession. In this case, it is a tongue-in-cheek letter from a recent social work graduate.

Dear Social Work Faculty:

Thank you for your letters of recommendation. I did get the job and by now I have been a professional social worker for one full month.

I don't want to sound critical but I must take this opportunity to say that my social work education did not prepare me for what I am facing in my new job. I have become very confused and I can hardly speak anymore.

I have discovered that the social workers in my office get real uptight about language and words. They are striving to be "politically correct." That means, I believe, that they are careful to select just the right word so they won't offend anyone. But that is really hard to do since we spend so much time talking about other people—who they are, what they believe, and how they behave.

Personally, I like political correctness because I don't like conflict, so I avoid offending anyone. But it is getting harder and harder to keep from accidentally using the wrong word. My relationships are becoming like mine fields and it's so easy to step on the wrong word. Nevertheless, I guess we should try. So, for example, rather than offend a man who is dead and call this limitation to his attention, it is probably best to refer to him as "metaphysically challenged."

We cannot be too careful about the words we use because words do strange things to people. Take, for example, the word <u>welfare.</u> This is a really great word. It represents a wonderful idea. According to my dictionary, <u>welfare</u> is defined as "health, happiness and general well-being." Yet, when I read the newspaper, I find that nearly everyone wants to do away with welfare. No one wants welfare and no one wants to pay for it. How can such a nice word upset so many people? People are really strange—I mean interesting.

I am also told I should avoid using the word <u>problem</u>. I am told I should use a word that is more positive, less negative. My dictionary defines a <u>problem</u> as "a question or situation that presents uncertainty, perplexity or difficulty." Actually that doesn't sound bad to me. I certainly have had a lot of perplexity and I don't think I have been terribly damaged so far.

Some in the helping professions manage to avoid the word <u>problem</u> by substituting the word <u>dysfunctional.</u> Seemingly, it is better to refer to a person or family that has a problem as a dysfunctional person or a dysfunctional family. My dictionary defines <u>dysfunction</u> as "disordered or impaired." I don't know about you, but I would rather have a problem.

Still other professionals are able to avoid the word <u>problem</u> by referring to a person's questions, perplexities, and difficulties as <u>issues, challenges,</u> or <u>concerns.</u> Thus, instead of saying "Tell me about your problem," they would say "Tell me about your issues, your challenges, and your concerns." Or perhaps they would say "Tell me about your unresolved issues" or "areas of concern" or "personal and family dilemmas."

Some say that I shouldn't focus so much on people's problems (i.e., uncertainties, perplexities or difficulties) and should instead focus on their strengths. I like that idea. However, the problem—I mean the challenge—with this suggestion is that when I look in my dictionary for a definition of <u>strength</u> I find that it means "(1) the state, quality or property of being strong; physical power; muscularity (2) the power of resisting force, attack, strain or stress; durability; solidity; impregnability.

Given that, I am not sure what to think of all this emphasis on a person's strengths. Being relatively small myself and out of shape, I think I would prefer to be around people with problems.

I am told to be very careful around children, especially children who have problems—I mean issues. It can be harmful to label a child with the wrong word. For example, instead of saying that a boy has a "problem" or a "serious problem," it is preferable to describe the child as being "at risk" or perhaps "seriously at risk." Such words have a nice ring but they are a bit confusing to me; I am never sure what "risk" we are talking about. And what about the word <u>at</u> in "at risk"? Does that mean the boy is approaching a risk, is about to meet the risk, or has now engaged the risk? Or does it mean he has a problem?

As I said, I am a bit confused about professional words and language. You might want to mention this to the students in your classes.

> Sincerely yours,
> Ben Goode, M.S.W.
> (Class of 96)

SELECTED BIBLIOGRAPHY

Blumenfeld, Ester, and Lynn Alpern. *Humor at Work.* Atlanta: Peachtree Publications, 1994.

Brown, H. S. *Some of My Best Friends are Social Workers.* Bloomfield, Conn.: H. S. Brown, 1976.

Fry, W. F., Jr., and W. A. Salameh, eds. *Handbook of Humor and Psychotherapy.* Sarasota, Fla.: Professional Resource Exchange, 1987.

Hageseth, Christian. *A Laughing Place: The Art and Psychology of Positive Humor in Love and Adversity.* Fort Collins, Colo.: Berwick Publishing, 1988.

Robinson, Vera. *Humor and the Health Professions.* Thorofare, N.J.: Slack Inc., 1991.

10.9   Making Ethical Decisions

PURPOSE: To clarify ethical issues and make practice choices that are consistent with social work's ethical principles and professional values.

DISCUSSION: Each day, social workers make decisions concerning complex ethical issues. Sometimes the task is to help clients sort out their own ethical concerns, and at other times it involves the social worker determining if an action he or she is about to take is appropriate from an ethical perspective. Sometimes all possible practice options will cause harm or distress to someone, creating an ethical dilemma for the social worker. Essentially, an ***ethical dilemma*** is a situation wherein the worker has two or more ethical obligations but cannot follow or adhere to one without violating another. For example, ethical dilemmas faced by social workers increasingly involve decisions on how best to allocate scarce resources in times of budget cutbacks or staff shortages. In such cases, the decision to provide services to one client may result in limiting or withholding the services needed by others.

A first step toward resolving such ethical dilemmas is to find answers to several questions that supply important background information. For example, consider the following:

- What aspects of the agency's activity or worker's roles and duties give rise to the dilemma (e.g., legal mandates, job requirements, agency policy, questions of efficient use of limited resources, possible harm caused by an intervention, etc.)?
- Who can or should resolve this dilemma? Is it rightfully a decision to be made by the client? Other family members? The worker? The agency administrator?
- For each decision possible, what are the short-term and long-term consequences for the client, family, worker, agency, community, and so on?
- Who stands to gain and who stands to lose from each possible choice or action? Are those who stand to gain or lose of equal or of unequal power (e.g., child vs. adult)? Do those who are most vulnerable or those with little power require special consideration?
- When harm to someone cannot be avoided, what decision will cause the least harm or a type of harm with fewest long-term consequences? Who of those that might be harmed are least able to recover from the harm?
- Will a particular resolution to this dilemma set an undesirable precedent for future decision making concerning other clients?

Once those questions have been answered, the worker must answer three additional questions.

- What ethical principles and obligations apply in this situation?
- Which, if any, ethical principles are in conflict in this situation and therefore create an ethical dilemma?
- Would certain ethical obligations be more important than others when resolving ethical dilemmas?

To answer these questions, two sources of help are available to the social worker. The first source of assistance is the National Association of Social Workers' *Code of Ethics.* Standards of ethical practice are expressed in the *Code,* which lists ethical principles and provides general guidelines for professional conduct. Perhaps nothing is more prescriptive in social work than the requirement to adhere to the *Code of Ethics.* Also, the *Code* is NASW's basis for evaluating and responding to any charges of unethical conduct that may be made against a social worker. To join NASW, a social worker must sign a statement indicating that he or she will abide by the *Code,* and each year, when membership is renewed, the social worker once again commits to uphold the *Code.*

NASW's *Code of Ethics,* therefore, is an important benchmark that may be used to survey a practice situation to determine if a specific alternative or action is ethically responsible. Since creative social workers regularly compare various alternative intervention strategies, the *Code* serves as an ethical screen or filter through which the acceptable practice alternatives should pass. The *Code of Ethics Checklist* (see Figure 10.1) is one tool for comparing the ethical dimensions of practice alternatives. It lists only those sections of the *Code* that apply most directly to working with

FIGURE 10.1
Code of
Ethics
Checklist

What options, actions, or decisions are being considered by social worker?

Option A: _____

Option B: _____

Option C: _____

Does the option place you in violation of any of the following "Code" requirements? (Answer with a Yes, No, or Cannot Determine)

I. *Conduct and Comportment as a Social Worker*

A. *Propriety:* The social worker should maintain high standards of personal conduct in the capacity or identity of a social worker (e.g., honesty, fairness, self-discipline).

Option A	Yes	No	Cannot Determine
Option B	Yes	No	Cannot Determine

B. *Competence and Integrity:* The social worker should act in accordance with the highest standards of professional integrity and impartiality.

Option A	Yes	No	Cannot Determine
Option B	Yes	No	Cannot Determine

II. *Ethical Responsibility to Clients*

F. *Primacy of Client's Interests:* The social worker's primary responsibility to his or her clients.

Option A	Yes	No	Cannot Determine
Option B	Yes	No	Cannot Determine

G. *Rights and Prerogatives of Clients:* The social worker should make every effort to foster maximum self-determination on the part of clients.

Option A	Yes	No	Cannot Determine
Option B	Yes	No	Cannot Determine

H. *Confidentiality and Privacy:* The social worker should respect the privacy of clients and hold in confidence all information obtained in the course of professional service.

Option A	Yes	No	Cannot Determine
Option B	Yes	No	Cannot Determine

IV. *Ethical Responsibility to Employers and Employing Organizations*

L. *Commitment to Employing Organization:* The social worker should adhere to commitments made to the employing organization.

Option A	Yes	No	Cannot Determine
Option B	Yes	No	Cannot Determine

VI. *Ethical Responsibility to Society*

P. *Promoting the General Welfare:* The social worker should promote the general welfare of the society.

Option A	Yes	No	Cannot Determine
Option B	Yes	No	Cannot Determine

clients, although ethical issues arise in work with colleagues and other professionals, as well as in relation to one's employing agency and the community.

To use the *Code of Ethics* Checklist, the worker should first list each practice option (i.e., each possible action or decision). For example, Option A might be "I will pressure my client to follow my advice in order to prevent him from making a serious mistake" and Option B might be "I will respect my client's decision even if his decision will get him into further trouble with the law." There could still be other options (e.g., an Option C, D, E, etc.). Second, the worker considers Section IA (i.e., Comportment, Propriety) on the checklist and decides if that particular section of the *Code* might be violated if the action depicted in Option A is taken. The worker circles either "Yes" (the *Code* is violated) or "No" (the *Code* is not violated). If it is not possible to decide this question without additional information, the worker circles "Cannot Determine" to flag the need for additional information and come back to the matter when such information is available. Third, the worker repeats this process for each of the options under consideration. Finally, for each "Yes" answer— each possible violation identified—the worker goes to the complete *Code* and studies all relevant subsections. For example, Section IA of the *Code* contains three subsections that are much more explicit about the expected behaviors. (See Appendix 10.1 for a complete copy of the NASW *Code of Ethics.*)

A limitation of the *Code of Ethics* as a tool for resolving ethical issues in practice is that all provisions of the *Code* are given equal weight. Thus, it is useful for the worker to also apply a second tool in making ethical decisions: the Ethical Issue Priority Checklist (see Figure 10.2). This checklist is derived from a ranking of priorities in making ethical choices developed by Loewenberg and Dolgoff (1996, 58–62). Basically, this is a ranking of seven guiding principles, with Principle 1 (i.e., the protection of life) viewed as most important and Principle 7 (i.e., telling the truth) considered least important among these seven obligations. Although an individual social worker might identify additional principles or develop a different ordering of the priorities, Loewenberg and Dolgoff provide a useful starting point.

The process followed in using this checklist is the same as the one used when completing the *Code of Ethics* Checklist. With this list, however, if "Yes" answers appear higher among the priorities (i.e., higher on the page) for one option as opposed to others, the worker should seriously question the appropriateness of using that practice option.

With the two checklists completed, the worker is better prepared to make a decision regarding which option to exercise—at least as far as the ethical issues are concerned. If an action must be taken that violates a provision of the *Code of Ethics* (i.e., a "Yes" answer), it is suggested that the worker document the reasons for selecting that action. Writing out the rationale not only helps one to become more precise in thinking about the matter but it may also prove to be useful documentation if the worker is subsequently charged with a *Code* violation as a result of this decision.

SELECTED BIBLIOGRAPHY

Levy, Charles. *Social Work Ethics on the Line.* New York: Haworth Press, 1993.

Loewenberg, Frank M., and Ralph Dolgoff. "Guides to Making Ethical Decisions." In *Tactics and Techniques of Community Intervention,* 3rd ed., edited by John Tropman, John Erlich, and Jack Rothman. Itasca, Ill.: F. E. Peacock, 1995, pp. 370–386.

FIGURE 10.2
Ethical Issue
Priority
Checklist

What options, actions, or decisions are being considered by social worker?

Option A: _____

Option B: _____

Option C: _____

Answer the following questions for each of the options you have identified with yes, no, or cannot determine. (Note: Avoid making too many assumptions about possible but unlikely long-range implications of the action.)

1. Does this option/action threaten or risk someone's life, physical well being or chances of survival?
   Option A   Yes   No   Cannot Determine
   Option B   Yes   No   Cannot Determine

2. Does this option treat someone in a fundamentally unjust, unfair, or unequal manner and/or violate basic human rights?
   Option A   Yes   No   Cannot Determine
   Option B   Yes   No   Cannot Determine

3. Does this option significantly and unreasonably limit someone's self-determination, autonomy?
   Option A   Yes   No   Cannot Determine
   Option B   Yes   No   Cannot Determine

4. Does this option cause someone significant personal distress or economic hardship.
   Option A   Yes   No   Cannot Determine
   Option B   Yes   No   Cannot Determine

5. Does this option decrease the quality of life for those of a neighborhood, community, or society as a whole?
   Option A   Yes   No   Cannot Determine
   Option B   Yes   No   Cannot Determine

6. Does this option cause someone to lose their right to privacy and confidentiality?
   Option A   Yes   No   Cannot Determine
   Option B   Yes   No   Cannot Determine

7. Does this option involve distorting or withholding the truth from an individual or a community?
   Option A   Yes   No   Cannot Determine
   Option B   Yes   No   Cannot Determine

———. *Ethical Decisions for Social Work Practice,* 4th ed. Itasca, Ill.: F. E. Peacock, 1996.

Reamer, Fredric. *Ethical Dilemmas in Social Services,* 2nd ed. New York: Columbia University Press, 1993.

Rhodes, Margaret L. *Ethical Dilemmas in Social Work Practice.* Milwaukee: Family Service Association of America, 1991.

10.10   Avoiding Malpractice Suits

PURPOSE: To minimize the possibility of being named in a lawsuit alleging professional negligence or misconduct.

DISCUSSION: A growing number of social workers are being sued for malpractice or professional negligence. Most social workers probably underestimate their legal vulnerability. Broadly speaking, a worker may be held liable if he or she did something or neglected to do something and these acts or omissions caused harm or injury to a client.

In general, the plaintiff in a successful malpractice suit must prove four points.

1. The defendant (e.g., the social worker) was obligated to provide the plaintiff with a particular standard of care or professional conduct.
2. The worker was derelict because he or she breached that obligation (or duty) by some act or omission that had a foreseeable consequence.
3. The client suffered some injury or harm (physical, financial, emotional, etc.).
4. The worker's conduct was a direct or proximate cause of the client's injury or harm.

The concept of obligation or duty refers to implicit or explicit promises or a contractual arrangement to deliver certain services or treatment. Whether a breach of duty has occurred is determined by measuring the allegedly harmful act or omission against published standards of practice, agency policy, and the performance of social workers in similar settings. The client's injury must be one that would not have occurred had it not been for the social worker's negligence. Despite this traditional "proximate cause" requirement, juries are increasingly finding liability without fault (i.e, finding providers of health and social services negligent even when they are not the proximate cause of the injury.)

The professional duties that, if breached, place social workers and social agencies at greatest risk of legal liability are the following:

- Duty to avoid sexual misconduct
- Duty to warn others when a client discloses intent to harm them (i.e., the Tasaroff Decision)
- Duty to prevent a client's suicide
- Duty to properly diagnose and treat a client
- Duty to ensure continuity of service to a client under the care of a worker or agency
- Duty to maintain and protect confidentiality
- Duty to maintain accurate professional records and a proper and legal accounting of payments and reimbursements

A number of allegations may give rise to lawsuits against social workers, such as the following:

- Providing or arranging the transportation that involves a client in a vehicular accident causing bodily injury
- Violating a client's right to confidentiality
- Failing to report or properly investigate suspected abuse or neglect
- Inappropriately placing of a child or adult into foster care, an institution, a hospital, or jail
- Inappropriately or prematurely releasing a client from foster care, a hospital, an institution, or another protective setting
- Placing or contributing to the placement of a client into a facility or foster home in which he or she is subsequently abused or neglected (i.e., failing to properly select or supervise the placement)
- Practicing while impaired by use of drugs or alcohol or failure to report a colleague known to be impaired
- Knowingly placing a client in the wrong diagnostic category in order to collect fees through third-party reimbursement (i.e., insurance fraud)
- Failing to prevent a client's suicide or contributing to a client's suicide
- Failing to warn others of a client's intention to cause them harm
- Failing to inform a client of eligibility rules or regulations, resulting in avoidable financial costs to the client
- Failing to consult with or refer a client to a specialist
- Failing to properly assess or diagnose a client's condition (e.g., not recognizing an obvious medical problem and not referring the client to a physician)
- Practicing medicine without a license (e.g., suggesting changes in the client's use of medications)
- Misrepresenting one's professional training and qualifications
- Using a radical or untested approach, technique, or procedure
- Providing inaccurate information or advice to a client
- Providing birth control information or abortion counseling to a minor without consent of the parent
- Acting in a prejudicial manner in the selection of an adoptive home or in the licensing of a foster home, day-care facility, or the like
- Failing to be available to a client when needed (e.g., failing to provide professional coverage during the worker's vacation)
- Inappropriately or prematurely terminating a treatment relationship
- Causing conflict or alienation between a parent and child or a husband and wife
- Failing to supervise a child or a person with a mental disability while he or she is participating in an agency program
- Failing to supervise the work of others, including the work of volunteers and students

Of course, there is a big difference between being named in a lawsuit alleging negligence and actually being found negligent by a jury. But even if the suit is eventually dropped or dismissed for a lack of evidence, the worker and/or the agency will have incurred legal expenses during their defense. Most of these lawsuits are settled out of court.

Most lawsuits name as defendants both the social worker and the employing agency because the agency is assumed to be indirectly responsible for the harm caused by an employee. A social worker employed by an agency can be found personally liable, although this is not likely if the worker was acting within his or her job description, was following agency policy, and did nothing of a criminal nature.

In some cases, a social worker is held liable for harm caused by a person under his or her supervision (e.g., another social worker, volunteer, or student). Also, a worker might be held liable if he or she somehow contributed to the harm caused by another professional. An example of this is when a worker refers a client to an incompetent professional or when a worker provides a social assessment report to a psychiatrist who then makes a poor decision based on that report.

A social worker who learns that he or she has been named in a malpractice suit should immediately contact an attorney (the worker's agency may provide legal representation) and also notify his or her supervisor, agency administrator, and insurance company. The social worker should not speak with anyone about the allegations before securing legal counsel. The worker must never alter case records or other documents related to the case. Such changes are easily detected and may constitute a crime. An attempt to alter a record will be viewed as an effort to destroy evidence and cover up a wrongdoing.

Legal experts explain that the key to avoiding a malpractice suit is adherence to reasonable, ordinary, and prudent practices. In order to defend one's self against allegations, the worker must show that his or her actions were fair, in good faith, and consistent with how other properly trained professionals would behave under similar circumstances. One of the best defenses is to be able to show that the client gave his or her informed consent to the professional's intervention. This underscores the need to document client involvement in problem identification, assessment, and case planning.

A number of additional guidelines will help the social worker avoid a malpractice suit or at least minimize its damage.

1. Because of the growing number of social work malpractice suits, the social worker should secure malpractice insurance. It can be purchased through the National Association of Social Workers by NASW members and from some insurance companies.

2. Adhere to the *Code of Ethics* and the *NASW Standards of Professional Practice* relevant to your area of practice. Also adhere to your agency's policies and procedures, as well as state and federal laws and regulations affecting your agency's program and services.

3. Do not become sexually or romantically involved with a client. Sexual misconduct toward a client is one of the most common allegations giving rise to malpractice suits in social work. Sexual involvement with a client is a clear violation of the NASW *Code of Ethics*, a violation of state professional licensing statutes, and, in some states, a violation of criminal law. Avoid situations that could be misinterpreted as sexually inappropriate or give rise to false allegations of sexual misconduct. For example, male workers should be very cautious about visiting a female client in her home. A third party (potential witness) should be within earshot whenever a male worker interviews a female adult or a child.

4. Do not engage in or create dual relationships. A dual relationship is one in which a second set of obligations or expectations is introduced into the social worker–client relationship. Examples include dating a client, renting an apartment to or from a client, loaning money to or borrowing money from a client, hiring a client to perform some service (e.g. repair worker's car), selling some item or product to a client, and so on. Dual relationships must also be avoided in supervisor-worker and faculty-student interaction.

5. Know your level of skill and ability and practice within those limitations. Secure the training and supervision needed to perform your job-related tasks and activities responsibly. Become aware of the types of clients or situations that touch your personal issues and lessen your ability to be objective. Obtain supervision and/or consultation when you are having unusual difficulties with a client. Consult with your peers, supervisor, and/or attorney when faced with difficult ethical or legal issues.

6. Be especially careful when dealing with clients or situations that present high legal risk. Examples include clients who may attempt suicide, clients who are violent and a threat to others, clients who have a history of filing lawsuits, clients who are very manipulative, and clients who always find fault or perceive bad intentions in the behavior of others.

7. Base your practice on a professionally recognized theory or model. Keep your client fully informed of decisions, plans, and any risks associated with the intervention. Be careful not to give your client false hope about what you will be able to do. Convey a realistic picture of what you and your agency's services can accomplish. Maintain records that document your actions and any events or circumstances that might have had an adverse impact on the client.

8. Inform clients of any circumstances that may affect confidentiality. Confidentiality must be broken in order to report suspected abuse or neglect, to warn others of your client's intention to harm them, and to alert others of your client's intention to commit suicide.

9. Reach out to the client who has been angered by your actions and attempt to rebuild the relationship and address his or her complaint. Many malpractice suits could have been prevented if only the worker or agency had followed up on client complaints. If you work for a fee-charging agency, make sure that financial arrangements are handled in a completely businesslike manner so as to minimize the possibility of misunderstanding regarding cost and the collection of insurance payments.

10. Adhere to agency policy whenever a client presents you with a gift. As a general rule, food and inexpensive gifts valued at not more than a few dollars can be accepted, but a more expensive gift should not be accepted before consulting with your supervisor.

11. Be very cautious about giving any advice that could have a significant impact on the client's life (e.g., advising a client to get a divorce, how to invest money, etc.).

12. Do not transport a client in your private car unless this is keeping with agency procedure and allowed under your auto insurance policy.

13. Adhere to rules and policies concerning confidentiality. If you receive a request from an attorney (or anyone else) for information about a client, say nothing before considering whether the information sought might be confidential. Even revealing that a record exists or that the client is, in fact, a client may violate the client's right to confidentiality.

14. If served a subpoena to release client records, immediately consult with your supervisor and agency attorney. Saltzman and Proch (1990, 406) note that "you are not required to yield your records just because a subpoena for the records has been issued by a court. . . . One must respond to a subpoena, but one may respond by claiming confidentiality. If the claim is contested, there will be a court hearing and a judge will decide if the claim is valid or if the records must be turned over."

15. Never agree to a interview with an attorney or other investigator before first consulting with your own attorney. (It is a common practice for attorneys to attempt to secure statements or information before you are even aware that you are the target of a lawsuit.)

16. Before accepting a job with an agency, check into the agency's record of providing legal defense for employees who are named in a lawsuit.

SELECTED BIBLIOGRAPHY

Barker, Robert, and Douglas Branson. *Forensic Social Work.* New York: Haworth Press, 1993.
Bullis, Ronald. *Clinical Social Worker Misconduct.* Chicago: Nelson-Hall, 1995.
Reamer, Frederic. *Social Work Malpractice and Liability.* New York: Columbia University Press, 1994.
Saltzman, Andrea, and Kathleen Proch. *Law in Social Work Practice.* Chicago: Nelson-Hall, 1990.
Schroeder, Leila. *The Legal Environment of Social Work.* Revised ed. Washington, D.C.: NASW Press, 1995.

10.11 Developing Self-Awareness

PURPOSE: To examine one's attitudes, personal habits, and interactional patterns to identify those that may obstruct work with clients.

DISCUSSION: The social worker uses himself or herself as a tool or an instrument in the helping process. Just as a physician must be attentive to the condition of medical instruments, the social worker must constantly examine the self to identify barriers to his or her effectiveness. Professional social workers have always emphasized the need to develop their self-awareness and self-knowledge. The term ***self-awareness*** refers to an accurate perception of one's own beliefs, attitudes, and behavioral habits and their usual effects on one's own decision making and behavior in social work practice. Efforts to develop self-awareness should focus on identifying both strengths and limitations. Many of the strengths that are of importance in social work practice are discussed in other parts of this book. Chapter 3, for example, describes the qualities of courage, compassion, hopefulness, empathy, genuineness, warmth, creativity, imagination, flexibility, energy, good judgment, knowledge, and so on (also see Chapters 2 and 8). In this section, the focus is mostly on factors that can interfere with effective practice. This is not to suggest that strengths are of less importance but rather to counter, in a straightforward manner, our common human tendency to deny and ignore personal limitations.

Many individuals are drawn to the helping professions (social work, nursing, medicine, counseling, etc.) because they believe the problems they have faced in life give them a special understanding or sensitivity to the problems of others. For example, many have grown up in alcoholic or otherwise dysfunctional families. Indeed, life's problems can be a powerful teacher and provide a degree of empathy that others do not have. However, this will be the case only after one has honestly examined those experiences and successfully worked through the residual feelings associated with them. If a professional denies or suppresses the emotions connected to painful life experiences and cannot come to peace with the past, efforts to help others will be plagued by misunderstanding, self-doubts, and feelings of failure.

Growing up in a dysfunctional family typically produces an individual who has low self-worth and a fear of strong emotions. According to Wegscheider (1981, 223–225), a professional helper with these characteristics will have serious problems in their work with clients:

- Because they fear emotion, they only give advice . . . rather than lead the client through their pain to find answers for themselves.
- Because they are not comfortable with certain feelings, they avoid topics that their client needs to discuss.
- Because they are preoccupied with defending their own fragile self-worth and defending against their own suppressed emotion, they cannot fully attend to the client nor hear the client's subtle messages. At the other extreme, they are unable to control their own emotions and they react inappropriately to their client's feelings.
- Because they have such a strong need to be liked by clients, they are unable to confront a client when necessary and they tell the client what he or she wants to hear and not what needs to be said.
- Because of their low self-worth, they are terribly afraid of being seen as incompetent in their work and may hide behind a facade of false professionalism and the use of endless jargon and intellectualizing in an attempt to convince others of their competence.

When a social worker becomes aware of some factor that interferes with client service, he or she must be willing to correct the problem or, if change is not possible, to seek a practice setting where the factor will not have a negative impact on clients. The following list outlines some of the factors that can interfere with the formation of a professional helping relationship and client service; use it as an aid in self-examination.

1. *Personal hang-ups and emotional problems.* To a considerable degree, our beliefs and behavior have been shaped by our childhood and early family experiences. Most people carry a certain amount of emotional "baggage" into their adult lives, including unresolved parent-child conflicts, prejudice, after-effects of traumatic events, and so on. Sometimes this "baggage" is carried to the workplace, where it has a negative impact on clients and work performances. For example:

- Preoccupation with personal problems, resulting in an inability to give one's full attention to the client
- Inability to control one's reactions or exercise self-discipline when in an emotionally charged situation or when under the ordinary pressure associated with direct social work practice
- Inability to demonstrate warmth, empathy, and genuine caring for clients served by the agency
- Inability or unwillingness to work cooperatively with persons in positions of authority (e.g., judges, physicians, administrators, supervisors, etc.)
- Difficulty separating personal experience (e.g., having been a victim of child abuse, growing up with alcoholic parents, etc.) from the concerns and problems presented by clients
- Extreme defensiveness that prevents a critical examination of one's own job performance
- Avoiding certain clients or difficult tasks
- Personalization of client anger and frustrations (i.e., inability to maintain an appropriate level of objectivity)
- Imposing one's values, political beliefs, religious beliefs or life-style on clients
- Inability to respect the religious beliefs and cultural values of a client
- Alcohol or drug abuse
- Misuse or abuse of one's authority over clients
- Extreme level of shyness or nonassertiveness resulting in an inability to express one's opinions and engage in the give-and-take of client work, peer supervision, and team decision making

2. *Appearance, clothing, and grooming.* To a large extent, people form impressions of others—especially the powerful first impression—on the basis of physical appearance. Thus the social worker must pay attention to his or her clothing and grooming because it matters to clients and will affect how they respond to the worker and their utilization of agency services. Of course, what is offensive to one client may be acceptable to another, and what is appropriate dress in one agency setting may be inappropriate in another. The staff in a particular setting must make decisions on what is acceptable. Many agencies and most hospitals establish dress codes as a way of providing guidance to staff. When examining your appearance and its possible impact on clients, remember the following:

- Some choices of clothing, hairstyle, makeup, perfume, or jewelry may offend or distract clients served by the agency.
- Deficiencies in grooming and personal hygiene may offend clients.
- Uncovered infections, skin irritations, and similar conditions may distract the client or cause him or her worry and anxiety.

3. *Behaviors that devalue or degrade others.* Social work values dictate that every client should be treated with respect. The social worker must avoid behaviors that are disrespectful, including the following:

- Using words, phrases, or gestures that are in bad taste or known to offend clients and staff (e.g., cursing, sexual overtones, etc.)
- Telling sexist, off-color, or ethnic jokes
- Telling disrespectful and disparaging stories about clients
- Demonstrating prejudice against particular client groups
- Making sarcastic, insulting, cruel, or disrespectful comments about clients

4. *Distracting personal habits.* Most people have some undesirable mannerisms and habits that their friends and families have learned to accept. However, the social worker must be willing to modify habits that annoy clients, including the following:

- Fidgeting, pencil tapping, knuckle cracking, nail biting, and the like
- Scratching, pulling, or twisting hair
- Chewing gum or tobacco and smoking
- Scowling, frowning, or other facial gestures that seem to express scorn, contempt
- Excessive nervous laughter, frequent clearing of throat, or other distracting mannerisms

5. *Difficulties in cognitive functioning.* A social worker must absorb information quickly and apply complex principles. A capacity for abstract thinking is essential. The following examples illustrate insufficient cognitive functioning.

- Difficulty processing new information, drawing logical inferences, and solving problems
- Lack of reading speed and comprehension needed to understand records and reports, agency policy, and professional books and journals
- Cognitive deficits that interfere with attention, memory, and judgment
- Inability to explain the assumptions and inferences behind one's professional judgments, conclusions, and decisions

6. *Difficulties in verbal communication.* The social worker's verbal communication must be understandable to clients and other professional persons. The following problems could hamper work with clients.

- Mumbling, speaking inaudibly, loud or penetrating voice tones, halting or hesitant speech, rapid speech
- Frequent use of slang not understood by or offensive to clients
- Errors of grammar or awkward sentence construction that confuse clients
- Inability or unwillingness to adjust vocabulary to client's age or educational level
- Uncorrected vision or hearing problems

7. *Problems in written communication.* Because so much of the social worker's service to a client involves the exchange of information with other professionals, the worker must be able to communicate in writing. If letters, reports, and agency records are carelessly written and difficult to understand, those attempting to read them will conclude either that the worker does not care enough to communicate clearly or is incompetent. The worker's effectiveness is seriously damaged if the client or other professional persons form such negative impressions. Serious writing problems that merit correction include the following:

- Inability to prepare letters, reports, and records that are understandable to clients, agency staff, and other professionals
- Problems recognizing and correcting errors of spelling, grammar, and syntax
- Difficulty selecting words that adequately express thought
- Inability to write at a speed sufficient to manage required paperwork

8. *Poor work habits.* Poor work habits may have a direct or indirect impact on the clients served by an agency. Some of the commonly observed problems are:

- Being late for client appointments, team meetings, case conferences, and other scheduled events
- Missing deadlines for the completion of written reports that are important to clients or other agencies and professionals serving the client
- Incomplete or sloppy recordkeeping
- Lack of preparation for meetings with clients and other professionals
- Not following through on assignments or tasks
- Distracting other staff members or keeping them from their work
- Unwillingness to seek and utilize direction and guidance from the supervisor
- Blaming clients or others for one's own ineffectiveness; inability or unwillingness to acknowledge mistakes or limitations of knowledge and skill
- Being more interested in diagnostic labels and theoretical issues than with clients as real people
- Unwillingness to follow established agency policies and procedures
- Behaviors occurring outside work hours that draw negative attention to the social worker and thereby lessen client and public respect for the social agency and/or the worker
- Unwillingness to share information and preoccupation with protection of professional or agency turf

SELECTED BIBLIOGRAPHY

Cory, Marianne, and Gerald Cory. *Becoming a Helper*, 2nd. ed. Pacific Grove, Calif.: Brooks/Cole, 1993.

Kottler, Jeffery. *Growing a Therapist.* San Francisco: Jossey-Bass, 1995.

Munson, Carlton. *An Introduction to Clinical Social Work Supervision*, 2nd ed. New York: Haworth, 1993.

Wegscheider, Sharon. *Another Change: Hope and Health for the Alcoholic Family.* Palo Alto, Calif.: Science and Behavior Book, Inc., 1981.

10.12   Dealing with Sexual Harassment

PURPOSE: To prevent sexual harassment in the academic setting or workplace.

DISCUSSION: Sexual harassment in education or employment covers a broad spectrum of behavior, ranging from sexual innuendoes and gender-based comments—sometimes in the guise of humor—to coerced sexual relations. Shank (1994) notes:

> Sexual harassment is an old problem but a new issue. Since the Clarence Thomas/Anita Hill hearings, sexual harassment has been the subject of increased attention in the media, the workplace, and the classroom. As a result, society is finally willing to acknowledge the existence of this problem, and victims are increasingly willing to confront the problem directly. (p. 12)

According to the Equal Employment Opportunity Commission (1980), unwelcome sexual advances, requests for sexual favors, and other verbal or physical conduct of a sexual nature can be defined as ***sexual harassment*** when:

- Submission to such conduct is explicitly or implicitly made a term or condition of an individual's employment or participation in an education program or activity.
- Submission to or rejection of such conduct by an individual is used as the basis for academic or employment decisions affecting that individual.
- Such conduct has the purpose or effect of substantially interfering with an individual's academic or work performance or creating an intimidating, hostile, or offensive working or educational environment.

Sexual harassment includes both heterosexual and homosexual advances. Most often, the offender is a male.

Since social workers often need to help clients deal with harassment and because they themselves may be victimized, they need to be knowledgeable about the appropriate responses. Two strategies are available for dealing with sexual harassment—organizational and individual. At the organizational level, it is advisable to create an agency policy that clearly prohibits sexual harassment and identifies procedures for making a complaint. That statement should be published in the agency's personnel manual, and the agency director should periodically post or circulate the statement. Periodic training that sensitizes all staff to the problem can help prevent harassment.

A number of steps are recommended for the individual who is subjected to sexual harassment.

1. Tell the harasser to stop. Clearly and firmly describe the troublesome behavior and its effects. Inform the harasser that the sexual harassment is a violation of federal law and/or agency or school policy. Also you may wish to deliver to the

harasser a letter that outlines your complaint. Sandler (1983) states that such a letter should include three parts:

a. *What happened.* Be as detailed and accurate as possible, providing dates (or approximate dates), places, and descriptions of the incidents. For example:

- "On [date of incident], when I met you for a conference about my work, you asked me to come to your house that evening and said it would 'help' my [evaluation]."
- "Several times this semester when I have talked to you after class, you put your arm around me. Once you also tried to fondle my breast."
- "Last week at the department party you asked me to go to bed with you."

b. *How you feel about what happened.* Express any feelings of dismay, misery, distrust, or revulsion, and include your opinions or thoughts about what happened. For example:

- "My stomach turns into knots when I come to class."
- "I cannot believe that you are able to evaluate my work fairly."
- "It is very difficult for me to concentrate on my work."

c. *What you want to happen next.* This part is usually short, since most victims just want the behavior to stop. For example:

- "I want our relationship to be purely professional from now on."
- "Don't ever touch me again or make remarks about my sexuality."

2. Keep a diary of the harassment, noting time, date, place, exactly what happened, and how you felt. Record names of any witnesses. Keep copies of all written materials received from the harasser as well as copies of your letters of complaint.

3. Consult with trusted co-workers. You may discover that they also are being harassed. A complaint by a group has more power and offers more protection from retaliation since the Federal Concerted Action Law protects two or more employees who take action to improve their working conditions.

4. Consult with your supervisor. If he or she is the harasser, go to the personnel department or affirmative action officer. Consult with your union representative, if applicable.

5. If in-house procedures to stop the harassment are nonexistent or ineffective, or if you are afraid to use them, contact your state human rights commission or the U.S. Equal Employment Opportunity Commission (EEOC). (*Note:* A complaint must be filed with the EEOC within 180 days of the incident; some employers may require an official complaint within 30 or 60 days of the incident.)

6. For further protection against retaliation, you may want to consult an attorney.

When you report harassment, be prepared for possible negative reactions from the harasser or others in the organization. The process can be stressful and expensive if you must hire an attorney and take legal action. Retaliation by an employer is illegal and should be reported. When you file a formal complaint, know how you want the problem resolved (e.g., stopping harassment, a job transfer, monetary award, medical bills paid, modification of an unfair performance evaluation, etc.).

SELECTED BIBLIOGRAPHY

Equal Employment Opportunity Commission. "Guidelines on Discrimination Because of Sex, Title VII, Section 703." Federal Register 45 (11 April 1980): 2505.

Paludi, Michelle, and Richard Barickman. *Academic and Workplace Sexual Harassment.* New York: SUNY Press, 1991.

Sandler, Bernice R. "Writing a Letter to the Sexual Harasser: Another Way of Dealing with the Problem." Washington D.C.: Association of American Colleges, February, 1983.

Shank, Barbara W. "Sexual Harassment: Definitions, Policy Frameworks, and Legal Issues." In *Sexual Harassment and Schools of Social Work: Issues, Costs, and Strategic Responses,* edited by Marie O. Weil, Michelle Hughes, and Nancy R. Hooyman. Alexandria, Va.: Council on Social Work Education, 1994.

Singer, Terry. "Sexual Harassment." In *Encyclopedia of Social Work,* 19th ed., Vol. 3, edited by Richard L. Edwards. Washington, D.C.: NASW Press, 1995, pp. 2148–2156.

Weil, Marie O., Michelle Hughes, and Nancy R. Hooyman, eds. *Sexual Harassment and Schools of Social Work: Issues, Costs, and Strategic Responses.* Alexandria, Va.: Council on Social Work Education, 1994.

10.13   Analyzing Research Reports

PURPOSE: To read research-based articles critically in order to assess their usefulness for practice.

DISCUSSION: Social workers increasingly rely on knowledge derived from research. Social work journals, monographs, and other sources regularly provide analyses of individual, family, group, and organizational behavior; the success of social policies; and the effectiveness of various practice approaches. Some of these studies are based on qualitative research methods (see Item 10.14), whereas others draw on quantitative data that have been subjected to statistical analyses (see Item 10.15). In either case, the effective practitioner must be prepared to intelligently consume the research literature.

When drawing ideas for practice from the research-based literature, it is important that they be based on more than one study. Recurrence (i.e., repetition of results) is a good indicator that the findings are trustworthy. Thus, when a potentially useful study is found, seek other reports on that same topic to see if other researchers arrived at the same conclusion. Also, remember that journal articles are usually an abbreviated version of a more lengthy research report; it is often necessary to read the original report in order to secure a complete understanding of the research effort and its findings. Another key to the proper use of the research-based literature is to use critical judgment to decide whether the research effort followed accepted procedures and methodology. The checksheet shown in Figure 10.3 can be used to guide an assessment of an article or research report.

FIGURE 10.3   Checksheet for Evaluating a Research Report

	Yes	No	??
1. Is the question under study clearly and accurately identified?	☐	☐	☐
2. Is the literature review thorough and does it reflect current thinking on this issue?	☐	☐	☐
3. Are the key terms, concepts, and assumptions clearly defined and key variables operationalized realistically?	☐	☐	☐
4. Is the design of the research sound?			
a. Is the study design and methodology clearly described?	☐	☐	☐
b. Is the method of sampling appropriate?	☐	☐	☐
c. Is the sample of sufficient size?	☐	☐	☐
d. Are data collection instruments valid (i.e., measuring what they said they were)?	☐	☐	☐
e. Are data collection instruments reliable (i.e., consistent from use to use)?	☐	☐	☐
5. Is the data analysis appropriate?			
a. If the data were *qualitative* in nature, was a systematic approach to recording and analyzing them used?	☐	☐	☐
b. If the data were *quantitative* in nature, are the statistical tests utilized correct for the type of sample and level of data?	☐	☐	☐
6. Are the results interpreted accurately and objectively?	☐	☐	☐
7. Are limitations to the study explained?	☐	☐	☐
8. Are the research questions answered satisfactorily?	☐	☐	☐
9. Are the conclusions stated clearly and adequately substantiated by the data?	☐	☐	☐
10. Are suggested applications to practice reasonable and realistic?	☐	☐	☐

SELECTED BIBLIOGRAPHY

Grinnell, Richard M., Jr. *Social Work Researach and Evaluation,* 4th ed. Itasca, Ill.: F. E. Peacock, 1993.

Hudson, Walter W., and Paula S. Nurius, eds. *Controversial Issues in Social Work Research.* Boston: Allyn and Bacon, 1994.

Royse, David. *Research Methods in Social Work,* 2nd ed. Chicago: Nelson-Hall, 1995.

Rubin, Allen, and Earl Babbie. *Research Methods for Social Work,* 2nd ed. Pacific Grove, Calif.: Brooks/Cole, 1993.

10.14   Understanding Qualitative Data

PURPOSE: To make sound judgments about the appropriateness of qualitative research studies reported in the social work literature.

DISCUSSION: In recent years, qualitative research has increasingly been viewed as a respectable form of data collection and analysis in the social sciences. As opposed to *quantita-*

tive research, which is focused on counting and statistically analyzing data (see Item 10.15), ***qualitative research*** is more concerned with describing the factors that are being studied.

Methods of quantitative research can collect an enormous amount of data from a large and representative sample of respondents. Statistical analysis may then be used to summarize and reduce those data to understandable generalizations and to identify relationships among the data. Qualitative research, by contrast, has the capacity to secure an in-depth understanding of the thoughts, values, and experiences of a smaller group of respondents.

Although some tend to view qualitative and quantitative research as competing methods, it is more useful to consider them as ends of a single continuum of approaches used in the development of knowledge. Qualitative research is most appropriate when the basic elements of the phenomenon being studied are still unclear and poorly defined. Qualitative methodologies are designed to assist in identifying the important characteristics of the phenomenon under study. On the other hand, quantitative research is most appropriate when the phenomenon is understood well enough to know what specific categories or types of information are needed to advance one's understanding of the phenomenon. In other words, a quantitative study must begin with a set of assumptions or beliefs about which data to collect. In many situations, the researcher lacks the knowledge base needed to formulate valid assumptions.

Several principles and concepts are unique to qualitative research. First, when formulating questions for inquiry, the researcher delays the in-depth literature review until the data have been collected, lest the researcher develop a bias or a predisposition in regard to what information is really important and what meaning should be assigned to the data. Second, the researcher acknowledges and owns up to his or her own perspectives on the matter under study as a means of providing the consumers of the research with evidence of possible bias that might have influenced how the data were collected and interpreted. In this approach, there is no pretense that the researcher is a completely objective or neutral party. Third, although it is hoped that the respondents will reflect a true cross-section of opinions and viewpoints, they need not be a scientifically selected sample nor is it necessary to have large numbers of respondents. Fewer respondents are asked to provide more in-depth data. In this approach, no preset limits determine when data collection is complete. Rather, the researcher continues to collect information until there is noticeable repetition. Finally, the concept of triangulation is central. *Triangulation* refers to the use of multiple (usually three) data-gathering methods, multiple observers or investigators, and/or multiple perspectives applied to the same data set. A particular interpretation of the data is accepted when a congruence emerges from these various ways of examining and thinking about the data.

The methods of data collection used in qualitative research are varied. The most basic is *interviewing* respondents to obtain their perceptions. Interviews with individuals will vary in the amount of structure allowed, but will always allow the interviewer the freedom to follow tangents in a respondent's discussion in order to capture the description as fully as possible. When interviewing groups of respondents, the focus-group technique (see Item 12.29) is commonly utilized. In both individual and group interviews, process notes and audio recordings are typically used to document the descriptions for later analysis.

A second method commonly used is *case study research.* This approach involves carefully documenting the experience of a single individual, family, organization, or community over time and identifying patterns, themes, and so on that emerge. In *ethnographic research,* the researcher gains an in-depth understanding of the perceptions, values, and experiences of others by immersing himself or herself in the repondent's physical, social, and cultural environment. *Sociometry* is a procedure used to examine the relationships (e.g., likes and dislikes, affinity and disdain) among people. A tool commonly used in such sociometric studies is the *sociogram,* which maps the nature and frequency of interactions among people in order to understand their relationships. The *Delphi Technique* provides a written dialog in which a statement about a subject is presented, each member of an expert panel comments, the statement is revised and circulated again along with the comments of each respondent, and a rating of relative agreement or disagreement with the statement is made. A Delphi study usually involves at least three cycles of this process until sufficient consensus among the respondents is achieved. Finally, a number of *unobtrusive measures,* such as archival data from existing records or recorded observations that do not require direct interaction with the subjects, provide another method of qualitative data collection.

Content analysis of the documented data is used to organize the data into categories. A first step is to code the data to form categories (i.e., *open coding*) combined with *axial coding* that is intended to facilitate discovering linkages among the categories. Several computer software programs (Weitzman and Miles 1995) have been developed to facilitate the reduction of massive data into categories for analysis. In addition, a goal of qualitative research is to buttress the summary results with sufficient description, usually in the respondent's own words, to make clear its meaning.

SELECTED BIBLIOGRAPHY

Berg, Bruce L. *Qualitative Research Methods for the Social Sciences,* 2nd ed. Boston: Allyn and Bacon, 1995.

Miles, Matthew B., and A. Michael Huberman. *Qualitative Data Analysis: An Expanded Sourcebook,* 2nd ed. Newbury Park, Calif.: Sage, 1994.

Sherman, Edmund, and William J. Reid. *Qualitative Research in Social Work.* New York: Columbia University Press, 1995.

Weitzman, Eben A., and Matthew B. Miles. *Computer Programs for Qualitative Analysis.* Newbury Park, Calif.: Sage, 1995.

10.15 Understanding Quantitative Data

PURPOSE: To make sound judgments about the appropriateness of quantitative research studies and to accurately interpret statistical data reported in the social work literature.

DISCUSSION: Much of the knowledge development activity in social work involves **quantitative research.** In their purest form, these methodologies seek to imitate the scientific methods used in the hard sciences. Key steps might include, for example: (1) hypothesize about the effectiveness of a certain type of intervention, (2) identify and isolate relevant elements for careful study, (3) select a statistically valid sample from the population being studied, (4) utilize control groups to reduce the influence of other factors on the outcome, (5) apply the intervention to an experimental group, (6) collect data and subject data to statistical analysis, and (7) draw conclusions. In Western society, where science is highly valued, this approach is often viewed as the most valid way to gain knowledge.

In research regarding human beings, it is always difficult and sometimes inappropriate to adhere rigidly to the principles of scientific inquiry. For example, can one ethically encourage or require a person to remain in an abusive family in order to be part of a control group during the study of a domestic violence intervention? As another example, consider how difficult it is to adequately match the people selected for a control and an experimental group; individuals, their life experiences, and their situations are very diverse. Despite the inherent difficulty of using rigorous study designs, it is possible to gain some understanding of the relationships between professional actions and client outcomes by collecting sufficient amounts of data from clients who have and who have not had the opportunity to experience a particular intervention or helping method. The application of statistical analysis is central to the task of sorting through such data and discovering and explaining the conections between various client characteristics, life experiences, circumstances and situations, the actions of a professional, the services of an agency, and client outcomes.

Few social workers consider themselves experts in statistical analysis, yet many journal articles present statistical analyses that must be understood if one is to base practice decisions on conclusions from that research. Like foreign languages, one must use statistical procedures on a regular basis before they become easy to read and interpret. Further, the title of one statistics book, *How to Lie with Statistics* (Huff 1954), signals an important caution—statistics are tools that help make decisions, but should not dictate practice choices. In other words, judgment is required to determine the usefulness and appropriateness of any statistical analyses.

Statistics are numerical representations of the characteristics of individual cases—in social work those cases are usually people. *Characteristics* or *variables* are attributes or properties of the cases that the researcher has chosen to define and observe in order to increase understanding of how that variable acts under certain conditions. The groups of cases selected for study may be either *samples* (part of a population) or the *populations* themselves (i.e., the total cases to which the researcher may want to generalize the results). At times, information about the total population actually exists and can be compared to a sample of the population. At other times, characteristics of the population are theoretical or estimated as part of the statistical analysis.

Statistical analysis involves assembling, analyzing, summarizing, and interpreting numerical data. Knowledge of relatively few statistical tests will allow the social worker to read most research reports that appear in professional journals. In fact, a review of three years' issues of NASW's journal, *Social Work,* indicated that knowledge of just 15 statistical procedures (see below) would make it possible to understand most of the research reported in the profession's primary journal. To interpret accurately this statistical information, it is useful to keep three guideposts in mind.

Guidepost 1: The Purpose of the Statistical Procedure

The reader of research reports should be aware of the reason the statistical procedure was applied. The most frequent reason statistics were used in the articles in *Social Work* was to describe the respondents or the responses. Those **descriptive statistics** permit the summarization of raw data into a more useable and communicable format. Descriptive statistics are often referred to as *data-reduction tools* because they reduce data from many responses to a single summary statistic. Some statistics consistently reported in the literature are frequency distributions, percentages, measures of central tendency (i.e., reflections of the most typical response from a group of respondents), and measures of variability (i.e., descriptions of the spread in the data or how the subjects are disbursed).

A second, and more complex, set of statistical tools are known as **inferential statistics.** They permit the researcher to draw certain conclusions from a randomly selected sample about the larger population from which the sample was drawn. These statistics include *measures of difference* that determine if the results from a sample were sufficiently different from an expected result to conclude that the finding was not due to chance and thus could be interpreted as being "statistically significant." Tests of significance are either reported at the exact level (e.g., $p = .02$, or the likelihood is 2 in 100 that the result would occur by chance) or that the result was greater or less than an established criterion for judging the result significant. In the social sciences the typical criterion for accepting a finding as significant is $p = .05$, meaning that the probability is equal to or less than 5 in 100 that the outcome would occur by chance.

A second frequently used set of inferential statistics are *measures of association.* This group of tests measure the correlation between two or more variables. In social research it is seldom possible to clearly establish a cause and effect relationship but it is possible to identify patterns of interaction among variables. If the relationships are completely random, they would show zero (0.00) correlation and one would conclude that the variables are unrelated. If there is a positive relationship (i.e., one variable increases when the other increases), the correlation coefficient would be somewhere between +0.01 and +1.00. When a negative relationship exists (i.e., one variable increases when the other decreases), the correlation coefficient would fall between –0.01 and –1.00. Although there is no established rule for interpreting correlation coefficients, Elifson, Runyon, and Haber (1990) suggest the following guidelines:

+ or – 0.01 to 0.30	=	a weak relationship
+ or – 0.31 to 0.70	=	a moderate relationship
+ or – 0.71 and above	=	a strong relationship

These guidelines for interpretation are predicated on the relationship having been judged "significant" from one's practice knowledge as well as on the basis of a test of significance (above) or a statistic derived from the measure of association. Further, depending on the nature of the data being examined and the experience of previous inquiries on this topic, these interpretations might appropriately be adjusted and should be noted by the author(s) of the research report.

In addition to the bivariant (two variables or two samples) statistical tests described next, there are additional tests for significant difference and measures of association that can be used when there are three or more variables or samples. These multivariant statistical procedures include multiple regression analysis, cluster analysis, and factor analysis. Except for the description of the Analysis of Variance (ANOVA) statistic provided below, a presentation of these more complex statistical tests is beyond the scope of this book and the reader is referred to a statistics text for further information.

Guidepost 2: Level of Measurement

The application of many statistical tests depends on the level of the data being analyzed. At the most basic level, data are simply grouped into different mutually exclusive categories, one category is not considered to have more or less value than another. Such information is termed *nominal data.* Gender, ethnicity, and various yes or no questions (e.g., parent or nonparent) are examples of nominal-level data. *Ordinal data* represent information that can be ranked from low to high, but for which it would not be reasonable to assume that there is equal value in each category. For example, many scales used in the social work literature are three- or five-point ratings of a factor (e.g., frequently, occasionally, seldom) but there is no assumption of equal intervals between ratings—only indication of more or less, or higher or lower. For example, a rating scale may be used to indicate that Client A has higher self-esteem than Client B, but in measuring a variable like self-esteem, one is not able to say that Client A has three times more self-esteem than Client B. *Interval or ratio data* on the other hand, assume the categories are divided into equal units and thus permit more precise measures. Interval-level data might include client age or the population of the community served by social workers. As the consumer of a research report or article, it is important to be sure that the statistical procedures selected were appropriate for the level of data collected in the study. Otherwise, the statistic may misrepresent the outcome.

Guidepost 3: Type of Sample

The type of sample (in combination with the level of measurement) determines which statistical procedures can be appropriately used. The most powerful (i.e., more rigorous in a mathematical sense) statistical tests are *parametric tests,* which require independent or random samples and interval- or ratio-level data for at least one of the variables. For a sample to meet the sampling criteria for parametric tests, the different cases being compared must have been independently assigned to groups or randomly selected and there must be reason to assume that the population from which the sample was drawn has a normal distribution. *Nonparamatric statistics,* in contrast, are less powerful predictors but allow work with data that are nominal and ordinal. Also, since they compare the outcomes observed in the study with expected outcomes for those respondents, they do not assume a normal distribution. Nonparametric statistics fit almost all research situations and are frequently used in social work research.

Some of the statistics commonly reported in the social work literature are described here. The reader is urged to see the Selected Bibliography or other statistics books to acquire more in-depth knowledge of these and other statistical tests. Each procedure is identified by the symbol that is commonly used in journal articles.

ANOVA
: *Analysis of Variance.* This test examines the variation in the means of two or more independent or predictor variables to determine the likelihood that the results could have occurred by chance. This parametric test requires that the dependent variable is measured by interval-level data, while the predictor variable or variables may be nominal or ordinal. The ANOVA is similar to the t-test (see below) but can also be applied when there are three or more groups of data being compared. By consulting an F table, the probability (e.g., $p < .05$) of a distribution occurring by chance can be estimated.

DF
: *Degrees of Freedom. DF* indicates the number of cells in a set of data that are free to vary. This freedom to vary is an important factor in estimating the probability of an outcome occurring by chance. *DF* is computed by multiplying the number of rows minus one in a table by the number of columns minus one. Thus a 2×3 table would have 2 *DF*, whereas a 3×4 table would have 6 *DF*. *DF* is reported to allow the reader to understand how the researcher interpreted the probability tables for the different statistical tests.

f
: *Frequency.* An *f* will usually be reported in a table and simply reflects the number of cases in each category or interval.

F-ratio
: *F.* Usually based on an ANOVA or a multiple regression analysis, this parametric test of significance is a measure of variability that requires interval or ratio data. It tests for difference between the standard deviations of two variables or samples. The *F*-ratio compares estimates of variance *between* the samples with variance *within* the samples. If the between-group variance is higher than the within-group variance, increasing the likelihood that the variance did not occur by chance, the *F*-ratio will be larger. The *F* value has little meaning until it is applied to a table that identifies the probability of that distribution occurring by chance.

Mdn
: *Median.* This is a measure of central tendency that may be used with ordinal- or interval-level data. It is the midpoint in a distribution (i.e., the score above which and below which 50 percent of the cases lie).

Mo
: *Mode.* This is a measure of central tendency that may be used with all levels of data. It reflects the value or category that includes the most cases in a distribution and thus can be applied to nominal

data. In some distributions more than one category may have the same number of cases, resulting in a bimodal or multimodal distribution.

N   *Number.* The *N* reports the total number of cases that are being considered in the statistical procedure. The *N* may vary in different analyses of a data set due to incomplete responses or test requirements that may necessitate the exclusion of some cases.

%   *Percent.* A percentage is a reflection of the share of the cases that would fall into a category if the total were 100. It is computed by dividing the frequency (*f*) in a category by the total number of cases (*N*) and multiplying by 100.

p   *Probability.* A *p*-value reports the likelihood of a particular distribution occurring by chance if a normal distribution is assumed. Thus, the lower the likelihood of a distribution occurring by chance, the more confidence can be placed in the assumption that the variables being tested indeed affected the outcome.

r   *Pearson Product-Moment Correlation Coefficient.* The *r* is a correlation coefficient (i.e., a number that represents the association between two variables). It reflects the tendency of high or low scores for one variable to regularly be associated with high or low scores for another variable. Therefore, it is possible to predict the value of one set of scores by knowing another. The nearer the *r*-score is to +1.00 or −1.00, the greater is the likelihood that the items vary together (i.e., are associated with each other). The *r* is a parametric test that requires interval-level data. (*Note: The Spearman Rank Order Correlation Coefficient* (r_s) is a similar nonparametric test that can be applied to ordinal or ranked data. It examines the association between pairs of variables and can be computed with a relatively small number of pairs [i.e., less than 30] in the sample.)

Range   *Range.* The range is a measure of variability that reports the span between the lowest and highest scores of the cases in the sample. Data must be at least ordinal to compute the range.

SD   *Standard Deviation.* SD tells how much dispersion from the mean exists in the scores of the sample or population being studied. The more the scores deviate from the mean, the greater the standard deviation score. When comparing samples or groups as part of a study, the ones with the largest SD scores have the greatest variability in distribution, whereas the respondents in groups with smaller SDs are more like the mean (or average) and thus are more homogeneous. In a normal distribution, about 68 percent of all cases fall within one standard deviation from the mean (34 percent above and 34 percent below) and 95 percent fall within two standard deviations from the mean.

t-test   *Student's t.* The *t*-test is a parametric test of significant difference between the means of two samples (or a sample and the population from which the sample was drawn). At times it is also used to test the significance of the difference between two coefficients of correlation. If the means differ substantially (i.e., a higher score), it is likely that the difference was not a result of sampling error or chance, and it is reasonable to assume that the difference is associated with actual variations in the factors being examined. A *t* table provides statistical estimates of the probability that the results might be due to chance (e.g., $p < .05$).

$\overline{X}$ *Mean.* The arithmetic mean is a measure of central tendency that requires interval- or ratio-level data. It is the sum of the values for a variable divided by the number (*N*) of cases.

X^2 *Chi Square.* X^2 is a nonparametric test of significance that may be applied with nominal data. In essence, it compares the observed and expected frequencies for a variable to determine if the differences found could be explained by chance. Until the chi square value is translated to a probability score (e.g., $p < .05$), it has little meaning.

SELECTED BIBLIOGRAPHY

Craft, John L. *Statistics and Data Analysis for Social Workers,* 2nd ed. Itasca, Ill.: F. E. Peacock, 1990.

DiLeonardi, Joan W., and Patrick Almond Curtis. *What to Do When the Numbers Are In.* Chicago: Nelson-Hall, 1988.

Elifson, Kirk W., Richard P. Runyon, and Audrey Haber. *Fundamentals of Social Statistics,* 2nd ed. New York: McGraw-Hill, 1990

Huff, Darrell. *How to Lie with Statistics.* New York: W. W. Norton, 1954.

Pilcher, Donald M. *Data Analysis for the Helping Professions: A Practical Guide.* Newbury Park, Calif.: Sage, 1990.

Vogt, W. Paul. *Dictionary of Statistics and Methodology: A Nontechnical Guide for the Social Sciences.* Newbury Park, Calif.: Sage, 1993.

Weinbach, Robert W., and Richard M. Grinnell, Jr. *Statistics for Social Workers,* 3rd ed. New York: Longman, 1995

10.16   Improving the Social Work Image

PURPOSE: To build public understanding and a more positive image of social workers.

DISCUSSION: Social work suffers from public misunderstanding and a negative image. The typical citizen has little understanding of what social workers actually do and the impressions they have are often erroneous or incomplete. On TV and in the movies, the social worker is often portrayed as either a judgmental and mindless busybody or someone who breaks up families by removing children for no good reason. All too often, the only newspaper or magazine articles that mention social workers are ones describing how the acts or omissions of an agency or a social worker contributed to a client's harm or distress. Additional image problems are created when the media uses the term *social worker* in a generic manner and applies it to all human services workers.

Social workers want a better image and want to be appreciated and understood by the public. They would also like the higher pay that comes with a high-status profession. However, such changes will not result from wishful thinking; they must be made to happen. The image will begin to change in a positive direction when it becomes evident to the public that social workers are truly experts in what they do and are able to get results that nonsocial workers are unable to match. The financial rewards and the status associated with certain other professions (e.g., medicine, engineering, accounting) came about not through exhortation but rather because their members completed long and difficult training, acquired a definite expertise, and assumed a legal responsibility for the outcome of their decisions and actions.

Social work's image problem is, in part, rooted in its history and its association with devalued groups (e.g., the poor) and with controversial and unpopular causes (e.g., the expansion of governmental programs to address social problems). However, individual social workers, by their own acts and omissions, also contribute to the problem. For example, many avoid describing themselves as social workers; they prefer to use titles such as therapists, counselors, administrators, and so on. Consequently, whatever the public finds positive and praiseworthy about their performance is associated with some other occupational title. In other words, by avoiding the title of social worker, they miss opportunities to inform the public about social work and to correct public misperceptions. Social workers cannot expect the public to change its attitude until social workers themselves are openly proud of their profession. In order to promote a greater public understanding, social workers should adhere to certain guidelines.

1. Use the title of social worker. If you must also use words such as *counseling* or *psychotherapy* to clarify your role, describe yourself as, for example: "I am a social worker—I provide psychotherapy to troubled youth," "I am a social worker specializing in the planning and development of services for persons with AIDS," "I am a social worker who administers a family support program," "I am a social worker who teaches at a university," and so on.

2. Assume a personal responsibility for improving the profession's image. Three actions are essential. First, provide the highest quality service possible—get results. Second, behave in a highly professional and completely responsible manner when dealing with clients and the public. Third, inform those observing your performance that you are a social worker.

3. When being interviewed for a news story, make sure the reporter understands that you are a social worker and that you have a degree in social work, and perhaps describe the special training that has prepared you for the work you do. Always operate on the assumption that reporters and the public at large have little or no idea that social work is a distinct profession. Otherwise, you will probably be termed a *sociologist, welfare worker, counselor, or agency worker.*

4. Speak of your work with respect. If you truly value what you do, others are more likely to adopt a positive attitude toward both you and your work. Avoid any action or association that would damage your credibility and trustworthiness.

5. Be very careful and thoughtful about what you say in public. Always anticipate how your words, manner, and actions will be perceived by the public and by the clients served by social workers and social agencies. Public statements must be accurate, clear, and respectful of others.

6. Work with other social workers and professional associations (e.g., the NASW) to plan and implement a media and public relations campaign aimed at educating the public about social work and social workers in your community.

7. Whenever a news story uses the term *social work* or *social worker* in an erroneous manner, send the newspaper, magazine, or radio or TV station a letter that explains the error. Also send a packet of informational materials that describes the nature of the profession and social work activities.

SELECTED BIBLIOGRAPHY

Barker, Robert. *Social Work in Private Practice.* Washington, D.C.: NASW, 1991.

Bromley, D. B. *Reputation, Image and Impression Management.* New York: John Wiley and Sons, 1993.

Hopps, June, and Pauline Collins. "Social Work Profession Overview." In *Encyclopedia of Social Work,* 19th ed., Vol. 3, edited by Richard Edwards. Washington, D.C.: NASW, 1995, pp. 902–908.

Lauffer, Armand. *Working in Social Work.* Newbury Park, Calif.: Sage, 1987.

APPENDIX 10.1

NASW Code of Ethics

Preamble

This code is intended to serve as a guide to the everyday conduct of members of the social work profession and as a basis for the adjudication of issues in ethics when the conduct of social workers is alleged to deviate from the standards expressed or implied in this code. It represents standards of ethical behavior for social workers in professional relationships with those served, with colleagues, with employers, with other individuals and professions, and with the community and society as a whole. It also embodies standards of ethical behavior governing individual conduct to the extent that such conduct is associated with an individual's status and identity as a social worker.

This code is based on the fundamental values of the social work profession that include the worth, dignity, and uniqueness of all persons as well as their rights and opportunities. It is also based on the nature of social work, which fosters conditions that promote these values.

In subscribing to and abiding by this code, the social worker is expected to view ethical responsibility in as inclusive a context as each situation demands and within which ethical judgment is required. The social worker is expected to take into consideration all the principles in this code that have a bearing upon any situation in which ethical judgment is to be exercised and professional intervention or conduct is planned. The course of action that the social worker chooses is expected to be consistent with the spirit as well as the letter of this code.

In itself, this code does not represent a set of rules that will prescribe all the behaviors of social workers in all the complexities of professional life. Rather, it offers general principles to guide conduct, and the judicious appraisal of conduct, in situations that have ethical implications. It provides the basis for making judgments about ethical actions before or after they occur. Frequently, the particular situation determines the ethical principles that apply and the manner of their application. In such cases, not only the particular ethical principles are taken into immediate consideration, but also the entire code and its spirit. Specific applications of ethical principles must be judged within the context in which they are being considered. Ethical behavior in a given situation must satisfy not only the judgment of the individual social worker, but also the judgment of an unbiased jury of professional peers.

This code should not be used as an instrument to deprive any social worker of the opportunity or freedom to practice with complete professional integrity; nor should any disciplinary action be taken on the basis of this code without maximum provision for safeguarding the rights of the social worker affected.

Reprinted with permission from NASW, *Code of Ethics.*

The ethical behavior of social workers results not from edict, but from a personal commitment of the individual. This code is offered to affirm the will and zeal of all social workers to be ethical and to act ethically in all that they do as social workers.

The following codified ethical principles should guide social workers in the various roles and relationships and at the various levels of responsibility in which they function professionally. These principles also serve as a basis for the adjudication by the National Association of Social Workers of issues in ethics.

In subscribing to this code, social workers are required to cooperate in its implementation and abide by any disciplinary rulings based on it. They should also take adequate measures to discourage, prevent, expose, and correct the unethical conduct of colleagues. Finally, social workers should be equally ready to defend and assist colleagues unjustly charged with unethical conduct.

The NASW Code of Ethics

I. *The Social Worker's Conduct and Comportment as a Social Worker*

A. *Propriety*—The social worker should maintain high standards of personal conduct in the capacity or identity as social worker.

1. The private conduct of the social worker is a personal matter to the same degree as is any other person's, except when such conduct compromises the fulfillment of professional responsibilities.
2. The social worker should not participate in, condone, or be associated with dishonesty, fraud, deceit, or misrepresentation.
3. The social worker should distinguish clearly between statements and actions made as a private individual and as a representative of the social work profession or an organization or group.

B. *Competence and Professional Development*—The social worker should strive to become and remain proficient in professional practice and the performance of professional functions.

1. The social worker should accept responsibility or employment only on the basis of existing competence or the intention to acquire the necessary competence.
2. The social worker should not misrepresent professional qualifications, education, experience, or affiliations.
3. The social worker should not allow his or her personal problems, psychosocial distress, substance abuse, or mental health difficulties to interfere with professional judgment and performance or jeopardize the best interests of those for whom the social worker has a professional responsibility.
4. The social worker whose personal problems, psychosocial distress, substance abuse, or mental health difficulties interfere with professional judgment and performance should immediately seek consultation and

take appropriate remedial action by seeking professional help, making adjustments in workload, terminating practice, or taking any other steps necessary to protect clients and others.

C. *Service*—The social worker should regard as primary the service obligation of the social work profession.

    1. The social worker should retain ultimate responsibility for the quality and extent of the service that individual assumes, assigns, or performs.

    2. The social worker should act to prevent practices that are inhumane or discriminatory against any person or group of persons.

D. *Integrity*—The social worker should act in accordance with the highest standards of professional integrity and impartiality.

    1. The social worker should be alert to and resist the influences and pressures that interfere with the exercise of professional discretion and impartial judgment required for the performance of professional functions.

    2. The social worker should not exploit professional relationships for personal gain.

E. *Scholarship and Research*—The social worker engaged in study and research should be guided by the conventions of scholarly inquiry.

    1. The social worker engaged in research should consider carefully its possible consequences for human beings.

    2. The social worker engaged in research should ascertain that the consent of the participants in the research is voluntary and informed, without any implied deprivation or penalty for refusal to participate, and with due regard for the participants' privacy and dignity.

    3. The social worker engaged in research should protect participants from unwarranted physical or mental discomfort, distress, harm, danger, or deprivation.

    4. The social worker who engages in the evaluation of services or cases should discuss them only for professional purposes and only with persons directly and professionally concerned with them.

    5. Information obtained about participants in research should be treated as confidential.

    6. The social worker should take credit only for work actually done in connection with scholarly and research endeavors and credit contributions made by others.

II. *The Social Worker's Ethical Responsibility to Clients*

F. *Primacy of Clients' Interests*—The social worker's primary responsibility is to clients.

    1. The social worker should serve clients with devotion, loyalty, determination, and the maximum application of professional skill and competence.

    2. The social worker should not exploit relationships with clients for personal advantage.

3. The social worker should not practice, condone, facilitate, or collaborate with any form of discrimination on the basis of race, color, sex, sexual orientation, age, religion, national origin, marital status, political belief, mental or physical handicap, or any other preference or personal characteristic, condition, or status.

4. The social worker should avoid relationships or commitments that conflict with the interests of clients.

5. The social worker should under no circumstances engage in sexual activities with clients.

6. The social worker should provide clients with accurate and complete information regarding the extent and nature of the services available to them.

7. The social worker should apprise clients of their risks, rights, opportunities, and obligations associated with social service to them.

8. The social worker should seek advice and counsel of colleagues and supervisors whenever such consultation is in the best interest of clients.

9. The social worker should terminate service to clients, and professional relationships with them, when such service and relationships are no longer required or no longer serve the clients' needs or interests.

10. The social worker should withdraw services precipitously only under unusual circumstances, giving careful consideration to all factors in the situation and taking care to minimize possible adverse effects.

11. The social worker who anticipates the termination or interruption of service to clients should notify clients promptly and seek the transfer, referral, or continuation of service in relation to the clients' needs and preferences

G. *Rights and Prerogatives of Clients*—The social worker should make every effort to foster maximum self-determination on the part of clients.

1. When the social worker must act on behalf of a client who has been adjudged legally incompetent, the social worker should safeguard the interests and rights of that client.

2. When another individual has been legally authorized to act in behalf of a client, the social worker should deal with that person always with the client's best interest in mind.

3. The social worker should not engage in any action that violates or diminishes the civil or legal rights of clients.

H. *Confidentiality and Privacy*—The social worker should respect the privacy of clients and hold in confidence all information obtained in the course of professional service.

1. The social worker should share with others confidences revealed by clients, without their consent, only for compelling professional reasons.

2. The social worker should inform clients fully about the limits of confidentiality in a given situation, the purposes for which information is obtained, and how it may be used.

3. The social worker should afford clients reasonable access to any official social work records concerning them.
4. When providing clients with access to records, the social worker should take due care to protect the confidences of others contained in those records.
5. The social worker should obtain informed consent of clients before taping, recording, or permitting third party observation of their activities.

I. **Fees**—When setting fees, the social worker should ensure that they are fair, reasonable, considerate, and commensurate with the service performed and with due regard for the clients' ability to pay.
1. The social worker should not accept anything of value for making a referral.

III. *The Social Worker's Ethical Responsibility to Colleagues*
J. *Respect, Fairness, and Courtesy*—The social worker should treat colleagues with respect, courtesy, fairness, and good faith.
1. The social worker should cooperate with colleagues to promote professional interests and concerns.
2. The social worker should respect confidences shared by colleagues in the course of their professional relationships and transactions.
3. The social worker should create and maintain conditions of practice that facilitate ethical and competent professional performance by colleagues.
4. The social worker should treat with respect, and represent accurately and fairly, the qualifications, views, and findings of colleagues and use appropriate channels to express judgments on these matters.
5. The social worker who replaces or is replaced by a colleague in professional practice should act with consideration for the interest, character, and reputation of that colleague.
6. The social worker should not exploit a dispute between a colleague and employers to obtain a position or otherwise advance the social worker's interest.
7. The social worker should seek arbitration or mediation when conflicts with colleagues require resolution for compelling professional reasons.
8. The social worker should extend to colleagues of other professions the same respect and cooperation that is extended to social work colleagues.
9. The social worker who serves as an employer, supervisor, or mentor to colleagues should make orderly and explicit arrangements regarding the conditions of their continuing professional relationship.
10. The social worker who has the responsibility for employing and evaluating the performance of other staff members, should fulfill such responsibility in a fair, considerate, and equitable manner, on the basis of clearly enunciated criteria.
11. The social worker who has the responsibility for evaluating the performance of employees, supervisees, or students should share evaluations with them.

12. The social worker should not use a professional position vested with power, such as that of employer, supervisor, teacher, or consultant, to his or her advantage or to exploit others.
13. The social worker who has direct knowledge of a social work colleague's impairment due to personal problems, psychosocial distress, substance abuse, or mental health difficulties should consult with that colleague and assist the colleague in taking remedial action.

K. *Dealing with Colleagues' Clients*—The social worker has the responsibility to relate to the clients of colleagues with full professional consideration.
   1. The social worker should not assume professional responsibility for the clients of another agency or a colleague without appropriate communication with that agency or colleague.
   2. The social worker who serves the clients of colleagues, during a temporary absence or emergency, should serve those clients with the same consideration as that afforded any client.

IV. *The Social Worker's Responsibility to Employers and Employing Organizations*

L. *Commitments to Employing Organization*—The social worker should adhere to commitments made to the employing organization.
   1. The social worker should work to improve the employing agency's policies and procedures, and the efficiency and effectiveness of its services.
   2. The social worker should not accept employment or arrange student field placements in an organization which is currently under public sanction by NASW for violating personnel standards, or imposing limitations on or penalties for professional actions on behalf of clients.
   3. The social worker should act to prevent and eliminate discrimination in the employing organization's work assignments and in its employment policies and practices.
   4. The social worker should use with scrupulous regard, and only for the purpose for which they are intended, the resources of the employing organization.

V. *The Social Worker's Ethical Responsibility to the Social Work Profession*

M. *Maintaining the Integrity of the Profession*—The social worker should uphold and advance the values, ethics, knowledge, and mission of the profession.
   1. The social worker should protect and enhance the dignity and integrity of the profession and should be responsible and vigorous in discussion and criticism of the profession.
   2. The social worker should take action through appropriate channels against unethical conduct by any other member of the profession.
   3. The social worker should act to prevent the unauthorized and unqualified practice of social work.
   4. The social worker should make no misrepresentations in advertising as to qualifications, competence, service, or results to be achieved.

N. *Community Service*—The social worker should assist the profession in making social services available to the general public.

1. The social worker should contribute time and professional expertise to activities that promote respect for the utility, the integrity, and the competence of the social work profession.
2. The social worker should support the formulation, development, enactment and implementation of social policies of concern to the profession.

O. *Development of Knowledge*—The social worker should take responsibility for identifying, developing, and fully utilizing knowledge for professional practice.

1. The social worker should base practice upon recognized knowledge relevant to social work.
2. The social worker should critically examine, and keep current with emerging knowledge relevant to social work.
3. The social worker should contribute to the knowledge base of social work and share research knowledge and practice wisdom with colleagues.

VI. *The Social Worker's Ethical Responsibility to Society*

P. *Promoting the General Welfare*—The social worker should promote the general welfare of society.

1. The social worker should act to prevent and eliminate discrimination against any person or group on the basis of race, color, sex, sexual orientation, age, religion, national origin, marital status, political belief, mental or physical handicap, or any other preference or personal characteristic, condition, or status.
2. The social worker should act to ensure that all persons have access to the resources, services, and opportunities which they require.
3. The social worker should act to expand choice and opportunity for all persons, with special regard for disadvantaged or oppressed groups and persons.
4. The social worker should promote conditions that encourage respect for the diversity of cultures which constitute American society.
5. The social worker should provide appropriate professional services in public emergencies.
6. The social worker should advocate changes in policy and legislation to improve social conditions and to promote social justice.
7. The social worker should encourage informed participation by the public in shaping social policies and institutions.

Part IV Techniques and Guidelines for Phases of the Planned Change Process

Many social work supervisors have heard practicum students and new social workers ask a question such as "Well, I think I understand the basic theory and the general principles of working with people, but what specifically should I do when I see Mrs. Jones and her daughter this afternoon?" Obviously, these social workers have discovered that there is a difference between the *knowing* and the *doing* in social work practice. They sense the need for some specific direction on what to do with the client.

Part IV of this book addresses this need. As was explained in the Preface, the authors chose to prepare a book that concentrates on techniques and guidelines rather than on theory. This decision reflects their belief that many texts do an excellent job of presenting the theoretical frameworks of practice, yet few provide the concrete guidance so often requested by students and new workers.

It is expected that a social worker will engage in providing both direct and indirect services. *Direct practice* includes those activities that involve face-to-face contact with a client or client group, as well as those activities that are planned to support specific clients. This might include, for example, social treatment, family counseling, case assessment, case management, advocating for services needed by a client, and so on. By contrast, *indirect practice* reflects the actions a social worker might take to prevent social problems from emerging or to improve the capacity of an agency or community to respond to existing problems. This form of practice includes activities such as public education, fund-raising, influencing legislative decisions, agency administration, and program evaluation. In Part IV, the direct practice techniques and guidelines are located in Section A of each chapter and those for indirect practice can be found in Section B.

The chapters in this part correspond to the phases of the change process described in Chapter 7. Chapter 11, "Intake and Engagement," is concerned with the beginning phase of a professional relationship. It focuses mostly on getting started with clients in the direct services, but it also gives attention to aspects of getting started as a practitioner in a new agency or new community and also with the process of bringing new employees and volunteers into an agency.

On occasion, getting started with a client in the direct services can be downright scary for the worker if he or she must deal with an angry, involuntary client or one who is potentially violent. The social worker must be able to engage a wide variety of clients, clarify their presenting problems, and help them connect to the agency. If the agency cannot provide the needed service, the worker must be able to use the referral process to link the client to a more appropriate resource.

Chapter 12, "Data Collection and Assessment," recognizes that within a relatively brief period of time, the social worker must gather information about the client and the presenting problem or concern and then draw inferences and formulate working hypotheses on what approaches might prove useful. These basic steps are required whether the client is an individual, a family, a small group, or an organization. Most of the techniques and guidelines presented are ones that help the worker gather information about individual and family functioning, but some items describe approaches to assessing groups, agencies, and communities.

Chapter 13, "Planning and Contracting," presents techniques and guidelines aimed at helping the worker and the client arrive at agreed upon intervention goals and objectives. The failure to formulate a clear and feasible plan is one of the most common errors made by human services professionals whether they are working with a family or an agency task force. A plan gives focus and direction to the change process. To be useful, that plan must grow from honest and open exchanges—and sometimes disagreement—among all involved.

Chapter 14, "Intervention and Monitoring," provides a sampling of both direct practice and indirect practice techniques and guidelines. These 55 separate items range from special approaches to interviewing a person with mental retardation to writing a grant proposal. Essentially, these are the "tools of the trade"—the action or behavioral component of a professional's performance. Interestingly, they are not given a lot of attention in the typical social work classroom, perhaps because there are so many that it is hard to decide which are important for all students to learn. All too often, these techniques are either not learned at all or learned in a rather haphazard manner, over many years, from a supervisor, from a co-worker, or at an occasional workshop. The selections included in Chapter 14 will alert the student and new social worker to the wide variety of techniques available for use in practice.

Chapter 15, "Evaluation and Termination," anticipates the practical problems associated with the evaluation of an intervention. Figuring out how to evaluate one's practice is a real struggle for most social workers. Few have either the time or agency support necessary to properly evaluate their work. Yet, the worker has an ethical obligation to determine if he or she has been effective. Chapter 15 provides some relatively simple evaluation techniques that will help the worker examine his or her own performance and the effectiveness of a program or agency.

Intake and Engagement

INTRODUCTION

This chapter presents guidelines and techniques for use during the beginning phase of the change process. In the direct services, this is often known as the *intake phase*. For indirect practice, this is thought of as the *start-up phase*. Including these activities in a single chapter is in keeping with a generalist perspective on practice and is intended to remind the reader that a social worker's intervention may take a variety of forms and move in a number of directions depending on the nature of the client's problem or concern.

SECTION A
TECHNIQUES AND GUIDELINES FOR DIRECT PRACTICE

The intake period and, in particular, the first meeting between worker and client tend to be pattern setting. This is a time when first impressions are formed. If things get off to a good start, positive interaction is likely to follow. If things get off to a bad start, a significant barrier to the helping process has been erected. It is during intake that the person seeking help decides whether to become a client. What happens in the first meeting strongly influences that decision and usually determines whether the client returns for a second interview or group session. In cases involving the involuntary client, what happens during the initial meeting will largely determine whether the social worker can eventually overcome the client's resistance to agency involvement.

For the inexperienced worker, the engagement of certain types of clients can be particularly difficult. For this reason, guidelines for working with the involuntary client, the hard-to-reach client, the chemically dependent client, the manipulative client, and the dangerous client are offered here. Also included in this chapter is guidance on using the in-home interview, obtaining information from other agencies, making a referral, and using problem checklists as a tool for facilitating engagement.

The social worker will be involved in most and possibly all of the following *activities during the intake and engagement phase.*

1. Greet for the first time and speak with the client in a way that is nonthreatening and puts the client at ease.
2. Demonstrate a genuine interest in the client and a concern for his or her problem or situation.
3. Learn about the client's expectations of the agency and worker.
4. Identify any fears or misunderstandings the client may have about the social worker, the agency, or its services.
5. Explain what the worker and agency can and cannot do to address the client's concerns.
6. Explain pertinent eligibility requirements and any special procedures that must be followed or fees that must be paid in order to receive services.
7. Address the client's possible ambivalence about talking with the worker or receiving agency services.
8. Decide if the client's concerns can be addressed by the worker and agency or if a referral to another agency is necessary.
9. Assess the urgency of the client's needs or presenting problem and attend to the crisis or emergency, if one exists.
10. Explain the responsibilities that both the client and worker will assume during the helping process.
11. Explain in what way and to what degree the client will be able to exercise control over the helping process.
12. Explain to the client that he or she will need to provide the information (in some cases, very personal information) needed to assess the problem or situation, formulate short-term and long-term goals, and decide what type of intervention is likely to be most effective.
13. Secure the client's signed release of confidential information (if one is needed) and explain the principles of confidentiality that apply.
14. Complete required agency paperwork associated with intake.
15. Reach tentative agreement on the minimum and, if possible, the maximum number of meetings that will probably be necessary.
16. Reach agreement on the time, place, and frequency of future meetings.

During intake and engagement, the social worker must be especially sensitive to the client's fear of the unknown and *resistance to change*. The need to make even small changes generates some degree of discomfort. Change can be particularly threatening to clients with rather rigid beliefs, attitudes, and behavioral patterns. Fear is at the heart of resistance.

The client typically moves through four *stages of resistance* during the helping process: conflict, defensiveness, resolution, and integration. In the first stage, the client senses a need to make some change; he or she recognizes that there is a different and perhaps a better way of thinking, behaving, or coping with a problem, yet the client wishes to hold on to familiar beliefs, attitudes, and behaviors. Thus, the client experiences ambivalence or a conflict between the old and the new.

When a familiar pattern is threatened, it is normal to feel defensive. If the need to change is apparent to the client, he or she may fairly quickly overcome these feelings. But some clients strongly defend against new ideas and new ways that, if accepted, would force them to acknowledge that their usual ways were ineffective or inappropriate. Feeling threatened, they may hold even tighter to their familiar patterns. Or they may use rationalization to justify themselves. Some may attack the new ways or discredit the social worker. If they feel very threatened, they may withdraw from the helping relationship.

If the client feels understanding and support from the worker, feels some discomfort with the current situation, and feels some hopefulness about the possibility of actually making a change, he or she may decide to take a risk and make at least some small change. As part of this experience, the client may decide it is safe to let go of the old and embrace the new.

In the final stage, the client emerges from this struggle by integrating the new idea or new behavior into other patterns of thought and behavior. It is important to note, however, that this new pattern soon becomes a familiar one; and in the future, the client will resist any threat to this established pattern. In other words, this cycle of conflict, defensiveness, resolution, and integration must be repeated over and over again as the client grows, develops, and makes changes in life.

11.1 The First Telephone Contact

PURPOSE: To engage the person contacting the agency by phone.

DISCUSSION: The first contact between the worker and client is often by telephone. Most clients feel nervous; many are confused and uncertain about what to expect. Others have a distorted idea about what the agency can or will do for them. Thus, the worker must use the time on the telephone to lessen the client's fears, secure at least a general understanding of what the client expects from the agency, and, if appropriate, arrange for the first face-to-face interview. Several guidelines should be kept in mind.

1. Remember that, during a telephone conversation, you cannot read the client's nonverbal behavior. You will not always know if the caller is becoming confused or fearful in response to what you are saying. Keep your messages clear and simple.

2. If speaking with a voluntary client, briefly explore the client's presenting concern or request so you can evaluate the appropriateness of this referral to your agency. However, avoid gathering detailed intake information by phone; that is best done during a face-to-face interview. Also, avoid overwhelming the client with extraneous information about your agency and its services and procedures. Explanations of complex or detailed concerns should also be saved for a face-to-face meeting.

3. If speaking to a involuntary client, it is usually best to confine the phone conversation to arranging the first face-to-face interview unless explanations and encouragement are needed to get the client to attend such a meeting. The involuntary client often has strong negative feelings about having to meet with a social worker. Such feelings are much easier to read and effectively address during a face-to-face interview. (See Item 11.7.)

4. When arranging the first office visit, make sure the client knows the location of your office and your name. Some clients may need guidance on how to use public transportation to reach the agency. In some cases, a follow-up letter should be sent to the client, repeating the time and place of the appointment.

5. Be aware of the client's relationships and roles (e.g., child, spouse, parent, etc.) and assess how family or household members will be impacted by the caller's decision to seek professional assistance. When taking a call from one member of a family or household, ask who else lives in the home and if they know about the caller's request for assistance. If the call is being kept secret from others, ask why secrecy is important. Determine if making the call places the caller in physical danger. Except in situations where secrecy is necessary to protect the caller, encourage the caller to consider involving others (e.g., spouse) in at least the beginning phase of the helping process. Explain that the assessment of the problem will be more accurate and intervention more effective if all persons affected share their perceptions of the problem, their thoughts on what might be helpful, and their views on what changes are possible. Explain that some agency services and interventions may be ineffective unless family members or significant others also become clients. If it sounds as if others might be willing to participate, hold out for such a meeting. If the caller insists that others will not or should not participate, respect his or her wishes and set up a meeting with the caller alone. Later in the helping process you should again try to involve the client's significant others.

SELECTED BIBLIOGRAPHY

Hartman, Ann, and Joan Laird. *Family Centered Social Work Practice.* New York: Free Press, 1983.
Hepworth, Dean, and Jo Ann Larsen. *Direct Social Work Practice,* 4th ed. Pacific Grove, Calif.: Brooks/Cole, 1993.

11.2 The First Face-to-Face Meeting

PURPOSE: To conduct the initial interview in a manner that lays the foundation for a good working relationship.

DISCUSSION: It is quite common to feel a bit nervous when meeting a client for the first time. It can be safely assumed that the client has similar feelings. It is during this first meeting that the worker and client size up each other and form initial impressions. Several guidelines can help the social worker get the interaction off to a good start.

1. Before beginning the first face-to-face session, anticipate what the client might be thinking and feeling. Be prepared to respond in an understanding way to the client's fears, ambivalence, confusion, or anger during a first meeting with a stranger whom the client may perceive as an authority figure.

2. Create a physical arrangement conducive to good communication. For a two-person meeting, chairs should face each other. Chairs for a family interview should be arranged in a circle. Make sure the room temperature is comfortable. Be aware that your body language, how you are dressed, your posture, facial expressions, and gestures all send messages to the client. Try to send a message of respect, caring, and professionalism.

3. If the client requested the meeting, begin with some introductory remarks and possibly some small talk, but soon move on to the concerns that brought the client to the agency. If you initiated the interview, begin by explaining who you are, who you represent, and why you need to speak to the person.

4. Explain the rules of confidentiality that apply and inform the client if what he or she says cannot be held in complete confidence. For example, you might say, "Before we begin, I want to make certain you understand that I will be preparing a report for the court that is based on our meetings. So, what you tell me may end up in my report to the judge. Do you understand that?"

5. If you have only limited time to spend with a client, explain this at the beginning of the session so those things of highest priority will receive sufficient attention.

6. Give serious attention to what the client describes as his or her concerns, but realize that many clients will test your competency and trustworthiness before revealing the whole story or the real problem. Begin with whatever the client considers important and wants to talk about.

7. Do not jump to conclusions about the nature or cause of the client's presenting problem. Check out your assumptions and perceptions. Do not display surprise or disbelief in response to what the client tells you.

8. Do not rush the client. Respect his or her need to be silent and pause before speaking. Convey the message, "I will give you the time necessary to develop your thoughts and decide what you want to say."

9. Adapt your language and vocabulary to the client's capacity to understand. If you do not understand what the client is saying, ask for clarification or examples.

10. Use open-ended questions, unless you need specific data. Do not ask a question that you believe the client will be unwilling to answer. This may force the client to lie and that may obstruct the further development of a working relationship.

11. When you do not know the answer to a service-related question asked by the client, explain this in a nonapologetic manner and offer to find the answer for the client. Be careful not to make promises that you may not be able to keep.

12. Some notetaking during the intake phase is usually necessary and appropriate. Writing down pertinent client information can demonstrate concern and a desire to remember important details. Notetaking can be distracting, however. If the client is bothered by notetaking, show him or her your notes and explain why they are needed. If the client still objects, cease taking notes. If you are completing an agency form, give the client a copy to follow along as you talk.

13. Plan the next meeting with the client, if one is necessary. Be sure the client has your business card that lists your name and phone number and that you have his or her full name, address, and phone number.

The social worker will encounter a number of **clients who have significant physical or sensory disabilities.** The place and usual patterns of first meetings may need to be altered in order to accommodate their special needs and limitations. A few guidelines should be kept in mind.

1. When interviewing a person in a hospital bed or using a wheelchair, sit or position yourself so that you directly face the client. Do not stand over him or her. Not only would this place the client in a psychologically inferior position but it may also force the client to strain his or her neck or body in order to look at you. If the client moves about in a wheelchair or by using crutches, a cane, or a walker, respect his or her wish to remain in control and move independently. Do not offer assistance unless it is needed, and respect the client's right to decline your assistance. Be patient if it takes him or her longer to complete tasks and movements. Avoid focusing on the client's medical equipment or prosthesis.

2. When you meet with a person who is blind and in an unfamiliar physical environment, you may need to provide information he or she needs to move about. When walking with a person who is blind and using a cane, simply stay at his or her side and let the person maneuver. Never grab or move the individual, for this is both insulting and frightening. If the client wants your assistance, he or she will ask or reach out; respond by offering your elbow to hold and then walk about a half-step ahead. It is appropriate to alert the person to an unusual obstacle or danger he or she might not detect and to mention things like overhead obstructions, sharp turns, or stairs. If the person is using a guide dog, never touch, feed, or speak to the dog. Guide dogs are trained to walk down the center of a sidewalk or hallway.

3. An individual with a hearing loss will easily confuse similar sounds and have difficulty accurately hearing the human voice, especially if there is background noise. Group conversations may be particularly troublesome. If possible, move to an area away from background noise. Since most hearing aids amplify all sounds, these limitations may exist even if the client is wearing an aid. If the client seems to be having difficulty, slow your pace slightly, speak as clearly as possible, but do not yell and do not exaggerate your sounds, since this makes speech reading (lip reading) more difficult. To facilitate speech reading, be sure to position yourself so he or she can see your face and do not speak while looking away or down at papers. Do not position yourself in front of a window or a bright light, for this too interferes with speech reading. Also, a heavily mustached mouth may impede lip reading. Check often to see if the person is able to follow the conversation. Do not mistake simple nodding and smiling as a sign of comprehension, for this may be the person's response to embarrassment and reluctance to say that he or she cannot understand. A person who is totally deaf is usually prepared to communicate in writing. Be aware that some people who are deaf use "hearing dogs"; these dogs usually wear an orange collar and leash. If the individual uses a sign language, find out what system he or she uses and secure the services of an interpreter who knows that system.

4. Increasingly, governmental offices, hospitals, and other essential services are equipped with devices that can be used by persons who have difficulty communicating because of blindness, hearing loss, or speech impairments. A social worker likely to encounter clients with these limitations should become familiar with amplifiers, signaling devices, puff-blow devices, electronic artificial larynx devices, telebraille, TDD (telecommunications device for the deaf), and TTY (teletypewriter).

SELECTED BIBLIOGRAPHY

Fox, Raymond. *Elements of the Helping Process.* New York: Haworth Press, 1993
Marziali, Elsa. "The First Session: An Interpersonal Encounter." *Social Casework* 69, No. 1 (January 1988): 23–27.
Shulman, Lawrence. *The Skills of Helping,* 3rd ed. Itasca, Ill.: F. E. Peacock, 1992

11.3 Making a Referral

PURPOSE: To link a client with an agency, program, or professional person that can and will provide the service needed by the client.

DISCUSSION: An important social work activity is to link the client with the community resources, services, and opportunities that he or she needs, wants, and can use. Many people view referral as a relatively simple task. However, studies indicate that many attempted referrals end in failure. This high rate of failure, possibly 50 percent, indicates that referral is actually very complex. By following these guidelines, the worker can increase the rate of success in the referral process.

1. Be clear about the reason why referral is under consideration. Remember that a referral is an action intended to help a client solve a specific problem. Thus, before considering a referral, it is important to help the client identify and clarify the problem as he or she sees it. Only after the problem has been clearly defined can you hope to make an appropriate and effective referral. The client must agree that the problem for which you are making the referral is in fact a high priority and one on which he or she wants to work. If the client is directed to an agency for help with what is, for the client, a low-priority concern, the referral will fail.

2. View the client as an expert on his or her problems and situation, on what services are needed, and on what will or will not work. Honor and respect the client's opinions and preferences.

3. Referral is appropriate when your agency cannot provide the service needed and wanted by a client. Referral is also appropriate when you do not have the knowledge or skills needed to work with a particular client and when you have reason to believe your own values, attitudes, religious beliefs, or language will be a barrier to developing an effective helping relationship. Attempting to rid yourself of responsibility for dealing with a difficult client is never an acceptable reason for referral. "Passing the buck" or "dumping" a client on another agency is unprofessional and unethical.

4. Before concluding that referral to another agency is necessary, make sure you have considered all sources of assistance available within your own agency. Because any attempted referral carries a risk of failure and may add to the client's frustration, the social worker should first use the resources of an agency to which the client is already linked.

5. Be realistic about what other agencies and professionals have to offer your client. Some workers tend to overestimate the worth of yet untapped resources and to undervalue the resources that the client is already using.

6. When helping a client select a provider of a professional service, such as counseling or psychotherapy, the social worker should ask himself or herself the following question: Would I refer my mother or my own child to this professional? The social worker must strive to help the client locate a service provider known to be competent and ethical.

7. Make sure you know of all the agencies already involved with a client before considering a referral. Some problems are best handled through interagency case coordination and improved case management rather than by expanding the number of agencies involved with the client. Professionals and other agencies already working with a client should be consulted prior to referring a client to yet another agency. The client's permission will usually be needed before this discussion can take place. Whenever necessary, obtain releases of information signed by the client prior to engaging in the referral process.

8. Before deciding on a referral to another agency, be sure to consider the client's friends, relatives, neighbors, natural helpers, and other informal resources as a source of assistance.

9. Whenever appropriate, the client's family and other significant individuals should be involved in the decision making related to a referral. This will, of course, increase the number of persons who have opinions about the referral, which may bog down the process. However, it will avoid having others unexpectedly throw up obstacles to the process because they "felt left out." In the long run, full involvement increases the chance that the referral will be successful.

10. Whenever considering a particular service that might prove beneficial to the client, give special attention to the practical problems that may be a barrier to its utilization (e.g., client's lack of transportation or phone, inability to read, lack of child care during appointments, fearfulness associated with travel in a high-crime area, inability to take time away from job, etc.).

11. Agency decisions concerning eligibility for services, benefits, and entitlement are usually tied to questions about whether the applicant fits into a legally defined category and meets established criteria. Thus, referral work requires skill in gathering information and documents related to, for example, citizenship, marriage, parent-child relationships, prior employment, income, household composition, medical conditions, and so forth. It is important to know how to verify information and obtain key documents such as citizenship papers, birth certificates, marriage certificates, divorce decrees, death certificates, Social Security numbers, tribal enrollment numbers, and military service papers.

12. Help the client tell his or her story about the agencies and resources he or she has used or rejected in the past. Also determine how the client approached and interacted with these resources; this will provide clues as to what needs to be done to facilitate the referral. A prior negative experience with an agency, a lack of time and energy, poor communication between client and agency, confusing agency policies and procedures, and a host of other factors can contribute to referral failure. Anticipate such possible barriers and take action to lay the groundwork for success.

13. Assume that the client is ambivalent about the referral. Although the client may see the logic of using the services of another agency or professional, he or she may be fearful. It is important to explore the client's ambivalence and help him or her express concerns and fears about using a particular resource.

14. The referral process is stressful and frustrating for many clients. They may encounter a harried agency receptionist, an overwhelmed intake worker, waiting lists, red tape, and illogical and confusing eligibility requirements. Thus, the client may need a great deal of emotional support during the referral process.

15. Acknowledge that the client has already invested emotion and energy in relating to you. A successful referral may mean terminating a satisfying and secure partnership. Be aware of these feelings and be prepared to deal with feelings of separation from you and a familiar agency.

16. Most communities have a clearinghouse and/or computerized database designed to help the user identify existing health and social service agencies, programs, and providers. The social worker should know how to access these listings for assistance in locating a needed resource.

17. Ordinarily, when telling a client about services available through another professional or agency, you should explain both the advantages and limitations of those services. However, with clients who are confused, fearful, or highly dysfunctional, it is best not to focus on the limitations. Doing so could create an added barrier to the client's use of a needed service. In some cases, it is even necessary to "sell" the idea of using a particular service. If the client asks for advice on whether to use a particular resource, you have an obligation to give your honest assessment of the appropriateness and quality of the services provided.

18. View the referral as the first step in a new helping process. It sets the stage for what will follow. If done well, the referral process itself will be an empowering and therapeutic experience for the client. Because the referral process involves the use of problem-solving skills such as problem definition, gathering information, and decision making, your involvement with the client during the referral process gives him or her an opportunity to learn these skills and how to secure needed resources. Many clients need to be coached how to approach an agency or apply for services.

19. All agencies and private practitioners have their own procedures, policies, and eligibility criteria. Do not expect them to suspend their ordinary procedures as a favor to you or your client. Be careful not to tell a client that he or she is eligible for a particular service unless you have the authority to make such eligibility decisions. Do not speak for another professional or agency.

20. When a client is in need of a professional or agency service for which there is a fee, the issue of cost and the client's ability to pay must be addressed. In some cases, the client will need assistance in obtaining information from the providers of the service, the client's health insurance company, a managed care organization, or a public program (e.g., Medicaid) in order to determine whether the client has a way of paying for the service.

21. Whenever possible, clients should make their own arrangements for the services they want. In some cases, however, the frightened, immature, or overwhelmed client will need help in setting up an appointment, securing transportation, arranging child care, and the like. As a general rule, the client should be expected to assume as much responsibility as possible, without, of course, placing the success of the referral in jeopardy. If a referral is critically important to a client, you should do whatever is needed to establish the linkage. Sometimes you will need to accompany clients if they are confused or fearful about going to an agency. Family members, friends, or volunteers may also be able to provide this support.

22. In order to make an effective referral, you must thoroughly understand existing community resources. Because much of social work practice involves linking people to needed resources, a social worker must invest the time and energy necessary to learn about available resources and keep up with the constant change that occurs within the community resource system. Just knowing that a resource exists is seldom sufficient. It is important for the worker to know someone on the agency staff who can be used as a contact point. Use interagency visits as well as NASW and other professional meetings as an opportunity to meet people working in the agencies to which you will be referring clients.

23. Make sure the client becomes linked to the resource. Weissman (1976) describes a number of techniques he calls **connection techniques** that can increase the likelihood that a referral will be effective.

> *Writing out* the necessary facts: the name and address of the resource, how to get an appointment at the resource, how to get to the resource and a specific explanation of what the client may expect to occur once he arrives. . . .
>
> Providing the client with the name of a specific *person to contact* at the resource. . . .
>
> Providing the client with a *brief written statement* addressed to the resource, describing in precise terms the nature of the problem and what the client would like done. The client should be involved in the composition of this statement. . . .

[Having the client call] the resource to make an appointment while he is in the worker's office. Alternately, the worker may place the call to ensure that the appropriate person is contacted, but the client then takes over the phone conversation. (p. 52)

With this last technique, it is important to remember that all too often the agency person on the other end of the phone does not really listen to the client and instead launches into a explanation of the service program, eligibility, and so on. Some instruction, support, and modeling for the client may be necessary to prepare the client to ask the right questions and be assertive during the phone conversation. There are multiple advantages to this technique.

- The client has support during the introductory contact.
- The social worker can assist with drawing out needed information and clarification from both sides, serving to repeat and reinforce instructions given, as well as express immediate appreciation to the accepting agency.
- The client and social worker share the experience. This can be especially valuable if the contact turns out to be disappointing, rude, abrupt, or inappropriate.

24. Even after the client has had a first interview with the other agency, take action to cement this connection. Weissman (1976) describes several *cementing techniques* designed to increase the chances that a client will continue with the agency beyond the first contact.

Checkback: the client is asked to call the worker after the initial contact at the resource to summarize what has been accomplished so far.

Haunting: the worker, with the client's approval, plans to contact the client by telephone after the initial contact at the resource and after each subsequent contact.

Sandwiching: a planned interview with the client before he or she goes for the initial interview at the resource and immediately after the interview.

Alternating: a planned series of interviews held intermittently during the period in which the client is involved in interviews at the resource. (p. 53)

These four cementing techniques will uncover any misunderstandings or problems the client may be having with the agency. If detected early, they can be corrected before causing the client to withdraw from the agency.

25. Evaluate your referral work. It is important to do a follow-up evaluation on referrals to assess whether the client actually received what he or she wanted from the agency, if the client is making progress, and if additional information is available to help guide the referral experience with other clients in the future.

SELECTED BIBLIOGRAPHY

Abramson, Julie. "Six Steps to Effective Referrals." In *Agency-Based Social Work,* edited by Harold Weissman, Irwin Epstein, and Andrea Savage. Philadelphia: Temple University Press, 1983, pp. 65–71.

Matthews, R. Mark, and Stephen Fawcett. *Matching Clients and Services: Information and Referral.* Beverly Hills, Calif.: Sage, 1981.

Weissman, Andrew. "Industrial Social Services: Linkage Technology." *Social Casework* 57 (January 1976): 50–54.

11.4   Obtaining Information from Other Agencies

PURPOSE: To secure client information from records maintained by other agencies and professionals.

DISCUSSION: It is often during intake that the social worker decides it is important to obtain client information contained in the records maintained by another agency or professional. For example, a social worker may conclude that it would be helpful to read a child's school record or medical report or perhaps read a child welfare agency record that describes how the child adjusted in a prior foster care placement. The process of gaining access to those records is controlled by a variety of federal and state laws and regulations. Different laws and regulations apply in different settings (e.g., hospitals, schools, adoption agencies, substance abuse programs, child protection agencies, etc.). Information concerning a client's treatment for drug and alcohol is very tightly controlled by federal law and regulation.

Generally speaking, client records belong to the client and therefore he or she can determine to whom they are released. Thus, if you want this information, it is necessary to secure the client's written permission. Similarly, you must not release client information to another agency or a professional outside your own agency without first receiving the client's written permission. There are, however, exceptions to this basic principle. For instance, a court order or a protective services agency investigator (i.e., investigation of child or elder abuse or neglect) may gain access to client records without the client's permission. In rare instances, the social worker will need to reveal selected client information when necessary to protect the client or others from imminent and serious physical harm.

The permission statement signed by the client is often called a *Consent for Release of Confidential Information.* Most agencies have developed a standard form for this purpose. A sample is presented in Figure 11.1. It should be noted that parents or legal guardians control the release of information concerning minor children.

The client's permission must constitute an *informed consent.* Thus, before signing a release, the client should:

- Know what information is being requested, by whom, and for what purpose.
- Have an opportunity to read the material to be released or, if necessary, have it read and explained in words he or she can understand.
- Have an opportunity to correct any errors in the record before it is released.
- Know whether the professional or agency that will receive the information is being given permission to pass it on to a third party (the client must be given the opportunity to prohibit this transfer).
- Be informed of any negative consequences that might occur if he or she decides not to sign the consent.
- Understand that when the consent form is signed, he or she has a right to revoke this consent at a later date.

FIGURE 11.1   Sample Release Form

DEPARTMENT OF HEALTH AND HUMAN SERVICES
PUBLIC HEALTH SERVICE
INDIAN HEALTH SERVICE

AUTHORIZATION FOR RELEASE OF INFORMATION

Each section must be completed.

I. I, _____ , hereby request the disclosure of information from my record.
(Name of Patient)

II. The information is to be released **from:**

Name of Facility _____

Address _____

City/State _____

and is to be provided **to:**

Name of Person/Organization/Facility _____

Address _____

City/State _____

III. The purpose or need for this disclosure is: _____

IV. The information to be released is from my: *(Check one)*

☐ Medical Record   ☐ Personnel Record   ☐ Other *(specify):* _____

and includes: *(Check as appropriate)*

☐ The entire record, including any information on alcohol or drug abuse contained therein.

☐ Only information related to *(specify):* _____

_____

☐ Only the period or events from: _____ to _____

V. I understand that I may revoke this authorization in writing at any time, except to the extent that action has been taken in reliance on this authorization. If this authorization has not been revoked, it will terminate one year from the date of my signature.

Signature of Patient: _____ _____
(Date)

Signature of Parent, Guardian
or Authorized Representative *(if necessary):* _____ _____
(Date)

Source: Privacy Act Procedures. Public Health Service, U.S. Department of Health and Human Services, Washington, D.C.: U.S. Government Printing Office, 1990.

In recent years, federal and state laws and regulations concerning client records have grown more complex. Their purpose is to provide citizens with greater privacy and make professionals and agencies more accountable for the records they keep. In general, they give social agency clients and hospital patients greater access to their own records, some control over what the record contains, and control over who else can read the record. In some instances, however, these laws and regulations may have the unintended effects of reducing confidentiality within the client-worker relationship, decreasing the usefulness of the professional record as a means of interprofessional communication, and decreasing interagency coordination.

The rules surrounding the release of client information can make it difficult for professionals and agencies to share information needed for an accurate diagnosis or assessment and can create an added barrier to proper case management and the coordination of services provided to the client by several different agencies. Laws giving clients easy access to their agency records have had a profound effect on what is placed into the record. Professionals may be reluctant to document information that could be upsetting or damaging to the client or family if they were to read the record. A school social worker, for example, may be reluctant to record the content of a discussion with a student about the parent-child relationship if the worker knows that the parent can review the school record and challenge what has been recorded. In reference to just such a situation, Kagle (1991, 188) observes that "it is ironic that in an effort to establish an important privacy safeguard (that is, by allowing parents to know what is in the record and therefore, know what is being communicated within the organization), the confidentiality of the worker-student relationship has been undermined."

The Federal Privacy Act of 1974, which applies to agencies receiving federal funds (except correctional agencies), assures a client access to his or her own records. The act defines a *record* as "any item, collection, or grouping of information about an individual that is maintained by an agency, including, but not limited to, his [or her] education, financial transactions, medical history, and criminal or employment history and that contains his [or her] name, or the identifying number, symbol, or other identifying particular assigned to the individual."

Deciding what is and is not part of an official agency record is more difficult than it might appear. For example, is a report prepared by a private psychologist part of the agency record just because it has been placed in the file? Or what about a report the social worker obtained from a school? The social worker must clearly understand agency policy and procedure concerning such questions before responding to a written request to release a client record.

In the absence of legal and policy guidance to the contrary, it is best to presume that records and reports prepared by and obtained from a third party (e.g., a doctor, another agency) are not a part of your own agency's record. In other words, the authors suggest that an agency record be defined as only the material written by agency staff. Thus, you should not release reports that were prepared by someone outside your own agency, even if your client previously gave you permission to obtain them from the third party. Also, when documenting service to a client, the social worker should always operate on the assumption that clients have a right to be told exactly what records are being kept, have full access to his or her record, and may copy, question, and correct the record.

Within the context of this discussion concerning the protection and release of client information, it is important that the reader understand a related concept. Some professional licensing laws provide for what is termed *privileged communication*. The extent of the privilege is governed by state statutes. It usually applies to doctor-patient, attorney-client, husband-wife, and priest-penitent relationships. Some laws might also extend the privilege to the social worker–client relationship. This privilege belongs to the client, not to the professional; it can be claimed by the client when he or she learns that information covered by the privilege has been sub-poenaed and could be disclosed in a trial. The client then asks the judge to recognize the privilege and prevent the disclosure. The judge makes the decision on the basis of whether there is a compelling need to reveal the information.

SELECTED BIBLIOGRAPHY

Gothard, Sol. "Legal Issues: Confidentiality and Priveleged Communication." In *Encyclopedia of Social Work*, 19th ed., Vol. 2, edited by Richard Edwards. Washington, D.C.: NASW, 1995, pp. 1579–1584.

Kagle, Jill. *Social Work Records*, 2nd ed. Belmont, Calif.: Wadsworth, 1991.

Public Health Service. *Privacy Act Procedures*. Washington D.C.: U.S. Department of Health and Human Services, August 1990.

Wilson, Suanna. *Confidentiality in Social Work*. New York: Free Press, 1978.

11.5 Problem Checklist

PURPOSE: To assist the client in identifying and explaining his or her problems or concerns.

DISCUSSION: At the beginning of the intake phase, many clients have difficulty defining their problems. Some are reluctant to verbalize their thoughts because they feel ashamed or embarrassed; others cannot find the words to describe their concerns. The use of a problem checklist can make it easier for a client to acknowledge a problem and put it into words. It can help to uncover problems and facilitate the exchange of information.

A problem checklist is simply a list of concerns commonly reported by a particular group of clients. The list is compiled by a social worker familiar with how people in certain situations typically think and feel. The client is asked to consider each item on the list and check those that come close to describing his or her own concerns. Because the list probably includes some of the client's private thoughts, it can prove reassuring to the client. It tells the client that he or she is not the first person to have a particular problem.

Figure 11.2 is an example of a problem checklist designed to facilitate communication with teen-aged mothers, many of whom are reluctant to verbalize their worries. Some clients, like the new mother who is hospitalized for only one or two

FIGURE 11.2
Sample
Problem
Checklist

Concerns of Young Mothers: A Checklist

The birth of a baby is a time of happiness and joy. But along with the good feelings are concerns about the changes in lifestyle and responsibility that lie ahead. A new mother often feels uncertain and a bit scared about the responsibility of caring for a baby. If we know about your concerns, we may be able to help you find ways to handle them.

Below is a list of worries and concerns that have been expressed by other new mothers who have had babies in this hospital. Please read through this list and place a check (✓) by all statements that are similar to the concerns you now have. Your responses will be held in strict confidence.

1. ____ Have worries about paying hospital and doctor bills.
2. ____ Have worries about my baby's health and physical condition.
3. ____ Have worries about my own health and physical condition.
4. ____ Uncertain about how to feed and care for an infant.
5. ____ Uncertain where to turn when I have questions about child care.
6. ____ Afraid I may become pregnant before I am ready to have another child.
7. ____ Worried about not having enough money to care for my baby.
8. ____ Concerned about whether I can finish school.
9. ____ Worried about getting or keeping a job when I have a baby to care for.
10. ____ Concerned when I feel resentment or anger toward my baby.
11. ____ Worried about the effects of drugs or alcohol on me and my baby.
12. ____ Worried that my friends will not accept me and my baby.
13. ____ Worried about my relationship with my baby's father.
14. ____ Concerned that I do not feel love toward my baby.
15. ____ Feeling sad and depressed about my situation.
16. ____ Worried that I will be a burden to my own parents.
17. ____ Worried about living alone with my baby.
18. ____ Concerned that my own parents and family will not accept me and my baby.
19. ____ Afraid I am going to lose my independence and freedom.
20. ____ In the space below, please describe or list any other concerns not covered by the checklist.

_____

_____

Now, look over all of those items you have checked and draw a circle around the one or two that seem most important. Please feel free to discuss these concerns with a hospital social worker.

Source: Charles Horejsi and Gloria Horejsi, "Practice Oriented Social Assessment Tools," Paper presented at the Sixth Biennial National Association of Social Workers Professional Symposium, San Antonio, Texas, 1979.

days after delivery of her baby, may be accessible to the hospital social worker for only one brief contact. A problem checklist can provide the focus needed to make the best possible use of very limited time.

Frequently, clients are unaware of the services that can be provided by the social worker. If the social worker and client examine a problem checklist together, the client begins to understand how the worker or agency might be of assistance. In this sense, the problem checklist serves as an educational tool. Also, the checklist can be used to provide focus and structure during an interview; this can be important in work with clients who are easily distracted. The problem checklist is most often used during the first face-to-face interview; however, it can be used as "homework" between the first and second meeting.

The advantage of the problem checklist is that it helps clients report their concerns. The disadvantage is that it does not give attention to client strengths. The worker must counterbalance this focus on problems with attention to client strengths. Also, it must be remembered that many clients have reading problems, in which case the checklist can be used verbally as a structured interview technique.

SELECTED BIBLIOGRAPHY

Horejsi, Charles. *Foster Family Care.* Springfield, Ill.: Charles C. Thomas, 1979.
———. *Assessment and Case Planning in Child Protection and Foster Care Services.* Englewood, Colo.: American Humane Association, in press.

11.6 The In-Home Interview

PURPOSE: To engage and deliver services to the client who cannot or will not meet in an office setting and/or to secure a more accurate assessment by observing the client in his or her natural environment.

DISCUSSION: The terms *in-home interview* or *home visit* refer to a meeting between social worker and client in the client's home. The in-home interview has become a lost art in many practice settings. In the early days of social work, home visiting was the *modus operandi* of the worker. In later years when social work was striving to attain professional status, the home visit was abandoned by many because it did not seem "professional" and did not fit the popular office-based models of therapy. Of course the home visit has always been used heavily by social workers in child protection and public health agencies and by those providing services to the elderly. The home visit is an essential component in all outreach activities and of critical importance in work with the hard-to-reach client (see Item 11.8). In recent years, the value of the in-home interview was rediscovered by family therapists and its use has increased.

Despite its usefulness and necessity in many cases, the in-home interview is a source of anxiety for many social workers. A number of guidelines can help the worker make proper use of this valuable diagnostic and treatment tool.

1. Understand the rationale for observing clients in their usual environment. Sherman and Fredman (1986) explain that

> information which is not readily presented in office visits may come across as the therapist interacts in a setting that is more natural to the family. Arranged home visits have the potential for decreasing family defensiveness and promoting the involvement of the entire family. It is a more natural setting for the family's functioning. It may also be possible that behavior change achieved in the home environment is both more adaptive to the family's reality and more likely to be retained. (p. 238)

The home visit is especially valuable in helping the worker develop empathy for the client and in understanding how the environment impinges on the client.

2. Appreciate the depth of understanding that can be gained from an in-home interview. Ebeling and Hill (1983) explain that a person's home is his or her "sacred" space and a reflection of the individual's personality and life-style.

> Within the walls of a home, people experience the intimate moments of their lives. They sleep, wake up, bathe, eat, drink, make love, raise children. They fight, scream, and rejoice; they cry, laugh, and sing. They may experience the warmth of positive object relationships, the anguish of negative ones, or isolation and loneliness. . . .
> Their outer space reflects their inner space. The way the homes are decorated and furnished can reveal either the chosen life-style of the occupants or their economic position. It can also indicate depression, despair, and disorganization. (p. 64)

3. Do not confuse the in-home interview with a purely social or friendly visit. This technique, like all others, is to be used in a purposeful manner. When it is the social worker who requests an in-home interview, the client should be given a clear explanation as to how and why it will make the service more effective.

4. An in-home interview should be scheduled at a mutually convenient time. Unannounced visits should be avoided but may be necessary when the client does not have a phone or is unable to read a letter, or when prior attempts to reach the client have failed. If you must stop by a client's home unannounced, explain immediately your previous efforts to reach him or her and use the conversation to set up a scheduled visit. (Often, the client will immediately invite you in.)

5. When you enter the home of a client, extend the same respect and courtesy you expect when someone enters your home. Ask where you are to be seated. Accept an appropriate offer of food or drink. Convey a genuine interest in family pictures and household furnishings that are an expression of the client's identity, interests, and culture. Ebeling and Hill (1983, 66) remind us that it is essential that the social worker never show shock or disapproval as he or she enters the client's home—their sacred space: "No matter what the condition of the building, . . . regardless of the number of dogs, the darkness of the halls, or the odors of the stairways; no matter how barren or cluttered or 'hospital' clean; even no matter what signs of impusivity, violence, or sexual acting out are encountered."

6. Obtaining sufficient privacy is often a problem during a home visit—children may run in and out of the house, neighbors may stop by, the telephone may ring, and the TV may be blaring. This will be distracting to you but possibly not to your client. On the positive side, such distractions provide an accurate picture of the family's real-life functioning and their ecosystem. Significant distractions are best dealt with directly by expressing a need for privacy and for attention to the interview's purpose. When friends or neighbors are in the home, the client should be asked if it is permissible to discuss private matters in their presence. Some clients may invite their informal helpers and supportive friends to sit in on the interview and this choice should be respected.

7. If your client lives in a high-crime neighborhood, it is important to schedule the home visit for a time when the risks are at a minimum. Ask your client if you should take some special precautions and to describe the safest route.

SELECTED BIBLIOGRAPHY

Ebeling, Nancy, and Deborah Hill, eds. *Child Abuse and Neglect.* Boston: John Wright, PSG, Inc., 1983.

Sherman, Robert, and Norman Fredman. *Handbook of Structured Techniques in Marriage and Family Therapy.* New York: Brunner/Mazel, 1986.

Wasik, Barbara. *Home Visiting: Procedures for Helping Families.* Newbury, Calif.: Sage, 1990.

Weiss, Marc. "Using House Calls in a Psychotherapy Practice." In I*nnovations in Clinical Practice: A Source Book,* Vol. 9, edited by Peter Keller and Steven Heyman. Sarasota, Fla.: Professional Resource Exchange, 1990, pp. 229–238.

11.7 Engaging the Involuntary Client

PURPOSE: To begin building a working relationship with a client who was forced into contact with a social worker and agency.

DISCUSSION: The term *involuntary client* refers to an individual who is required or mandated to seek professional help. The coercive force bringing them into contact with the worker may be a legal authority such as a judge, probation officer, or child protection agency; a powerful family member; or an employer. Such clients are often resentful, angry, and sometimes belligerent. Needless to say, social workers would much rather work with a client who asks Who am I? rather than the client who asks Who are you? What are you doing here? and When are you going to get out of here? It is a challenge to engage the involuntary client in the helping process, but it can be done.

In most cases involving an involuntary client, the social worker will possess some degree of official authority. For example, social workers employed in child protection, probation, and parole are granted authority by law to impose a certain course of action on a client. Many social workers are uncomfortable with such authority and avoid using it; others overuse or misuse legitimate authority. Workers who are in positions of legal authority must learn to use it in ways that are helpful to the client. In fact, a worker's compassionate and fair exercise of legitimate authority can be a therapeutic experience for clients who associate authority with abuse and exploitation.

An experienced probation and parole officer (Hardman 1960), offers the following advice on the appropriate use of authority:

> I will make crystal clear, in defining my role, where my authority begins and ends, and I will consistently function within these limits. I will avoid veiled threats, bluffing, or any behavior that might be so interpreted, since this clouds, rather than clarifies my limits. This rule will eliminate a vast amount of testing by the client. I will further clarify which decisions are mine to make and which the client must make. . . . Once I have made a decision, I will steadfastly resist all client efforts to alter my decision by threats, tantrums, seduction, illness, etc. I will just as steadfastly defend his right to make his decisions and stand by them. By the same token, if a client shows me rational evidence that I have made a hasty or unwise decision, I will alter it and will tell him so. Common terms which [clients] . . . use to describe authority are "arbitrary, inconsistent, and unfair." For this reason I must demonstrate that authority can be considerate, consistent and fair. (p. 17)

Filip, McDaniel, and Schene (1992) remind child protection workers (CPS) of the therapeutic use of authority with the following:

- Use your authority in a warm, personal, supportive manner and show an understanding of the parents' feelings about the problem.
- A family may feel less fearful of your authority if you demonstrate a non-threatening and non-coercive attitude.
- Help your client to see that you represent a reasonable authority so that (s)he can learn that other authority figures can also be reasonable.
- Demonstrate your authority in a manner which indicates that you have no hidden agenda, that is, be honest.
- Clarify your protective service role and function. Do not retreat from your responsibility; make the family aware of the expectations for change and the consequences of no change in their behavior. Make them aware that you will develop a plan for your work together and that there are consequences should the changes in their behavior not occur and their child be considered at-risk.
- Make the family aware of your knowledge that CPS intervention can be traumatic and you will do your best to minimize that trauma. Remember the experience may be traumatic for both children and parents. . . .
- Avoid insensitivity to parental feelings since insensitivity may create anger, hostility, and resistance and will make it difficult for you to establish a helping relationship.
- Avoid excessive reliance on your legal authority. (p. 45)

Also, consider the following guidelines when working with the involuntary client.

1. Before meeting your client for the first time, be very clear as to what requirements are nonnegotiable and what choices and options are available to the client. Anticipate how the client may feel about his or her loss of freedom.

2. When you first meet with your client, reveal the factual information you have about why the client is involved with your agency, and ask the client to correct any misunderstandings you may have about this information. Seek clarification from the referring source if there is a significant discrepancy between what the client has been told about why he or she must seek professional help and what you have been told by the referring person.

3. Provide a clear and completely honest explanation of both your role and responsibility and what you or your agency expect of the client. Also, explain the rules of confidentiality that apply. For example, if you are expected to prepare a report to the court, the client has a right to know that what he or she tells you is not confidential.

4. Inform the client of any adverse consequences that may occur if he or she does not cooperate. However, respect the client's right to choose the consequences rather than your services. Remind the client who decides not to cooperate that he or she is, in effect, giving up the control he or she has to influence the outcome.

5. Assume that the client has negative feelings about being forced into contact with a social worker. Be prepared to encounter hostility, anger, and a number of defensive reactions, but do not take the client's reactions personally (see Item 8.7). Foremost, you need to address the client's negativism. Do not ignore or avoid these feelings; deal with them directly. Use basic interviewing skills to help the client express negative feelings. Do not ask questions that could be construed as an attempt to trap the client or catch him or her in a lie. Demonstrate an empathetic understanding of what it is like to be forced to do something you do not choose to do.

6. Discuss the client's previous experience with professionals or the "system," along with any preconceived notions he or she has about social workers, counselors, or other professional helpers. Be aware of the client's cultural background or experience with discrimination and how this might add to his or her feeling of being overpowered by or alienated from social institutions. Provide the client with as much choice and self-determination as can be allowed within the legal constraints.

7. Consider trying to engage the client with the "let's make a deal" strategy. In this approach, the worker agrees to do something that will lessen the client's discomfort (e.g., talk to the prosecuting attorney about reducing a criminal charge) or help the client get something he or she wants (something legal and legitimate) in exchange for the client's cooperation in the helping process.

8. There is no such thing as an unmotivated client. All clients are motivated—all have wants, needs, and preferences. When a social worker labels a client "unmotivated," he or she is simply acknowledging that what the client wants is different from what the worker wants for the client. Successfully engaging the involuntary client requires that the worker tap into the client's own needs and wants and establish intervention goals that are at least partially consistent with the client's own wishes and inclinations. Some workers call this "going with the flow" or "moving with the motive." Work hard to identify something that both you and the client agree is a problem or a desirable course of action (e.g., getting off probation or not having to see a social worker anymore). Once there is an agreed upon goal, you can more easily engage the client in problem solving aimed at making change. For example, you might say, "Well, we both want you to get off probation so you won't have to see me each week. What ideas do you have on how we can work together to reach that goal?"

9. Highlight the client's strengths and make frequent use of the reframing technique (see Item 14.12). Use the problem search technique (see Item 13.2) if you and the client cannot agree on the problems that need to be addressed.

10. With most clients, some degree of self-disclosure by the worker has the effect of breaking down client defensiveness. However, when working with a prison inmate population, sociopathic individuals, or persons who are skilled manipulators, you should avoid sharing personal information (see Item 11.10). The use of self-disclosure with these individuals will usually have unwanted consequences, as many have an uncanny ability to spot and exploit a helper's personal weakness. For similar reasons, you must never break or even bend agency rules as a favor to the client; even a minor concession quickly leads to further requests or a "blackmail" situation (e.g., "Look, if you won't do . . . for me, I'll tell your supervisor that you violated program rules when you allowed me to. . . .").

SELECTED BIBLIOGRAPHY

Filip, Judee, Nancy McDaniel, and Patricia Schene, eds. *Helping in Child Protective Services.* Englewood, Colo.: American Humane Association, 1992.

Hardman, Dale. "The Functions of the Probation Officer." *Federal Probation* 24 (September 1960): 3–10.

Harris, George, ed. *Tough Customer: Counseling Unwilling Clients.* Laurel, Md.: American Correctional Association, 1991.

Ivanoff, Andre, Betty Blythe, and Tony Tripodi. *Involuntary Clients in Social Work Practice.* New York: Aldine de Gruyter, 1994.

Rooney, Ronald. *Strategies for Work with Involuntary Clients.* New York: Columbia University Press, 1991.

11.8   Engaging the Hard-to-Reach Client

PURPOSE: To build a working relationship with a client who is distrustful and reluctant to become involved.

DISCUSSION: The term *hard to reach* is used here to describe a client with whom it is extremely difficult to build a relationship. Most of these clients are socially isolated, fearful, and distrustful. Many suffer from serious mental illness and/or are extremely uncomfortable in interpersonal relations. The term *hard to reach* should not be confused with the term *involuntary client;* some hard to reach clients are, in fact, voluntary, and many involuntary clients are actually quite easy to engage. In working with the hard to reach, the greatest challenge is to break through the client's distrust. Several guidelines should be followed.

1. You must be willing to use unconventional methods. The techniques that are most effective are usually not ones drawn from the traditional approaches to psychotherapy and counseling, nor ones used by conventional mental health and social service agencies. Homebuilders, a program operated by Behavioral Sciences Institute based in Federal Way, Washington, has a remarkable record of effective work with highly dysfunctional, multiproblem, and hard-to-reach families in imminent risk of having a child placed into foster care. Among the methods and principles that contribute to the success of Homebuilders are: (a) reaching out to families while they are in crisis; (b) responding to the family within 24 hours of referral; (c) being available to families 24 hours a day, seven days a week; (d) meeting with families in their home, not in an office setting; and (e) a willingness and ability to provide a wide variety of services (e.g., helping to clean the kitchen floor, meeting basic needs for food and shelter, case coordination, and applying the most sophisticated of psychotherapeutic techniques, such as individual and family therapy, assertiveness training, behavior management, etc.).

2. Remember that first impressions are extremely important to these clients. They are quick to form judgments; more often than not, they interpret situations in the most negative way possible. To be effective, you must be a warm, giving, and dependable person. Use a liberal dose of self-disclosure to help the client see you as a real and genuine person. In many ways, you must become a good parent figure to the client—loving but firm. That firmness and concern may express itself in the gentle setting of limits on what is and is not acceptable behavior.

3. Be prepared to tolerate a great deal of testing behavior, and be patient when progress is slow. Many hard-to-reach clients have been so beaten down by life that they feel hopeless about ever making a change in their situation.

4. Be very tactful. The feelings of hard-to-reach clients are easily hurt and many are supersensitive to any hint of rejection. Do nothing that could be construed as criticism. If you accidentally do something that is hurtful to the client, discuss it immediately and repair the damaged relationship; if you do not, the client may withdraw from the relationship, once again convinced that no one can be trusted.

5. In the early stages of relationship building, you will probably need to do many things *for* the client before reaching the point where you do things *with* the client. Strive to demonstrate your good will and usefulness to the client in a concrete way. Home visits, sending birthday cards, sharing food, and other tangible expressions of concern are usually necessary. By doing things for the client and by "feeding" the client's dependency needs, you provide assurance that you are "safe." By becoming useful to the client, you become attractive and thereby gain some psychological leverage. Unless you become attractive and a reinforcer, the client's distrust will keep him or her from entering into even a superficial relationship. Do not worry about creating overdependency. That problem can be addressed later. Remember, your first objective is simply to build a human bond or connection.

6. Encourage frequent contacts. As a general rule, the more often people interact, the more important they become to each other. Use frequent phone calls and brief letters to supplement face-to-face interviews.

7. Place only minimal demands or expectations on the client until you have developed a meaningful relationship. This does not mean you should be completely permissive, however. You need to help the client understand that the two of you are to work on the client's problems and that you will not tolerate destructive or manipulative behavior.

8. If the client announces that he or she does not want to talk about certain topics, explain that his or her decision is acceptable and that you will not ask the client to talk about those topics. But then follow up with an effort to engage the client in a discussion of general reasons why some topics might be hard for people to discuss and why people often want to withhold and protect certain information. These reasons might include feelings of shame and embarrassment, not knowing what words to use, not knowing how the social worker will react, not knowing if the worker would understand, fear that the worker might be judgmental, fear of a lack of confidentiality, fear that the information will be used to exploit the client, and so on. Very often this general discussion of common fears and concerns will reveal to the client that the worker can be trusted and the client will then decide to talk about previously protected topics.

SELECTED BIBLIOGRAPHY

Harris, George, and David Watkins. *Counseling the Involuntary and Resistant Client.* Laurel, Md.: American Correctional Association, 1987.

Kaplan, Lisa. *Working with Multiproblem Families.* Lexington, Mass.: Lexington Books, 1986.

Kinney, Jill, David Haapla, and Charlotte Booth. *Keeping Families Together: The Homebuilders Model.* New York: Aldine, 1991.

11.9   Engaging the Client Who Is Chemically Dependent

PURPOSE: To engage the chemically dependent client in a way that increases the chances he or she will seek treatment.

DISCUSSION: Many of the individuals receiving services from social agencies suffer directly or indirectly from the effects of alcoholism and drug abuse. The abuse of chemicals is related to many other problems, including marital discord, parent-child conflict, spouse abuse, child abuse and neglect, suicide, homicide, financial problems, crime, and auto accidents. The use of alcohol and drugs by a pregnant woman can cause damage to the unborn child. Use and abuse also contribute to the spread of AIDS due to intravenous injections and indiscriminate sexual behavior related to the disinhibiting effects of drugs and alcohol.

Most social workers consider the actively drinking alcoholic and active drug user to be difficult clients, in part because of the extreme denial, rationalization, and self-centeredness that is so much a part of the addictive process. A social worker's response to this type of client must be based on an understanding of how these chemicals affect mind and body and on the realization that it is nearly impossible for an individual to break a dependency or addiction without specialized treatment.

Some professionals find it useful to distinguish between dependency and abuse. *Chemical abuse* refers to occasional use that causes problems in only one or two areas of functioning. In contrast, *chemical dependency* refers to a pattern of frequent use that is affecting several areas of functioning.

A *chemical dependency* can be defined as a pathological relationship with a mood-altering substance. The dynamics of this relationship resemble those of a neurotic love affair, but in this case the love object is a chemical. The chemicals likely to be abused share a common characteristic—each has the capacity to alter a person's mood. Each time the chemical is used, its mood-altering effects reinforce usage, and over time this learning process results in *psychological addiction*. In addition, many drugs alter body chemistry, and this can lead to a *physical addiction* and such symptoms as craving and withdrawal. Central to the physical addiction process is the gradual development of *tolerance* (i.e., more and more of the chemical is necessary to create its desired mood-altering effect).

Generally speaking, the chemicals most sought after are those with the most rapid onset of action. Onset of effect is related to chemical properties, dose, method of intake, and characteristics of the user. The effect of a chemical is also influenced by the psychosocial setting of its use.

There are local and regional differences in the popularity of certain chemicals, terminology, and preferred methods of intake. There are continual changes in the street lingo applied to illegal substances and new chemical combinations appear frequently. Provided here are brief descriptions of the legal and illegal substances most often abused and that serve as the basic ingredients for new combinations.

Nicotine

Although legal, the nicotine found in tobacco is a highly addictive substance. Because this stimulant is so widely used and is a contributing cause in cancer and heart and lung disease, nicotine may lead to more serious illness and death than all of the illegal street drugs combined. It is usually smoked but is also chewed or placed next to the gums in the form of "snuff."

Alcohol

If one considers the number of individuals and families affected, the number of injuries and deaths caused by drunken driving, and the number of health problems either caused or exacerbated by drinking, the abuse of alcohol (a legal drug) is the number one drug problem in the United States. It is estimated that of every ten adults who drink at all, one has a serious drinking problem.

Because alcohol depresses the central nervous system (CNS), it can be very dangerous when used with other drugs or medications that also depress the CNS. Alcohol consumption by a pregnant woman can cause serious problems for the unborn child, including mental retardation, curvature of the spine, facial abnormalities, and other birth defects. The greater the consumption, the greater the impact on the fetus. Damage to the brain of the fetus by alcohol is one of the major causes of mental retardation. From 2 to 3 newborns per 1,000 are now diagnosed as having full-blown *Fetal Alcohol Syndrome*—a cluster of physical and mental abnormalities. Additional newborns are also affected by alcohol but to a lesser degree.

In 1990, the National Council on Alcoholism and the American Society of Addiction Medicine approved the following definition of *alcoholism:*

> A primary, chronic disease with genetic, psychosocial, and environmental factors influencing its development and manifestations. The disease is often progressive and fatal. It is characterized by continuous or periodic: impaired control over drinking, preoccupation with the drug alcohol, use of alcohol despite adverse consequences, and distortions in thinking, most notable denial.

So long as the alcoholic continues to drink, his or her condition becomes worse. There is no cure; at best, alcoholism can be controlled through complete abstinence. Experts generally agree that it is not possible for an alcoholic to become a social drinker; if the alcoholic tries, he or she soon slips back into a pattern of problem drinking.

In its early stage, alcoholism is difficult to recognize because its symptoms are subtle. However, one may observe that the person drinks a lot and that alcohol has a part in many of his or her activities. The incipient alcoholic can consume a great deal without showing the effects; this phenomenon may be genetic in origin. At this early stage, the consumption of alcohol does not significantly interfere with job or family functioning and may be almost indistinguishable from the person who only occasionally drinks too much.

In the middle stage, the alcoholic is physically addicted. When his or her blood alcohol level is lowered, the alcoholic will experience withdrawal symptoms, including anxiety, agitation, and tremors. Family and job functioning are now affected. At this stage, it is common for family and friends to pressure the alcoholic to cut back. Concerned family members may reach out for help, but typically the alcoholic denies there is a problem. He or she may quit for weeks or months at a time but eventually starts again. These short periods of abstinence convince the alcoholic that he or she can quit at any time and that alcohol is not a problem.

In the later stage of alcoholism, the existence of a serious problem is apparent to all but the alcoholic. Although family, job, and health are affected, the denial continues, at least until some major crisis occurs (e.g., an accident, loss of job, health problems, divorce, etc.). It may take from 5 to 15 years of drinking for an adult to develop alcoholism. This illness may develop in an adolescent after only 6 to 18 months of heavy drinking.

The following list identifies a number of the *symptoms of alcoholism.* Usually, the alcoholic will display several of these:

- Inability to stop at one or two drinks; increase in the amount of alcohol consumed; "gulping" drinks
- Increased dependency on alcohol; hiding and protecting liquor supply
- Inability to remember what occurred while drinking (blackouts); passing out when drinking
- Drinking alone; needing a drink the next morning
- Lateness and absenteeism at work; neglect of financial obligations
- Neglect or indifference to personal appearance

- Deterioration of moral and ethical behavior
- Family quarrels and family tensions over drinking
- Lateness in returning home (growing number of excuses or none at all)
- Changes in eating and sleeping habits; grandiose beliefs; hallucinations; persistent remorse; increased irritability
- Suspiciousness of family and friends; loss of friendships
- Hostile and belligerent behavior when drinking
- Hand tremors and increased nervousness; falling and stumbling
- Repeated unsuccessful attempts at abstaining from alcohol
- Angry denial that there is a drinking problem, usually accompanied with a strong "alibi system" to excuse or minimize drinking
- In its terminal phases, health problems affecting such vital organs as the brain, liver, and gastrointestinal system

Amphetamines

There are several forms of amphetamines. As CNS stimulants, they have similar effects on the body but differ in strength and method of manufacture. Some amphetamines (e.g., Dexedrine, Benzedrine, Methedrine) are manufactured by pharmaceutical companies and prescribed in the medical treatment of conditions such as narcolepsy, brain dysfunction, and obesity. When these drugs are sold illegally on the street, they are often called *uppers, dexies, bennies,* and so on. As new laws placed tight controls on the prescription use of these drugs, related forms (i.e., the methamphetamines) were produced illegally and are now widely used because of their strength, low cost, and the ease with which they can be manufactured in very simple laboratories.

Among the various forms of methamphetamine are methamphetamine sulfate (i.e., "crank"), methamphetamine hydrochloride (i.e., "crystal meth"), and dextromethamphetamine (i.e., "ice," "glass," "batu," and "shabu"). These drugs produce an intense and long-lasting euphoria. The powerful "crystal meth" and "ice" produce a high similar to that of crack cocaine but one that lasts many hours. Because these drugs are relatively inexpensive, they have been called the "poor man's cocaine." Depending on their form, they may be snorted, swallowed, smoked, or injected.

In general, the abuse of a these stimulants is indicated by hyperactivity, nervousness and anxiety, dilated pupils, irritability, and going for long periods without sleep or food. Some users experience a dry mouth, sweating, headache, blurred vision, dizziness, and sleeplessness. Extremely high doses can cause dangerously rapid or irregular heartbeat, tremors, loss of coordination, and physical collapse. Long-time and heavy use can lead to malnutrition, skin disorders, ulcers, weight loss, kidney damage, depression, and speech and thought disturbances. An amphetamine injection causes a sudden increase in blood pressure that can precipitate a stroke or heart failure. If taken during pregnancy, these drugs, especially "crank" and "ice," can do serious damage to the fetus.

Heavy use can also result in an amphetamine psychosis involving hallucinations (seeing, hearing, and feeling things that do not exist), delusions (having irrational thoughts or beliefs), and paranoia (feeling as though people are out to harm you). In such a state, the person may exhibit bizarre and sometimes violent behavior. Methamphetamine use is a major factor in some cases of severe child abuse, domestic abuse, and other forms of violence.

Related to the amphetamines are the so-called designer drugs—drugs whose molecular structure has been modified slightly for the purpose of producing a stronger effect and/or escaping legal sanctions.

Cocaine

Cocaine, like the amphetamines, is a CNS stimulant. It is smuggled into the United States as a fine, white, crystalline powder (cocaine hydrochloride). This powder is then diluted or "cut" to increase its bulk and stretch the supply for sale.

The most common method of administration is intranasal, or "snorting" the diluted powder, which may be about 15 to 25 percent cocaine. When snorted, the euphoric effects begin within a few minutes, peak within 15 to 20 minutes, and disappear within about 45 minutes. During this brief period, the user often feels confident, energetic, talkative, and omnipotent. To sustain these pleasant feelings, additional cocaine is needed.

A couple of chemical procedures can be used to separate or free the pure cocaine from the other usual additives in powdered cocaine. This results in "freebase" that can be smoked—a more direct and rapid way to transmit the chemical to the brain. Smokeable "crack" or "rock cocaine," which can be 90 percent pure cocaine, is particularly potent and highly addictive.

The smoking of "crack" produces a short but very intense "high." Thus, it is even more addictive and increases the risks associated with this drug (e.g., confusion, slurred speech, anxiety, and hallucinations and paranoid delusions). Whereas the users of powdered cocaine may develop their addiction over many months or even years, "crack" smokers can become addicted in a matter of days. Children born to mothers using "crack" during pregnancy often suffer from neurological damage.

Since freebase cocaine is water soluble, it can also be injected. This is the most dangerous method of administration. Because it produces an immediate and intense euphoria, intravenous cocaine use is highly addictive.

Regular users of cocaine often report feelings of restlessness, irritability, anxiety, and sleeplessness. Cocaine causes physical and mental damage similar to that caused by the amphetamines (see "Amphetamines" earlier). High doses over a long period may precipitate a "cocaine psychosis" with hallucinations of touch, sight, taste, or smell. Because cocaine stimulates the body and its nervous system, it is not uncommon to experience a physical "crash" and a mental depression following a period of use. The depressions can be debilitating and last from a few hours to several days.

Marijuana

Marijuana is the common name for a drug made from the plant *cannabis sativa*. The main psychoactive ingredient in marijuana is THC (delta-9-tetrahydrocannabinol). The amount of THC in the marijuana determines how strong its effects will be on the user. Hashish, or hash, is made by taking the resin from the leaves and flowers of the plant and pressing it into cakes; it may contain 5 to 10 times more THC than crude marijuana. Marijuana and hash are usually smoked but sometimes taken orally.

In the past, marijuana was regarded as a substance with a low addictive potential and unlikely to cause serious problems, but recent research and the clinical experience of drug treatment programs identify several adverse effects. Some individuals do become psychologically addicted and heavy users may develop "amotivational syndrome," a general loss of interest in life's activities and an increase in passivity and sluggishness.

An individual who is "high" on marijuana or hashish will feel euphoric and may speak rapidly and loudly and have dilated pupils. Some individuals experience sensory distortions. The drug can impair short-term memory, alter sense of time, and reduce the ability to do things that require concentration and quick reactions such as in driving a car or operating machinery. A possible response to marijuana is an acute panic reaction, which is an extreme fear of losing control. These symptoms disappear in a few hours.

PCP

PCP (phencyclidine), often called "angel dust," was developed as an anesthetic in the 1950s but later taken off the market for human use because it sometimes caused hallucinations. It continues to have use in veterinary medicine. PCP is easily manufactured and is available in a number of forms (i.e., white crystal-like powder, tablet, or capsule). It can be swallowed, smoked, sniffed, or injected. PCP is sometimes sprinkled on marijuana and smoked. It is sometimes sold as mescaline or THC, thus the user of those drugs may get PCP by mistake.

The sought-after effect is euphoria. For some, small amounts act as a stimulant. For many users, PCP changes how they perceive their own bodies and things around them; movements and time are slowed. The effects of PCP are unpredictable and for this reason many "experimenters" abandon its use. Others, unfortunately, become dependent. Negative effects include increased heart rate and blood pressure, flushing, sweating, dizziness, and numbness. When large doses are taken, effects include drowsiness, convulsions, coma, and sometimes death. PCP can produce violent or bizarre behavior. Regular use affects memory, perception, concentration, and judgment. Users may show signs of paranoia, fearfulness, and anxiety. When under the drug's influence, some users become aggressive; others withdraw and have difficulty communicating. A PCP-induced psychosis may last for days or weeks.

Hallucinogens

Hallucinogens, or psychedelics, are drugs that affect a person's perceptions, sensations, thinking, self-awareness, and emotions. Hallucinogens include such drugs as LSD, mescaline, psilocybin, and DMT. *LSD* is manufactured from lysergic acid, which is found in a fungus that grows on grains; it is one of the most potent mood-changing chemicals. It is odorless, colorless, and tasteless. LSD is sold on the street in tablets, capsules, or occasionally in liquid form. It is usually taken by mouth but sometimes is injected.

DMT is similar to LSD. *Mescaline* comes from the peyote cactus and, although it is not as strong as LSD, its effects are similar. Mescaline is usually smoked or swallowed in the form of capsules or tablets. *Psilocybin* comes from certain mushrooms. It is sold in tablet or capsule form or the mushrooms themselves may be eaten.

The effects of psychedelics are unpredictable and depend on dosage as well as the user's personality, mood, expectations, and the surroundings. Usually, the user feels the first effects 30 to 90 minutes after taking it. They may feel several different emotions at once or swing rapidly from one emotion to another. The person's sense of time and self change. Sensations become mixed and seem to "cross over," giving the user the feeling of hearing colors and seeing sounds. For some users, these strange sensations are frightening and cause a "bad trip" that may last a few minutes or several hours and involve confusion, suspiciousness, anxiety, feelings of helplessness, and loss of control. Physical effects include dilated pupils, higher body temperature, increased heart rate and blood pressure, and often sweating, irregular breathing, and tremors. Some users may sit in a stupor, whereas others become agitated.

Taking a hallucinogen can unmask mental or emotional problems. Flashbacks, in which the person experiences a drug's effects without having to take the drug again, can occur. Heavy users sometimes develop impaired memory, loss of attention span, confusion, and difficulty with abstract thinking.

Sedative Hypnotics

Sedative hypnotics are prescription drugs often referred to as tranquilizers, sleeping pills, or sedatives. Because they depress the central nervous system, they have a calming effect and promote sleep. An individual who has taken a higher than prescribed dosage may give the appearance of being drunk (e.g., staggering, slurred speech, sleepiness, etc.) but not smell of alcohol. At high doses or when taken with alcohol (also a depressant), these drugs can cause unconsciousness and death.

Barbiturates and benzodiazepines are the two major categories of sedative hypnotics. Some well-known barbiturates are secobarbital (Seconal) and pentobarbital (Nembutal). Diazepam (Valium), chlordiazepoxide (Librium), and chlorazepate (Tranxene) are examples of benzodiazepines. A few sedative hypnotics do not fit in either category; they include methaqualone (Quaalude), ethchlorvynol (Placidyl), chloral hydrate (Noctec), and mebrobamate (Miltown).

Sedative-hypnotic drugs can cause both physical and psychological dependence. Regular use over a long period of time may result in tolerance. When regular large dose users suddenly stop, they may develop withdrawal symptoms, ranging from restlessness, insomnia, and anxiety to convulsions and death. Barbiturate overdose is a factor in nearly one-third of all reported drug-related deaths; these include suicides and accidental poisonings.

Babies born to mothers who abuse sedatives during their pregnancy may show withdrawal symptoms shortly after birth. Many sedative hypnotics pass through the placenta easily and may cause birth defects and behavioral problems in newborns.

Inhalants

Inhalants are chemicals that produce psychoactive vapors. They are grouped into four classes (1) volatile solvents (e.g., certain glues, gasoline, paint thinner, nail polish remover, lighter fluid); (2) aerosols (e.g., spray paints); (3) anesthetics (e.g., ether, chloroform, nitrous oxide); and (4) amyl and butyl nitrates. Nearly all of the abused inhalants act to depress the body's functions. At low doses, users may feel slightly stimulated and some, like butyl nitrite, produce a "rush" or "high" lasting for a few seconds or a couple of minutes. Young people are likely to abuse inhalants, in part because these chemicals are readily available and inexpensive.

Possible negative effects include nausea, sneezing, coughing, nosebleeds, fatigue, bad breath, lack of coordination, and a loss of appetite. Solvents and aerosols decrease the heart and breathing rates and affect judgment. Deep breathing of the vapors may result in a loss of self-control, violent behavior, and unconsciousness. Inhalants can cause death from suffocation by displacing oxygen in the lungs and also by depressing the central nervous system to a point that breathing stops. Long-term use can damage the brain, liver, kidneys, blood, and bone marrow.

Opiates

Opiates (narcotics) are a group of drugs used medically to relieve pain, but they also have a high potential for abuse. Some opiates (opium, morphine, heroin, and codeine) come from the Asian poppy. Others, such as meperidine (Demerol), are manufactured. Heroin accounts for 90 percent of the opiate abuse in the United States.

Opiates are often ingested, snorted, or smoked. Some are injected intravenously. After causing an initial rush, they tend to relax the user. Indicators of opiate abuse include needle scars on the arms and the backs of hands, drowsiness, frequent scratching, red and watering eyes, sniffles, and a loss of appetite overall but an attraction to sugar and candies. In contrast to the effects of most other abused drugs that dilate the eye's pupils, the opiates constrict the pupils. When an opiate-dependent person stops taking the drug, withdrawal symptoms begin within 4 to 6 hours; symptoms include anxiety, diarrhea, abdominal cramps, chills, sweating, nausea, and runny nose and eyes. The intensity of these symptoms depends on how much was taken, how often, and for how long. Withdrawal symptoms for most opiates are stronger approximately 24 to 72 hours after they begin but subside within 7 to 10 days.

Most of the physical dangers of opiate abuse are caused by overdose, the use of unsterile needles, contamination of the drug by other chemicals, or combining the drug with other substances. Over time, opiate users may develop infections of the heart lining and valves, skin abscesses, and congested lungs. Babies born to mothers using an opiate often experience withdrawal symptoms and are at high risk of other health problems.

Guidelines

The social worker should follow a number of guidelines during their initial contact with the chemically dependent individual and his or her family.

1. Because the abuse of alcohol and other drugs is such a pervasive problem in our society, assume that it will be a contributing cause to many of the individual and family problems you encounter in direct practice. The existence of a chemical dependency must be considered a possibility even when there has been no mention of the problem by the client and his or her family.

2. There is no great mystery surrounding the question of why people use drugs. Drugs and alcohol are attractive because they make people feel better, even if but for a short time. Curiosity and peer pressure also play a role in the initial stages. The powerful reinforcement provided by the chemical's mood-altering effects often leads to psychological dependence. No one starts using a drug with the intention of becoming dependent or addicted; in fact, beginners usually believe they are invulnerable to addiction. There is a steady supply of both legal drugs (e.g., alcohol, nicotine) and illegal drugs because so much money can be made in this market.

3. Never underestimate the psychological power of alcohol and drugs. The addictive process can turn an otherwise kind and honest person into a self-centered individual who is willing to lie, cheat, and even injure loved ones in order to protect and maintain his or her love relationship with a chemical. Typically, the user is adamant in denying any dependence on a substance and denies any connection between his or her problems and his or her use of alcohol or a drug.

4. Be alert to *signs of abuse and dependency.* An individual with a significant drug (or alcohol) problem will probably exhibit at least a few of the following behaviors and patterns:

- Takes more of the substance and takes it for a longer period of time than was intended
- Experiences frequent intoxication and withdrawal symptoms that interfere with performance of work, school, or family roles
- Uses substance to relieve withdrawal symptoms
- Develops tolerance to drug (i.e., more and more of substance is needed in order to attain the desired mood-altering effect)
- Has a persistent desire to quit and/or has experienced one or more unsuccessful efforts to quit
- Spends much time securing, protecting, and taking the substance
- Gives up previously valued and important activities (e.g., family, work, recreation, etc.) in favor of drinking and drug use
- Continually uses substance even though aware that its use is causing family, social, or health problems
- Experiences unexplained changes in behavior and role performance at work, in school, or within the family (e.g., avoidance of friends and loved ones)
- Neglects physical appearance, bodily hygiene, and dress
- Experiences a decrease in physical and intellectual capacities (e.g., ability to concentrate, stay on track, think logically)
- Participates in illegal activities (e.g., stealing, prostitution, etc.) when there has been no prior history of such activities
- Makes efforts to cover needle scars on arms
- Uses sunglasses to protect dilated eyes from light

5. Assess the degree to which your client's psychosocial functioning is impaired by his or her drug use. If it is a problem, referral to a treatment program is imperative. Consult with treatment specialists on how best to overcome the client's denial and resistance.

6. Learn about the 12-step recovery programs by attending "open" meetings and talking with members. Members are usually eager to consult with professionals who are trying to decide how best to approach problems presented by the chemically dependent client.

7. Be patient and nonjudgmental but do not be afraid to be confrontive in your communications. You will not help the chemically dependent client by accepting his or her denials, alibis, rationalizations, or manipulations—all of which are part of the addictive process.

8. If you are a recovering alcoholic or drug abuser, share this fact with the client. Emphasize that you know from personal experience that controlling the problem is a difficult, day-by-day struggle, but that it is possible.

9. Do not lend the client money, and do not become part of the enabling system that "covers" for the client by protecting him or her from the real-life consequences of chemical abuse.

10. If your client comes to an interview intoxicated, realize there is no point in trying to gather detailed psychosocial data or to engage the client in a counseling process. Explain in a polite but firm manner that you need accurate information to do your job and must, therefore, postpone the interview, rescheduling it for a time when the client is sober. Expect the client to become angry but remain calm and firm.

11. If an intoxicated individual appears unexpectedly at your agency, secure only basic identifying information (name, age, address, etc.) and then give attention to the individual's physical condition. Be alert to the immediate life-threatening dangers of delirium tremens or drug overdose and the need for detoxification under medical supervision.

12. Encourage family members to make use of Al-Anon and Alateen groups, along with other resources such as COA (Children of Alcoholics), ACOA or ACA (Adult Children of Alcoholics), and programs that address the problem of codependency.

13. Learn about the behavioral pattern of *codependency* that develops as a result of living for many years with someone who is chemically dependent. Typically, the codependent assumes responsibility for the behavior of others (e.g., the alcoholic) while neglecting his or her own needs and ignoring responsibility for his or her own behavior. Persons who have taken on a pattern of codependency are often hostile because of how they have been treated by someone they love, controlling because their situation is so out of control, manipulative because manipulation seems to be the only way to get things done, and indirect and vague in their communication because they live in a family system that cannot tolerate honesty.

14. The assistance and support of the client's family and friends will probably be needed in making a referral to a treatment program. Thus, it is important to reach out to these individuals and engage them in the assessment, planning, and helping process. However, be alert to the possibility that they too may have a drug problem and/or may be contributing to your client's problem through denial, enabling, or codependency behaviors.

When appropriate, consult with family members and others deeply concerned for the person who is chemically dependent and determine if they would be willing to participate in a professionally guided confrontation of the individual. This procedure (known as an ***intervention***) is used to convince the person who is locked into the denial pattern that he or she has a major problem and that there will be serious and immediate consequences if he or she does not immediately enter treatment. If it is well planned and properly implemented, it can break through the denial and help the individual accept treatment. The intervention must be planned under the direction of an experienced chemical dependency counselor who is skilled in using this procedure.

The intervention requires detailed preparation and rehearsal by the people who mean most to the client or those who exert power or control (e.g., spouse, children, employer, close friends, etc.). Each person prepares a list of specific incidents of destructive drinking or drug-related behavior and vividly describes how he or she and the client are being hurt by the chemical abuse. It is important that these feelings be conveyed in a nonjudgmental and caring manner. During several practice sessions, each person reads his or her list and rehearses the presentation until he or she feels confident enough to directly face the chemically dependent person. Such rehearsals are critical to the success of the emotionally charged encounter. The group as a whole decides when to confront the chemically dependent person. It must be unannounced and arranged at a time when the individual will be as sober and lucid as possible. Those involved gently insist that the individual listen and hear them out. The individual's usual denials and promises are not accepted, and no one comes to the person's rescue. Instead, everyone insists that the chemically dependent person must immediately—today—enter a treatment program. Prior to the confrontation, necessary arrangements are made so a treatment program is ready to accept the individual on the very day of the confrontation. Thus, all details (cost, insurance coverage, leave of absence from work, etc.) must have been worked out in advance.

If the use of an intervention is not feasible and if the chemically dependent person engages in behavior very dangerous to self or others, a court-ordered involuntary commitment to a treatment facility should be considered.

15. Realize that successful treatment usually involves three phases: (a) detoxification in a hospital or as an outpatient (i.e., supervised withdrawal from drug dependence, either with or without medication); (b) inpatient treatment within a highly structured therapeutic community where the client's denial system can be broken down and he or she begins to use counseling and self-help groups; and (c) outpatient, drug-free programs that provide counseling and self-help groups using the 12-step approach. Following these three phases, the client enters the most difficult and most important part of his or her recovery: the day-by-day and life-long struggle to rebuild his or her life and remain drug free. To be successful, the chemically dependent person must take responsibility for his or her own recovery.

The various *12-step programs* (e.g., Alcoholics Anonymous, Cocaine Anonymous, Narcotics Anonymous, etc.) have the best record of success in facilitating this long-term recovery process. These self-help programs provide encouragement and teach methods of day-by-day coping. They emphasize the development of one's spirituality and help the individual reorient his or her philosophy of living and lifestyle.

16. Once the individual stops using chemicals, special attention must be given to planning for relapse prevention. This involves helping the individual develop a plan for coping with those times and situations when he or she will be at risk of resuming the use of alcohol and drugs.

17. Because drugs alter mood, individuals with low self-esteem, feelings of powerlessness or loneliness, and emotional pain are especially prone to misuse drugs. Because they do not value themselves, they do not believe they are capable of changing their situation, so they look to things outside themselves (e.g., drugs) for relief from life's problems and pain. Effective recovery programs counteract these beliefs and help the individual develop self-esteem, learn problem-solving skills, rely on inner resources, and create drug-free relationships with others.

18. Be aware that hundreds of over-the-counter medicines and grocery store products contain alcohol (e.g., vanilla extract, certain cough syrups, cold medicines, and some mouthwashes). This fact may be important in the identification of substance abuse problems and especially for recovering alcoholics who are using *anabuse* in their treatment and will, therefore, have a violent physical reaction to alcohol in any form.

19. Be alert to problems caused by the misuse of other drugs and medications. For example, it is estimated that about one million individuals, mostly male, use *anabolic steroids* to boost their athletic strength and physical appearance; more than half of these people are under age 18. Steroids are not addictive like the other drugs discussed in this section, but they do pose a serious problem. Steroids are attractive because they build muscles, but they also cause tumors, high blood pressure, shrunken testicles, liver and kidney disorders, and erratic sleep disorders. In young users, steroids can retard growth. In some cases, steroid use leads to violent mood shifts, aggression, and violence. Steroids are easy to obtain and inexpensive.

SELECTED BIBLIOGRAPHY

American Psychiatric Association. *DSM-IV.* Washington, D.C.: APA, 1994.

Cermak, Timmen. *Diagnosing and Treating Co-Dependence.* Minneapolis: Johnson Institute Books, 1986.

Doweiko, Harold. *Concepts of Chemical Dependency,* 2nd. ed. Pacific Grove, Calif.: Brooks/Cole, 1993.

Inaba, Darryl, and William Cohen. *Uppers, Downers, All Arounders,* 2nd ed. Ashland, Ore.: CNS Productions, 1993.

Levin, Jerome. *Introduction to Alcoholism Counseling*, 2nd. ed. Washington, D.C.: Taylor and Francis, 1995.

McNeece, C. Aaron, and Diana Dinitto. *Chemical Dependency: A Systems Approach.* Englewood Cliffs, N. J.: Prentice Hall, 1994.

Miller, William, and Stephen Rollnick. *Motivational Interviewing: Preparing People to Change Addictive Behavior.* New York: Guilford Press, 1991.

Schlaadt, Richard, and Peter Shannon. *Drugs: Use, Misuse and Abuse,* 4th ed. Englewood Cliffs, N. J.: Prentice Hall, 1994.

11.10   The Manipulative Client

PURPOSE: To respond appropriately to the client who frequently manipulates other people.

DISCUSSION: Most people, at least occasionally, attempt to manipulate others as a way of getting what they want. However, some individuals rely on manipulation and "conning" as a primary means of coping with life. These individuals can be difficult clients, primarily because they are so skilled and subtle in "using" other people. Social workers who are unable to detect a manipulation may quickly find themselves in legal and ethical difficulties.

Some of the most practiced manipulators are labeled as "sociopaths," "psychopaths," or as having an "antisocial personality disorder." Many have a long history of criminal activity. Hare (1993) explains that the hallmark of the psychopath is their lack of a conscience; they do not experience genuine remorse or guilt. They also lack empathy and are unable to appreciate the feelings of other people. Additional common characteristics include a glib and superficial manner of relating, egocentric and grandiose thinking, shallow emotions, impulsiveness and poor self-control, a strong need for excitement and risk taking, and antisocial behavior. For them, truth is whatever fits their purpose at the moment. Many grew up in environments where manipulation was the key to their physical and psychological survival; thus, it is useful to view manipulation as the continuation of behavioral patterns that proved effective in the past. Included here are a few guidelines.

1.   The manipulative client, like all clients, is deserving of respect. With this client, however, you need to be much more cautious, deliberate, and careful in your actions. You must be explicit in outlining your role, what you can and cannot do as a professional person, and your expectations of the client. You must demonstrate firmness and strength of conviction. Yochelson and Samenow (1985) remind us that the habitual manipulator is always behaving in ways that help him or her gain control of others.

He tries to determine what others want to hear and feeds it to them. He finds and uses opportunities for digression and diversion. He discloses as it suits his purposes. He slants his version of events to make himself a victim and blames others for his plight in life. He tries whatever he thinks will impress the [change agent], enlist his sympathy and compassion, or convince him of a particular point of view. Failing this, he uses a variety of tactics to put [the change agent] on the defensive. These may be couched in highly intellectual terms as the criminal argues the meaning of a word, disputes a philosophic issue, and generalizes a point to absurdity. However, there are also open power plays as he intimidates, threatens, ridicules and erupts with angry reactions.

The agent of change has no hope of being successful if he allows a criminal to set the conditions of a meeting. . . . The [agent of change] must stand firm. . . . [A professional] who is indecisive or lacks confidence does not instill confidence or respect in a criminal. Nor can [a professional] who is permissive later establish himself as a firm authority. Many criminals have had experience with permissive change agents and have exploited them. A person who is shy, timid, or reserved may do well in many endeavors, but he will fail to effect change in criminals. (p. 541)

2. Suspect a manipulation whenever your client takes an inordinate interest in your personal life or your feelings about your job. Be especially cautious when your client says such things as, "You are the only person that really understands me," "No one else has ever been as helpful as you," "You are the most caring person I have ever met," "If you could just do this one thing for me (often something illegal or unethical), I can get my life straightened out," "I have a wonderful opportunity to pull my life together—I just need a small loan," or "I need to tell you something but you must promise not to tell this to anyone else." Also, be alert to the possibility of manipulation if your client makes frequent use of the word *but* as a way of avoiding responsibility or downplaying the seriousness of a behavior (e.g., "Well yes I did steal some money but only 30 dollars" or "I hit him with a chair but not very hard").

3. If you suspect a manipulation, consult with another professional and examine your actions and feelings. If you are part of a team, raise your concerns with team members. Often you will find that the client is saying very different things to other team members. An elevated level of communication and coordination is necessary to keep team members from being drawn into a manipulation where one is played against another.

4. Inform your client that above all else, you do not want him or her to lie. Say, for example, "I want to be very clear on one point. If I ask you a question that you do not want to answer, tell me so. Do not lie to me. If you lie, it will only confuse our relationship; it will not help you and it will not help me." Remember that there are no completely reliable ways of knowing when a person is lying. It is very difficult to detect a lie offered by a person who is practiced in the art of lying. It is especially difficult if you have not previously observed this person with others in a variety of situations. A few generalizations can help detect a lie:

- Most people feel at least a bit uncomfortable when they lie. Consequently, when lying, their voices often become higher in pitch and they are more likely to stumble over words.
- When lying, people tend to use fewer descriptive phrases and fewer hand motions than when they are not engaged in deception. Also, when lying, they are more prone to frequent blinking and fidgeting.
- Engage the person in several minutes of friendly small talk before addressing a topic about which they may lie and before asking pointed questions aimed at detecting a deception. An obvious change in voice, facial expressions, or other body language suggests a deception.

- Even a clever, confident, and experienced liar cannot completely control his or her facial expressions. Thus, they may exhibit a momentary look of panic when they fear they have been detected.
- The experienced liar has prepared and practiced responses to commonly asked questions, but his or her response often sounds emotionally flat. A really unusual or unexpected question may catch such a person off guard.

5. Be fair but unwavering in your expectations of these clients. Hold manipulative clients responsible for their behavior and do not rescue them from the natural consequences of their choices. Before deciding to change their behavior, they usually need first to experience the punishing consequences of their actions.

6. Professionals who are usually nonjudgmental in their relationships with clients may become judgmental when they encounter the manipulative client, especially one who knows how to "work the system"—meaning that the client can accurately predict how agencies, social workers, and other professionals will respond under certain circumstances. You can increase your tolerance for these clients and decrease your judgmentalness by remembering that manipulation is essentially a coping strategy. This client uses manipulation because it works better than anything else he or she knows how to do. Although there may be something particularly irritating about people who use deception and lies to manipulate caring professionals, it is important to remember that in other areas of society, being able to "work the system" is a mark of competence. For example, the lawyer, businessperson, or social worker who knows how to get the "system" to do what he or she wants is viewed as someone with great skill.

SELECTED BIBLIOGRAPHY

Allen, Bud, and Diana Bosta. *Games Criminals Play.* Sacramento: Rae John Publishers, 1981.

Doren, Dennis. *Understanding and Treating the Psychopath.* New York: Wiley, 1987.

Hare, Robert. *Without Conscience: The Disturbing World of the Psychpaths Among Us.* New York: Simon and Schuster, 1993.

Harris, George, ed. *Tough Customers: Counseling Unwilling Clients.* Laurel, Md.: American Correctional Association, 1991.

Yochelson, Samuel, and Stanton Samenow. *The Criminal Personality,* Vol. II. Northvale, N.J.: Jason Aronson, 1985.

11.11   The Dangerous Client

PURPOSE: To respond to a potentially violent client in a manner that reduces the danger inherent in the situation.

DISCUSSION: Social workers in correctional settings and child protective services, more than those in other fields of practice, are frequently in contact with persons who are potentially violent. For example, the removal of a abused child from an abusing parent always carries some risk of being physically assaulted. When interacting with an extremely angry and potentially violent person, the social worker should adhere to the following guidelines.

1. Never enter a situation believed to be dangerous without first consulting with others about your plans. Consider the situation to be high risk whenever you are to meet with individuals who have a history of violence or who possess firearms or other lethal weapons, and whenever you are to meet an unfamiliar client in a non-public or isolated place. An inadvertent encounter with illegal activity such as drug dealing is also dangerous. If you must enter a dangerous situation, do not hesitate to call for police protection.

2. A history of violent behavior is the best predictor of future violence. Statistically speaking, individuals with certain characteristics and certain life experiences are more likely to commit violent acts, such as:

- Has a history of committing violent acts
- Is violent when under the influence of alcohol or drugs
- Is or was the target of violence and/or observed family violence during childhood
- Is or was the target of violence in his or her community
- Has been publicly humiliated
- Is part of a violent peer group
- Is experiencing a high level of stress
- Is a male teen or a young adult
- Has experienced a tramatic brain injury

3. An agency's recordkeeping system should utilize color coding or some other method of flagging the case record of a potentially dangerous client so the social worker who is to meet the client for the first time can take appropriate precautions. Your agency should have a preestablished emergency communication code so all staff will recognize a disguised request for assistance. For example, in a telephone message such as, "Hello Bob. This is Jim. Would you please send a copy of our red resource book to my office?" the phrase *red resource book* might be code for "send the police to my office."

4. When making a home visit that could develop into a dangerous situation, always keep your office aware of your concern and informed of your itinerary, and check in by phone according to a prearranged schedule. Before entering a home or building, take a few seconds to look around and think about your safety. Are you alone? Where are the escape routes? Do you hear a violent argument in process? Do the people inside sound out of control?

5. Never move through a doorway as a response to an invitation to "come in" unless you can see the person who is speaking and he or she has seen you. (Being mistaken for someone else can be dangerous.) When entering a room containing an angry person, move in slowly. Remain on the periphery until you can assess the situation and then move in slowly. Do not move into the person's space. Intrusive movement may trigger violent behavior.

6. Be alert to anything about the situation that feels or looks unusual or out of place. We all possess an unconscious "danger detector." Thus, trust your "gut feelings." If you feel afraid, assume that you are in danger even if you cannot pinpoint why you are feeling this way.

7. Most people who become angry will vent for 2 or 3 minutes and then begin to calm down. However, some individuals are further stimulated and aggravated by what they say and think in anger. If an angry individual is not calming down after a few minutes, assume that the situation has become more dangerous.

8. Do not touch an angry person; do nothing that could be interpreted as a threat. If possible, sit rather than stand, because sitting is a less aggressive stance. Also encourage the client to sit, as it usually has a calming effect. However, avoid sitting in a overstuffed chair or sofa because it can be difficult to rapidly get up and out of a well-cushioned chair. Rather, pick a hard, movable chair that could be used for protection if you are attacked.

9. Be alert to signs of imminent attack such as flaring nostrils, rapid breathing, dilated pupils, pulsing veins, grinding teeth, pointing fingers, clenching fists, choppy movements and speech, crouching upper body, and bobbing or dipping movements of the body. Do not turn your back to an angry or distraught person nor let that person walk behind you. If the danger of the situation escalates, leave.

10. When in the home of a potentially violent person, be alert to the fact that guns are usually kept in the bedroom and that the kitchen contains numerous potential weapons. If the person has threatened you and then moves quickly to one of these rooms, leave immediately.

11. An attack on others is often a reaction to being afraid; thus, do what you can to lessen the person's need to be afraid of you. Remain composed and speak in a gentle and soothing manner. Do not argue, accuse, or give advice. Demonstrate empathy for the person's feelings of frustration and anger. Use active listening skills (see Item 8.3) to secure an accurate understanding of his or her feelings. If an inappropriate statement on your part causes the client to become angry, admit your error and apologize. Use I-messages (see Item 8.5) when expressing your concerns or explaining your intentions, role, and responsibilities. Allow the angry client to ventilate; this can drain off some of the emotional intensity.

12. Aggressiveness and attacks often arise out of a feeling of being controlled by others. Thus, for an office interview, position your furniture and yourself so you have easy access to an escape route; make sure that the client also has easy access to the door so he or she does not feel trapped. To the extent possible, increase the client's sense of being in control by offering options and choices and using language such as, "Of course, it is up to you to decide what is best" or "Think about what we have discussed and decide which course of action you want to follow."

13. Select clothing and shoes that permit running and rapid movement. Do not wear long earrings that can be easily grabbed. Maintain a neat, well-groomed appearance and an attitude of confidence that projects the impression that you take your job seriously and are able to handle the situation. An angry person is more likely to attack someone who appears weak, afraid, and insecure.

14. Do not attempt to disarm a person with a weapon. Leave that to the police! If your client has a weapon, calmly explain that you intend no harm and then slowly back away or otherwise extricate yourself from the situation.

15. The social worker's family (e.g., spouse, children) may become the target of a client's anger and violence. Thus, family members should be informed and prepared for that possibility.

16. If you work in a dangerous neighborhood, secure guidance from experienced peers, local merchants, and the police on how to protect yourself. If you are likely to encounter dangerous clients, ask your agency for in-service training on nonviolent self-defense. You must be able to protect yourself from harm without inflicting physical injury on your clients. If you secure training in self-defense be sure to select an instructor who has had personal experience with violent persons. Remember, even excellent training does not adequately prepare you for the real thing. Never overestimate your ability to handle a situation or underestimate the paralyzing effect of fear.

SELECTED BIBLIOGRAPHY

Cambell, Jacquelyn, ed. *Assessing Dangerousness.* Thousand Oaks, Calif.: Sage, 1995.
Griffin, William. "Social Worker and Agency Safety." In *Encyclopedia of Social Work,* 19th ed., Vol. 3, edited by Richard L. Edwards. Washington, D.C.: NASW, 1995, pp. 2293–2305.
Kaplan, Stephen, and Eugenie Wheeler. "Survival Skills for Working with Potentially Violent Clients." *Social Casework* 64 (June 1983): 339–346.
Schoborn, Karl. *Dealing with Violence: The Challenge Faced by Police and Other Peacekeepers.* Springfield, Ill.: Charles C. Thomas, 1975.

SECTION B
TECHNIQUES AND GUIDELINES FOR INDIRECT PRACTICE

Most new social workers begin with jobs that primarily involve working directly with clients. Later, many master's-level workers move into supervisory, administrative, and other positions in which they devote much of their attention to the functioning of human services agencies and working with the network of agencies in the community. This book is not intended for that more experienced social worker. Rather, the indirect-service techniques and guidelines have been selected to support the activities of the direct-service practitioner who must develop the necessary background knowledge and skills to work effectively with or in behalf of clients.

At the intake and engagement phase of indirect practice, the focus is on getting the appropriate staff in place, whether professional or volunteer, and learning about the agency and the community. Perhaps the first task is to learn about the agency's culture. This process begins at the point the worker applies for a job (see Item 10.1), but must be expanded once employment begins. An ***organization's culture*** consists of the set of beliefs and behavioral expectations that shape its norms and operating procedures. Workers are rewarded when their actions are appropriate to the culture and are penalized when they violate that culture. Thus, an agency's culture has a profound effect on worker performance, and the new worker must take the steps to understand these norms and expectations as he or she becomes a part of the agency.

The methods for selecting and orienting professional and volunteer staff members is also important for the worker to understand. The people who make up a human services agency are the most important feature of its operation. The process of personnel selection is therefore critical and should be carefully planned and executed. Every social worker should be knowledgeable about what makes a sound and fair screening and selection process (see Items 11.13 and 11.14) and attempt to improve that process if it does not meet those criteria.

Because social workers are concerned with the environment as well as the person, they must also have a thorough knowledge of the community in which they work. The local community is the context in which clients (as well as the social workers) live out their lives, the agency gains its sanction to provide its services, social problems emerge, and responsive programs are created. Knowing one's community is essential, both for understanding the nature of the issues and for facilitating change when problems exist.

11.12   Learning about Your Agency

PURPOSE: To become knowledgeable about an agency's purpose, structure, and procedures.

DISCUSSION: Most social workers are employed by either a private or a public agency. ***Public agencies*** (whether at the city, county, state, or federal level) are established by legislation adopted by elected officials and are funded by tax dollars. By contrast, most ***private agencies*** (also called *voluntary agencies*) are nonprofit corporations funded primarily by voluntary contributions and possibly by fees, grants, or contracts. It should be noted that some of the organizations providing mental health and substance abuse treatment may be ***for-profit corporations*** designed to yield income for investors and stockholders. Some private agencies enter into the purchase of service contracts with public agencies and are paid to deliver specified services; thus, such private agencies are funded, in part, by tax dollars. The term ***membership agency*** refers to a private agency that derives a significant portion of its funds from membership fees (e.g., a YMCA). The term ***sectarian agency*** is often used to describe a private agency that is under the auspices of a specific religious body (e.g., Jewish Community Services, Catholic Social Services).

Social agencies and programs have typically been created in response to some need or problem as perceived by elected officials, powerful community leaders, or investors. Professional social workers may have some influence on an agency's program and operating procedures but they seldom have an opportunity to determine an agency's overall direction and mission.

In order to deliver social services and programs effectively, the social worker must understand the agency's mission, structure, funding, policies, and procedures. The following activities will help the worker learn about his or her agency.

1. Ask your supervisor and experienced agency staff for guidance on how best to become familiar with the agency's purpose, policies and operation. Study the agency's organization chart and determine how you and your immediate supervisor and your department or unit fit into the chain of command.

2. If your agency is a public agency, read the law(s) that established the agency and those describing the specific programs that the agency is to administer (e.g., state child protection laws) and examine relevant state and federal administrative rules and regulations.

3. If your agency is a private agency, read the agency's bylaws that describe the agency's purpose and the functions of the board of directors and its officers and committees and how board meetings are to be conducted. The bylaws will also describe the responsibilities assigned to the executive director.

4. Examine your agency's manual of policies and procedures. Pay special attention to any ethical guidelines that prescribe employee behavior, as agencies may differ in what they believe to be unethical activities. For example, many agencies will have guidelines for such potential ethical issues as:

- Use of time at work for personal matters or a private practice
- Use of agency property (e.g., telephones, fax, automobiles, copy machines, computer, office space) for personal use or private practice
- Receipt of gifts from clients, other employees, or persons who are in a position to receive referrals of fee-paying clients from agency employees
- Use of the agency's name or the worker's affiliation with the agency in outside activities
- Provision of agency services to friends and family
- Situations wherein personal or financial interests might conflict, or appear to conflict, with official duties
- Publication and dissemination of research reports or other information prepared or developed during agency employment
- Sale of materials prepared on agency time or with agency resources

5. Read documents that describe your agency's history, mission, and philosophy. Find out how the agency has changed during the past 5 to 10 years and what community or political forces are having a significant impact on the agency. Seek information about the agency's goals and objectives for the current year and its goals and plans for the next 3 to 5 years.

6. Examine the agency's personnel policies, the tools or forms that will be used in the evaluation of your job performance. Read the union contract, if one exists.

7. If your agency must conform to standards issued by a national accrediting organization (e.g., Child Welfare League of America, Council on Accreditation of Rehabilitation Facilities), review those portions of the accreditation standards that apply most directly to your areas of service.

8. Examine your agency's budget. Pay special attention to the sources of income, because the agency must be responsive to these sources if it is to continue to attract needed funding and remain solvent. Also, review any purchase of service agreements, interagency agreements, or protocol statements that tie the services and operation of your agency to other agencies or funding sources. If your are working on a project funded by a grant or a contact, read the relevant documents so you know what the funding source is expecting of the project.

9. Examine statistical reports compiled by your agency and determine which of its programs and services are most used and least used by clients and consumers. Also, examine data that describe the people served by your agency in terms of their ages, genders, social-economic status, races, ethnicities, religions, and so on.

10. Determine what procedures are used to evaluate agency performance and the quality of services provided. Also determine how the agency's clients and consumers are involved in evaluation and planning services and programs.

11. Identify the agencies and organizations with which your agency frequently interacts. Determine what community or state planning agencies have an impact on your agency and how the services and programs provided by your agency are to be coordinated with other agencies in the community.

12. Determine what specific roles, tasks, and activities are assigned to the agency's social work staff and those assigned to persons of other disciplines and professions. Also, find out what practice frameworks guide service delivery (see Chapter 6).

13. Talk to community leaders and professionals outside your agency to ascertain how your agency and its programs are perceived by others. Determine the public image attached to your agency and how it acquired that reputation.

SELECTED BIBLIOGRAPHY

Flynn, John. *Social Agency Policy,* 2nd ed. Chicago: Nelson-Hall, 1992.
Weinbach, Robert. *The Social Worker as Manager,* 2nd ed. Boston: Allyn and Bacon, 1994.

11.13   Staff Recruitment and Selection

PURPOSE: To conduct a fair and effective search for agency staff.

DISCUSSION: The quality of staff is critically important in the provision of human services. Thus, the skill or ability to provide the agency's services should be the key consideration in selecting new staff. Social work values require that a search is open, fair, and does not discriminate on the basis of race, national origin, gender, age, disability, or sexual orientation. It is important, therefore, that social workers who participate in recruiting and selecting new staff be familiar with the elements of a good affirmative action search. This understanding is also valuable because social workers too are persons being hired for positions in human services organizations and knowledge of the search process helps them to successfully compete for available positions (see Item 10.1).

The Search Committee
One of the most important elements of a search is the membership of the search committee. If the members all reflect a particular viewpoint (such as being from the same age, gender, or ethnic group), it is more likely that the person selected for the position will also reflect those characteristics and associated perspectives. Thus, the membership should include a mix of persons in ethnic background, age, and gender. It should also reflect a range of perceptions of the agency, including those of staff, board, and clientele. Usually a committee of four or five persons is sufficient; it is small enough to be efficient yet large enough to represent a range of perspectives.

Contents of a Position Announcement
The search committee (often with input from other staff and board members) must prepare a position announcement. It should be prepared very carefully, as it must serve to attract qualified applicants and, at the same time, become the basis on which applicants will be evaluated. At a minimum, a position announcement should contain the following:

1. *A description of the major tasks of the position.* In most cases, this can be adapted from the job description. Any changes in that description should be identified before the position announcement is finalized. Applicants are expected to prepare a cover letter that specifically identifies their preparation for this job.

2. *A statement of legitimate requirements for the position.* In order to avoid discriminating against potential applicants, and particularly against population groups that have less access to advanced education, it is important that the qualifications are appropriate to the work to be performed. For example, a M.S.W. degree should not be required when a B.S.W. is sufficient; five years of practice experience should not be required of an entry-level position; and so on. It is important to separate those characteristics that are *required* from those that are *preferred.*

3. *The closing date for applications.* Provide enough time between the date the announcement is published and the closing date to allow potential candidates to learn of the opening, prepare application materials, get permission from potential references, and permit the mail to reach the search committee. A minimum of four weeks is suggested.

4. *A description of how to apply.* Clearly identify the materials that will constitute a completed application. Usually, this will include a resumé, names and addresses of three to five persons who could be contacted as references (or letters of reference supplied with the application), and sometimes an application form. The announcement should include the name, address, and phone number of the person responsible for the search or a person who can be contacted for answers to questions.

5. *The salary range and starting date.* If these factors are known, include them, as they help to screen out persons who would not consider the position if this information were known. Such self-screening saves time and energy for both the applicant and the selection committee.

Advertising

It is important to advertise the position widely. The most commonly used sources are the local newspaper, the *NASW News* (national), and the state chapter or local program unit of NASW's newsletter. It may also be productive to circulate a flyer to local agencies and to contact any coalitions of minority social workers that exist in the community or region. In addition, the committee, board, and staff should identify and encourage applications from qualified persons with whom they are familiar. It takes only one strong applicant to conclude a successful search, but the chances are vastly improved when selection can be made from a pool of strong candidates.

Paper Screening

When the closing date has passed, the completed applications are reviewed by the committee. This "paper screening" involves independently reading the candidates' files and evaluating each according to the criteria identified in the position announcement. Prior to examining individual files, the committee should develop an evaluation form to score the applications. This form should list the required and preferred characteristics, and sometimes numerical weights are assigned to represent the importance of a specific characteristic for the job. A narrative statement of impressions of the candidate should be recorded to serve as a basis for committee discussion and as documentation in case the search process is challenged by an unsuccessful candidate.

When this review of applications is completed, the committee is then prepared to meet, compare evaluations, discuss differences in perception, eliminate unacceptable candidates from consideration, and develop a priority list to invite for interviews. It is a professional courtesy to inform applicants not placed on the priority list that they are no longer under consideration.

Interviewing

Usually, three to five candidates are interviewed for a position, although the priority list may include backup candidates. The interviews should be carefully planned and hosted by members of the committee. However, other members of the staff and board should participate in the interviews. A list of questions to be asked of all candidates should be prepared by the committee in order to provide a fair comparison between the finalists. All persons involved in interviews should be warned against asking inappropriate personal questions about a candidate's marital status, plans for having children, child care arrangements, sexual orientation, and other such topics. It should be assumed that professionals will make appropriate provision for their personal lives and keep that separate from professional responsibilities. The interview should be a time of give and take between the candidate and the agency. It is important to remember that not only is the agency determining if the candidate is suitable for the job, but the candidate is also making a decision about accepting the position, should it be offered.

Selection

Following the interviews, feedback from the various participants should be collected and reviewed by the committee. At this point, the committee should be prepared to conclude the search and recommend one or more persons (preferably in rank order) to the executive director or those responsible for hiring. The committee's frank evaluation of the candidates' strengths and limitations should be shared with this person. The job can then be offered and negotiated. When the position is filled, all persons left from the priority list should be informed of the decision and thanked for their interest. Records of the search should be maintained for a minimum of three years.

SELECTED BIBLIOGRAPHY

Pecora, Peter J., and Michael J. Austin. *Managing Human Services Personnel,* 3rd ed. Newbury Park, Calif.: Sage, 1987.

Pecora, Peter. "Personnel Management." *In Encyclopedia of Social Work,* 19th ed., Vol. 3, edited by Richard Edwards. Washington, D.C.: 1995, pp. 1828–1836.

11.14   Selecting and Training Volunteers

PURPOSE: To screen and prepare volunteers to provide human services as caregivers and as an adjunct to the agency staff.

DISCUSSION: Social workers often have the responsibility to recruit, train, and supervise the work of volunteers. Throughout the history of social welfare in the United States, volunteers have played a central role. Volunteers can help to maximize scarce agency and professional resources. In addition, experienced and informed volunteers often become effective advocates for the agency and its programs. Volunteers can perform a wide variety of important tasks, ranging from office work and fund-raising to activities involving client contact. The key to using volunteers successfully is being able to match the task to the volunteer's special interests and abilities. However, if volunteers are not carefully selected, prepared, and supervised, they become frustrated and may quit. In some cases, they may harm agency clients and damage the agency's reputation.

Volunteers are especially active in the area of youth services. Examples include the work of volunteers in YMCA/YWCA and Big Sister/Big Brother programs, Scouting, 4-H, foster care, tutoring programs, and so forth. Increasingly, the various forms of caregiving are popular areas of volunteer activity. Typically, these volunteers are assigned duties that will support or supplement the services provided by professionals. Examples include providing transportation, companionship, or personal care to people who are elderly or disabled, helping such an individual write letters and pay bills, delivering or preparing meals, and so on. Such volunteer-supported home care is far less expensive than nursing home or other forms of institutionalized care.

Recruitment

Reaching out to the community and attracting volunteers to the work of the agency must be an ongoing activity. Because there is always some turnover, new volunteers must be found to replace those who leave. In general, volunteers are the best recruiters of other volunteers. If agency volunteers enjoy their work, they will tell their friends and attract them to the idea of volunteering. On the other hand, if an agency treats its volunteers poorly, it will soon have a bad reputation and will find it very difficult to recruit volunteers.

Screening

One of the most difficult and sensitive tasks is to screen volunteers. Maintaining the goodwill of people who express an interest in volunteer work must be balanced against the agency's responsibility to protect its clients from harm and exploitation. This is especially true when the agency's clients are highly vulnerable, such as children and the frail elderly. It must be remembered that the agency assumes a legal liability for the work of its volunteers; improper screening can leave the agency open to a costly lawsuit.

Several questions might be asked to assess a person's motivation and capacity for volunteer work, such as:

- Why are you interested in being a volunteer in this agency?
- What type of activity is of greatest interest?
- Are there certain tasks or activities that are of little or no interest?
- Are you hoping to have direct contact with agency clients? If yes, with what type of clients? If yes, what type of relationship do you want to have with clients?
- What do you expect to gain personally from this experience?
- Have you been a volunteer for other agencies? If yes, when and where? Can you provide references?
- For about how long do you expect to serve as a volunteer?
- How much time can you contribute each week or month? Can you commit to being at the agency on certain days of each week or month?
- What special skills and experience would you bring to the agency? Do you have certain limitations that the agency should know about?
- What type of training and supervision do you expect from the agency?
- How will you maintain confidentiality concerning the agency and client information you may obtain while working as a volunteer?

Throughout the screening process, special attention needs to be given to the person's attitudes toward the agency's clients and the problems or concerns the clients bring to the agency. References should be obtained and checked on those volunteers who will have direct contact with agency clients. Police checks for a history of child molestation are important on volunteers who will work with children.

Job Description

Being able to provide a clear description of the agency's expectations and the volunteer's duties is critical to successful recruitment and selection. The agency should prepare a written job description for the position to be filled by a volunteer. That description should address at least the following:

- Specific tasks and activities to be performed
- Time required each week or month and perhaps the duration of the activity (e.g., volunteer must commit to one year)
- Training and skills needed by the volunteer
- Name and title of person who will supervise the volunteer

A signed contract with the volunteer may be used to further define duties and responsibilities.

Training

Volunteers must be adequately trained for the specific tasks and work they are assigned. The staff member to whom the volunteer is responsible is usually the best person to provide this training. Demonstrations of how the tasks should be performed and ongoing coaching are often necessary. Volunteers need to be constantly reminded of the importance of confidentiality.

New volunteers should be oriented to the agency's structure, operations, and programs. Part of this orientation can be conducted with groups of volunteers. In these sessions, it is helpful to use case examples and allow the volunteers to share ideas and interact with agency staff. Staff observations may be useful to the screening and selection process.

Support and Monitoring

Volunteers must be supervised and supported to make sure they are meeting agency expectations, are properly prepared for their work, and are finding satisfaction in their work. Because volunteers are not paid, they must receive recognition for the work they do. They must feel appreciated. Many volunteers quit because they do not receive the recognition, support, and supervision they expect of agency staff.

Some types of volunteer work is stressful. For example, those who work in hospice programs, nursing homes, or foster-care programs find their work to be emotionally draining. Such volunteers may become too attached to their clients and experience a sense of loss and grieving when a client dies or is transferred to another facility. Agency staff must be able to help the volunteers work through painful experiences.

SELECTED BIBLIOGRAPHY

MacDuff, Nancy. *Designing Programs for the Volunteer Sector.* Walla Walla, Wash.: MacDuff/Bunt Associates, 1989.

Moore, Larry, ed. *Motivating Volunteers.* Vancouver, B.C.: Vancouver Volunteer Center, 1985.

Navarre, Ralph G. *Professional Administration of Volunteer Programs.* Madison, Wis.: "N"-Way Publishing, 1986.

11.15   Learning about Your Community

PURPOSE: To conduct an informal assessment of a community in order to understand the context in which an agency's services are delivered.

DISCUSSION: Essentially, a community is a group of people who feel a bond with each other because they share an identity, common interests, and a sense of belonging. Thus, it is possible to speak of the social work community, the business community, or a particular ethnic community. Communities are also defined as geographic entities such as neighborhoods or barrios and as legal entities such as towns or cities. Given the usual activities and responsibilities of social workers, *community* is defined as a social system, operating in a particular locality, that performs certain functions for the people living in that area. The basic functions that such communities are expected to perform are the following:

1. *Provision and distribution of goods and services.* Water, food, housing, garbage disposal, medical care, education, transportation, recreation, social services, information, and the like are provided.

2. *Location of business activity and employment.* Commerce and jobs exist from which people earn the money needed to purchase goods and services.

3. *Public safety.* Protection from criminal behavior and hazards such as fires, floods, and toxic chemicals is provided.

4. *Socialization.* Opportunities are available to communicate and interact with others and to develop a sense of identity and belonging beyond that provided by the family system.

5. *Mutual support.* Tangible assistance and social supports beyond those provided by one's family are available.

6. *Social control.* Rules and norms necessary to guide and control large numbers of people (e.g., laws, police, courts, traffic control, pollution control, etc.)are established and enforced.

7. *Political organization, and participation.* Governance and decision making related to local matters and public services are in place (e.g., streets, sewer, education, public welfare, public health, economic development, zoning of housing and businesses, etc.).

By conducting an informal study of the community, a social worker will obtain information about existing resources, identify gaps in the availability of human services, and better understand the behavior and attitudes of clients. As compared to a formal study that would be used in a large-scale community planning effort, the informal community study is intended for use by the social work practitioners. Such an assessment has three purposes.

1. *To understand the context of one's practice.* The social worker must become knowledgeable about the community's history, as well as its economic and political structures and the prevailing values, norms, and myths that affect decision making and intergroup behavior.

2. *To evaluate the existing human services system.* The social worker needs to know what services are available and to understand community attitudes toward people who have psychosocial problems and utilize the human services. Communities differ in their willingness to respond to human needs and fund social agencies. Communities also differ in regard to how well the local professionals and agencies work together.

3. *To acquire understanding of the community decision-making structure.* At some point, the social worker's desire for more adequate human services should lead to efforts to bring about changes in the community's response to a particular problem or need. To succeed in those efforts, the social worker must understand the power structure operating in the community, the beliefs and values of the leaders and key actors who decide what programs and services will be provided and funded, and the formal and informal processes used to reach those decisions.

The social worker's study and assessment of his or her community is an ongoing activity that must be continually updated as new information surfaces. However, it is essential that this process be initiated when beginning work in a new community. This might be done in collaboration with several other professionals who are also new to the community.

Information that describes a community and its functioning can be gleaned from documents such as census tract data, economic forecasts, public health reports, prior studies of a community problem, reports related to community planning projects, directories of health and human services agencies, and the like. Helpful documents may be available from the local library, Chamber of Commerce, United Way, and government offices. Supplemental data might be obtained by reading historical accounts of how the community grew and developed and how it responded to recent problems, by interviewing long-time residents, and by closely following current issues and controversies reported in the local news. It is important to record the names of the organizations and individuals who are important decision makers, especially those associated with human services concerns.

Although the social worker's area of practice will determine the nature and depth of information sought in relation to particular aspects of the community and its service systems, certain general information is essential. The following points will help the social worker develop a profile of the community in which he or she is working.

1. *Identifying information*
   - Name(s) of city, community, or neighborhood
   - Names used to refer to neighborhoods, sections, or areas of the community
   - Social, legal, and physical boundaries that define the community
   - Distance from other cities or communities

2. *Demographics*
   - Total population and number per square block or square mile
   - Age distribution (e.g., number of preschoolers, number in grade school and high school, persons over age 65, etc.)
   - Minority and ethnic groups; languages spoken by various groups
   - Religious affiliations and traditions
   - Size of families and types of households (e.g., married couples, single parents, people living alone)

3. *History of area*
   - When, why, and by whom was area developed
   - Major events that shaped area's development and the attitudes of it's people
   - Changes in characteristics of population over time
   - Reasons why newcomers moved to area; reasons why do people move away

4. *Geography and environmental influences on community*
   - Effect of climate, mountains, valleys, rivers, lakes, and so forth on local transportation patterns, economic development, and population distribution
   - Effect of highways, railroads, truck routes, and other corridors and barriers on neighborhood patterns, social interaction, agency location, and service delivery
   - Effect of natural resources and environmental concerns on current and future development (e.g., water supply, pollution, sewage treatment, sources of electricity and energy, distance from markets)

5. *Beliefs and attitudes*
   - Dominant values, beliefs, and attitudes of population and its various subgroups
   - Types of human services agencies and programs that are valued and respected and that attract community support, favorable publicity, and funding
   - Types of agencies and programs that have been rejected by the community or viewed in an unfavorable light, and underfunded
   - Residents' sense of "belonging" to the community
   - Identification with and a sense of loyalty and responsibility toward the community

6. *Local politics*
   - Form of local government
   - Relative power and influence of political parties and various interest groups
   - Level of voter participation
   - Types and level of taxes used to secure public funds
   - Current debates, issues, and controversies at local level

7. *Local economy and businesses*
   - Major industries, businesses, and products of area
   - Area's businesses and corporations that are locally owned and those controlled from outside the community

- Types of jobs and work available in area (wages; part time or full time; seasonal or year-round; hours and times of work)
- Job skills required by major employers
- Reasons why new businesses move to area; move away from area
- Percentage of labor force employed; unemployed
- Forecast of future economic growth and job opportunity

8. *Income distribution*
   - Median income for women; for men; for minority groups
   - Number of persons/families below official poverty line
   - Number of persons/families/children receiving various types of public assistance such as AFDC, Medicaid, food stamps, etc.

9. *Housing*
   - Most common types of housing (e.g., single-family dwellings, apartments, public housing)
   - Cost and availability of housing
   - Percentage of housing units occupied and vacant
   - Percentage of units overcrowded or substandard

10. *Educational facilities and programs*
    - Locations and types schools (i.e., public, private, neighborhood, magnet, etc.)
    - Sufficient and appropriate school programs for children with special needs
    - Schools sensitive to problems and strengths of persons from minority and ethnic groups; schools with bilingual programs
    - Minority and ethnic groups of the community represented on school boards, school staffs, etc.
    - Dropout rate for all students; for members of various socio-economic and minority groups
    - Availability of college-level, adult education, vocational, and job-training programs

11. *Health and welfare systems*
    - Names and locations of providers of health care (e.g., emergency services, acute care, home health programs, long-term care, public and private hospitals, public health programs, private clinics, etc.)
    - Names and locations of agencies providing social and human services (e.g., housing, substance abuse treatment, child welfare, protection from child abuse and domestic abuse, financial assistance, etc.)
    - Comprehensiveness, availability, accessibility, and adequacy of local health and human services programs; organizations exist to promote the improvement and coordination of these services
    - Service providers sensitive to special needs or concerns of minority and ethnic groups; bilingual staff members; clients treated with respect
    - Self-help groups and informal helping networks exist in the community
    - Numbers of children and youth in out-of-home placements

12. *Public safety and justice system*
    - Adequacy of police and fire protection and public health safeguards (i.e., people feel safe)
    - Public attitudes toward local police, courts, and correctional programs
    - Responsiveness of these agencies to concerns of minority groups in community
    - Numbers of adults in jail or on probation and parole
    - Numbers of youth in correctional facilities and juvenile justice programs

13. *Sources of information and public opinion*
    - Influential TV and radio stations and newspapers to which the people look for information and perspectives on current events
    - Key leaders and spokespersons for various segments of the community, including racial or ethnic and religious groups

14. *Major problems and concerns in community*
    - Assessment of major social problems within the community (e.g., inadequate housing, inadequate public transportation, lack of jobs, youth gangs, crime, poverty, racism, teen pregnancy, domestic abuse, etc.)
    - Efforts underway to address these concerns; leaders in these efforts
    - Major gaps among existing social, health care, and educational services

SELECTED BIBLIOGRAPHY

Devore, Wynetta, and Elfriede G. Schlesinger. *Ethnic-Sensitive Social Work Practice,* 4th ed. Boston: Allyn and Bacon, 1996.

Fellin, Phillip. *The Community and the Social Worker,* 2nd ed. Itasca, Ill.: F. E. Peacock, 1995.

Homan, Mark. *Promoting Community Change.* Pacific Grove, Calif.: Brooks/Cole, 1994.

Rubin, Herbert J., and Irene S. Rubin. *Community Organization and Development,* 2nd ed. New York: Macmillan, 1992.

Warren, Rochelle, and Donald Warren. "How to Diagnose a Neighborhood." In *Tactics and Techniques of Community Practice,* 2nd ed., edited by Fred Cox, John Erlich, Jack Rothman, and John Tropman. Itasca, Ill.: F. E. Peacock, 1984.

12 Data Collection and Assessment

INTRODUCTION

Data collection and assessment are essential steps in the helping process, whether the client is an individual, family, group, organization, or community. They are key elements of every intervention and problem-solving effort. *Data collection* refers to the gathering of the information, whereas *assessment* refers to the intellectual activity of interpreting and drawing inferences from the data. Both activities are concentrated in the beginning stages but continue throughout the helping process.

Assessment is an activity directed toward understanding the client's concern and situation and then developing a plan of action. It is a joint effort; together, the client and worker try to make sense out of available facts, observations, and other information and use that understanding as a basis for deciding what can be done about the client's concerns. Broadly speaking, an assessment should answer the following questions: What is the problem, issue, or concern? Who does it affect? Where and when does it occur? Why does it exist? How can it be resolved or mitigated?

SECTION A

TECHNIQUES AND GUIDELINES FOR DIRECT PRACTICE

In direct practice with individuals, families, and small groups, a social worker's data-gathering and assessment activities are characterized by an especially heavy emphasis on the *person-in-environment configuration.* As explained in Chapters 1 and 3, this refers to the fit or match between the needs, wants, and abilities of the person and the demands of his or her environment or external world. This match is usually achieved through exchange, negotiation, and compromise. Unfortunately, sometimes the needs of one person are met at the expense of others and some individuals meet their needs by using coercion and violence.

Traditionally, social workers have been concerned about the ability of individuals, families, and communities to meet basic human needs (e.g., food, shelter, income, safety, belonging, self-respect, etc.). A social work assessment will be cognizant of such fundamental needs. In addition, it will focus on how these needs are expressed and on whether their expression is physically and psychologically normal. For example, a client may have a "need" for cocaine or perhaps a psychological need to control others. These are needs of a sort, but they are destructive; consequently, the social worker would try to change these needs rather than searching for ways to meet them. During assessment, the social worker also examines the willingness and capacity of the people and systems making up the client's environment (e.g., family, social network, employment, community, governmental agencies, etc.) to recognize and address client needs.

Social work assessments give at least some attention to all ***dimensions of the whole person*** and the human experience and how these relate to an individual's motivation, capacity, and opportunity to meet his or her basic needs and perform social roles. Consider the following:

- *Volitional* (e.g., personal choices and decisions, processes used to make a decision, impact of choices on self and others, etc.)
- *Familial* (e.g., interaction with family members, sense of belonging to a group of concerned people, sense of loyalty and obligation to relatives, one's personal history and traditions, etc.)
- *Social* (e.g., interaction with friends and peers; one's place in the community; one's roles, status, and ethnic identity; use of various formal and informal resources to meet needs and solve problems)
- *Spiritual* (e.g., one's beliefs concerning the meaning and purpose of life; relationship with one's Creator, views as to what is right and wrong, sense of responsibility for self and others, meaning assigned to pain and suffering)
- *Emotional* (e.g., feelings or moods such as joy, love, sadness, anger, fear, shame, etc.; inclination to move toward or away from certain experiences and persons)
- *Intellectual* (e.g., ideas, knowledge, and beliefs used to make decisions and to understand one's self, others, and the world; ability to interpret and give conceptual order to what one's senses reveal, etc.)
- *Economic* (e.g., one's material resources and capacity to secure money and compete for necessary goods and services, etc.)
- *Physical* (e.g., one's energy, health, illness, pain, vision, hearing, ease of movement, nutrition, etc.)
- *Legal* (e.g., one's rights, responsibilities, protections, and entitlements as a citizen)

Because an assessment can be only as good as the data on which it is based, the social worker must know how to gather accurate and useable data. Data are useful when they can actually make a difference in decision-making and practice activity. There are several ***modes of data collection,*** as in the following:

1. Direct verbal questioning of the client by the social worker (e.g., the face-to-face interview)

2. Direct written questioning of the client by the social worker (e.g., use of problem checklists, questionnaires, inventories, etc.)
3. Indirect or projective verbal questioning of the client by the social worker (e.g., story completions, discussion of vignettes, etc.)
4. Indirect or projective written questioning of the client by the social worker (e.g., sentence completions)
5. Observation of the client in the client's natural environment by the social worker or other trained observer (e.g., home visit, observation of child at school, having a meal with the family)
6. Observation of the client by the social worker in a simulated situation that is analogous to real life (e.g., role-play of a job interview or role-play of how parent handles a child discipline situation)
7. Client self-monitoring and self-observation by means of a written recording tool, logs, or journals
8. The use of existing documents (e.g., agency records, newspapers, school records, medical records, committee reports, etc.)

Since each method of data collection has limitations, the social worker should use more than one whenever possible. This tends to increase the accuracy of the inferences drawn from the data.

Most social workers receive training in verbal questioning (i.e., face-to-face interviewing) but few are adequately prepared to use other modes. Thus, this chapter presents several examples of direct written questioning and projective written questioning. These techniques make use of checklists, questionnaires, and vignettes. Some can be used during face-to-face interviews; some can be used to gather data by mail. Most are simple, inexpensive, and understood by clients. The reader is encouraged to view them as illustrations or models; several can be adapted to specific agencies and client groups.

Whereas a *data-gathering tool* like an interview schedule or questionnaire simply records raw data, an *assessment tool* goes one step further and incorporates some type of scaling procedure that informs the user about the probable meaning of the data. Most often, this involves comparing the client's responses to the collective responses of others to whom the instrument was administered. This chapter includes only a sampling of the assessment tools developed by social workers; there are dozens more. Also presented here are a few not developed by social workers but ones used frequently by social workers. Psychologists have been particularly active in the development of such instruments. Literally hundreds of assessment tools are potentially useful to the social worker.

Assessment tools should not be confused with *research instruments* (i.e., those designed to collect data for purposes of research). A good research tool is seldom a good practice tool because most are too complex or too long to administer in direct-service situations. The instruments that most practitioners find useful are those that are brief, simple to administer, and easily understood by the client.

As the social worker thinks about issues related to data collection and assessment, he or she should remember that the client also engages in these activities. The client is constantly gathering information about the worker and pondering such questions as: Can this social worker really help me? Does this person know what he or she is doing? Can I trust this professional?

12.1   The Social Assessment Report

PURPOSE: To convey to other professionals a basic understanding of relevant social information about a particular client.

DISCUSSION: A *social assessment report* (often called a *social history*) is frequently prepared by social workers in direct practice. As contrasted, for example, to a report prepared by a physician that focuses on physical functioning, the report prepared by a professional social worker focuses primarily on social functioning—the social, relational, or interactional aspects of the client's functioning and his or her situation. The word *social* refers to the interactions between and among people and between people and the significant systems of their social environment (e.g., family, school, job, hospital, etc.). Social workers are particularly concerned about the match (or lack thereof) between client needs and the resources (formal and informal) available to meet those needs. A good social assessment report will reflect this interactional focus.

Past behavior is the best predictor of future behavior; this fact is the rationale for compiling a social history. If a social worker can gather accurate descriptions of how a client previously thought, felt, behaved, handled stress, and coped with problems, and can also identify patterns in those prior responses, the worker can then make an informed prediction about how the client will respond to similar situations in the future. A social history or assessment is especially useful to professionals responsible for making decisions concerning the type of program or service that would be most appropriate for a particular client and to those responsible for facilitating a client's adjustment to a new environment (e.g., treatment program, foster home, nursing home).

Most reports contain two types of information: (1) the social data and (2) the worker's assessment or thoughts about the meaning of that data. Social data are the basic facts; the social assessment is a statement summarizing the worker's impressions and hypotheses that give added meaning to the data and their implications for social work intervention. The information presented in a report should lay a foundation for doing something with the client about his or her problem or situation.

The organization, format, and content of a report will vary from agency to agency and reflect the agency's purpose and program. Also, the content will vary depending on the audience for which it is prepared: doctors, judges, psychologists, school personnel, interdisciplinary teams, and so on. A good report is characterized by a number of qualities, which are outlined in the following list.

1. *Shortness.* The report should say no more than needs to be said to those who will use the report. Everyone is busy. Do not ask others to read more than is necessary.

2. *Simplicity.* Select the least complicated words and phrases. Avoid jargon and psychiatric labels. Rather than use labels, describe and give examples of the behavior you want the reader to know about.

3. *Usefulness.* Keep the report's purpose in mind while you are preparing it. Ask yourself who will read the report and what they need to know. Do not include information merely because it is interesting or sensational.

4. *Organization.* Use numerous headings to break the information into easy-to-find topical categories. Here are some of the headings commonly used in social assessment reports:

- Identifying Information (name, date of birth, address, etc.)
- Reason for Report
- Reason for Social Work or Agency Involvement
- Statement of Client's Problem or Concern
- Client's Family Background (family of origin)
- Current Family Composition and/or Household Membership
- Relationships to Significant Others
- Ethnicity, Religion, and Spirituality
- Physical Functioning, Health Concerns, Nutrition, Home Safety, Illness, Disabilities, Medications
- Educational Background, School Performance, Intellectual Functioning
- Psychological and Emotional Functioning
- Strengths, Ways of Coping, and Problem-Solving Capacities
- Employment, Income, Work Experience, and Skills
- Housing, Neighborhood, and Transportation
- Current and Recent Use of Community and Professional Services
- Social Worker's Impressions and Assessment
- Intervention and Service Plan

The sample social assessment report presented in Figure 12.1 illustrates the use of various topical headings.

5. *Confidentiality and Client Access.* Respect the client's privacy. Assume that the client may want to read the report and has a right to do so. Think carefully before including information that you would not want the client or family (or their lawyer) to read.

6. *Objectivity.* Select words that express your observations in an accurate and nonjudgmental manner. Beware of value-laden words and connotative meanings such as, for example, "AFDC mother," "chauvinist," "The client admits he doesn't attend church," and "He claims to have completed high school." Label your opinions and personal judgments as such and support your conclusions with data. Do not present an opinion as if it were a fact. The best way to do this is to place your

Greystone Family Service Agency

Identifying Information

Client Name: ___Shirley McCarthy___	Case Record #: ___3456___
D.O.B: _July 4.1976_ Age: _20_	Date of Referral: ___Oct. 8, 1996___
Soc. Security #: _505-67-8910_	Social Worker: ___Jane Green. BSW___
Address: ___2109 B Street,___	Report Prepared: ___Oct. 13, 1996___
___Greystone, Mt. 09876___	
Phone: ___591-0123___	

Reason for Report

This report was prepared for use during consultation with Dr. Jones, the agency's psychiatric consultant, and for purposes of peer supervision. (The client is aware that a report is being prepared for this purpose.)

Reason for Social Work Involvement

Shirley was referred to this agency by Dr. Smith, an emergency room physician at City Hospital. Shirley was treated there for having taken an unknown quantity of aspirin in an apparent suicide attempt. She is reacting with anxiety and depression to her unwanted pregnancy. The father is a former boyfriend with whom she has broken off. She does not want him nor her parents to learn that she is pregnant.

She does not want an abortion and does not want to care for a child. She has thought about adoption but knows little about what would be involved. She agreed to come to this agency in order to figure out how she might deal with her dilemma.

Source of Data

This report is based on two one-hour interviews with the client (Oct. 9 and 11), and a phone conversation with Dr. Smith.

Family Background and Situation

Shirley is the youngest of three children. Her brother, John, age 30, is a chemical engineer in Austin, Texas. Her sister, Martha, age 27, is a pharmacist in Seattle. Shirley does not feel close to either sibling and neither knows of her pregnancy.

Her parents have been married for 33 years. They live in Spokane, Washington. Her father, Thomas, is an engineer for a farm equipment company. Her mother, Mary, is a registered nurse.

Shirley describes her parents as hard-working, honest people who have a strong sense of right and wrong and a commitment to family. The family is middle class and of Irish heritage. The McCarthy's are life-long Catholics. The three children attended Catholic grade and high schools. Shirley says that if her parents knew of the pregnancy "it would just kill them." Her wish to keep her parents from learning of the pregnancy seems motivated by a desire to protect them from distress.

Physical Functioning and Health

Shirley is 5'7" tall and weights 105 pounds. She is about three months pregnant. Dr. Smith reports that she is underweight but otherwise healthy. He has concern about her willingness to obtain proper prenatal care; he had referred Shirley to Dr. Johnson (an OB/GYN physician), but she did not keep that appointment.

Shirley says that she is in good health, eats well, exercises minimally, and reports no medical problems. She is not taking any medication.

Intellectual Functioning

Shirley completed two years at the University of Washington and then transferred to the University of Montana where she is currently a junior in computer science. She has an overall GPA of 3.8. Despite her good grades, Shirley describes herself as a "mediocre student."

She is attracted to subjects where there is a clear right and wrong answer. She does not like courses such as philosophy, which seems "wishy-washy" to her. Although she values the logical and precise thinking that is part of computer science, she explains that she tends to make personal decisions impulsively and "jumps into things without considering the consequences."

Emotional Functioning

Shirley describes herself as "moody." Even before the pregnancy, she had bouts of depression when she would sit alone in her room for hours at a time. She never sought treatment for the depression. In describing herself, Shirley uses the words *childish* and *immature;* she has always felt younger than others her age.

She often feels anger and sadness, but tries to keep her feelings from showing. In this sense, she is like her father, who always keeps things to himself until he finally "blows up."

In spite of her accomplishments, Shirley seems to have poor self-esteem and focuses more on her limitations than her strengths.

Interpersonal and Social Relationships

Shirley has no "close friends." She says it is difficult for her to interact with others and she wishes she had better social skills. She has held various part-time jobs during high school and college, but socialized only minimally with co-workers. In college, Shirley had trouble getting along with her roommates in the dorm, so she moved to an apartment so that she could be alone.

When she drinks alcohol, she feels more outgoing and friendly. However, this fact scares her because several uncles are alcoholic. For the past year, she worked hard at not drinking at all. She was not drinking when she took the aspirin.

Her former boyfriend, Bob (father of her baby), was the first person she ever dated for more than a few months. The relationship ended one month ago. Bob is also a student.

Religion and Spirituality

Shirley was raised as a Catholic and retains many of the beliefs and values she learned as a child. She describes herself as a spiritual person and one who prays quite often. She has clear ideas of right and wrong but also feels she is in a stage of life when she is trying to decide what she really believes and is in the process of constructing a system of values, morals, and ethical principles.

(continued)

**FIGURE 12.1
Continued**

Strengths and Problem-Solving Capacity

Although Shirley tends to minimize her strengths, she exhibits intelligence, an ability to work hard, a desire to make friends, a loyalty to her family while also wanting to make her own decisions, and a moderate motivation to deal with her situation constructively. She displays a good vocabulary and expresses herself in a clear manner.

She tends to avoid making hard decisions and lets things pile up until she is forced by circumstances to follow the only option still open to her. She usually knows what she "should do" but does not act; she attributes this to a fear of making mistakes. When faced with interpersonal conflict, she is inclined to withdraw.

Economics/Housing/Transportation

Shirley's parents are assisting her with the costs of her education. She also works about 30 hours per week at the Baylor Department Store, earning minimum wage. With this money, she pays rent and keeps her eight-year-old car running.

Aside from her college student health insurance, she has no medical coverage. She does not know if that policy covers pregnancy. Shirley lives alone in a two-room apartment which she says is located in a "rough area" of town. She is afraid to be out alone after dark.

Use of Community Resources

This is the first time Shirley has had contact with a social agency. During our sessions, she asked many questions about the agency and expressed some confusion about why she had been referred here by Dr. Smith. She acknowledged that feelings of embarrassment and shame make it difficult for her to talk to about her concerns.

Impressions and Assessment

This 20-year-old is experiencing inner conflict and depression because of an unwanted pregnancy. This gave rise to a suicide attempt. In keeping with her tendency to avoid conflict, she has not told others of the pregnancy, yet the father (Bob) will need to be involved if she chooses the legal procedure of relinquishment, and her parents' involvement may be needed for financial support. Prenatal care is needed, but it too has been avoided. Abortion is not an acceptable solution to Shirley, and she is ambivalent about adoption and how to manage her life while pregnant.

Goals for Work with Client

In order to help Shirley make the necessary decisions to deal with this pregnancy, I hope to engage her in pregnancy options counseling. Issues to be addressed include making a further assessment of her depression and suicide attempt, obtaining and paying for medical care, and deciding on whether to inform Bob and her own parents. She will need emotional support, some structure, and a gentle demand for work so she can overcome her avoidance, make decisions, and take necessary action.

Note: The names in this report are fictitious.

conclusions, opinions, and hypotheses under a separate topical heading called "Worker's Impressions and Assessment."

When it is necessary to include information or draw conclusions that might offend the client/family, do so, if possible, by using the client's own words. Note these examples:

Inappropriate: It is apparent that Jane is a hostile and uncaring individual who is too self-centered and immature to cope with the demands of her elderly father.

Acceptable: While I was talking with Jane, her father requested a glass of water. She responded in a loud voice and said, "Go to hell, you old fool."

7. *Relevance.* The information included in the report should have a clear connection to the client's presenting concern and/or the reason the social worker and agency are involved with the client.

8. *Focus on client strengths.* Avoid preoccupation with psychopathology and family disorganization, personal weakness, and limitation. To the extent possible, emphasize whatever strengths exist. Focus on what the client/family can do, not on what they cannot do. Successful intervention is built on client strength; the social assessment report must identify these strengths (see Item 12.8).

SELECTED BIBLIOGRAPHY

Kagle, Jill. *Social Work Records,* 2nd ed. Belmont, Calif.: Wadsworth, 1991.
Wilson, Suanna. *Recording: Guidelines for Social Workers.* New York: Free Press, 1976.
Zuckerman, Edward. *The Clinician's Thesaurus: The Guide for Wording Psychological Reports and Other Evaluations,* 3rd ed. Sarasota, Fla.: Professional Resource Press, 1993.

12.2 The Dual Perspective

PURPOSE: To graphically depict barriers and supports that affect a person's interactions with his or her social environment.

DISCUSSION: Among the helping professions, one of social work's unique contributions is its emphasis on understanding the client within the context of his or her social environment. Norton's (1978) dual perspective brings this conceptualization alive in practice. She identifies two distinct sets of influences that make up a person's social environment: the nurturing environment and the sustaining environment.

One's **nurturing environment** (or immediate environment) is composed of family, friends, neighbors, and close associates at work or school. These are people with whom a person interacts frequently and often in an intimate manner. It is in and through these relationships that a person develops a sense of identity, belonging, and self-worth. These relationships have a profound effect on one's functioning.

A person's *sustaining environment* is made up of the people through which one encounters the wider community and broader society such as the people who represent political organizations, economic resources, labor unions, the media, educational systems, health care facilities, and human services programs. (A social worker and a social agency are also part of this sustaining environment.) Ideally, the individual is accepted, respected, and valued within both environments, but this is often not the case.

Of special concern during the assessment phase of the change process is the question of whether an intervention should be directed toward elements of the nurturing environment or toward the sustaining environment. The dual perspective helps to answer that question. For example, if the nurturing system is positive but the messages from the sustaining system are negative (e.g., a minority child from a supportive family who feels devalued when in school), the social worker needs to focus on changing aspects of the school experience. If the messages from the nurturing system are negative (e.g., the child abused by his parents), arranging a positive sustaining system experience can help compensate for these negative influences but the social worker must focus primarily on changing interactions within the family. Finally, and most difficult, are those situations where both the sustaining and nurturing environments give negative messages to the person. An example of this double negative would be a gay or lesbian adolescent who is rejected by his or her family, by peers at school, and by the wider society. In that situation, change efforts would need to be simultaneously directed toward helping the adolescent cope with the rejection, helping the family understand and accept the adolescent, and changing community attitudes toward gays and lesbians.

The concepts of a nurturing and a sustaining environment can be translated into a simple assessment tool for identifying the location of both the supports and problems a person experiences in the social environment. To make a dual perspective assessment, one begins by recording on a chart (see Figure 12.2) the positives and negatives in the client's situation as you understand them. Begin with the person. List in the inner-most circle the characteristics and capacities of the client and indicate with a (+) or (–) the effects they have on his or her situation. Make a few notes in the margins to explain the reasons for arriving at this conclusion. Next, move to the center circle—the nurturing environment. Write in the names of all key actors in the client's situation and again indicate if they are a positive, negative, or neutral (0) influence. Once again, add some description to clarify the rationale for your judgments. Finally, do the same for the circle representing the sustaining environment. Some social workers have found it useful to conduct a dual perspective assessment directly with clients to check the accuracy of the judgments and help them gain insights into the issues they face.

Examination of the completed dual perspective worksheet will reveal both the areas that need to be changed (i.e., the – notations) and the areas of strength (i.e., the + notations) that might be resources for accomplishing change. With an accurate problem and resource assessment completed, it is then possible to begin planning appropriate interventions.

**FIGURE 12.2
Dual
Perspective
Worksheet**

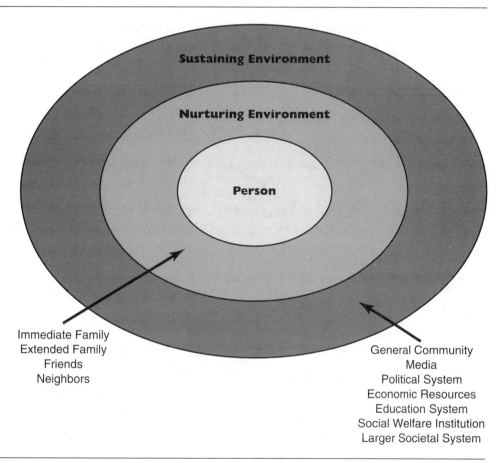

SELECTED BIBLIOGRAPHY

Norton, Dolores. *The Dual Perspective: Inclusion of Ethnic Minority Content in the Social Work Curriculum.* New York: CSWE, 1978.

12.3	**Genograms and Ecomapping**

PURPOSE: To graphically depict family and interactional data as an aid in the social assessment process.

DISCUSSION: A *genogram* is a diagram very similar to a family tree. It can describe family relationships for two or three generations (an attempt to depict more than three generations becomes very complex). The *ecomap* drawing places an individual or a family within a social context.

In addition to their value in assessment, the genogram and ecomap can shorten the case record. Family descriptions that might require two or three pages of narrative can often be reduced to a single page of genogram and ecomap diagrams. For example, a typical record or social history will focus on information such as the following:

- Age, sex, marital status, and household composition
- Family structure and relationships (e.g., biological children, stepchildren, parents, etc.)
- Job situation, employment, and responsibilities
- Social activities and interests (hobbies, recreational activities, etc.)
- Formal associations (church membership, participation in union, membership in service club, etc.)
- Sources of support and stress in social interactions (between people and between people and community systems)
- Utilization of community resources (Medicaid, economic assistance, public health, mental health, schools, Social Security, doctors, etc.)
- Informal resources and natural helpers (extended family, relatives, friends, neighbors, self-help groups)

All of these data can be "drawn" into a one-page ecomap.

Although the user of these diagrams can create his or her own symbols and abbreviations, certain symbols are commonly used, as shown in Figure 12.3. Words and notations—such as "m" for "married," "div" for "divorced," and "d" for "died"— may also be used in the family diagram and ecomap.

Figure 12.4 is a diagram of a reconstituted family, which appears within the dotted circle (boundary). It indicates that a man (age 45), his wife (age 33), and three children (ages 3, 1, and 10) live in the household. The 10-year-old is from his mother's former marriage; the boy's biological father died in 1987. The 45-year-old husband was divorced from his former wife (age 42) in 1986. Also, we see that he has two daughters (ages 20 and 18) by this former wife and is now a grandfather, since his 20-year-old daughter has a 1-year-old daughter. The former wife is now married to a man who is age 44.

An ecomap places the family or client within their social context by using circles to represent organizations or factors impacting their lives. Various symbols or short phrases are used to describe the nature of these interactions. Figure 12.5 is an ecomap of Dick and Barb and their two children, John and June.

Usually, an ecomap is developed jointly by the social worker and client and helps both to view the family from a system's or ecological perspective. Ecomapping can be used by the worker to build a relationship and demonstrate a desire to learn about the client and his or her situation. It has been used in adoption and foster-care home studies and in marriage and family counseling. Many clients report that doing an ecomap helps them see their situation more clearly and sort out what they can do about their problems.

**FIGURE 12.3
Symbols for
Ecomaps and
Genograms**

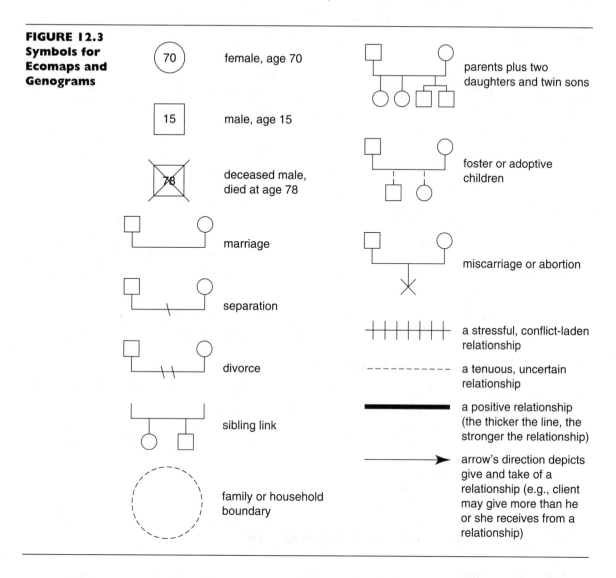

When examining an ecomap, consider a number of basic questions: Does the family have an income adequate to cover basic needs such as food, shelter, transportation, and health care? Are family members employed? Do they enjoy their jobs? Does the family live in a neighborhood that is safe? Does the family interact with relatives, friends, and neighbors? Does the family participate in social, cultural, religious, and community activities? Are the family's values, beliefs, or life-style in conflict with those dominant in the neighborhood? Do the children have access to needed educational resources? Do they enjoy their school experience? Are some of

**FIGURE 12.4
Sample
Genogram
of a Recon-
stituted
Family**

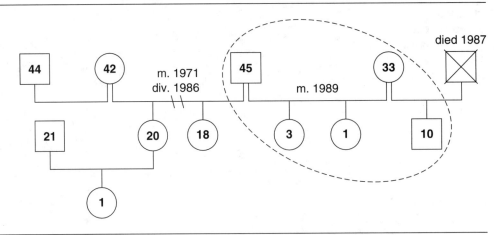

the family members experiencing high levels of stress? Answers to such questions yield important information for assessment and intervention.

SELECTED BIBLIOGRAPHY

Holman, Adele. *Family Assessment: Tools for Understanding and Intervention.* Beverly Hills: Sage, 1983.

Mattaini, Mark. *More than a Thousand Words: Graphics for Clinical Practice.* Washington, D.C.: NASW, 1993.

McGoldrick, Monica, and Randy Gerson. *Genograms in Family Assessment.* New York: W. W. Norton, 1985.

12.4   Social Support Assessment

PURPOSE: To identify persons to whom a client might turn for various types of social support.

DISCUSSION: Gottlieb (1983, 28) defines *social support* as "verbal and/or nonverbal information or advice, tangible aid, or action that is proffered by social intimates or inferred by their presence and has beneficial emotional or behavioral effects on the recipient." Social supports are a component of one's *social network*—the people and groups with which one interacts on a regular basis. It is important to remember that although social supports are a positive influence, some other parts of a client's social network may add to his or her stress or have a harmful influence on client functioning. Many of the clients seen by social workers have few, if any, social supports. Whittaker and Tracy (1987, 1) explain that "paradoxically, many of the families that are most in need of the social support that relatives, family and friends can pro-

**FIGURE 12.5
Sample
Ecomap**

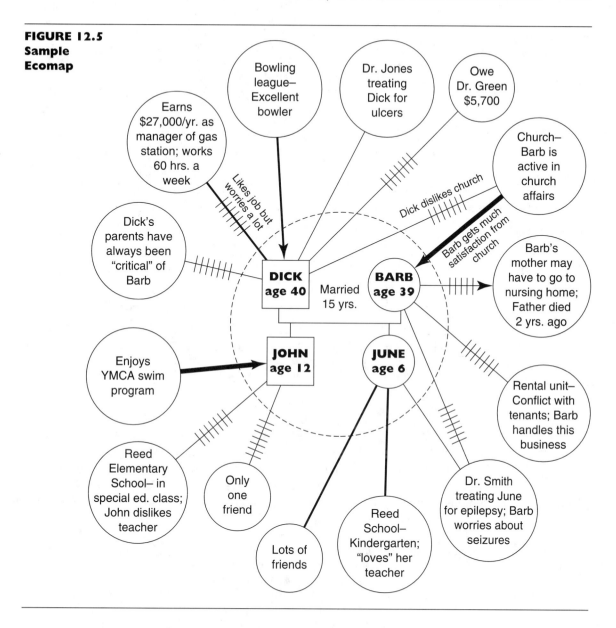

vide are also the same families that are most isolated from relatives, family and friends. . . . Other families are surrounded by social networks that are themselves beset by multiple problems."

In order to help clients make appropriate and effective use of social supports, it is necessary to engage them in the identification and assessment of potential social supports. The *Social Network Map* (Figure 12.6) and its accompanying *Social Network Grid* (Figure 12.7) are tools for that purpose. This assessment process was de-

FIGURE 12.6
Social Network Map

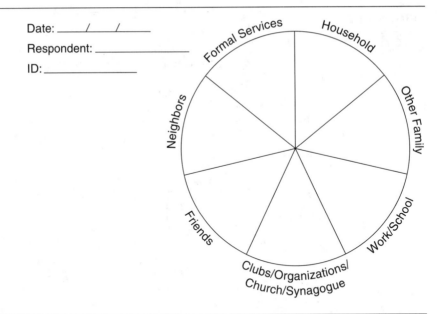

Date: _____ / _____ / _____

Respondent: _____

ID: _____

Source: Family Support Project, University of Washington, School of Social Work and Behavioral Sciences Institute. James K. Whittaker, Principal Investigator; Elizabeth M. Tracy, Project Coordinator. Reproduced with permission of Elizabeth M. Tracy.

veloped and piloted by Tracy as part of the Family Support Project based at the University of Washington (Whittaker, Tracy, and Marckworth 1989). The map and the grid are especially attractive because they use sort cards that draw the client into a visual and tactile activity. Tracy (undated) presents a sample script as a way of describing how a social worker might communicate with a client as they work together on the Social Network Map and the Social Network Grid.

> *Step One: Developing a Social Network Map**
> Let's take a look at who is in your social network by putting together a network map. (Show network map—Figure 12.6.) We can use first names or initials because I'm not that interested in knowing the particular people and I wouldn't necessarily be contacting any of the people we talk about.
>
> Think back to this past month, say since [date]. What people have been important to you? They may have been people you saw, talked with, or wrote letters to. This includes people who made you feel good, people who made you feel bad, and others who just played a part in your life. They may be people who had an influence on the way you made decisions during this time.
>
> First, think of people in your *household*—that includes who?
>
> Now going around the map, what *other family members* would you include in your network?

*Reproduced with permission of Elizabeth Tracy.

FIGURE 12.7 Social Network Grid

ID _____

RESPONDENT _____

NAME	#	Area of Life 1. Household 2. Other Family 3. Work/School 4. Organizations 5. Other Friends 6. Neighbors 7. Professionals 8. Other	Concrete Support 1. Hardly Ever 2. Sometimes 3. Almost Always	Emotional Support 1. Hardly Ever 2. Sometimes 3. Almost Always	Information/ Advice 1. Hardly Ever 2. Sometimes 3. Almost Always	Critical 1. Hardly Ever 2. Sometimes 3. Almost Always	Direction of Help 1. Goes Both Ways 2. You to Them 3. Them to You	Closeness 1. Not Very Close 2. Sort of Close 3. Very Close	How Often Seen 0. Does Not See 1. Few Times/Yr 2. Monthly 3. Weekly 4. Daily	How Long Known 1. Less Than 1 Yr 2. From 1–5 Yrs 3. More than 5 Yrs
	01									
	02									
	03									
	04									
	05									
	06									
	07									
	08									
	09									
	10									
	11									
	12									
	13									
	14									
	15									
		1–6	7	8	9	10	11	12	13	14	15

Source: University of Washington, School of Social Work and Behavioral Sciences Institute. James K. Whittaker, Principal Investigator; Elizabeth M. Tracy, Project Coordinator. Reproduced with permission of Elizabeth M. Tracy.

335

How about *people from work or school?*

People from clubs, organizations or religious groups? Who should we include here?

Other friends that haven't been listed in the other categories?

Neighbors? (Note: Local shopkeepers may be included here.)

Finally, list professional people or people from formal agencies (like DSHS) that you have contact with.

Look over your network. Are these the people you would consider part of your social network this past month? (Add or delete names as needed.)

Step Two: Completing the Social Network Grid

(If there are more than 15 people in the network, ask the client to select the "top fifteen," and then ask the questions about only those network members. For each of the questions, use the appropriate sorting guide card. Once the client has divided up the cards, put the appropriate code number for each person listed on the network grid.)

Now, I'd like to learn more about the people in your network. I'm going to write their names on this network grid [see Figure 12.7], put a code number for the area of life, and then ask a few questions about the ways in which they help you. Let's also write their names on these slips of paper too; this will make answering the questions a lot easier. These are the questions I'll be asking (show list of social network questions), and we'll check off the names on this grid as we go through each question.

The first three questions have to do with the *types of support* people give you.

Who would be available to help you out in real *concrete ways*—for example, would give you a ride if you needed one, or would pitch in to help you with a big chore, or would look after your belongings for awhile if you were away? Divide your cards into three piles—those people you can hardly ever rely on for concrete help, those you can rely on sometimes, and those you'd almost always rely on for this type of help.

Now who would be available to give you *emotional support*—for example, to comfort you if you were upset, to be right there with you in a stressful situation, to listen to you talk about your feelings? Again, divide your cards into three piles—those people you can hardly ever rely on for emotional support, those you can rely on sometimes, and those you almost always can rely on for this type of help.

Finally, who do you rely on for *advice*—for example, who would give you information on how to do something, help you make a big decision, or teach you how to do something? Divide your cards into the three piles—hardly ever, sometimes, and almost always—for this type of support.

Look through your cards and this time select those people, if any, in your network that you feel are *critical* of you (or your lifestyle, or you as a parent). When I say "critical," I mean critical of you in a way that makes you feel bad or inadequate. Divide the cards into three piles—those people who are hardly ever critical of you, sometimes critical of you, and almost always critical of you. Again we'll put the code numbers next to their names.

Now look over your cards, and think about the *direction of help*. Divide your cards into three piles—those people where help goes both ways (you help them just as much as they help you), those where it's mostly you helping them, and those where it's mostly them helping you. OK, let's get their code numbers on the grid.

Now think about how *close* you are to the people in your network. Divide the cards into three piles—those you are not very close to, those you are sort of close to, and those you are very close to—and then we'll put a code number for them.

Finally, just a few questions about *how often* you see people, and *how long* you've known the people in your network.

Divide the cards into four piles—people you see just a few times a year, people you see monthly, people you see weekly, and people you see daily. (*Note:* If you see someone twice or more than twice a week, count that as "daily.") OK, we'll put their numbers on the grid.

This is the last question. Divide the cards into three piles—those people you have known less than a year, from 1–5 years, and over 5 years.

Now we have a pretty complete picture of who is in your social network.

It is important to remember that the Social Support Map and the Social Network Grid do not objectively describe the client's support but rather reflect the client's perceptions and beliefs. It is quite possible that a client may exaggerate or underestimate the importance of some people and simply forget to name others.

Once the map and grid have been completed, the social worker engages the client in a discussion of how the client might reach out to and use identified social supports. Whether the supports are likely resources will depend on the nature of the client's problem or needs and the client's willingness to use them.

SELECTED BIBLIOGRAPHY

Gottlieb, Benjamin. *Social Support Strategies: Guidelines for Mental Health Practice.* Beverly Hills: Sage, 1983.

Tracy, Elizabeth. *Social Support Assessment.* Seattle: University of Washington School of Social Work, Family Support Project (mimeograph, undated).

———, and James Whittaker. "The Evidence Base for Social Support Interventions in Child and Family Practice: Emerging Issues for Research and Practice." *Children and Youth Services Review* 9 (1987): 249–270.

———, and James Whittaker. "The Social Network Map: Assessing Social Support in Clinical Practice." *Families in Society* 71 (October 1990): 461–470.

Whittaker, James, and Elizabeth Tracy. "Supporting Families: Linking Formal and Informal Helping in Family Preservation Services." *Permanency Report* 5, No. 1 (Winter 1987).

———, Elizabeth Tracy, and Peg Marckworth. *The Family Support Project: Identifying Informal Support Resources for High Risk Families.* Seattle: School of Social Work, University of Washington, 1989.

12.5 Life History Grid

PURPOSE: To graphically depict significant events in a client's life and/or the development of significant problems through time.

DISCUSSION: The *life history grid* is a method of organizing and presenting data related to the various periods in a client's life. The grid is especially useful in work with children and adolescents, where an understanding of life experiences during a particular stage of development may shed light on current functioning. Data from a variety of sources (interview, agency records, hospital records, etc.) are brought together in a life grid.

Figure 12.8 is a grid prepared on David, a 14-year-old referred to a social worker because of behavior problems. When one examines David's life history grid,

FIGURE 12.8   Sample Life History Grid

Client: David

Year	Age	Location	Family	School	Health	Activities	Problems
1981	DOB: 3-23-81	Chicago, IL	Father 21, Mother 18	—	Normal birth	—	—
1982	1						
1983	2		Karen born				
1984	3	Billings, MT			Asthma, hospital, 3 days		
1985	4						
1986	5	Denver, CO	Donald born	K—Lewis & Clark School	Asthma, in hospital 3 times		
1987	6		Dad drinking a lot	I	Car accident, broken leg		Did not like school Frequently sick
1988	7	Butte, MT		II—new school			Lots of fights at school
1989	8		Dad fired from job	III		Cub Scouts	
1990	9		Mother takes job	IV	Asthma attack		Steals money from mother
1991	10			V	Appendectomy		Ran away from home
1992	11	Denver, CO	Parents separate and mother moves	VI—grades poor	Asthma attack/ hospital		Breaks classmate's nose in fight
1993	12			VII—truancy		Paper route	Alcohol & fighting
1994	13	Mother & kids move to Helena, MT	Parents divorce	VII—new school			Hits teacher, suicide gesture
1995	14		Dad killed in car accident	Freshman at Big Sky HS		Tried out for football	Pot smoking, arrest for shoplifting, poor grades

it becomes apparent that his problems have grown worse in reaction to his parents' escalating marital conflict and eventual divorce. Also, there appears to be a relationship between his asthma attacks and significant family changes. Thus, we see that a life history grid can help a social worker formulate hypotheses about the causes of problem behavior and suggest focal points for intervention.

SELECTED BIBLIOGRAPHY

Anderson, James, and Ralph Brown. "Life History Grid for Adolescents." *Social Work* 25 (July 1980): 321–322.

12.6 Life Cycle Matrix

PURPOSE: To graphically depict the developmental stage of all persons in a household.

DISCUSSION: An assessment should consider the client's stage in the life cycle and the developmental tasks common to that stage. This is especially important in work with families because the various members are at different points in the life cycle. The use of a matrix can help the social worker organize his or her thoughts about the family members and the physical, psychological, social, and spiritual needs associated with a particular stage of life.

Figure 12.9 depicts a household made up of a father, mother, three children, and a grandmother. The importance of considering the developmental stage of each member of a household becomes apparent when we recognize that certain tasks need to be accomplished and certain developmental crises must be resolved during

FIGURE 12.9 Sample Life Cycle Matrix

Family Member	Developmental Stage								
	0–1	2–4	5–7	8–12	13–17	18–22	23–34	35–60	61+
Margaret (Grandmother)									✗
John								✗	
Mary								✗	
John (Jr.)					✗				
Jimmy			✗						
Mary		✗							

TABLE 12.1   The Life Cycle

Stage	Common Developmental Tasks	Developmental Crisis
Prenatal (conception to birth)	▪ In utero physical development	
Infant (birth–2 years)	▪ Bonding and attachment ▪ Differentiation of emotions ▪ Maturation of nervous and motor systems ▪ Concept of object permanence ▪ Beginning understanding of causality	Basic trust versus mistrust of others
Toddler (2–4 years)	▪ Fantasy and play ▪ Language ▪ Self-control ▪ Locomotion ▪ Use of symbols in thought	Basic sense of worth and autonomy versus shame and self-doubt
Early school age (5–7 years)	▪ Group play ▪ Early gender identification ▪ Beginning moral standards ▪ Learning of classification, combination, and other basic intellectual skills	Taking initiative versus only reacting to or imitating others
Middle school age (8–12 years)	▪ Cooperation with others ▪ Team play ▪ Same sex peer identification ▪ Introspection	Self-confidence and industry versus inferiority
Early adolescence (13–17 years)	▪ Physical and sexual maturation ▪ Membership in peer group ▪ Boy-girl relationships ▪ Abstract thought processes ▪ Coping with strong emotions	Group identity versus sense of alienation
Late adolescence (18–22 years)	▪ Dating and mate selection ▪ Sex-role identity ▪ Internalization of moral principles ▪ Career choice ▪ Separation from parent	Individual identity versus role diffusion and confusion
Early adulthood (23–34 years)	▪ Marriage ▪ Childbearing ▪ Work ▪ Developing life-style apart from parents	Intimacy versus isolation
Middle adulthood (35–60 years)	▪ Childrearing ▪ Career development ▪ Management of home and financial resources	Expansion of life experience and concern for society versus stagnation and self-absorption
Late adulthood (61 + years)	▪ Coping with physical change and health problems ▪ Acceptance of one's own life choices ▪ Redirection of energy after retirement ▪ Developing a perspective on one's death	Integrity versus despair

each stage. Within a family system, the developmental struggles of one member may interfere with the developmental tasks and crises faced by another.

Table 12.1 presents an overview of the life cycle intended to remind the social worker how developmental tasks change over time. The concept of developmental crisis reflects the belief that psychosocial development proceeds by stages; each stage represents a time to decide between hanging on to the old or letting go and moving on to a new way of thinking and behaving.

SELECTED BIBLIOGRAPHY

Berger, Kathleen. *The Developing Person Through the Life Span,* 3rd ed. New York: Worth Publishers, 1994.

Rice, F. Philip. *Human Development: A Life Span Approach,* 2nd Ed. New York: Macmillan, 1994.

12.7 Family Life Cycle

PURPOSE: To identify developmental tasks and changes common to various stages in the life of a family.

DISCUSSION: Just as an individual can be described in terms of his or her stage in the human life cycle (see Item 12.6), it is possible to describe stages that occur throughout the life of a family unit. Although the stages of family development are less distinct and more variable than the stages of individual development, such a conceptualization can help the worker assess a family's functioning in a broader context, and better understand the family's strengths and problems.

Table 12.2 outlines the stages commonly observed within the nuclear family (i.e., married man and woman with their biological children) based on ones identified by Carter and McGoldrick (1989). Needless to say, the structure, functioning, and life cycle of many families vary significantly from that of the nuclear family; examples include extended family structures and the various types of single-parent families such as ones headed by an unmarried mother or father, divorced or widowed parents, and single adoptive parents.

Given the high rate of divorce in the United States, it is important to understand how phases in the family life cycle are impacted by the dissolution of a marriage and by remarriage. Table 12.3, also developed by Carter and McGoldrick (1989), describes the family both prior to and after a divorce. A high percentage of those who divorce eventually remarry and start another family unit. A remarriage often gives rise to the so-called *blended family,* which is particularly complex because the two adults entering this new marriage may bring with them biological children and sometimes stepchildren from one or more previous marriages, and, subsequently, they may bear additional children. Multiple sets of grandparents, stepparents, and other relatives are significant figures in the dynamics and develop-

TABLE 12.2   Family Life Cycle

Family Life Cycle Stage	Emotional Process of Transition: Key Principles	Second-Order Changes in Family Status Required to Proceed Developmentally
1. Leaving home: Single young adults	Accepting emotional and financial responsibility for self	a. Differentiation of self in relation to family of origin b. Development of intimate peer relationships c. Establishment of self re work and financial independence
2. The joining of families through marriage: The new couple	Commitment to new system	a. Formation of marital system b. Realignment of relationships with extended families and friends to include spouse
3. Families with young children	Accepting new members into the system	a. Adjusting marital system to make space for child(ren) b. Joining in childrearing, financial, and household tasks c. Realignment of relationships with extended family to include parenting and grand-parenting roles
4. Families with adolescents	Increasing flexibility of family boundaries to include children's in-dependence and grandparent's frailties	a. Shifting of parent child relationships to permit adolescent to move in and out of system b. Refocus on midlife marital and career issues c. Beginning shift toward joint caring for older generation
5. Launching children and moving on	Accepting a multitude of exits from and entries into the family system	a. Renegotiation of marital system as a dyad b. Development of adult to adult relationships between grown children and their parents c. Realignment of relationships to include in-laws and grandchildren d. Dealing with disabilities and death of parents (grandparents)
6. Families in later life	Accepting the shifting of generational roles	a. Maintaining own and/or couple functioning and interests in face of physiological decline; exploration of new familial and social role options b. Support for a more central role of middle generation c. Making room in the system for the wisdom and experience of the elderly, supporting the older generation without overfunctioning for them d. Dealing with loss of spouse, siblings, and other peers and preparation for own death. Life review and integration

Source: From Betty Carter and Monica McGoldrick, *The Changing Family Life Cycle: A Framework for Family Therapy,* 2nd ed. Copyright © 1989 by Allyn and Bacon. Reprinted by permission.

TABLE 12.3 Family Life Cycle and Divorce

Phase	Emotional Process of Transition: Prerequisite Attitude	Developmental Issues
Divorce		
1. The decision to divorce	Acceptance of inability to resolve marital tensions sufficiently to continue relationship	Acceptance of one's own part in the failure of the marriage
2. Planning the breakup of the system	Supporting viable arrangements for all parts of the system	a. Working cooperatively on problems of custody, visitation, and finances b Dealing with extended family about the divorce
3. Separation	a. Willingness to continue cooperative coparental relationship and joint financial support of children b. Work on resolution of attachment to spouse	a. Mourning loss of intact family b. Restructuring marital and parent-child relationships and finances; adaptation to living apart c. Realignment of relationships with extended family; staying connected with spouse's extended family
4. The divorce	More work on emotional divorce: overcoming hurt, anger, guilt, etc.	a. Mourning loss of intact family: giving up fantasies of reunion b. Retrieval of hopes, dreams, expectations from the marriage c. Staying connected with extended families
Postdivorce Family		
5. Single-parent (custodial household or primary residence)	Willingness to maintain financial responsibilities, continue parental contact with ex-spouse, and support contact of children with ex-spouse and his or her family	a. Making flexible visitation arrangements with ex-spouse and his family b. Rebuilding own financial resources c. Rebuilding own social network
6. Single-parent (noncustodial)	Willingness to maintain parental contact with ex-spouse and support custodial parent's relationship with children	a. Finding ways to continue effective parenting relationship with children b. Maintaining financial responsibilities to ex-spouse and children. c. Rebuilding own social network

Source: From Betty Carter and Monica McGoldrick, *The Changing Family Life Cycle: A Framework for Family Therapy*, 2nd ed. Copyright © 1989 by Allyn and Bacon. Reprinted by permission.

ment of the blended family. The schema presented in Table 12.4, from Carter and McGoldrick (1989), presents important elements of the remarried family formation.

Poverty, when combined with parenthood at an early age, often creates a truncated family life-cycle consisting of only three major stages: (1) adolescent/unattached young adult; (2) family with children, often in a three- or four-generation

TABLE 12.4   Remarried Family Formation

Steps	Prerequisite Attitude	Developmental Issues
1. Entering the new relationship	Recovery from loss of first marriage (adequate "emotional divorce")	Recommitment to marriage and to forming a family with readiness to deal with complexity and ambiguity
2. Conceptualizing and planning new marriage and family	Accepting one's own fears and those of new spouse and children about remarriage and forming a stepfamily. Accepting need for time and patience for adjustment to complexity and ambiguity of the following: 1. Multiple new roles 2. Boundaries: space, time, membership, and authority 3. Affective issues: guilt, loyalty conflicts, desire for mutuality, unresolvable past hurts	a. Work on openness in the new relationships to avoid pseudomutuality. b. Plan for maintenance of cooperative financial and coparental relationships with ex-spouses. c. Plan to help children deal with fears, loyalty conflicts, and membership in two systems. d. Realignment of relationships with extended family to include new spouse and children. e. Plan maintenance of connections for children with extended family of ex-spouse(s).
3. Remarriage and reconstruction of family	Final resolution of attachment to previous spouse and ideal of "intact" family: Acceptance of a different model of family with permeable boundaries	a. Restructuring family boundaries to allow for inclusion of new spouse-stepparent. b. Realignment of relationships and financial arrangements throughout subsystems to permit interweaving of several systems. c. Making room for relationships of all children with biological (noncustodial) parents, grandparents, and other extended family. d. Sharing memories and histories to enhance stepfamily integration.

Source: From Betty Carter and Monica McGoldrick, *The Changing Family Life Cycle: A Framework for Family Therapy,* 2nd ed. Copyright © 1989 by Allyn and Bacon. Reprinted by permission. This table is a variation on a developmental scheme presented by J. W. Ransom, S. Schlesinger, and A. Derdeyn, " A Stepfamily in Formation," *American Journal of Orthopsychiatry* 49 (1979).

household; and (3) a stage when the grandmother has a central role in the direct care of grandchildren and other young people in the household.

SELECTED BIBLIOGRAPHY

Carter, Betty, and Monica McGoldrick. "The Changing Family Life Cycle." In *The Changing Family Life Cycle: A Framework for Family Therapy,* 2nd ed., edited by Betty Carter and Monica McGoldrick. Boston: Allyn and Bacon, 1989.

12.8 Identifying Client Strengths

PURPOSE: To identify individual and family strengths.

DISCUSSION: A social worker's assessment of a client's functioning and situation should empha-size strengths rather than weaknesses and pathology. It should identify positive and functional patterns rather than only the dysfunctional ones. In short, the assessment should focus mostly on what the client can do and wants to do, rather than on what the client cannot do or will not do. This is not to suggest a Pollyannaish approach that ignores or overlooks real problems, but it does ask the worker to search for strengths even in the most dysfunctional, difficult, and chaotic of cases. The reason for this emphasis is simple: To be successful, *an intervention must be built on and around client strengths*. Numerous studies underscore this principle. If the worker focuses only on problems and on what is going wrong in the client's life, the client will soon feel even more frustrated and discouraged and the worker will feel pes-simistic about being able to be of help.

For many in the helping professions, focusing on client strengths requires a paradigm shift—a whole new way of thought and analysis. Several forces encourage and reinforce a focus on problems and limitations rather than on strengths. Con-sider the following:

- *Agency policy and funding.* Most human services agencies are created for the purpose of addressing or correcting some personal or family problem, pathol-ogy, deficiency, or dysfunction. Thus, agency staff may assume that their pri-mary "duty" is to identify and focus on problems.
- *Diagnostic labels.* Commonly used terminology and reference books (e.g., *DSM IV*) focus attention on pathology and on all that is wrong and troublesome in a person's life. Frequent use of this terminology creates a rather negative mind-set that looks for and finds only problems and pathology.
- *Lack of skill.* Identifying personal and family problems can be described as a beginning level or elementary skill. Most people can do it with little or no for-mal training. On the other hand, identifying strengths is an advanced or high-level skill. It is a skill that many seem unable to learn.
- *Personality and temperament.* Many people tend to be negative in their out-look. They see the glass as "half empty" rather than "half full." They just natu-rally focus on what is missing and on what is wrong. Some sociobiologists be-lieve that the human tendency to notice quickly what is wrong and out of place has a survival or protective value for animals and the human species. Conse-quently, evolution has "wired" our senses and perceptual processes so we will quickly notice things that are unusual, because doing so helps us to detect and avoid dangers in our environment.

As suggested earlier, a strength is something positive and important that an in-dividual or a family can do and will do. The social worker can identify strengths by carefully observing individual and family behavior. Examples of *individual strengths* include the following:

- Taking responsibility for one's actions
- Showing a willingness to take risks in order to make needed changes
- Demonstrating loyalty and concern for family, relatives, and friends
- Showing affection, compassion, and concern for others; assisting and encouraging others
- Protecting others from harm
- Seeking employment, holding a job, being a responsible employee, meeting one's financial obligations
- Exercising self-control and making thoughtful decisions and plans
- Being trustworthy, fair, and honest in dealing with others
- Demonstrating sorrow and guilt and making amends for having hurt others; showing a willingness to forgive others
- Seeking to understand others and their situations and accepting differences among people
- Showing a willingness to keep trying despite hardship and setback; following one's dreams
- Participating in social, community, or religious organizations and showing concern for and interest in improving one's neighborhood and community
- Expressing one's point of view and standing up for one's own rights and the rights of others
- Making constructive use of special abilities and aptitudes (e.g., mechanical, artistic, interpersonal, athletic, etc.)

Important *family strengths* include the following:

- Members trust, respect, and enjoy each other.
- Members listen to and respect each other's opinions, even when they disagree. Their communication is clear, positive, and productive.
- The family has clear and reasonable rules that govern interaction.
- Each member's ideas, preferences and needs are considered before making a decision that would affect the family.
- The family has traditions, rituals, and stories that provide a sense of history, belonging, and identity.
- Family members share what they have and make personal sacrifices in order to help each other; members stick together and support each other in times of adversity.
- Conflicts are acknowledged and resolved.

Additional client strengths are listed in Items 12.9, 12.16, and 12.17.

Strengths can be identified by asking the client questions such as: Can you tell me about times when you successfully handled problems similar to those you now face? Where did you find the courage and energy to deal with those problems? How have you managed to cope up to this point? What kept you going? Despite you current problems, what parts of your life are going fairly well? What do other people like about you? What strengths do others see in your approach to life? What would you not change about yourself, your situation, and your life?

Building on client strengths may require looking at a client's problems from a different angle. For example, consider the man who has been labeled uncooperative and unmotivated. If one views this so-called uncooperative behavior from another perspective, one uncovers a strength: He is asserting his rights to disagree and resist doing what does not make sense. In other words, he is being logical and assertive. When problems are reframed in way that reveals strengths, one usually also discovers more effective ways of helping. (See Item 14.12 for other examples of redefining a problem as a strength.)

Another way of orienting your approach to one that recognizes and builds on client strengths is to operate on the assumption that within all people, there are innate tendencies toward psychological health and prosocial behavior. Just as there are natural processes that are constantly repairing the human body, there appears to be natural psychological, family, and interpersonal forces that, over time, tend to heal and repair psychological damage, ruptured relationships, and the many other hurts that are part of human life and living. If such a belief is a reasonable one, it lends hope to the worker's helping efforts. It informs the social worker of the importance of supporting those natural forces and creating conditions and environments that allow the client's natural healing processes to work.

Drawing on some of the suggestions made by Cowger (1994), several guidelines are offered that will help the worker maintain a focus on strengths.

1. Believe the client. Assume that he or she is honest and trustworthy, unless it is proven otherwise. Assume that all people are capable of making positive changes in how they cope with the challenges of life and in how they interact with others.

2. Display an interest in strengths. Listen for and call to the client's attention all indicators of the client's competence, skill, resourcefulness, and motivation to make his or her situation better.

3. Strive to help the client identify, clarify, and articulate what he or she expects from you and your agency. Assist and encourage the client to describe specifically what he or she wants to change about his or her situation.

4. Assume that the client is an "expert" on his or her behavior, life, and situation, and knows best what will and will not work in a change effort or treatment plan. Give primary attention to the client's own perceptions and understanding of his or her situation. View the client as the "director" of the helping process.

5. View the assessment and the service planning processes as joint worker-client activity. Both the client and the professional share responsibility for determining what concern or issue needs to be addressed and how this can be done most effectively.

6. Assess but do not diagnose. Avoid the use of diagnostic labeling, for it draws attention away from client strengths and places the focus on pathology, deviance, and deficits.

7. Avoid discussions of blame and what the client or others should or should not have done previously. Attempts to assign blame lead nowhere and use time and energy better spent on problem solving. Rather, focus on what can be done now. Also, avoid pointless discussions of cause and effect. Typically, problems of social functioning arise from many complex and interrelated factors. Trying to figure out the exact cause of a problem is usually nonproductive. Time is better spent on here-and-now problem solving.

8. View the client's family, social network, and community as an "oasis" of potential resources, both formal and informal, that can be drawn into the helping process. Every family, every neighborhood, and every community contains people who are willing and capable of being helpful and supportive of others.

9. Formulate an intervention plan that is specific and individualized to the client and his or her situation. Because every individual and every family is unique and unlike every other one, all treatment plans or service plans should be unique and unlike any other one.

SELECTED BIBLIOGRAPHY

Cowger, Charles. "Assessing Client Strengths: Clinical Assessment for Client Empowerment." *Social Work* 39 (May 1994): 262–268.

Kaplan, Lisa, and Judith Girard. *Strengthening High Risk Families.* New York: Lexington Books, 1994.

Saleebey, Dennis. *The Strengths Perspective in Social Work Practice.* New York: Longman, 1992.

12.9   Coping Strategies and Ego Defenses

PURPOSE: To identify a client's usual methods of coping and defenses in order to anticipate how the client will respond to difficult situations.

DISCUSSION: Some people use the terms *coping strategy* and *ego defense mechanism* interchangeably, but the authors find it useful to make a distinction based on the degree to which the response is under conscious and voluntary control and whether self-deception and reality distortion is involved. A ***coping strategy*** is a fairly deliberate and conscious effort to solve a problem or handle personal distress. By contrast, an ***ego defense mechanism*** is often a habitual or unconscious problem-avoiding maneuver.

Coping strategies have two functions: to solve a problem (task-focused coping) and to reduce the emotional discomfort caused by stressors (emotion-focused coping). Often, an individual must first deal with emotional reactions before moving on to problem solving, but emotion-focused and task-focused coping frequently occur simultaneously.

Individuals vary widely in the type of emotion-focused strategies they use to cope with intense feelings and stressful situations. For example, given a situation that causes much anxiety, some individuals might elect to go off by themselves, others might visit friends, some pray and meditate, and still others might engage in a brisk physical workout. Other coping strategies—some functional, some not so functional—include ignoring the problem, sleeping more, eating more, and absorption in work. Since an individual tends to use certain coping strategies habitually, the social worker can get a pretty good idea of a client's usual coping strategies by asking how he or she behaved previously in response to stressful situations.

In their initial reactions to intense emotional pain, people, regardless of culture, use certain ***emotion-focused coping strategies,*** such as the following:

- *Crying.* Crying is a common and normal means of alleviating tension and responding to loss. It is a necessary part of successful grief work.
- *Talking it out.* People who have undergone traumatic experiences often need to repeatedly describe and talk about the experience. As a result of this natural desensitization process, they eventually learn to accept and tolerate the painful thoughts and feelings associated with the traumatic experience.
- *Laughing it off.* Joking and viewing painful experiences with a sense of humor serves to release tension and place the matter in perspective. In successful grieving, for example, there is often a good mix of crying and laughter among those adjusting to the death of a loved one.
- *Seeking support.* It is natural for both children and adults to seek support, attention, and affection from others as a means of regaining emotional equilibrium.
- *Dreaming and nightmares.* These do not fit the authors' definition of a coping strategy (i.e., conscious and voluntary) but they are a common reaction to traumatic experience. Dreams and nightmares are often repetitive. And, like the desensitization process involved in talking it out, the recurring dream encourages the individual to grapple with the experience.

If a client has recently had a traumatic experience (rape, death of a loved one, etc.), the social worker should be especially attentive to the coping strategies just mentioned and, where possible, facilitate their utilization by the client. In working with clients who have moved beyond these initial, emotion-focused responses or who have not had a recent traumatic experience, the social worker's assessment should give more attention to task-focused strategies.

The more ***task-focused coping strategies*** involve deliberate action to make changes in one's self, one's environment, or both. As compared to the emotion-focused strategies, these are more rational and planned. Listed here are coping strategies of a rather general nature, but they illustrate what the social worker would be looking for in data collection and assessment. A client with good task-oriented coping strategies will have the motivation, the capacity, and the opportunity to:

- Express thoughts and feelings in a clear, positive, and, when necessary, assertive manner.
- Ask questions and gather new information, even when the new information may challenge current beliefs.
- Identify one's personal needs and learn socially acceptable means of meeting those needs.
- Model one's own behavior after persons who behave in an effective and responsible manner.
- Recognize that one does have choices and can exert influence on one's own behavior, feelings, and life events.
- "Cut one's losses" and withdraw from relationships or situations that are unhealthy or stressful and unchangeable.
- Examine the religious and spiritual dimension of life and draw on one's beliefs for insight, strength, and direction.
- Identify early signs or indicators of a developing problem so action can be taken before the problem becomes serious.
- Take positive and appropriate steps to solve problems even when such actions are a source of fear and anxiety.
- Release pent-up emotion in ways that do not verbally or physically harm self or others.
- Take care of one's body and maintain one's health.
- Delay immediate gratification in order to stick with a plan that will attain a more distant but desired goal.
- Use mental images of future actions or events to mentally rehearse how to handle anticipated difficulties.
- Make fair and appropriate changes in one's daily activities of living so as not to interfere with the needs of others.
- Ignore unjustified criticism by others and remove one's self from situations that lead to self-defeating or harmful outcomes.
- Seek out and use additional skills training and needed professional services.

If the assessment reveals that a client lacks necessary coping strategies, the intervention plan should focus on helping the client learn specific *coping skills*. Of course, the skills needed will depend on the client's problem, situation, and goals. For example, an abusing parent may need to learn parenting skills, an individual in need of a job will need to focus on job finding skill, a married couple in conflict may need communication skills, and a youth leaving the foster-care system will need to acquire independent living skills.

The concept of ego defense mechanisms is part of psychodynamic theory. Although this theoretical framework is not as popular as it once was, defense mechanism terminology continues to be used by many practitioners. Defense mechanisms frequently mentioned in the professional literature include denial, projection, repression, reaction formation, rationalization, displacement, intellectualization, fantasy, and acting out. The *DSM-IV* (American Psychiatric Association 1994, 765) defines *defense mechanisms* as "automatic psychological process that protects the individual against anxiety and from awareness of internal or external stressors or dangers." Coleman (1993, 123) explains that "a person tends to be fairly consistent in the specific use of such mechanisms. While their reactions may serve useful defensive functions, they usually involve some measure of self-deception and reality distortion; . . . [and] are considered maladaptive when they become the predominant means of coping with stress."

We all use defense mechanisms, singly or in combination, as we cope with anxiety, stress, and the problems of living. It is clear, however, that defensiveness impairs a person's ability to accurately perceive reality and get along with others. The rigid or excessive use of defenses is a barrier to realistic problem solving. High levels of defensiveness and distortions of reality are characteristic of disturbed personalities.

An individual who uses the ego defense of *denial* screens out certain realities by unconsciously refusing to acknowledge them. Denial is often used in combination with *rationalization,* which involves the justification of inappropriate behavior by manufacturing logical or socially acceptable reasons for the behavior. An example is the abusing parent who justifies physical abuse on the basis that "the only thing he understands is pain." Although clearly a distortion of the truth, a rationalization is not the same as a lie because the defensive pattern is so habitual that the person is not consciously and deliberately trying to fabricate a falsehood. Denial and rationalization are predominant defenses used by people who are chemically dependent.

In *projection,* others are seen as being responsible for one's own shortcomings or unacceptable behavior. For example, the child molester may believe that he was seduced by the young child and sees himself as the victim rather than the offender.

Repression refers to a mental process in which extremely threatening and painful thoughts or experiences are excluded from consciousness. This concept is used to explain certain forms of amnesia and conversion reactions. For example, it is not uncommon for a child to repress experiences of sexual abuse and not remember them until many years later.

Emotional insulation is a maneuver aimed at withholding an emotional investment in a desired but unlikely outcome. This defense creates a shield that protects the individual from loss or a recurrence of previous pain and disappointment. For example, a child who is moved frequently from foster home to foster home learns to use emotional insulation as a defense against the pain of separation and loss; unfortunately, such a child often carries this pattern into adulthood and is then unable to develop emotional attachments to a marriage partner or to his or her own children. This defense is closely related to the concept of "learned helplessness"—after a long period of frustration, many people simply give up and quit trying to escape their misery. These are the "broken" individuals who become passive recipients of whatever life brings them. Emotional insulation is commonly used by persons who have grown up in extreme deprivation.

Intellectualization involves the use of abstractions as a way of avoiding feelings and distancing one's self from emotional pain. The impact of disappointment is softened by theoretical explanations and platitudes. For example, the individual who is turned down for a much desired job may avoid feelings of disappointment by discussing our economic system and employment conditions.

Regression involves a retreat from one's present status or level of maturity to one that has fewer demands and stressors. For example, when a new child is born to a family, the 5-year-old may begin behaving like an infant (e.g., wetting pants, sucking thumb) as a way of getting more attention and coping with fears of being overlooked by his or her parents. Regression is common among physically ill persons who are experiencing much fear or pain.

When using *reaction formation,* a person defends against troublesome thoughts, feelings, or impulses by rigidly adhering to exactly the opposite set of thoughts and behaviors. An example is an individual who discovers he is sexually attracted to children. In response, such a person becomes obsessed with the dangers of child sexual abuse and campaigns endlessly for prevention programs. Another example is the individual who is filled with anger and the desire to strike out at others but denies these feelings and rigidly holds to a philosophy of nonviolence that does not allow even the killing of a mosquito.

Displacement refers to transferring troublesome emotions (often hostility) and acting-out behaviors (e.g., violence) from the person(s) who arouses the emotion to another less threatening and less powerful person or thing. The classic example is the man who kicks his dog because he is angry with his boss.

When using *fantasy* as a defense, a person day dreams imaginary achievements and pleasant situations as a way of meeting personal needs or counteracting painful feelings of inadequacy. Serious problems develop when the person finds his or her reality so painful that much of the time is spent in a fantasy world. Excessive fantasy and the inability to distinguish between fantasy and reality are often symptoms of serious mental illness.

Acting out is not a defensive maneuver like the mechanisms described above, but it is a pattern of thought and behavior designed to alleviate stress and inner conflict. For example, an angry and frustrated individual may seek release from inner tension by attacking the person he or she views as the source of trouble. An example of another form of acting out is the battered wife who feels the tensions build and knows she will soon be beaten by her husband, so she proceeds to provoke him so she can "get it over with." Combat soldiers who can no longer handle the stress of waiting for an attack have been known to leave the safety of their foxhole and blindly charge the enemy.

Several guidelines can be offered to assist the social worker in assessing and responding to a client's defense mechanisms.

1. When using defense mechanism terminology, certain precautions are necessary. The patterns we call defenses are only hypothetical constructs inferred from the way people behave. At best, they are a shorthand language for describing behavior. Labeling a client's behavior as projection or rationalization, for example, in no way explains the behavior. You must look behind the surface behavior and identify the unmet needs and personal pain that causes the client to rely on the defense mechanism.

2. Because defenses are mostly learned and habitual, an individual tends to utilize those defenses he or she has used in the past. For example, if, in the past, an individual frequently used denial and rationalization, you can expect him or her to use those same defenses when again faced with anxiety or conflict.

3. People hold tightly to their defensive patterns. The more anxiety they experience, the more rigidly they use the defense. People do not easily give up these habits of thought and behavior. It is usually only within a relationship characterized by empathy, warmth, and genuineness that a person can feel safe enough to let down his or her defenses and examine the underlying pain.

4. Sometimes it can be difficult to tell where a true description leaves off and rationalization begins. Behaviors that suggest rationalization by a client include: (a) groping for reasons to justify an action or belief, (b) inability to recognize inconsistencies in his or her own "story," and (c) unwillingness to even consider alternative explanations and becoming angry when one's "reasons" are questioned.

SELECTED BIBLIOGRAPHY

American Psychiatric Association. *Diagnostic Statistical Manual of Mental Disorders, DSM-IV,* 4th ed., revised. Washington D.C.: American Psychiatric Association, 1994.
Coleman, James. *Abnormal Psychology and Modern Life,* 9th ed. Scott, Foresman, 1993.
Conte, Hope, and Robert Plutchik. *Ego Defenses: Theory and Measurement.* New York: Wiley and Sons, 1995

12.10 Assessing Clients' Role Performances

PURPOSE: To clarify and describe the nature of a client's difficulty in performing role-related behaviors.

DISCUSSION: As used here, a problem in role performance refers to a significant discrepancy between a client's behavior and that considered appropriate to one of his or her assigned roles (e.g., employee, parent, spouse, etc.). A number of concepts borrowed from role theories can help the social worker assess and describe role behavior. These concepts are especially useful because they bridge psychological and social perspectives on human behavior and deepen the understanding of social functioning.

The concept of *social role* derives from the observation that within a society's social structure and institutions, certain behaviors and norms are prescribed for certain relationships. For example, in the parent-child relationship, the parent is expected to provide the child with food, shelter, supervision, guidance, and so on. In a teacher-student relationship, the teacher is expected to teach, and the student is expected to learn that which the teacher judges to be important. The term *role,* borrowed from the world of theater, implies that a script, an actor, and an audience are components of interactional behavior.

The term ***role expectation*** suggests that for a given role (e.g., parent, social worker), there is a cluster of behaviors that are deemed appropriate and acceptable by a reference group or by society as a whole. In other words, the reference group (e.g., a peer group, organization, community) expects the individual to behave in a certain way and will either approve or disapprove of the person, depending on whether he or she conforms to those norms or expectations. Role expectations define the limits or the range of acceptable and tolerated behavior.

Role performance (or role enactment) refers to a person's actual behavior, which may or may not conform to role expectations. ***Role conception*** (or subjective role) is an individual's beliefs about a role and how he or she expects to behave in that role. One's expectation of self in a particular role may or may not conform to role expectations, as defined by other social systems and wider society. The term ***role demands*** refers to the specific knowledge, values, skills, physical and mental abilities, and other personal attributes necessary to perform a particular role successfully.

A number of terms are used to describe problems in role performance. ***Inter-role conflict*** refers to an incompatibility or clash between two or more roles. For example, a woman may experience a conflict between her role as parent to a young child and her role as a corporate executive who is expected to make frequent out-of-town business trips. ***Intrarole conflict*** exists when a person is caught up in a situation where two or more sets of expectations are assigned to a single role. For example, a high school boy may not be able to reconcile the role of student as defined by his teacher with how the role is defined by his peers. ***Role incapacity*** exists when, for some reason, an individual cannot adequately perform a role; possible reasons include physical or mental illness, lack of needed knowledge or skills, drug addiction, mental retardation, and so on. ***Role rejection*** occurs when an individual refuses to perform a role; an extreme example is when a parent abandons his or her child.

A problem of ***role ambiguity*** (or role confusion) exists when there are few clear expectations associated with a role—a condition most likely to occur in times of rapid social change. Consequently, the individual is unsure of what is expected and is unable to evaluate his or her own performance. ***Self-role incongruence*** exists when there is little overlap between the requirements of a role and the individual's personality. For example, an individual may occupy the role of a professional but not feel comfortable in that role. Another example is when an individual finds that his or her values, ethics, or life-style is at odds with the expectations of a role. The problem of ***role overload*** exists when a person occupies more roles than he or she can perform adequately. In reality, most individuals are unable or do not choose to conform to the expectations of all their social roles. Thus, most people live with some degree of ***role strain,*** a situation that necessitates making compromises and trade-offs, setting priorities, and using the various defense mechanisms and coping strategies to reconcile role demands with limited time, energy, and commitment.

A number of questions can help the social worker analyze problems of role performance and make decisions concerning the type of intervention needed. The questions are based, in part, on ones proposed by Mager and Pipe (1970) for the analysis of job-related performance problems.

1. *What is the nature and degree of the discrepancy between actual performance and role expectation?*
- How does the client's behavior differ from that considered appropriate or "normal" for persons in this particular role?
- What observations, events, or experiences have caused you and/or the client to conclude that a discrepancy exists?
- Why are you and/or the client dissatisfied or concerned about the client's role performance? Why is this role important? What will happen if there is no change in the client's role performance?

2. *Is the discrepancy caused by a lack of knowledge or skill?*
- Does the client possess the knowledge or skill needed to perform this role?
- Could the client adequately perform this role if he or she really had to or really wanted to? Could he or she do it if life depended on it?

3. *If the discrepancy is caused by a lack of knowledge and skill, how best can the problem be addressed?*
- Was there a time when the client could perform this role? If so, what experience or condition has caused the client to lose the capacity or motivation to perform this role?
- What can be done to help the client regain a capacity that has deteriorated?
- Is the client now able to learn the behaviors needed to perform the role?
- What teaching methods or techniques will help the client learn the behaviors needed to perform this role?

4. *If the discrepancy is caused by a rejection or a lack of interest in the role, how can the problem be addressed?*
- Does this role really matter to the client? Is it important to the client?
- What roles or activities does the client consider more important?
- Does the client see any benefits in performing this role?
- Is the client rewarded or reinforced for the performance of this role? If not, how can rewards be increased?
- Is the client punished by others or the social environment for attempting to perform this role? How can the client be helped to avoid this punishment?

SELECTED BIBLIOGRAPHY

Davis, Liane. "Role Theory." In *Social Work Treatment,* 3rd ed., edited by Francis Turner. New York: Free Press, 1986, pp. 541–563.

Mager, Robert, and Peter Pipe. *Analyzing Performance Problems.* Belmont, Calif.: Pitman Learning, 1970.

Perlman, Helen. *Persona: Social Role and Personality.* Chicago: University of Chicago Press, 1968.

12.11   Assessing Clients' Self-Concepts

PURPOSE: To understand a client's perceptions and thoughts about herself or himself as a person.

DISCUSSION: As used here, the term *self* refers to that private world of perceptions and thoughts that each of us has about ourselves and our life experiences. Basically, one's sense of self answers the question: Who am I? Meador and Rogers (1984, 158) explain that the term *self-concept* refers to a set of perceptions of the characteristics of the 'I' or 'me' and the perceptions of the relationship of the 'I' or 'me' to others and to various aspects of life, together with the values attached to those perceptions." This sense of self is of critical importance to our social functioning because how we respond to others and react to events is strongly influenced by how we think and feel about ourselves. However, Nurius and Berlin (1995, 517–518) remind us that each of us has not one, but rather "multiple concepts about who she or he is, sometimes is, was, should be or could be." They also state that the concept of self that is activated is, to some degree, responsive to the situation and the circumstances or tasks most salient at that time.

Several other terms and concepts are used to explain and describe various aspects of the private, inner world of the self. *Self-identity* is how we define and describe ourselves to ourselves and differentiate ourselves from other people. It is important to recognize that what we think about ourselves (our private thoughts) may be different from the image we present to other people. Thus, we have a private self and a public self. Others may view us quite differently than we view ourselves. *Self-efficacy* has to do with our feelings of being competent and effective and in control of one's life. The term *self-worth* (self-esteem) refers to our evaluation of our own value or adequacy as human beings. Self-worth is a very subjective evaluation, not an objective one. The term *self-acceptance* can be thought of as the degree to which we are satisfied and at peace with our qualities and attributes, assets and limitations. The term *ideal-self* (self-expectation) refers to our inner thoughts about who we could be, should be, or want to be. *Body image* refers to our perceptions of our bodies. Deeply personal thoughts and the core beliefs that are part of the self have much to do with the meaning and purpose we assign to our lives and our life experiences; thus, a person's sense of self is closely related to his or her *spirituality.*

To a large degree, one's sense of self is formed during early childhood but experiences during adolescence also exert a strong influence. However, experiences throughout one's lifetime can lead one to reevaluate and modify the answer to the questions: Who am I? and How did I come to be the person I am?

It is helpful for the social worker to approach the assessment process as an effort by one human to appreciate the inner world of another. Whether a particular aspect of a client's self-concept needs to be discussed depends on the client's concern and situation and the reasons why the client and social worker are meeting together. The exploration of a client's sense of self must be approached with great sensitivity. However, because people generally want to tell their story and describe meaningful life experiences, many clients respond nondefensively to questioning that is organized around five dimensions of experience that are common to the human condition. These dimensions are love, loss, fear, being hurt, and hurting others.

- *Who and what do you love?* Who do you really care for? What is most important to you? For whom do you make personal sacrifices? For what purposes do you donate your time and money? Are you able to love others as you want to?
- *Who and what have you lost?* Have you lost parents, children, and close friends to death or separation? Have loved ones become disabled or seriously ill? Have you lost your hopes and dreams because of divorce, abandonment, or relocation? Have you lost some physical abilities as a result of illness or injury (e.g. mobility, vision, hearing, etc.)? Have you lost your sense of emotional security and personal safety as a result of abuse, exploitation, violence, or war? Have you lost purpose and meaning in life? Have you lost contact with your homeland or native language? Have you lost touch with meaningful religious and cultural activity? Have you lost a home or important possessions to a flood, fire, or natural disaster?
- *Who and what do you fear?* Do you live with a fear of hunger, violence, illness, pain, disability, or death? Do you fear that no one cares for you? Do you fear that you are incapable of loving others? Do you fear the loss of respect and status? Do you fear the loss of important relationships, a job, money, or a home?
- *How have you been hurt in life?* How and when were you hurt by others (physically, emotionally, financially, etc.)? How do you explain these painful life experiences? Who is responsible? Have these past hurts given rise to fears of being hurt again or a desire for revenge? How have these experiences affected the way you think and feel about yourself and others?
- *Whom have you hurt?* How and when have you hurt others, deliberately or inadvertently? Why did it happen? How do you explain these experiences? How has your hurting of others shaped the way you think and feel about yourself? What have you done to correct or make amends for the pain and injury you caused?

Included next are some other lines of questioning that might be used, in one form or another, to explore a client's sense of self.

1. *Family membership.* Who is your family (tribe or clan)? For whom do you feel responsible and obligated to help or look after? With whom do you live? Where do other family members live? How often do you talk to with these family members? To which members of your family do you feel especially close? Are you comfortable with your membership in this family?

2. *Identity.* How do you define yourself in terms of the groupings and labels commonly used to describe people? (For example: Gender? Sexual orientation? Occupation? Nationality? Ethnicity? Religion? Socioeconomic class? Language? Political orientation?)

3. *Body image.* What do you notice most about your body? What do others see when they look at you body? Are you satisfied with your body? To what extent do you worry about illness and a loss of physical capacity? What specifically do you worry about?

4. *Self-acceptance.* To what degree are you comfortable with your answer to the question: Who am I? Do you enjoy times when you are alone? When by yourself, are you comfortable with your thoughts and feelings? Are you usually at ease or usually tense when you are with people you know? If you could change yourself, what, if anything, would you change?

5. *Self-worth.* What criteria do you use when you judge the worth or value of another person? How do you measure up on those same criteria? Do you like yourself? What are your major strengths, talents, and abilities? In what ways are you a unique person?

6. *Ideal-self.* To what degree are you doing or accomplishing what you expect of yourself? Are your hopes and dreams within reach? How do you define personal success? In what areas are you successful? In what areas are you falling short of your expectations? What do you want to accomplish or achieve in your lifetime? What contributions do you want to make to others, your family, or your community? How do you want to be remembered after you die?

7. *Self-efficacy.* Do you feel that you are in control of your life? Which has more influence in your life: the decisions that you make or the decisions that others people make? Do you usually respond to change with anticipation and enthusiasm or with fear? Are you hopeful about your future? Is what you expect to happen mostly good or mostly bad?

8. *Spirituality.* Do you have spiritual or religious beliefs or particular moral standards that I should know about in order to better understand your concerns and situation? Do you have a set of beliefs that help you find meaning and purpose in your life? How do you explain or make sense out of the pain and suffering that you and others experience in life?

9. *Past self and future self.* Do you see yourself as about the same or somewhat different from who you were one year ago? Five years ago? Ten years ago? Do you have regrets or guilt feelings about the past? Do these feelings have a significant impact on your life? Do you expect that you will be a different person in five years? Will this be a desirable or an undesirable change for you?

10. *Sense of place.* In what kind of a physical environment are you most comfortable? To what degree are you satisfied with your home? Your neighborhood? Your community? Is there some place you really want to live? Where? Why?

SELECTED BIBLIOGRAPHY

Bracken, Bruce, ed. *Handbook of Self-Concept.* Somerset, N. J.: John Wiley and Sons, 1995.
Meador, B. D., and Carl Rogers. "Person-Centered Therapy." In *Current Psychotherapies,* 3rd ed., edited by R. J. Corsini. Itasca, Ill.: F.E. Peacock, 1984, pp. 142–195.
Nurius, Paula, and Sharon Berlin. "Cognition and Social Cognitive Theory." In *Encyclopedia of Social Work,* 19th ed., Vol. 1, edited by Richard Edwards. Washington, D.C.: NASW, 1995, pp. 513–524.

12.12   Family Dynamics and Family Functioning

PURPOSE: To identify the nature and structure of interactions among those who make up a family system.

DISCUSSION: Given the dramatic societal changes of recent decades, it is increasingly difficult to define and describe the family in the United States. The U.S. Census Bureau defines a *family* as "two or more persons related by birth, marriage or adoption who reside in the same household" and it defines a *household* as "all the persons, related or not, occupying a housing unit." For purposes of planning human services and maintaining a family-centered approach in the delivery of these services, the authors prefer a definition based on family functions. Thus, the authors define a *family* as a group of persons related by biological ties, a legal relationship, and/or long-term expectations of loyalty and commitment, often comprising at least two generations and usually inhabiting one household; moreover, some of the adults of this group must have the intention and also the capacity to carry out all or most of the *functions common to a family,* as in the following:

- *Provide for the rearing and socialization of children* (e.g., prepare children for adulthood; teach children what they need to know in order to function within a particular culture and society; teach and model basic values, morals, and social skills such as honesty, responsibility, cooperation, compassion, trust, sharing, communication, and self-acceptance).
- *Provide its members with intimacy and a sense of belonging* (e.g., acceptance and love).
- *Provide an emotionally secure environment for sexual expression among consenting adults.*
- *Provide its members with a place of privacy and respite* (e.g., respite from other and more formal and more public social roles such as those related to community, work, and school responsibilities).
- *Provide its members with a legal and social identity* (e.g., an identity and location for the purposes of legal transactions, especially those related to parental rights and responsibilities).
- *Serve as an economic unit* (e.g., make decisions concerning the purchase of goods and services, budget and plan for future, and manage and care for possessions and property).
- *Protect, assist, and care for those family members who are vulnerable or cannot care for themselves* (e.g., young children, the frail elderly, the sick or disabled).
- *Serve as an advocate for family members in need of community resources* (e.g., parent identifies her child as being ill or disabled and seeks out medical care, parent makes sure his child gets a proper education, etc.).

In addition to nuclear and extended family structures, other variations in family form are increasingly common. These include *single-parent families* (i.e., one biological parent or adoptive parent or foster parent plus children), *blended families* or stepparent families (i.e., two married adults plus each one's children from a prior marriage and possibly children born to them as a couple), and *functional families* (i.e., two or more unmarried and unrelated adults plus their children). We are also seeing a growing number of families headed by what some call *second-time-around-parents*, referring to grandparents who have assumed primary responsibility for rearing their grandchildren. In part, this is due to the growing number of biological parents whose functioning is seriously impaired by addiction to drugs and alcohol.

As people create or join a new family, there is a tendency for them to repeat the behavioral patterns they learned as a child in their family of origin. Moreover, when people live together for an extended period, their interactions become habitual. Once the patterns are well established, there is a tendency for family members to preserve the status quo and repeat that which is familiar, even when there are obvious problems in the family's functioning.

The family is indeed a complex system and it is a challenging task to identify and assess its interactional patterns. Following are questions that the social worker should keep in mind as he or she gathers information about a family's functioning.

1. *How is family membership defined?* One can view membership in a number of ways. For example, who are members of the *biological family* (e.g., bio-parents, biological offspring)? Who are members of the *legal family*, as defined by marriage, divorce, and adoption laws and by court orders affecting child custody? What is the composition of the *functional family* (i.e., who is part of household and who assumes responsibility for child care and other tasks of daily living)? Who belongs to the *perceived family* (i.e., those who the members consider as belonging to the family regardless of biological and legal ties)? And finally, who belongs to the *family of long-term commitments*, as defined by an expectation of lifelong loyalty, duty, and "being there for me" regardless of changes in household composition or legal definitions?

2. *What facts and realities describe the family?* What are the names, sex, and ages of the members? How is the family's functioning impacted by the various developmental stages of its members, such as the presence of young children, teens, and the elderly (see Item 12.6)? How does the family's functioning relate to the family life cycle (see Item 12.7)? Does the family have a particular religious, ethnic, or cultural identity? What is the source of income? Are family members employed? Where? What are their occupations? How do the demands of these jobs affect family roles and functioning? What personal and social circumstances surrounded the marriage or the formation of the family and the birth of the children? Is there a history of divorce, abandonment, or violence? Is the family's functioning affected by a member's physical or mental illness, disability, or addiction?

3. *Is family functioning supported by the community?* In what neighborhood and community does this family live? How is the family affected by living there? Is it a safe place to be? Is decent and affordable housing available? Are jobs available? Are basic public utilities and services available (e.g., police protection, sanitation ser-

vices, transportation, library)? Do the local schools provide the educational programs needed by the children?

4. ***How well are family functions performed?*** How does the family function as an economic unit (i.e., secure income, pay bills, etc.)? Does it successfully manage tasks of daily living (e.g., cooking, cleaning, laundry, etc.)? Does the home serve as a place of rest, recuperation, and privacy for its members? Does the family provide its members with a sense of identity and belonging? Does it provide nurturing, love, companionship, and intimacy? Do the children receive the encouragement and guidance needed to prepare for success in school and work roles? Does the family provide appropriate socialization experiences for its children so they learn the interpersonal and social skills they will need in adulthood? Is the family able to adhere to customs, traditions, and religious beliefs it considers important?

5. ***What are the boundaries, subsystems, rules, and roles governing family interaction?*** A family system may consist of four subsystems: the *spouse subsystem* (i.e., two adults that usually involves a sexual relationship); the *parental subsystem* (i.e., those family members responsible for childrearing); the *parent-child subsystem* (i.e., a special closeness between a particular parent and child); and the *sibling subsystem.* The various rules, communication channels, and behavioral patterns that define and regulate these subsystems are termed *boundaries.* In a healthy family, these boundaries are fairly clear and in keeping with societal norms. By contrast, for example, in an incest family, the child has been drawn into the spouse subsystem. In many cases of physical child abuse, a child will move into the parental subsystem and engage in role reversal behavior wherein the young child cares for his or her parent—often in an effort to keep the parent calm.

When boundaries are unclear and defuse, members become intrusive and overly involved in the lives of family members. Such family relationships are termed *enmeshed,* fused, or merged. The opposite condition is where there is little meaningful interaction among family members or between the family's subsystems. Such families are said to have a *disengaged* pattern of relationships. A boundary also exists between a family and its social environment. The nature of that boundary determines whether the family will be *open* or *closed* to outside influences. (See Chapter 6 for more information on systems theory.)

Special attention must be given to the family's *role structure.* Roles are those patterns of thought and action that define who we are, how we behave toward others in the family, and, of course, how they behave toward us. Certain role sets guide the common tasks of living, such as who drives the car, who pays the bills, and who cares for the children. It is important for the social worker to determine why such tasks are assigned to certain family members. The role structure may be strongly influenced by the family's culture and religion. The family-related roles we take on during the course of growing up in a family tend to be more permanent, less flexible, and less conscious than other social roles, such as those of student, employee, social worker, or supervisor. Pet expressions for common family roles include "black sheep," "the happy one," "peace maker," "the banker," "golden boy," "disciplinarian," "family worrier," "lone wolf," and "daddy's little girl." In professional literature, one often finds references to the family roles of scapegoat, identified patient, infantalized child, parentified child, hero, mascot, lost child, rescuer, and message boy.

Essentially, *family rules* are explicit or implicit principles that maintain the family's organization or "systemness" and that govern member interaction. Rules are reflected in the seating arrangement during meals and in family regulations, such as "always clean the bath tub when finished." Most family rules are necessary and innocuous and some can appear silly to the outsider, such as "Don't take a trip in the car without first changing your underwear." By contrast, it is the unspoken or hidden rules that contribute most to family dysfunction. Rules that suppress emotion, cover up irresponsible behavior, promote dishonesty, or generate feelings of shame are especially harmful. Examples include: "When Dad is drinking, never mention his brother Ed" or "Pretend you don't see Mom and Dad fighting" or "Only an evil person would ever feel anger toward a parent." The children of parents who are alcoholic often grow up with the rules of "don't talk" (about the drinking or other real issues), "don't feel" (suppress all feelings), and "don't trust" (always be on guard and keep people at a distance). The social worker must identify family rules and, more importantly, observe whether they can be openly discussed and what happens when rules are broken.

The boundaries, rules, and roles at work within a family can only be inferred after careful observation. Some family members may be able to articulate family rules, but most of these patterns are so ingrained that they seem natural and normal and are never questioned.

6. *How well does each member fit within the family system?* Although there is great value in viewing the family from a systems perspective, it is important to remember that this dynamic system is made up of separate human beings, each of which has a unique genetic makeup, biology, personality, and life experience. Thus, the worker needs to be cognizant that each member has his or her own thoughts and feeling; hopes, expectations, and obligations; talents; sense of identity; spirituality; coping strategies and ego defenses; special emotional needs; and physical or mental limitations. It is useful to consider whether there is a good match or a possible mismatch between each family member and the norms, values, and rules of his or her family system.

7. *What are the moral and ethical dimensions of the family's functioning?* This dimension of family dynamics refers to issues such as obligation, loyalty, fairness, sacrifice, accountability, and entitlement that relate rather directly to a person's moral standards, religious beliefs, notions of good and evil, and spirituality. Many of the conflicts among family members revolve around moral and ethical issues.

8. *What aspects of life are considered beyond human control?* In order to understand a client's behavior and decisions, it may be necessary to understand his or her sense of the sacred—that which is in the sphere of the mysterious, the awesome, the uncontrollable, and the supremely important. These views and beliefs are in contrast to views concerning aspects of life that one can control or at least attempt to control. An individual's or family's sense of the sacred is closely related to their religious beliefs, spirituality, concepts of God, and the meanings assigned to life, death, and human suffering.

9. *How does the family make decisions?* All families develop patterns or styles of decision making. In some families, all members can express opinions and participate in decision making. On the other extreme are families in which one member makes all major decisions. Some practitioners learn about a family's way of making decisions by meeting with the whole family and asking them to perform a task (e.g., plan a vacation or family outing) and then observing how they reach a decision.

10. *What is the mood of the family?* Much like an individual, a family is often characterized by a prevailing mood. Is the family warm and caring? Optimistic? Pessimistic? Excitable? Outgoing? Depressed? Fun loving? Angry? Controlled? Spontaneous?

11. *How do family members handle "differentness"?* Everyone is unique and everyone must learn to live with others. A common source of interpersonal difficulty is the inability to accept others as being different from oneself and/or the inability to accept oneself as being different from others. Thus, when assessing a family, consider how each member deals with differentness. There are four basic ways of handling differences:

- *Eliminating others.* Attempting to deal with differentness by beating down or suppressing the individuality of others (e.g., finding fault with others, blaming, attacking, etc.)
- *Eliminating self.* Handling differentness by suppressing one's individuality (e.g., always agreeing, submitting to others, accommodating, hiding one's true feelings)
- *Avoiding issues.* Attempting to handle differentness by denying or avoiding issues that would reveal differences (e.g., keeping family communication on "safe" topics, etc.)
- *Open and honest communication.* Dealing with differentness by acknowledging the existence of differences, discussing them in a respectful manner, and working to resolve whatever conflicts exist

Systems theory postulates the existence of system forces that resist change and maintain a state of dynamic equilibrium. When other maneuvers do not work, a family may attempt to preserve itself and protect its systemness by scapegoating one family member. A related phenomena, often termed *re-peopling,* refers to the family system's efforts to regain stability by either adding or excluding a member. A request by parents to have their disruptive teenager placed in foster care can be viewed as a re-peopling maneuver.

12. *How clearly do family members communicate their own expectations and needs?* In order for family members to respond appropriately to each other's needs, there must be communication concerning those needs. Sometimes we are unwilling or unable to communicate our wants and needs but still feel angry and disappointed when others do not respond in the desired way. Problems arise when family members expect others to be skilled at mind reading.

13. *What communication patterns exist within the family?* A pattern of verbal and nonverbal communication develops whenever two or more people interact on a regular basis; certain unwritten rules begin to guide interaction. The pattern reveals

how each member regards himself or herself in relation to the others. There are many forms of workable communication patterns. What is functional for one family may not work for another. As with so many aspects of family functioning, culture and ethnicity have a strong impact on family communication and on what works for the family. To decipher this pattern, the worker needs to observe: Who speaks to whom? Who speaks first? Who responds? Who listens to whom? Who speaks most? Who speaks least? Who speaks last? Who sits next to whom? Are messages directed to one person but meant for someone else? Are the messages clear? Do the words say one thing but mean another? Are the family's communications characterized by respect, openness, and honesty or by evasiveness, denial, double messages, blaming, threats, hurtful jokes, interruptions, or defiance?

14. *Do family members allow other members to get close emotionally?* Everyone has a need for intimacy, but at the same time most of us have some fear of closeness. Sometimes people avoid getting close to others because they fear that if they reveal their vulnerabilities, others will take advantage of their weakness. Some people hide behind a facade because they fear others will not care for the "real" them. Even within a family, members may keep others at a distance. Within a well-functioning family, members are able to reveal many of their inner thoughts and feelings but also maintain a comfortable level of privacy.

15. *What are the interpersonal payoffs of "troublesome behavior"?* To understand a troubled family, the social worker must see beyond the problem behavior and develop working hypotheses about why members repeatedly engage in interactions that create so much distress and misery. Two interrelated themes of family interaction explain many problem and nonproblem behaviors: the desire by a member for closeness versus his or her desire for distance and the member's desire for belonging versus his or her desire for independence. People want intimacy but not to be oppressed by the closeness. Also, people want to be part of a family but not to be consumed or controlled by family loyalty. When observing the family's struggle with a problem, the worker should constantly ask: How does this behavior bring the family members closer emotionally or create a feeling of belonging? How does this behavior promote a sense of separateness and independence?

16. *Who supports and who opposes change?* Whenever a change is being considered, some degree of resistance can be expected. However, family members will differ in the degree to which they will oppose change. In order to assess support and opposition, the social worker might ask the family members to speculate on the effects of a hypothetical change.

SELECTED BIBLIOGRAPHY

Karpel, Mark. *Evaluating Couples: A Handbook for Practitioners.* New York: W. W. Norton, 1994.

Karpel, Mark, and Eric Strauss. *Family Evaluation.* New York: Gardner Press, 1983.

Kaslow, Florence, ed. *Handbook of Relational Diagnosis and Dysfunctional Family Patterns.* Somerset, N. J.: John Wiley and Sons, 1996.

Walsh, Froma, ed. *Normal Family Processes,* rev. ed. New York: Guilford Press, 1993.

12.13 Multiworker Family Assessment Interviews

PURPOSE: To utilize more than one social worker in the assessment process in order to secure a more detailed understanding of how each family member views the family's problem.

DISCUSSION: There are many advantages to using an approach that brings additional social workers into the assessment process. This is especially true when working with whole families. Kinney, Haapala, and Gast (1981) report that a multiworker model of assessment is particularly helpful when providing intensive family crisis services designed to prevent out-of-home placements.

A multiworker assessment interview is conducted after the social worker assigned to the case (i.e., the primary worker) has conducted an initial interview with the family. If this worker decides to use a multiworker assessment, it is explained to the family. Once the family agrees, secondary social workers are temporarily assigned to each family member (e.g., if there were four family members, four additional workers would be needed). Each secondary worker then spends an hour or so listening to their assigned family member's perspective on the family's problem and attempts to understand how that member sees himself or herself within the context of the family system. After these individual interviews are completed, the secondary social workers and the primary social worker meet for about an hour and share what they have learned about each family member. Meanwhile, the family members spend this time together without a social worker being present.

Next, all of the social workers and all of the family members meet together. Each secondary social worker sits next to his or her family member and speaks for that person; each speaks as if he or she were the family member and uses I-messages to describe his or her thoughts and feelings about the family's functioning. During this phase, the family members are not to speak or respond to what is being said. If a family member does not like what is being said, he or she and the social worker can leave the room, discuss the difference, and then rejoin the group. After all of the social workers have spoken for the family members, the family members are asked to react to what they have heard.

The last part of this session is used to plan the next steps in the family's effort to secure help with their problem. After this multiworker assessment, the primary social worker continues to provide service.

Although this assessment process may take from three to five hours, it has important advantages, such as the following:

1. A great deal of information is gathered and each family member's point of view is expressed and explored. The workers are often able to say things that the individual is afraid of saying, thus the issues are out in the open.

2. The family members usually leave this lengthy assessment session feeling they have been listened to and understood. Typically, the process yields a firmer commitment by the family members to work on the problem, a feeling of hopefulness, and ideas on how to make changes.

3. The process has the effect of creating several consultants who have firsthand knowledge of the family, which can be helpful to the primary social worker.

SELECTED BIBLIOGRAPHY

Kinney, Jill, David Haapala, and Elizabeth Gast. "Assessment of Families in Crisis." In *Treating Families in the Home,* edited by Marvin Bryce and June Lloyd. Springfield, Ill.: Charles C. Thomas, 1981.

12.14   The ABC Model and the Behavior Matrix

PURPOSE: To achieve greater precision in observation and the analysis of behavioral interactions.

DISCUSSION: Social workers often look to behavioral analysis and behavior modification for techniques of helping clients learn new behaviors or eliminate problem behaviors. The influence of behavior-oriented approaches has done much to help practitioners be more precise in data gathering and assessment. Two tools commonly used in behavioral analysis, the ABC model and the behavior matrix, are particularly useful.

The ABC's of Behavior

In the *ABC model,* the letter *A* stands for *antecedent, B* for *behavior,* and *C* for *consequences.* For example, when assessing a problem behavior, such as a child's temper tantrum, the worker first clearly identifies and operationally defines the behavior under study. In this example, the tantrum is the *B* (i.e., target behavior).

Next, the worker looks for the *A,* or the antecedent, which are the various situational factors or cues that set up the behavior. In the tantrum example, it might be a particular action by the parent that sets the stage for the child's tantrum; perhaps the parent begins to work in the kitchen or turns on the TV news.

Finally, the worker looks for the immediate consequences of the behavior, which is the *C* in the model. This may identify factors that reinforce or reward the behavior. For example, once the tantrum starts, the parent may try to comfort the child and, in the process, reinforce the tantrum behavior. By using the ABC model, the worker may be able to identify those factors that can be changed in order to reduce or eliminate a problem behavior.

Behavior Matrix

A second tool, actually an observational aid, is a three-cell matrix known as the *Behavior Matrix* (see Figure 12.10). After observing the interactions of an individual client, family, or small group, the worker records his or her observations in the appropriate cell. What emerges will be a picture of what positive behaviors should be reinforced, what negative behaviors should be extinguished, and what new positive behaviors will need to be learned by the client.

**FIGURE 12.10
Behavior
Matrix**

	Behavior Exists	Behavior Does Not Exist
Positive or Appropriate Behavior	1	2
Negative or Inappropriate Behavior	3	

As an example, assume that the worker is attempting to help a man who is developmentally disabled learn to interact more appropriately when greeting other adults. While observing and using the matrix, the worker sees that when introduced to another person, the client giggles, reaches for a handshake, and fails to look directly at the person he is greeting. The worker would record his or her observations as follows:

1. The giggle is an existing inappropriate behavior—enter comment in cell 3.
2. The handshake is an existing appropriate behavior—enter comment in cell 1.
3. Eye contact when shaking hands is a nonexisting appropriate behavior—enter comment in cell 2.

Having made such observations, the next step is to develop an appropriate intervention strategy. Table 12.5 matches recommended behavioral techniques to findings derived from the matrix. (See Items 14.4, 14.5, and 14.6 for information on behavior techniques.)

TABLE 12.5   Behavioral Observations and Intervention Techniques

Observation	Possible Intervention
Desired behaviors do not occur at all	Instruction, modeling, prompting, shaping
Desired behaviors occur but infrequently	Additional reinforcement, shaping behavioral rehearsal
Behaviors occur but not at appropriate time	Behavioral contracting, prompting, and other reminders
Desired behavior occurs so frequently as to be inappropriate	Reduce frequency of reinforcement, differential reinforcement, removal from reinforcing environment
Behaviors that occur are dangerous to self or others	Removal from reinforcing environment, reinforcement of an incompatible behavior

SELECTED BIBLIOGRAPHY

Cautela, Joseph. *Behavior Analysis Forms for Clinical Intervention.* Vol. 1. Champaign, Ill.: Research Press, 1977.

———. *Behavior Analysis Forms for Clinical Intervention.* Vol. 2. Champaign, Ill.: Research Press, 1981.

Cautela, Joseph, Julie Cautela, and Sharon Esonis. *Form for Behavioral Analysis with Children.* Champaign, Ill.: Research Press, 1983.

Sundel, Sandra, and Martin Sundel. *Behavior Modification in the Human Services,* 3rd ed. Newbury Park, Calif.: Sage, 1993.

12.15   Homemade Data-Gathering Tools

PURPOSE: To create data-gathering questionnaires, checklists, vignettes, and other data-gathering tools for use with clients in a particular practice setting.

DISCUSSION: The major advantage of using commercially available data-gathering and assessment instruments is that they have been field-tested and can be easily ordered from a publisher. Their major disadvantages are that they can be expensive and may be too complex, too long, or too limited in their application. As an alternative to using ones that are copyrighted and commercial products, social workers should consider designing their own so the tools will be tailored to the types of clients served and the agency setting. With a bit of trial and error, most workers can create simple and practical tools such as the questionnaire, checklist, and vignette.

Figure 12.11 is a sample *questionnaire* developed for use during initial interviews with couples seeking assistance with marital problems. Because it is short and takes only a few minutes to complete, clients do not find it burdensome. As with a problem checklist (see Item 11.5), this type of questionnaire can be used to zero in on the client's primary concerns. The basic format has wide application. Items can be rewritten to focus on other relationships, problems, or concerns. The reader can use this sample questionnaire as a model for developing tools for his or her own practice.

The checklist is a simple format for data gathering. It demands little of the client. With a little creativity, the worker can develop a checklist related to a specific set of client concerns. Figure 12.12 is an example of a *checklist* designed especially for the parents of children involuntarily placed in foster care by a child protection agency. It was developed by Horejsi, Bertsche, and Clark (1981) to help parents express their feelings about their child being placed into foster care.

Information about a person's attitudes and values cannot be easily obtained through direct verbal or written questioning. Projective or indirect methods are more effective. Think, for example, about the child welfare worker responsible for deciding whether or not a couple should be licensed as foster parents. In order to assess the couple's capacity for foster parenting, the worker needs to learn about their beliefs and attitudes surrounding child care. The worker could ask a direct question,

FIGURE 12.11   Sample Homemade Questionnaire

Questionnaire on the Husband-Wife Relationship

Explanation: This is a questionnaire about how satisfied you are with what goes on between you and your spouse (between husband and wife). Your answer will help us identify possible sources of stress and worry. Place a check (✓) on the line under the phrase that best describes the degree of satisfaction you have in relation to the item. If an item does not apply to you, simply put NA next to the item.

	Very Satisfied	Mostly Satisfied	Mostly Dissatisfied	Very Dissatisfied
The way we make decisions				
The way we divide up responsibility for child care				
The way we handle and budget money				
The amount of money we earn				
The way we resolve conflict				
The way we divide up housework and other home-related jobs				
The way we get along with our children				
The way we discipline our children				
The way we get along with in-laws and other relatives				
The way we use our free time				
The way we talk to each other				
The way we care for our home				
The amount of time we have together				
The amount of alcohol used				
The way we give each other emotional support				
The amount of privacy we have				
The way we handle birth control				
The sexual part of our relationship				
The way we plan for our future				
The way we get along with the neighbors				
The way we deal with moral or religious concerns				
The way we handle anger and frustration				

Please list here any other concerns you may have about your marital relationship:

_____

What do you consider to be the major strengths in your marriage?

_____

What do you consider to be the one or two major problems in your marriage?

_____

FIGURE 12.12   Sample Homemade Checklist

Understanding the Parents' Feelings

Explanation: Below is a list of feelings that have been expressed by other parents who have had their children placed in foster care. Your feelings may be similar or they may be different from those of other parents who have had a similar experience. Please place a check (✓) by those statements that come close to expressing how you feel.

_____ I feel stunned and numb.

_____ I feel like this whole thing is a bad dream; I cannot believe this is really happening.

_____ I feel preoccupied with the thoughts of my child and the separation; I cannot seem to think of anything else.

_____ I feel shaky and nervous—as if a friend had suddenly died.

_____ I feel overwhelmed; I can't think clearly or do what I know I should do.

_____ I feel everyone blames me for what happened, even though it was not all my fault.

_____ I feel I was singled out unfairly and that I am being accused of being a "bad" parent.

_____ I feel like I have been railroaded and treated unfairly by the agency and the court.

_____ I feel like I cannot face my own child.

_____ I am afraid of what others think of me.

_____ I feel resentment toward everyone.

_____ I fear what I tell my social worker will be used against me.

_____ I feel afraid that I will never get my child back.

_____ I feel confused over why my child was placed in foster care.

_____ I feel that my other children will be placed in foster care.

_____ I feel depressed and sad.

_____ I feel alone and isolated; I feel everyone has abandoned me.

_____ I feel cut off from family and friends.

_____ I feel like running away and never coming back.

_____ I feel God is punishing me.

_____ I feel placement was necessary even though it was painful.

_____ Given time and help, I feel I can put things back together again.

_____ I am pretty sure of what I need to do in order to deal with the situation.

_____ I feel much better than I did when my child first went into foster care.

_____ I have mixed feelings about foster care-sometimes I want my child back and sometimes I think he/she is better off if we are not together.

Please describe here any feelings you have that do not appear on the above list.

_____

_____

_____

Source: From Horejsi, Bertsche, and Clark, *Social Work Practice with Children in Foster Care* (1981), Appendix D, pp. 236–37. Courtesy of Charles C Thomas, Publisher, Springfield, Illinois.

such as: Do you believe in spanking a child who misbehaves? or How do you feel about children who wet the bed? Such pointed questions, however, tend to elicit rather superficial responses, which do not reveal the underlying attitudes that are so important in parenting.

An alternative approach is to use a series of carefully written vignettes as springboards for discussion and exploration. Basically, a *vignette* is a brief description of a real-life problem or situation. It provides an indirect method of gathering information and facilitates the expression of feelings and personal viewpoints. Figure 12.13 presents two samples developed by Horejsi (1979) for use in the foster home study process. Needless to say, the worker using this projective tool must create vignettes that will elicit the type of information needed to understand the client.

In general, social workers underutilize aids like questionnaires, checklists, and vignettes in their data collection. The reader is encouraged to develop and experiment with these tools. A number of guidelines will help those willing to give it a try.

1. Be clear about the purpose to be served by the tool, the reasons for using it, the type of information sought, and the type of client for whom it is being prepared.

FIGURE 12.13 Sample Vignettes

The Brown Family: A Situation to Discuss

Mr. and Mrs. Brown are foster parents to Johnny, age five. Johnny is mentally retarded and has poor arm and hand coordination. Consequently, he has some trouble eating. Because today is Mrs. Brown's birthday, the Browns have decided to go out for an evening meal at a restaurant. While eating, Johnny drops food on the floor and is generally messy. In addition, he has a temper tantrum, cries, and throws food. This gets stares and disapproving looks from the other people in the restaurant.

a. What do you think of this situation?
b. How should this behavior be handled?

The Patterson Family: A Situation to Discuss

The Pattersons are very religious people. They have been foster parents to fifteen-year-old Alfred for the past five years. The Pattersons go to church services and participate in other church activities on a regular basis. It means a lot to them. Until a few months ago, Alfred went to church with them, even though he was raised in another religious denomination. Now Alfred refuses to go to church. He says that religion is foolishness and that he should not be forced to go to the Pattersons' church when his parents belonged to a different one. The Pattersons feel that religion is central to their life, and they expect everyone living in their family to participate in religious activities.

a. What do you think of this situation?
b. How should a conflict of this type be handled?

Source: From Horejsi, *Foster Family Care* (1979), pp. 165–166. Courtesy of Charles C Thomas, Publisher, Springfield, Illinois.

2. The completion of the questionnaire should be a relatively easy task and not tax the client's physical or mental capacity. A simple, short, and focused questionnaire is more likely to be completed than a long one.

3. Rather than attempt to develop an all-purpose questionnaire, it is better to design several, each with a specific purpose or focus.

4. In general, the higher the client's level of education and motivation, the more likely he or she is to deal successfully with a written data-gathering tool. Remember that many people lack basic reading skills.

5. Open-ended questions may be necessary when it is difficult to anticipate probable responses. However, written responses to open-ended questions are often difficult to read and understand. Consequently, tools with many open-ended questions offer few advantages over the interview.

6. The construction of precoded or close-ended questions (multiple choice, checklists, etc.) requires knowledge about the kinds of responses clients are likely to give. However, a good close-ended question is easy on the client and can be read quickly by the worker.

7. When possible, the questionnaire items should follow a uniform format (i.e., each item has similar wording, and structure). This helps the client move easily from question to question and minimizes the chance that the client will misunderstand a question.

8. The sequence of questions should follow a logical order. The most sensitive or probing questions should appear toward the end of the questionnaire.

9. Each question or item should contain a single idea. Avoid two- or three-part questions. Questions should be free of bias. The language used should be simple, clear, and concise. Avoid jargon.

10. A pretest should be used to determine whether clients can understand all of the questions, can complete it in a reasonable amount of time, and whether the data obtained are indeed useful.

11. Tools developed for use in multidisciplinary or interdisciplinary settings should be understandable to and useable by all members of the team.

12. Whenever possible, tools should be designed so that the data collected can be represented in a visual or graphic manner for rapid comprehension.

SELECTED BIBLIOGRAPHY

Horejsi, Charles. *Foster Family Care.* Springfield, Ill.: Charles C. Thomas, 1979.
———. *Questionnaire on Husband-Wife Relationship.* Missoula: University of Montana, 1982.
Horejsi, Charles, Anne Bertsche, and Frank Clark. *Social Work Practice with Parents of Children in Foster Care: A Handbook.* Springfield, Ill.: Charles C. Thomas, 1981.
Jordan, Cathleen, and Cynthia Franklin. *Clinical Assessment for Social Workers.* Chicago: Lyceum Books, 1995.

12.16 Assessment of Adult Social Functioning (AASF)

PURPOSE: To measure and record levels of adult social functioning.

DISCUSSION: The *AASF (Assessment of Adult Social Functioning)* is designed to assist social workers in data gathering, assessment, and case recording. Application of the AASF involves ranking the client on each of 33 items using a four-level index that ranges from a desirable level of functioning to one in which there are major problems. The instrument provides descriptive statements of client functioning to facilitate this ranking. Each item focuses on a type or an area of social functioning that may concern the practitioner and client. Only those items applicable to the client are rated.

The following is one of the six AASF items in Section 2, "Care of Self." This item, termed "Control of Time and Energy," and its four levels of functioning illustrate the rating and recording format used in the AASF.

AASF Item: Control of Time and Energy

Level		Now	Goals	Later
4	Sets clear conditions and bargains assertively concerning demands on personal time and energy.	4	P S	4
3	Sets unclear conditions in bargaining for use of personal time and energy.	3	P S	(3)
2	Allows demands on personal time and energy to be made without setting conditions.	(2)	(P) S	2
1	Reacts to demands on personal time and energy by withdrawing passively or aggresively.	1	P S	1

Note that under the *Now* column, the number *2* is circled, and alongside it the *P* is circled. This indicates that, at the start of intervention, the client was rated at level 2 for "control of time and energy" and this dimension of functioning was selected as a primary (P) target of intervention (the letter *S* refers to secondary). Note that, after a period of intervention (i.e., later), the client was rated at level 3. The change of rating, if any, between the *Now* (before) and the *Later* (after) records the client's progress toward an intervention goal.

The user should not attempt to summarize the rankings on the individual items. MacNair (1981, 88) warns that "the instrument was not constructed with this intention in mind. In fact, both the number of items and the frequent use of 'not applicable' render any summary score misleading, if not useless." The AASF is not a research tool.

Because the individual items of the AASF serve to remind the social worker of the various dimensions of functioning that need to be considered in the social assessment process, included here is a brief description of all 33 items. The descriptions are paraphrased versions of those provided by MacNair (1981, 13–36) to depict the highest level of functioning. These positive statements can also be viewed as client strengths and successful coping strategies. Many of these statements can be useful in the preparation of a service plan (see Items 13.4 and 13.5) and in identifying client strengths (see Item 12.8).

Client's Crisis Prevention and Management

1. *Response to illness or injury.* Client seeks out and uses appropriate treatment for illness or injury. Client's attitude and behavior serve to restore health.
2. *Recovery from anxiety or depression.* Client recovers at a relatively rapid rate from anxiety or depression brought on by crisis episode. Work and family's functioning continue without serious interruption.
3. *Coping with loss or separation.* Client carefully and purposely rebuilds alternate intimate relationships following a divorce, separation, or death of spouse or other significant person. Maintains satisfaction with self despite the loss.
4. *Safety or legality of behavior.* Client avoids behavior that could produce a crisis, arrest, or injury. Stays clear of daredevil high-risk activities, physical fighting, theft, property damage, and abuse of drugs and alcohol.
5. *Maintaining balanced budget.* Client balances income and expenditures and also has income adequate to purchase food, clothing, shelter, transportation, and other essentials.
6. *Job stability.* Client shows commitment to job and achieves reputation as good and productive worker. Changes jobs only for reasons of career improvement.

Client's Care of Self

1. *Physical care.* Client engages in health-building behaviors, including appropriate hygiene, diet, exercise, and sleep, and avoids misuse or abuse of medicines, harmful foods, drugs, and alcohol.
2. *Reductions of anxiety or depression.* Client is able to control anxiety, worry, and depression within normal limits. Personal satisfactions not reduced by anxiety or depression.
3. *Relationships that are encouraging.* Client selects companions who provide acceptance and encouragement and have qualities of warmth and genuineness. Avoids companions who are pervasively discouraging or manipulative.
4. *Control of time and energy.* Client is able to set priorities and reasonable limits on demands by others for client's time and energy. Has adequate time and energy to carry out essential responsibilities.
5. *Home environment.* Home and neighborhood meet basic standards of safety and health.
6. *Career choice.* Client chooses career that holds promise for earning needed income, promotions, and increasing responsibility and recognition. Career choice is good match between abilities and occupational requirements.

Client's Family Life

1. *Sexual satisfaction.* Mutual and nonexploitative sexual activity is frequent enough and sufficiently enjoyable to satisfy self and partner.
2. *Partnership with spouse.* Marital relationship is mutually satisfying and meets need for intimacy and emotional expressiveness.
3. *Attention to children.* Relationship with children is accepting, supportive, and encouraging. Parent able to meet child's need for nurturing, guidance, and protection.
4. *Response of children to parent(s).* Children consider guidance, limits, and discipline by parents to be fair and reasonable.
5. *Family encouragement for public life.* Spouses encourage each other and parents encourage children to participate in community, school, job, recreation, religious, civic, or other activities within the limits of energy and demands of other responsibilities necessary to maintain a healthy family life.

Client's Personal Satisfaction

1. *Self-acceptance.* Client has positive self-image and an attitude of self-confidence. Has realistic picture of own strengths and limitations.
2. *Relationship with friends.* Client communicates a sense of belonging and a feeling of closeness to a variety of different people. Maintains satisfying interactions with friends, relatives, neighbors, and co-workers.
3. *Assertiveness.* Client can initiate interactions with others and influence them to cooperate and/or meet his or her own legitimate needs.
4. *Productivity.* Client is able to successfully complete tasks required on the job, in school, and at home.
5. *Learning.* Client is able to assess own learning needs, seek out instruction, and learn that which is needed for work, home, and school. Client is free of cognitive or sensory difficulties that impede learning process or can compensate for deficits.

Client's Adjustments to Disability

1. *Use of prescribed physical or chemical supports.* Client makes full and appropriate use of supports such as hearing aid, artificial limbs, and medications.
2. *Control of frustration.* Client's expressions of anger over disability do not offend family members, friends, relatives, and other helpers. Frustration is expressed in ways that reduce rather than increase tension. Client appreciates those trying to help him or her overcome frustration.
3. *Participation in relationships.* Client with disability remains involved in intimate relationship and with family, relatives, and friends.
4. *Willingness to talk about disability.* Client willing and able to discuss disability and need for assistance without embarrassment or apology. Client lets others know what he or she can and cannot do.
5. *Participation in occupation and public life.* Client is willing to learn and implement rehabilitation techniques that facilitate involvement in work activities and make possible a life-style as near normal as possible.
6. *Ability to plan for emergencies.* Client recognizes disability-related vulnerabilities and plans how to handle possible emergencies or accidents.

Client's Coping with Deviance or Addiction

1. *Control over deviance or addiction.* Client has successfully overcome or controlled previous deviance or addiction and now maintains nondeviant lifestyle.
2. *Awareness of deviance or addiction.* Client recognizes nature of deviance or addiction and faces up to its personal and social consequences. Client is free of tendency to deny or rationalize.
3. *Relationships with nondeviant peers.* Client has overcome social barriers to meaningful relationships with nondeviant relatives, friends, and co-workers. Client interacts with wide variety of people and prior deviant behavior no longer limits range of associations.
4. *Participation in nondeviant leisure activities.* Client participates in diverse social and leisure activities. Activities no longer limited by pursuit of deviance or addiction.
5. *Career involvement.* Client pursues career and income completely free of hindrance by addiction or deviance.

SELECTED BIBLIOGRAPHY

MacNair, Ray. *Assessment of Social Functioning: A Client Instrument for Practitioners. Vol. 6, Human Services Series.* Athens: Institute of Community and Area Development, University of Georgia, 1981.

12.17 Assessment of Child and Adolescent Functioning (ACAF)

PURPOSE: To measure and record levels of adolescent and child social functioning.

DISCUSSION: The *ACAF (Assessment of Child and Adolescent Functioning),* developed by MacNair and McKinney (1983), is similar in purpose, format, and rating system to the Assessment of Adult Social Functioning (AASF), which is described in Item 12.16. The ACAF consists of 45 items divided over nine sections.

The individual items of the ACAF serve as useful reminders of the many dimensions of functioning that should be considered when completing a social assessment of a child or adolescent. Thus, paraphrased versions of all 45 items are presented. Statements are based on those offered by MacNair and McKinney (1983, 9–37) to describe an item's level-4 rating (i.e., the highest and most positive level of child and adolescent functioning).

Child's Coping with Problem Behavior

1. *Awareness of problem behavior.* Child acknowledges that the behavior is a problem. Recognizes that problem is blocking positive interactions and neither underestimates nor exaggerates its effect.

Note: As used here, the term *deviance* refers to such behaviors as delinquency, criminality, and abuse of others; *addiction* refers to abuse of alcohol and drugs, overeating, and other compulsive behaviors.

2. *Self-control over problem behavior.* Child exercises control over the problem behavior or perhaps shows the behavior only at certain times and places and with certain people.
3. *Planning actions that eliminate problem behavior.* Child plans clear and specific actions that will avoid any occurrence of the problem behavior.
4. *Action that replaces the problem behavior.* Child almost always chooses alternative actions that replace or avoid the problem behavior.

Child's Crisis Prevention and Management

1. *Clarity of emotional responses.* Child clearly and accurately expresses the feelings suitable for the crisis event.
2. *Expression and control of emotions.* Child is able to express intense emotions without letting these emotions interfere with the activities of everyday living, such as responsibilities at home, school activities, and personal health habits.
3. *Learning from experience.* Child confidently uses past crises experiences to deal with a current crisis event.
4. *Coping with loss or separation.* Child chooses suitable, helpful, and caring persons for support in experiences of loss and separation.
5. *Response to new parent figures.* Child accepts the emotional support and guidance offered by the new parent figures such as stepparents, guardians, or foster parents.

Child's Adjustment to Disabilities

1. *Use of prescribed physical or chemical supports.* Child shows correct applications of supports prescribed for a disability (e.g., hearing aid, artificial limb, or medicines) to achieve the greatest level of activity possible.
2. *Control of frustration.* Child expresses frustrations in a manner that reduces tension and that does not negatively affect social interaction.
3. *Communication about disabled self.* Child lets others know clearly, consistently, and without embarrassment what he or she can and cannot do without help; seeks help when necessary.
4. *Adaptation to disability.* Consistent with the limitations imposed by the disability, the child moves through the activities of daily living with relative ease. Learns new adaptive skills when necessary.
5. *Participation in public life.* Child is willing to learn about and participate in activities outside the home and school, such as shopping, recreation, entertainment, and community affairs.

Child's Family Life

1. *Response to parental expectations.* Child responds to reasonable parental expectations and accepts household and schoolwork responsibilities. Almost always meets parents' reasonable expectations and appears to understand the reasons for those expectations.
2. *Sibling relationships.* Child consistently maintains close supportive relationship with siblings; quarreling is not bitter or hostile.

3. *Activities with family group.* Child frequently joins in family's recreational, so-cial, or spiritual activities, such as going to church, shopping, watching TV, and so on.
4. *Relationships with extended family.* Child regularly interacts with extended family members such as grandparents, aunts, uncles, and cousins.

Child's Sexuality

1. *Acceptance of sexuality.* Child consistently expresses contentment and comfort with biological, social, and psychological aspects of his or her own sexuality.
2. *Friendships with opposite sex.* Child consistently relates to members of the op-posite sex in a way that contributes to meaningful friendships.
3. *Sexual interest.* Child desires to know more about the biological facts pertain-ing to sex; accepts information about sex and expresses comfort with this in-formation.
4. *Sexuality in dating (adolescent).* Adolescent perceives sexual activity in dating as a mutual, respectful activity. Respects dating partner and self and makes de-cisions about sexual activity accordingly. Sexual activity is kept within the lim-its of partner's and own sense of morality. No indication of compulsion or forced participation.
5. *Relationship with parents concerning sexuality.* Child or adolescent frequently talks with parents about feelings, thoughts, and questions about sexual facts and experiences.

Child's School Life

1. *Academic performance.* Child's performance is consistent with ability. (Evi-dence of ability includes responses to school work, responses to classroom ex-ercises, intelligence shown in discussion, and standardized tests.)
2. *Response to academic activities.* Child is self-directed in pursuing activities and assignments.
3. *Relationship with faculty.* Child communicates with authority figures (e.g., teachers, principals) concerning both academic and personal matters and de-sires to exchange ideas.
4. *Participation in school social life.* Child appears outgoing and self-directed; participates in both planned social activities and in the more spontaneous ac-tivities involving other students (i.e., sports, dances, clubs).
5. *Awareness of career possibilities.* Child knows future prospects in career choices and/or employment, according to age level. Expresses interest in ca-reer objectives.

Child's Neighborhood/Community Life

1. *Satisfaction with neighborhood.* Child is content with the neighborhood's ac-tivities, residents, and physical environment.
2. *Stability of commitment.* Child has strong neighborhood ties through parents and relatives as well as through cultural identification.
3. *Mutual aid relations in neighborhood.* Child takes initiative to help neighbors; is willing to help and be helped by others in the neighborhood.

4. *Opportunities to play.* Child looks for and initiates many fun things to do with friends and others in the community.
5. *Participation with peers in decision making.* Child or adolescent joins with friends in peer network to lead, plan, and make decisions for activities within the neighborhood or community.
6. *Association with adults in community.* Child voluntarily communicates, relates, and interacts with adults in community.

Child's Care of Self

1. *Physical care.* Child eats a balanced daily diet, gets adequate sleep, exercises regularly, and avoids practices such as smoking, using drugs and alcohol, overuse of medicines, and overeating.
2. *Reducing anxiety or depressions.* Child actively prevents or reduces the conditions triggering anxiety and depression; actively controls anxiety or depression through relaxation or another activity or by means of self-control. Anxiety or depression does not reduce personal satisfactions.
3. *Friendships that are encouraging.* Child selects friends who provide encouragement, acceptance, warmth, and help develop a positive self-image.
4. *Control of personal time and energy.* Child sets reasonable limits on use of time and energy that avoids constant imposition or disruption by other children or adults.
5. *Balance of work and fun.* Child achieves a balance between work, school, and household requirements and other activities that provide recreation and enjoyment.
6. *Game playing related to work.* Child creatively plays housekeeper, doctor, carpenter, storekeeper, and so on, and thus develops an ability to imagine work roles; builds self-confidence in ability to perform adult roles.

Child's Personal Satisfaction

1. *Self-acceptance.* Child accepts self openly and confidently; expresses feelings of self-worth.
2. *Friendships.* Child can make friends with many different kinds of people: male, female, old, young, passive, aggressive; members of other socioeconomic groups and races.
3. *Assertiveness.* Child handles himself or herself confidently and effectively in order to have needs met. Exercises personal rights without denying others their rights.
4. *Ability to carry responsibility.* Child completes tasks or responsibilities in various areas of life such as school, home, and neighborhood with no reminders or supervision.
5. *Learning outside of school.* Child shows interest in learning new things and finds ways to pick up the necessary knowledge and skill.

SELECTED BIBLIOGRAPHY

MacNair, Ray, and Elizabeth McKinney. *Assessment of Child and Adolescent Functioning: A Practitioner's Instrument for Assessing Clients.* Athens: Institute of Community and Area Development, University of Georgia, 1983.

12.18   WALMYR Assessment Scales (WAS)

PURPOSE: To measure various dimensions of client functioning.

DISCUSSION: The **WALMYR Assessment Scales (WAS)** consist of more than 20 short-form scales designed for use in assessing a variety of personal and relational problems. The scales were designed for use by practitioners and researchers in need of reliable and valid measures that are easy to administer. Each scale is a paper-and-pencil, self-report tool that measures the severity or magnitude of a distinct area or problem in personal or social functioning. The WALMYR scales and the area measured by each are listed here.

Scale Name	*Measurement Construct*
Personal Adjustment Measures	
Generalized Contentment Scale (GCS)	Depression
Index of Self-Esteem (ISE)	Self-esteem problems
Index of Clinical Stress (ICS)	Personal stress
Clinical Anxiety Scale (CAS)	Anxiety
Index of Alcohol Involvement (IAI)	Alcohol abuse
Index of Drug Involvement (IDI)	Drug abuse
Index of Sexual Harassment (IHS)	Sexual harassment
Index of Peer Relations (IPR)	Peer discord
Sexual Attitude Scale (SAS)	Sexual conservatism
Index of Homophobia (IHP)	Homophobia
Global Screening Inventory (GSI)	Problem array
Problems with a Spouse or Partner	
Index of Marital Satisfaction (IMS)	Marital discord
Index of Sexual Satisfaction (ISS)	Sexual discord
Partner Abuse Scale: Non-physical (PASNP)	Nonphysical abuse
Partner Abuse Scale: Physical (PASPH)	Physical abuse
Non-Physical Abuse of Partner Scale (NPAPS)	Nonphysical abusiveness
Physical Abuse of Partner Scale (PAPS)	Physical abusiveness
Family Relationship Problems	
Index of Parental Attitudes (IPA)	Discord with child
Child's Attitude toward Mother (CAM)	Discord with mother
Child's Attitude toward Father (CAF)	Discord with father
Index of Brother Relations (IBR)	Discord with brother
Index of Sister Relations (ISR)	Discord with sister
Index of Family Relations (IFR)	Intrafamilial stress
Children's Behavior Rating Scale (CBRS)	Behavioral disorder

Each of the scales consists of 20 to 25 brief statements. The client is asked to read each statement and respond with one of five to seven possible answers as a way of indicating the degree to which he or she is described by the statement. For example, the first five items from the Index of Parental Attitudes (IPA) are as follows:*

1. My child gets on my nerves.   _____
2. I get along well with my child.   _____
3. I feel that I can really trust my child.   _____
4. I dislike my child.   _____
5. My child is well behaved.   _____

The seven possible answers are: (1) none of the time, (2) very rarely, (3) a little of the time, (4) some of the time, (5) a good part of the time, (6) most of the time, and (7) all of the time.

A score can be calculated in just a few minutes, and each scale uses the same scoring procedure. Thus, only one scoring formula is needed. Each scale has a score range from 0 to 100, where low scores indicates the relative absence of the problem being measured and higher scores indicate the presence of a more severe problem.

Another characteristic of the WALMYR scales is that many of them have a clinical cutting score of 30. That is, it is generally found that persons who obtain a score above 30 have a clinically significant problem in the area being measured, whereas those who score below 30 are generally free of such problems. Such a clinical cutting score provides a diagnostic benchmark against which to judge the effectiveness of treatment. The scales should not be used with children under the age of 12 or with clients who may receive important rewards or punishments as a consequence of their scores on the scales, such as prisoners seeking parole or mental hospital patients seeking discharge.

Each of the scales has a reliability of at least 0.90. All have good face, content, construct, and discriminant validity. The scales were designed for repeated use with the same client in single-subject designs; thus, the scales can be used to measure the outcome of an intervention. Their shortness and ease of use make them attractive to social work practitioners.

Most of the scales are described in Fischer and Corcoran (1994). The complete set of WALMYR scales, related scoring manuals, and computer software known as the *Clinical Measurement Package* (Hudson and Hudson, 1995) are available from the WALMYR Publishing Co., P. O. Box 24779, Tempe, AZ, 85285-4779.

SELECTED BIBLIOGRAPHY

Fischer, Joel, and Kevin Corcoran. *Measures for Clinical Practice,* 2nd ed. New York: Simon and Schuster, 1994.

Hudson, Walter, and Hudson, Kirk. *The Clinical Measurement Package.* Tempe, Ariz.: WALMYR Publishing, 1995.

Nurius, Paula, and Walter Hudson. *Human Services Practice, Evaluation and Computers.* Pacific Grove, Calif.: Brooks/Cole, 1993.

*IPA items reproduced with permission from Walter Hudson.

12.19   Assessing Mental Status

PURPOSE: To determine if the client's thought and behavior indicate serious mental illness and the need for a psychiatric referral.

DISCUSSION: Regardless of agency setting, the social worker will encounter clients who suffer from mental illness. Thus, it is important to be able to recognize symptoms of mental illness so that the client will be promptly referred for a competent psychiatric and medical examination. Some mental disorders are caused by dramatic changes in the brain (e.g., tumors, neurological diseases, etc.). In such cases, prompt referral can mean the difference between life and death. (See Items 14.35 and 14.36.)

Mental status exams consist of a set of simple questions aimed at gauging orientation to time and place, short- and long-term memory, and appropriateness of affect. Typical questions are: How old are you? In what year were you born? What did you have to eat at your last meal? Can you count backwards from ten? What is the name of the building we are in?

When gathering information for purposes of assessing mental status, it is important to work the questions into the ordinary flow of conversation. If asked one question after another, the client may be offended, and if the client cannot answer the questions, he or she will feel embarrassed. Engaging the client in a description of his or her typical day—from awaking to bed time—provides a context for asking specific questions. Daiches (1983) describes eleven categories of information that should be considered in assessing mental status.

1. *General appearance and attitude* considers whether the client's appearance is appropriate and consistent with his or her age, social, and economic status. The client's dress, hygiene, speech, facial expressions, and motor activity provide information about his or her self-perception and awareness of others. Marked inappropriateness in appearance may be associated with psychological disturbance, particularly if these characteristics have changed over a short period of time.

2. *Behavior* is concerned with the appropriateness of the client's conduct during the interview and with any reports of bizarre behavior by others or the client. Irrational behaviors, such as compulsions (repeated acts that the client feels compelled to do) and phobias (avoidance of places, persons, or objects because of unfounded fears) are characteristics of many disorders.

3. *Orientation to time and place* refers to whether the client is aware of who he or she is, where he or she is, and what time it is (year, month, date, and day). Disorientation is a symptom of brain dysfunction.

4. *Memory* deficits may be associated with psychiatric as well as physical disorders. Four types of memory may be assessed.
   - Immediate recall refers to the ability to recall things within seconds of their presentation.

- Short-term memory is generally defined as covering events transpiring within the last 25 minutes.
- Recent memory refers to the client's recollection of current events and situations occurring within the few weeks preceding the interview.
- Remote memory refers to events and situations transpiring before that period and to significant life events (e.g., marriage, first job, etc.).

Immediate and short-term recall are generally assessed by instructing the client to remember something (a word, number, or object) and then asking him or her to recall that item after the lapse of a few minutes. Recent memory can be tested by asking questions such as: Where do you live? and How long have you lived there? Remote memory can be tested by asking: Where were you born? Where did you go to school? and Who was president of the United States when you got married?

5. *Sensorium* refers to an individual's ability to utilize data from his or her sense organs (hearing, vision, touch, smelling, and taste) and more generally to his or her overall attentiveness and alertness to the surroundings. If a client cannot comprehend visual symbols (and has no visual impairment), touch, or ordinary conversation (and has no hearing impairment and can be presumed to understand the language) or otherwise demonstrates an inability to respond to sensory stimuli, he or she may be affected by an organic brain disorder.

6. *Intellectual functioning* is screened by evaluating the client's abilities to read, write, and follow simple instructions, to do simple arithmetic, to think abstractly (e.g., How are an apple and orange alike?), and his or her awareness of common knowledge consistent with his or her level of education. Poor comprehension as well as deficits in abstract thinking and intellectual performance are commonly noted as symptoms of various psychological disorders. Gauging educational attainment is important because low levels of intellectual functioning may be attributable to a lack of education. Poor intellectual functioning among educated persons, however, may be indicative of organic disorders. Intellectual deterioration is most apparent among individuals with central nervous system disorders but may also be evident in other disturbed individuals.

7. *Mood and affect* refer to the client's prevailing emotional state and the range of emotions displayed during the interview. Moods include such emotions as anger, irritability, elation, exhilaration, anxiety, fear, depression, sadness, apathy, and indifference. In assessing mood and affect, two questions are important.

- Is the client's emotional state a reasonable response to his or her situation? For example, it is important to determine whether a client's depression is the result of recent events (e.g., the death of a spouse).
- Does the client show emotions that correspond to the topic being discussed? A person's expression of mood will usually correspond to the subject matter being discussed. Inappropriate smiling or laughter when talking about sad events or rapid changes in emotional expression, such as laughing or crying without relevance to the conversation or circumstances, may be indicative of a more serious psychiatric disorder. Emotional lability can also have an organic origin (e.g., after a stroke).

8. *Perceptual distortions* may be exhibited by some psychologically impaired individuals. Two of the most significant perceptual problems are illusions and hallucinations. Illusions are misinterpretations of actual stimuli. Hallucinations are perceptual experiences in the absence of external stimuli (e.g., hearing voices).

9. *Thought content* refers to the logic and consistency of an individual's attitudes, ideas, and beliefs. Examples of thought content problems include delusional thinking (false beliefs that cannot be altered by logical arguments) and obsessions (fixed or repetitive ideas that the client cannot get out of his or her mind).

10. *Insight* can be evaluated by asking questions that determine whether the client understands and is aware that he or she has a problem or is exhibiting behavior that is of concern to family members, the social worker, or a physician, and whether the client can describe reasons why he or she might be having this problem. Ironically, the more severe the disorder, the more likely it is that the client will be unaware of that his or her behavior is unusual or symptomatic of a mental disorder.

11. *Judgment* refers to the individual's ability to make responsible and rational decisions in relation to obvious problems. It also refers to a client's mental capability to make decisions related to daily living and particularly his or her physical well-being and survival.

SELECTED BIBLIOGRAPHY

Daiches, Sol. *Risk Assessment: A Guide for Adult Protective Service Workers.* New York: The City of New York, Human Resources Administration, Project Focus, 1983.

Kaplan, Harold, and Benjamin Sadock. *Synopsis of Psychiatry.* Baltimore: Williams & Wilkins, 1991.

Sommers-Flannigan, John, and Rita Sommers-Flannagan. *Foundations of Therapeutic Interviewing.* Boston: Allyn and Bacon, 1993.

12.20   Identifying Developmental Delays

PURPOSE: To identify a young child's developmental problems.

DISCUSSION: The social worker is often in a strategic position to observe preschool-aged children and conduct at least a cursory assessment of the child's physical and mental development. Once children enter school, teachers will usually detect developmental delays. Children who are malnourished or chronically ill, many who are abused and neglected, and, of course, those who have mental retardation will fall behind developmental norms. Early identification and intervention are of critical importance. Table 12.6 presents a listing of developmental milestones by Martin (1979, 32–33). If a child is not able to accomplish two or three of the milestones for his or her age level, the child should be referred for an in-depth evaluation.

TABLE 12.6   Developmental Milestones*

Age	Motor	Mental	Language	Social
3–6 months	will bear weight on legs can roll over stomach to back engages hands in midline when pulled to sit, head is steady, doesn't fall back when on abdomen, can lift shoulders off mat when on abdomen, can lift head and look about will begin to reach for and grasp objects sits with support	looks at objects in hand looks after a toy which is dropped uses a 2-hand approach to grasp toys looks at objects as small as a raisin turns head to voice, follows with eyes	coos gurgles chuckles laughs aloud squeals has expressive noises	has a social smile will pat a bottle with both hands anticipates food on sight
6–9 months	rolls from back to stomach gets feet to mouth sits alone, unsupported, for extended period (over 1 minute) stands with hands held on back, can lift head up beginning attempts to crawl or creep when sitting, reaches forward to grasp without falling	bangs toys in play transfers objects from hand to hand reaches for a toy with one hand picks up a toy he/she drops is persistent in obtaining toys would pull a toy to self by attached string	responds to name vocalizes to social stimulus has single consonants, i.e., ba, ka, ma combines syllables, i.e., da-da, ba-ba likes to make sounds with toys imitates sounds	expects repetition of stimulus likes frolicky play discriminates strangers smiles to mirror image takes some solid food to mouth bites and chews toys beginning to enjoy peek-a-boo
9–12 months	crawls well can sit steadily for more than 10 minutes stands holding on to furniture can pull to sitting position walks, holding on to a hand or to furniture	will uncover a toy he/she sees covered up can grasp object small as raisin with thumb and one finger beginning to put things in and out of containers goes for an object with index finger outstretched likes to drop objects deliberately shows interest in pictures	understands no, or inflection of "no!" uses mama, or dada, first inappropriately, then with meaning by 12 months has at least one other word knows meaning of 1–3 words	cooperates in games will try to roll ball to another person plays patacake and peekaboo waves goodbye will offer toy without releasing it likes to interact in play with adult

(continued)

385

TABLE 12.6 Continued

Age	Motor	Mental	Language	Social
12–18 months	by 18 months, walks well alone creeps up stairs can get to standing position alone can stoop and recover an object walking, pulls a pull-toy seats self on chair	looks at pictures in a book will scribble spontaneously with pencil or crayon uses spoon drinks from cup will follow one or two directions, i.e., take a ball to . . .	has 3–5 words will point to one body part will point to at least one picture uses jargon, i.e., unintelligible "foreign" language with inflection imitates some words	cooperates in dressing holds own bottle or cup finger feeds points or vocalizes to make desires known shows or offers a toy
18–24 months	can run, albeit stiffly walks up and down stairs with one hand held hurls a ball can kick a ball or object jumps with both feet stands on one foot with one hand held	can tower 2 or more one-inch blocks turns pages of a book, even if 2–3 at a time will try to imitate what an adult draws with pencil can point to 2–3 body parts	by two years, has at least 20 words by two years, is combining two words in a phrase jargon, which was elaborate by 18 months, is gone by 24 months verbalizes desires with words	uses spoon, spilling very little removes one piece of clothing imitates housework more and more handles a cup quite well
2–3 years	can walk up stairs without hand held can balance on one foot for one second can jump in place can walk on tiptoe can jump from the bottom step kicks ball forward can throw a ball	can tower 6 one-inch blocks can dump a raisin from a bottle to attain without hints can imitate a vertical line, possibly a horizontal line, with pencil can anticipate the need to urinate or defecate if worked with, can toilet self	uses 2–4 word phrases uses plurals names at least one picture talks incessantly vocabulary 100–300 words by 3 years uses some personal pronouns, i.e., I, me, mine points to several parts of a doll on request identifies over 5 parts of own body	puts on some clothing washes and dries hands has parallel play with peers can pour from a pitcher

Age	Gross motor	Fine motor / Adaptive	Language	Personal–social
3–4 years	rides a tricycle / alternates feet when going up stairs / can stand on one foot for 2–5 seconds / can broad jump / uses scissors / swings and climbs	can tower 8–10 one-inch blocks / says full name / can match colors / has sense of round, square, and triangular shaped figures and can match them / copies a circle, line, cross with pencil / can repeat 3 digits	can answer some questions / knows rhymes and songs / asks questions / has understanding of on, under, and behind	knows own sex / beginning to play with other children / unbuttons / dresses with supervision
4–5 years	runs well and turns / can hop on one foot 1–2 times / beginning to skip / stands on one leg for 10 seconds / throws ball well overhand / walks down stairs one foot to each step	can copy a cross with a pencil / can pick the longer of two lines / can copy a square with pencil	vocabulary over 1000 words / can match colors, and by 5 years, name 3–4 colors / counts 3 objects with pointing / 90% of speech intelligible / can define words in terms of use / can answer questions like, what do you do when you are cold . . . hungry . . . tired . . . ?	can separate from mother easily / dresses with little supervision buttons / likes to play "dramatic" play, make-believe / imaginative play with a doll
5–6 years	skips on both feet alternately / can catch a bounced ball / can walk heel to toe on a line / can hop on one foot for 10 feet	can copy a square or triangle from looking at a copy / gives age / knows morning from afternoon / draws a person with a body, with 3–6 parts / prints simple words	can repeat 4 digits / asks questions about meaning of words / counts 10 objects / names coins / can tell what some things are made of / can define some words	no supervision necessary for dressing / plays "dress-up" / elaborate dramatic play / does simple chores unattended at home

*If child is not accomplishing two or three of these milestones, consider developmental consultation.

Source: Harold Martin, Treatment for Abused and Neglected Children, Washington, D.C.: National Center on Child Abuse and Neglect, U.S. Department of Health Education and Welfare, DHEW Publication No. (OHDS) 79–30 199, U.S. Government Printing Office, 1979.

SELECTED BIBLIOGRAPHY

Martin, Harold. *Treatment for Abused and Neglected Children.* Washington, D.C.: U.S. Department of Health Education and Welfare, DHEW publication No. (OHDS) 79–30 199, U.S. Government Printing Office, 1979.

Newman, Barbara, and Philip Newman. *Development Through Life,* 6th ed. Pacific Grove, Calif.: Brooks/Cole, 1995.

12.21   Referral for Psychological Testing

PURPOSE: To make appropriate use of psychological testing in the assessment of client functioning.

DISCUSSION: Not infrequently, the social worker will refer a client to a psychologist for testing. Such testing can provide information on the client's intellectual capacity, patterns of motivation and coping behavior, self-concept, level of anxiety or depression, and general personality integration. It is important to remember that psychological tests focus on certain variables while neglecting others that may be of importance. Cronbach (1990), an authority on testing, reminds us that the value of test information should be judged by how much it improves decisions over the best possible decisions made without the test. A psychological test can provide valuable information on which to base a decision, but one should not rely exclusively on standardized test results, especially if based on a single test instrument. Presented here are brief descriptions of some of the tests often aministered by psychologists.

Infant Development Scales

- *The Brazelton Neonatal Behavioral Assessment Scale* tests an infant's (1) neurological intactness, (2) interactive behavior (including motoric control such as putting the thumb in the mouth and remaining calm and alert in response to stimuli such as a bell, a light, and pinprick), and (3) responsiveness to the examiner and need for stimulation.
- *The Bayley Scales of Infant Development* test mental abilities, including memory, learning, and problem-solving behavior; motor skills; and social behaviors, such as social orientation, fearfulness, and cooperation.
- *The Gesell Developmental Schedules* test for fine and gross motor behavior; language behavior; adaptive behavior, including eye-hand coordination, imitation, and object recovery; and personal/social behavior, including reaction to persons, initiative, independence, and play response.
- *The Denver Developmental Screening Test* is widely used and can be administered by a person with only limited training. It is a screening tool, not a dianostic test. It is used to discover possible developmental delays in the four areas of personal/social, fine motor/adaptive, language, and gross motor skills that should be more carefully evaluated with other tests.

Intelligence Tests for Preschool- and School-Aged Children

- *The Stanford-Binet IV* can be used with both preschool- and school-aged children and is usually administered to children between the ages of 2 and 8. Examples of what is required include remembering where an object was hidden, building a four-block tower to match an existing tower, explaining the uses of common objects, and identifying pictured objects by name. The test is best suited for middle-class, English-speaking children; it may not provide a fair assessment of bilingual or bicultural children. Depending on the child's age, the test requires vision, eye-hand coordination, hearing, and speech.
- *The Wechsler Scales* include separate forms for preschool- and school-aged children. The preschool form is called the *Wechsler Preschool and Primary Scale of Intelligence (WPPSI),* and the school-aged form is called the *Wechsler Intelligence Scale for Children (WISC-III).* The WISC III is the test most likely to be used to assess the cognitive functioning of school-aged children. It has six verbal and six performance subtests.
- *The System of Multicultural Pluralistic Assessment (SOMPA),* a test based on the WISC, was designed to take into account a child's handicapping condition and sociocultural background and thus be nondiscriminatory.

Intelligence Tests for Adults

- *The Wechsler Adult Intelligence Scale–Revised (WAIS–R)* is usually considered to be the best general intelligence test for persons aged 16 and older. Six subtests (information, digit span, vocabulary, arithmetic, comprehension, and similarities) make up its verbal scale, and five subtests (picture completion, picture arrangement, block design, object assemble, and digit symbol) make up the performance scale.

Special Abilities Tests

- *The Bender Visual Motor Gestalt Test* is used to assess visual perceptual skills and eye-hand coordination. The client is given nine geometric figures, one at a time, and asked to copy each.
- *The Peabody Picture Vocabulary Test* assesses familiarity with vocabulary words without requiring the child to speak. The client is shown four pictures at a time and must point to the one that corresponds to the word the examiner says. The test was originally designed to be used with persons who are nonverbal, mentally retarded, and/or have cerebral palsy.
- *The Detroit Test of Learning Aptitude* measures auditory and visual memory and concentration.

Testing for Cognitive Delay

An IQ score below 70 indicates that a client may have cognitive delay or mental retardation. However, a low IQ score by itself is not sufficient for diagnosis; the client's adaptive behavior must also be measured. *Adaptive behavior* refers to the person's ability to carry out everyday living skills, such as dressing, eating, washing, playing, functioning independently, and cooperating with others. Several instruments measure age-appropriate adaptive behavior: *The Vineland Adaptive Behavior Scale (VABS), The American Association on Mental Retardation's (AAMR) Adaptive Behavior Scales,* and *The Adaptive Behavior Inventory for Children.*

Personality Tests

Objective-type personality tests are pencil-and-paper tests designed to determine predominant personality traits or behaviors.

- *The Minnesota Multiphasic Personality Inventory (MMPI-2)* is probably the most often used objective personality test. It consists of 567 self-descriptive statements to which the client answers either true, false, or cannot say. It is used with persons 16 years of age or older.
- *The Personality Inventory for Children (PIC)* is one of the few objective tests for younger children.

Projective tests provide a stimulus (e.g., inkblots, a set of pictures, or incomplete sentences) and ask the client to respond to the stimulus. These tests rest on the assumption that the client's responses will reveal his or her unique view of the world, including issues of concern and emotional needs. Another type of projective test provides instructions for the client to draw a picture, again with the idea that the drawing will reveal information about the inner self.

- *The Rorschach Test* was the first inkblot test and the one still most commonly used.
- *The Holtzman Inkblot Technique* is another projective test that may substitute for the Rorschach.
  The most common picture-story tests are:
- *The Thematic Apperception Test (TAT)*
- *The Children's Apperception Test (CAT)*
- *The Michigan Picture Test*
- *The Tasks of Emotional Development Test*
- *The Make-a-Picture-Story Test*

Referring a Client for Psychological Testing

1. Before deciding on a referral, be very clear about why you are seeking a psychological evaluation of your client.
2. When making a referral to a psychologist for testing, explain how and why you and your agency are involved in providing service to this client, the case management decisions you face, and the type of information that would be helpful. List the questions you would like the psychologist to answer.
3. Provide the psychologist with information concerning the client's age, sex, education, occupation and employment history, ethnicity, and any special disabilities, such as hearing or visual problems or physical limitations. Also provide the results of any previous testing, including the dates of testing and the names of the tests used.

4. After consulting with the psychologist who will do the testing, prepare the client by giving him or her basic information on what to expect, where the testing will be done, and about how long it will take.

5. Have realistic expectations of psychological testing. In many cases, the results of testing will simply confirm the conclusions already reached by people who have observed the client for a matter of weeks or months.

6. Ask the psychologist to explain the strengths and limitations of the testing procedures used with your client, so you can decide how much faith to place in the results.

SELECTED BIBLIOGRAPHY

Anastasi, Anne. *Psychological Testing,* 6th ed. New York: Macmillan, 1988.
Baily, Thelma, and Walter Baily. *Psychological Evaluations—An Aid to CPS Assessment.* Denver: American Humane Association, 1986.
Cronbach, L. J. *Essentials for Psychological Testing,* 5th ed. New York: Harper & Row, 1990.

12.22 The Person-in-Environment Classification System (PIE)

PURPOSE: To describe, classify, and code problems in adult social functioning.

DISCUSSION: The PIE system is designed for use by social workers and is built around two key social work concepts: social functioning and the person-in-environment construct (see Chapter 1 for discussion of these concepts). According to Karls and Wandrei (1994), the PIE provides social workers with the following:

- common language . . . to describe their clients' problems in social functioning.
- a common capsulated description of social phenomena that could facilitate treatment or amelioration of the problems presented by clients.
- a basis for gathering data required to measure the need for services and to design human services programs and evaluate effectiveness.
- a mechanism for clearer communication among social work practitioners and between practitioners and administrators and researchers.
- a basis for clarifying the domain of social work in the human services field. (p. 7)

The PIE system groups client problems into four classes or "factors." Basically, a factor is a category or a general type of problem. The terminology used for Factor I (social functioning problems) and Factor II (environmental problems) is unique to social work practice. Factor III (mental health problems) utilizes the clinical syndrome and personality and developmental disorders terminology found in the *DSM-IV.* Factor IV (*physical health problems*) records diseases and health problems that have been diagnosed by a physician or reported by the client or others. It should be noted that the PIE is not intended as a substitute for the *DSM-IV* but rather is a complementary system (see Item 12.23 for information about the *DSM IV*).

An abbreviated outline of Factor I and Factor II categories and subcategories is presented here.

PIE Factor I: Social Functioning Problems

1. Social role in which each problem is defined (four categories and numerous subcategories):
   - Familial roles (parent, spouse, child, sibling, other family member, and significant other)
   - Other interpersonal roles (lover, friend, neighbor, member, and other)
   - Occupational roles (worker-paid, worker-home, worker-volunteer, student, and other)
   - Special life situation roles (consumer, inpatient/client, outpatient/client, probationer/parolee, prisoner, immigrant-legal, immigrant-undocumented, immigrant-refugee, and other)
2. Type of problem in social role (nine types: power, ambivalence, responsibility, dependency, loss, isolation, victimization, mixed, and other)
3. Severity of problem (rated on a 6-point scale)
4. Duration of problem (six categories)
5. Ability of client to cope with problem (six levels)

PIE Factor II: Environmental Problems

1. Social system where each problem is identified (six major systems and numerous subcategories):
   - Economic/Basic needs system problems
   - Education and training system problems
   - Judicial and legal system problems
   - Health, safety, and social services problems
   - Voluntary association system problems
   - Affectional support system problems
2. Specific type of problem with in each social system (71 subcategories; number varies for each of six social systems. Examples of social system problem subcategories: lack of regular food supply, absence of shelter, lack of culturally relevant education, discrimination, lack of police services, unsafe conditions in home, regulatory barriers to social services, absence of affectional support system, lack of community acceptance of religious values, etc.)
3. Severity of problem (rated on a 6-point scale)
4. Duration of problem (six categories)

SELECTED BIBLIOGRAPHY

Karls, James, and Karin Wandrei. "Person-in-Environment." In *Encyclopedia of Social Work*, 19th ed., vol. 3, edited by Richard Edwards. Washington, D.C.: NASW, 1995, pp. 1818–1827.

———, eds. *Person-In-Environment*. Washington, D.C.: National Association of Social Workers, 1994.

———. *Pie Manual*.Washington, D.C.: National Association of Social Workers, 1994.

12.23 The Diagnostic and Statistical Manual for Mental Disorders (DSM-IV)

PURPOSE: To use proper terminology and classifications when exchanging information about a client's mental disorder.

DISCUSSION: In order to communicate accurately with other professionals about a client's mental disorder and to understand reports prepared by psychologists and psychiatrists, the social worker must be familiar with a book titled the *Diagnostic and Statistical Manual for Mental Disorders*, or the *DSM-IV*, published by the American Psychiatric Association (1994). An increasing number social workers and agencies look to third-party payments (e.g., Medicaid, Medicare, private health insurance, etc.) as sources of payment for the psychotherepy they provide to clients; prior to submitting a claim for such payments, the client must be assigned to a specific diagnostic category from the *DSM-IV*.

In the *DSM-IV* system, over 200 disorders are classified within 17 broad categories, Each disorder is described in terms of symptoms, diagnostic criteria, age of onset, prevalence, level of impairment, and so on. The major categories are the following:

1. Disorders Usually First Diagnosed in Infancy, Childhood, or Adolescence
2. Delirium, Dementia, and Amnestic and Other Cognitive Disorders
3. Mental Disorders Due to a General Medical Condition
4. Substance-Related Disorders
5. Schizophrenia and Other Psychotic Disorders
6. Mood Disorders
7. Anxiety Disorders
8. Somatoform Disorders
9. Factitious Disorders
10. Dissociative Disorders
11. Sexual and Gender Identity Disorders
12. Eating Disorders
13. Sleep Disorders
14. Impulse-Control Disorders Not Elsewhere Classified
15. Adjustment Disorder
16. Personality Disorders
17. Other Conditions That May Be a Focus of Clinical Attention

The American Psychiatric Association (1994) warns of the inherent difficulties of assessing the behavior of a person from an ethnic or cultural group different from that of the clinician: "a clinician who is unfamiliar with the nuances of an individual's cultural frame of reference may incorrectly judge as psychopathology those normal variations in behavior, belief, or experiences that are particular to the individual's culture" (p. xxiv).

A number of social workers have reservations about the appropriateness of this diagnostic manual for social work practice. Many are bothered by the labeling inherent in the *DSM* system, by the manual's exclusive focus on pathology, and by its lack of attention to environmental context. Fortunately, the *Person in-Environment (PIE)* is now available as a supplement to the *DSM-IV* (see Item 12.22).

SELECTED BIBLIOGRAPHY

Abramovitz, Robert, Janet Williams, and Mark Mattaini. "The Pros and Cons of the Diagnostic and Statistical Manual for Social Work Practice and Research." *Research on Social Work Practice* 2, No. 3 (July 1992).

American Psychiatric Association. *Diagnostic Statistical Manual of Mental Disorders (DSM IV)*, 4th ed. Washington, D.C.: American Psychiatric Association, 1994.

Kirk, Stuart, and Herb Kutchins. *Selling DSM III: The Rhetoric of Science in Psychiatry*. New York: Aldine de Gruyter, 1992.

12.24   Assessment of Suicide Risk

PURPOSE: To form an opinion about whether a client is at risk of suicide.

DISCUSSION: Given the high rate of suicide among teenagers, young adults, and the elderly, the social worker will encounter clients who are at risk of taking their own lives. *Warning signs of suicide* include depression, preoccupation with death and pain, giving away prized possessions, personality change, sudden increase in the use of drugs and alcohol, and impulsive or reckless behavior. Clinical data indicate that most suicide victims have consulted with a physician within six months of their suicide. Although not all people who end their lives are clinically depressed, studies reveal that depression is often present. *Symptoms of depression* include lack of interest in activities, expressions of hopelessness, loss of appetite, withdrawal from others, early waking from sleep or erratic sleep patterns, irritability, and unexplained crying. Whereas depression in adults usually results in a retardation of activity, depression in children and youth is often expressed in agitation.

Legally and ethically, the social worker must make every reasonable effort to prevent a client's suicide. This includes providing counseling, staying with the person during times of high risk, and, if necessary, calling the police and arranging for involuntary hospitalization. If one has reason to believe that a client is at risk of suicide, consult with other professionals in making a decision on how best to proceed. The social worker must not allow himself or herself to be "hooked" by the suicidal client into a promise of complete confidentiality. Ordinary rules of confidentiality must be broken in order to prevent a death or a serious injury.

The following guidelines will help the worker in assessing suicide potential.

1. Take every message about suicide seriously. It is significant that the person is talking about harm to self rather than expressing frustration in other ways. It is a myth that people who talk about suicide will not kill themselves. However, the messages may be subtle; unfortunately, in some cases, it is not until after the death that their meaning becomes clear. In 10 to 20 percent of suicides, there are no real warnings prior to the death.

2. Listen for indirect statements of suicidal intent such as: I won't be around much longer or There is nothing worth living for anymore or I can't stand it anymore. Be especially alert to such clues if the person has recently experienced a loss of an important relationship or a loss of status among peers, an episode of family violence, or is in the throes of adjusting to chronic pain, a life-threatening illness, or a serious physical limitation.

3. Keep in mind that suicidal persons are experiencing intense feelings of ambivalence—the desire to live and, at the same time, the desire to escape pain, even if by death. They do not really want to die but want desperately to get away from their pain. Thus, assume that a person talking about suicide is ambivalent and hoping for your assistance. Reach out and support that part of the person holding to life.

4. Ask simple and direct questions when communicating with the suicidal person. Do not be afraid to ask if he or she is thinking about suicide. Speaking openly about a person's wish to die will not increase the likelihood of suicide. Direct questioning tells the suicidal person that you are concerned and not afraid to talk straight. Also, direct questioning is a way of eliciting the information needed to help. Examples of questions include: Are you thinking of killing yourself? Can you tell me why suicide seems like the answer? and Who else knows you are thinking about suicide?

5. Try to understand why life now seems so painful and futile to the individual. Always remember that suicide is seen by the person as a solution to a problem. It is of critical importance to identify the problem. Do not argue or become judgmental—the suicidal person already feels helpless and hopeless. Do nothing that would add to his or her feelings of inadequacy.

6. Determine whether the person has chosen a specific suicide method (shooting, hanging, pills, etc.). Also determine if the person has access to the method. The person who has selected a method and has access to it is at high risk.

7. Determine whether the person has worked out a specific suicide plan. Most persons who kill themselves have a plan; suicide is not usually an impulsive, unplanned action. Ask questions such as: Do you have a plan for killing yourself? How do you plan to get the gun you intend to use? Where do you plan to kill yourself? and What time of day or night do you plan to kill yourself? The more detailed and specific the person's plan, the higher the risk of suicide. Many suicidal persons have thought about their suicide plan, but most have not thought about an alternative or a "plan B." Thus, if you can interfere with a key element of their plan, you can often thwart their suicide.

8. Determine the lethality of the method. Highly lethal methods include shooting, jumping, hanging, drowning, carbon monoxide poisoning, car crash, or taking high doses of barbiturates, sleeping pills, or aspirin. Less lethal methods include wrist cutting, natural (cooking) gas, or taking tranquilizers and nonprescription drugs (excluding aspirin and Tylenol). The more lethal the method, the higher the risk and the greater the chance that a suicidal gesture will result in death.

9. Determine whether the person has attempted suicide in the past. Ask questions such as: Have you attempted suicide in the past? How did you try to kill yourself in your prior attempt? What kind of help did you receive? and Was it helpful? A history of previous attempts increases the risk.

10. Determine what has happened recently that causes the person to think more and more of suicide. For example, ask: What has happened that makes you feel so hopeless now? Determine what this event means to the person: Is his or her perception of the event realistic? Is the person too upset to understand the situation clearly? Will the event continue to trouble the individual or will things change in time? Ask: Why do you believe your situation will not improve? How might your situation be different six months from now?

11. Most suicidal persons have "tunnel vision"—they can think only about their pain and helplessness. It is important to help them identify and consider alternative methods of dealing with the pain they feel. How has the individual managed stressful situations in the past? Will any of these methods work in the present situation?

12. Determine whether the suicidal person has anyone to rely on during a time of crisis. Many of the people who commit suicide feel ignored or cut off from the significant people around them. The risk of suicide increases when a person is widowed, divorced, or separated. It is important to help significant others come to the support of the suicidal person.

13. Help the person see that suicide is a permanent solution to a temporary problem. Identify other possible solutions to dealing with the pain the individual is experiencing but do not lie or offer false hope. Ask the client to immediately enter counseling as an alternative to suicide. If necessary, ask him or her to agree not to commit suicide for a specific period (e.g., two weeks) or promise not to commit suicide before talking to you one more time. If a referral for counseling is made, you or someone else should accompany the client to the initial interview. Follow-up is necessary to ensure that the client is making use of the service.

14. Realize that it may not be possible to prevent the suicide of a person who is genuinely committed to taking his or her own life. Counseling, close monitoring, and hospitalization may delay a suicide but such efforts will not always prevent a suicide.

SELECTED BIBLIOGRAPHY

Hack, Thomas. "Suicide Risk Assessment and Intervention," In *First Steps in the Art of Intervention,* edited by David Marlin and Allan Moore. Pacific Grove, Calif.: Brooks/Cole, 1995.

Hoff, Lee Ann. *People in Crisis: Understanding and Helping,* 4th ed. San Francisco: Jossey-Bass, 1995.

Patros, Philip, and Tonia Shamoo. *Depression and Suicide in Children and Adolescents.* Boston: Allyn and Bacon, 1989.

12.25   Assessing a Child's Need for Protection

PURPOSE: To identify a child who has been abused or neglected and to determine if the child is at risk of further harm.

DISCUSSION: Nearly every social worker has some involvement with cases of child abuse and neglect. State laws require social workers to report cases of suspected abuse or neglect. (Many states also mandate the reporting of elder abuse.) The observation of several of the physical and behavioral indicators suggest the possible existence of child abuse or neglect. These indicators are summarized in Table 12.7.

In the United States, over 50 percent of all cases of child maltreatment are cases of neglect. Moreover, about 50 percent of all child maltreatment-related fatalities are caused by neglect. A high percentage of the neglect cases occur in families where the parents are abusing alcohol or addicted to drugs.

Many parents believe in and utilize corporal punishment as discipline. Thus, in assessing a situation, the social worker must be able to differentiate physical abuse from ordinary spanking or corporal punishment. That decision will, of course, be tied to the definition of abuse found in a states legal code. In addition, we offer three criteria for making that distinction.

1. In corporal punishment, the child experiences some pain and discomfort. In abuse, there is injury to body tissue.
2. In using corporal punishment, the parent maintains self-control and is aware of where and how hard the child is being hit. In an abusive situation, the parent loses control over his or her emotions and strikes the child with excessive force or hits the child in places that are easily injured.
3. Nonabusive parents using corporal punishment may occasionally get carried away and hit too hard but they quickly realize what has happened and are able to make changes in how they discipline the child so this does not happen again. In situations of abuse, there are repeated episodes of excessive corporal punishment and injury because the parents are unable to gain control of their anger and make changes in how they respond to the child.

It is tragic but true that child sexual abuse is not an uncommon occurrence in our society. Most children who are sexually abused do not tell anyone because they are either afraid or feel great shame. Most cases of child sexual abuse involve fondling and masturbation but *not* penetration. Penetration might be of the mouth, vagina, or rectum; oral penetration is probably the most common form. Even if there has been penetration, there will be no observable physical evidence in most cases.

It is also important to understand that the majority of sexually abused children do *not* exhibit unusual sexual behavior. However, sexually abused children are more likely than nonabused children to display adultlike sexual behavior.

The social worker must report suspected cases of child sexual abuse. However, he or she must also be alert to the fact that false or mistaken accusations do occur. Both children and adults are suggestible and may misinterpret facts, and occasion-

**TABLE 12.7   Physical and Behavioral Indicators
of Child Abuse and Neglect**

Indicators of Physical Abuse

- Unexplained bruises or welts, especially if on both sides of face or body, or on back, buttocks or torso.
- Bruises in different stages of healing.
- Multiple bruises clustered in one area, forming symmetrical patterns or reflecting the shape of an instrument (e.g., loop marks, lineal or parallel marks, punch marks).
- Bruises regularly appear after a weekend or a visit.
- Bruises on shoulders or neck displaying shape of hand and fingers (e.g., grab marks)
- Unexplained burns, such as those caused by cigarettes, and especially if on palms, soles, back, or buttocks.
- Hot water immersion or dunking burns (e.g., socklike, glovelike, doughnut shaped on buttocks or genitalia)
- Burns patterned like electric stove burner, hot plate, curling iron, etc.
- Rope burns on wrists or ankles (i.e., tie marks)
- Unexplained mouth injuries such as frenulum tears or broken teeth (caused by rough feeding)
- Human, adult-size bites to child's body.
- Unexplained broken bones or head injuries such as skull fractures, subdural hematoma.
- Retina detachment or whiplash injuries to neck caused by violent shaking.
- Internal injuries caused by punch.
- Poisoning caused by ingestion of street drugs, alcohol, prescription medicines, or household chemicals.
- Child attempts to hide injuries with clothing; embarrassment or shame over injury, reluctance to talk about injury (nonabused children proudly display injuries)
- Hyper-vigilant, fearful, and guarded around adults; avoids physical contact with people including his parents (i.e., fearful of human touch).
- Often exhibits overly adaptive behavior in an attempt to meet parents' needs (i.e., by taking care of and comforting parent, the child seeks to keep things calm and prevent abusive episodes).
- Becomes uneasy when another child cries or acts up (i.e., has learned to associate crying with pain of abuse).
- Serious behavioral problems at young age (e.g., runs away, self-mutilation, suicide attempts, violent, withdrawn).

Indicators of Neglect

- Begging, stealing, or hoarding food; underweight; failure to thrive; bald patches on scalp.
- Poor school attendance (sometimes the neglectful parent is so lonely he or she keeps the child home for company; sometimes the child remains home to care for younger siblings).
- Identified medical and dental problems go untreated even though parent has resources to get medical services.
- Unsocialized and primitive in eating and toilet behaviors.
- Unusual fatigue and listlessness; falling asleep at unusual times.
- Stays at school, in public places, or at other homes for extended periods.
- Poor hygiene, filthy clothing, clothing inappropriate for weather.
- Child not supervised or protected from dangerous activity.

Indicators of Sexual Abuse

- Bruises, scaring, or tissue tears around vagina and anus; bruised or swollen penis (caused by rough fondling and masturbation).
- Blood on child's underwear.
- Redness or rash in genital area in child not wearing diaper (caused by frequent fondling).
- Redness or abrasions between upper legs (caused by penis placed between child's legs).
- Recurrent bladder infections (i.e., bacteria from rectum introduced into vagina when there is both anal and vaginal intercourse).
- Pregnancy or a sexually transmitted disease in younger child.
- Semen in vagina, rectum, or mouth (can be detected by medical exam within three days of intercourse).
- Child exhibits inappropriate masturbation that has a driven or compulsive quality.
- Unusual sexual play and exploration of pets or dolls.
- Child exhibits aggressive and forced sexual activity with other children, usually of a younger age.
- Inappropriate sexual behavior toward adults.
- Unusual level of knowledge about sexual activity (e.g., can describe sexual movement, smells, taste, feelings).
- Preoccupation with sexual matters or unusual fear of anything sexual.
- Unusual fear of showers, bathrooms, bedrooms.
- Unwilling to change clothes for gym or to expose body (caused by extreme shame of body).
- Frequent and patterned absences from school that are justified by one adult, the offender.
- Unusual or bizarre sexual themes in art work.
- Wearing many layers of clothing (protection of body).
- Frequent use of dissociation as coping mechanism.
- Unusually close relationship with adult that has secretive or sexual overtones.
- Extreme protectiveness of child by an adult who keeps child from talking to or getting close to responsible adults.

---

ally false accusations are used as a means of hurting someone. False allegations by a child are relatively rare but the rate increases if the child's accusation is being encouraged or prompted by a parent and the rate becomes even higher in cases involving child custody fights between parents.

Once a case of abuse or neglect has been identified, the question of risk must be addressed. In other words, is the child at risk of serious harm and in need of immediate protection? Presented in Table 12.8 are factors that should be considered in the assessment of risk. When assessing risk, it is well to remember that prior behavior is the best predictor of future behavior.

In some cases, the removal of the child from his or her own home is necessary. However, because the separation of parent and child is so traumatic to the child and so disruptive to the family, an out-of-home placement should be used only in those cases where the child is at high risk of serious harm and there is no less drastic

TABLE 12.8 Risk Assessment Factors

Child-Related Factors

- Child's young age and/or presences of serious illness or physical or mental disability (i.e., vulnerable and unable to protect self, need for medication, etc.)
- Prior history of being target of abuse
- History of severe or frequent abuse or neglect
- Injuries to child at vulnerable body locations (e.g., head, face, genitals, etc.)
- Injuries are of a nature that require medical attention or hospitalization
- Child's behavior and special needs (e.g., disability or illness) place great and stressful demands on caregiver
- Perpetrator has access to child
- Child's relationships with siblings or others in the household are strained or troubled (i.e., decreasing chances that others will offer protection).

Parent/Caregiver-Related Factors

- Presence of condition that limits ability of caregiver to care for or protect child (e.g., existence of a serious physical or mental illness, mental retardation, extreme immaturity, etc.)
- Presence of serious drug or alcohol dependency
- History of domestic violence (e.g., spouse abuse) or other violent criminal activity
- History of having abused or neglected other children
- Lack of basic parenting skills or knowledge
- High levels of anger, hostility, or rejection toward child
- Existence of other serious family problems that place added stress on family (e.g., marital conflict, financial, health, chaotic life-style, etc.)
- Unrealistic and unreasonable expectations of child
- Denial of problem; evasiveness or refusal to cooperate with agency personnel or other helpers
- Prior efforts to work with family have been rejected or ineffective

Environmental Factors

- Physical conditions of home presents serious danger to child (e.g., exposed electrical wiring, unprotected household chemicals, etc.)
- Family is socially or physically isolated from social supports and other forms of assistance in times of emergency

method of protecting the child. The following principles should guide placement decisions.

- If a child must be placed into foster care, it is to be done for one reason only: to protect the child from harm. For example, it would be unethical and unprofessional to place a child in order to coerce the parent into taking some action.
- A child should be placed in the least restrictive alternative; moreover, the parent(s) and child should, to the extent possible and appropriate, participate in the placement decision and the preparation of the child for the placement.

- Efforts to assure protection for child are to be those that are the least intrusive and least disruptive for both the child and family.
- During the placement, respect and maintain the child's cultural heritage and religious beliefs (*Note:* See the special requirements and provisions of PL 95-608, the Indian Child Welfare Act.)

SELECTED BIBLIOGRAPHY

Monteleone, James. *Recoqnition of Child Abuse for Mandated Reporters.* St. Louis: G. W. Medical Publishing, 1994.

Tower, Cynthia. *Understanding Child Abuse and Neglect,* 3rd ed. Boston: Allyn and Bacon, 1996.

Veltkamp, Lane, and Thomas Miller. *Clinical Handbook of Child Abuse and Neglect.* Madison, CN: International Universities Press, 1994.

Yakpo, Michael. *Suggestions of Abuse: True and False Memories of Childhood Sexual Trauma.* New York: Simon and Schuster, 1994.

12.26 The 4 Ps, 4 Rs, and 4 Ms

PURPOSE: To assist the social worker in assessing the client's behavior and functioning within a social context.

DISCUSSION: For many years, Perlman's (1957) *4 Ps* (person, problem, place, and process) have proven useful to many social workers as a way of organizing their thoughts about a client, his or her situation, and the agency context of social work intervention. Doremus (1976) suggested the *4 Rs* (roles, reactions, relationships, and resources) as a way of conceptualizing assessment in health care settings. In addition, the authors offer the *4 Ms* (motivation, meanings, management, and monitoring) as further reminders of important elements in social work intervention. A blending of the 4 Ps, 4 Rs, and 4 Ms results in a 12-item, easily remembered conceptual tool that helps a worker sift through available data, organize it, and begin formulating an intervention plan. As used here, the word *client* refers to an individual. However, the underlying ideas that make up the 4 P/4 R/4 M can be applied to work with other client systems, including couples, families, or small groups.

The 4 Ps

1. Problem
   - What is the nature of the client's problem (intensity, frequency, duration)?
   - How does the client define the problem as compared to how others (including the worker) define the problem?
   - Can the problem or situation be changed, solved, or ameliorated? What parts of the problem or situation can feasibly be addressed in a change effort?
   - How effective have previous agency efforts been in dealing with the client's problem or situation?
   - Is the problem or situation an emergency that requires a rapid response?

- What will the consequences be if the worker or agency takes no action and does nothing for or with the client?

2. Person
   - What dimensions of the whole person (physical, emotional, mental, spiritual, etc.) and what behavioral patterns are relevant to the current problem or situation?
   - What aspects of the client's usual ways of coping interfere with efforts to deal effectively with new problems or situations?
   - What is the relationship between the client's usual ways of thinking and behaving and his or her role performance, reactions, relationships to significant others, and use of resources or services?

3. Place
   - What meaning does the client assign to his or her involvement with the agency (e.g., hopefulness, stigma, fear, humiliation, etc.)?
   - Can the agency provide the services needed by the client? If not, is referral to another agency likely to be effective?
   - Are agency programs, policies, or procedures contributing to the client's problem or situation?

4. Process
   - What type of helping approach is the client likely to find acceptable?
   - What approach is most likely to be effective?
   - How will the requirements of the helping process impact on the client's current role performance and relationships with significant others?

The 4 Rs
5. Roles
   - What roles and responsibilities does the client have in life (e.g., as a parent, spouse, employee, etc.)?
   - What do others (e.g., family, employers, etc.) expect of the client?
   - What capacities, behavioral patterns, and strengths has the client previously used to perform his or her roles, solve problems of role performance, and cope with the demands of roles?
   - How satisfied is the client with his or her role performance?

6. Reactions
   - What are the client's reactions (psychological, emotional, behavioral, physical, etc.) to the current problem or situation? How do these reactions compare to the client's usual or previous behavioral patterns? Is the client in a state of crisis?

7. Relationships
   - What people are significant in the client's life (family, peers, friends, etc.)?
   - How are they being impacted by the client's problem or situation?
   - What is the relationship between the behavior of significant others and the client's current problem or situation?

8. Resources
   - What formal and informal resources has the client used effectively in the past to cope with problems?
   - What additional resources are needed now to address the current problem or situation?
   - Does the client have access to these needed resources and is he or she willing and able to use them? Is the client eligible for needed formal resources?

The 4 Ms

9. Motivation
   - What does the client want to do about his or her problem or situation and how much does he or she want to do it?
   - What discomfort or aversive factors are pushing the client toward action?
   - What factors of hope and optimism are pulling the client toward action?
   - What can be done to increase client motivation?

10. Meanings
    - What meaning does the client assign to his or her life, situation, and problems? What ethnic, cultural, and religious beliefs and values are important to the client and relevant to the current problem or situation?

11. Management
    - How can the worker best use his or her limited time, energy, and resources to help the client deal with the problem or situation?
    - What overall plan or strategy will guide the worker's activity with the client?
    - How will work with this client affect the worker's other responsibilities?

12. Monitoring
    - How will the worker monitor his or her impact on the client and evaluate the effectiveness of the intervention?
    - How can the worker use peers, supervisors, or consultants to monitor and evaluate intervention?

SELECTED BIBLIOGRAPHY

Doremus, Bertha. "The Four R's: Social Diagnosis in Health Care." *Health and Social Work* 1 (1976): 121–139.

Perlman, Helen. *Social Casework: A Problem Solving Process.* Chicago: University of Chicago Press, 1957.

SECTION B

TECHNIQUES AND GUIDELINES FOR INDIRECT PRACTICE

Like direct practice, indirect social work practice requires that careful data collection and thoughtful analysis precedes planning and action. The social worker interested in changing an agency or the human services delivery system in a community must do his or her homework before launching into action.

The first step in preparing for agency or community change is to collect sufficient information to be well informed. In an agency, for example, change requires working through, or sometimes around, the agency's decision-making structure. To do this, the social worker needs to know what options are possible and feasible, given the agency's administrative structure, its sources of sanction and funding, the way decisions are usually made, and the agency's history of change.

At the community level, the social worker is often involved in data gathering and assessments intended to better understand unmet needs for services and possible ways to create new programs or improve existing ones. Although community-wide assessments should be conducted periodically to aid in adjusting human services programs and systems to changing needs and circumstances, such studies are a major undertaking and too large in scope for one or even a few social workers to carry out. However, social workers should understand the basic elements of large-scale, comprehensive studies and be prepared to be active participants in such efforts.

Short of full studies of agency or community functioning, insights can quickly and inexpensively be obtained through interviews with persons who have experience with the manner in which they operate. One useful technique for collecting such information is the focus group. In addition, when change is anticipated, it is important to analyze the manner in which decisions are made and assess the strength of various actors and issues associated with the change. Techniques for analyzing community decision making and the Force Field Analysis technique are examples of tools that facilitate this activity.

Once collected, information must be analyzed in order to identify the probable affects of various social policy alternatives. A variety of helpful formats for policy analysis exist in the social work literature. In this chapter, one example of an outline a social worker might use for undertaking a social policy analysis is included.

12.27 Assessing Agency Structure

PURPOSE: To identify alternative ways to structure staff roles and responsibilities in order to achieve efficient and effective agency operation.

DISCUSSION: The organizational structure of an agency has a significant impact on the ability of the social worker to provide effective services. In any type of organization, the structure can be expected to vary according to the complexity of the tasks being performed, the amount of authority for central decision making, and the degree to which policies, rules, and procedures are formalized. For example, many successful industrial organizations are based on the bureaucratic model. That model is most viable when the work requires the performance of relatively simple tasks (e.g., putting together parts on an assembly line) that are coordinated through a carefully structured process and very specific rules of operation. The bureaucratic organizational model, however, is much less viable in human services agencies where the work (i.e., the practice activities) is complex and must be adapted to the unique needs of clients. This work requires individualized judgments by professionals that cannot be readily subjected to centralized control and formalized rules and procedures.

In human services agencies, a variety of structures exist that range from highly bureaucratized operations to those that permit considerable worker autonomy. For example, public agencies are relatively inflexible because they are constrained by the laws that establish and sanction their operation, are dependent on a budget allocation from a legislative body, tend to be large with multiple functions, and are governed by elected or politically appointed boards that are often only vaguely familiar with the agency's day-to-day operation. Consequently, these agencies tend to be bureaucratized, allowing the policymakers and program administrators to maintain a high degree control over agency functioning. Private nonprofit agencies, by contrast, are usually smaller, offer fewer programs, and are governed by volunteer boards that are at least moderately familiar with the internal operation of the agency. These agencies tend toward decentralized authority and a minimum of rules and regulations, thus allowing staff members more control over their practice activities and substantial flexibility in how they perform their jobs.

For social workers in all types of human services organizations, it is useful to recognize that various degrees of bureaucratization can exist and that adaptations can be made that create a balance between management and worker in order to facilitate the provision of high-quality services. At times, workers must advocate for structural changes when they find that the agency's structure interferes with service to clients. To inform these advocacy efforts, it is useful to examine several structural formats commonly found in human services agencies.

Bureaucratic Model

At one end of the continuum of organizational structures is the bureaucratic model. In their pure form, bureaucracies have an elaborate *division of labor* in which work activities are clearly defined and assigned to specialized workers. A *hierarchy* of several of layers of managers, supervisors, and front-line workers is developed; a formalized set of very specific *rules and regulations* is rigidly applied; and the work carried out in a *spirit of impersonality* that is not adjusted to accommodate individual uniqueness. Bureaucracies are characterized by fairness and equal treatment, but they suffer from lack of flexibility and the ability to individualize. They are stable and consistent, yet slow to change.

Adhocracy

At the other end of the continuum of organizational structures is the adhocracy (i.e., the organization that forms internal structures on an issue-by-issue basis with various collectives of staff members addressing each issue). The ad hoc groups have considerable authority and operate with few agencywide rules and regulations. These organizations have a "flat" administrative structure in which all staff positions are somewhat equal. Ad hoc agencies are weak on both structure and stability, but are able to respond to new issues and undergo change rapidly. They are particularly effective when the nature of the work is dynamic or fluid. In social work, group private practice perhaps best illustrates adhocracy.

Other Organizational Structures

In reality, most human service agencies fall somewhere between a fully developed bureaucracy and a completely ad hoc structure. In smaller agencies, it is possible to have a relative flat, *simple structure* with an executive director heading the organization (e.g., representing the staff with the board and community) and the other staff member reporting directly to that executive.

As agencies become larger and more complex and when the span of control or number of contacts becomes too great for one person to manage, the work must be divided into segments. In this situation, a *functional structure* is likely to serve the agency well. In the functional model, a second-level administrative layer reports to the director and also leads a program unit or supervises a group of workers. A family services agency, for example, might have a counseling unit, a day treatment unit, a social action unit, and an administrative support unit—each with its own unit manager. The executive director would facilitate coordination of these units and oversee the work of the unit managers.

At times, an agency may temporarily supplement one of these structures with a *project-team* approach. This model provides for groups of staff to be organized around specific tasks for limited periods of time. In addition to being assigned to a specific unit or supervisor for their primary job, workers may be temporarily assigned on a full- or part-time basis to a team that cuts across units to address a specific problem. For example, staff from a family agency's clinical and day treatment units may temporarily join with a staff member from the social action unit to plan and carry out a strategy of public education and legislative advocacy to reduce the incidence of spouse abuse.

SELECTED BIBLIOGRAPHY

Kettner, Peter, Robert M. Moroney, and Lawrence L. Martin. *Designing and Managing Programs: An Effectiveness Based Approach,* Newbury Park, Calif.: Sage, 1990.

Robbins, Stephen P. *Organization Theory: The Structure and Design of Organizations.* Englewood Cliffs, N. J.: Prentice-Hall, 1983.

Weiss, Richard M. "Organizational Structure in Human Service Agencies." In *Managing Human Service Organizations,* edited by Lynn E. Miller. New York: Quorum Books, 1988.

12.28   Assessing Human Services Needs

PURPOSE: To provide data on the utilization of and/or need for specific human services offered in a community or region, or to an identified population group.

DISCUSSION: Although the perspective of the agency board and staff is a valuable source of information for determining agency goals and services, it is also important that decisions be based on a formal evaluation of the need for these services. Agencies should periodically conduct needs assessments.

The Minnesota State Planning Agency (Franczyk 1977, 4) observes that the term *needs assessment* usually refers to "the process of identifying the incidence, prevalence and nature of certain conditions within a community or target group. The ultimate purpose is to assess the adequacy of existing services and resources in addressing those conditions. The extent to which those conditions are not adequately addressed denotes a need for different services or resources."

When conducting a needs assessment, two judgments must be made by those conducting the analysis and those who will use the findings (e.g., agency board, city council, United Way). First, there should be agreement about what constitutes a need. Second, there must be a willingness to take action if an unmet need is identified. It is not a good use of time or resources to conduct a needs assessment if there is not recognition in advance that if needs are discovered some corrective action is both possible and probable.

Methods and Steps of a Needs Assessment

Several methods may be used to gather needs assessment data:

1. Community forums attended by concerned and interested members of the community
2. Caseload counts (i.e., counts of persons utilizing various services)
3. Opinions expressed by experts or other professionals having relevant knowledge or experience
4. Public opinion and attitude surveys
5. Social indicators (e.g., suicide rates, poverty rates, divorce rates, etc.)

Franczyk (1977) identifies six steps in the needs assessment process.

Step 1. *Selecting units and topics for analysis.* This step involves the identification of target groups (populations at risk) and/or the geographical area about which information is to be gathered. These target groups and geographical areas are known as the units of analysis. The kinds of information desired about each of these units are the topics of analysis.

Step 2. *Selection of one or more methods for gathering data.* On one level, a choice must be made between establishing an ongoing, agency based, informational system and implementing a short-term data collection project. On another level, the advantages of using existing data must be weighed against the costs of generating new data.

Step 3. *Gathering data/generating information.* Information about the needs of the specific units of analysis is generated from the aggregation and analysis of the individual bits of data collected.

Step 4. *Identifying unacceptable social or human conditions.* Having formulated a composite picture of the conditions experienced by the units of analysis, certain conditions are judged to be in violation of acceptable standards.

Step 5. *Comparing observed conditions to existing services.* Step five involves the gathering of information about the availability, adequacy and effectiveness of existing services in meeting identified needs.

Step 6. *Recommending changes in existing services.* The product of a well done needs assessment should be a confirmation of existing services as adequate or recommendations for change to cope with the observed inadequacy. (p. 6)

Guidelines for Conducting a Needs Assessment

The following guidelines should be kept in mind when conducting needs assessment:

1. It is essential to have a clear understanding of the policy issues and administrative concerns that prompted the decision maker to recommend the use of a needs assessment. In other words, what problems do the decision makers hope to solve through the use of a needs assessment?

2. The goals and objectives of the needs assessment must be clear before it is possible to select appropriate methods of data collection and analysis. All too often, those planning a needs assessment jump ahead to the question of What questions should we ask the people we are going to interview? before they are clear on exactly what kind of data they can and will use in the planning of new services or the modification of existing services.

3. It is helpful to know how other communities or agencies have approached the task, but it is usually a mistake to borrow someone else's objectives and methodology. Those who are in a position to use the data should decide what approach would be useful and work best in their community. Such decisions should not be made by outside consultants or by persons or agencies that have a vested interest in seeing the assessment yield certain findings.

4. In planning a needs assessment, it is important to anticipate possible reasons why situations of unmet need might exist. For example:
- No services are available in the community.
- Existing services are not accessible because of transportation problems, eligibility criteria, and the like.
- Persons in need are not aware that services exist.
- Existing services are not integrated to provide a continuity of service to multiproblem individuals and families.
- Existing programs do not have adequate resources to provide quality service.
- Existing services are unacceptable to residents of a particular community. For example, they may be perceived as degrading, threatening, or in conflict with existing ethnic, religious, or cultural norms and values.

5. A needs assessment should not only identify unmet service needs but also shed light on the quantity, quality, and direction of existing services. For example:
- *Quantity.* Does the level of service meet the need? This involves some assessment of the number of persons in need of service compared with the capacity of providers to serve those persons.
- *Quality.* Are the services effective? Do they accomplish what they are intended to do? Do they work?
- *Direction.* Are the approaches used in service delivery appropriate or possibly out of touch with the real needs of clients? Does the philosophy that gave rise to existing programs coincide with the generally accepted philosophy espoused by current experts in the field?

6. Do not attempt a needs assessment until there is evidence that the agency(s) and community possess the administrative and political readiness to use the data once it is gathered. If they are not ready, the report will gather dust on a shelf.

SELECTED BIBLIOGRAPHY

Franczyk, James J. *Needs Assessment: A Guide to Human Service Agencies.* St. Paul: Minnesota State Planning Agency, 1977.

Slaght, Evelyn, and Janice H. Schopler. "Are Quick and Dirty Needs Assessments Better Than No Needs Assessments?" In *Controversial Isues in Communities and Organizations,* edited by Michael J. Austin and Jane Isaacs Lowe. Boston: Allyn and Bacon, 1994, pp. 142–157.

Soriano, Fernando I. *Conducting Needs Assessments: A Multidisciplinary Approach.* Newbury Park, Calif.: Sage, 1995.

Witkin, Belle Ruth, and James Altschuld. *Planning and Conducting Needs Assessment.* Newbury Park, Calif.: Sage, 1995.

12.29   Leading Focus Groups

PURPOSE: To acquire in-depth responses from a group of human services consumers or research subjects regarding an agency, program, service, or other topic.

DISCUSSION: Human services agencies and qualitative researchers have followed the marketing branch of the business community in the use of focus groups as a technique for collecting valuable information. A *focus group* is a small group of people (usually 8 to 12) who have had a common experience or share common knowledge and are led through a one- to two-hour discussion of a particular topic. The goal is to explore the topic by allowing the ideas of participants to create a synergy that promotes in-depth discussion until the points of agreement or disagreement emerge and become clear. Focus groups are particularly useful in identifying why the participants think or feel as they do about the subject.

When used for administrative purposes, focus groups can supply information that may be helpful in activities such as planning new services, assessing the needs of current consumers of services, developing marketing strategies, or identifying the implications of terminating a particular program. This technique might be used with existing groups such as agency boards, advisory committees, and staff members or with groups of clients or community members. In research, focus groups are used in association with qualitative approaches (see Item 10.14) in which content analysis of transcriptions of the meetings serve as a data source for the identification of important themes and fleshing out the meaning participants attribute to them. In addition to the snowball effect of members extending their thinking from the ideas presented by others, focus groups are a relatively inexpensive and, usually, a readily available source of data.

There are four essentials of a successful focus group meeting. First, the participants should be selected carefully. They should represent a broad range of the people who are familiar with the topic and should be people willing to speak their minds. The atmosphere of the meeting and the meeting place should be conducive to freewheeling discussion, and the participants should be protected from retribution for any remarks they might make. It is not usual procedure to follow a scientific sampling process in selecting the participants. Thus, the results should be viewed cautiously and considered only one data source for making decisions.

Second, the moderator should be well prepared. It is the leader's responsibility to introduce the topic without suggesting a bias and to facilitate open discussion of the topic. The moderator must listen carefully and explore the meaning behind the participants' statements, constantly probing for greater depth and clarity. He or she must also be flexible in allowing the group to explore the topic as the flow of their discussion leads, but at the same time be able to bring the group back to the topic when tangents are no longer productive. The moderator must assure that no one member dominates the session and that everyone has a opportunity to speak on each dimension of the topic being explored.

Third, there should be a carefully developed plan for the meeting that includes a series of open-ended questions or statements that stimulate discussion of the topic. The persons planning the focus group meeting should develop an outline known as a "moderator guide" that introduces the subject matter in a logical order (i.e., usually from the most general areas to the most specific) and probes for what the participants perceive to be the relevant dimensions of the topic. The "moderator guide" can be used as a checklist during the meeting to assure that all important aspects of the topic are addressed before the meeting is concluded. Time should be reserved at the end of the meeting for participants to add topics that may have been omitted and for the moderator to summarize what he or she saw as important themes in the discussion, allowing participants to reply to that summary.

Finally, the information provided by the group members must be assessed and accurately interpreted. Often, audiotapes or videotapes of the sessions are used, along with notetaking by observers, to record the information that emerges in the meeting. Again, it is important to minimize any biases or self-interests when interpreting the information.

SELECTED BIBLIOGRAPHY

Greenbaum, Thomas L. *The Handbook of Focus Group Research,* rev. and expanded ed. New York: Lexington Books, 1993.

Krueger, Richard A. *Focus Groups: A Practical Guide for Applied Research,* 2nd ed. Newbury Park, Calif.: Sage, 1994.

Toseland, Ronald W., and Robert F. Rivas. *An Introduction to Group Work Practice,* 2nd ed. Boston: Allyn and Bacon, 1995.

Webster, Susan. *Focus Groups: An Effective Marketing Research Tool for Social Service Agencies.* Portland, Maine: National Child Welfare Resource Center for Management and Administration, 1992.

12.30   Community Decision-Making Analysis

PURPOSE: To assess the factors that influence the actions of elected officials and other decision makers.

DISCUSSION: As social workers seek to influence decisions that affect the quality of human services in a community, they must develop a strategy for convincing the person or persons in authority that a particular course of action is the best choice among the possible options. Ideally, decisions should be made on the merit of the proposal; in reality, however, decision makers usually respond to external pressures and various personal considerations. The social worker must be alert to the factors and forces that may sway a decision maker.

Research on community decision making and community power structures does not yield a consistent picture of the forces that lead to these decisions. However, several generalizations can be made regarding variables that at least partially explain why some communities tend to center the decision making in a small, elite group of people while others are more pluralistic and involve a broader spectrum of the community.

1. *Size.* Large cities tend to be pluralistic. They are likely to become more diverse and competitive as they grow, resulting in a greater range of people and interest groups involved in making decisions.

2. *Population diversity.* Communities that have more varied and complex class and ethnic structures develop more special interest groups and more community organizations that compete for power and resources. Consequently, there are more challenges to any dominant elite group and a tendency to increase pluralism in decision making.

3. *Economic diversity.* More diversified communities in terms of varied sources of employment, high levels of industrialization, and the presence of absentee-owned industry (as opposed to local people owning the major industries) all tend to make communities more pluralistic in how decisions are made.

4. *Structure of local government.* Reformed governments (i.e., cities with council-manager format, nonpartisan-at-large elections) tend to be more elitist than those partisan governments with representatives elected by districts. Further, the greater the competition or balance among political groups, the more likely the community will have a pluralistic decision-making structure.

Increasingly, communities in the United States have a pluralistic type of decision-making structure. Few are under the influence of a small elite group. Meenaghan, Washington, and Ryan (1982, 131) explain that within pluralist communities, social workers can expect to observe the following:

1. The key decision makers tend to specialize in terms of which issues get their attention. In other words, certain powerful individuals and interest groups will become actively involved in the decision-making process when the decision relates to their occupation, profession, or organizational affiliations but will ignore decisions that are outside their rather narrow range of concerns.

2. With regard to a specific decision, relatively few people are actually involved in making the decision.

3. The powerful decision makers usually come from three institutional sectors: industry and business, government, and the professions. No one of these three sectors routinely dominates the decision-making process.

The literature identifies three factors that should be assessed in determining a strategy for influencing community decision makers.

1. Decision makers are responsive to the personal characteristics of the people who seek to influence their decisions.
2. Decision makers are impacted by the institutional base (e.g., control of money, jobs, information and votes) from which that person speaks. The person who can combine these personal and institutional sources of influence can be especially effective in influencing decisions.
3. Decision makers are also influenced by their own personal judgment of the matter and their assessment of the personal gains and losses from acting on the various options. (Dahl 1960, 39–40)

Using a method like the Force Field Analysis technique (see Item 12.31) the social worker should carefully assess the strength of these factors and seek to counterbalance those that do not support the desired position. Figure 12.14 identifies the influence factors that should be considered.

**FIGURE 12.14
Factors Influencing
Community
Decision Makers**

**Personal Influence
Characteristics**
1. Status, social standing
2. Charisma, popularity
3. Knowledge, expertise
4. Skill in use of self

**Institutional Power
Characteristics**
1. Control of financial resources
2. Control of jobs
3. Control of mass media
4. Control of special-interest groups
5. Control of voting blocks

External Influences

Decision Maker

Internal Influences

The Decision Maker's Personal Considerations
1. Material interests: income, reelection, advancement
2. Self-esteem: pride, self-respect
3. Social esteem: status, position, social standing
4. Trade-offs: exchange for support on other issues
5. Solidarity: loyalties, sense of belonging, love
6. Perception of the importance of the matter
7. Assessment of the merits of the proposed action

SELECTED BIBLIOGRAPHY

Dahl, Robert. "The Analysis of Influence in Local Communities." In *Social Science and Community Action,* edited by Charles R. Adrian. East Lansing: Michigan State University 1960.

Meenaghan, Thomas, Robert Washington, and Robert Ryan. *Macro Practice in the Human Services.* New York: Free Press, 1982.

Rubin, Herbert J., and Irene S. Rubin. *Community Organization and Development,* 2nd ed. New York: Macmillan, 1992.

12.31   Force Field Analysis (FFA)

PURPOSE: To identify and assess the various forces that may affect a decision regarding a social problem or issue.

DISCUSSION: *Force Field Analysis (FFA)* is a technique that organizes data concerning the forces that may affect the outcome of a change effort. Basically, FFA helps the social worker identify and examine the forces that may either foster or restrain a particular change. Although this technique is most commonly used in organizational or community change, the basic concepts of FFA can be applied in work with individuals and families. Five steps are involved in conducting a force field analysis.

1. *Specify the desired change or objective.* Describe the change you hope to achieve (e.g., to develop emergency shelter facilities for 100 homeless families).

2. *Identify the driving and restraining forces that will probably determine whether the change or objective is achieved.* Those doing the FFA must identify the people (individuals, groups, coalitions, organizations, etc.) that will be interested in the issue. Some of these can be expected to work for the change; these are termed *driving forces.* Some can be expected to work against the proposed change; these are the *restraining forces.* On a sheet of paper (see Figure 12.15), list on the left side each driving force (D-force) and on the right side list each restraining force (R-force).

3. *Assess the strengths of each driving and restraining force.* Each D-force and each R-force on the list must be examined and assessed in terms of its potency, consistency, and amenability. *Potency (P)* refers to the power of a particular force. Some may be very strong, others may be weak. *Consistency (C)* refers to the stability of the position taken. In other words, is the position taken by a particular D-force or R-force solid or might it weaken over time? *Amenability (A)* refers to how open a particular force might be to outside influence and pressure. In other words, to what degree is a particular force vulnerable to the influence of those who may ask it to strengthen or weaken its position?

   The potency, consistency, and amenability of each D-force and R-force are rated as either high (H) or low (L). Codes can be used to depict these ratings. For example, the code R-HP-LA would refer to a restraining force of high power and one unlikely to be influenced by outside influence.

**FIGURE 12.15
Sample
Force Field
Analysis**

Current Level

Driving Forces ———▶	◀——— Restraining Forces
1.	1.
2.	2.
3.	3.
4.	4.
Etc.	Etc.

P = Potency   C = Consistency   A = Amenability

4. *Identify the actors.* As used here, an *actor (ACT)* is a person or organization that might be called on to influence a particular driving force or restraining force and thereby alter its strength. Once identified, the probability that the actor will exercise its influence is rated as either high (H) or low (L).

5. *Select a strategy for change.* Given your analysis of the various forces that may be working for or against the change and an assessment of the various actors that might be able to modify these forces, a plan is formulated. The plan will, of course, seek to strengthen the D-forces and weaken the R-forces by enlisting the help of key actors and asking them to exercise their influence. The R-forces targeted for weakening would, most likely, be those that are powerful but are thought to have low consistency and/or high amenability. The plan would also seek to strengthen D-forces, especially those with low consistency and high amenability. In some cases, the FFA may reveal that the chances of success in making the desired change are so small that it is best to delay action and wait for a more favorable mix of forces and actors.

SELECTED BIBLIOGRAPHY

Brager, George, and Stephen Holloway. *Changing Human Service Organizations.* New York: Free Press, 1978.

Lauffer, Armand. *Assessment Tools for Practitioners, Managers, and Trainers.* Beverly Hills: Sage, 1982.

12.32   Social Policy Analysis

PURPOSE: To make an accurate assessment of social policy and program issues in order to guide community change activities.

DISCUSSION: The analysis of public social policy issues can be a difficult and time-consuming task. Fortunately, several good models that can guide such an analysis exist within the social work literature. Depending on the social worker's role and preparation for making an analysis, it is possible to approach this task in greater or lesser depth. Social workers who are not engaged in full-time community change activity usually do not have the time or resources available to apply the more complex models.

When examining a public social policy, it is important to recognize that social policies and social programs are a response to some social problem as perceived by those groups who formulate program proposals and have the political power to pass the laws or policies that establish them as part of an agency's program. To a large extent, every policy and program reflects the beliefs, values assumptions, and self-interests of those able to influence the process of program design and policy development. Also, it is helpful to recognize that a policy is a reflection of how a problem is understood at a particular point in time. As knowledge of a problem accumulates, existing policies may become outdated and require revision.

Chambers (1993, 7–49) has developed an approach to public policy analysis that is relatively simple and straightforward. As such, it is helpful in identifying the key questions that should be addressed by the occasional policy analyst.

1. *Social problem analysis.* The first step in the analysis of a social policy or program is to have a clear understanding of the problems that created the situation requiring such a policy. To make this assessment, it is useful to undertake the following activities.

- *Identify how the problem is defined and locate estimates of its magnitude.* For example, what definition of poverty, mental illness, or unemployment is commonly used? Are there other definitions that might be more appropriate? How many people experience this problem as it is defined? What particular subpopulations are most likely to experience this problem?
- *Determine the causes and consequences of the problem.* What forces or factors have caused the problem? Are there multiple causes? Are there multiple consequences from a single cause?
- *Identify the ideological beliefs or basic principles embedded in the description of the problem.* The definition of a problem is influenced by beliefs about what "ought to be," or the values one holds. Is there a difference of opinion about the seriousness of the problem? Do different groups hold varying views about the nature and cause of the problem?
- *Identify the gainers and losers in relation to the problem.* Who gains from the existence of the problem? What do they gain and how much? Who loses? What do they lose and how much? How serious are the negative consequences on the lives of the losers?

2. *Social policy and program analysis.* Once the problem is understood, the second step is to assess the social policy and/or program being considered as a means of addressing the problem or offering relief to the victims of the problem. The following are useful for this analysis.

- *Search out the relevant program and policy history.* Is this a new problem? Have conditions, values, or perceptions changed over time? What is different about the proposed program or policy from past efforts to deal with the problem?

■ *Identify the key elements or operating characteristics of the proposed policy or program.* What are the goals and objectives of the proposal? Who would be eligible to benefit from the plan? What benefits or services would be delivered if this proposal gains approval? What administrative structure would be required and how would it work? How would the program be financed and how much money would be required? Are there any undesirable consequences from interactions among the characteristics already listed?

3. *Draw conclusions.* After the information identified above has been collected, it is necessary to judge the merits of the policy or program under analysis. Ultimately, it is the weight of the evidence matched with one's beliefs about what the quality of life should be for members of the society that results in a recommendation favoring or opposing the proposal—or suggesting modification.

Answers to the following questions might be considered in arriving at conclusions about this program or policy proposal: Is it appropriate for addressing the problem identified? Does the remedy proposed adequately deal with the causes as well as the consequences of the problem? Will it yield an outcome different from ones attempted in the past? Would the costs associated with the proposed remedy justify the possible outcomes? Are there better remedies that might be proposed?

When addressing a social policy, it is particularly important to be conscientious about using accurate data. If challenged by those with competing interests, credibility can be lost by not having sufficient and accurate data to support conclusions and underpin recommendations for change.

With a solid analysis of the policy or program proposal in hand, the social worker is prepared to influence the legislation that would impact the problem under consideration. At times, the social worker will work through committees or other groups to affect these decisions; on other occasions, it is appropriate to contact a legislator directly and express a position on the proposal.

SELECTED BIBLIOGRAPHY

Chambers, Donald E. *Social Policy and Social Programs: A Method for the Practical Public Policy Analyst,* 2nd ed. New York: Macmillan, 1993.

DiNitto, Diane, and Thomas Dye. *Social Welfare Politics and Public Policy,* 3rd ed. Englewood Cliffs, N.J.: Prentice Hall, 1991.

Dobelstein, Andrew H. *Social Welfare: Policy and Analysis.* Chicago: Nelson-Hall, 1990.

Ginsberg, Leon. *Understanding Social Problems, Policies, and Programs.* Columbia: University of South Carolina Press, 1994.

Meenaghan, Thomas M., and Keith M. Kilty. *Policy Analysis and Research Teachnology: Political and Ethical Considerations.* Chicago: Lyceum, 1994.

13 Planning and Contracting

INTRODUCTION

Once the client and social worker have engaged in data gathering and agreed on an initial assessment of the client's problem or situation, they reach a stage in the helping process called *planning and contracting*. During this stage, they must come to an agreement on intervention goals and objectives and formulate a plan to achieve those ends. Essentially, this plan must identify:

1. Problems or concerns to be addressed by the intervention
2. Objectives or expected outcomes of the intervention
3. Actions to be taken by worker and client during intervention
4. Timelines (i.e., beginning and projected ending of intervention)

As with all phases in the problem-solving or helping process, joint decision making is emphasized during planning and contracting. During this stage, even subtle disagreements between worker and client on the nature of the problem and how to proceed will become evident. If there are disagreements, they must be discussed and resolved before proceeding.

SECTION A
TECHNIQUES AND GUIDELINES FOR DIRECT PRACTICE

This section presents selected techniques and guidelines pertinent to planning and contracting activity with individuals, families, and small groups. In particular, it offers information on the selection of target problems, the formulation of goals and objectives, written service contracts, client needs lists, the use of informal resources, and the use of the small group as a resource.

In keeping with the social work principle of client self-determination, the client has the right to be fully informed about any intervention or professional decision that may impact his or her life situation. More specifically, the client has a right to:

- Make decisions and have input concerning the intervention goals and objectives and the general approach to be used to reach those ends.
- Know what approach the worker proposes to use, the likelihood of success, and if there are any risks or adverse effects associated with the proposed intervention.
- Know how long the intervention will last and/or about how long it will take to achieve the agreed upon objectives.
- Know how much time and money (if any) will be required of the client.
- Know of any consequences for terminating the intervention against the advice of the social worker or agency.
- Know what rules of confidentiality apply and know who else (e.g., court, probation officer, parent, etc.) will have access to information about the client's participation and the effectiveness of the intervention.
- Know how the effectiveness of the intervention will be evaluated.
- Know of appeals or grievance procedures that can be used to challenge a decision made by a social worker or agency.

The worker's activities during the planning and contracting phase must be guided by a genuine respect for these client rights.

The social worker must make numerous decisions during all stages of the helping process, but some of the most critical ones occur after assessment and during planning and contracting. Some such decisions can have lifelong consequences for a client—for example, whether to separate an abused child from his or her parents, whether to recommend probation or incarceration for a youth, and so on. An awareness of common errors in reaching a decision can prevent bad decisions.

A major cause of poor decision making is spending insufficient time defining the problem to be addressed and clarifying what issues need to be resolved or what questions need to be answered. If, from the beginning, there is a lack of clarity about what needs to be addressed, decisions are bound to be faulty. Another common source of poor decision making is deciding on the basis of unrecognized or unexamined assumptions. This happens when one does not look beyond surface concerns or does not consider data that might contradict preconceived ideas.

Errors often result because the decision maker considered only a narrow range of alternatives. This can occur because of parochialism, bias, adherence to the "party line," political pressure, or a rigid interpretation of agency policy. Many poor decisions are caused by unclear or incomplete communication among those having information critical to the decision, In this instance, the information needed for a good decision is available but does not get to the person who needs it or it gets distorted in the exchange.

The overuse or misapplication of a particular practice theory or model can also cause bad decisions. Conceptual frameworks tend to create a mindset as to the nature and cause of problems and their solutions. A person committed to a certain way of thinking may overlook or disregard information that does not "fit" the theory.

Attention to detail is important but a preoccupation with the detail slows the decision making and can also narrow one's vision of what is possible. On the other extreme is the pitfall that comes from being so creative or visionary that important details, uncertainties, and real barriers are overlooked. When that happens, the implementation of the decision proves impractical.

A reliance on only intuition or hunch in decision making can be disastrous. On the other hand, giving attention only to hard data and neglecting "gut feelings" can also result in a poor decision. Studies suggest that people differ greatly in the amount of data needed to make good decisions. Some must have much information, whereas others seem more able to perceive quickly the whole of the situation, even with very incomplete information.

In summary, several guidelines can assist in making good decisions.

1. Give ample attention to the definition and formulation of the problem or question. Remember that a partial answer to a good question is better than a perfect answer to the wrong question.
2. Consider every alternative, even ones that are unusual or uncommon.
3. Be explicit about the assumptions on which a particular decision will rest.
4. Use a theory or model that fits the problem or situation; never redefine the problem so it fits a preconceived idea or a preferred theory.
5. Use interdisciplinary teams whenever possible or consult with a colleague.
6. Be explicit about the uncertainties and limitations inherent in a given decision. Anticipate the consequences, especially the harmful ones, that may be associated with a particular decision.
7. To the extent possible, base the decision on hard facts and objective evidence. Strive to avoid bias and the influence of untested assumptions, but do not neglect or discount intuition and "gut feelings."

13.1   Selecting Target Problems and Goals

PURPOSE: To select the target problems and goals that will give direction to the social work intervention.

DISCUSSION: A *goal* is a desired end toward which an activity is directed. Broadly speaking, the goal of an intervention with a specific client is the desired end toward which that client and his or her social worker are working. This goal logically flows from the data-gathering and assessment phase. The intervention goals can take many forms. For example, the client might seek to:

- *Learn a skill or acquire needed knowledge* (e.g., learn how to interview for a job, manage time, make decisions, resolve interpersonal conflict, manage stress, take care of a child, etc.).
- *Make an important decision* (e.g., decide on a college major, whether to get a divorce, whether to relinquish custody of a child, whether to seek help for an emotional problem, etc.).

- *Gather the information* needed to make a plan or make a decision.
- *Assess a problem or concern* (i.e., conduct a careful assessment of some concern in order to decide if it is a serious problem needing attention, what the nature of the problem is, etc.).
- *Make a plan* (e.g., formulate a plan on how best to address some concern or problem).
- *Change a behavior* (e.g., increase a desirable behavior, decrease or eliminate a troublesome behavior).
- *Alter feelings and attitudes* about self or about some other person(s).
- *Gather information about availability of certain types of services or programs.*
- *Become linked to or enrolled in a program or service* provided by some agency or professional.
- *Rebuild a damaged relationship* (e.g., reach out to and reestablish relationship with estranged parent or child, improve husband-wife relationship, etc.).
- *Change the way life circumstances or a life event is perceived or interpreted* (i.e., learn to assign new meaning to events and circumstances, view things from a different angle, develop new perspectives).

Sometimes the social worker and client can quickly agree on the goal. This is likely when the client's need or problem is readily apparent. However, in many cases, the social worker and client will see things differently and they must struggle to clarify the nature of the problem and come to an agreement on what should be done about it. Often, the worker and client must also devote considerable time to the task of priority setting in order to decide which of the client's many problems should become target problems for intervention. Until those decisions are made, they cannot formulate a feasible intervention plan.

The principle of *client self-determination* dictates that the client has the right to select the concerns to be addressed. There are also practical reasons related to motivation for expecting the client—rather than the social worker—to select the target problems and goals. Epstein (1992, 174) observes, "It is unlikely that a client's motivation can be readily enhanced, or that [he or] she can be maneuvered into a genuine commitment for a personal change not wanted, not sought, and not accepted. [However] clients seek and value help help that makes sense to them, is useful in their daily lives, and gets or keeps them out of trouble." Even with the nonvoluntary client, it is important to give the client as much choice as possible. In such cases, the worker or agency might mandate one target problem but allow the involuntary client to select the second or third.

Most clients have multiple problems. Both research and practice wisdom show that, in order to be effective, the helping process must concentrate available time and energy on just one, two, or three problems at a time. If priorities and a clear focus are not established, the helping effort flounders and usually ends in frustration for both client and worker. The following steps will help the client and worker set *priorities*.

1. The client identifies and lists what he or she sees as problems or concerns (i.e., what client wants to change).

2. The social worker offers his or her recommendations, if any, and explains why they also need to be considered. The worker makes sure that any mandated problems are included (mandated problems are ones imposed on the client by some legitimate authority such as a court, probation officer, or child protection agency).

3. The problems and concerns are reviewed and sorted into logical groupings or combinations so that interrelatedness is identified.

4. The client examines his or her list and selects the two or three problems or concerns of highest priority.

5. The worker selects the two or three items he or she considers to be of highest priority.

6. Together, the client and worker discuss those identified in steps 4 and 5 and examine them against the following criteria.

- Which ones weigh most heavily on the client's situation (e.g., which ones cause the most worry and anxiety)?
- Which ones, if not addressed and corrected, will have the most negative and far-reaching consequences for the client?
- Which ones, if addressed and corrected, would have the most positive effects on the client (e.g., provide the client with greatest sense of relief, make it easier to solve other problems, etc.)?
- Which ones are of greatest interest to the client (e.g., which ones the client is most motivated to work on at this time)?
- Which ones can be addressed and corrected with only a moderate investment of time, energy, and other resources?
- Which ones are relatively unchangeable or would require a extraordinary investment of time, energy, or resources?

7. After considering these criteria, the three problems of highest priority are selected. As mentioned earlier, both experience and research suggest that it is usually counterproductive to try to address more than three problems at one time. Task-centered practitioners have termed this principle *the rule of three.*

8. It is important for the social worker to remember that the client's problems and concerns will almost always affect or involve significant others (e.g., spouse, children, parents, close friends, employer, etc.). Unless these individuals, who are either part of the problem or part of the solution, are considered in the intervention planning, there is good chance that they will—knowingly or unknowingly—become an obstacle to the change process. In some cases, they may actively sabotage the client's attempt to make desired changes.

SELECTED BIBLIOGRAPHY

Epstein, Laura. *Brief Treatment and a New Look at the Task-Centered Approach.* New York: Macmillan, 1992.
Gambrill, Eileen. *Critical Thinking in Clinical Practice.* San Francisco: Jossey-Bass, 1990.
Seligman, Martin. *What You Can Change and What You Can't.* New York: Alfred Knopf, 1994.

13.2   **The Problem Search**

PURPOSE: To engage the reluctant client in a process designed to identify a problem on which he or she is willing to work.

DISCUSSION: Not infrequently, the social worker encounters the nonvoluntary client who has been forced by either a court or a powerful family member to seek professional help. Typically, these clients deny the existence of a problem and resent having to speak with a social worker(see Item 11.7). With the court-ordered, nonvoluntary client, involvement can sometimes be secured with arguments such as, "Well, it looks like we are stuck with each other. Since we have to talk to each other, let's figure out what we can do together to get me and the probation department off your back." With a resistant adult client being pressured by other family members, there are two options: Terminate the contact or suggest the use of a problem search. The ***problem search*** can be viewed as a "minicontract" or an agreement to spend a couple of sessions trying to determine whether a problem exists and, if so, whether it should be addressed.

The problem search procedure is used either when (1) the client has been referred by an authoritative agency or by his or her family but does not acknowledge the existence of a problem as defined by others or (2) the client has requested a specific agency service but, in the worker's opinion, it is desirable to help the client expand that request or redefine the presenting problem. In this later situation, the social worker is concerned that the client's definition of the problem is not accurate or realistic and/or that his or her request for a specific service will not resolve the problem. An example might be the father who requests foster care placement for his children because he and his wife are having serious marital problems.

Essentially, the problem search asks the reluctant client to participate in one or two additional sessions in order to explore the situation in more depth. The client is asked to withhold judgment about the need for service and the worker's usefulness until after these meetings. In using this technique, the social worker moves through several steps.

1. *Explain why you are suggesting a further exploration of the client's situation.* Briefly identify your concerns and the advantages of an additional session or two. For example: "I realize that you see no problems that deserve my attention, but what you have said about getting fired leads me to believe that you really try to get along but for some reason you and your supervisors often clash on how best to do the work. Because of that, I suggest we meet two times and talk more about your job experiences. If, after the second session, we cannot figure out what might be done to improve the situation, we will stop meeting."

2. *Solicit the client's thoughts and feedback on the proposal.* For example: "What do you think about my suggestion that we meet two times to review and discuss the stress you experience on the job?" (If client responds with a no, say, for example, "Well, I can understand your reluctance and I will respect your decision, but let me give you one other reason why I think it is a good idea. . . .")

3. *Set up a plan for a future meeting.* For example: "I am glad that you agreed to meet again. As I said, we will meet two times. If it proves useful, that will be great. But, if after the second session, it doesn't seem useful, then we will not continue. How about meeting the next two Wednesdays at 4 P.M.?"

4. *Identify two or three topics to be discussed.* For example: "When we meet next week, let's start with a discussion of the jobs you have really liked and why. Second, I would like to discuss the type of supervision you expect to get on the job. Does that sound like a reasonable place to begin?"

SELECTED BIBLIOGRAPHY

Doel, Mark, and Peter Marsh. *Task Centered Social Work.* Brookfield, Vt.: Ashgate Publishing, 1992.

Epstein, Laura. *Brief Treatment and a New Look at the Task-Centered Approach.* New York: Macmillan, 1992.

13.3 Using Checklists in Goal Selection

PURPOSE: To assist the client in identifying and selecting intervention goals.

DISCUSSION: Some clients have difficulty conceptualizing and articulating the goals they hope the social work intervention will achieve. In such cases, a checklist may be useful. A worker familiar with the problems and concerns of a particular client group can easily construct a simple checklist and tailor it to the type of client served and the practice setting. For example, Figure 13.1 is a goal checklist developed by Horejsi, Bertsche, and Clark (1981, 239) for use with parents of children who have been placed in foster care for reasons of abuse or neglect. This tool was designed to help these parents discuss and identify changes that need to occur before the parent and child could be reunited (also see Item 15.5).

SELECTED BIBLIOGRAPHY

Horejsi, Charles. *Assessment and Case Planning in Child Protection and Foster Care Services.* Englewood, Colo.: American Humane Association (in press).

Horejsi, Charles, Ann Bertsche, and Frank Clark. *Social Work Practice with Parents of Children in Foster Care: A Handbook.* Springfield, Ill.: Charles C. Thomas, 1981.

13.4 Formulating Intervention Objectives

PURPOSE: To develop objectives that are measurable and relevant to the client's concerns.

DISCUSSION: A key attribute of an effective intervention is an objective that is sharply defined. Unless objectives are clear, the helping process flounders and the evaluation of outcome is impossible. Although many people use the terms *goals* and *objectives* inter-

FIGURE 13.1   Sample Goal Checklist

A List of Goals for Parents
with Children in Foster Care

Explanation: Sometimes problems related to the parent's own behavior or conflicts between parent and child need to be solved before parents and child can be reunited. Having a clear goal in mind is one important step in successfully solving problems. Once there is agreement on a goal, it is possible to develop a plan of work toward the goal. Below is a list of goals that have been mentioned by parents with children in foster care. Place a check (✓) by those goals that are close to ones that make sense for you and your situation. This checklist can help you and your social worker formulate a plan of action.

_____ Learn to talk to people about my concerns.

_____ Learn to like myself.

_____ Learn how to budget my money.

_____ Learn to prepare meals.

_____ Learn to take care of the house.

_____ Learn to find and make use of services such as daycare, counseling, legal services.

_____ Learn to cope with daily pressures and demands.

_____ Learn to show affection toward my children.

_____ Learn to make friends, mix, and feel comfortable with people.

_____ Learn skills needed to get a job.

_____ Learn how to have good visits with my child in foster care.

_____ Learn to get along with my spouse (husband/wife).

_____ Learn to control my anger and temper.

_____ Learn to talk with my child and make him/her feel secure.

_____ Learn ways of disciplining my child without using physical punishment.

_____ Learn how to talk and plan with the foster parents.

_____ Learn how to talk with my social worker and make use of the help he/she can provide.

_____ Learn to share my feelings and worries with other people, such as other parents who have had similar problems.

_____ Learn to find friends, or groups that may understand my situation and help me deal with problems.

_____ Learn what to expect from children and find out what is "normal" behavior for my child.

_____ Learn to be more assertive in making my thoughts and feelings known to other people.

_____ Learn how to get along without alcohol or drugs.

_____ Learn how to deal with conflicts with my parents and relatives.

_____ Learn how to deal with emergency situations or times when I get overwhelmed.

_____ Learn to cope with strong emotions like guilt and sadness.

Source: From Horejsi, Bertsche, and Clark, *Social Work Practice with Children in Foster Care* (1981), p. 239. Courtesy of Charles C Thomas, Publisher, Springfield, Illinois.

changeably, they do not mean the same. A statement of *goals* is usually broad and somewhat abstract (e.g., "to better cope with the demands of a child who has a disability"). Not infrequently, a goal is simply a restatement of a problem in a way that suggests a solution. For example, if a family's lack of money creates stress that erupts in violence against children, a logical goal would be to increase that family's financial resources in order to reduce stress.

As compared to a goal, an *objective* is more specific and concrete. In addition, an objective is measurable, whereas a goal is not. It is helpful to think of an objective as one of many measurable steps that must be taken in order to reach a goal. A properly written objective answers a five-part question:

1. Who . . .
2. will do what . . .
3. to what extent . . .
4. under what conditions . . .
5. by when?

For a better understanding of objectives, it is helpful to compare a poorly written one with a well-stated objective.

Objectives Prepared by a Hospital Social Worker

Poor: Improve responsiveness of social work staff to new referrals.

Good: To conduct at least 80 percent of initial patient or family member interviews within four hours of receiving a referral from a doctor or nurse.

Objectives Prepared by an Administrator of a Big Brother/Big Sister Program

Poor: Obtain more big brothers and big sisters for our children.

Good: To recruit, train, and match 35 new volunteers before August 1.

Objectives Prepared by a Child Welfare Worker

Poor: To enhance the development of parent-child relationships.

Good: To encourage and facilitate parental visitation so that by January 15 at least 70 percent of parents in my caseload visit their children in foster care at least once a month.

When developing an objective, it is important not to confuse *input* with *outcome*. This common error results in statements like "Mr. Jones is to obtain counseling," which describes an input (counseling) but says nothing about the intended outcome. In this example, counseling is presented as an end, but in reality, it is only a means to an end. What is the intended outcome of the counseling? What is the counseling to accomplish? A better statement would be "Mr. Jones will obtain counseling focused on his physical abuse of his son, Johnny, and designed to help him learn to use time out and positive reinforcement as alternatives to harsh spanking and screaming as discipline."

In writing an objective, *positive language* should be used whenever possible; the words used should describe what the client will do, not what the client will not do (e.g., "learn and follow table manners" versus "stop being so messy when eating").

In direct-service work, it is especially important that objectives be formulated in *behavioral language*—using words that describe observable actions in terms of their frequency, duration, and intensity. The following examples do not use behavioral wording:

> Client will work to improve self-esteem.
> Client will look for a job.
> Improve quality of child care.

Such statements are vague and impossible to evaluate. The next examples use behavioral language:

> To greet at least two people per day between June 1 and June 10 with the words "Hi" or "Hello" while smiling and making eye contact.
>
> To submit at least four completed job applications for janitorial work before July 1.
>
> To spend 15 uninterrupted minutes per day reading stories to Bobby while he sits on my lap.

A *timeframe* is an essential part of an objective. In interpersonal helping, for example, an objective should not take more than a few weeks to accomplish. Thus, an objective that would probably take a couple months to accomplish should be broken down into several smaller ones. This is important because the client needs to see evidence of progress. If the client can perceive he or she is making concrete gains (i.e., reaching an objective), even if the steps are small, he or she will feel more hopeful and more motivated to continue.

The concept of *task*, as used by social workers favoring the task-centered approach, is both similar to and different from the concept of objectives, as presented here. Reid (1992) defines a task as a type of problem-solving action, sometimes of a general nature and sometimes highly specific, but always an activity that can be evaluated in terms of whether it was achieved or completed. Still another way of conceptualizing a task is to define it as one of the many highly specific and short-term activities necessary to achieve an objective. Thus, in working toward a single goal, a client may need to achieve several objectives, and in order to achieve objectives, he or she may need to complete numerous tasks (see Figure 13.2).

Generally speaking, an objective is something that a client might achieve in a matter of weeks (e.g., "Learn new methods of discipline with the help of a parent training program"), whereas a task is something that can be completed in a matter of days (e.g., "Call a friend to arrange transportation to the parent training program"). Regardless of the terminology used, the point to remember is that an intervention must have a clear purpose and direction.

**FIGURE 13.2
Relationship
of Goals,
Objectives,
and Tasks**

Objectives are intended to give direction, structure, and relevance to the helping process, but objectives should never stifle the humanness and individualization that are essential ingredients in effective helping. A willingness to revise objectives to meet changing circumstances is critical to effective helping. In summary, a properly developed objective meets the following criteria.

1. It usually starts with the word *to,* followed by an action verb.
2. It specifies a single key result to be accomplished.
3. It specifies a target date for its accomplishment.
4. It is as specific and quantitative as possible and, hence, measurable and verifiable.
5. It is readily understandable by the client and others who will be contributing to or participating in the intervention.
6. It is realistic and attainable but still represents a significant challenge.
7. It is willingly agreed to by both client and worker without pressure or coercion.
8. It is consistent with agency policies and procedures and with the social work *Code of Ethics.*

SELECTED BIBLIOGRAPHY

Pipe, Peter. *Objectives—Tools for Change.* Belmont, Calif.: Fearon, 1975.
Reid, William. *Task Strategies: An Empirical Approach to Clinical Social Work.* New York: Columbia University Press, 1992.

13.5 Written Service Contracts

PURPOSE: To provide direction and focus during intervention.

DISCUSSION: Increasingly, social workers use written service contracts (or service agreements) in their work with clients. The American Public Welfare Association (1979, 82) defines a *service agreement* as "a written document which specifies the behavioral objectives of service and describes, in concrete terms, the actions that will be taken within established time frames to facilitate accomplishment of the objectives. The agreement is signed by all those involved in the service planning process, as appropriate. . . . The agreement constitutes a non-legally binding commitment to pursue mutually agreed-upon goals." While the authors prefer the term *service contract,* other practitioners or agencies may use the terms *service agreement, case plan, treatment plan, intervention plan,* or *individual family support plan* when referring to this document. Often these terms are used interchangeably.

A service contract should answer the following:

- What is the desired outcome of the worker's and/or agency's service to the client?
- What is to be done by the client? By when?
- What is to be done by the client's significant others (family, friends, neighbors, etc.)? By when?
- What is to be done by the worker and other agency staff? By when?
- What services are to be obtained from other agencies? By when?
- What events will trigger a reassessment of the client's situation and/or a revision of the service contract?
- What are the consequences, if any, for not adhering to the plan?

Service contracts should not be confused with *behavioral contracts* (see Item 14.6). The two have similarities but also important differences. A behavioral contract is much more specific and covers a shorter period of time, often a matter of days or, a week or two. The period covered by a service contract may be several months, although it is ordinarily renegotiated and rewritten every three or six months.

Consider the following guidelines on the utilization of written service contracts:

1. Be clear about your agency's policy and legal requirements related to the use of written service contracts. Workers in fields such as child welfare and developmental disabilities will find that written plans are required by law and agency policy. It should be noted that in the fields of child protection and probation it is common for service contracts to be incorporated into a court order. The following statement, taken from a public agency manual concerning the handling of certain cases of child abuse and neglect, is fairly typical of agency policy on written service contracts:

> The tasks of identification, assessment and formulation of treatment recommendations rest primarily with the social worker working with the family. The results of these formulations are set forth in the written treatment plan to advise the parents and the court of the problems identified and the course of action recommended to remedy these problems. The treatment plan should contain the following elements:
>
> - Identification of the problems or conditions which resulted in the abuse or neglect.
> - Treatment goals for the family which address the needs identified and which, when attained, will assure the adequate level of care for the child.
> - Specific treatment objectives, or tasks, which outline in detail the series of steps which must be taken by each member of the household to reach the treatment goals. These objectives should clearly define the separate roles and responsibilities of all of the parties involved in the treatment process. Objectives should clearly state the actions which are necessary, and the time period in which the objective should be ac-

complished. The objectives should be reasonably attainable and designed to fit the capabilities and existing circumstances of the family involved.

2. Understand both the advantages and disadvantages of using written service contracts. A contract can clarify purpose and thereby reduce client-worker conflict, set priorities, delineate roles and responsibilities, and provide an agreed upon means of measuring progress. Reid and Epstein (1977) point out that service contracts are especially important in work with involuntary clients.

> Contracting . . . works best when the client has an active interest in getting help and some notion of what he wants to accomplish. Unfortunately many if not most of the clients of social work do not fall into this category. Forming contracts becomes far more difficult when the client is reluctant to accept the services of a social worker or is uncertain about the nature of his problems or the kind of help he wants. Although contracts are hard to develop with such clients, we would argue that they are even more important with this group. . . . Most important, use of contracts with the unmotivated or uncertain clients provides some assurance that he will not be treated "behind his back" for conditions that have not been made clear to him. (p. 9)

An obvious disadvantage of such contracts is the time required to prepare a clearly written contact. Other problems associated with written contracts include their uncertain legal status, the possibility of concentrating on trivial but easily conceptualized objectives while avoiding complex objectives or ones that require risk taking in order to achieve success, and the danger of powerless clients agreeing to a contract out of a fear of being punished. This later danger is of special concern whenever a contract is written into a court order. Despite these potential problems, Epstein (1992) concludes that written contracts

> can and should be used in the bulk of ordinary practice. However, written contracts should not be viewed as a remedy for all difficulties nor as rigid machinery for pushing a case toward some hard and fast end. If a contract has been agreed upon and put into writing, it represents a degree of commitment to an arrangement worked out between the client and practitioner—a promising basis for positive movement. . . . Without mutual agreement and continuous work, the contract has little force for change. (p. 198)

3. Develop the contract only after a thorough social assessment during which you and the client study and agree on the problems to be tackled. The terms of the contract should be consistent with the client's capacities, the worker's skill, and the agency's mission.

4. By definition, a contract specifies what the client will do and what the worker/agency will do. A contract must never be one-sided and list only that which the worker or agency expects of the client. A written statement that neglects to specify what the worker and agency will do is not a contract at all.

5. The contract should be phrased in simple, clear language so that the client will know exactly what it says. The wording should not confuse or intimidate the client. Avoid legal or social work jargon. It may be necessary to prepare the contract in the client's first language (e.g., Spanish) if he or she has a poor understanding of English. In cases where the client cannot read, the worker should consider recording the agreement on a cassette tape, in addition to preparing a written statement.

6. A contract should be developed in a way that makes success probable without, of course, sacrificing relevance. If the worker believes that the client will be unable to meet the terms of a particular contract, that alone is an indication that its objectives are too ambitious, or the timeframe is too short.

7. The objectives identified in the contract must be realistic and worth achieving from the client's viewpoint. Since the purpose of the contract is to facilitate change, it must focus on behaviors or situations that can, in fact, be changed. Do not waste time on things that are beyond anyone's control.

8. When selecting and formulating objectives, logical sequences must be anticipated and built into the plan. New behaviors may need to be learned in a particular sequence, and some problems must be tackled one step at a time. For example, the client who wants a job must first learn how to complete a job application. (Additional information on goals and objectives is presented in Items 13.1 and 13.4.)

9. Do not do anything for clients that they are able to do for themselves. Sometimes a busy social worker is tempted to do something for a client rather than taking the time to teach or encourage the client to do it himself or herself. Unnecessarily doing things for a client can also occur when a worker is overly eager to be helpful or when the worker overlooks client strengths.

10. Provisions of the contract should be modified as necessary to stay in step with changing realities of the situation. This flexibility is important in maintaining the trust of the client.

SELECTED BIBLIOGRAPHY

American Public Welfare Association. *Standards for Foster Family Services Systems for Public Agencies.* Washington, D.C.: American Public Welfare Association, 1979.

Epstein, Laura. *Brief Treatment and a New Look at the Task-Centered Approach*, 3rd. ed. New York: Macmillan, 1992.

Reid, William, and Laura Epstein. *Task-Centered Practice.* New York: Columbia University Press, 1977.

Rooney, Ronald. *Stratagies for Work with Involuntary Clients.* New York: Columbia University Press, 1992.

13.6 Client Needs List

PURPOSE: To remind the worker and client of concerns and needs that should be addressed in a service contract or case plan.

DISCUSSION: A *needs list* is a tool used to guide case-planning and case-management activities related to a certain category of clients. Basically, it is a checklist that reminds all involved of concerns that should be addressed. Such lists are most often used in work with clients who are highly dependent on the services of social agencies (e.g. the frail elderly, children in foster care, and persons who have a serious developmental disability or mental illness). A needs list is especially useful when the case planning is done by a multidisciplinary and/or multiagency team because potential interagency and interprofessional disagreements must be anticipated and resolved if the plan is to succeed. Those involved in formulating a service plan—including the client—must decide how the needs can best be met and who will be responsible for seeing that they are met.

Figure 13.3 is an example of a needs list used in work with adults who have a developmental disability but are capable of functioning in an independent living situation. Note that the needs on the list are concrete expressions of fundamental human needs, such as:

- *Physical and life-sustaining needs.* The need for food, water, warmth, sexual gratification, elimination of bodily wastes, and so on
- *Physical safety.* The need for protection from physical attack and disease
- *Love.* The need to be cherished, supported, and aided by others
- *Self-esteem.* The need to have a sense of personal worth and value, to respect and value one's self
- *Self-realization.* The need to be creative and productive and to attain worthwhile objectives.

**FIGURE 13.3
Sample
Needs List**

Needs List for Independent Living

1. Housing suitable for client's level of mobility and physical limitations (consider stairs, wheelchair accessibility, etc.)
2. Safe heating and electrical system and usable toilet facilities
3. Home furnishing (chairs, tables, TV, radio, etc.)
4. Bed, blankets, sheets, etc.
5. Clothing for all seasons of the year
6. Food, food storage, stove
7. Telephone or other means of requesting assistance
8. Items needed for food preparation (e.g., utensils, pots, pans)
9. Items needed to maintain personal hygiene (razor, soap, sanitary napkins, etc.)
10. Financial resources/money management system
11. Transportation
12. Medical and dental care
13. Medication and monitoring of dosage, if needed
14. Social contacts and recreational activities
15. Concern and interest shown by family, friends, and neighbors
16. Protection from harm or exploitation
17. Appropriate level of supervision
18. Training (job-related, community, survival skills, etc.)
19. Employment or work-related activity
20. Adaptive aids (e.g., eyeglasses, hearing aids, leg braces, etc.)
21. Therapy and other special treatments (e.g., physical therapy, speech therapy, etc.)
22. Maintenance of cultural and ethnic heritage
23. Participation in spiritual or religious activities
24. Legal assistance

FIGURE 13.4
Sample of
Skills
Needed
by Elderly
Person for
Semi-
Independent
Living

Meal Preparation

- Ability to identify nutritious foods and plan a meal
- Ability to use a stove and other cooking appliances
- Ability to wash dishes and maintain clean kitchen area
- Ability to recognize spoiled or unsafe food items

Personal Safety

- Ability to recognize unsafe behavior or conditions (e.g., lighted stove, smoking in bed, unlocked doors, etc.)
- Ability to call for help (e.g., use phone, contact neighbor, use fire extinguisher, etc.)
- Ability to recognize attempts by others to manipulate, exploit, or cheat

Shopping and Money Management

- Ability to get to store and bring home purchase
- Ability to compare prices and negotiate a purchase
- Ability to count money and make change
- Ability to maintain record of income and expenditures
- Ability to make check deposit

Mobility and Transportation

- Ability to climb stairs, open doors, unlock doors, etc.
- Ability to read a map, find an address, etc.
- Ability to use public transportation (bus, subway, taxi, etc.)

Illness Management

- Ability to recognize signs and symptoms of illness
- Ability to recognize different medications and take prescribed dosage
- Ability to call a doctor or other professional and understand and follow his or her directions

Some social workers and case-planning teams may prefer to use a list that focuses on a client's skills and abilities. Figure 13.4 presents a sampling of items that might be included in a needs list used in assessment, formulating a service plan, and coordinating services for persons who are elderly but able to remain in their own homes if helped to perform selected tasks of self-care and daily living.

SELECTED BIBLIOGRAPHY

Bertsche, Ann, and Charles Horejsi. "Coordination of Client Services." *Social Work* 25 (March 1980): 94–98.

Moxley, David. *The Practice of Case Management.* Newbury Park, Calif.: Sage, 1989.

Rose, Stephen. *Case Management and Social Work Practice.* New York: Longman, 1992.

Rothman, Jack. *Practice With Highly Vulnerable Clients.* Englewood Cliffs, N.J.: Prentice Hall, 1994.

13.7 Making Use of Informal Resources

PURPOSE: To assist the client in identifying and utilizing informal resources.

DISCUSSION: The intervention plan should draw on resources available within the client's social network, such as the extended family, friends, neighbors, church groups, and service organizations. These resources are often termed *informal resources,* as contrasted to *formal resources,* such as agencies, hospitals, and trained professionals. Informal resources can provide emotional support, material assistance (e.g., money, loans, food, housing), physical care (e.g., child care, supervision of frail elderly persons living in their own home), information and referral, and the mediation of interpersonal conflict.

Self-help groups, such as Alcoholics Anonymous and Parents Anonymous, are usually considered to be informal resources, even though they are part of a national organization and may use professionals as advisors. Another important informal resource is the *natural helper,* an individual who has often resided in the community for a long time and is known for his or her ability to help others. An example is the "neighborhood Mom" to whom children gravitate for nurturing, advice, and friendship. Other natural helpers include respected elders, religious leaders, and healers. Another informal resource—one often overlooked by professionals—is other agency clients. Clients can often be of help to each other; however, in some cases, they can also exacerbate each other's problems.

Although informal resources are the oldest and most common form of helping activity, some professionals are reluctant to encourage or assist their clients in using these resources. Possible reasons include the following:

- Traditional education and training in social work and the other helping professions have not given much attention to informal resources. Consequently, social workers perceive professional helpers and formal services as inherently more valuable and more effective than nonprofessionals, regardless of the client's problem or situation.
- Informal helping is often an "invisible" activity. Unless the social worker grew up in a particular neighborhood or community, he or she will have little awareness of the informal network and how to gain access to it.
- It has often been assumed that clients make use of informal resources, as a matter of course. Thus, it was believed that agency clients did not need to be encouraged to explore and make use of informal resources.
- It has been assumed that the client's involvement with a formal resource was a clear indicator that informal resources did not exist for the client or that the client had chosen not to use them.
- The use of informal resources has been judged inappropriate because of the professional's need to protect client confidentiality.

Many people prefer to use informal resources over the formal ones, for several reasons.

■ No stigma is attached to receiving help from an informal resource.
■ Informal helping is available 24 hours a day, seven days a week and at no cost.
■ You do not have to be categorized, labeled, diagnosed, or otherwise meet eligibility requirements in order to secure needed help.
■ Informal helping involves a reciprocal relationship—the give and take among two equals or peers—rather than the expert-client relationship that is part of a professional helping process.

When considering the use of informal resources, the social worker should keep the following guidelines in mind.

1. The goal of practice is to help clients improve their social functioning. The resources used—whether formal, informal, or a mix of both—are simply the means to that end.

2. Informal resources must never be viewed as a panacea or an inexpensive alternative to formal services. Both may be needed and both are important; one should support and supplement the other. A professional should not feel threatened by a client's use of or preference for informal resources.

3. During the assessment and planning phases, the client's social network should always be viewed as a potential source of assistance. The client's relationship—past and present—with relatives, friends, neighbors, churches, and service organizations should be explored to identify possible informal resources that are relevant to the client's current situation. If identified, the advantages and disadvantages of attempting to use the resource need to be discussed. In the final analysis, it is the client who decides which resources, whether informal or formal, he or she will use. Clients may need guidance on how to reach out to an informal resource, establish a relationship, and handle the expectation of reciprocity (see Item 12.4).

4. The ethical and legal codes concerning confidentiality need not be a barrier to the use of informal resources. Most often, the client first approaches the informal resources. Thus, the client is in control of what he or she chooses to reveal. In cases where the social worker needs to talk with an informal resource, he or she must, of course, first secure the client's permission, just as is done when the worker communicates with another professional or agency.

5. Do not attempt to "professionalize" informal resources. Generally, they work best when they are left alone. Efforts to train informal resources in the use of helping skills tend to disrupt the natural helping process.

6. Learn about self-help groups available in your community. You may wish to seek information from the National Self-Help Clearinghouse, 25 W. 43rd Street, Room 620, New York, N.Y. 10036 (212/642-2944).

SELECTED BIBLIOGRAPHY

Gitterman, Alex, and Lawrence Shulman, eds. *Mutual Aid Groups, Vulnerable Populations and the Life Cycle.* New York: Columbia University Press, 1994.

Maguire, Lambert. *Social Support Systems in Practice.* Washington, D.C.: NASW, 1991.

Powell, Thomas, ed. *Working with Self-Help.* Washington, D.C.: NASW, 1990.

13.8   The Small Group as a Resource

PURPOSE: To develop groups that can be a resource to clients.

DISCUSSION: Small groups are an invaluable resource to clients. They can provide a sense of belonging and support, information, new perspectives, awareness that others have similar problems and concerns, role models for learning new behaviors, and opportunities to be helpful to others. Despite these advantages, social workers in many practice settings do not make groups available to their clients. One reason is that some workers presume that clients are not interested in being part of a group. Another reason is the difficulty of bringing several clients together at a convenient time and place. Still another barrier to the use of groups is the erroneous belief that the members of a group must all have the very same problem or concern; such a belief makes it nearly impossible to ever find enough participants for a group. And finally, some workers avoid groups because they fear that they will not be able to handle a group. While it is true that the development and utilization of a group experience can pose some challenges, the authors urge social workers to expand their use of groups in practice.

A group made up of individuals who meet several times and discuss some issue can be expected to move through various *stages of group development:* (1) preaffiliation, (2) power and control, (3) intimacy, (4) differentiation, and (5) separation. It is during the *preaffiliation stage* that members size each other up, consider what they have in common, and decide whether they want to belong to the group. Unless the members feel they have something in common and share the same goals for the group, they will resist further involvement. During this stage, members tend to be dependent on the leader for direction.

During the *power and control stage,* members test each other and the leader and come to a decision of where they fit in the group. They may challenge each other for position and leadership. Also, members tend to challenge the designated leader. At this time, a number of informal rules develop to govern what is and is not acceptable behavior within the group.

As the members get to know each other, they gradually let down their defenses and the group enters the *intimacy stage.* Members recognize and value what they have in common. Next, the group moves to the stage of *differentiation,* wherein differences of opinion and behavior are exhibited but respected and valued. Members begin to understand that each has a life and important roles outside the group and may behave quite differently in other settings. As the life of the group approaches its ending, it enters the *separation stage* and each member must struggle with the loss of meaningful relationships.

For those who want to make a group experience available to their clients, the following guidelines are suggested.

1. Before deciding to form a group, be clear as to its purpose and why it will be of benefit to your clients. Answers to most other questions about forming a group relate directly to the question of purpose and desired outcome.

As a general rule, the more focused and specialized the group's purpose, the better it serves the members. If all members share a common reason for being in the group and all agree on the group's purpose, they will feel more comfortable and better understood in the group and more willing to discuss issues in greater depth.

2. Decide which clients are to be offered the group experience. Some social group workers hold definite beliefs about the mix of personalities they want in the group (e.g., having outgoing and verbal members to offset members who are quiet and shy). Also, some group workers may want to eliminate from consideration those who are reputed to be resistant or uncooperative. However, in many practice settings, the worker does not have the luxury of using detailed selection criteria and must simply select for possible membership those who have a need for a group experience, have some ability to tolerate differences of opinion, and have at least a basic capacity to enter into relationships. Once in the group, a voluntary member should feel free to drop out if he or she feels uncomfortable or if the group is not meeting his or her needs.

When screening or selecting potential members, the group worker must balance the needs of the individual with the needs and safety of other members. Persons exhibiting bizarre or truly dangerous behavior should be eliminated from consideration for membership unless the meetings occur within an institutional setting that provides close supervision. In addition, individuals who are at high risk of suicide and persons who are actively using or selling illegal drugs may not be appropriate for inclusion.

3. It is often not possible to predict accurately how an individual will behave and function as a group member. As a general rule, however, people will behave in a formal group about as they do in other situations. For example, if an individual has difficulty demonstrating warmth or expressing positive feelings with family members, he or she will usually carry these same patterns into the group. Likewise, the person who controls and dominates others at work can be expected to try to dominate and control the group.

4. Decide what is an appropriate group size. Size depends on such factors as the age of the clients, concerns to be addressed by the group, and your experience as a leader or facilitator. You will want the group to be small enough so all members have a sense of belonging and a chance to participate, but large enough to yield a variety of opinions and minimize pressure on those who are fearful of interaction. You will also need to consider the developmental abilities of the members. For preadolescents, a group of only 3 or 4 is often workable. For adolescents, a group of 6 to 10 is preferred. Most adults seem comfortable in a group of about 8 to 10. You must also anticipate the inevitable problem of nonattendance and dropouts. In the beginning, the group must be large enough to continue functioning when some members miss a meeting and after a member or two decides to drop out.

5. Decide on the frequency of meetings and the length of each session. For most adults, a meeting lasting one and one-half to two hours is about right. Because of limited attention span, shorter but more frequent meetings are usually best for children and adolescents. The practice setting will also dictate the frequency of meetings. In an institutional setting, daily meetings are often possible and desirable. When members are drawn from the larger community, it may not be feasible to meet more often than weekly or monthly.

6. Decide when and where the group will meet. A meeting space should be quiet, private, comfortable, and large enough for people to move around and to accommodate a circle of chairs. The decision of when to meet must consider each member's work and family responsibilities and matters of personal convenience.

7. Decide on the approximate number of times the group will meet. This is, of course, tied to purpose. An information sharing or training group might meet only once or twice, whereas a support or therapy group might meet weekly for several months or longer. Consider setting a limit (e.g., 3, 5, or 10 meetings) with the understanding that at the end of that period, you and the group will decide whether the group should continue for a longer period. This can help to keep members involved because they know there is a planned time to terminate and it can prevent a group from continuing to meet even when there is no longer a clear purpose.

8. Decide whether the group will be open or closed to additional members. This is sometimes a decision for the group to make. If it is to be decided by the group, the decision needs to be made during the first or second meeting. Incorporating new members into an already functioning group has the advantage of maintaining group size if some members drop out. Also, new members may bring fresh perspectives. However, the frequent introduction of new members is a barrier to the development of group cohesion and it may limit the intensity of interaction.

9. Decide if the group is for voluntary clients, involuntary clients, or both. Obviously, there are advantages to limiting membership to persons who want to attend. Although involuntary members can be forced by court order to attend, they cannot be forced to interact in a meaningful and productive manner. Nevertheless, the successful utilization of group methods in correctional, chemical dependency, and child abuse treatment programs demonstrates that groups made up of involuntary clients are feasible and can be effective. However, the leader of such groups must be strong and skilled in confronting resistant and manipulative members.

The addition of involuntary members to a basically voluntary group will usually work if the group has been functioning quite well for a time and the involuntary member is willing to cooperate to at least a minimal degree. On the other hand, it is not likely to work if the group is newly formed or has not been functioning well and/or if the involuntary member is highly resistant and disruptive. Before adding a new involuntary member, it is best to wait until the group has reached the intimacy stage. The addition of new members, especially resistant ones, should be avoided during the power and control stage.

10. When extending an invitation to join a group, be prepared to explain how the group will be of benefit, what will happen during the meetings, and the atmosphere you hope to create (e.g., informal, fun, learning, sharing, etc.). Also, be prepared to offer information that might raise interest and reduce fears about participating in a group.

11. As the group moves through the usual stages of development, assess the functioning of each group member and consider the use of various techniques to deal with identified problems (see Item 8.3 and 14.41). The answers to the following questions will help the worker in this assessment.

- Is the member in agreement with the group's purpose and format?
- Is the member personally involved—sharing feelings, opinions, and experiences?
- Does the member attend on a regular basis and participate in discussion or activities?
- Does the member enjoy being with other members?
- Does the member engage in a mix of confrontation and support of others?
- How might the group's activities be modified to address the problems or concerns identified?

12. Be prepared to establish rules (possibly written) to govern the behavior of group members. Possible rules include the following:

- Members are expected to attend all meetings.
- Members are expected to maintain confidentiality.
- Members cannot smoke or do drugs during the meeting.
- Members are not allowed to remain at the meeting if they arrive under the influence of alcohol or drugs.
- Minor-aged members must have parents' written consent to participate.
- Members are to avoid dating and having sexual relationships with other members.
- Members who bring weapons, threaten violence, or engage in sexual harassment will be excluded.

13. Select activities (programs) for each meeting (e.g., introductions, ice breakers, refreshments, structured discussion, free and open discussion, role-play, guest speaker, etc.). These activities should be consistent with the group's overall purpose and encourage the type of activity relevant to the group's stage of development (see Item 14.23).

14. Anticipate how you can handle the numerous practical problems associated with a meeting, such as the room is too hot or cold or too large or small; the leader must miss a meeting; members arrive late; members bring uninvited friends; will there be refreshments and, if so, who pays; conflict between smokers and nonsmokers; who will remind members of next meeting; and so on.

SELECTED BIBLIOGRAPHY

Brown, Leonard. *Groups for Growth and Change.* New York: Longman, 1991.
Garvin, Charles. *Contemporary Group Work.* Englewood Cliffs, N.J.: Prentice Hall, 1987.
Henry, Sue. *Group Skills in Social Work,* 2nd ed. Pacific Grove, Calif.: Brooks/Cole, 1992.
Reid, Kenneth. *Social Work Practice with Groups: A Clinical Perspective.* Pacific Grove, Calif.: Brooks/Cole, 1991.
Rose, Sheldon, and Jeffrey Edleson. *Working with Children and Adolescents in Groups.* San Francisco: Jossey-Bass, 1988.
Toseland, Ronald, and Robert Rivas. *An Introduction to Group Work Practice,* 2nd ed. Boston: Allyn and Bacon, 1995.

SECTION B
TECHNIQUES AND GUIDELINES FOR INDIRECT PRACTICE

As systems become more complex, it becomes increasingly difficult and time consuming to create meaningful change in a system's ways of operating. When working with organizations and communities, the social worker must be constantly aware of the fact that a change in one system will reverberate not only through that system but also through related systems as well. It is especially important, therefore, that change efforts in these large complex systems are carefully planned and that the responsibilities of each actor in the change process are clearly identified.

Much of the planning in work with organizations and communities requires that the social worker is prepared to compare various alternatives for remedying a problem, to determine which alternatives for change will have the most positive outcomes, and to plot the schedule of change activities to make the process as efficient and effective as possible. Another purpose of planning activity involves the delicate task of facilitating the development of interagency collaboration and instituting formal working relationships among human services agencies. The effectiveness of the social worker engaged in both types of planning can be enhanced through use of the techniques discussed here.

13.9　Establishing and Changing Organizations

PURPOSE:　To establish or modify agency goals, policies, and programs.

DISCUSSION:　Social agencies must stake their claim to specific areas of service provision. They must clearly state their mission, the goals they intend to achieve, the services they will provide, and the policies and procedures they will follow. Only then can the public be accurately informed about the nature of the agency, can clients know what services to expect, can unplanned duplication and overlap of services be minimized, and can staff members plan and coordinate their work.

An effective social agency is dynamic; it must constantly adapt to community and societal changes, to new knowledge about the nature of personal and social problems, to changes in public attitudes, and to ever-changing fiscal and political realities. Thus, a social worker can expect to participate, to some degree and at some level, in efforts to modify agency goals, structure, and operations.

Public agencies are particularly reactive to any change in the state and federal laws relevant to their areas of service and to budget modifications. In response to such changes, the agency's own policies and procedures may need to undergo significant change during a short period of time.

Private agencies, too, must be capable of responding to a variety of forces. When a private agency is created, the bylaws spell out its mission and decision-making structure. Although the original bylaws may capture the intent of the founders, such agencies must change over time to keep pace with changing community needs and new concepts of service. Leadership for needed change by a private agency often falls first to the executive director and the staff, with the board and/or a broader membership group subsequently amending the bylaws to reflect the proposed changes.

Although change is inevitable, an agency, like all social systems, will resist change; in fact it may take considerable effort to make needed change. The following guidelines suggest several factors to consider when planning and initiating organizational change.

1. Begin by describing as precisely as possible the change that is needed and why. Then secure and study all documents that may pertain to the desired change. These may include, for example, federal and state laws and regulations, administrative and personnel manuals, union contracts, accreditation standards, agreements and contracts involving other agencies, agreements with national parent organizations, and so on. The information drawn from these sources will determine, to some degree, what changes are possible, how the change process must proceed, and who else must support or approve the change.

2. Assess the organization's readiness for change. Review its prior experience in accepting change. The people of an organization are likely to resist change if prior change efforts have been misguided, ineffective, or frustrating. On the other hand, they will tend to accept change if they trust those promoting or leading the change effort, when they believe the proposed change is needed and feasible, and when the proposal has addressed their questions, concerns, and fears about changing.

3. Determine if the desire for change is shared across the various levels, departments, and units of the organization. Pay special attention to the views of those who will be affected most directly by the proposed change. A common and serious error in planning change is to overlook or disregard the opinions of line workers and clerical staff—those who may know most about how the proposed change will impact on day-to-day agency operations and on agency clients.

4. Assess the degree to which the change is compatible with the agency's mission, traditions, and current goals. Determine the degree to which the change is desired and supported by top management and the board of directors.

5. Use a Force Field Analysis (see Item 12.31) to identify and assess the relative strength of the organizational subsystems and individuals who are likely to favor the change and those who will oppose it. Determine who stands to gain and who stands to be hurt by the proposed change. The strategy most likely to overcome resistance is one that either (a) increases the power of those within the agency that favor the change or (b) introduces new resources into the organization that will minimize the impact of the change on those who are resistant.

6. The agency, or a unit of the agency, is most likely to adopt a proposed change if it can be shown that the change will result in an increase in scope, authority, autonomy, or funds and other resources. A change that decreases power and resources will be resisted. People will favor a change that makes their work easier; they will resist a change that makes their work more complex or demands more of their time.

7. The members of an organization will strongly resist a change that they perceive as a threat to their jobs, advancement, or opportunities within the organization. Also, they will be resistant to change whenever they suspect others are withholding information about the true intentions of the change.

8. An organization will be more open to a proposed change if it can be demonstrated that other similar organizations have successfully made this change.

9. A change is most likely to be accepted by the organization after its advantages have been demonstrated in a trial run or as a demonstration project within only a part of the organization. Thus, it is desirable that the first phase of a more far-reaching change effort begin by focusing on a problem or situation of limited scope. It might, for example, involve a specific program, activity, or unit of the agency and should be achievable in a three-month period. Subsequent efforts would then deal with more complex changes. It is advisable to start small and then, by building on success, gradually widen the scope of the change effort.

10. Whenever possible, changes should be integrated into current structures and procedures so as to minimize the disruption of existing relationships and patterns.

SELECTED BIBLIOGRAPHY

Dalziel, Murray, and Stephen Schoonover. *Changing Ways: A Practical Tool for Implementing Change within Organizations.* New York: American Management Institute, 1988.

Frey, Gerald A. "A Framework for Promoting Organizational Change." *Families in Society* (March 1990): 142–147.

Gummer, Burton. *The Politics of Social Administration: Managing Organizational Politics in Social Agencies.* Englewood Cliffs, N.J.: Prentice Hall, 1990.

Kettner, Peter, John M. Daley, and Ann Weaver Nichols. *Initiating Change in Organizations and Communities.* Monterey, Calif.: Brooks/Cole, 1985.

Netting, F. Ellen, Peter M. Kettner, and Steven L. McMurty. *Social Work Macro Practice.* New York: Longman, 1993.

Rothman, Jack, John L. Erlich, and Joseph G. Teresa. *Changing Organizations and Community Programs.* Beverly Hills: Sage, 1981.

Weinbach, Robert. *The Social Worker as Manager,* 2nd ed. Boston: Allyn and Bacon, 1994.

13.10   The Process of Agency Planning

PURPOSE: To formulate plans to guide an agency's operations and to maximize its performance.

DISCUSSION: In order to operate in an effective and efficient manner and to grow and develop as an organization, a social agency must formulate both short-range and long-range plans that will guide its ongoing activity and decision making. All too often, agencies neglect long-term planning and then find that they must make hasty decisions and rapid changes in agency operations in response to a situation or crisis they did not anticipate and for which they were unprepared.

Ideally, an agency's planning process is proactive and forward looking. The plan it constructs will therefore be a truly useful and accurate description of how it will utilize its resources (i.e., staff time, money, knowledge, skills, etc.), how it can capitalize on its strengths and opportunities, how it will correct its weaknesses, and how it can respond to certain unwanted but possible future events such as a lawsuit, increased demand for service, loss of staff, or a reduction in funding.

A fruitful planning process is complex and time consuming. It can be especially difficult because all planning decisions rest on a set of predictions as to what will happen in future months and years. Unfortunately, few agencies are able to predict accurately the ever-changing political, economic, and public opinion forces that may impact on agency operation. Given the reality of constant community and societal change, only three things are known about the future.

- The future will be different from the past.
- The future is difficult to predict.
- Future changes will occur faster than ever before.

Given these uncertainties, even the best of plans must be constantly reviewed and revised.

Despite all the challenges inherent in planning, an agency must devote time and energy to this activity. Broadly speaking, there are three types of planning processes: (1) problem-solving planning, (2) operational planning, and (3) strategic planning. They differ primarily in terms of the time period covered.

Problem-solving planning has a life span of 60 to 90 days. It focuses on some specific problem that is having an adverse effect on the agency's usual activity. The process involves (1) identifying and examining the problem, (2) selecting a set of corrective actions or measures, (3) planning the implementation of these measures, and (4) monitoring the effectiveness of the corrective action. If the agency is successful in its operational and strategic planning (discussed next), the need for problem-solving planning will be minimized.

Operational planning refers to short-range planning covering a period of 6 to 12 months or perhaps one budget cycle. This planning process formulates objectives, details performance standards, and prepares an action plan to reach the stated objectives.

Strategic planning may cover a period of 3 to 10 years. Basically, the strategic planning process strives to develop a plan for achieving the agency's mission or long-term goals. This type of planning calls for the identification and analysis of broad social and economic trends, for speculation on what challenges and opportunities the agency will face in several years, and for creativity in deciding how best to use agency resources. Strategic planning is based on the belief that it is important to have a plan that considers all conditions and factors that may significantly impact the agency, regardless how uncertain the future must be. Because it is so speculative and based on so many uncertain variables, a strategic plan must be revised if there are unexpected changes in the internal or external environment.

Adherence to the following guidelines will enhance the planning process.

1. Make certain that adequate and accurate data are readily available to those engaged in the planning process. Such data should describe:
   - The agency's mission and goals
   - Current and projected budgets and a history of the agency's fiscal condition
   - Programs and services provided and the number of clients/consumers participating in each program or service area
   - Characteristics of the persons served by the agency (e.g., age, income, ethnicity, religion, etc.)
   - Profile of the agency staff (e.g., education, training, interests, skills, etc.)
   - The agency's relationship with other agencies in community
   - Requests and concerns voiced by staff
   - Requests and concerns voiced by clients/consumers and other agencies and community groups
   - Trends and projections (i.e., demands for services, capacity to raise funds, demographic changes in community)
   - Special problems faced by the agency

2. Keep the planning process as simple as possible so that all those who should participate can do so despite the day-to-day pressures of their other responsibilities. Do not demand more of their time than is absolutely necessary. Keep the number of meetings and the paperwork requirement to a minimum.

3. Make sure that all who might be impacted by a decision or proposed change are invited to participate in the discussion and encouraged to voice their thoughts and concerns. It is critically important to avoid "top-down planning" (i.e., decision-making and planning by only the upper level administrative personnel).

4. Gather and organize ideas and promote creativity by performing a SWOPA analysis of the agency. The acronym *SWOPA* stands for Strengths, Weaknesses, Opportunities, Problems, and Action.

- *Strengths.* Identify the services, programs, and activities currently provided at a level of quality that meets or exceeds professional standards.
- *Weaknesses.* Identify the services, programs, and activities that fall below acceptable levels of quality or needed levels of quantity.
- *Opportunities.* Identify the service or program activities that are promising for development or expansion because of a favorable environment, growing demand, available funding, staff interest, and so on.
- *Problems.* Identify the areas of agency performance that are especially troublesome.
- *Actions.* Identify the possible activities or changes that would build on agency strengths, exploit opportunities, address areas of weakness, or better manage the problems faced by the agency.

5. Perform a *competition analysis.* This requirement asks those participating in the planning process to examine the activities of other agencies, organizations, or professional groups to determine if they present a threat to the agency's current programs and services. For example, are other organizations developing services that would attract your agency's clients or staff or are other agencies making requests for the funds now utilized by your agency?

6. Perform a *stakeholder's analysis.* As used here, stakeholders are those individuals, groups, or organizations that have an interest in the agency. Their beliefs, values, and possible reactions to changes in the agency must be given serious consideration. Examples of *internal* stakeholders are clients/consumers, agency staff, unions representing staff, members of the board of directors, and so on. Examples of *external* stakeholders include professional associations, politicians, other agencies, businesses and corporations, local newspapers, citizen groups, taxpayers, contributors, former clients, and the like.

7. Perform a *threat analysis.* A threat is some possible future circumstance or action by others that could harm the agency. Examples might include a lawsuit against the agency, an employee strike, loss of funding, loss of key staff, rapid change in community demographics, significant changes in the laws or regulations that impact the agency, damaging news stories, and so forth.

8. Make sure that the many facets of the planning process are coordinated and well integrated. For example, decisions concerning budget, staffing patterns, performance standards, and the programs and services to be offered are all interrelated. In particular, financial planning must be incorporated into all other areas of planning. If the many components of the process are not properly coordinated and integrated, much time will be wasted, much confusion will occur, and the planning process will be doomed to failure.

SELECTED BIBLIOGRAPHY

Kettner, Peter M., Robert M. Moroney, and Lawrence L. Martin. *Designing and Managing Programs: An Effectiveness-Based Approach.* Newbury Park, Calif.: Sage, 1990.
Rapp, Charles, and John Poertner. *Social Administration: A Client-Centered Approach.* New York: Longman, 1992.
Weinbach, Robert. *The Social Worker as Manager,* 2nd ed. Boston: Allyn and Bacon, 1994.

13.11 Project Planning and Evaluation

PURPOSE: To plan, coordinate, and schedule project activities.

DISCUSSION: The introduction of a new service or special project into the day-to-day operation of a social agency can be a disruptive experience unless it is carefully planned and integrated to the life of the organization. Efficient planning of new activities involves selecting the most effective strategy for accomplishing objectives, scheduling activities to maximize efficiency, and carefully planning the manner in which tasks are completed so as not to disrupt other parts of the agency.

Strategy Selection

Achieving the goals and objectives of a new project calls for the selection of the best possible course of action or strategy from among available alternatives. Craig (1978) identifies five criteria that should be considered in this selection.

1. *Appropriateness.* Is this strategy consistent with the agency's overall mission and goals? Is it consistent with the agency's experience and usual methods and standards of operation? Does the use of this strategy raise any legal or ethical concerns?
2. *Effectiveness.* Given the nature of the problem or issue being addressed by the project, is this strategy likely to be successful?
3. *Efficiency.* Given the agency's current resources (e.g., funding, available staff time, expertise), is this strategy an efficient use of those resources?
4. *Adequacy.* Are the actions called for by this strategy ones that will have a real and lasting impact on the problem or issues to be addressed by the project?
5. *Side effects.* What positive and negative side effects could result from using this strategy?

By charting each alternative according to these five criteria, it is possible to compare the advantages and disadvantages of each. Table 13.1 is an example of a chart that might be developed to compare strategies for increasing the number of minorities and women on the staff of a human services agency.

TABLE 13.1   Example of an Alternative Comparison Chart

Objective: To create a process for recruiting and promoting minorities and women that has the support of employee unions and minority/women's groups

Strategy	Appropriate *Yes/No/Maybe*	Adequacy *Hi/Med/Low*	Effectiveness *Hi/Med/Low*	Efficiency *Hi/Med/Low*	Side Effect *Good/Bad*
A. Develop task force of employees and advocates to write Affirmative Action plan.	Maybe	Hi	Hi	Med (probable benefits high, so is cost)	*Good*—precedent for better decision-making process. *Bad*—too much citizen involvement; time consuming
B. Ask for suggestions first, then circulate plan, ask for comments.	Yes	Med	Med	Hi (probable benefits high, cost not so high)	*Good*—precedent for more input in decision making. *Bad*—hostility if we don't adopt their comments.
C. Write plan, then circulate for comments.	Yes	Low	Low	Med (probable benefits low, but so is cost)	*Good*—avoid direct confrontation *Bad*—plan may not have real support.
D. Copy plan from another city where it was implemented without conflict.	Maybe	Low	Low	Low (low cost, but low benefit too)	*Good*—maybe no one would know we'd done a plan. *Bad*—plan might never be used.

Source: Craig 1978, p. 52. A Learning Concepts Publication, distributed by University Associates, San Diego.

Scheduling

A variety of techniques have been developed to help schedule specific project activities. One frequently used scheduling tool is the **Gantt chart.** This chart provides a visual means of depicting the relationship between the activities required for a project and the time frame for completing each. The activities are listed down the left column and the periods of work on each activity, charted by month or week, are across the top of the page (see Figure 13.5). The usefulness of a Gantt chart is that it helps to identify the sequencing required for the entire project and helps to keep track of the completion dates for specific activities.

The Program Evaluation and Review Technique (**PERT chart**) is a second useful scheduling tool. This chart is especially helpful for sorting out the proper sequencing of events and estimating the amount of time required to complete each

**FIGURE 13.5
Sample
Gantt Chart**

Activity

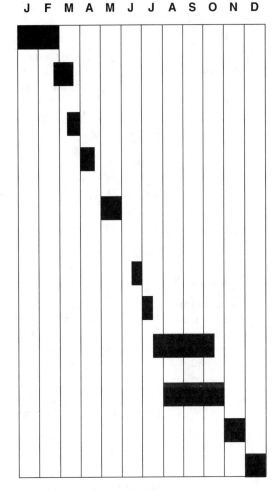

1. Collect literature on parent-effectiveness training.

2. Secure permission to initiate parent-effectiveness training group from supervisor.

3. Interpret parent-effectiveness training in staff meeting.

4. Request all workers in unit to nominate families for parent-effectiveness training.

5. Send letters to nominated families, inviting them to participate and asking for preference on which night to meet.

6. Set meeting times, reserve room, and notify families of first meeting.

7. Make day-care plans for children of the participants.

8. Prepare presentations and materials for parent-effectiveness training sessions.

9. Hold 12 weekly meetings with participants.

10. Assess the value of the sessions to the participants.

11. Report results to supervisor and other staff members.

activity or event. When developing a PERT chart, an *activity* is defined as requiring staff time to complete. Thus, by adding up the days or hours devoted to the various activities, it is possible to estimate the cost in staff time to carry out the project. An *event* is an action taken by someone other than staff on a target date that affects the timeline of the project. By first identifying the dates on which various events are likely to be completed and then charting the activities that must occur to prepare for each event, it is possible to start with the intended completion date for the project and work backwards to build the PERT chart. Figure 13.6 illustrates a section of a PERT chart developed for a client survey regarding the effectiveness of an agency's services.

FIGURE 13.6   Sample PERT Chart for Client Survey Proposal

Task Planning

A final step in completing a special project is to identify and carry out the activities required to implement the strategy that has been selected. This activity involves identifying the tasks to be completed and the rationale for engaging in this activity, noting when it must be completed and who should be involved, and specifying the time or other resources required for completing the task. Table 13.2 is an example of a chart that might be developed for this purpose when establishing a task force.

SELECTED BIBLIOGRAPHY

Brody, Ralph. *Problem Solving: Concepts and Methods for Community Organization.* New York: Human Services Press, 1982.

Craig, Dorothy. *Hip Pocket Guide to Planning and Evaluation.* San Diego: University Associates, 1978.

Schaefer, Morris. *Implementing Change in Service Programs: Project Planning and Management.* Newbury Park, Calif.: Sage, 1987.

TABLE 13.2   Example of a Task Planning Sheet

Staff Member: Personnel Manager

Strategy: Form task force to develop Affirmative Action Plan

Activity: Get agreement of members to serve on task force

Tasks	Why?	When?	Who?	Resources?
1. List key groups and potential task force members.	Make sure all possibilities are considered.	Jan. 3	Self	3 hrs.
2. Go over list with department director and agree on whom to approach.	Get director's perspective and approval.	Jan. 4	Self and director	2 hrs.
3. Review overall strategy with department director.	Make sure we're on same wavelength, confirm commitment to strategy.	Jan. 4	Self, director, and key clerical staff	same meeting as #2
4. Arrange meetings with some potential members for preliminary discussion.	Person-to-person, informal approach most likely to succeed.	Jan 15–22	Self and potential members	6 hrs.
5. Etc.				

Source: Craig 1978, p. 80. A Learning Concepts Publication, distributed by University Associates, San Diego.

13.12   Decision Trees

PURPOSE: To examine alternative choices for improving agency functioning or strengthening human services programs.

DISCUSSION: To remain viable in a changing society, human services agencies must regularly make decisions about how to adjust their programs and methods of operation to better serve community needs. These decisions must be made carefully and social workers should be prepared to assist the agencies in making the best choices from the available alternatives.

A *decision* is the outcome of a process whereby a choice is made regarding how to solve a problem or achieve a desired goal (Gibson, Ivancevich, and Donnelly 1988). Most decisions made in human service agencies are in-house decisions regarding ways to make the agency more efficient or effective. For example, decisions must be made regarding what information to collect on the agency's intake form or what content to include in a volunteer training program. These decisions are typically made by middle-level managers, supervisors, and direct-service practitioners. Other decisions are more far reaching and represent the agency's efforts to make a major change in direction or respond to a unique need or opportunity. Such decisions might include responding to another agency's request to provide collaborative services in a low-income neighborhood or to terminate a program. The latter decisions are typically made by top-level management, boards, and/or legislators.

Both types of decisions can have an important impact on clients and the services they receive from the agency. Such decisions must be made carefully following a study process that involves the clear explication of the problems or issues of concern, the collection and assessment of relevant data, the selection of the best plan of action, the implementation of that plan, and the evaluation of the results with the recognition that if the desired result is not achieved the change should be modified or rescinded. One technique that reveals the likely implications of selecting various alternatives is the decision tree.

A *decision tree* diagrams the choices available in a given situation, forces a projection of possible events that may lead to differing outcomes, and helps explicate the payoffs from each choice. A decision tree can be applied as a relatively simple tool for visually listing possible actions for achieving a desired goal, identifying obstacles to those actions, and then considering countermeasures to overcome the obstacles. Decision trees can also be quite sophisticated using various weighting systems regarding the probability of outcomes, the cost effectiveness of various choices, and the possible impact of risk factors. In the work of most social workers, the more simple decision trees are likely to be used.

Following are the basic steps in developing a decision tree.

Step 1   *State the goal.* For example, determine the value of creating a home visitation program staffed by volunteers.

Step 2   *Identify possible obstacles.* Select approximately three significant impediments to reaching the goal. In the example of the home visitation program, these might be (1) difficulty in recruiting a sufficient pool of qualified people, (2) difficulty in finding time and resources to train the volunteers, and (3) difficulty in providing for the personal safety of volunteers when they visit homes.

Step 3   *Identify countermeasures* (i.e., ways or methods of overcoming obstacles identified in Step 2). In relation to Obstacle 2 in Step 2, for example, countermeasures might be (a) hire a new staff member to develop a training curriculum and offer it to the volunteers, (b) release a staff member from current responsibilities to develop and provide training, or (c) contract for the training from a nearby university.

Step 4   *Identify obstacles that may be needed to overcome each countermeasure.* Regarding countermeasure (a) in Step 3, for example, obstacles might be (i) difficulty of securing funds for a new staff member and (ii) inability to recruit a staff member competent to develop this training curriculum.

**FIGURE 13.7
Illustration
of a Decision
Tree**

Essentially, a decision tree diagrams the analytic process set in motion by the preceding steps. In Figure 13.7, the path of arrows reflects the branches of the partial decision tree described here. The tree can branch indefinitely, but usually after four or five steps are completed, the most viable options will emerge. If each obstacle and countermeasure is fully developed, a thorough assessment of the implications for each option can be made and the quality of the decision-making process enhanced.

SELECTED BIBLIOGRAPHY

Delp, Peter, Arne Thesen, Juzar Motiwalla, and Neelakantan Seshadri. *System Tools for Project Planning.* Bloomington: Indiana University, International Development Institute, 1977.
Gibson, James L., John M. Ivancevich, and James H. Donnelly, Jr. *Organizations: Behavior, Structure, and Processes*, 6th ed. Homewood, Ill.: BPI/IRWIN, 1988.

13.13   Interagency Coordination and Collaboration

PURPOSE: To improve services to clients through the exchange and sharing of agency resources.

DISCUSSION: It is useful to visualize the relationships among agencies as existing on a continuum, potentially ranging from competition to collaboration.

competition ↔ cooperation ↔ coordination ↔ collaboration

When in *competition* with other agencies, an agency engages in actions necessary to secure and hold on to the financial resources and the community and political support it needs to continue operation. It does not share resources or information with other agencies because doing so might place it at a disadvantage in the competition. Mattessich and Monsey (1992) distinguish between cooperation, coordination, and collaboration:

Cooperation is characterized by informal relationships that exist without any commonly defined mission, structure, or planning effort. Information is shared as needed, and authority is retained by each organization. . . . Resources are [kept] separate, as are rewards.

Coordination is characterized by more formal relationships and understanding of compatible missions. Some planning and division of roles are required, and communication channels are established. Authority still rests with the individual organizations. . . . Resources are available to participants and rewards are mutually acknowledged.

Collaboration connotes a more durable and pervasive relationship. Collaborations bring previously separated organizations into a new structure with full commitment to a common mission. Such relationships require comprehensive planning and well defined communication channels operating on many levels. Authority is determined by the collaborative structure. Risk is much greater because each member contributes its own resources and reputation. Resources are pooled or jointly secured and the [rewards] are shared. (p. 39)

Although most agencies speak to the importance of working together, a number of factors keep them from doing so. These include the following:

- Competition is significant for scarce resources, especially when organizational or program survival depends on securing money that could be allocated to other agencies.
- Categorical funding and other restrictions on how funds can be spent make it difficult to share resources or assign them to some new purpose.
- An overburdened and underfunded service system severely limits the staff time and resources available for planning and implementing complex cooperative or collaborative activities.
- The desire for agency and professional status and power create "turf" problems that are barriers to cooperation, conflict resolution, and planning.
- Differences in agency philosophies, values, and practice frameworks become barriers to agreement on a common purpose and approach.

Indeed, finding ways to work together can be a challenge because each agency has its own special mission and constituency, its own policies and procedures, and its own restrictions on how its funds and staff time may be used. Despite these difficulties, coordination and collaboration are both necessary and possible. Here are some examples.

- *Purchase of services.* One agency contracts with another to provide certain services; for example, a public agency purchases group home services from a private agency.
- *Joint budgeting.* Two or more agencies commit a portion of their budgets to a specific activity, often for the purpose of creating the match needed to secure a grant.
- *Joint funding.* Two or more agencies pool their funds to achieve an objective beyond the reach of a single agency.
- *Joint studies.* Two or more agencies fund and or conduct research or a needs assessment desired by both.
- *Centralized information processing.* Two or more agencies share data-processing systems used in recordkeeping, program planning, grant management, or case management.
- *Public relations.* There is joint planning and dissemination of publicity and information about agency programs and community needs.
- *Procedural integration.* Two or more agencies adopt a uniform system of recordkeeping, utilize the same intake forms, use the same computer program, and so on as ways of facilitating interagency communication, program planning, or the evaluation of services.
- *Shared program evaluation resources.* Several agencies hire a specialist to examine their interagency coordination or conduct evaluations of individual programs.
- *Centralized information and referral.* Several agencies operate and fund a centralized service needed to guide clients to the proper agency.
- *Interagency coordination of client services.* Several agencies agree to exchange information and share in the decision making necessary for case management, case coordination, the handling of grievances by clients, and so on.
- *Sharing of special services.* Several agencies pool resources in order for all to gain access to outside consultants, case assessments by specialists, transportation for clients, or needed staff training.
- *Standards and guidelines.* Several agencies jointly develop standards of service quality or staff performance.
- *Loaner staff.* A staff person with special expertise from one agency is "loaned" to another for a special project.
- *Outstationing of staff.* A staff member from one agency is housed in another agency in order to more easily reach certain clients or to better achieve interagency coordination of services.
- *Volunteer bureaus.* Several agencies share in the recruitment and training of the volunteers needed by the individual agencies.

Several preconditions are beneficial to successful interagency coordination and collaboration.

- A prior history of these agencies working together exists, as do mutual trust and respect.

- There is clear support for interagency cooperation and collaboration by the media or others who shape community opinion and by the decision makers who control the resources needed by the agencies.
- The group planning the cooperative or collaborative effort includes representatives from each agency and each segment of the community who will be affected by these activities.
- The agencies really understand each others' goals, values, methods of operation, and the clients/consumers served by each agency.
- Key administrators and participants know and trust each other and communicate clearly
- The staff of each agency involved truly believe that working together is in their self-interest.
- Agencies enter into a written agreement that specifies their roles, rights, and responsibilities in their joint activities (see Item 13.14).
- Agencies agree on concrete and attainable goals and objectives, but ones that are at least partially different from those held by each agency individually.
- Sufficient funds or in-kind contributions and staff time are available to support the needed effort and activity.
- At least one energetic, inspiring, and highly motivated individual is committed to making the collaborative arrangement work.

Those wishing to promote interagency coordination and collaboration should consider the following guidelines.

1. Carefully examine your agency's purpose and programs and its funding base in an effort to identify those areas of service or activity that require a competitive strategy and those areas that offer an opportunity for coordination and collaboration.

2. Identify the new programs or services that you want to see developed but that are beyond your own agency's capability, yet might be possible if several agencies worked together and shared resources. Bring together representatives from all the agencies that might be interested in discussing the idea of pooling resources in order to reach a goal that is desired by all but is beyond the reach of each agency acting alone. Identify how all these agencies and their clients stand to benefit.

3. Conduct the research necessary to answer the many fiscal, administrative, legal, organizational, and staffing questions that will arise in discussions of coordination and collaboration. Obtain information on how similar agencies in other communities have successfully addressed these issues.

4. Recognize that coordination and collaboration activities involve some degree of risk for your organization and for all others involved. Before entering any serious discussions or negotiations on how agencies might share resources, each one must be clear as to what resources it can and cannot afford to give up or reallocate.

5. Assemble a team of agency representatives that have the authority to sanction and plan the coordination or collaboration activity. It is critically important that this team secure suggestions and guidance from all of those affected by this plan and from those who will be expected to carry out its provisions.

6. Sign an agreement that describes in detail the goals and objectives of the planned activity and the rights and responsibilities of each agency affected. Included in the agreement is a plan for monitoring and evaluating the activity and making necessary improvements.

SELECTED BIBLIOGRAPHY

Gray, Barbara. *Collaborating.* San Francisco: Jossey-Bass, 1989.

Haeuser, Adrienne. *Factors Influencing Successful Collaboration: Examples from the NCCAN Prevention Consortium Projects.* Chicago: National Committee to Prevent Child Abuse, 1994.

Mattessich, Paul, and Barbara Monsey. *Collaboration: What Makes It Work—A Review of Research Literature on Factors in Successful Collaboration.* St. Paul, Minn.: Amherst H. Wilder Foundation, 1992.

Rossi, Robert, Kevin Gilmartin, and Charles Dayton. *Agencies Working Together.* Newbury Park, Calif.: Sage, 1982.

Winer, Michael, and Karen Ray. *Collaboration Handbook.* St. Paul, Minn.: Amherst H. Wilder Foundation, 1994.

13.14 Using Protocol Statements

PURPOSE: To improve service to clients through the use of protocol statements that specify the responsibilities of participating agencies.

DISCUSSION: When two or more agencies are involved in a particular case or other practice activity, it is critical to the well-being of the client that each clearly understands its own responsibilities and those of others involved. Increasingly, agencies formalize such relationships by using protocol statements. A ***protocol*** is a concise, written description of the steps to be taken by a professional or agency in a situation where mistakes or omissions can have serious negative consequences. Levy (1980) explains the use of protocols by hospital social workers as follows:

> The protocols are designed to ensure consistent and complete provision and documentation of social work services. Separate protocols have been developed for the specific types of social work problems encountered at the medical center. Each protocol lists the necessary steps in social work intervention for a particular problem. Both the appropriate intervention process and the necessary documentation are indicated by the protocol; that is, the social worker is to perform each activity listed and also document those activities for which documentation is required. (p. 21)

The following excerpts are from a 13-step protocol developed by Bertsche, Francetich, and Horejsi (1985) for use in a state child protective services agency during the investigative phase of child sexual abuse cases. The key actors in this example are Child Protective Services (CPS), law enforcement, and the County Attorney's Office (prosecutor). Because criminal prosecution of the offender is common in sexual abuse cases, it is critical that these three agencies understand who is responsible for specific activities and know the preferred sequence of activities.

Protocol: Child Sexual Abuse Investigation

1. *Receive Referral* (i.e., report of alleged abuse)
   - CPS social worker speaks with referral source if possible. Obtain specifics (i.e., location of alleged incident, quotations from child). Make collateral contacts such as: individuals with knowledge of the sexual abuse as mentioned by referral source; school; doctors or other medical information sources; and the police department to discover if the offender named has a past arrest record for sexual molestation.
   - Contact County Attorney and advise of referral and that it will be investigated. If County Attorney is not available, a message left with the secretary.

2. *Interview with Child* CPS worker conducts interview with the child but obtains only enough information to determine that, most likely, abuse has occurred. Interview will be conducted in a manner appropriate to the developmental level of the child.

3. *Assessment* Based on information gathered from the child in Step 2, worker assesses need for:
   - Emergency placement.
   - Medical exam (non-offending parent may arrange this if parent believes and is supportive of child).
   - Action concerning other siblings in the home.

4. *County Attorney/CPS Consultation* CPS worker advises the County Attorney of action taken thus far. In conjunction with County Attorney, CPS worker arranges formal interview using one of the following:
   - Social worker and mental health therapist.
   - Social worker and law enforcement representative.
   - Any combination determined to be most appropriate.

5. *Formal Interview* (In some instances the non-offending parent is interviewed first, and if supportive of child, is present at the formal interview but seated behind the child.)
   - The interview is conducted in the manner determined most appropriate by the social worker and County Attorney. Emphasis should be on making this interview as non-threatening and non-traumatic for child as possible.
   - A tape recorder supported by written notes will suffice, if video equipment is not available. There should be two methods of recording used in case one malfunctions. Once taken, the report (tape, film, notes, etc.) forms evidence and needs to be appropriately protected. (Usually the Sheriff's Office or Police Department maintains the tapes.)

6. *Interview with Non-Offending Parent(s)* In this interview the worker assesses the non-offending parent's ability to protect the child from further abuse, the level of support for the child, and the need for out-of-home placement. If alleged offender is present, he/she is told that the referral will be made to law enforcement. (pp. 2.1–2.3)

The other steps in this 13-step protocol are (7) "Request for Legal Action Via Civil Court (when appropriate)," (8) "Separation of Alleged Offender from Child," (9) "Interview with Offender," (10) "Follow-Up," (11) "Prosecution," (12) "Ongoing Casework," and (13) "Treatment Plan."

SELECTED BIBLIOGRAPHY

Bertsche, Jon, Sherry Francetich, and Charles Horejsi. *Protocol Notebook for Child Welfare Workers.* Missoula: University of Montana, Department of Social Work, 1985.

Horejsi, Charles, Jon Bertsche, Sherry Francetich, Bill Collins, and Russell Francetich. "Protocols in Child Welfare." *Child Welfare* 66 (September/October 1987): 423–431.

Levy, Louis. "An Integrated Data Management System for Social Service." *Quality Review Bulletin* 6 (October 1980): 20–25.

14 Intervention and Monitoring

INTRODUCTION

Once the client and social worker have agreed on a plan intended to address the client's concern and bring about some specified change, they enter into a phase termed *intervention and monitoring*. During this phase, they strive to implement their plan of action. The concept of monitoring coupled with intervention is used because the worker is constantly observing the client's response to the change process and assessing whether there is progress toward the agreed upon objectives. If progress is lacking, the worker suggests needed modifications in the intervention plan and may reopen discussions on the nature of the client's concern or problem and how best to address it.

It should be noted that the authors' decisions concerning the placement of certain techniques and guidelines in this or another chapter are somewhat arbitrary. For example, the use of a single-subject design or task achievement scaling that are described in Chapter 15 (see Items 15.1 and 15.3) may be used to monitor client progress. Also, some of the assessment tools included in Chapter 12 lend themselves to a monitoring function. Likewise, such activities as the referral process described in Item 11.3 and the problem search discussed in Item 13.2 could logically be classified as interventions.

SECTION A

TECHNIQUES AND GUIDELINES FOR DIRECT PRACTICE

The direct-service techniques included in this section of the chapter have been drawn from several theoretical orientations. This is consistent with the authors' belief that the social worker must look to many sources for ideas and helping techniques that can be applied in diverse practice situations.

Regardless of what specific techniques are used to help the client, the social worker should remember certain *dos and don'ts of helping people*.

1. Helping is not the sterile application of techniques. Rather, it is a very human struggle. Be willing to participate in that struggle.

2. Remember that your job is to facilitate problem solving. You are to help the client search for a solution with which he or she can live. In a great many cases, the solution your client chooses will not be the one you would choose for yourself.

3. Problem solving is not solution given by a professional. To the contrary, problem solving is mostly a search and a process of considering options and making decisions; each client must struggle with problems in his or her own unique way. The solution to a client's problem must grow out of his or her own values, belief system, and usual methods of coping with life.

4. A client is only motivated to change that which he or she perceives to be a real problem. The individual is motivated to work on a problem only when he or she feels hopeful that a solution is possible. No matter what you want for your client, it is only what he or she wants that makes change possible.

5. Remember that your client's behavior is always purposeful. Even dysfunctional behavior serves a purpose by meeting a need or mitigating some conflict or other problem—often a problem you know nothing about.

6. View your client holistically and in context. People do not live in a vacuum. Everything affects everything else. Life is complex; do not act as if it were totally logical or completely controllable. Help your client take control of those things he or she can control and to give up efforts to control those things over which her or she has no control.

7. Emphasize empathy. Strive to view the world through your client's eyes. Remember, his or her world is not your world, nor does it have to be. Realize that your client is probably doing the best he or she knows how.

8. Always demonstrate genuine respect and caring for your client, even if his or her behavior is abrasive, obnoxious, or repulsive. Do not be afraid to let your client know you care—if you don't care, then be afraid for yourself.

9. Remember that it is not your responsibility nor right to judge or punish a client in any way for his or her problems or troublesome behavior. Most clients have already received an abundance of disapproval from others. Disapproval from you will only dampen communication and harm your relationship. Seek to accept and understand. Because acceptance and understanding are in such short supply, they will have great value to your client.

10. Do not moralize or preach. You do not need to argue the "rightness" of your choices in life. If your moral character is indeed worthy of emulation, your client will be influenced by your behavior; your explanations will not be necessary.

11. Reach for and explore your client's feelings. Do not be afraid of emotion. Struggling with confusing and conflicting feelings is what helping is all about. When emotions are high, they must be dealt with before problem solving can proceed. If feelings scare you, work with things, not people.

12. Maintain confidentiality. Respecting your client's desire for privacy is critical to the establishment of trust. Trust is essential in helping.

13. Expect a client who is struggling with serious psychosocial problems to feel frustrated and overwhelmed. His or her anger may be directed toward you,

even when you are not the true source of the frustration. When this happens, do not take it personally nor react defensively.

14. Develop self-awareness and self-discipline. Do not allow your own problems to distort the helping process. Meet your emotional needs and handle your personal problems outside your professional relationships. Your client already has a fair share of life's problems. Do not ask him or her to worry about yours.

15. Listen much more than you talk. What your client has to say is much more important and helpful than what you have to say to your client. Keep your own message short, simple, and clear. Leave the jargon in your textbooks and at professional conferences.

16. Do not take sides in your client's conflicts with others. If you do, you will almost always destroy the relationship you have with your client.

17. Search for your client's strengths and for positives in the situation. Build on those strengths. Give more attention to what your client can do rather than to what he or she is unable to do.

18. Do not allow yourself or your client to become discouraged by the labels others have attached to your client. View all labeling by professionals and diagnostic statements with a degree of skepticism.

19. Believe in the possibilities of change. Remain hopeful—especially when your client is feeling hopeless. Expect him or her to work toward agreed upon goals; do not be afraid to challenge and confront the client when reasonable progress is not being made.

20. A client should participate as much as possible in the professional and agency decisions that impact his or her life. Keep your client informed of what you are doing on his or her behalf.

21. To the greatest extent possible, a client should be encouraged to make use of the informal resources that exist within his or her own social network (e.g., family, friends, neighbors, natural helpers, etc.).

22. Avoid creating dependence; a client should be encouraged to make his or her own decisions. Plan and conduct interventions so your client can learn problem-solving skills that will be useful in the future. The help you provide should prepare and empower your client to cope without your assistance.

23. Recognize your limitations but do not underestimate your abilities. Consult with another professional when confronted with a situation you do not know how to handle. Refer your client to another professional only when he or she has needs that are beyond the scope of your agency's program or your own skills.

24. Do not defend an agency procedure or policy that is illogical or unfair. Doing so only makes you look foolish and insensitive. It is best simply to acknowledge that the policy or procedure in question needs to be changed but that it is a reality that cannot now be changed and, therefore, must be followed.

25. Remember that human beings are incredibly resilient and adaptive. They can put up with a great deal of pain and discomfort if they understand why it is necessary in order to reach a goal they desire.

14.1 Planning an Interview

PURPOSE: To formulate a tentative plan for an interview or contact with a client.

DISCUSSION: One of the most common errors made by new workers is to go into a session without a clear purpose. Just as there should be an overall intervention plan, there should be a plan for each contact the worker has with the client. Of course, this plan must be tentative and flexible in order to respond to client concerns that could not be anticipated. The following questions can help the worker formulate such a plan.

1. What are the overall goals and objectives of the intervention with this client? How will my next contact relate to these goals and objectives?

2. What needs to be accomplished during the interview? What decisions need to be reached during the interview? Who needs to be present?

3. Should the next contact be a face-to-face or a telephone interview? One-on-one, family, or group session?

4. Will other professionals and/or concerned individuals participate in the interview (e.g., a family conference in a medical setting)? What objectives do these other participants have and how might differences in expectations be resolved?

5. How much time do I have to devote to the interview? How much time can the client devote to the interview?

6. Where and when will the interview take place? What arrangements are necessary prior to the interview (e.g., scheduling interviewing room, transportation, child care for client's children)?

7. What specific techniques might be used during the interview to achieve specific tasks and work toward intervention goals and objectives?

8. What factors related to the client's values or religious beliefs and social and family network need to be considered in preparing for the interview?

9. What factors related to the client's current emotional state (e.g., anger, fear, confusion, depression, etc.) need to be considered in preparing for the interview?

10. What factors related to the client's current physical functioning (e.g., mobility, pain, discomfort, hearing problems, effects of medication, etc.) need to be considered in preparing for the interview?

11. What documentation on this contact is necessary for the agency record?

SELECTED BIBLIOGRAPHY

Fox, Raymond. *Elements of the Helping Process.* New York: Haworth Press, 1993.
Kadushin, Alfred. *The Social Work Interview,* 3rd ed. New York: Columbia University Press, 1990.
Lukas, Susan. *Where to Start and What to Ask: An Assessment Handbook.* New York: W. W. Norton, 1993.

14.2   Information and Advice

PURPOSE: To enhance the client's problem-solving capacity by providing needed information and guidance.

DISCUSSION: *Information giving* refers to providing a client with information he or she needs to make a decision or carry out a task. As used here, the term ***advice giving*** refers to worker statements that recommend or suggest what a client should do. In information giving, the client feels free to use the information as he or she sees fit; in advice giving, the client clearly senses the social worker's preference.

One of the common errors made by inexperienced social workers is to give advice when the client has not asked for it. This is an understandable error because often the worker has known other clients with similar problems or has had personal experience with the problem now faced by the client, and, naturally, the worker wants the client to benefit from those experiences. However, there are many pitfalls in advice giving, and the worker needs to be very cautious in using this technique. Follow these ***guidelines for advice giving.***

1. Before giving advice, reflect on how you feel when someone gives you advice. Remember that most people do not follow advice, even when they have requested it. On those rare occurrences when someone does follow advice, it was usually offered by a person he or she has known for a long time and trusts completely.

2. Whether or not the giving of advice is appropriate depends largely on the purpose of the worker-client interaction. If it is a counseling-therapy relationship, giving advice is rarely appropriate. If the purpose relates to referral, brokering, or advocacy, advice giving may be appropriate and necessary. Never give advice on a topic outside your area of training and expertise.

3. Do not offer advice unless you have determined that the client genuinely wants your opinions and suggestions. Test the client's receptivity to advice by asking questions such as: Are you looking for some suggestions? or If you want, I could give you a few ideas about that.

4. When you do give advice, present it in a way that says, "This is what I would do" or "This is what others have done." But leave the responsibility for deciding what to do to the client. Explain the reasoning behind the guidance you offer.

5. Consider the issue of legal liability if you advise a client and he or she later suffers an adverse personal or financial consequence as a result of your recommendation. For example, beware of advising a client who asks questions such as: Do you think I should get a divorce? Do you think I should quit my job and look for another? Do you think it would be OK if I cut down on my medicine?

6. Be alert to the dangers of giving advice to a manipulative client, who may then hold you responsible if things do not turn out well (e.g., "I did what you said and it didn't work, so it's your fault"). Also be alert to the danger of encouraging dependency in a client who can and should take responsibility for decision making.

When providing information to a client, keep these *guidelines for information giving* in mind.

1. Carefully consider the client's current state of mind when giving information. Adapt what you say to his or her educational background, level of intelligence, command of the language, fears, and the like. If it is likely that the client will misunderstand, make sure that you give the same information to the client's significant others.

2. Provide information or directions in a logical, organized, step-by-step fashion. If you are haphazard in your presentation, the client will become confused. Give the client time to think about what you are saying, and invite him or her to ask questions to clarify any uncertainty. Never assume that the client understands what you have said. Look for nonverbal signs of misunderstanding. After giving information to a client, it is desirable to end your message with something like: " Now I want to make sure that I was clear in what I have been telling you. Would you please repeat back to me what you heard me say?" Do not simply ask, "Do you understand?" All too often, people will answer by saying that they understand even when they do not. It is important to always check that your message was completely understood.

3. Complicated, multistep instructions (e.g., how to get to another agency) may need to be written down. Also write out names, addresses, and phone numbers needed by the client.

4. Use pronouns (e.g., *it, this, that, those, them*) with caution. For example, the statement, "Fill out the form and take it to the person at the desk over there" could be very confusing to someone who does not know what the "form," "it," "person," or "over there" mean specifically. It is best to use the exact word rather than a pronoun, or provide sufficient description so there can be no mistake about what or to whom you are referring.

5. Speak distinctly. Avoid talking fast or using words the client may not understand. Remember that poor grammar and awkwardly constructed sentences result in confusion and misinterpretation.

SELECTED BIBLIOGRAPHY

Haley, Jay. *Problem Solving Therapy*, 2nd ed. San Francisco: Jossey-Bass, 1987.

Middleman, Ruth, and Gale Goldberg Wood. *Skills for Direct Practice in Social Work*. New York: Columbia University Press, 1990.

Shulman, Lawrence. *The Skills of Helping: Individuals, Families, and Groups*, 3rd ed. Itasca, Ill.: F. E. Peacock, 1992.

14.3   Encouragement, Reassurance, and Universalization

PURPOSE: To enhance the client's problem-solving capacity by providing supportive and encouraging statements.

DISCUSSION: The interrelated techniques of encouragement, reassurance, and universalization are especially useful and important in work with children and with clients who lack self-confidence. *Encouragement* often takes the form of worker statements that express confidence in the client's capabilities and is a means of recognizing and supporting client strengths (see Item 12.8). When using this technique, the worker must be genuine and send a clear, targeted message that explains why the worker has confidence in the client—for example: "On the basis of your performance on your job over the past six months, I think you are capable of handling the new responsibility even though you are feeling scared."

Overgeneralizations such as "You're the greatest" or "I am sure you can do anything you want to do" are seldom perceived by the client as genuine because he or she knows they are exaggerations. At best, the client accepts such a statement as a gesture of politeness; at worst, he or she takes it as a put-down. By always being realistic and tying words of encouragement to some facts, the worker will avoid sounding phony.

Reassurance is used when the client is feeling doubtful about his or her thoughts or decisions when they are, in fact, reasonable and realistic. However, inexperienced workers are often too quick to use reassurance. Woods and Hollis (1990, 107) warn that reassurance "must be used with delicacy and discrimination. Yielding to the temptation to overuse reassurance in an attempt to build up a relationship or because the worker cannot endure the client's anxiety may merely leave the client with the feeling that the worker does not fully comprehend the reasons for guilt or anxiety, or that the worker is deficient in moral discrimination and therefore is not a person whose judgment matters."

Universalization is a form of reassurance that consists of statements explaining to the client that his or her thoughts, feelings, or behavior are similar to those of other people—for example: "I have known a lot of people who had to place their parent in a nursing home and they described the same kind of feelings that you are expressing." This technique is intended to counteract the client's feelings of being different or deviant.

In every session, the worker should take some time to focus the discussion on client choices and experiences that make clients feel good about themselves. This is important because so many sessions end up focusing mostly on client problems and on things the client does not like about himself or herself or his or her situation. To counterbalance this attention to the negative, workers should create opportunities that encourage clients to recognize and verbalize their positive personal traits, strengths, and successes.

SELECTED BIBLIOGRAPHY

Gorden, Raymond. *Basic Interviewing Skills.* Itasca, Ill.: F. E. Peacock, 1992.
Woods, Mary, and Florence Hollis. *Casework: A Psychosocial Therapy,* 4th ed. New York: Mc-
    Graw-Hill, 1990.

14.4 Reinforcement and Related Behavioral Techniques

PURPOSE: To modify the frequency, intensity, or duration of a specific behavior.

DISCUSSION: Behavioral techniques are some of the most powerful available to the social worker when the intervention objective is to help the client learn a new behavior or alter an existing one. They are especially useful when dealing with child behavior problems. The social worker usually employs behavioral techniques when trying either to strengthen (increase) or weaken (decrease) a particular target behavior. The term *target behavior* refers to an operationally defined and measurable behavior that is the focus of the intervention. The *strength* of a target behavior can be described in terms of its frequency, intensity, or duration.

    Reinforcement is any event or activity that increases the likelihood that a target behavior will occur more frequently than in the past. Thus, a reinforcer is anything that strengthens a target behavior. There are two forms of reinforcement: positive and negative. *Positive reinforcement* involves adding, presenting, or giving something to the client (such as attention, objects of value, or privileges) that has the effect of increasing the target behavior. Ordinarily, a positive reinforcer is a pleasurable event or an obvious reward, but sometimes even a painful event can prove to be a positive reinforcer. Thus, only by observing the effects of what you believe is a reinforcer can you know for sure that it is a reinforcer. For this reason, it is important to establish a *baseline measurement* that describes the frequency, intensity, or duration of the target behavior prior to intervention. As a general rule, what a person does when he or she does not have to do something else is an indicator of what is positively reinforcing for that person (e.g., how a person spends extra time and money).

    There are two kinds of positive reinforcers: primary and secondary. *Primary reinforcers* are inherently rewarding and almost universally reinforcing. Examples include food, water, sex, warmth, and so on. *Secondary reinforcers* are learned, usually as a result of having been associated with primary reinforcers. Examples include money, tokens, and new clothes. Social reinforcers—such as praise, attention, and hugs—are usually considered to be secondary reinforcers, but there is some evidence that they are universally reinforcing.

    Both positive and negative reinforcement increase the frequency, intensity, or duration of a target behavior. *Negative reinforcement* involves subtracting or removing some condition that is aversive or unpleasant to the client, which has the effect of increasing the target behavior. Negative reinforcement is often confused with punishment, but they are not the same. Punishment weakens the target behavior, whereas negative reinforcement strengthens the behavior.

As a technique of behavior change, **punishment** involves the presentation of a painful or unpleasant stimulus that has the effect of suppressing a target behavior or reducing its strength. For ethical and legal reasons, the social worker must usually avoid the use of punishment. Most agencies and treatment programs prohibit the use of punishment for one or more of the following reasons.

1. Often, the results of punishment are short term. When the threat of punishment is not present, the target behavior often recurs.
2. The use of punishment provides a poor behavioral model for the client.
3. Punishment can be excessive or reach truly dangerous levels when administered by an angry or frustrated person.
4. Punishment may also suppress desirable behavior and make the client afraid to respond.
5. The use of physical punishment may make the worker vulnerable to a civil lawsuit or criminal charges (e.g., assault).

A behavior that is not reinforced tends to decrease in frequency, duration, or intensity. The term *extinction* describes the planned withdrawal of whatever reinforces a target behavior so as to eliminate or reduce the frequency of that behavior.

There are two basic **reinforcement schedules:** continuous and intermittent. *Continuous reinforcement* constitutes providing a reinforcer each time the desired target behavior occurs. In *intermittent reinforcement,* the target behavior is not rewarded every time it occurs. Continuous reinforcement is almost always used in the first stages of a program designed to teach a new behavior because it allows faster learning than intermittent reinforcement. However, a behavior that has been continuously reinforced is comparatively easy to extinguish. To make the newly learned behavior resistant to extinction, continuous reinforcement should be replaced by intermittent reinforcement.

A behavior that is maintained by a completely *random reinforcement schedule* (e.g., slot machine, bingo, fishing, etc.) or learned during a time of high emotion or personal crisis is highly resistant to change and difficult to extinguish.

When one behavior is described as being incompatible with another, it means that a person cannot perform both behaviors concurrently. For example, a child cannot play basketball and watch TV at the same time. A highly useful procedure in planned behavior change is to recognize such an incompatibility and ignore an unwanted target behavior while at the same time reinforcing an incompatible desired behavior and thereby encourage a new desired behavior. This technique is often called *differential reinforcement.*

The techniques of chaining, prompting, fading, and shaping are useful when the objective is to help a client learn a new behavior. These techniques are frequently used in training programs for the mentally retarded, in speech therapy, and in certain aspects of physical rehabilitation. **Chaining** refers to a procedure that breaks down a complex behavior (e.g., dressing) into many separate steps or components and teaches only one of these steps at a time. As new components are learned, they are "chained," or linked, to the ones already learned. The number of steps needed to teach a particular behavior will depend on the complexity of the behavior and the capacity of the client. There are two types of chaining: forward and backward.

In *forward chaining*, the first step in a chain is taught first. For example, in teaching a client to put on his trousers, the client would first be taught how to pick up and hold his pants. All subsequent steps are taught in order of their "natural sequence." This sequence is determined by observing several people perform the behavior and noting the most common sequence of steps.

In *backward chaining*, the last step in the chain is taught first. Thus, all of the steps in the sequence would be done for the client except the one being taught. For example, in dressing training, the first step to be taught would be "pulls pants up to the waist." One advantage of backward chaining is that the last step in the chain is always the one that is reinforced. Thus, the client is always reinforced at the very end of the behavior chain (e.g., when he has finished putting on his pants). For some self-help skills, such as hand and face washing, backward chaining is not feasible.

The term ***prompting*** describes any form of assistance given by the worker to help the client perform the target behavior. A prompt may be a verbal cue or instruction, a gesture or other nonverbal cue, or physically moving or guiding the client through the behavior. Prompting should be used only when necessary.

Fading is the process of gradually withdrawing prompts and decreasing the frequency of reinforcement as the client begins to learn the desired behavior. In the first steps of a training program, the worker will use continuous reinforcement and frequent prompting to help establish the new behavior. Later, when the client begins to perform the target behavior, the worker will gradually "fade out" or decrease the frequency of reinforcement and prompting.

Shaping is a technique of building a new behavior by reinforcing close approximations of the desired response. For example, a speech therapist teaching a child to say "cookie" may reward the child when he says "gowk." Perhaps later, the child is reinforced for saying "gook-koo" and still later, "gookie." Finally, after many days or weeks of reinforcing the child for closer and closer approximations of the desired sound, the child is able to say "cookie."

Much of what one learns—especially one's social or interactional behavior—is learned by observing others and subsequently imitating their behavior. This learning process is termed ***modeling***. Needless to say, both functional and dysfunctional behaviors are learned this way. A social worker can enhance the learning of functional behavior by keeping several principles in mind.

- Individual A is most likely to imitate the behavior of individual B if he or she views B as having some valued status (e.g., power, prestige, attractiveness, etc.) and if he or she observes B being rewarded for the behavior.
- In addition, individual A must in some way identify with B and feel similar. If A views B as being completely different, A may conclude there is no chance he or she could actually perform the behavior and/or that there was little or no chance that it would be rewarded.

■ Individual A is most likely to learn B's behavior if he or she has an opportunity to perform or practice the behavior soon after observing it and is then rewarded for the behavior.

Under ordinary conditions, licensed foster parents and child care staff working in hospitals, treatment centers, and group homes are prohibited from using any form of physical punishment. The procedure termed *time out* is an alternative to physical discipline. Its purpose is to reduce or eliminate a problem behavior by temporarily removing the client from an environment that is reinforcing the unwanted behavior. Consider this set of instructions given to a foster parent who is learning methods of nonviolent child care for use with a 10-year-old, male, foster child.

1. Find an area in your home that can be used for time out. If he kicks, throws things, or has tantrums, be sure to choose an area that has no breakable or dangerous objects. You might use his bedroom or other quiet area that is well lighted and ventilated.

2. Identify the behaviors that will always result in time out (i.e., clearly define the target behavior). For example, you may decide to use time out whenever he hits other children or screams at you.

3. Each time a target behavior occurs, use the time-out procedure immediately. Walk up to the child, explain what rule was broken, and tell him or her what must now happen. For example, "Johnny, whenever you hit your sister, you must go on time out." Accompany the child to the time-out area; don't look at or talk to him on the way. If the child resists, carry him there as quickly as possible.

4. Leave him in the time-out area for a preselected period of time. As a rule of thumb, use the formula of one minute per year of the child's age. At the end of the time period or when he is quiet and behaving well, go to the door and ask if he is ready to come out and behave correctly. For example, if Johnny threw toys, ask him, "Are you ready to come out and put your toys away?" If he hit his sister, ask, "Are you ready to come out and be friendly to your sister?"

5. If he answers this question "yes," have him come out and correct the earlier behavior. Reinforce the correct behavior with praise. For example, say, "I like the way you are picking up your toys."

6. If he does not answer "yes" or screams, cries, throws a tantrum, or displays other undesirable behavior, walk away from the door and wait until he is again quiet and behaving appropriately. Then go back and repeat the question.

7. At first, you may have to question him several times before he is ready to come out and correct the bad behavior. Don't be discouraged—just continue to follow these rules. If you follow the rules carefully, chances are that he will soon learn to follow them, too.

8. Try to arrange a special activity, privilege, or treat at the end of each day that he did not have to be taken to the time-out area, and tell him that the reward is for his good behavior.

SELECTED BIBLIOGRAPHY

Bellac, Alan, Michael Hersen, and Alan Kazdin, eds. *International Handbook on Behavior Modification and Therapy,* 2nd ed. New York: Plenum, 1990

Sanders, Matthew, and Mark Dadds. *Behavioral Family Intervention.* Boston: Allyn and Bacon, 1993.

Sundel, Sandra, and Martin Sundel. *Behavior Modification in the Human Services,* 3rd ed. Newbury Park, Calif.: Sage, 1993.

Watson, David, and Ronald Tharp. *Self-Directed Behavior: Self-Modification for Personal Adjustment,* 6th ed. Pacific Grove, Calif.: Brooks/Cole, 1993.

14.5 Behavioral Rehearsal

PURPOSE: To assist the client in learning a new behavior to better cope with a particular situation.

DISCUSSION: *Behavioral rehearsal* is a technique drawn from behavioral therapy that teaches a client how to handle a specific interpersonal exchange for which he or she feels unprepared. This technique helps reduce anxiety and builds the client's self-confidence about being able to handle the situation. Essentially, it is a form of role-playing that makes use of modeling and coaching. Like other forms of role-play, behavioral rehearsal provides the client with an opportunity to try out new behaviors in a protected environment and without risk of failure. For example, the technique can be used to prepare a client for a job interview (e.g., the social worker takes the role of the employer and conducts a simulated job interview). As the client practices the behavior, the worker provides feedback and offers suggestions and alternative ways of behaving. The worker may demonstrate or model the behavior, so it can be imitated by the client. Whether used during a one-to-one interview or during a group session, the steps are basically the same.

1. The client identifies the problem or concern and then describes or demonstrates how he or she would usually behave in that situation.
2. The worker (and/or group members) makes suggestions on how the situation might be handled more effectively.
3. The client is given an opportunity to provide additional information about the problem or concern and to ask the worker (or group members) to further explain the suggestions.
4. A role-play is used to demonstrate the behavioral changes suggested to the client. The worker (or group members) will usually take the role of the client. However, the client may enact the behavior if he or she feels ready and understands the changes being suggested.
5. After the role-play, the worker (or members) first identifies the positive aspects of the performance, then makes additional suggestions for improvement. If necessary, the role-play is repeated to further illustrate the preferred way of behaving.

6. When the client understands how he or she ought to behave, he or she practices the behavior until satisfied with the performance.

7. Homework outside the session can be used to further the client's learning of the new behavior.

The major limitation of behavioral rehearsal is that the client may successfully learn what to do in the presence of the worker but may not be able to generalize it to the real world. Sometimes the real situation poses problems that cannot be anticipated during a practice session.

SELECTED BIBLIOGRAPHY

Curran, James, and Peter Monti, eds. *Social Skills Training.* New York: Guilford Press, 1982.
Garvin, Charles. *Contemporary Group Work,* 2nd ed. Englewood Cliffs, N.J.: Prentice Hall, 1987.
Rose, Sheldon. *Group Therapy: A Behavioral Approach.* Englewood Cliffs, N.J.: Prentice-Hall, 1977.

14.6   Behavioral Contracting

PURPOSE: To modify a behavior through the mutual exchange of reinforcers.

DISCUSSION: A *behavioral contract* is an written agreement designed to bring about a change in a person's behavior. Usually, the contract involves an exchange of rewards or positive reinforcements between two or more persons. DeRisi and Butz (1975, 1–2) explain that behavior contracting "is a technique used to structure behavioral counseling by making each of the necessary elements of the process so clear and explicit that they may be written into an agreement for behavior change that is understandable and acceptable to everyone involved."

A behavioral contract can follow one or two forms: a contingency contract or a reciprocal behavioral contract. In a *contingency contract,* one person sets up a consequence associated with the behavior of another. For example, a group home manager may agree to take a resident to a movie if the resident cleans his or her room five days in a row. By contrast, the *reciprocal behavior contract* is an agreement between the members of a dyad (e.g., husband-wife), in which each agrees to reward the other for a specific desired behavior. For example, the husband agrees to take his wife to a movie of her choice if she will take the car to the repair shop, and she agrees to cook his favorite meal if he will clean the house.

Thus, we see that a behavioral contract might be negotiated between the social worker and the client, or the worker may help two or more clients (e.g., a husband and wife, parent and child) negotiate their own behavioral contract. Any behavior can become the focus or target of a contract so long as the behavior can be described clearly and is agreed to by everyone affected by the contract. Target behaviors should, of course, be described in positive terms. In other words, the contract should describe what a person *will* do rather than what he or she *will not* do. The contract should be developed in a way that makes success likely, for success sustains motivation.

When helping to formulate a reciprocal behavioral contract to be used by a couple or family, several guidelines are important.

1. Assist all parties named in the contract to select tasks that will provide some immediate reward or relief from their problems. Make sure that each person stands to receive some desired payoff for participating and completing the tasks.
2. Select tasks that everyone agrees are worthwhile and possible, given the current circumstances.
3. Select tasks that are easily observed by others so there will be no disagreement as to whether a task was completed.
4. Select tasks that allow for approximation. In other words, it should be possible to observe even a partial success and a person's genuine effort to complete the task.
5. Set up a simple plan for recording task completion and the exchange of rewards. The plan should be one that can be easily monitored by the practitioner.
6. Before the participants leave the negotiation session, ask each one to describe and explain the contract and the tasks he or she has agreed to carry out. Make sure there is no misunderstanding.

Variations of the contingency behavioral contracting, often called *point systems* or *token economies*, are often used in certain types of special educational settings and residential treatment facilities. Under such systems, a client earns points or tokens for performing specific behaviors (e.g., completing homework, saying thank you, cleaning one's room) and can then use the tokens to "purchase" desired objects, privileges, or rewards.

When using a contingency contract, the reinforcement (rewards) for compliance, along with any adverse consequences for noncompliance, should be clearly described and understood by all. Whenever noncompliance can have serious consequences for a client (e.g., when used in a probation or child protective services agency), the contract should be in writing. In other situations, a verbal agreement may suffice.

SELECTED BIBLIOGRAPHY

DeRisi, William, and George Butz. *Writing Behavioral Contracts*. Champaign, Ill.: Research Press, 1975.

Gambrill, Eileen. *Casework: A Competency Based Approach*. Englewood Cliffs, N.J.: Prentice Hall, 1983.

Stuart, Richard. *Helping Couples Change: A Social Learning Approach to Marital Therapy*. New York: Guilford Press, 1980.

14.7   Role Reversal

PURPOSE: To assist the client in understanding the viewpoint and feelings of a significant other.

DISCUSSION: In a *role reversal,* a person is asked to assume the role of another and try to see things from the other person's perspective. The technique is especially useful during marriage or family counseling. The social worker may elect to use role reversal when two clients, such as husband and wife or parent and child, are in conflict, and when it is apparent that one or both has little awareness of how the other feels. The best time to use role reversal is when the two people have reached an impasse and keep repeating the same dialogue or when one is "stuck" on a particular perception.

The worker might initiate the role reversal by saying something like, "Joe and Susan, would you two be willing to try something? I would like you to reverse roles to see how it feels being the other person." The two people are then asked to switch chairs; if the clients do not change chairs, they often become confused as to which role they are playing. The worker should explain, "In this chair, you are yourself. In that chair, you are Joe."

Once they are in the role of the other, the social worker might get the discussion going by focusing attention on a particular line of repetitious or contentious dialogue. For example, "Joe, I want you to start playing Susan's part in this conflict and begin with the line 'Joe, you don't care about me.'" "And Susan, in the role of Joe, I want you to respond by saying how those words make you feel." As the discussion unfolds, the worker uses various interviewing techniques to encourage the expression of thoughts and feeling.

After a few minutes of role reversal, the worker has each person return to his or her own chair and perspective. The content of the role reversal is discussed in a way that helps each understand how and why the other thinks and feels about the issue that causes conflict.

When working with couples and families, the role reversal technique may be adapted for use as homework, asking the couple or family members to take an hour at home prior to the next session and reverse roles. It also allows the individual to experience how his or her own behavior, as dramatized by another, affects others. It can provide insight and maybe even a little humor if the clients are instructed not to take the task too seriously.

SELECTED BIBLIOGRAPHY

Ohlsen, Merle. *Marriage Counseling in Groups.* Champaign, Ill.: Research Press, 1979.

Sherman, Robert, and Norman Fredman. *Handbook of Structured Techniques in Marriage and Family Therapy.* New York: Brunner/Mazel, 1986.

Sprafkin, Robert, N. Jane Gershaw, and Arnold Goldstein. *Social Skills for Mental Health.* Boston: Allyn and Bacon, 1993.

14.8 Managing Self-Talk

PURPOSE: To assist the client to manage emotional reactions by modifying distorted interpretations of reality.

DISCUSSION: Social work places much emphasis on viewing the client within an environmental context. The profession is particularly concerned about how the realities of life and external influences affect one's social functioning. However, in many situations, the client is more influenced by his or her interpretation of reality than by objective reality itself.

The term *self-talk* refers to the messages that we give ourselves. What we "say" to ourselves reflects our unique interpretation of what we have experienced. Social workers who adhere to the theoretical assumptions of cognitive therapy emphasize that self-talk evokes emotional reactions, which, in turn, give rise to behaviors. Emery (1981) explains the basic principle of cognitive therapy:

> How you evaluate or think about your experiences determines how you react emotionally. If you think you've lost something, you'll feel sad; if you think you're in danger, you'll feel anxious; if you think others have treated you wrongly, you'll feel angry. Recent research has found that people with emotional disorders systematically distort their experiences. The direction and type of cognitive distortion determines the nature of the emotional disorder. (p. 23)

Our ways of thinking become habitual. If a person habitually thinks about his or her experiences in distorting and irrational ways, he or she generates much inner turmoil and also creates problems in interpersonal relationships. Following are some common types of distortions.

- *All or nothing.* Experiences are evaluated in terms of the extremes of black and white, all right or all wrong; there is no grey area or middle ground (e.g., we conclude that a single mistake proves we are a complete failure).
- *Jumping to conclusions.* An unsupported and unrealistic conclusion is made on the basis of little or no evidence (e.g., we conclude that something is undesirable or unworkable even before we have gathered information).
- *Selective Attention.* Attention is given to only those facts that support our preconceived ideas; facts that point to a different conclusion are overlooked or dismissed.
- *Catastrophizing.* We anticipate and look for the worst possible outcome; we always expect something bad to happen.
- *Magnification of failure.* The meaning or importance of a setback or mistake is exaggerated (e.g., at work we have ten successes and one failure but we only pay attention to the failure).
- *Minimization of success.* The importance of a positive experience or success is disregarded or played down (e.g., we attribute our success to dumb luck).

- *Negative beliefs about self, others, and the world.* We hold enduring and negative beliefs that everything and everybody, including ourselves, are bad, unchangeable, and hopeless.
- *Personalization.* Every problem or negative happening is caused by our inadequacy. We take responsibility for things over which we have little or no control.
- *External locus of control.* We have no control over our lives; we believe that others control our lives or that whatever happens is a matter of fate.

Many dysfunctional emotional reactions and problem behaviors are the result of unclear thinking or faulty beliefs about how we or others should behave. McMullin (1986, 55–56) lists numerous examples of irrational thoughts that create problems for clients. These include beliefs such as: "Home is safe. Thus, the farther away from home I travel, the greater the danger"; "I must fit in with everybody else's values and behavior, otherwise I will be totally alone and rejected by everyone"; and "I must try as hard as I can in everything I attempt." By helping a client learn to think more precisely, the worker can help him or her control troublesome emotions and behave more effectively. This is, of course, more difficult than it sounds. Patterns of thinking are habits; they are not easily changed and are themselves a barrier to change.

The social worker can use a five-step approach to help a client modify distortions in self-talk. Ask the client to do the following:

1. Identify what you are feeling and thinking right now.
2. Get in touch with your self-talk. Pay attention to extremes in thinking, as suggested by the use of words such as *never, can't, always, everybody, completely,* and so on.
3. Examine the objective reality of your situation. Once the facts have been identified, relax, take a deep breath, and repeat them out loud three times.
4. Notice that, when you hold to the facts and avoid using inaccurate words, you begin to feel differently and things do not seem as bad as before.
5. Keeping the facts of your situation clearly in mind, consider what you can do about it.

This five-step method is illustrated below in a dialogue between a social worker and a college student who has just learned that he failed a math exam.

Client: I cannot believe I am so stupid. I had a B average in math and got an F on the last test. I might as well leave school and get a job as a dishwasher. I am a complete failure. I don't deserve to be in school.

Worker: Wait a minute! You have said before you wanted to learn how to stop putting yourself down. Let's try something. Start by telling me again what you are feeling and thinking right now.

Client: Well, I just can't pass math tests. I'm stupid. I am embarrassed and I hate myself. I am never going to get through college. My parents are going to kill me for this. This is the worst possible thing that could have happened. My future is down the drain. Everything is just awful.

Worker: Let's take a look at that kind of self-talk. Try to recognize what you are saying to yourself; notice your extreme language. Let's take a look at the way things are in reality. Is it true you cannot pass math tests?

Client: Well, not really. I passed all of them before this one and I still have a B average in college.

Worker: Are your parents really going to kill you?

Client: Well, no, but they will be disappointed.

Worker: Is failing a test really the worst possible thing that could happen to you?

Client: Well, no, but it seems awful right now.

Worker: Does failing this test really mean you have no future?

Client: Well, I still have a future. I know what you are saying, and I agree that I am overreacting. But I don't know how to put a lid on those thoughts and feelings.

Worker: Do this for me. Repeat outloud the truth—the reality—of your situation, which is as follows: I flunked one math test. My parents will be unhappy. I have a B average in college. I can remain in college. My life is not over.

Client: (repeats above)

Worker: Now take a couple of deep breaths and relax. Now say that outloud again, three times.

Client: (client follows instruction)

Worker: How do you feel when you change your self-talk?

Client: Well, I guess it isn't as bad as I thought. I feel less upset than before.

Worker: Our emotions react to what we tell ourselves about our experiences. If your self-talk is distorted, your emotions are going to be more extreme and more negative than they need to be. You can use this technique yourself when your feelings start to get out of control. Certainly, your situation is not as bad as it seemed when you were telling yourself those awful things. But you still have to make some plans on how to prepare for your next math test. Now let's talk about that.

Once a client is able to describe his or her pattern of maladaptive self-talk, the cognitive restructuring techniques of self-instruction and visualization may prove helpful. *Self-instruction* (also termed *positive self-talk, covert speech,* and *countering*) refers to a set of statements that are repeated by the client on a regular basis, perhaps three times a day, and especially in times of distress. Often they are said aloud in front of a mirror. These messages are incompatible with the client's habitual negative self-talk and are intended to counteract the dysfunctional pattern and to foster self-acceptance and self-confidence. The use of this technique rests on the observation that when an individual actively argues against his or her own irrational thoughts, those thoughts are weakened.

This technique should not be confused with blindly optimistic "positive thinking" that may gloss over important realities and allow self-deception. Rather, self-instruction requires that the messages be truthful and realistic, given the client's abilities and situation. Also, the messages should be as specific as possible and tied directly to the client's concerns. Self-instruction works but it works slowly. Frequent and consistent practice for a year or more may be needed to effect a significant and lasting change.

Ingrained dysfunctional and irrational core beliefs are highly resistant to change. As an example, consider the client who avoids taking a better job because her dysfunctional self-talk tells her: "If I make a mistake on the job, people will think I am stupid and will criticize me". This woman might be taught to repeat the following message: "Each time I make a mistake on the job, I have an opportunity to learn something very important. If someone criticizes me, he or she is either right or wrong. If the person is right, I have learned something. If he or she is wrong, I can ignore it."

In using the technique of *visualization,* the client is taught to prepare himself or herself to deal with a specific, worry-causing event by repeatedly imagining this event and mentally rehearsing the specific steps necessary to handle it successfully. It is important that the images are ones of action and activity; the more vivid and detailed, the better. For many individuals, visualization reduces their fear of the event and builds confidence in their ability to do what they know they must do. For example, a client might prepare for a frightening job interview by visualizing being asked hard questions and giving clear and appropriate answers. Such a visualization would need to be practiced dozens of times before the interview.

The technique of *journaling* asks the client to keep a daily log or a diary of significant thoughts and feelings. It is especially useful for clients who like to write and it often helps them recognize recurring themes and patterns in the meaning assigned to their experiences. As a way of structuring this homework, the client might be instructed to respond in writing to specific questions such as the following: What have I learned about myself today? What feelings and moods did I experience? What thoughts gave rise to these feelings? What were the two most significant events of the day? What thoughts and feelings did I have in relation to these events? What personal strengths did I observe in myself today? What troublesome thoughts do I need to work on and what is my plan for doing so? How will my plan build on my personal strengths?

SELECTED BIBLIOGRAPHY

Emery, Gary. *A New Beginning.* New York: Simon and Schuster, 1981.
Lazarus, Arnold. *In the Mind's Eye.* New York: Rawson Associates. 1977.
McMullin, Rian. *Handbook of Cognitive Therapy Techniques.* New York: W. W. Norton, 1986.

14.9 Building Self-Esteem

PURPOSE: To assist the client in coming to a more positive evaluation of self.

DISCUSSION: The term *self-esteem* refers to one's beliefs about one's own worth. Low self-esteem is an important contributing cause of unhappiness and problems of social functioning. Individuals who do not value or respect themselves lack self-confidence and struggle with a multitude of self-imposed barriers and limitations. Often they engage in self-defeating behaviors and are vulnerable to exploitation and abuse by others.

Because the effects of low self-esteem are so far reaching and so painful to observe, social workers have wished for a magic wand that could transform a client's negative self-evaluation into a more realistic and positive one. Unfortunately, no such magic exists. Movement toward self-esteem is a slow journey. By following several guidelines, the social worker can help the client during that journey.

1. It is important to help clients understand that one's feelings of personal worth is a perception—a subjective personal opinion about one's self. Consequently, Person A, who is violent and dishonest, may have high self-esteem; whereas Person B, who others view as a truly wonderful human being, may have low self-esteem.

2. Help clients to understand that self-awareness and self-acceptance are the basic building blocks of self-esteem. Humans cannot come to know and accept ourselves without support and encouragement from others. We need other people. Thus, the client will need to form new relationships even when that is scary. Self-acceptance requires that we recognize our own goodness and also our weakness, woundedness, and incompleteness. To truly accept ourselves, we need to acknowledge our need to love and be loved. Self-esteem begins to grow when we begin to believe that our lives are valuable and valued, despite our imperfections.

3. A change in self-esteem must grow from within. Self-esteem cannot be taught, but it can be learned, and certain types of experiences encourage a growth in self-esteem. Efforts to help others elevate their self-esteem involves creating situations of cognitive dissonance wherein they must reconcile a seemingly positive outcome or experience with their negative opinions of self. A willingness to reevaluate one's beliefs about self is the first step toward a growth in self-esteem.

4. Encourage clients to identify the specific conditions and circumstances, if they occurred, that they believe would help to elevate their feelings of self-worth. Then engage the clients in an examination of the underlying values reflected in those conditions and whether they are truly worthwhile and suitable criteria for measuring the worth of a person. For example, many people assume they would have higher self-esteem if they were more attractive, were better athletes or had more money or higher social status. A closer look at those desires reveals that they are the values of a society obsessed with physical appearance, competition, and self-aggrandizement. Other values—such as generosity, compassion, friendliness, and honesty—are more appropriate and lasting measures of personal worth.

5. Low self-esteem often derives from unfavorable comparisons of self to others. Persons with low self-esteem tend to compare themselves with the "best in the field" (e.g., with the best musician, the best student, the most attractive person, etc.). Given that mode of thinking, they always suffer by comparison and this reinforces their beliefs that they are not as good as other people. Help clients to understand that this is a self-defeating pattern of thinking. Help clients view others in a more realistic manner. For example, another individual may indeed be outstanding in a certain area but he or she is not outstanding in all areas.

6. Encourage clients to participate in a support group, personal growth group, or church group where they will be accepted and respected by others, learn they have much in common with others, and learn that everyone has both strengths and limitations. Such group experiences are usually more effective than individual counseling but both may be necessary for some clients.

7. Encourage clients to take steps necessary to place themselves in new situations where they will have an opportunity to discover and develop their abilities and reassess their beliefs and assumptions about self; this may involve taking a job, changing jobs, returning to school, joining an organization, building a friendship, and so on. People with low self-esteem are inclined to reject the opportunities and avoid the experiences they need most.

8. Encourage clients to examine the way they think, especially how they tend to see the negative rather than the positive, and how they are overly influenced by what others say and do. Also help clients understand that their value as a person is not dependent on the approval or actions of others and that they, not others, control how they will think and feel about life.

9. For some clients, low self-esteem is tied to one or more significant separation and loss experiences (e.g., separation from bio-family, loss of one's childhood through sexual abuse, loss of respect from valued others, etc.). Help these clients to recognize and grieve for what they have lost.

10. Encourage and assist clients to develop a vision—a sense of purpose and meaning in life. Self-worth grows from knowing that you are living in accord with a set of ideals and values. For this reason, clients should be encouraged to do what they think and feel is the right thing to do.

SELECTED BIBLIOGRAPHY

Branden, Nathaniel. *Six Pillars of Self Esteem*. New York: Bantam Books, 1994.
Burns, David. *Ten Days to Self Esteem*. New York: Quill-William Morrow, 1993.
Frey, Diane, and C. Jesse Carlock. *Enhancing Self-Esteem*. Muncie, Ind.: Accelerated Development, Inc., 1989.
McKay, Matthew, and Patrick Fanning. *Self-Esteem*, 2nd ed., Oakland, Calif.: New Harbinger Publications, 1993.

14.10   The Empty Chair

PURPOSE: To help the client understand his or her feelings toward self or a significant other.

DISCUSSION: The *empty-chair technique,* sometimes called the *double-chair technique,* is borrowed from Gestalt therapy. It is usually used to clarify the issues involved in an interpersonal conflict. It helps the client view the conflict from a different angle and gain insight into why he or she is feeling and behaving in a certain way. Some skilled practitioners are able to use the technique to clarify intrapersonal conflict.

The social worker may elect to employ this technique after recognizing a specific conflict that needs to be explored with the client. To get started, the worker pulls up an empty chair and places it opposite the client. The chair becomes the person or situation with which the client is in conflict. The client is asked to speak to the chair, explaining his or her perceptions and feelings. The client is then asked to sit on the chair (assuming the role of that person or situation) and respond to what was just said. The client may move back and forth several times throughout this dialogue. The worker uses other interviewing techniques to explore the exchange as it unfolds.

As an example of application, consider Mary, a 40-year-old woman, who has exhaustingly high housekeeping standards. Even though she does not enjoy housework, she spends hours each day cleaning all rooms in her house, including her children's rooms and the garage. When asked how she became so devoted to cleaning and housework, Mary says that her mother emphasized the importance of housework. The worker pulls up an empty chair and asks Mary to sit on it, assume the role of her mother, and tell Mary about the importance of doing housework. In the role of her mother, Mary explains that cleanliness is next to Godliness, that the oldest child should take care of the younger ones, and that a good wife is devoted to her home. Then, the worker has Mary switch chairs, become herself, and respond to what her "mother" had to say. Her first response is, "Yes, ma'am." Exploration reveals that this response covers much hostility. What Mary really wants to say aloud is, "No, I don't want to do it. I am tired of working all the time. I am tired of doing things for other people." The worker then uses the empty chair to represent Mary's husband and invites Mary to express her feelings to him. During the course of this dialogue, Mary may realize that, as an adult, she now has choices that she did not have as a child. Moreover, she realizes that she has never told her husband how she feels.

The technique can be adapted to many situations. In the hands of a skilled social worker, it can be very powerful. It can be combined effectively with behavioral rehearsal and role reversal techniques.

SELECTED BIBLIOGRAPHY

Cory, Gerald. *Theory and Practice of Counseling and Psychotherapy*, 4th ed. Pacific Grove, Calif.: Brooks/Cole, 1991.

Fagan, Joen, and Irma Shepherd. *Gestalt Therapy Now: Theory, Techniques, Applications*. Ben Lomond, Calif.: Science and Behavior Books, 1970.

Sherman, Robert, and Norman Fredman. *Handbook of Structured Techniques in Marriage and Family Therapy*. New York: Brunner/Mazel, 1986.

14.11   Confrontation and Challenge

PURPOSE: To increase the client's self-awareness, especially in regard to self-imposed barriers to change.

DISCUSSION: Egan (1975, 158) has described *confrontation* as "a responsible unmasking of the discrepancies, distortions, games and smoke screens the client uses to hide both from self understanding and from constructive behavioral change." In his more recent writings, Egan (1994, 158) concludes that the word *challenge* is now preferred. He defines **challenge** "as an invitation to examine internal (cognitive) or external behavior that seems to be self defeating, harmful to others, or both—and to change that behavior."

A challenge or confrontation is initiated by the social worker. Thus, its focus will depend on the worker's judgment as to what changes are essential for a client and what stands in the way of those changes. Most often the challenge will focus on the client's avoidance or self-deception, such as failure to acknowledge or "own" an obvious problem; rationalizations, evasions, distortions, and game playing; unwillingness to recognize consequences of one's behavior; discrepancies between what the client says and what he or she does; unwillingness to take steps to correct a problem or deal with an important issue.

For a challenge to be effective, it must be done with concern for the client's feelings and perceptions. The worker must avoid using this technique when angry or frustrated with the client. Egan (1975, 166) explains that the motive of the professional "should be to help the client, not to be right, not to punish, to get back at the client, or to put him in his place." Highly defensive clients will usually reject its message by rationalizing, verbally attacking the worker or minimizing the situation. If challenged, depressed clients may withdraw from the relationship. Several guidelines need to be considered in the use of this technique.

1. Do not challenge when you are feeling angry. Unless you have a genuine concern for the client, its use may be little more than an expression of frustration or a desire to punish a difficult client.

2. Do not challenge or confront a client if you cannot or do not intend to become more deeply involved. Once offered, it is the responsibility of the worker to help the client deal nondefensively with the message, to understand it, and to consider what it means for future choices. Unless you have the time to help the client make use of the information, do not use this technique.

3. A challenge offered by someone for whom the client has no positive feelings will have no beneficial impact whatsoever. It will be effective only if the client feels care and respect from the social worker and if the client has similar feelings toward the worker. If those feelings are not there, the information will be discounted.

4. Couple the challenging message with positive observations about the client. In other words, present the message within a context of recognizing and supporting the client's strengths.

5. Make sure your message is descriptive and nonjudgmental. Be prepared to give a detailed description of the client's self-destructive or negative behavior, and provide concrete examples of how this behavior creates problems. Vague, general statements are often misunderstood. Moreover, judgmental statements tend to trigger anger, whereas descriptive statements provide information that can be used in problem-solving efforts.

6. Present the observations or data on which your inferences are based. For example, an observation should be stated directly: "I saw you . . ." or "You told me . . ."

An inference is the conclusion based on your observations. Because an inference is really an opinion, it should be stated tentatively: "Because of what I have seen you do, it seems to me that . . ." or "I sense that . . ." For example, if the confrontation focuses on self-defeating behavior, present descriptions of the behavior before explaining how the behavior is counterproductive for the client and make sure the client understands the distinction between your observations and your inferences.

7. Use I-messages throughout the challenge (see Item 8.5).

SELECTED BIBLIOGRAPHY

Cormier, William, and L. Sherilyn Cormier. *Interviewing Strategies for Helpers,* 3rd ed. Monterey, Calif.: Brooks/Cole, 1991.
Egan, Gerald. *The Skilled Helper,* 5th ed. Monterey, Calif.: Brooks/Cole, 1994.
———. *The Skilled Helper.* Monterey, Calif.: Brooks/Cole, 1975.
Hepworth, Dean, and Jo Ann Larsen. *Direct Social Work Practice,* 4th ed. Pacific Grove, Calif.: Brooks/Cole, 1993.

14.12 Reframing

PURPOSE: To assist the client in viewing the behavior from a different perspective and in a more positive light.

DISCUSSION: The technique known as *reframing,* sometimes called *relabeling* or *redefining,* is used to help a client modify the meaning he or she assigns to a particular event, behavior, or life experience. Its purpose is to gently persuade a client that the event or behavior can be viewed in a different and more positive light. Reframing recognizes the wisdom of the first-century philosopher Epictetus, who said, "It is not the things themselves which trouble us, but the opinions we have about these things."

This technique is especially useful in work with persons having interpersonal conflicts, such as a couple or family. It encourages family members to reexamine their definitions of the problem and their beliefs about why others are behaving as they do. It promotes interpersonal understanding and helps each person feel more favorable about the other. When a person perceives things in a new way, he or she usually feels differently and begins to behave differently.

The following example illustrates a social worker's use of reframing.

Foster Parent: I get so upset with Mary (foster child). So often, she blows up and gets angry with me. But I haven't done anything to make her angry!
Social Worker: That must be frustrating—to know you do not deserve to be the target of her anger. As you know, Mary is an angry child because of the severe abuse she experienced last year. But, in one way of looking at it, Mary is paying you a big compliment. When she gets angry in your presence, she is demonstrating that she feels safe when with you and she trusts that you will not retaliate and hurt her.

Another example of reframing is illustrated in the following statement made to a 35-year-old client who has experienced a lifetime of physical and emotional pain related to a disabling car accident and having been physically and sexually abused as a child.

> *Social Worker:*   I have been thinking about your life and all that you have experienced. Despite all you have been through, here you are at age 35 still alive and still struggling to do the best you can. In the school of life, you have received a very expensive and a very good education—much better than what a Harvard or a Yale could provide. You have learned things about people and about life that most people never learn, no matter how long they go to school, no matter how much money they spend on college tuition. Your tuition has been paid in the form of personal pain and suffering but in return you have received a high-quality education.

An alternative to the social worker providing the client with a new perspective is to encourage the client to brainstorm several different interpretations. For example, the worker might begin by explaining that there is a difference between the factual reality that describes a particular life experience and the story an individual tells himself or herself about that experience. The client will usually agree that five people will most likely tell five slightly different stories about the same experience. Using that agreement as a foundation, the worker can encourage the client to come up with additional stories (interpretations) about the particular behavior being discussed. After thinking up several alternative perceptions, the client will usually soften his or her position and at least acknowledge that there may indeed be a different way to interpret his or her situation.

Still another approach to reframing is to redefine a client's problem or irresponsible action as a basically positive behavior taken to an extreme. In other words, a problem is redefined as a strength that is spinning out of control. For example, consider the young mother who has injured her three year old child as a result of using excessive spanking as discipline. The discussion of her behavior might be approached by first recognizing that the mother wants to teach the child proper behavior but in this situation her motive to be a good mother jumped the track or went out of control.

When the worker can redefine a problem as a strength that is spinning out of control or as a positive behavior that has jumped the track, the client feels less defensive and more hopeful. Somehow it seems easier to tone down a strength than to get rid of a problem behavior or to correct a dysfunction. The words a helper uses do make a difference.

SELECTED BIBLIOGRAPHY

Berg, Insoo Kim. *Family Based Services.* New York: W. W. Norton, 1994.

Minuchin, Salvador, and H. Charles Fishman. *Family Therapy Techniques.* Cambridge, Mass.: Harvard University Press, 1981.

Watzlawick, Paul, John Weakland, and Richard Fisch. *Change: Principles of Problem Formulation and Problem Resolution.* New York: W. W. Norton, 1974.

14.13   Family Sculpting

PURPOSE: To help a client or family system understand their own feelings and behavior and those of other family members by acting out significant family events.

DISCUSSION: *Family sculpting* is a technique designed to help a client (within a group session) or a client family reenact and thus relive some important aspects of their family's behavior. It is a tool for assessment as well as treatment. The term *sculpting* is an artistic analogy that describes how one of the family members physically arranges or molds the family in a way that conveys a certain meaning, much like a sculptor working with clay.

The social worker begins by explaining the technique to the family. Baron and Feeney (1976) offer a sample explanation.

> We're going to do something a little different today that will help us learn what's happening in the family. First of all, it involves everyone getting up out of their seats (worker stands as an example). Now we need someone who will make a family sculpture. What I mean is, I want someone, without talking, to arrange the family into a picture which if I were walking through the park would tell me something about who you are. Who's close to whom, who is far away, might be a way to start. The rest of the family has to let the sculptor sculpt. That means being as much like clay as possible. Some sculptors have sculpted the parents with Mom standing over Dad ruling the roost. Others show us kids who are still sitting on Momma's lap even though they are teenagers. You get the idea. Who wants to try it? (p. 82)

After such an explanation, someone will usually volunteer to do the first sculpture. In the beginning, this family member may need support and encouragement from the worker. The worker watches to make sure that the sculptor really sculpts and does not just verbalize instructions. Verbalizing can result in arguments and keeps members from touching. Playful touching and a bit of silliness are some of the positive aspects of this technique.

Hartman (1984) offers the following guidance on family sculpting.

> It may be suggested that the sculptor imagine the family at home in the evenings. Where will each person be? What will they be doing? Chairs and other props may be used. Placement of the members should include not only where they are in relationship to other members but also where they are looking and how their bodies are positioned.
>
> As the sculpture develops, family members may object because they see themselves in the family system in a different way. For example, if a child placed dad in the corner behind the newspaper he might not like that picture of himself, nor what his son or daughter is communicating through the sculpture. It is important, however, to allow the sculptor to finish without interruption and to assure other family members that they will be able to sculpt the family later in the way they see it if they so wish.
>
> The worker should give the sculptor support and help as needed, encouraging him or her to take whatever time is needed and asking enabling questions like, "Do you want mom to be looking in any particular direction?" or "Is that the way you want it? Are there any changes you want to make?"

After the sculptor has completed the sculpture to his or her satisfaction, and taken his or her place in the tableau, the worker assumes the role of monitor and while the actors maintain their positions asks each member how they are experiencing their place in the sculpture. This invitation surfaces disagreements on the part of the family members as to how they see the family. It surfaces how they are feeling about current family structure and may expose points of stress and tension. (p. 24)*

In a variation of the family sculpture, the sculpting member gives each person a sentence to say, something typical of their relationship. This further reflects how the sculptor sees himself or herself in the family.

The instructions for a family sculpture can be done within the context of the family's past or present. It can also vary from visualizing the ideal to portraying the most feared circumstances. And the technique can be used as part of a group therapy session. In this latter application, the sculptor chooses group members to play the roles of the sculptor's family, including the sculptor. Once the sculpture is developed, the worker asks the client to assume his or her own role and everyone discusses their feelings and perceptions.

By using 3×5 name cards to represent family members, another form of sculpting can be conducted within a one-to-one interview. The basic procedure is as follows:

1. The client and worker identify all family members and write each of their names on a separate 3×5 card. The client's name is also written on one of the cards.
2. The client is asked to imagine being with his or her family members in a room and then to arrange the cards in a way that shows where each would be sitting or standing in relation to others. This arrangement is then discussed.
3. The client is asked to rearrange the cards in a way that illustrates the various emotional ties, subsystems, and interpersonal conflicts within the family. This arrangement is then discussed.
4. The client selects one of the cards representing another family member and then rearranges all the other cards showing how that particular member experiences the family system. This step can be repeated with other cards.
5. The client is asked to rearrange the cards in a way that depicts the relationship he or she desires for his or her family. Discussion then focuses on what it would take to create this more desirable family interaction.

SELECTED BIBLIOGRAPHY

Baron, Roger, and Floyd Feeney. *Juvenile Diversion Through Family Counseling.* Washington, D.C.: National Institute of Law Enforcement and Criminal Justice, U.S. Government Printing Office, 1976.

Hartman, Ann. *Working with Adoptive Families: Beyond Placement.* New York: Child Welfare League of America, 1984.

Vondracek, Fred, and Sherry Corneal. *Strategies for Resolving Individual and Family Problems.* Pacific Grove, Calif.: Brooks/Cole, 1995.

*Reprinted by special permission of CWLA from *Working with Adoptive Families: Beyond Placement,* 1984.

14.14 The Talking Stick

PURPOSE: To structure discussion within a group session or family interview.

DISCUSSION: For centuries, many American Indian tribes have used the "talking stick" to govern small group discussion and encourage listening behaviors. Instead of a decorated stick some tribes use an eagle feather or other sacred object. During a discussion, the talking stick is passed around the group, from person to person. Whoever holds it has permission to speak; all others are to give that person their undivided attention. This ensures that everyone has a chance to speak and is heard by the others. Reverence for the object serves to limit the verbose members and encourage the timid and those less inclined to speak.

This method of structuring discussion can be used with a small group or a family. It may be especially useful if members tend to talk all at once or do not listen to each other. In place of the talking stick or feather, a family might use some other object that illicits reverence and respect (e.g., a family picture, a Bible, etc.).

SELECTED BIBLIOGRAPHY

Locust, Carol. "The Talking Stick." Tucson, Ariz.: Native American Research and Training Center. (undated)

14.15 Homework Assignments

PURPOSE: To assist the client in learning a new behavior by assigning specific tasks and activities to be worked on between counseling sessions.

DISCUSSION: Learning a new skill or developing a new behavioral pattern is essential to the solution of many problems in social functioning. Moreover, the new skill and/or behavior needs to be practiced in the client's natural environment, not just during sessions with the social worker.

The term *homework* refers to assignments given to the client that are to be carried out by the client between sessions. Needless to say, homework should be directly related to the client-worker contract and the objectives of intervention. The worker and client should jointly select and plan homework. It is important that the homework make sense to the client. For example, given a client whose problem revolves around low self-esteem and an inability to interact comfortably with others, a homework assignment might be to strike up at least two conversations per day while riding to and from work on the bus.

When using homework assignments, the worker should give the client a precise set of instructions. Often, these need to be written. A worker can prepare the instructions before the session. If possible, they should be written on NCR (no carbon required) paper or duplicated so both the client and the worker will have a copy.

Shelton and Ackerman (1974) explain that homework instructions contain one or more of the following:

1. *A do statement.* "Read, practice, observe, say, count . . . some kind of homework."
2. *A quantity statement.* "Talk three times about . . . ; spend thirty minutes three times . . . ; give four compliments per day . . . ; write a list of at least ten . . . ."
3. *A record statement.* "Count and record the number of compliments; each time he hits, mark a _____ on the chart; whenever that thought comes to you, write a _____ on the . . . ."
4. *A bring statement.* "Bring . . . your list; the chart; the cards; your spouse . . . to the next appointment."
5. *A contingency statement.* "Call for your next appointment after you have done . . . ; for each activity you attend, one dollar will be deducted . . . ; each minute spent doing _____ will earn you _____ ; one-tenth of your penalty deposit will be forfeited for each assignment not completed." (p. 16)

Homework is not appropriate for all clients. As a technique, it works best with an approach that emphasizes client training and skill building. The use of homework presumes that the client is willing to accept direction from the worker and practice new behaviors outside sessions with the social worker. Thus, a client must be willing and able to work independently.

SELECTED BIBLIOGRAPHY

Hudson, Barbara, and Geraldine MacDonald. *Behavioural Social Work.* Chicago: Dorsey Press, 1986.

Reid, William. *Family Problem Solving.* New York: Columbia University Press, 1985.

Shelton, John, and J. Mark Ackerman. *Homework in Counseling and Psychotherapy.* Springfield, Ill.: Charles C. Thomas, 1974.

Shelton, John, and Rona Levy. *Behavioral Assignments and Treatment Compliance.* Champaign, Ill.: Research Press, 1981.

14.16   Envelope Budgeting

PURPOSE: To assist the client in money management.

DISCUSSION: Many of the clients served by social workers are economically poor. They find it difficult to stretch a very limited income to cover the bare essentials. Most of their money transactions are in cash; few have checking accounts. *Envelope budgeting* can be taught to clients who need a simple method for keeping track of their money and expenses.

The first step in setting up this budgeting system is for the client to identify the key categories of expenditure: rent, food, clothing, transportation, household supplies, and so on. The next step is to determine how many dollars need to be spent on each category during a spending cycle, such as a one- or two-week period. An envelope is prepared and labeled for each category, and all of the envelopes are kept together in a box. In the "food envelope," for example, the client places the money allotted for food.

As money is removed from an envelope and spent, the client has a tangible measure of cash outflow and the balance that remains. The client is encouraged to resist the temptation to shift money from one category to another, but this may sometimes be necessary. When the client obtains additional income, cash is again placed in the envelopes for the new spending cycle.

This technique can be used with clients who have limited computational skills. If the client can only count, he or she can usually use envelope budgeting. Subtraction and addition skills are helpful but not essential. This technique helps people plan and monitor expenditures but it is not a permanent solution for clients who are overwhelmed by debt or have expenditures that far exceed their income. In such cases, more complex approaches—such as consumer credit counseling, debt consolidation, or even bankruptcy—may be necessary.

SELECTED BIBLIOGRAPHY

American Association of Retired Persons. *A Primer on Personal Money Management for Midlife and Older Women.* Washington, D.C.: AARP, 1991.

Vosler, Nancy. "Assessing Family Access to Basic Resources: An Essential Component of Social Work Practice." *Social Work* 35, No. 5 (September 1990): 434–441.

14.17 Managing Personal Debt

PURPOSE: To assist the client in handling large bills and debt.

DISCUSSION: An individual or family with too many bills and too little money experiences much stress. A shortage of money can be made up by borrowing money or buying on credit, but this only makes the problem worse. Paying some bills while neglecting others may be necessary, but this soon results in a damaged credit rating and possible legal ramifications.

There is no easy way to climb out of debt, but several things can be done to gain control of the situation. Offer the following suggestions to a client who is trying to deal with financial problems.

1. Recognize that financial problems are often more complex that the simple lack of money. The problem is often rooted in a set of personal values, attitudes, and shopping behaviors that lead to overspending. The power of advertising, peer-group influences, and feelings of low self-esteem push many people into buying more than they can afford. The ease of obtaining and using credit cards is a pitfall for many. In order to get out of debt, some significant changes in behavior are usually required.

2. When bills always exceed income, you must find a way to decrease spending, increase income, or both. Begin immediately to cut spending. Since accumulating additional debts makes the problem even worse, avoid purchasing items on credit. Eliminate revolving credit accounts at stores, so you are not tempted to buy something whenever in the store. If the overuse of credit cards is a cause of your financial problems, destroy the cards and use only cash. If you must use credit cards, buy only what you can pay for within 30 days and avoid interest charges.

3. Make a careful analysis of what you owe. Begin by making four columns on a piece of paper. In column 1, list all of the items for which you are billed on a regular basis (e.g., loan and credit card bills, utilities, rent, car payments, dental and medical, phone, insurance, and the like). In column 2, list the expected monthly payment for each item in column 1. In column 3, list the amount you actually pay each month toward each item. In column 4, total the amount owed for all items. Begin your analysis by marking all items for which interest is charged; these should become high-priority targets for payment. If you must skip payments or reduce the amount paid toward a bill, do so on items that do not involve interest charges or overdue charges. Also, prioritize the interest-related bills according to the amount still owed; concentrate on paying off those on which the least amount is owed, which will eliminate all credit charges associated with that bill and free up money for other bills. Completely paying off a bill also provides a feeling of making progress on debt reduction and this record of progress can be used to argue for payment extensions because it demonstrates ability to pay bills.

4. If you cannot pay a bill, do not avoid the problem. Never miss a payment without first explaining the problem to your creditor. If they understand your situation, if your explanation is reasonable, and if they believe you intend to pay, they may be willing to make an adjustment. Be sure to describe the actions you are taking to solve your financial problems. Some lenders and businesses have emergency plans that can provide temporary relief. They might rewrite your loan at a lower rate of interest or spread the loan over a longer time period, both of which will lower the monthly payment.

5. Do not avoid bill collectors. A frank discussion may result in an acceptable solution. Remember that collection agencies do not really want your possessions. Moreover, they do not want to do anything that will cause you to lose whatever income you do have. What they want is money. If you can demonstrate a genuine desire to pay and actually pay even a little each month, often a creditor will find this acceptable. However, if you avoid bill collectors or show no effort to pay the bill, they seldom hesitate to do whatever is legal to recover something of value and make your life miserable.

6. Sell possessions you do not need. Consider selling your car unless it is needed for work-related transportation. Getting rid of a car is especially important if it has not been paid for and you are buying it on an installment plan. A car loan creates a vicious cycle of debt because by the time it is finally paid off, the car must often be replaced. Look seriously for a less expensive means of transportation.

7. Make use of credit-counseling resources, but before using a particular program, be sure to find out: (a) who sponsors the program; (b) what, if any, charges are involved; and (c) how the program operates. If possible, use the services offered by nonprofit agencies. Do not confuse the credit-counseling services available for little or no cost with the for-profit businesses that do debt adjustment for a high fee. A good consumer credit-counseling program can reduce your worry, help you develop the self-discipline needed to handle debt, and help you avoid bankruptcy.

8. When other less drastic methods fail to impact the debt problem, loan consolidation or bankruptcy must be considered. When utilizing a ***consolidation loan*** strategy, you take out a new loan and immediately pay off all other loans and overdue accounts. The single payment on this new loan is designed to be smaller than the total for prior monthly payments, and it is easier to keep track of payments on just one loan. However, a consolidation loan stretches your payments over a longer period of time. You must still pay the whole amount before you are debt free, and you will be paying interest during the life of the consolidation loan. Another disadvantage of consolidation is that it is easy to forget how much is actually owed and you may be tempted to take on new credit obligations because the new monthly loan payment seems small in comparison to previous bills.

9. ***Bankruptcy*** may be necessary in cases of extreme financial difficulty, when creditors are unwilling to renegotiate debts, when a consolidation loan cannot be obtained, and when informal loans cannot be obtained from family or friends. For individuals and married couples, the Federal Bankruptcy Act provides two types of bankruptcy. The most common type is a Chapter 7—*straight bankruptcy* or liquidation proceeding. After a petition is filed with the U.S. District Court, a bankruptcy judge notifies the people to whom you owe money (i.e., your creditors) of their rights to file a claim against you and to question you on the witness stand. Creditors have an opportunity to object to your not having to pay what you owe. If there are no objections, the bankruptcy judge will grant what is called a "discharge in bankruptcy," which relieves you from legal liability for the payment of all debts owed at the time of bankruptcy. All of your possessions, with the exception of those exempt by state or federal law, are turned over to a trustee to be sold. The proceeds from this sale are distributed to the creditors who filed claims. The remaining debt is legally erased. Debts such as child support or alimony, taxes, unlisted debts, fines, and/or debts obtained under false pretenses cannot be discharged.

Another bankruptcy option, called a Chapter 13 or *wage earner plan*, allows you to keep your possessions while paying off your debts under an installment plan monitored by a court-appointed trustee. You develop a plan for repaying your debts over a period of three years (sometimes five years) and if your plan is approved by the judge, your creditors must stop all collection efforts. They must also stop charging you interest and late charges on most types of debts. Each payday, a fixed amount of your wage or other income is turned over to the trustee, who then pays your creditors. Creditors will usually agree to this plan because they are more likely to be paid under this arrangement than under straight bankruptcy.

Bankruptcy has a number of negative consequences. For example, a bankruptcy remains on your credit report for 10 years and will affect your credit rating. A person considering bankruptcy should seek the advice of an attorney and/or a credit-counseling agency. Information can be obtained from the Division of Bankruptcy, Administrative Office of the United States Courts, Washington, D.C. 20544.

SELECTED BIBLIOGRAPHY

Bamford, Janet. *Consumer Reports Money Book.* Novi, Mich.: Consumer Union of United States, 1995.
Leonard, Robin. *Money Troubles,* 3rd ed. Berkeley, Calif.: Nolo Press, 1995.
Poduska, Bernard. *For Love and Money.* Pacific Grove, Calif.: Brooks/Cole, 1993.

14.18   Decision-Making Worksheets

PURPOSE: To assist the client in considering alternatives and making a decision.

DISCUSSION: Helping clients make difficult decisions is an important social work activity. A social worker familiar with key issues and common feelings surrounding a particular decision can facilitate the client's decision making by constructing a ***decision-making worksheet,*** which provides direction and focuses the client's attention on factors that need to be considered prior to arriving at a decision.

Figure 14.1 contains excerpts from a decision-making worksheet designed for use with pregnant teenagers considering whether to relinquish their babies for adoption. As can be seen from this sample, a worksheet is simply a format for raising questions and helping the client analyze his or her situation. Obviously, skilled interviewing could accomplish the same thing, but the worksheet can provide added structure and can be used as homework between sessions.

SELECTED BIBLIOGRAPHY

Lutheran Social Services. "Decision-Making Plans for the Baby." Missoula, Mont.: Lutheran Social Services. (Mimeo.)
McClam, Tricia, and Marianne Woodside. *Problem Solving in the Helping Professions.* Pacific Grove, Calif.: Brooks/Cole, 1994.
Winkler, Robin, Dirk Brown, Margaret vonKeppel, and Amy Blanchard. *Clinical Practice in Adoption.* New York: Pergamon Press, 1988.

14.19   Distinguishing Means from Ends

PURPOSE: To assist the client in problem-solving efforts by making a clear distinction between the problem to be solved and possible solutions.

FIGURE 14.1
Sample
Decision-
Making
Worksheet

Planning for My Baby

I. Questions about my relationship with my baby's father.
   A. Can I count on him for financial support?
   B. Can I count on him for emotional support?
   C. Has my relationship with him changed since I got pregnant?
   (and so on)

II. Questions about my relationship with my parents.
   A. What do my parents want me to do?
   B. Can I go against their wishes?
   C. If my mother helps take care of my baby, is it possible the baby will become "her baby"?
   (and so on)

III. Questions about my life after having the baby.
   A. If I keep the baby, how will this affect future dating, marriage, and children?
   B. If I give my baby up for adoption, how will this affect my future dating, marriage, and children?
   (and so on)

IV. A daydream exercise.
   A. If I could pick the ideal time for having a baby, when would it be? Where would I be? What would the baby's father be like?
   B. How does the above ideal situation compare with my real situation?
   (and so on)

V. Picturing myself.
   A. Draw a picture of yourself one year ago. Around your picture, indicate in words or pictures the things that were important to you then. What were your activities, how did you use your time? What were your goals and aspirations one year ago?
   B. Think about yourself now. Change the above picture of yourself one year ago to fit things today. Cross out those activities in which you are no longer involved. Have your goals and aspirations changed?
   C. Draw a picture of yourself one year from now. Again, around your picture, write in those things that you will be involved in one year from now. How will you spend your time? In one year, what will be your goals and aspirations?
   (and so on)

Source: Lutheran Social Services, mimeographed item (no date), pp. 1–2, 4–5.

DISCUSSION: When helping a client solve a problem, it is necessary to distinguish between the problem and the means of solving that problem. For example, a client may request a worker's assistance on figuring out how to get money to buy a car because of the need to get to and from a new job. In this case, the client has confused means and ends. The client's problem is a lack of transportation, not the lack of a car. A car is only one means of transportation; others might include public transportation, paying a private car owner for a ride, walking, or taking a taxi.

A simple listing may help the client keep the ends and means separate. The following list was developed during an interview with a young single mother who had requested foster care placement for her child because she could not care for the child while holding a job.

End	*Means*
Child care while mother works in order to secure money to support self and child.	Licensed day-care center
	Paid babysitter
	Informal babysitting exchange with friend
	Babysitting (relative)
	Change jobs or hours of work
	AFDC

As can be seen, once the client's presenting problem was redefined as a need for child care, rather than a need for placement, several new options emerged.

SELECTED BIBLIOGRAPHY

Kaufman, Roger. *Identifying and Solving Problems.* La Jolla, Calif.: University Associates, 1976.

Priestley, Philip, James McGuire, David Flegg, Valerie Hemsley, and David Welham. *Social Skills and Personal Problem Solving: A Handbook of Methods.* London: Travistock Publication, 1978.

Sprafkin, Robert, N. Jane Gershaw, and Arnold Goldstein. *Social Skills for Mental Health.* Boston: Allyn and Bacon, 1993.

14.20   Priorities-Weighting Grid

PURPOSE: To help the client make a decision when there are four or more options.

DISCUSSION: The *priorities-weighting grid* is a decision-making tool that can help an individual, family, or small group make a difficult decision by systematically examining each option in relation to every other option. It is useful when those who need to make a decision have numerous options but cannot see that any one choice is better than another. Essentially, this technique moves the client through a series of forced choices; from this process, the preferred option will emerge.

This technique can be used with a client during an interview, or taught to clients so they can use it at home to make personal and family decisions. The grid can focus on decisions as diverse as prioritizing one's personal values or something as mundane as deciding which of five used cars to buy. In this latter example, choices would have to be made between the relative importance of price, condition, size, and so on. The grid is not an effective tool if a choice is to be made between only two or three options.

FIGURE 14.2   Sample Priorities-Weighting Grid

Priorities	Priorities Grid										Options/Alternatives
1.	1	1	1	1	1	1	1	1	1	____	1. _____
	2	3	4	5	6	7	8	9	10		
2.		2	2	2	2	2	2	2	____	2. _____
		3	4	5	6	7	8	9	10		
3.			3	3	3	3	3	3	____	3. _____
			4	5	6	7	8	9	10		
4.				4	4	4	4	4	____	4. _____
				5	6	7	8	9	10		
5.					5	5	5	5	____	5. _____
					6	7	8	9	10		
6.						6	6	6	____	6. _____
						7	8	9	10		
7.							7	7	____	7. _____
							8	9	10		
8.								8	____	8. _____
								9	10		
9.									9	____	9. _____
									10		
10.										____	10. _____

Figure 14.2 is a sample priorities-weighting grid. Directions for completing the grid are the following:

1. List the options you are considering down the right side of the page. Assign each a number; order is not important.
2. Compare option 1 with option 2, circling your preference on the grid. Next, compare option 1 with option 3; again, circle your preferred option on the grid.
3. When you are finished comparing option 1 with every option listed, proceed in the same manner comparing option 2 with 3, then 4, and so on through the list.
4. When finished, count the number of times you circled each number. Remember to count both horizontally and vertically.
5. Finally, list your options in the priorities column on the left side of the paper according to their score: highest number as 1, lowest as 10. In the case of a tie score, examine the grid and determine which option you chose when you compared the two.

SELECTED BIBLIOGRAPHY

Carkhuff, Robert. *The Art of Problem-Solving.* Amherst, Mass.: Human Resource Development Press, 1973.

14.21   Decision-Making Matrix

PURPOSE: To help a client make a decision when there are two or three options.

DISCUSSION: Many of the problems faced by clients revolve around decision making. For example, a 60-year-old woman must decide whether to place her 83-year-old mother in a nursing home or try once again to care for her at home. Decision making can be especially difficult for the client who has multiple problems and is under much stress. Many individuals either avoid making decisions or they make decisions impulsively without considering the advantages and disadvantages of each option.

A *decision-making matrix* can help a client think through the pros and cons of each option and arrive at a decision. The matrix has three columns: (1) Alternative, (2) Cost, and (3) Benefit. In the Alternative column, the client lists the two or three options being considered. Then, across from each alternative, in the other columns, the client describes both the drawbacks (costs) and the advantages (benefits) associated with each option. Finally, after all the pros and cons have been outlined, the client compares each option and makes a decision.

Figure 14.3 is an example of a matrix completed by a social worker and a battered wife during an interview focusing on the decision of whether she should return to her husband or end her marriage.

SELECTED BIBLIOGRAPHY

Kaufman, Roger. *Identifying and Solving Problems.* La Jolla, Calif.: University Associates, 1976.
Nelson-Jones, Richard. *Lifeskills Helping.* Pacific Grove, Calif.: Brooks/Cole, 1993.

FIGURE 14.3   Sample Decision-Making Matrix

Alternative	Cost	Benefit
1. Return to John	a. Abuse would probably continue b. Children are fearful c. Would have to face same hard decisions in the future d. I could get seriously hurt or killed e. Medical costs	a. Preserve family b. Hard decision is delayed until later c. Would have place to live and money d. John says he cares for me
2. Leave John and end the marriage	a. Fear of the unknown—(I need to be with somebody) b. Trauma of divorce for me and kids c. Would have less money to live on d. Might be forced on AFDC e. Legal costs f. Custody battle over children	a. Abuse, pain, and fear would end b. Decision would have been made and I could try to put my life together c. Children would be less nervous and upset d. I could find out if I can function on my own e. Opportunity for fresh start

14.22   Indirect Discussion of Self in Small Groups

PURPOSE: To make it easier for group participants to discuss personal concerns.

DISCUSSION: This technique is designed to stimulate and structure small-group discussion of the participants' problems and concerns while at the same time protecting individual privacy. It allows clients to discuss matters that they would not ordinarily share with others. Moreover, this technique can engage a reluctant client in group discussion. Essentially, the technique calls for each participant to respond to a set of questions by writing answers on 3 × 5 cards. The unsigned cards are collected, shuffled, and randomly passed out to the group members. The members then discuss and analyze the responses, problems, or concerns found on the cards.

To begin the process, each participant is given three 3 × 5 cards; each card is labeled A, B, or C. The participant will use each card to write a response to a specific question: question A, question B, question C. Instruct the participants not to put their names on the cards. And before they write, tell them exactly how the cards will be collected, shuffled, and then redistributed randomly for discussion. Warn participants against writing a response in a way that might reveal their identity. Encourage the group to be honest in answering the questions, since the identity of the person writing the card will be protected.

The social worker using the technique preselects the questions. The following is a sample set of stem sentences used in a group session with physically abusing parents.

On Card A: (complete the statement) "Before a hitting episode, I feel . . . ."

On Card B: (complete the statement) "The thing I feel most after a hitting episode is . . . ."

On Card C: (complete the statement) "One thing I could do to decrease the hitting episodes is . . . ."

The technique is also useful in training sessions. The next sample is a set of stem sentences used in a training session for foster parents concerned with improving their work with the biological parents of children in foster care.

On Card A: (complete the statement) "In my work with biological parents, I find it most difficult to . . . ."

On Card B: (complete the statement) "I know I shouldn't have this negative feeling toward biological parents, but I feel . . . ."

On Card C: (complete the statement) "The thing that would help me to improve my work with biological parents is . . . ."

After all of the participants have finished writing their responses, collect the cards in sequence: first, all of the A cards, then the Bs, then the C cards. Shuffle each stack separately. Then pass out all of the A cards randomly, then the Bs, then the Cs. This procedure ensures that each participant receives a response to each of the three questions or stem sentences.

The next step is to have groups of three or four members, if part of a large group, study and discuss the cards they have been given. They might be asked to summarize what the cards seem to be saying. For example, the foster parents might be asked to study the cards and answer the following:

1. Identify the difficulties experienced in work with biological parents.
2. Identify the possible causes of these difficulties.
3. Identify methods of improving relationships with biological parents.

After a small group has studied their cards, participants are encouraged to trade their cards with other small groups in order to obtain even more data. Typically, the participants discover that they share common worries, problems, and feelings. This can be reassuring. Use of the technique helps counteract feelings of isolation and the belief that "no one else feels like I do."

The technique works best in groups larger than about fifteen, but it can be adapted for use in smaller groups and even with families. When used with a small group, the social worker should also submit a set of cards. Sometimes, the worker can help things along by writing responses that are sure to provoke discussion.

SELECTED BIBLIOGRAPHY

Brandler, Sondra, and Camille Roman. *Group Work*. New York: Haworth Press, 1991.
Zastrow, Charles. *Social Work With Groups*, 3rd ed. Chicago: Nelson-Hall, 1993.

14.23 Programming in Group Work

PURPOSE: To encourage individual and group development by selecting and arranging group activities that promote specific types of interaction.

DISCUSSION: The technique of *programming* originated within the group work tradition of social work. It refers to the planful selection and use of recreation, nonverbal media, and other activities to create opportunities for clients to learn new behaviors or experience positive interpersonal relationships and to move the group in certain directions. Participation in an activity can have a profound effect on how members feel about themselves and each other and on the structure and norms that develop within the group.

A broad range of activities can be used in programming: camping, puppet shows, drama, care of animals, art, dance, music, crafts, cooking, basketball, parties, and the like. Games can be useful in work with clients of all ages but they are especially important with children. According to Schaefer and Reid (1986), games are helpful for six reasons.

1. Playing a game is an enjoyable activity.
2. Games have an "as if" quality that separates them from real life and allows for fantasy experience.

3. Rules exist or are created that define and restrict the behavior of the players and add organization and structure to the game.
4. A contest is implied or explicit in games, in that players compete either with each other or with themselves in order to win the game.
5. Games, by virtue of their structured, competitive makeup pose a challenge to the participants. At the lowest level, the challenge is to play with other people in a self-controlled, cooperative fashion. More complex games require more in terms of emotional control, intellect, and social skills.
6. Game-playing usually involves interaction between two or more players. (p. 4)

An individual's behavior during a program activity can provide important assessment and diagnostic information. For example, a child's interaction with peers during a game may garner insights into the child's behavior that could not be obtained from a battery of psychological tests.

The type of programming used will depend on the social worker's assessment of individual members, the functioning of the group as a whole, and the group's purpose. Guidelines include the following:

1. The usefulness of a particular activity is related to the stage of group development. For example, in the get acquainted stage, you would use activities that promote friendly interaction but avoid ones that would require a member to assume a leadership role (see Item 13.8).

2. The selection of an activity is always tied to the question: What behaviors do I want to encourage? Select an activity that elicits or teaches the behaviors you want to encourage in the group. Schaefer and Reid (1986, 9) explain a particular activity may elicit one or more of nine behaviors: communication, respect for rules, self-discipline, independence, cooperation, awareness and handling of norms and expectations, competition, control of aggression, and handling issues of power and authority. Consider how the activity will fit with the group's purpose. Select activities that call forth behaviors that will advance the group's development and help it achieve its purpose.

3. When selecting an activity, consider such factors as the members' ages, developmental levels, physical capacities, motor skills, endurance, interests, attention spans, needs for control and protection, social skills, and so forth. Also group size needs to be considered.

4. An activity needs to be attractive and interesting to the members. It should offer a challenge but not generate excessive frustration.

5. When selecting an activity, carefully consider what prerequisite skills it demands of the members. For example, does it require oral communication, writing, reading, cooperation, competition, movement, initiative, memory, judgment, self-control, ability to follow directions? Avoid activities for which members do not have prerequisite abilities.

6. Carefully consider what the activity will require of the social worker. For example, does the activity require the worker to function as a teacher, leader, advisor, planner, police officer, umpire, time keeper, transporter, supplier of food, or what?

7. Consider how the rules of the activity will impact on the members. For example, does a game involve the selection or ranking of participants, the choosing of sides, or the elimination of a "loser" from further competition? Can the members cope with whatever frustration the rules may create?

8. Consider how the activity fits with scheduling constraints and the physical environment. How much time is required? How much space? Is it safe? Is it noisy?

SELECTED BIBLIOGRAPHY

Middleman, Ruth. *The Non-Verbal Method in Working With Groups.* New York: Association Press, 1968.

Middleman, Ruth, and Gale Goldberg Wood. *Skills for Direct Practice in Social Work.* New York: Columbia University Press, 1990.

Schaefer, Charles, and Steven Reid. *Game Play: Therapeutic Use of Childhood Games.* New York: Wiley & Sons, 1986.

14.24 Resolving Interpersonal Conflict

PURPOSE: To assist people in resolving conflicts and disagreements.

DISCUSSION: The social worker is frequently in the position of trying to help clients resolve conflicts (e.g., between parent and teenager, husband and wife, etc.) and sometimes in the position of trying to help two professionals resolve a conflict. An important first step in helping others resolve a conflict is to realize that the dynamics of the conflict may be complex and that the conflict is often about issues no one is mentioning. People often fight over a minor issue because they are afraid to face the real one. If true resolution is to take place, the real issue must be identified.

Bisno (1988, 31) alerts us to various motives behind a conflict by identifying six types of conflict: those characterized by a clash of opposing interests or commitments; those created in order to achieve some hidden purpose; those related to errors of attribution and unknowingly misdirected to the wrong party or wrong issue; those deliberately directed to the wrong party or wrong issue in order to avoid the real issue; those based on misperceptions, misunderstandings, and poor communications; and, finally, those created for the purpose of expressing hostility or other strong emotion.

A worker trying to mediate a conflict should keep several guidelines in mind.

1. Do not take sides. Be fair and respect the views and feelings of everyone involved. Remind the parties in conflict of the things they already agree on, such as certain values, concern for a third party, desire to avoid further pain, and so on.

2. Appeal for a demonstration of mutual respect and a willingness to at least listen and try to understand differences in perception and needs. Attempt to get those in conflict to agree that during the discussion, they will avoid issuing threats, name calling, moralizing, attacking sensitive spots, or bringing up past hurts and disagreements that are unrelated to the current conflict.

3. Urge those in conflict to ask themselves four questions before they speak:
   - Do I want to resolve this conflict or am I really after some other hidden goal that I am afraid to talk about?
   - Is what I am going to say true, or is it an exaggeration or only a partial truth that will invite an angry response?
   - Is what I am going to say relevant to the issue we are discussing?
   - Is what I am going to say constructive—something that will move us closer to mutual understanding?

4. Help those in conflict to clearly identify and define the problems and issues. But urge them to avoid taking a definite stand on what they want as a solution, for doing so sets the stage for a struggle of wills. Ask each person to state briefly his or her concerns and needs as clearly as possible. Ask the others to repeat what they have heard. If they have not understood, repeat this process. The objective here is to help each person understand what the other is really saying and to gain empathy for each other's perspective and feelings.

5. Use techniques of reflection, clarification, paraphrase, and summarization to assist each to express his or her point of view, needs, and concerns (see Chapter 8). Help each to use I-messages in expressing his or her side in the conflict.

6. Once the issues are on the table and there is some degree of mutual understanding, use brainstorming to identify several potential solutions. Look for solutions or compromises that provide some benefits to both sides.

7. Throughout the discussion, recognize and reinforce efforts to control anger, to understand the other party, and to honestly express needs and concerns—even if these are only feeble efforts.

8. Remember that the person who is labeled a troublemaker or the one who is causing the problem is very often a person who feels powerless. People who feel powerless often strike out, directly or indirectly, at others. In response, others may strike back or withdraw from the relationship, thereby creating a vicious cycle. It is important to directly address the feelings that may be giving rise to a sense of powerlessness.

9. Those who want to resolve an interpersonal conflict are advised to *do what comes unnaturally.* The person who feels the desire to retreat from the conflict really needs to directly confront the issue. The person who wants to talk actually needs to listen. The person who would like to vent frustration and inflict pain really needs to develop compassion and empathy.

SELECTED BIBLIOGRAPHY

Bisno, Herb. *Managing Conflict.* Newbury Park, Calif.: Sage, 1988.
Folberg, Jay, and Alison Taylor. *Mediation: A Comprehensive Guide to Resolving Conflicts Without Litigation.* San Francisco: Jossey-Bass, 1986.
Hocker, Joyce and William Wilmot. *Interpersonal Conflict.* Madison, Wis.: W. C. B. Brown and Benchmark, 1995.

14.25   The Feelings List

PURPOSE: To assist a client in the identification and expression of feelings.

DISCUSSION: Many of the clients seen by social workers are persons who grew up in dysfunctional families (e.g., alcoholic, abusive, etc.) where they learned to suppress their feelings. Often they were severely punished for expressing emotion or for asking the "wrong" questions. Many were exposed to a childrearing pattern that allowed the expression of feelings but at the same time invalidated or discounted these feelings (e.g., when a mother tells her angry child, "You're not really angry; you're just tired"). As these individuals grow older, they carry with them a tendency to suppress, misinterpret, or mistrust their own emotions and feelings. Many are unsure of their true feelings; many cannot distinguish one emotion from another and can speak of feelings in only broad terms such as *sad, upset* or *OK*.

Simplistic as it sounds, a written list of feeling words can help a client identify and express feelings. As the client struggles to identify and sort out personal feelings, he or she is encouraged to review the list as an aid in finding the words needed to describe feelings. Even a short list of 25 to 50 words can serve as a starting place and help the client distinguish one feeling from another. Here are sample feeling words drawn from lists used by Porter (1986), Black (1981), and Mayer (1983).

controlled	embarrassed	attached	abandoned
excited	courageous	worthless	serene
concerned	tender	secure	curious
manipulated	tough	lost	ashamed
hateful	sarcastic	protected	guilty
desperate	competitive	isolated	vulnerable
joyful	confident	relieved	apathetic
disloyal	fearful	detached	warm
attractive	assertive	defensive	unfeeling

While discussing feelings, the client should be helped to understand that feelings and emotions are a normal human experience. Because feelings are real and important, they should not be hidden or denied. Although some feelings are pleasant and some unpleasant, they are neither good or bad. How one chooses to behave in response to feelings may be appropriate or inappropriate, but the feelings themselves simply exist and are neither right and wrong in a moral sense.

A feelings list can prove useful in work with individuals, families, and groups. If you believe the use of a feelings list would be helpful to your clients, the authors suggest that you prepare one consisting of words that will be meaningful to persons served by your agency. A client's age, life experience, culture, and educational level need to be considered when compiling a list. (Also see Item 8.6 for additional information on emotion.)

SELECTED BIBLIOGRAPHY

Black, Claudia. *It Will Never Happen to Me.* Denver: MAC Publishing, 1981.

Mayer, Adele. *Incest: A Treatment Manual for Therapy with Victims, Spouses and Offenders.* Homes Beach, Fla.: Learning Publications, 1983.

Porter, Eugene. *Treating the Young Male Victim of Sexual Assault.* Syracuse,: N.Y. Safer Society Press, 1986.

14.26   The Life Book

PURPOSE: To help a child in a foster care or adoption placement develop a sense of identity and understand his or her experiences with separation and placement.

DISCUSSION: The *life book* is both a therapeutic tool and a personalized record of a child's life experience. Backhaus (1984) explains that

> a Life Book is an individually made book covering the child's life from birth to present, written in the child's own words. It generally includes a narrative describing what has happened to the child, when, and why, as well as what the child's feelings are about what has happened. The book may also incorporate photos, drawings, report cards, awards and certificates, letters from previous foster or adoptive parents and birth parents, a birth certificate, a genogram, and anything else a particular child might want to include. It is current practice to assemble a Life Book for older children who are being adopted as part of their preparation. Life Books . . . can be invaluable for those being adopted, living in foster or residential care, or returning to birth parents. (p. 551)

The life book is especially useful in helping a child:

1. Develop a sense of continuity and identity.
2. Understand past separations and placements and reduce confusion and misconceptions about these and other disruptive experiences.
3. Avoid the unhealthy use of fantasy and denial in trying to cope with painful life experiences.
4. Remember significant people and childhood events.
5. Maintain in one place a record of important personal data (i.e., birth and medical information, pictures of family and significant others, school records, etc.).

The worker involves the child in the creation of the book and refers to it when discussing the child's life experience and his or her feelings about those experiences.

SELECTED BIBLIOGRAPHY

American Foster Care Resources. *The Book About Me.* King George, Va.: American Foster Care Resources, 1984.

Aust, Patricia. "Using the Life Story Book in Treatment of Children in Placement." *Child Welfare* 60 (September 1981): 535–560.

Backhaus, Kristiana. "Life Books: Tool for Working with Children in Placement." *Social Work* 29 (November–December 1984): 551–545.

14.27   Client Advocacy

PURPOSE: To secure services that the client needs and is entitled to but unable to obtain on his or her own.

DISCUSSION: When the social worker performs as a ***client advocate,*** he or she speaks, argues, manipulates, bargains, and negotiates on behalf of the client. At the direct-service level, an advocacy stance may be necessary in order to secure benefits or services that the client is entitled to but, for one reason or another, is unable to obtain. As compared to other tactics for securing services (e.g., referral/brokering, mediation), advocacy is essentially a confrontation. Because the worker's advocacy may threaten another professional or agency, the risks must be carefully considered. Remember these guidelines:

1. Make sure your client wants you to become his or her advocate. Do not engage in advocacy unless you have an explicit agreement with your client and he or she understands both the potential benefits and risks. To the extent possible, involve your client in all decisions concerning the actions you will take. If possible, help your client to argue the case rather than speak on his or her behalf.

2. Realize that your advocacy can damage your relationship or your agency's relationship with another agency or professional and that this damaged relationship may create problems in the future when you need their cooperation to serve other clients. Do not use advocacy until you have tried approaches with fewer risks or that are less likely to polarize the affected parties.

3. Your willingness to assume the role of client advocate should arise from a desire to help your client, and never from a motive of dislike for another professional or agency or a desire for self-aggrandizement.

4. Before you engage in a confrontational tactic, be sure you understand the facts of the matter. Do not base your decisions on hearsay or on one-sided descriptions of the situation. For example, realize that many clients do not understand the explanations given by agency representatives and often they are confused by complex eligibility requirements. Get the facts before you decide how to proceed.

5. Successful advocacy requires a high level of interpersonal skill and empathy. You need to be able to put yourself in the shoes of those you are confronting. Try to understand the feelings and position of the opposing party. Communicate your concerns in a factual and nonabrasive manner, but speak in a tone that conveys that you feel strongly about the matter. Face-to-face meetings are almost always more effective than phone calls and letters.

6. Before you speak with a representative of an agency or organization that you are confronting, write down exactly what you intend to say and the questions you will ask. For example, begin your conversation with a courteous request for an expla-

nation of why your client was not able to secure desired services. Write down the answers. If the answers you receive are significantly different from your prior understanding, discuss the matter with your client and seek clarification. Keep a record of who you talked to, their position, their responses, and the time and date of the communication.

7. Do not assume that you know the inner workings of another agency or its policies, procedures, or eligibility requirements. Appreciate the real limitations and complexities that exist within human services agencies. Respect the other agency's chain of command (e.g., do not ask to speak with a supervisor until you have spoken to the line worker; do not ask to speak with an administrator until you have spoken with the supervisor).

8. If the information you have gathered indicates that the agency should be able to provide the needed service—or wants to but cannot because of a technicality or a policy—ask the representative for information on how the decision can be appealed and who else you should speak to about the matter. Consider asking if the top administrator, board members, or a legislative committee should be informed of the difficulty faced by your client or perhaps consulted on how the matter can be resolved. Consider using a measured expression of anger to demonstrate your resolve.

9. When pursuing an appeals process, prepare detailed documentation of the client's need and what was done, step by step, to try to secure needed services. List names, dates, and content of all communication. Include copies of all letters sent and received.

SELECTED BIBLIOGRAPHY

Kirst-Ashman, Karen, and Grafton Hull. *Understanding Generalist Practice.* Chicago: Nelson-Hall, 1993.

Mickelson, James. "Advocacy." In *Encyclopedia of Social Work,* 19th ed., Vol. 1, edited by Richard L. Edwards. Washington, D.C.: NASW, 1995, pp 95–100.

Sunley, Robert. *Advocating Today: A Human Service Practitioner's Handbook.* New York: Family Service Association of America, 1983.

Weissman, Harold, Irwin Epstein, and Andrea Savage. *Agency-Based Social Work: Neglected Aspects of Clinical Practice.* Philadelphia: Temple University Press, 1983.

14.28   Empowerment

PURPOSE: To assist a client to develop a sense of control and power.

DISCUSSION: Many of the clients served by social workers feel helpless to change their situation. This is especially so among groups that have experienced discrimination and oppression. In our society, there is an attitude that blames the individual, even for problems caused by social and economic forces beyond the control of the individual. Unfortunately, many who are victims of these forces adopt this same attitude and blame themselves totally for the difficulties they experience.

Victims of exploitation and abuse—especially spouse abuse and child abuse—are often carefully taught by the abuser that they deserve the abuse. Often, they accept this interpretation and perceive themselves as the perpetrator, not the victim. Such an interpretation adds to their feelings of self-blame and helplessness.

In order to counter feelings of powerlessness, social workers need to emphasize empowerment in their interventions. Guterrez (1990, 149) defines **empowerment** as a "process of increasing personal, interpersonal or political power so individuals can take action to improve their life situation." In this definition, *power* refers to an individual's or a group's ability to influence the behavior of others and change public opinion and social institutions.

Empowerment places an emphasis on helping a client secure access to and control over needed resources, on client involvement in decision making, and on helping the client acquire the knowledge and skills needed to function independently. This approach rests on the assumption that the individual in question already possesses or has the potential to learn necessary competencies and that the client's difficulty is created primarily by a social barrier or a lack of resources. The strategy of empowerment will not prove beneficial if this assumption is not valid in a given case.

In some circles, the term *empowerment* has become little more that a buzzword. Even in social work, there is some debate over whether empowerment is a new paradigm for practice or only a new word for well-established concepts and methods of working with people. Whether a new or old idea, a truly empowering approach requires that the social worker adhere to certain guidelines.

1. View your helping role as that of a partner, or consultant to the client, not as an authority or source of directives to be followed by the client. Also, view the client as the only true expert on his or her problem or situation. Thus, it is the client's definition of the problem and the client's thoughts on what should be done about it that are most relevant and hold the greatest promise for success.

2. Recognize that people cannot begin to solve their problems or take control of their lives until they are given responsibility for defining the problems they face, for selecting the solution, and can gain access to the resources they deem important to that solution. In order to accurately define their problem and assess their situation, clients need complete access to information relevant to their situation.

3. Give attention to helping clients build self-esteem and self-confidence, increase their willingness to take the personal risks necessary to break out of self-defeating patterns, build a positive social network, and learn problem-solving and communication skills such as assertiveness and negotiation.

4. Develop a group consciousness so individuals do not feel alone. Encourage clients to participate in groups. According to Guterrez (1990, 151), the small group is the ideal environment for "raising consciousness, engaging in mutual aid, develop-

ing skills and solving problems and an ideal way for clients to experience individual effectiveness in influencing others."

5. Uncover potential sources of power. Assist the client in making an inventory of his or her power sources such as knowledge derived from life experience, motivation, time, energy, knowledge of the community, understanding of particular problems, sense of humor, willingness to take risks, verbal ability, voting, writing letters to persons in authority, feelings of solidarity with others, membership in groups and organizations, and the like.

6. Help your clients to understand the individuals, organizations, and systems with which they must interact. Provide or help them obtain information needed to understand why and how others arrived at their decisions.

7. Assist the client to make a planned and disciplined use of the power they have. Recognize that persons who finally discover that they have some power do not always use this power in an appropriate manner. Sometimes they are overly eager or aggressive and as a result they alienate others and create unnecessary opposition. While encouraging clients to use their power, help them to understand that numerous realities will limit how others can respond. For example, an agency may not be able to respond completely to their requests because of time limitations, rules, regulations, and the needs of other clients.

8. Make frequent use of active teaching techniques (e.g., coaching, role-play) that provide the client with experience in communication, decision making, and problem solving. Find opportunities for the client to practice newly learned skills.

9. Recognize and build on client strengths. Search for the positive in the situation. Provide encouragement and a sense of hope. Make generous use of reframing (see Item 14.12) to help the client view mistreatment and injustice from a different angle. For example, help the client let go of anger by viewing the past as a painful but invaluable source of wisdom regarding what is really important in life and how and why people behave as they do. Help the client see that if one chooses to be taught rather than hurt, one can accept "mistakes" as opportunities to grow as a person. Help your client to recognize that even distress can be beneficial if it pushes a person to carefully reexamine his or her situation and take action to change those things that are causing pain and discomfort.

10. Help clients experience a sense of personal power and control by allowing and encouraging them to make decisions and follow through on those decisions. Be prepared to respect their choices and allow them to experience the consequences of those choices—both the positive and the negative.

11. Help your clients understand how they came to view themselves as helpless. Help them understand the social forces that contributed to their feelings of powerlessness. It should be noted, however, that individuals who seriously examine how they have been mistreated or held back may become engulfed by rage. Some get "stuck" at this point and become prisoners of their own anger. Help your clients express their feelings and then move beyond feelings of bitterness.

12. Use advocacy where necessary (see Items 14.27 and 14.47) but avoid taking an action yourself if clients can be taught or helped to take action themselves. Fully involve the client in all decisions concerning whether and how to engage in advocacy.

SELECTED BIBLIOGRAPHY

Dunst, Carl, Carl Trivette, and Angela Deal. *Enabling and Empowering Families.* Cambridge, Mass.: Brookline Books, 1988.

Guterrez, Lorraine. "Working With Women of Color: An Empowerment Perspective." *Social Work* 35, No. 2, (March 1990): 149–153.

Guterrez, Lorraine, and Paula Nuris, eds. *Education and Research for Empowerment Practice.* Seattle: University of Washington School of Social Work, Center for Policy and Practice Research, 1994.

Lee, Judith. *The Empowerment Approach to Social Work Practice.* New York: Columbia University Press, 1994.

14.29   Crisis Cards

PURPOSE: To help a client manage a recurring troublesome situation.

DISCUSSION: Crisis cards are a set of 3 × 5 cards on which the client has written various suggestions to himself or herself on how to cope with and manage a situation that could easily escalate out of control. For example, if the client is a father who is easily angered by his son's rebellious behavior, crisis cards might be used to help the father maintain self-control.

The suggestions written on the cards are ones identified by the client during discussions with the worker. Brainstorming may be used to identify the various options. They must be ones that make sense to the client and are likely to work, given the client's patterns and circumstances. For example, the father just mentioned might prepare the following seven cards:

> *Card 1:*   Remember that this will pass. Don't do anything foolish! Remember the times when I was a kid and also drove my parents nuts.
>
> *Card 2:*   Look at the family photo album and think of happier times.
>
> *Card 3:*   Read my Bible and pray.
>
> *Card 4:*   Call my friend Jim (555-6789) and ask him to listen to my frustration.
>
> *Card 5:*   Work out on my weight-lifting set.
>
> *Card 6:*   Cook one of my favorite meals.
>
> *Card 7:*   Walk to the store and back.

When the father finds himself getting angry and in danger of losing control, he refers to the cards and looks for a suggestion that might help him control his anger.

In addition to helping the client prepare a set of crisis cards, it is usually important to help the client work out a system for recognizing when he or she needs to use the cards. For example, the father could be helped to formulate a 10-point anger scale, ranging from 0 (no anger) to 10 (potentially violent). As the father learns to monitor his level of anger, he comes to recognize that at point 5 on the scale, he is to refer to the crisis cards.

The crisis cards technique can be adapted for use in work with whole families. For example, during a family meeting, the members might brainstorm various options on how they could better handle recurring conflicts or misunderstandings. A set of cards might also be used by someone learning to cope with a newly acquired disability or a difficult job-related task. Such cards and self-messages can also be used by someone working to maintain sobriety or trying to change a behavior pattern (e.g., keep to a diet, stick with a program of physical exercise).

SELECTED BIBLIOGRAPHY

Kinney, Jill, David Haapala, and Charlotte Booth. *Keeping Families Together: The Homebuilders Model*. New York: Aldine de Gruyter, 1991.

14.30 The Client in Crisis

PURPOSE: To assist the client in coping with a personal crisis.

DISCUSSION: The social worker will encounter many individuals who are in a state of crisis. Although the word *crisis* is widely used, it has a specific meaning within the mental health field. Gilliland and James (1993, 23) define a **crisis** as "a perception of an event or situation as an intolerable difficulty that exceeds the resources and coping mechanisms of the person." Among the events that can precipitate a crisis are the death of a loved one, loss of a job, marital separation, birth of a child with a severe disability, serious illness or accident, house fire, rape or mugging, or other traumatic event.

A crisis is a time of both danger and opportunity. It is dangerous because if the crisis is not resolved constructively, it can set in motion a downward spiral that leads to a level of functioning lower than that which existed prior to the crisis. On the other hand, a crisis can be an opportunity to learn new coping skills and make life changes that actually elevate one's level of functioning. A crisis is *time limited* and it is expected that, within a matter of weeks, the person will come to some level of adjustment. And, as suggested, that adjustment may be either positive or negative, depending, in part, on how others respond to the person during the crisis.

It is important to distinguish a personal crisis from a particular coping pattern that Kagan and Schlosberg (1989) term "perpetual crisis" or "crisis oriented." They explain that

> living in a crisis-oriented family is like riding a roller coaster 24 hours a day: terrifying, energizing and addicting. . . . Real, rather than perpetual crisis, puts us into acute grief. . . . For families in 'perpetual crisis' the grief process is blocked. . . . Crisis becomes a way of life. . . . Instead of becoming vulnerable and facing change, crisis-oriented families protect themselves from facing difficult issues. (pp. 2–3)

The following practice guidelines apply when working with a person in a real crisis but not with persons in "perpetual crisis."

1. Realize that this state of disorganization will diminish over time; with or without professional help, the crisis will typically be over within about four to six weeks. The purpose of crisis intervention is to help the client deal with the crisis in a positive way and prevent the development of more serious and long-standing problems.

2. Listen actively and offer emotional support. A person in crisis is in a heightened state of either anxiety or depression and also feels a sense of failure because he or she is unable to cope. The client is probably preoccupied with the precipitating event and will have difficulty focusing attention on anything else. Before the client can consider alternatives, make decisions, or plan ways for resolving problems, he or she will need much emotional support from the worker and significant others. This support may range from simply acknowledging the existence of the problem to offering strong verbal reassurance (e.g., "You did the right thing in leaving your house and coming to our shelter").

3. Involve others in the helping process. People in crisis are often most receptive to assistance provided by those whom they know and trust (e.g., family, friends, employer, minister, neighbors, etc.). Encourage the client to reach out to others, or, with his or her permission, contact these significant others and enlist their help on behalf of the client.

4. Allow the client to express emotion. Calmly allow the client to cry or express feelings of fear or anger while you continue to provide emotional support and acceptance. The client's strong feelings will lessen with time.

5. Communicate hope. A hopeful attitude is an essential element in responding to a person in crisis. If you communicate a belief in the client's ability to cope, he or she will be less fearful and will gradually regain self-confidence.

6. To most people in crisis, their own problems are of utmost importance. They have tunnel vision and can think of little else. Consequently, they are not able to step back and objectively analyze their situation. You will need to ask questions and actively examine the details of their situation.

7. Use partialization. The person in crisis feels as if he or she is facing a giant and completely unmanageable problem. By breaking the problem down into several smaller ones, to be addressed one at a time, the client will feel more hopeful about regaining control.

8. Provide factual information. Often, a crisis arises because the person has misconceptions about his or her situation or because intense feelings have distorted his or her perception of reality (e.g., "I just know that I'm going to lose my job" or "This goes to prove that no company is going to hire someone in a wheelchair like me"). Provide factual information related to the person's concern (e.g., "No, I don't think it is because you are in a wheelchair that you weren't hired; there are laws against discrimination of that kind"). When appropriate, give honest feedback needed to cor-

rect misunderstandings (e.g., "Mr. Jones told me that you weren't hired because you were belligerent and sarcastic during the interview").

9. A person in crisis has difficulty making decisions and anticipating the consequences of his or her actions. Thus, you may need to provide highly specific directions as to what the person needs to do or what will probably happen if he or she takes a certain course of action. It is especially important to help the client anticipate the consequences of destructive behaviors (e.g., "If you lose control and again injure your child, she will be placed in a foster home").

10. Reinforce adaptive behavior. Help the individual identify what kinds of coping behaviors worked in the past; encourage the client to take similar actions to address their current problem. An important part of crisis intervention is to encourage clients to take action so they begin to regain a faith and trust in their own capabilities.

11. Consider using a behavioral contract (see Item 14.6) as a means of providing the client with structure and direction. This helps the client mobilize inner resources, and it also sends the message that you have confidence in his or her ability to take the steps needed to get through the crisis.

SELECTED BIBLIOGRAPHY

Gilliland, Burl, and Richard James. *Crisis Intervention Strategies,* 2nd ed. Pacific Grove, Calif.: Brooks/Cole, 1993.
Greenstone, James, and Sharon Leviton. *Elements of Crisis Intervention.* Pacific Grove, Calif.: Brooks/Cole, 1993.
Hoff, Lee Ann. *People in Crisis,* 4th ed. San Francisco: Jossey-Bass, 1995.
Kagan, Richard, and Shirley Schlosberg. *Families in Perpetual Crisis.* New York: W. W. Norton, 1989.

14.31   The Client Who Is a Child

PURPOSE: To adapt basic social work techniques and approaches to the special needs of the child under age 12.

DISCUSSION: Children are not miniature adults. Because many of the interviewing techniques that are effective with adults may not work with children, some new skills, such as the use of play, need to be added to the worker's repertoire. Several guidelines should be considered when working with a child.

Planning the Interview

1. Anticipate how the child's level of development will affect his or her capacity to understand and use language. How and what children think and feel are closely tied to their developmental stages. Realize, however, that there is much variation among the children in a particular age group.

2. Be clear about why you are meeting with the child and what you need to accomplish during the meeting. Plan several alternative methods to accomplish your goal. Anticipate what might go wrong (e.g., child will not talk, child cries, child will not leave parent, etc.) and plan how you will handle such situations.

3. Plan to use some form of play to facilitate communication. Play is a normal activity for children; it is a child's natural means of communication. Prior to the interview, assemble play materials that may be needed. For young children, provide art materials (e.g., finger paints, clay, building blocks) as well as objects that can be used to portray family themes (e.g., dolls, puppets, doll house, toy animals). For older children, consider simple card or board games, puzzles, or electronic games. The skillful interviewer of children is someone who can be playful and think or feel like a child.

4. Conduct the interview in a room that is familiar and comfortable to the child. If that is not possible, consider an open space that affords some privacy (e.g., a public park or school playground).

Introducing Yourself and Getting Started

5. When first meeting a child, explain who you are and how you want to be addressed (e.g., "My name is John Smith. Please call me John. My job is to help children who are having problems at home."). If the child seems fearful or unwilling to talk, try doing something unexpected (e.g., "Jimmy, we are going to be doing a lot of talking and we may get thirsty. Should we get some juice now or should we wait until later?"). Place yourself at the child's level physically; sit or squat so you do not tower over the child. Initiate some friendly interaction by showing an interest in items the child is wearing or carrying or ask about the child's school or favorite games or TV shows. If the child refuses to interact, engage in a parallel activity and then gradually initiate conversation about the activity. For example, if the child does not talk but begins to play with a doll, pick up another doll and engage in similar play. This will often prompt some interaction and an opportunity for verbal exchange.

6. If the child appears frightened of the interview, attempt to normalize the situation (e.g., "When I was your age, I was afraid to talk to new people"). It may be necessary to ally the child's fears that he or she is in trouble or that the interview is some kind of punishment. Many young children will relax and open up to a "dumb" adult. By playing the role of a bumbling adult and asking some ridiculous questions (e.g., "Are you married?" "Do you know how to fly an airplane?" "Do you own a candy store?"), you may get the child to respond. You might also fumble the spelling of the child's name so he or she has to correct you and thereby take control and feel more powerful.

7. If the child is as least 6 or 7 years of age, ask what he or she knows about the purpose of the interview. This will reveal what the child is expecting. Then explain why you want to speak with the child. Ask if he or she has talked to anyone else about the meeting and what others have said about the meeting or perhaps what instructions the child was given about what to say and do.

8. Do not disguise the interview as recreation; this may confuse the child about who you are and your role. Also be cognizant that little or no confidentiality can be provided to a child. Do not promise to keep secrets. If the child appears reluctant to talk for fear of retaliation by others, you may need to describe what you can do to keep him or her safe.

Gathering Information from a Child

9. If the child is below about age 6, much of the information you gather will be from your observations of the child's play and interactions with you and others. At this young age, a child will often act out his or her thoughts and feelings. However, in order to draw valid inferences from observations, it is important to observe the child in several different settings and at different times of the day. Conclusions should not be based on a single session.

10. Children between the ages of 3 and 6 are eager to please adults, quite suggestible, and easily influenced by an adult's leading questions. Children this age are very sensitive and reactive to an adult's nonverbal communication; they may modify their story to make it fit what they believe the adult wants to hear. It is important to be warm and accepting or children may judge that you disapprove of what they are saying and cease talking. Young children are influenced more by the social context of the message (i.e., who said it and how, when, and where it was said) than by the literal meaning of the words.

11. Children under about age 6 will often project their own thoughts and feelings onto dolls or pictures. Thus, consider using dolls or pictures to set up a make-believe situation relevant to the topics you wish to explore and then ask the child to complete the story or describe what the dolls or characters in the picture are doing, thinking, and feeling. You may need to initiate the storytelling about the dolls or pictures, but once the child is attentive, you can ask the child to continue the story. The techniques of active listening (e.g., paraphrase, summarization, etc.) do not work with children below age 6 or 7.

Young children are easily distracted and tend to move quickly from topic to topic. Consequently, they may describe only once or with just a few words what they think or feel about an important topic and then they are ready to move on to something else. Asking them to stick with one topic is seldom successful; however, you may initiate a return to the original topic at a later time. Children often become noncommittal (e.g., not answering, shrugging) if pressured and when uncomfortable or unsure how to respond. Thus, it is important to facilitate the child's expression without being so directive that the child withdraws.

12. If the child is older than about 6 years, he or she will be better able to use words to express thoughts and feelings and answer questions—if the questions are simple and age appropriate. Children of this age frequently need assistance to fully describe a situation or event. For example, you may need to ask: What happened next? Then what did you do? Where did this happen? Who else was with you? However, because it is difficult for them to describe reasons behind their behavior, you should avoid "why" questions.

13. By age 9 or 10, children are able to describe others by describing patterns of behavior and using concepts to describe personality traits and attitudes. Because they can now think conceptually, they pay more attention to the words of a message. Also, they are able to detect phony or insincere messages and they become suspicious when they observe incongruency between a person's words and behavior.

Story completions, dolls, and drawing may still be necessary interviewing techniques for children between about ages 7 and 9, but many children older than 9 years will respond thoughtfully to an interviewer's questions if the interviewer is nonthreatening and unhurried. Children of this age group find it easier to talk about personal matters if they can do so while playing a simple card game or a board game like checkers that does not require a great deal of concentration. Puppet-to-puppet interaction will often facilitate communication and talking on play telephones usually works well. Sentence completions are also useful (e.g., When at home, I am afraid that . . .). Many 7- to 10-year-olds respond well to humor, if it is not subtle.

Understanding How Children Think

14. Children between the ages of about 3 to 6 are very subjective, concrete, and egocentric in their thinking. For example, they believe an event that makes them happy will have the same effect on all other people. They report their feelings in a global manner and their thinking is characterized by an "all-or-nothing" pattern. For example, things are either good or bad; the child is unable to understand mixed feelings or ambivalence. The child may describe a person as mean and minutes later describe the same person as nice or fun. Such thinking in extremes and absolutes causes them to categorize both themselves and others as either good or bad, smart or dumb, and so on. Children of this age describe themselves and others in terms of external characteristics (e.g., age, hair color, grade in school, etc.); they do not mention personality traits except in global terms such as "she is happy" or "he is a bad person."

15. Beginning at about age 6, the child's thinking becomes more objective and logical. Gradually the child acquires the ability to imagine himself or herself in the role of another person and to understand that everyone can be different in how they think, feel, and respond. However, even a 7-year-old may still believe that he or she is the total cause for how others, especially parents, feel and behave. It is not until about age 9 or 10 that children truly understand that they do not cause all of the behaviors and emotions they observe in others.

16. By about age 10, the child no longer thinks in absolutes, and views himself or herself as a separate person and a mixture of characteristics and abilities (e.g., someone who is skilled at some things but not others or good sometimes and bad at other times). At this age, he or she understands it is possible and normal to simultaneously feel opposing emotions (e.g., to be angry at someone you love). Also, the child now has the ability to reflect on his or her own thoughts and actions and can figure out how others will probably react in a particular situation or react to certain information. Thus, the child can now manipulate words and information in order to influence how others will behave.

Assessing Truthfulness of Child's Statements

17. Social workers who investigate reports of abuse and neglect and those who conduct child custody evaluations frequently find themselves in situations where they must form a judgment about whether a child is telling the truth. Children from 4 to 6 years old can and will tell a simple lie in order to avoid punishment (e.g., "I didn't break the cup"), but they do not have the cognitive abilities necessary to fabricate a complex story having several interrelated elements, actions, or actors. In trying to describe something that happened, they can often recall central actors or central events but not the connecting details, such as what happened before and after and how one action lead to another. They have what some call a "script memory." For example, they can remember events (e.g., a birthday party) and rituals (e.g., going to bed, mealtime) but do not accurately remember events that are not part of their usual routines. Children this age frequently exaggerate events or boast when describing their abilities and experiences; however, when asked, "Is that pretend or real?" or "Is that an 'I wish' story or is it true?" they generally can articulate the difference between what was true and what was an exaggeration.

18. Children between the ages of 7 and 11 value honesty and fairness and generally avoid telling a lie. It is rare for them to fabricate. However, they have the cognitive abilities necessary to add or selectively withhold information and will use deception as a means of avoiding punishment or getting what they want. Children in this age group tend to embellish on the truth in order to tell an exciting story. Children aged 9, 10, or 11 are eager to please adults and inclined to say what they believe adults want to hear. They have good memories of central actors and events and good free recall (i.e., able to recall and describe without the aid of detailed questioning by an interviewer).

19. As a general rule, the younger the child, the less likely he or she is to fabricate a falsehood. However, it is important to remember that children—like adults—can and do misunderstand and misinterpret their experiences and will, at times, lie. In cases where a child self-reports sexual abuse, deliberate false reports are rare among children below age 12, and also quite rare among teenagers. Most efforts to study this matter conclude that about 5 percent of self-reports by children are erroneous and arise from misinterpretations of nonsexual behavior and psychological disturbance. However, the rate of false reports becomes higher when the child is the focus of custody or visitation disputes and is encouraged by one parent to accuse the other of some wrongdoing.

20. Sometimes a parent or parent figure will pressure a child to lie to a social worker. Certain behaviors indicate that a child is reciting a fabricated story in order to please or protect a parent—for example, inconsistency regarding the major elements of the story or extreme consistency regarding major events but with no supporting detail; flat affect (i.e., absence of anxiety, fear, guilt, shame, anger, etc.); use of adult phrases and terminology; the only emotion expressed is anger (i.e., suggests motive of revenge); and visual description only (i.e., child describes what was seen but is unable to describe smell, sounds, and touch associated with the situation described). If a parent has coached a child, the parent is usually threatened by the social worker's request for a private interview with the child.

21. One must be cautious about interpreting the meaning of a child's play. Indeed, young children incorporate their thoughts, feelings, and recent experiences into their play. However, children also incorporate into their play various themes drawn from TV programs and books, from incidents described by their friends, and from events they have observed outside the home. Thus, it may be difficult to pinpoint the exact source of the themes that appear in a child's play.

22. Themes of violence are common in the stories told by normal, nonabused, young children. For example, among nonabused 3-year-olds, about 66 percent of girls and 90 percent of boys include acts of violence and destruction in the stories they tell to other children and adults. Thus, talk about violence is not, by itself, an indicator of physical abuse.

23. The social worker should not assume that a young child can accurately describe when an event happened. Young children do not use clocks or calendars to measure time. In fact, preschool children do not grasp the concept of time and younger grade school-age children typically use events such as nap time, lunch time, Christmas, start of school, and other events as markers of time. Such markers, rather than clock times and dates, should be used to establish time frames.

Additional Suggestions

24. Realize that during an interview, you get only a sample of the child's behavior. The child may behave differently in other situations and with other people. The farther removed the child is from his or her usual social and family context, the more cautious you must be in drawing conclusions about the child's behavior. For example, the child who appears anxious or withdrawn during an office interview may simply be fearful of an unfamiliar environment. In-home interviews are important to an accurate assessment of a child's functioning.

25. Allow the child to set the pace of the interview. Follow his or her lead. Allow the child to move around and explore the room. Children—especially young children—have short attention spans and are easily distracted. Excessive squirming and a lack of attention probably indicates that the child is tired and the interview should end.

26. The vocabulary you use should be appropriate to the age of the child. For example, with a 12-year-old, you can use words and expressions similar to those used with adults. But with a 4-year-old child, your expressions must be very simple and concrete.

27. Because young children are especially responsive to nonverbal communication, it is helpful to make frequent use of nonverbal messages (e.g., facial expressions, simple touch, gestures, etc.) in your communication. However, do not kiss or caress the child; this makes most children uncomfortable, and it opens the door to a misinterpretation of your intentions and a possible accusation of sexual abuse. Touch can be especially confusing and threatening to a child who has been physically or sexually abused.

28. Answer a child's question honestly, directly, and correctly (e.g., "I believe you will be in foster care until the school term ends"). Do not use euphemisms; do not beat around the bush. Avoid giving elaborate explanations. When providing important information, try to give it in phases and small doses.

29. When behavior-control rules are necessary during an interview, explain the rules, along with any consequences for breaking them (e.g., "You are not permitted to hit me; if you do hit me, I will put away the toys and today's meeting will end").

30. During an interview, give the child as much choice and control as possible. But be sure to offer choices among alternatives that you can accept. This point is illustrated in the following statements: *Misleading:* "Well, Jimmy, what would you like to do? We can do whatever you like." *Correct:* "Jimmy, today you can use the finger paints or the crayons. Which one do you want to use?"

31. Outings, treats, or gifts should be used judiciously. Although they are an extension of normal adult-child interaction and may be helpful in building a relationship, they are easily misinterpreted. Also, be careful that your gift of even a small toy is not viewed as competition with the child's parents.

32. Do not express criticism of the child's parents. Children are protective of their parents. A child will usually defend his or her parents even if they have been abusive. Be objective and concrete in talking about the parent-child relationship and the parents' behavior (e.g., "Your dad does has a problem with alcohol. He gets drunk about once a week. He cannot stop drinking. That is why your parents are getting a divorce.").

33. A series of interviews should usually have structure and a routine, depending on each child's needs. For example, some children like interviews that have definite beginning and ending rituals. Others, however, may want relief from structure and need freedom to do more of what they feel like doing.

The Child in Out-of-Home Placement

34. Many of the children known professionally to social workers are in out-of-home placement (i.e., foster family care, group homes, institutional care, etc.). Realize that placement is always disruptive and emotionally traumatic to a child. Many children blame themselves for the family problems that led up to the placement. Consequently, many view placement as a punishment for some real or imagined wrongdoing.

35. Be sensitive to the pain of their separation and loss experiences. Relationship losses, especially a series of losses, have long-lasting, negative effects on a child. Thus, it is critically important to minimize the number of separations experienced by a child. If a child must be separated from someone to which he or she is emotionally attached, the move should be as gradual as possible, thus giving the child an opportunity to prepare and time to adjust. A ritual such as a going-away party helps the child make this transition by symbolically ending one relationship and beginning another. Without such a ritual, the child might feel as if he or she was given away or rejected; a transition ritual gives the child permission to let go of one relationship and begin a new one. After the physical separation, it is important that the child be able to return to his or her former home for occasional visits.

36. Remember that the child's biological parents are central to his or her identity. Do everything possible to maintain frequent contacts and visits between the child in placement and his or her parents, siblings, and other close relatives. In the long run, frequent visitation is helpful to the child, even if the visits are at times upsetting to all.

37. Some children make a fairly good adjustment to placement but most experience much inner turmoil. The child in placement usually feels insecure and uncertain about why he or she is in placement. Thus, assume that the child has many questions about his or her past, present, and future; make it easy for the child to ask these questions. If a child does not understand why he or she is separated from his or her parents and has little or no contact with the parents, the child will usually create an elaborate fantasy that explains the situation. Be factual and honest when describing the child's current situation and possible changes in the future. It is better for the child to struggle with an unpleasant reality than to adjust to a pleasant fantasy.

38. Because foster children experience so much change and because their lives are so unpredictable, you must be prepared to become a predictable figure in their lives. The foster child is especially sensitive to any hint of rejection. Contacts should occur on a regular basis. If you must miss an appointment, explain the reason directly to the child. If you may not be able to keep a promise, do not make it!

39. Children often feel shame and embarrassment about being in foster care, and consequently they fabricate a story to explain their situation. When the fabrication is discovered, the child acquires a reputation for being a spinner of tall tales or a liar. Thus, it is important to help these children develop a clear, understandable, and socially acceptable explanation of why they are in an out-of-home placement so they can comfortably describe their living situation to teachers, friends, and others.

40. When speaking with foster parents, adoptive parents, or group care staff, be truthful about the child's behavior, situation, and history. Efforts to conceal the child's life experience in an attempt to protect the child or because you fear others will not understand almost always backfire.

SELECTED BIBLIOGRAPHY

Allen-Meares, Paula. *Social Work with Children and Adolescents*. White Plains, N. Y.: Longman, 1995.

Garbarino, James, and Frances Stott. *What Children Can Tell Us: Eliciting, Interpreting and Evaluating Information from Children*. San Francisco: Jossey-Bass, 1989.

LeVine, Elaine, and Alvin Sallee. *Listen to Our Children: Clinical Theory and Practice*. Dubuque, Iowa: Kendall/Hunt, 1986.

Maluccio, Anthony. "Children: Direct Practice." In *Encyclopedia of Social Work*, 19th ed., Vol. 1, edited by Richard L. Edwards. Washington, D.C.: NASW, 1995, pp. 442–447.

Ney, Tara, ed., *True and False Allegations of Child Sexual Abuse*. New York: Brunner/Mazel, 1994.

O'Connor, Kevin, and Charles Schaefer. *Handbook of Play Therapy*, Vol. II. New York: John Wiley, 1994.

14.32   The Client Who Is an Adolescent

PURPOSE: To adapt basic social work techniques and approaches to the needs of the adolescent.

DISCUSSION: The developmental period between ages 12 and 18 is a stormy one. Many parents experience serious conflicts with their adolescent children; most of these revolve around issues of authority and control. Parents typically worry that their adolescent children will become involved with drugs and irresponsible sex or become injured by recklessness. Some parents become so upset and angered that they physically abuse their adolescent children or kick them out of the home.

The problems most likely to bring the adolescent to the attention of a social worker include family conflict, running away, violence, delinquency, pregnancy, drug abuse, threat of suicide, and the need for foster care or residential treatment. The following guidelines are useful for working with adolescents.

1. Adolescents are typically idealistic, painfully self-conscious, in conflict with parents over authority issues, fiercely attached to peers, preoccupied with bodily changes and their sexuality, seeking popularity and conformity within their peer group, and desperately trying to develop an identity apart from their family. These behaviors and feelings are not abnormal or deviant.

2. Remember that adolescents are resilient and have great capacity to grow and change. An effective social work intervention can have a positive, lifelong impact. Because these are often lively, inquisitive, and questioning clients, work with adolescents can be stimulating and genuinely fun. The helping relationships and environments that workers create for adolescents must provide models of fair and responsible adult behavior.

3. Adolescents have an intense need to be heard. However, you must listen for the underlying meaning rather than to the words used, because often the words themselves are offensive and shocking. Listen nonjudgmentally and encourage them to talk about life—as they experience it—about their needs, hopes, and dreams.

4. Adolescents need an environment that is predictable and provides structure and limits. However, adolescents will usually test the rules and limits put in place by an adult. Expect all the rules to be challenged. Before you create a new rule, be sure it is really necessary, can be enforced, and is worth fighting over. Inform adolescents of rules and the consequences for violating a rule. Be fair and consistent in enforcing rules and imposing consequences.

5. Because of their high energy level, interaction with adolescents should allow for movement and activity. If possible, avoid office interviews; rather, try talking with adolescent clients while walking, shooting baskets, working out in a gym, or riding in a car. Movement makes it easier for adolescents to talk and express feelings.

6. Because the peer group is so important during adolescence, group approaches (e.g., group discussion, psychodrama, group counseling) can be useful. Most adolescents are more accepting of a group-related intervention than a one-to-one interview. Adolescents in need of out-of-home placement usually do better in a group home setting than in foster family care. Behavioral contracting works fairly well with adolescents (see Item 14.6).

7. Keep parents informed and involved in your work with their child while providing the adolescent with as much confidentiality as is legally permissible. By helping parents recall and talk about their own adolescence, you can often increase their understanding and acceptance of their teenager.

8. Adolescents are sensitive to any hint of artificiality in others, even though they themselves may pretend to be someone they are not. Thus, it is important to be genuine. Do not try to talk and act like their peers. It is nearly impossible to keep up with the latest adolescent fads, music, and slang. Imitating adolescent talk is likely to make you appear phoney.

9. Be alert to the fact that when you work with adolescents, your own unresolved parent-child and authority issues often rise to the surface and you may project them onto your client.

10. Many adolescents are involuntary clients. Given the authority struggle common to this period, this is a very uncomfortable situation for adolescents. Silence is their usual means of resisting adult intrusion. Also, adolescents challenge adult authority by being rude, contradictory, and using abusive language.

11. Because adolescents' emotions are so intense and characterized by ambivalence, many adolescents find it difficult to verbalize how they are feeling, at least in ways that others can tolerate. Allow them to express private thoughts and feelings but do not push them toward such expressions since this will be perceived as control and invite further resistance.

12. Most adolescents are preoccupied with the here and now. Many have a sort of tunnel vision and seem unable to think beyond today or maybe tomorrow. Gently encourage adolescents to examine their current decisions and actions in light of their hopes and dreams, opportunities, and goals. When their thinking is clearly unrealistic or dangerous, it is usually best to tell them so in a respectful but firm manner.

13. It is during adolescence that some individuals are attracted to and drawn into gang activity. Goldstein (1993) explains that

> youth join gangs and commit illegal activities therein to satisfy needs no different from those motivating all youths, gang or nongang. Adolescents of all types seek recognition from peers, status, clarification of their identity, pride, tangible resources, self-esteem, excitement, camaraderie. Such needs are age-appropriate, developmentally desirable, and to be encouraged, not thwarted. It is of course, the *means* by which such need satisfaction is sought that is at issue. Effective gang interventions will provide means for satisfying such needs in prosocial, growth-enhancing, and societally acceptable ways—and not ignore or deny their pressing reality. (pp. 477–488)

Youth gangs or street gangs have existed in major U.S. cities since the late nineteenth century. In the past, their illegal activity was mostly theft. In recent years, many youth gangs have adults as leaders, have grown more violent, and they are often involved in serious criminal activity such as drug dealing and murder. Economic gain from drug dealing has become a driving force behind the expansion of gang activity across the country and into even small communities. Consequently, it is increasingly difficult to distinguish between some youth gangs and organized crime.

SELECTED BIBLIOGRAPHY

Aldgate, Jane, Anthony Maluccio, and Christine Reeves. *Adolescents in Foster Families.* Chicago: Lyceum Books, 1989.

Carrell, Susan. *Group Exercises for Adolescents: A Manual For Therapists.* Newbury Park, Calif.: Sage, 1993.

de Anda, Diane. "Adolescence Overview." In *Encyclopedia of Social Work,* 19th ed., Vol. 1, edited by Richard L. Edwards. Washington, D.C.: NASW, 1995, pp. 16–33.

Goldstein, Arnold. "Gang Interventions: Issues and Opportunities." In *The Gang Intervention Handbook,* edited by Arnold Goldstein and C. Ronald Huff. Champaign, Ill.: Research Press, 1993.

LeCroy, Craig. *Handbook of Child and Adolescent Treatment Manuals.* New York: Lexington Books, 1994.

14.33   The Client Who Is Elderly

PURPOSE: To adapt social work techniques and approaches to the special needs of the elderly.

DISCUSSION: By the year 2000, about 13 percent of the U.S. population will be age 65 or older. By the year 2030, this percentage will grow to about 21 percent. Social workers must give increasing attention to the needs of older people, especially those in their seventies, eighties, and nineties. The following guidelines will help the worker serving the elderly client.

1. Most elderly people actively strive to maintain their independence. As a person ages, he or she experiences many losses (e.g., death of loved ones, loss of health, etc.); becoming staunchly independent is a normal coping mechanism. Consequently, elderly clients may be resistant or ambivalent about receiving services they perceive as limiting their freedom. To the greatest extent possible, enable elderly clients to retain control, make choices, and maintain independence.

2. A good way to break the ice and get the relationship with an older person off to a good start is to show an interest in the furnishings in his or her room or home, such as family pictures, unique pieces of furniture, homemade items, and the like.

3. In the beginning, always focus on the older client's most obvious and concrete needs, which are the ones he or she can most easily discuss. Like most other clients, the elderly person understands and can easily talk about needs like transportation, housing, medical care, and home maintenance, but finds it difficult to express feelings to a stranger.

4. Allow and even encourage the client to reminisce. The past means a lot to an elderly person. Thinking and talking about the past is a normal activity for the elderly—it is not a sign of deteriorating mental abilities. Listen carefully to the reminiscence; it will reveal much about the client's values, feelings, and current concerns.

5. As individuals grow older and closer to death, they think more about their life's achievements and disappointments. Typically, their religious beliefs and spirituality take on added importance and many desire to communicate what they have learned from life. Look for opportunities that allow the elderly to teach what they have learned.

6. During their later years, elderly persons typically become intensely aware of their unique relationship to children and grandchildren. It may be of great importance for them to stay in contact with offspring or reactivate relationships that have deteriorated. Some older persons may want to reach out to estranged offspring and patch up differences or make amends for the harm they caused. Do everything possible to facilitate intergenerational family communication.

7. If the elderly client is much older than you, the two of you probably have very different mores, values, and attitudes. For example, "taking charity" is difficult for many older people, and they usually find it harder than younger persons to accept counseling and psychotherapy. Many elderly are concerned about the cost of services. Early in your contact, clarify any financial implications. Many older clients will simply reject services rather than inquire about the cost or reveal their inability to pay.

8. Most elderly people suffer from some degree of vision and hearing loss. Thus, it is important to speak clearly and repeat the message as often as necessary. Your nonverbal communication is especially important as a means of compensating for the client's auditory deficit. Also, the pace of an interview will usually be slower with an elderly person, and the client's lack of energy may limit the length of the interview.

9. For both physical and psychological reasons, an interview in the client's home is usually more comfortable than an office interview. Elderly clients may be especially bothered by unusual clothing or hairstyles worn by a worker.

10. Given the impact of racism, discrimination, and prejudice on people, be especially sensitive when interacting with the elderly person who is a member of a racial or ethnic minority. Lowy (1985) offers a number of suggestions:

- Respect the elder's interactional style. This may mean spending more time in initial interviews so that the client has "sufficient time to look them over."
- Bureaucratic coolness in interpersonal exchange is likely to antagonize some minority elders, while addressing a Black elder by his or her first name may be regarded as demeaning and disrespectful rather than informal and friendly. Workers must be

sensitive to the fact that their presence in initial contacts will be evaluated by the client in terms of his or her prior experience with authority and power, and may reflect experience with discrimination and oppression. . . .

- [Recognize] the importance of working with minority aged within their own homes, which serves as a leveling factor in the relationship and allows the worker to observe how environmental and familial variables affect the client. . . .
- In general, minority elderly prefer intimate types of service provision (i.e., needs met by self or family). However, care must be taken not to assume that this is the case for any individual client for . . . ethnicity alone is not a good predictor of service preferences. It must be considered together with age, level of education, cohort effects and "family member living status." (pp. 230–231)

The values common to a particular ethnic group may make life either more or less difficult for the aging person. For example, the elderly of certain ethnic groups (e.g., Chicano, Chinese, Native American) usually occupy a position of respect and influence within families, and the importance of hard work as a value within an ethnic group (e.g., Slavic-American) may cause the nonworking elderly person to feel particularly unworthy and unimportant.

11. Be alert to *indicators of elder abuse and neglect* (especially self-neglect), such as bruises, cuts, burns, or untreated injuries that are explained in a vague or defensive manner; improper clothing for the weather; wandering outside at odd hours or into dangerous areas; mail, newspapers, or other deliveries that are not picked up; unusual activity or no signs of movement from their home; unpleasant odors associated with hygiene or housekeeping; the person does not recognize you or does not know where he or she is or the day or time; the person has means to meet basic needs but is facing an eviction, utility shutoff, or has many unpaid bills; or the person is dependent on a stressed, chemically dependent or mentally ill caregiver and basic needs are not being met.

SELECTED BIBLIOGRAPHY

Burlingame, Virginia. *Gerocounseling: Counseling Elders and Their Families*. New York: Springer, 1995.

Dunkle, Ruth, and Theresa Norgard. "Aging Overview." In *Encyclopedia of Social Work*, 19th ed., Vol. 1, edited by Richard L. Edwards. Washington, D.C.: NASW, 1995, pp. 142–153.

Lowy, Louis. *Social Work With the Aging*, 2nd ed. New York: Longman, 1985.

Toseland, Ronald. *Group Work with the Elderly*. New York: Springer, 1995.

14.34 The Client with Mental Retardation

PURPOSE: To adapt basic social work techniques to the special needs of persons with mental retardation.

DISCUSSION: Mental retardation is one of several conditions included in the legal and programmatic classification known as developmental disability. A *developmental disability* is a severe disability caused by physical or mental impairment that limits a person's development, appears before the age of 22, is likely to last a lifetime, and affects the person's functioning in self-care, learning, self-direction, language, independent living, mobility, and/or economic self-sufficiency. The developmental disabilities include mental retardation, cerebral palsy, autism, severe dyslexia, and epilepsy. Increasingly, the term *cognitive delay* is used in place of mental retardation, especially when speaking about children.

Roughly 3 percent of the U.S. population has some degree of mental retardation. Of those, about 80 percent are in the mild to moderate range and 20 percent are in the range of severe to profound retardation. The vast majority of persons with mental retardation are never institutionalized.

Various signs and symptoms of cognitive delay are usually apparent early in childhood. However, in some cases of mild retardation, the condition may go undetected until the child enters school. Early diagnosis and early medical and educational intervention are of critical importance to minimize the effects of the condition. (See Item 12.20 on identifying developmental delays and Item 12.21 on psychological testing.)

Most adults with mental retardation hold jobs (albeit low-paying ones) and many marry and have children. However, people with mental retardation live in a society that values material success, education, and physical attractiveness. Consequently, many are devalued. Although society shows concern for children with cognitive delays, it tends to reject or avoid the adults with this condition.

The following guidelines will aid the social worker in serving an adult client with mental retardation.

1. Individualize the client; discard any preconceived notions or stereotypes concerning persons with mental retardation. They have the same physical, emotional, social, sexual, and spiritual needs as everyone else. Unfortunately, they encounter much frustration in trying to meet these needs, and because of this frustration and social rejection, many individuals with mental retardation develop an overlay of emotional problems.

2. Adapt your approach to the abilities of the client (e.g., his or her intellectual level, language skills, etc.). As much as possible, a client should participate in making decisions that affect his or her own life. However, this may be limited in the case of an individual who has a severe level of retardation. On the other hand, the client with only a mild or moderate level of retardation should participate in the decision making.

3. A person with mental retardation has difficulty with abstract thinking and often has limited verbal skills. Thus, be prepared to utilize alternatives to verbal interviewing and counseling. Behavioral techniques and related teaching methodologies, nonverbal group work techniques, role-playing, modeling, and the creative arts are examples. (This is not to say that verbal techniques cannot be effective with some clients.)

4. Because the client's attention span may be short, the length of interviews will need to be adjusted accordingly. And because the client's memory may be limited,

each contact and communication should be planned as a discrete event rather than as a continuation of previous conversations. When you give explanations, you may need to repeat them and use several concrete examples and illustrations. Your language must be clear, straightforward, and simple but never childish or patronizing.

5. Because the client's life situation is so impacted by the attitudes of others toward persons with disabilities, be prepared to formulate intervention plans that give much attention to the decisions and actions of others in the client's environment (e.g., family, neighbors, employers, landlord, etc.). The social work practice roles of advocate, case manager, broker, and mediator are especially important in work with persons with mental retardation.

6. In your interactions with your client, do nothing to reinforce inappropriate behaviors. For example, hugging is not a conventional greeting among adults who do not know each other very well. Thus, initiate a handshake rather than allow yourself to be hugged in an inappropriate manner.

7. Be especially careful to avoid demeaning behavior, such as referring to an adult as a "kid." Address adults with retardation as you would any other adult. For example, always use "Mr." or "Miss," unless you know each other so well that your are on a first-name basis. These are normalizing activities that display respect for the client.

8. Learn more about mental retardation. There are many types of mental retardation and for many of these there are associated behavioral patterns and medical disorders. Such knowledge is of critical importance in assessment and planning activities and in working as part of a team with other disciplines, such as psychology, physical therapy, occupational therapy, medicine, speech therapy, special education, and vocational rehabilitation.

9. The principles of normalization should guide the delivery of social services and the formulation of client habilitation plans. *Normalization* refers to the utilization of approaches and services that are as culturally normative as possible. The phrase *culturally normative* means "typical" or "conventional." Normalization does not refer to being "normal" but rather to attempts to decrease deviance (i.e., differences that are socially created). Moreover, normalization does not imply that the person with a disability would be placed in situations that generate unusual frustration or impossible competition just because those situations are typical for the "average" person. However, it does call for actions that remove all forms of overprotection and recognizes that learning and living one's life involve a degree of risk taking and possible failure.

10. It is in relation to clients with severe disabilities that a social worker is likely to encounter the legal procedures known as guardianship and conservatorship. In a ***guardianship*** arrangement, a court has found a person to be legally incompetent because of age or mental or physical incapacity, and therefore invests another person (the guardian) with the power to manage the incapacitated person's money and property and to make certain other decisions. In a ***conservatorship,*** the court appoints another (the conservator) for the more limited purpose of managing the legally incompetent person's estate. Neither of these two procedures should be confused with ***power of attorney,*** which does not involve a court finding of legal incompetence but simply involves the use of a notarized document in which one legally competent person voluntarily gives to another the legal power to take certain actions such as selling a property, depositing or withdrawing funds from a bank, or paying bills.

SELECTED BIBLIOGRAPHY

Baroff, George. *Developmental Disabilities: Psycho-social Aspects.* Austin, Tex.: Pro-Ed, 1991.

Beirne-Smith, Mary, James Patton, and Richard Ittenbach. *Mental Retardation,* 4th ed. New York: Merrill, 1994.

Freedman, Ruth. "Developmental Disabilities: Direct Practice." In *Encyclopedia of Social Work,* 19th ed., Vol. 1, edited by Richard L. Edwards. Washington, D.C.: NASW, 1995, pp 721–729.

14.35   The Client with Brain Injury

PURPOSE: To consider the aftereffects of a brain injury in assessment and case planning.

DISCUSSION: A growing number of individuals in U.S. society suffer the effects of brain injury. Brain injury results in significant but often subtle alterations in memory, judgment, impulse control, perception, emotionality, speech control, and motor control. Such changes can have a profound effect on the person's capacity for social functioning, employability, and family relationships.

The most common causes of brain injury are blows to the head and strokes. The actual effects of an injury depend primarily on what parts of the brain are damaged and the type of damage. For example, the effects of stroke (cerebral vascular accident or CVA) can be quite circumscribed because a blocked blood vessel will cause damage to a very specific area of the brain. For this reason, once the location of stroke-caused damage is known, the aftereffects can be predicted with some accuracy. By contrast, the aftereffects of a traumatic brain injury, such as one acquired in an auto accident or a beating to the head, can be defuse and unpredictable because the tearing and shearing of tissue occurs in several areas of the brain.

Stroke

Typically, the most visible sign of a stroke is a paralysis on one side of the body. Damage to the left side of the brain results in right-sided paralysis and problems with speech and language (termed *aphasia*). In addition, the person tends to be slow, hesitant, and disorganized when faced with an unfamiliar situation.

CVA damage to the right brain results in left side paralysis and causes difficulties in perception. The person tends to be impulsive, have poor judgment, and overlook his or her limitations. This individual can often describe and explain tasks that need to be done but is not able to do them. He or she has trouble both expressing emotions and perceiving the emotional signals of others.

Many of those who have had a stroke have what is termed *one-sided neglect,* meaning that they may have lost sections of their visual field or have lost sensory signals to parts of their bodies. For example, a man with a paralyzed arm may repeatedly allow it to dangle dangerously near the spokes of his wheelchair. Another illustrative example is the woman who looks at her own leg and then becomes confused and upset because she concludes someone is laying in bed beside her. Persons with such perceptual problems can easily become confused while traveling or moving about.

Other problems commonly associated with a stroke include (1) the person becomes careless and neglectful of personal grooming and appearance); (2) loss of memory retention span (i.e., a decrease in the number of things that can be retained and attended to at one time); (3) decreased capacity for short-term memory, which makes new learning difficult; (4) difficulty in generalization (i.e., applying what was learned in one situation to another); (5) emotional lability (i.e., laughing or crying for little or no reason); (6) sensory deprivation (i.e., loss in the ability to taste, hear, see, perceive touch, etc.); and (7) fatigue.

Traumatic Brain Injury

As indicated earlier, brain injury caused by a blow to the head tends to affect more areas of the brain than an injury caused by stroke. Trauma to the brain may result in paralysis or other physical symptoms such as seizures and a decrease in strength and coordination; however, it is common for the person to appear physically normal but experience a number of cognitive, behavioral, and emotional problems. Difficulties in memory, judgment, attention, perception, and impulse control can result in major problems in social interaction and job performance and can be especially troublesome if others assume these problems are caused by laziness or intellectual deficit rather than impaired brain functioning.

For the social work practitioner who may encounter a client who has had a stroke or a traumatic brain injury, several guidelines are important.

1. Be alert to the possibility of brain injury whenever presenting problems that involve personality changes, impulsiveness, poor memory, poor judgment, and so on. Inquire as to a history of a concussion, coma, stroke, skull fracture, or other injuries to the head caused by, for example, car accidents, sports injuries, or violence.

2. If there is reason to suspect the existence of a brain injury, consult with a rehabilitation specialist, neurologist, or neuropsychologist concerning the symptoms and determine if a referral for an in-depth evaluation is indicated. A medical doctor who specializes in physical rehabilitation and in treating the aftereffects of stroke and head injury is called a *physiatrist.* This medical specialty is known as physiatry (not to be confused with psychiatry).

3. Realize that rehabilitation programs can be successful in teaching patients how to compensate for some of the deficits caused by brain injury. Rehabilitation is most beneficial when started as soon as possible after the brain damage has occurred.

4. The family of a person who has had a stroke or acquired a head injury will need information, guidance, and support in learning to cope with the many changes they face in relating to a loved one who may seem like a "different person." Support groups exist in most communities.

5. Individuals with brain injury may fabricate an explanation or make up a story in order to cope with or hide their problems of poor memory and learning difficulties. They may hold tightly to false beliefs because the beliefs help them to make sense out of the unorganized bits of information they possess and the confusion they experience. The family may be distressed and angry when the person with brain injury insists that an obviously false belief is true.

6. The family should be encouraged to review relevant legal documents, contracts, wills, financial agreements, and the like and to develop legal protection against impulsive decisions and poor judgments made by a family member who experiences the effects of a head injury.

7. National organizations such as the National Head Injury Foundation and the National Stroke Association provide information as well as support to the survivors of head injury and stroke and their families.

8. State departments of vocational rehabilitation may have special employment programs for persons with serious cognitive deficits caused by head injury. Such services may include job coaching and extended or supported employment programs. Cognitive deficits that preclude competitive employment may qualify a person for Social Security Disability Income benefits.

SELECTED BIBLIOGRAPHY

Goldberg, Stephen. *Clinical Neuroanatomy Made Ridiculously Simple.* Miami: Med Master Inc., 1990.

Miller, Laurence. *Psychotherapy of the Brain-Injured Patient.* New York: W. W. Norton, 1993.

Williams, J. M., and T. Kay, eds. *Head Injury: A Family Affair.* Baltimore, Md.: Paul H. Brooks, 1991.

14.36   The Client with a Serious Mental Illness

PURPOSE: To adapt social work techniques and approaches to the special needs of a client with a serious mental illness.

DISCUSSION: There are three major categories of serious mental illness: schizophrenia, bipolar disorder, and major depression. All three are diseases of the brain caused primarily by biochemical and structural changes in the brain tissue. Each may be episodic and vary in intensity and the degree to which it impairs a person's functioning. Some of those who experience these illnesses may lose touch with reality (i.e., become psychotic), whereas others may only have trouble with memory, judgment, or feelings of low self-worth. Social work interventions must be sensitive to the highly subjective nature of a person's mental illness.

Schizophrenia is a baffling and debilitating illness. About 1.5 percent of the population is afflicted with this disturbance of the thinking processes. Research suggests that the tendency to develop schizophrenia is hereditary. The usual age of onset is between 15 and 25 years old, when the frontal lobes of the brain are rapidly maturing. Symptoms frequently appear between the ages of 18 to 21 and are exacerbated by the stress of emancipation from the family. Many experts believe that a stressful environment, viral infections, and other physiological conditions may trigger the onset of this illness in those predisposed by heredity.

An individual with schizophrenia will exhibit several of the following symptoms.

- *Delusions* (i.e., has false beliefs that have no factual basis)
- *Hallucinations* (Hearing voices is the most common hallucination; visual hallucination [seeing nonexistent things] is relatively rare but is more likely if the individual is also abusing illegal drugs or psychiatric medications; olfactory and tactile hallucinations are less common but possible.)
- *Disordered thinking* (i.e., making loose or illogical connections between thoughts; shifting rapidly from one topic to another; making conclusions that are unrelated to facts or logic; making up words or using sounds or rhythms that have no meaning to others)
- *Blunted or inappropriate affect* (i.e., narrow range of emotional reactions; the emotions or feelings do not fit the situation; speaks in monotone)
- *Extreme withdrawal* (i.e., withdrawal from ordinary life experiences and social interaction; deterioration in work or school performance; apathy in regard to appearance and self-care)

About one-fourth of those who have a schizophrenic episode get well and never have another episode. Some have occasional relapses. Between 20 to 30 percent develop symptoms that are persistent throughout life.

The other two types of serious mental illness—major depression and bipolar disorder—are known as *mood disorders* or *affective disorders*. Individuals suffering from a **major depression** experience persistent feelings of sadness and melancholy. They often become tearful, irritable, or hostile for no apparent reason. Other symptoms common to depression include:

- Poor appetite and weight loss or increased appetite and weight gain
- Change in sleep pattern (sleeping too little or too much)
- Excessive fatigue; loss of energy
- Change in activity level (either increased or decreased)
- Loss of interest in being with others
- Loss of interest or pleasure in usual activities
- Decreased sexual drive
- Diminished ability to think, concentrate, or make decisions

- Anxiety and rumination over problems
- Feelings of worthlessness or excessive guilt that may reach delusional proportions
- Recurrent thoughts of death or self-harm; wishing to be dead or contemplating or attempting suicide

About 1 percent of the population suffer from *bipolar disorder,* which is characterized by swings between periods of depression and mania (a hyperactive state). Mania is often characterized by:

- An exaggerated or irritable mood
- Decreased need for sleep
- Inflated self-esteem and grandiose ideas
- Increased energy and activity
- Overoptimism, poor judgment, quick and impulsive decision making
- Unusually high levels of involvement in work, pleasurable activities, and sexuality
- Rapid and pressured speech and racing thoughts
- Distractibility

Most often, the depressive phase follows the manic phase. Sometimes, the two phases are separated by periods of near normal functioning. These episodes may come and go and last from several days to several months. Without treatment, there is usually an increase in the severity of the symptoms and the frequency of the episodes.

Some individuals experience the bipolar disorder with only the depressive or manic symptoms rather than both. These are termed *bipolar disorder, depressive type* and *bipolar disorder, manic type.* Often, a person's mental health history will indicate how the bipolar disorder will manifest itself in the future. For example, a person who historically experiences depression in the autumn may continue to experience more severe symptoms during these months of the year.

There are strong indicators that the bipolar disorder has a basis in heredity. About 80 to 90 percent of the persons with this disorder have relatives that suffer from depression. If one parent has the bipolar illness, a child has a 30 percent of developing a depressive disorder; if both parents suffer from the manic-depressive illness, the child has a 75 percent chance of developing a depressive illness.

When working with a client with a serious mental illness, the social worker should follow several guidelines.

1. These illnesses, especially the mood disorders, can usually be treated effectively with proper medications. Thus, an individual with a serious mental illness should be under the care of a physician, preferably a psychiatrist, who can administer medications and monitor their effects. A combination of medication and other forms of mental health care, such as psychotherapy and supportive services, is the preferred treatment for most persons with a serious mental illness. (See Item 14.37 on psychotropic medication.)

2. Because depression gives rise to intense emotional pain and feelings of hope-lessness, the risk of suicide must always be considered. (See Item 12.24 on suicide risk.) Of those with schizophrenia, about one in four attempts suicide and about one in ten dies of suicide. Thoughts of suicide or self-mutilation by someone suffering from schizophrenia place him or her at extremely high risk.

3. Delusions are a common symptom in schizophrenia. By definition, a *delusion* is a set of ideas and beliefs that remain fixed, even in the face of clear evidence to the contrary. Be very cautious about how you respond to a person's delusions. Remember that a delusion serves a purpose; it helps the individual cope with or make sense out of some mental or perceptual confusion. The person believes in the delusions because they make sense and feel right. Listen carefully to the delusion and try to understand the assumptions on which it is built, but do not judge and do not criticize. Do not argue or use logic in an effort to eliminate this symptom. Do not challenge or confront the delusional thoughts, for that will probably destroy the relationship you have with the individual and cause him or her to feel angry and misunderstood. Also, confronting a delusion increases the risk that you will become part of the delusional system of thought and perhaps defined as an enemy or part of a plot or conspiracy.

4. A very small percentage of persons who become psychotic will experience *command hallucinations,* which are voices that tell these people to hurt themselves or others (e.g., a voice telling them to jump off a bridge or kill the mayor). These command hallucinations, although rare, are very dangerous. All threats to personal safety must be taken seriously. If this symptom cannot be controlled by medication, the individual should be hospitalized.

5. The individual with a persistent and serious mental illness is usually in need of services that will assist him or her with the everyday tasks of living. Such services include case management, counseling, case advocacy, budgeting, and assistance in securing income, a job, housing, transportation, medical care, and the like. The *clubhouse model*—which provides peer support, acceptance, meaningful work and activity, and other services—is especially helpful and important to persons with a persistent mental illness (see Chapter 6).

6. A family member's mental illness has a profound impact on others in the family. The social worker should address the concerns of the family by doing the following:
- Help family members grieve the loss of their loved one who, because of mental illness, may now seem like a stranger.
- Provide practical information about mental illness. Ask about their possible fear of physical assault and worry over irresponsible financial decisions by the family member who is mentally ill.
- Encourage family members to join a self-help or support group such as the National Alliance for the Mentally Ill.
- Remain accessible to the families, especially during family crises that can be precipitated by relapses.

- Help the parents and siblings recognize their own rights to a life apart from the anguish and worry they feel toward the family member who is mentally ill.
- Assist family members to secure services such as case management and respite care to relieve them of the daily responsibility of care giving and provide opportunities for rest and renewal.
- Inform family members of legal issues and rights related to securing and refusing treatment.

7. It should be noted that the treatment and management of a mental illness can be further complicated by the presence of another serious problem such as substance abuse, a personality disorder or a developmental disability. The term *dual diagnosis* is applied to such a situation. A *personality disorder* is a deeply ingrained, inflexible, lifelong, and maladaptive pattern of emotional responses and behaviors that are often harmful or distressful to others. However, individuals with a personality disorder seldom see anything unusual about their own behavior and typically blame others for whatever difficulties they encounter in life. Because they do not feel inner pain or anxiety, they do not usually seek treatment voluntarily. There are several types of personality disorders. They are not brain disorders and appear to develop in response to family and social influences.

SELECTED BIBLIOGRAPHY

American Psychiatric Association. *Diagnostic and Statistical Manual of Mental Disorders* (*DSM IV*). Washington D.C.: American Psychiatric Association, 1994.

Austrian, Sonia. *Mental Disorders, Medications and Clinical Social Work*. New York: Columbia University Press, 1995.

Kaplan, Harold, Benjamin Sadock, and Jack Green. *Synopsis of Psychiatry*, 6th ed. Baltimore, Md.: Williams and Williams, 1994.

Psychosocial Rehabilitation Journal. Vol. 16, No. 2 (October 1992). (Special issue on the Clubhouse Model).

Torry, E. Fuller. *Surviving Schizophrenia: A Guide for Family and Friends*, 3rd ed. New York: HarperCollins, 1995.

14.37 The Client on Psychotropic Medication

PURPOSE: To provide appropriate guidance to the client taking psychotropic medication.

DISCUSSION: The social worker will encounter many clients who take medication to control psychiatric symptoms. These medications fall into discrete groups, each of which alleviates a particular set of symptoms. The major groups are antipsychotic, antidepressant, antianxiety, antimanic, psychomotor stimulants, and sedative-hypnotics. Each medication has a chemical name, a generic or general name (e.g., Fluoxetine), and a registered trade or brand name (e.g., Prozac). Each has a specific target symptom, contraindications, potency, and potential side effects. The selection of a specific medication is based on the patient's medical history, physical exam, laboratory tests, use of other medications, use and abuse of alcohol or street drugs, and, of course, the disorder being treated. Physicians generally advise against taking psychotropic medications during pregnancy.

When an individual is hospitalized and/or experiencing disabling symptoms, he or she may be started on a quick-acting medication or given a fairly large dose. Most will not need to take the same dosage after leaving the hospital or after the severe symptoms subside, and a physician may want to reduce the dosage or switch to a medication that is slower acting but has other advantages. Usually, it is desirable for physicians to reduce the dosage but reductions are best done gradually—a process that may take weeks or months. Even when on a "maintenance dose," some people find that their symptoms worsen from time to time. This may be due to stress, biochemical changes, or some other factors.

Some patients are frightened when their doctor suggests they take less medication because they fear a return of symptoms. On the other hand, some individuals are very resistive to the use of medication because they fear side effects or because it is perceived as a loss of control or a blow to their self-esteem.

All of the antipsychotic medications can have side effects that include sedation; weight gain; spasms of eye, face, neck, and back muscles; blurred vision; shuffling gait; and tremors. These effects are dose-related and diminish if the amount taken is reduced. *Tardive dyskinesia* is a troublesome side effect seen most often in patients who have been taking antipsychotic medications for many years. Symptoms include involuntary twitching, lip smacking and jaw and tongue movement, and a blunting of normal emotional responses. In some individuals, these symptoms persist long after the drug that caused them has been withdrawn.

Side effects associated with other drug groups include dry mouth, weight gain, drowsiness, oversensitivity to the sun, and menstrual cycle disturbance. Children and the elderly are particularly vulnerable to side effects. A psychotropic medication may exacerbate nonpsychiatric medical problems such as hypertension, liver disease, epilepsy, and glaucoma. Despite these troublesome side effects, it must be remembered that symptom control is of critical importance to persons suffering from a major mental illness. There is a benefit-risk balance with all medications. In general, a physician will reduce the side effects by prescribing the lowest dosage that produces the desired effects, discontinuing a problematic medication and trying another, avoiding the simultaneous use of two medications that have a similar effect, and, whenever possible, treating only one symptom at a time.

When working with a client taking psychotropic medications, several guidelines should be kept in mind.

1. The decision to prescribe a medication is a complex medical judgment to be made only by a competent physician, preferably a psychiatrist. For ethical and legal reasons, a social worker must never give medication instructions outside the physician's directions.

2. Encourage your client to maintain regular contact with a physician so the effects of the drug can be monitored and dosage can be properly regulated. If you observe what appears to be unusual or unexpected side effects, but your client is un-willing to see a physician, get the name and dosage of the medication and consult with a physician. Also, inform the physician if your client is no longer taking a med-ication as prescribed.

3. Make sure your client and your client's family and friends understand the dan-gers of modifying the prescribed daily dosage and of exchanging medications with others. Also, alert your client to the dangers of using alcohol or street drugs while taking any medication. If your client takes more than one medication, an adverse drug interaction could occur. This happens when the two drugs mixed together have an effect very different than when each is taken alone. Side effects can also occur when the client mixes a psychotropic medication with nonprescription drugs like a cold medicine. Some foods (e.g., aged cheese) may cause adverse reactions when eaten by a person on certain medications.

4. As in the case of other forms of medical treatment, an adult has a right to refuse psychotropic medications. Exceptions are when a court has declared that the indi-vidual is legally incompetent to make that decision and/or when his or her behavior constitutes an imminent threat to self or others. Because the decision to reject a needed medication can have tragic results when symptoms recur, you should do everything possible to inform the patient and his or her family and close friends of the possible consequences. In the final analysis, however, the decision of a legally competent adult must be respected.

SELECTED BIBLIOGRAPHY

Libassi, Mary. "Psychotropic Medications." In *Encyclopedia of Social Work*, 19th ed., Vol. 3, edited by Richard L. Edwards. Washington D.C.: NASW, 1995, pp. 1961–1966.
Maxmen, Jerrold, and Nicholas Ward. *Psychotropic Drugs: Fast Facts.* New York: W. W. Norton, 1995.
Preston, John, John O'Neal, and Mary Talaga. *Handbook of Clinical Psychopharmacology for Therapists.* Oakland, Calif.: New Harbinger, 1994.

SECTION B

TECHNIQUES AND GUIDELINES FOR INDIRECT PRACTICE

The activity that creates change in organizations and communities may be a sus-tained effort over a long period of time or intensive work on a project during a some-what limited time period. The effective social worker should be prepared for both forms of change and develop a repertoire of intervention and monitoring techniques to serve these purposes.

Sustained change effort is often hardly perceptible. The effective social worker builds a working relationship with decision makers and encourages actions that pre-vent crises, contributes to an environment in the agency that supports and sustains high-quality social work practice, helps solve the inevitable issues that arise on a daily basis before they become problems, and performs literally hundreds of tasks that assist in the ongoing operation of agencies and communities. We sometimes neglect to consider these activities as part of the intervention or monitoring activity of social workers, yet they constitute the bulk of practice with these large social structures.

The more dramatic change activities are those that attempt to solve immediate problems. That form of intervention might include raising funds for a special project, developing a grant application, or influencing decision makers when they allocate funds or establish social policies and programs.

These actions require aggressive advocacy that often pits the social worker's preferred outcome against that of others. Should a social worker advocate for one group when it might be to the detriment of another? It is here that involving the persons who are most affected by the outcome of the change effort in the process becomes a check to be sure that the effort is aimed at benefiting those who are most vulnerable. Also, by adhering to the basic social work principles elaborated in Chapter 5, one can be relatively sure that both the purpose and process of the change activity is consistent with the social goals the profession promotes.

14.38 **Working with a Governing or Advisory Board**

PURPOSE: To understand the responsibilities of governing and advisory boards in the operation of human service organizations.

DISCUSSION: Human services agencies operate at the will of the people. If they are public agencies, they are created and at least partially funded through the actions of elected officials. Some private agencies are business concerns operated for the profit of owners or stockholders, but most are incorporated as nonprofit organizations and exist because the people of a community recognize the need for the agency's services.

Maintaining linkage to the community is important to the agency's continued sanction and success. An agency must have community support to adequately fulfill its needs for resources (e.g., funding, volunteers, public image) and must also be responsive to the community's changing service needs. One means of sustaining community linkage is through effective utilization of an advisory board, if a public agency, and the appropriate functioning of its governing board, if a private, nonprofit agency.

Since boards play a central role in making the social agency a positive environment in which to offer services, it is important that social workers are able to work effectively with them.

In private or nonprofit social agencies, the ***governing board*** is the body that is sanctioned to manage the organization. Legally, the board is responsible for the total management of the organization and the members are personally liable for its financial security. However, board members cannot and should not be present on a day-to-day basis to manage the operation of the agency. That is the job of the executive director or administrator. When a governing board shares its authority with the executive director, who then engages other staff members to provide the services, it is important that the lines of authority are clearly drawn so that there is no confusion that interferes with the provision of client services. A governing board typically is responsible for the following activities.

1. *Policy making.* The governing board is legally charged with formulating the goals, objectives, operating policies, and programs of the agency. It should periodically review and revise the agency bylaws to assure that the operation of the agency conforms to the established goals and procedures.

2. *Planning.* As a link between community interests and agency, the board should engage in long-range planning that helps the agency project community needs and evolve programs appropriate to its mission.

3. *Funding.* A governing board is legally responsible for procuring the funds needed to operate the organization, budgeting the use of those resources, establishing procedures for the allocation of those funds, and overseeing fiscal operation of the organization. The board, then, can be expected to engage in preparing and/or approving budgets and grant applications and in representing the agency in appeals for funds from foundations, public fund allocation committees, and other funding agencies such as the United Way.

4. *Staffing.* In discharging the authority to operate the agency, the board hires an administrator (i.e., executive director) to manage the day-to-day operation of the organization. Within the hiring guidelines and personnel procedures established by the board, the administrator assures that qualified staff provide the agency's services.

5. *Facilities.* The board is responsible for assuring that the organization has appropriate housing for the operation of the established programs. If a capital campaign is required to secure needed space for program activities, for example, the board should play a major role in this activity.

6. *Community interpretation.* The board is a critical liaison with the community. It not only interprets community needs to the agency but also helps the community learn about the agency's programs and services. The board typically serves in the capacity of planning the agency's public relations activities.

7. *Evaluation.* Ultimately, the governing board must be accountable for all aspects of agency operation. Therefore, it must assess the effectiveness of the services provided and periodically evaluate the efficiency of the agency's operations.

Particularly in private agencies, the composition of the board is important. It should be representative of the community but also bring expertise or resources that are needed. Some agencies, but not all, select members with the expectation that they will be major fund-raisers or donors (i.e., the principle of the 3Gs applies: get money, give money, or get off the board). Board members can be especially helpful in working with the media, securing space, and lobbying for issues that affect the agency.

In a public agency, by contrast, the ***advisory board*** (also called an *advisory council* or *advisory committee*) has no legal authority or responsibility for the operation of the organization. It is established either because the public officials responsible for the operation of the organization desire citizen input and/or because public law requires an advisory body as a channel for citizen participation. As the name implies, it offers advice, but that advice may or may not be heeded by administrative staff—at times a point of confusion if board and staff alike are not clear about the differences between governance and advisory functions. Azarnoff and Seliger (1982, 124) identify the following as typical responsibilities of an advisory board.

1. *Recommend policies and practices to the body legally created to govern the organization.* Consultation from an advisory board serves to inform the decision-making process. While usually the advisory function is found in public agencies, it can also serve the private agency regarding specific issues or special programs or projects.

2. *Evaluate agency services and recommend improvements.* Where staff are oftentimes too close to the services to offer an objective view of service provision or when the credibility of the staff to accurately assess the agency's functioning is in question, advisory committees can perform this valuable function.

3. *Assist in determining the needs of consumers.* Advisory boards are in a good position to represent the interests of the agency's clientele or potential clientele. For this reason, among others, it is important that clients or people familiar with client needs serve on advisory committees.

4. *Publicize agency activities.* Like the governing board, the advisory committee can inform the public of the agency's programs and methods of service delivery.

The members of both governing and advisory boards volunteer their time and talents to the agency. The motivations of board members may vary from a desire to help others, to a desire to use their special knowledge to benefit the community, to seeking personal recognition and social status. It is important to understand these motivations and use this resource in a manner that both serves the agency and satisfies the board member's need.

SELECTED BIBLIOGRAPHY

Azarnoff, Roy S., and Jerome S. Seliger. *Delivering Human Services.* Englewood Cliffs, N.J.: Prentice Hall, 1982.

Child Welfare League of America. *Board Self-Assessment Checklist.* Washington, D.C.: CWLA, 1992.

Conrad, William R., Jr., and William E. Glenn. *The Effective Voluntary Board of Directors: What It Is and How It Works,* rev. ed. Athens, Ohio: Swallow Press, 1983.

Herman, Robert D., and Richard D. Heimovics. *Executive Leadership in Nonprofit Organizations: New Strategies for Shaping Executive-Board Dynamics.* San Francisco: Jossey-Bass, 1991.

14.39   Conducting Effective Staff Meetings

PURPOSE: To design and conduct efficient staff meetings that promote intraagency communication.

DISCUSSION: An important factor in the successful operation of a social agency is the quality of staff communication, making the staff meeting a critically important tool in agency management. Properly used, the staff meeting enhances communication and can prevent organizational problems caused by staff who act on inaccurate or incomplete information. Improperly used, staff meetings can be both costly for the agency and frustrating for the staff. A one-hour meeting involving a staff of eight, for example, is the equivalent of a day's salary for one person. The cost of the meeting should be justified by its benefits for achieving the agency's purpose, as compared to the staff providing service to clients during that time.

It is important to distinguish between a staff meeting and other types of meetings, such as case staffings and consultations and the meetings used for case assignments or by special committees and project teams. The distinction between staff meetings and team meetings can be made in terms of *purpose* (e.g., exchange of information regarding the agency versus practice techniques related to specific cases); *content* (e.g., discussion of policies, procedures, organizational maintenance, and professional practice issues versus a specific issue of practice activity regarding a case situation); *formality* (i.e., formal versus informal); *membership* (e.g., inclusive of practitioners and support staff versus involving only practitioners who are members of the team); and *size* (e.g., typically large and somewhat impersonal versus small, intensive, and personally disclosing interaction).

Staff meeting time should not be spent on routine or easily understood information that can be disseminated by other means such as memos or routing documents among the staff. Staff meeting time is best spent only on matters that require verbal clarification, feedback from staff, or a staff decision. It should be noted, however, that research by Barretta-Herman (1989) suggests that social agency staff tend to resist both written and electronic communications in favor of face-to-face contact.

Staff meetings should be held at the same time each week or month, have a set starting and ending time, and should last not more than one hour. Attendance should be mandatory and the leader should prepare and circulate an agenda in advance of the meeting and take responsibility to keep the discussion moving. However, staff meetings are not solely a management responsibility. All staff should be expected to contribute agenda items, be prepared for discussion of those items, and assume responsibility for following through on items that require their attention. If an issue requires extensive discussion or if in-service training is the best way to deal with a problem, a separate meeting should be scheduled. In many settings, the preparation of minutes is useful to disseminate information and properly record staff decisions in order to keep upper levels of administration informed of the activities of this unit.

Barretta-Herman's (1990, 145) analysis of staff meetings in human services organizations identifies three elements of successful meetings.

- They fulfill their objectives as defined jointly by management and practitioners.
- They provide a forum for active discussion, creative problem solving, and participation of staff members.
- The structure of the meeting ensures decisions made are followed through with action.

SELECTED BIBLIOGRAPHY

Barretta-Herman, Angeline. "The Effective Social Service Staff Meeting." In *Business Communication: New Zealand Perspectives,* edited by Frank Slegio. Auckland: Software Technology, 1990, pp. 136–147.

———. "Computer Utilization in the Social Services," *New Zealand Journal of Social Work* 7 (Fall 1989).

Brody, Ralph. *Effectively Managing Human Service Organizations.* Newbury Park, Calif.: Sage, 1993.

14.40 Building Teamwork and Cooperation

PURPOSE: To encourage and develop interagency and interprofessional cooperation.

DISCUSSION: In many cases, no one professional and no one agency can provide all of the services needed by the client. Thus, if the client is to be served, several professionals must work as a team. Teamwork and cooperative behavior grow from a proper mix of values, attitudes, and interpersonal skills. For example, Motz and Schultz (1988, 37) observe that effective members on interagency child protection teams have certain characteristics: (1) assertiveness, (2) ability to listen and maintain an openness to differing ideas, (3) willingness to support other team members, (4) ability to offer criticism in a constructive manner, (5) strong commitment to the team approach, and (6) consistent attendance at team meetings.

The following guidelines can encourage cooperation and teamwork.

1. In general, individuals and organizations cooperate with each other when it is of benefit to do so. Those benefits may be personal, professional, organizational, political, or financial. An increased frequency of interaction usually leads to increased cooperation if the parties have similar goals, beliefs, and values. Cooperation is fostered by emphasizing what the parties have in common and how they will benefit from working together.

2. Genuine teamwork and interagency cooperation does not occur by accident; they must be encouraged and nurtured. Statements of thanks, recognition, praise, and taking a personal interest in other team members help to reinforce cooperative behavior. Where appropriate, invite other members of the team to office parties and

social gatherings as a way of building relationships and promoting goodwill. Do not engage in gossip or any other activity that might diminish respect for other professionals or agencies.

3. Teamwork and cooperation is built on a common purpose. That purpose is to serve the client and to accomplish what no one professional or single agency can achieve alone. Whenever necessary, help the team members or agency representatives revisit the question: What are we trying to achieve for our clients?

4. When functioning as part of a team, encourage the selection of a leader or chairperson who is nondefensive, supportive of others, and respected by the group. Strive to be proactive and willing to plan and prepare carefully for team meetings and assume a leadership role when appropriate.

5. Concern for client confidentiality is a reason commonly given for not working closely with other agencies and professionals. Sometimes this issue is more imagined than real. Clients can be asked to sign a release of information, thus removing this barrier. If professionals or agencies want to work together but are hesitant to do so because of the confidentiality issue, they should ask their agency's legal counsel to recommend a workable procedure.

6. Be alert to the fact that many interagency conflicts center on questions of which agency has primary fiscal responsibility for providing a particular service. In other words, many disagreements boil down to the question of whose budget is to be used to pay the cost of services. Be prepared to address these questions.

7. Understand your role and responsibility and those of the people with whom you are working. Make sure everyone knows what they can and cannot expect of each other. Consider developing interagency agreements that will clarify these relationships (see Items 13.13 and 13.14). Several forms of documents might be used to define interagency expectations such as contracts, letters of agreement, protocol statements, purchase of service agreements, and policy manuals.

8. Remember that even under the best circumstances, teamwork can be challenging. This is especially true when the team is attempting to make difficult, value-laden decisions and to formulate plans concerning highly dysfunctional individuals and families. If the team is unable to communicate clearly and resolve its own conflicts, it may end up behaving much like the dysfunctional families it is trying to serve.

9. Be willing to address directly and openly the conflicts or hidden agendas that disrupt team efforts. Conflict that arises from thoughtful differences of opinion is healthy. However, conflict that stems from prejudice, displaced hostility, or thoughtless loyalty to actions of the past is disruptive and must be addressed. Attempts to suppress or avoid conflicts or significant differences of opinion by denial, capitulation, or domination often make the problem even worse. When it is necessary to express a difference of opinion, use I-messages (see Item 8.5) and other communication skills that convey your message in a clear, straightforward, and non-threatening manner. Try to resolve interprofessional and interagency conflicts by focusing on shared values and goals and by using negotiating skills.

10. Realize that some of those with whom you must work may not be committed to teamwork. When this is evident, be firm but diplomatic in expressing the need for cooperation and for putting the good of the client before other considerations.

SELECTED BIBLIOGRAPHY

Garner, Howard. *Helping Others Through Teamwork.* New York: Child Welfare League of America, 1988.

Hagebak, Beaumont. *Getting Local Agencies to Cooperate.* Baltimore: University Park Press, 1982.

Motz, Janet, and Michael Schultz. "Rural Child Protection Teams." In *The New Child Protection Team Handbook*, edited by Donald Bross et al. New York: Garland, 1988.

14.41   Leading Small-Group Meetings

PURPOSE: To schedule and conduct efficient and productive committee and group meetings.

DISCUSSION: Group decision making has become increasingly popular in the human services. Therefore, social workers spend considerable time participating in groups, agency staff meetings (see Item 14.39), interagency team meetings, and various agency and community committees. In their study of task group decision making, Toseland, Rivas, and Chapman (1984, 343–344) state that "the reliance of agencies on groups for making decisions regarding agency policies, practices, and business is warranted. [And] even if group leaders or group members do not act on the decision made by a group in which they participated, they are likely to make a better independent decision because they participated in a group."

While group consideration of issues may have inherent benefits, group meetings, without proper planning and direction, can waste much valuable time and reduce the opportunity for making significant community or organizational change. As the leader of a small group, the social worker is responsible for making the meeting as productive and efficient as possible. Barker and associates (1979), Brilhart (1995), and Bertcher (1979) identify a number of principles and guidelines that should be followed by the worker when he or she is in a leadership position.

1. *Prepare for the meeting by engaging in the following activities:*
   - Clearly identify the purpose of the meeting. *Never have a meeting unless there is a real need for one.*
   - Decide who should participate.
   - Identify objectives for the meeting and anticipate what the participants will and should expect. You may want to involve them in the planning.
   - Decide the best time and place for the meeting, and determine how participants will be notified of the purpose, agenda, time, and place of the meeting.
   - Decide how much time will be required for the meeting and construct a realistic agenda. Plan to address high-priority items first.
   - Decide what physical arrangements are necessary (e.g., room reservations, seating arrangements, audiovisual equipment, refreshments).

- Decide if a written report will be needed and, if so, who will prepare it and how it will be distributed.
- Decide if a follow-up meeting will be needed.

2. *Get the discussion off to a good start.*
   - Make sure that all members are introduced to each other. This might be done with formal introductions or a coffee hour. Use name tags if members do not already know each other.
   - Explain the purpose of the discussion and its relevance to the participants.
   - Distribute materials needed for the discussion (e.g., fact sheets, outlines, case examples).
   - Create an atmosphere that helps the participants feel unthreatened and responsible for contributing to the discussion.

3. *Keep the discussion orderly, efficient, and productive.*
   - Make sure the goal is understood by all and that it is a goal that makes sense to the group. Keep the participants oriented toward that goal. For example, occasionally ask: Are we still on target for reaching our objectives?
   - Be alert to extended departures from the topic. If the group is drifting away from the topic, call this to everyone's attention. Ask if the digression means that there is disagreement on the goal or if it is an indication that the group is ready to move on to another topic.
   - If there is much repetition in the discussion, ask if the group has exhausted the subject at hand. If so, help them get started on a new topic.
   - Be the group's timekeeper. Keep the group informed of the time limits so high-priority topics will get the attention they deserve.
   - Bring the discussion to a conclusion, which might include:
     a. A summary of progress made by the group
     b. Comments about planning and preparation for another meeting
     c. Assignments for follow-up and implementation
     d. Commendations when appropriate
     e. Request an evaluation of the meeting in order to improve future ones

4. *Give all members an equal opportunity to participate.*
   - Explain in your opening remarks that the role of the group leader primarily will be that of coordinator to ensure that all members have an opportunity to be heard.
   - Address your comments and questions to the group as a whole, rather than to specific individuals, unless specific information is needed from a particular person.
   - Make sure that all members have a chance to participate. While no one should be forced to speak, neither should anyone be prevented from speaking.
   - Scan the group every minute or two. Look for indications that a member wants to speak. If this is seen and the member has been quiet, bring that person into the discussion by asking if he or she would like to add something to the discussion.
   - If the group contains members who dominate the discussion, try to control them for the benefit of the group. A number of techniques can be used;

begin with a more subtle approach and become directive only if necessary. Some possible ways to deal with such members are:

  a. When possible, seat the talkative members where they are more easily overlooked by other members.
  b. When a question is asked of the group, meet the eyes of those members who have spoken infrequently and avoid eye contact with the dominant talkers.
  c. When a frequent talker has made a point, cut in with something like: How do the rest of you feel about that idea?
  d. Adopt a rule that each person can make but one statement per topic.
  e. In private, ask the excessive talkers to help in getting the quiet members to speak more often.
  f. Point out the problem and ask others to contribute more—for instance: We have heard a lot from John and Mary, but what do the rest of you think about . . . ?

- If asked by a member to express a personal opinion about a controversial issue, try to bounce the question back to the group, unless members already have expressed their opinions. Say, "Well, let's see how others feel about this first." If you must express a personal opinion, do so in a manner that will not inhibit others from speaking on the topic.
- Don't comment after each member has spoken; it is too easy to get into a "wheel" pattern of communication, with the leader becoming the hub of the wheel.
- React to what members say with acceptance and without judgment, showing only that a point is understood or that it needs clarification. If evaluation seems necessary, invite it from others with a question such as: Does that fit with your perception on the matter?
- Use nonverbal communication to promote discussion. Nods and gestures can be used to encourage participation, especially from the quiet members.

5. *Promote cooperation and harmony in a small group.*
   - Be alert to the possibility of hidden agendas, and call them to the attention of the group. The group usually can solve a problem of conflicting purposes if it is brought into the open for discussion.
   - Emphasize the importance of the mutual sharing of ideas and experiences and the need for clear communication.
   - Use the word *we* often to stress the group's unity of purpose.
   - Keep conflicts focused on facts and issues. Stop any attacks on a member's personality.
   - Do not let the discussion become so serious that the members do not have some fun. Humor can reduce tension. Effective discussion is characterized by a constant shifting between the serious and the playful.

6. *Use questioning techniques to maintain attention on a topic and stimulate analytical thinking.*
   - Use open-ended questions rather than closed-ended ones.
   - Questions should be understandable to all. Vague or obtuse questions frustrate the members.

- Questions should be asked in a natural and conversational tone of voice.
- Questions should usually be addressed to the group as a whole, rather than to a particular individual. This motivates everyone to think and respond.
- Questions occasionally should be asked of persons who are not giving their attention to the discussion. This usually stimulates the individual and the whole group to redirect its attention to the topic.
- Questions should be asked in a manner that indicates the leader's confidence in the person's ability to respond.
- Questions should be selected to maintain the focus on the topic under discussion. Avoid questions that would cause the group to leave its task and go off on a tangent.

7. *Encourage critical thinking.*
   - Ask for more detail and specification. Dig for the rationale and assumptions behind an opinion or a belief. Help those offering opinions to furnish evidence for the positions they take.
   - See that the evidence offered for a position is tested and not accepted at face value.
   - Assign one or two members of the group to challenge ideas and play devil's advocate so that differences are aired openly.

SELECTED BIBLIOGRAPHY

Barker, Larry, Donald Cegala, Robert Kibler, and Kathy Wahlers. *Groups in Process.* Englewood Cliffs, N.J.: Prentice Hall, 1979.

Bertcher, Harvey. *Group Participation Techniques for Leaders and Members.* Beverly Hills: Sage, 1979.

Brilhart, John. *Effective Group Discussion,* 8th ed. Madison, Wis.: Brown and Benchmark, 1995.

Fatout, Marian, and Steven R. Rose. *Task Groups in the Social Services.* Newbury Park, Calif.: Sage, 1995.

Hildreth, Richard A. *The Essentials of Meeting Management.* Englewood Cliffs, N.J.: Prentice Hall, 1990.

Toseland, Ronald W., Robert F. Rivas, and Dennis Chapman. "An Evaluation of Decision-Making Methods in Task Groups." *Social Work* 29 (July–August 1984): 339–346.

Tropman, John E. *Making Meeting Work: Achieving High-Quality Group Decisions.* Newbury Park, Calif.: Sage, 1995.

14.42   The RISK Technique

PURPOSE: To facilitate committee or group members in expressing their fears or concerns about an issue or proposed action.

DISCUSSION: At times, committees (and especially staff committees) need to address fears and concerns related to some perceived risk or threat. For example, when new policies are adopted by a board, when new legislation is passed that affects a social program and/or the resources available, or when administrators establish a change in routine, it becomes important to identify and clarify the facts and issues in the situation and set aside rumors and fantasized outcomes. In these situations, the RISK technique can be useful.

To use this technique, the leader must take a nondefensive posture and communicate an interest in having the group members express all fears, issues, concerns, complaints, and anticipated problems. By maintaining this approach, the leader encourages members of the group to express their views and to listen and understand one anothers' fears.

For example, assuming that a proposed change in a social agency is that all workers would double the number of days they are on 24-hour call each month, the agency supervisor might elect to use the **RISK technique** by taking the following steps.

1. The leader (i.e., the supervisor) schedules a meeting with all agency workers and presents a detailed description of the proposed change in the "on-call" section of the agency's personnel policy.

2. The leader explains that he or she will utilize the RISK technique to help workers identify all of their concerns about this proposed change.

3. The leader begins by asking workers to voice any and all fears, concerns, and worries they have in relation to the proposed change. These "risks" are written on newsprint for all to see, with the wording of the statement acceptable to the person raising the concern. Discussion of the items is not permitted at this time. (Note that up to this point, the RISK technique is similar to brainstorming, Item 14.46.)

4. The leader continues to encourage workers to voice additional concerns about the proposed change. It is important to allow adequate time for this session because the concerns that are most disturbing and threatening often will not surface until late in the session.

5. The initial session ends and the leader schedules a second meeting to occur in the next three to seven days. Meanwhile, all workers receive a written listing of the risk items identified during the meeting.

6. At the second meeting, the leader encourages workers to voice any additional risks they may have thought of since the initial meeting or to change the wording of any risk statements. The group is then asked to discuss and react to each risk item and decide if it is, indeed, a serious and substantive concern or issue. The risks considered to be minor or of little concern are dropped from the list. Those remaining are further discussed and clarified. At this point, the second meeting is ended with the understanding that the identified risks are viewed as those of the group as a whole, and not the person who first identified any risk.

7. The leader places the group's identified risks (i.e., the final list from the second meeting) on an agenda for a meeting between the workers and administrators.

SELECTED BIBLIOGRAPHY

Brilhart, John K., and Gloria J. Galanes. *Effective Group Discussion*, 8th ed. Madison, Wis.: Brown and Benchmark, 1995.

14.43   The Nominal Group Technique (NGT)

PURPOSE: To help consensus-oriented groups arrive at decisions.

DISCUSSION: Committees that depend on a consensus approach sometimes get stuck in reaching a decision. One technique that helps bring issues into the open and moves the group toward consensus is the Nominal Group Technique (NGT). It is particularly suited for groups of six to nine people; if used with a larger group, it should be divided into smaller subgroups. The main elements of the NGT process are the following:

1. The individuals generate ideas in writing.
2. Round-robin feedback is given from group members with each idea recorded in a terse phrase on a flipchart.
3. Group discussion of each recorded idea is held for clarification and evaluation.
4. Individual voting establishes priorities among ideas with a group decision being mathematically derived through rank ordering or rating.

This approach is especially useful with groups addressing direct-service issues, such as identifying and sharing experiences about a practice problem or an organizational or community issue. Depending on the scope and complexity of the matter being addressed, it might take from as little as an hour and a half to as much as nine hours to complete the process.

The following guidelines are designed for the social worker using the shorter form of the NGT.

1. The chair acts as facilitator and does not vote.

2. The issue is stated on a flipchart.

3. The pros and cons are freely discussed for 10 minutes.

4. Each person is asked to spend 5 to 15 minutes working silently, writing down ideas or solutions on a piece of paper. The chair polls each committee member for one idea or solution.

5. Each idea or solution is listed on the chart and numbered. The chair then polls each member for a second idea or solution and repeats this process until the lists have been exhausted.

6. Ten more minutes are allowed for clarification of the ideas or solutions presented—not for defense of the position.

7. All members vote on a secret ballot, ranking their top five choices 1, 2, 3, 4, 5. By adding the scores for each idea or solution, the lowest scores will reflect the most favored positions by the committee.

8. Have a full evaluation discussion of the several items at the top of the list. Encourage critical thinking, invite disagreement, and seek careful analysis of the items.

9. If a clear consensus is not reached, revote and then discuss the items again. This can be repeated until a synthesis of ideas is developed or there is clear support for one idea.

The NGT encourages active involvement by all committee members as they consider and write down their ideas. Too often, in a group process, a few members carry the discussion and others do not actively and creatively think about the issues from their own perspective. The interactive presentation of the issues allows all committee members an opportunity to express themselves and respond to the ideas from both the verbal and less-verbal members.

SELECTED BIBLIOGRAPHY

Brilhart, John K., and Gloria J. Galanes. *Effective Group Discussion*, 8th ed. Madison, Wis.: Brown and Benchmark, 1995.

Toseland, Ronald W., and Robert F. Rivas. *An Introduction to Group Work Practice*, 2nd ed. Boston: Allyn and Bacon, 1995.

14.44   Chairing a Committee

PURPOSE: To effectively serve as chair of a committee and lead it to successful action.

DISCUSSION: The committee is a particular type of small group for which the social worker might assume a leadership function. As chairperson of a committee, the social worker should make use of the guidelines for working with small groups (see Item 14.41). In addition, chairing a committee requires the use of a formal task-oriented approach to groups that can be facilitated by the selective use of Items 14.42 and 14.43.

Essential knowledge for both the chairperson and committee members is familiarity with parliamentary procedures. For almost a century, *Robert's Rules of Order* (Robert 1990) has been the accepted procedures to be followed in formal committee proceedings. A copy should be on every social worker's bookshelf. Table 14.1 provides a summary of these rules of order.

Above all else, a committee chair must believe in the worth and wisdom of group decision making. The decisions made by a small group, as compared to those made by a single individual, are more likely to be based on accurate and complete information and on a wider range of considerations; thus, the decisions are more likely to be the best ones possible. That is not to say that committees do not make bad decisions. They do. But a group is less likely to make a bad decision or a serious error in judgment than is an individual acting alone.

Tropman, Johnson, and Tropman (l992) remind us that the committee chair must be alert to the danger of *groupthink*, a situation of false agreement or false consensus that arises when a powerful committee member takes a strong stand on an issue and other members simply acquiesce rather than argue an opposing point of view. Soon after the meeting, the other members will usually complain and agree

TABLE 14.1 Summary of Parliamentary Procedure

Guidelines/ Description	Type of Action	Purpose of Action	Interrupts Debate?	Requires Second?	Debatable?	Amendable?	Vote Required?
	PRIVILEGED MOTIONS						
■ #1–12 in order of priority	1. Fix time to adjourn	Establish plan to discontinue meeting	No	Yes	No	No	Majority
■ #1–4 supersede all other actions	2. Recess	Temporary break in meeting	No	Yes	Yes	Yes	Majority
	3. Question of privilege	Challenge rights of assembly or a member to take an action	Yes	No	No	No	None
	4. Point of order	Clarify or challenge process	Yes	No	No	No	None
	SUBSIDIARY MOTIONS						
■ #5–12 facilitate action on other motions	5. Table the motion	Delay action to a specified meeting	No	Yes	No	No	Majority
	6. Previous question	Close debate and vote immediately	No	Yes	No	No	2/3
	7. Limit debate	Set limits on future debate	No	Yes	No	Yes	2/3
	8. Postpone definitely	Temporarily delay action to a specified time	No	Yes	Yes	Yes	Majority
■ Each may be made while motion below is on the floor	9. Refer to committee	Delay until committee can review matter and report back	No	Yes	Yes	Yes	Majority
	10. Amend the amendment	One amendment to primary amendment is permitted at a time	No	Yes	Yes	Yes	Majority
	11. Primary amendment	Propose change in main motion	No	Yes	Yes	Yes	Majority
	12. Postpone indefinitely	Remove motion from consideration	No	Yes	Yes	No	Majority

Process Starts Here →

- Routes to opening main motion
- No order of precedence
- Arise from process of debate and may occur at any time
- Yeild only to privileged motions

MAIN MOTION OR RESOLUTION

Motion	Description					
New motion	Introduce action for first time	No	Yes	Yes	Yes	Majority
Reconsider prior action	Reconsider previous vote	Yes	Yes	Yes	No	Majority
Resume consideration	Take up motion previously tabled	No	Yes	Yes	No	Majority

INCIDENTAL MOTIONS

Motion	Description					
Move to appeal	Challenge ruling of the chair	Yes	Yes	Yes	No	Majority
Move to suspend rules	Override existing procedures	No	Yes	No	No	2/3
Request point of order	Correct parlimentary process error	Yes	No	No	No	None
Withdraw motion	Remove motion from consideration	Yes	No	No	No	None
Division of question	Act on parts of motion or amendment	No	No	No	No	None
Division of assembly	After voice vote, request vote count	Yes	No	No	No	None
Request for information	Seek clarification	Yes	No	No	No	None

among themselves that the decision reached was a bad one. Needless to say, this conflict could have been avoided if the chair had made sure all points of view were expressed and debated and no one member or faction dominated the meeting.

People are usually willing to serve on a committee if they believe their time will be used efficiently and the committee's work will result in a real and positive change. On the other hand, many people have reasons for disliking and avoiding committee work. Among their reasons are the following:

- There is a lack of clear purpose (e.g., members are not sure why they are meeting or what they are to accomplish).
- There is a lack of leadership and direction by the chairperson (e.g., the chair does not keep the group moving and focused; real issues are not addressed or difficult decisions are avoided).
- The chair and/or members do not take the assignment seriously (i.e., lack of motivation or interest in the work of the committee).
- The committee's work is disregarded by top management (e.g., a committee is asked to study an issue and make a recommendation but the recommendation is ignored; sometimes the committee discovers that there was never an intention to follow the committee's recommendation).
- Committee discussion is controlled or dominated by one individual or a clique.
- There is a lack of preparation for the meetings (e.g., no agenda, needed information is not made available, etc.).
- There is a lack of follow through (e.g., members or the chair promises to do something but fails to do so).
- The chair or members have a hidden agenda (e.g., some members have an ax to grind or will accept only one outcome, regardless of majority opinion).

One means of helping a committee avoid pitfalls that can lead to unproductive meetings is to engage the members in setting goals and operating procedures for the committee. Whether it is new or a committee that has continued over an extended period of time, it is useful for the chairperson or other members to periodically review and renegotiate the objectives and methods of operation so that all members can fully participate in the work. Dyer (1977, 76–81) identifies several steps that should be followed in building a productive committee.

1. *Develop a realistic priority level.* It is important to give members a chance to discuss why they are serving on the committee, clarify the relative importance of this work in the context of their total responsibilities, and indicate the amount of time they are able to commit to this activity. Sharing these matters helps to establish the pace at which the committee can operate and allows the chair to identify persons who have the time and interest to carry major responsibilities.

2. *Share expectations.* Each person should be asked to identify his or her greatest concerns about working on this committee, how he or she sees it functioning, and what actions are necessary to ensure positive outcomes.

3. *Clarify goals.* The committee members should collectively discuss and write down a statement that represents the group's *core mission.* Subgoals can then be developed to reflect the intermediate or short-range objectives necessary to accomplish this mission. Each decision and action should be examined for its contribution to the mission or subgoals that have been established.

4. *Formulate operating guidelines.* The committee members should then establish procedures for their operation. Answers to the following questions will provide guidance for the chair and allow members to know how to proceed.

- How will we make decisions?
- What will be our basic method of working as a group?
- How do we make sure everyone gets a chance to discuss issues or raise concerns?
- How will we resolve differences?
- How will we ensure that we complete our work and meet deadlines?
- How will we change methods that are not producing results?

In addition, it should be recognized that the formality with which a committee operates often depends on its size, the existing relationships among the members, and the speed with which it needs to make decisions. The purpose of some committees is best served by a very open dialogue that explores topics in depth before action is taken. For others, the work is more task oriented, with subcommittees considering the issues and preparing reports of their deliberations on which the full committee will act.

SELECTED BIBLIOGRAPHY

Dyer, William G. *Team Building: Issues and Alternatives.* Reading, Mass.: Addison-Wesley, 1977.
Robert, Henry M. *Robert's Rules of Order,* 9th ed. Glenview, Ill.: Scott Foresman, 1990.
Tropman, John E., Harold R. Johnson, and Elmer J. Tropman. *Committee Management in Human Services,* 2nd ed. Chicago: Nelson-Hall, 1992.

14.45 Problem Solving by a Large Group

PURPOSE: To help a large group of people arrive at a decision.

DISCUSSION: At times, it is necessary for a social worker to initiate problem-solving activity within a large group. The technique described here is intended to elicit ideas from all members and provide an opportunity for participation, even when as many as thirty or more people are involved.

The technique begins with the group leader explaining the purpose of the meeting; for example: We need to come up with a method of collecting information from the agencies in town on trends in the number of homeless people applying for help. The following steps should then be followed.

1. *Each individual is asked to think privately about the problem and possible solutions.* Members are asked to make written notes on their thoughts.

2. *Dyads are formed.* Each person in the dyad is instructed to interview his or her partner and to try to understand that person's perspective on the problem and proposed solutions. The dyads work for 10 minutes.

3. *Quartets are formed.* For 15 minutes, each group of four people discusses the problem and possible solutions. Each quartet records the key points of its deliberation on a large piece of paper, which is hung on the wall for all to see.

4. *Each individual studies the papers for 10 minutes.*

5. *The whole group reassembles and shares their analysis of the problem and proposed solutions.* This final step sets the stage for the prioritizing of proposed solutions to be explored in more depth.

SELECTED BIBLIOGRAPHY

Brody, Ralph. *Effectively Managing Human Service Organizations.* Newbury Park, Calif.: Sage, 1993.

Kahn, Si. *Organizing: A Guide for Grassroots Leaders.* New York: McGraw-Hill, 1982.

Rivira, Felix G., and John L. Erlich. *Community Organizing in a Diverse Society.* Boston: Allyn and Bacon, 1992.

14.46   Brainstorming

PURPOSE: To help a client identify several possible solutions to a problem.

DISCUSSION: Problem solving includes the important step of identifying all possible alternatives or solutions. Too often, some potential solutions are overlooked because they do not fit preconceived notions or expectations. Rigidity and following old habits of thought can limit creativity during the problem-solving process. The technique of *brainstorming* is designed to overcome this limitation. It can be applied to any problem for which there may be a range of solutions. The objective of brainstorming is to free persons temporarily from self-criticism and from the criticism of others in order to generate imaginative solutions to a specific problem. However, it should not be used until the problem has been clearly defined. Confusion will result when the technique is applied to a vaguely stated problem or question.

Although brainstorming is most often used when a group is in search of a problem's solution, it can be used in other phases of the problem-solving process, such as: What information do we need? Where or how can we get this information? How will we evaluate proposed solutions? Brainstorming is most often used in work with groups or committees, but many workers adapt its principles for use in one-on-one counseling sessions.

A brainstorming session begins with the identification and listing of a wide variety of possible solutions. Many may be unrealistic, but it is only after all alternatives have been identified that the participants are permitted to evaluate the proposed solutions in search of those that are feasible. A social worker setting up a brainstorming session will give the participants several instructions.

1. Participants are encouraged to develop a large number of solutions. The goal is to generate a quantity of solutions—quality will be determined later.
2. Participants are encouraged to be freewheeling in their thinking. Even wild ideas are welcomed and accepted without judgment.
3. Participants are encouraged to combine and elaborate on the solutions that are offered.
4. Participants are not permitted to criticize or evaluate one another's proposed solutions.

During the brainstorming session, a recorder writes down all the ideas as fast as they come up. If possible, do this on a blackboard or flipchart so the visual record stimulates additional ideas. The leader of the session should quickly stop any criticism of ideas, whether verbal or implied by tone of voice or nonverbal gesture. Also, the group leader needs to keep the participants focused on the problem under consideration.

Once all of the proposed solutions or ideas have been heard and recorded, the session moves to a second stage: the critical examination of each idea. De Bono (1992) suggests a useful technique for ensuring that six types of questioning and thinking are applied during the evaluation stage. Each of these six categories of thinking is called a "hat" and each hat has a color. Thus, for example, when the group is asked by the group leader to "put on your red hats," the group is being asked to evaluate the proposed solutions in terms of hunches, intuition, and gut feelings. If asked to put on the "black hat," the group is to view the solutions in a highly critical and skeptical manner.

The six thinking hats are as follows:

White hat (focus on objectivity and data): What information do we have? How reliable is this information? What additional information do we need?

Red hat (focus on hunches and intuition): What are our gut feelings about this proposed solution? Does it "feel" right? Let's trust our instincts!

Black hat (focus on caution and risk): What are the legal, policy, political, and funding problems we will encounter? This cannot be done and will not work because . . . .

Yellow hat (focus on optimism): It needs to be done, so let's try! Who cares if it has never been done before? Let's try something different! It will work if we really want it to work!

Green hat (focus on creativity and other combinations of ideas): Are there still other ways of thinking about this? Can we combine the best parts of several different proposals?

Blue hat (focus on the big picture and holistic thinking): How does this idea fit with other things we know about this issue? Are we missing something important? Let's summarize the conclusions we have reached and the decisions we have made so far. Is our way of discussing and approaching this issue working for us? Are we making progress toward a decision or solution?

A brainstorming session, plus the evaluation of each proposed solution (50 might be generated in a single session), could take several hours.

SELECTED BIBLIOGRAPHY

De Bono, Edward. *Serious Creativity* New York: HarperCollins,1992.
Kottler, Jeffery. *Advanced Group Leadership.* Pacific Grove, Calif.: Brooks/Cole, 1994.
Zastrow, Charles. *Social Work with Groups*, 3rd ed. Chicago: Nelson-Hall, 1993.

14.47 Class Advocacy

PURPOSE: To advance the cause of a group in order to establish a right or entitlement to a resource or opportunity.

DISCUSSION: The term *class advocacy* refers to actions on behalf of a whole group or class of people. This is in contrast to *client advocacy* (see Item 14.27), in which the advocacy is on behalf of a specific individual. Because class advocacy seeks change in law and public policy at either the local, state, or national level, it is essentially a political process aimed at influencing the decisions of elected officials and high-level administrators. It entails building coalitions with other groups and organizations that share concerns about a social issue. The social worker typically participates as a representative of an organization, rather than as an independent practitioner.

Since the goal is to bring about a change, resistance, opposition, and conflict should be expected. Those with power can and will use their power to resist change, creating some risk for the advocates. When a person sets out to alter the status quo, there is a good chance that he or she will ruffle some feathers, lose some friends, create some enemies, or get labeled as a troublemaker. Thus, not everyone is comfortable with this type of advocacy. Further, each organization must examine the pros and cons of taking on an advocacy role and decide whether having its representatives perform this role fits with the purpose of the organization.

For those who become engaged in class advocacy, the following guidelines may increase the chances of success.

1. Realize that advocacy can make a difference. You can bring about needed changes in laws, policies, and programs. Bringing about change is difficult—but not impossible.

2. Remember that you cannot do it alone. Individual social workers will need to join with others. A group has more power than an individual. Also, your organization needs to join with other organizations that share your concerns. Several organizations, working together, have more power than a single organization working alone.

3. Working with other organizations will mean that your own organization will have to share some resources, make some compromises and perhaps do things differently than it prefers. In the long run, however, your organization will accomplish more as part of a coalition than it will by working alone.

4. Many improvements are needed in our human service systems. Since you cannot do everything that needs to be done, you must decide which concern has the highest priority. Choose your cause very carefully. If you or your organization take on several causes at one time, you may be spread too thin. It is better to make real gains in just one area than to make minimal gains or fail completely in several.

5. It is also important to choose a cause where success is possible. Be realistic! Do not waste your organization's time and energy on a lost cause. That will only result in frustration. As in other aspects of life, a successful experience generates hope and a feeling that other successes are possible. If the members of an organization can see even small successes, they will be more willing to invest themselves in future advocacy efforts and be more motivated to work on other needed changes in the system.

6. Anticipate the many problems that will arise and plan for their solution. Sunley (1983, 154–156) identifies a few of the common problems that advocates for change might experience.

- Advocates do not have sufficient time and proposed actions fall behind schedule.
- Advocates and supporters begin to have doubts and second thoughts about actions after they are underway.
- Advocates are thrown off course or demoralized by the delaying tactics used by opponents of change.
- Advocacy efforts founder because the purpose lacks clarity and the persons involved do not share common goals.
- Factional disputes and power struggles develop within the action system.
- Dissatisfied, undisciplined, or uncooperative individuals create personnel and morale problems among advocates.

7. Successful advocacy is built on a foundation of careful analysis and planning. It is important to define what you see as a problem and carefully study the problem—before you make a decision on what to do about it. Do not launch an effort to change something until you know exactly what has to be changed, why it has to be changed, and what will be involved in bringing about the change.

8. Before you take action, carefully assess what achieving your goal will require in the way of time, energy, money, and other resources. Do you have the resources? If not, it is best to scale down your goals or wait until later when you are better organized and more capable of reaching your goal.

9. Try to understand those who oppose you. There is always resistance to change. Analysis of the situation to be changed should include understanding why there is resistance. The advocate needs to know how opponents think and feel when asked to change. You need to be able to put yourself in your opponent's shoes (i.e., you must have empathy). People always have reasons for opposing change. You may not agree with their reasons, but you must understand them if you are to figure out a way to successfully overcome that resistance.

10. Successful advocacy requires self-discipline. It is important to think before you act. Class advocacy requires that you build coalitions and those coalitions are built on mutual trust and mutual self-interest. One of the most serious errors one can make in advocacy is to act impulsively. If that happens, the other organizations in the coalition may pull back or be reluctant to cooperate because they fear that your recklessness will cause damage to their organization or to the coalition. Also, if you act impulsively, those who oppose you can more easily discredit your organization.

11. Advocacy involves the use of power. You may not have as much power as you want, but do not overlook the power you do have. Essentially, *power* is the ability to make others behave the way you want them to behave. Think of power as a resource that can be used or "spent" for a particular purpose. There are different kinds of power. It is important to study your own organization and its membership in order to discover the type of power that you do possess.

Among the types of power social workers have is the power that comes from knowledge and expertise. For example, if you are advocating on behalf of children, you have detailed information about children and troubled families, and you know how the system works or does not work for the benefit of children and families. Information, if carefully assembled and presented, can have a powerful impact on legislators, agency administrators, and the public.

No doubt some members of your organization are highly respected in the community. They are held in high esteem by the public because of their past achievements. They have credibility that gives them a type of power. Individuals who are respected can have a significant influence on legislators and administrators. You need to encourage and help those respected individuals to become spokespersons for your organization.

Do not forget that personal commitment, time, and energy are also types of power. Much can be accomplished just by sticking with a task and seeing it through to the end. Organizational solidarity is also a type of power. If legislators and decision makers can see that members are solidly behind their organization, they will pay attention to what the organization's leaders have to say.

Within your organization are members who are natural leaders. Some may be charismatic and articulate. They can excite people and get them to work together on a cause. Charisma is a rare quality, but it is definitely a type of power. Identify those individuals in your organization and let them speak for your cause.

12. There are times when class advocacy must take the form of a lawsuit (Morales and Sheafor 1995). Many changes and reforms would never have happened without lawsuits and court decisions. For example, within the past 25 years, most of the reforms in the areas of mental health and mental retardation grew out of lawsuits. An organization committed to advocacy will, at times, need to encourage and support lawsuits that have potential for bringing about a needed change.

13. Most people in the United States depend on television and newspapers for information. If one wants the public to understand and support a cause, it is important to learn to work with the media (see Item 14.51). If there is someone associated with the organization who knows how to work in advertising and the use of media, make use of that person. If not, approach an advertising agency or perhaps a school of journalism and ask if it would be willing to help you get your message on TV or in the newspapers.

SELECTED BIBLIOGRAPHY

Austin, Michael J., and Jane Isaacs Lowe. *Controversial Issues in Communities and Organizations.* Boston: Allyn and Bacon, 1994.

Morales, Armando T., and Bradford W. Sheafor. *Social Work: A Profession of Many Faces,* 7th ed. Boston: Allyn and Bacon, 1995.

Rubin, Herbert, and Irene Rubin. *Community Organizing and Development.* Columbus, Ohio: Merrill, 1986.

Sunley, Robert. *Advocating Today: A Human Service Practitioner's Handbook.* New York: Family Service Association of America, 1983.

14.48 Teaching and Training

PURPOSE: To guide and assist others in the acquisition of information, knowledge, or skills.

DISCUSSION: Social workers do a lot of teaching. They frequently teach skills related to parenting, interpersonal communication, stress management, job seeking, independent living, and so on. Their teaching may be directed to clients, volunteers, colleagues, or concerned citizens. It may occur within the context of a one-to-one relationship, a workshop, or a formal classroom situation. In direct work with clients, the teaching activities usually resemble a tutorial or coaching relationship, but nevertheless is teaching. Several guidelines can help the social worker increase his or her effectiveness as a teacher.

1. The adage "It hasn't been taught until it has been learned" underscores the difference between teaching and learning. Teaching activities are planned and controlled by the teacher, but learning is not. Learning occurs within the learner and is tied to such factors as motivation, ability, and readiness. The teacher's job is to find a way of engaging and motivating the learner to examine and consider the materials to be taught.

2. That which we teach and learn falls into three broad categories: *knowledge, beliefs and values,* and *skills.* Of these three, knowledge is the easiest to teach because there is an agreed upon language to explain facts, concepts, and theories. This is not so when we focus on values and attitudes. In fact, values and attitudes cannot be taught directly, but they can be "caught" or learned from a teacher. If the teacher models or exhibits the desired beliefs, values, and attitudes, the learners may modify their own in order to imitate those of the teacher. Skills, too, are best learned through modeling and demonstration. They then can be performed and practiced in a real or simulated situation in order to master the behaviors or actions related to the skill.

3. It is said that the truly educated person is one who has learned how to learn. Unfortunately, no one is sure how to teach others to learn, because everyone seems to develop a unique approach to learning. What works for one person may not work for another. The uniqueness of how we learn relates to such factors as our sensory preferences (hearing, seeing, kinesthetic, etc.), our need for or resistance to structure and direction, our desire for either competition or cooperation, our tendency to

move from the specific (parts) to the general (whole) or vice versa, our tendency to either break apart or build concepts, our need to read and write in order to learn, our preferences for either solitary or group learning, and so forth. An important first step in teaching, then, is to plan for differences in how people learn. An effective teacher must be prepared to use several different methods when teaching a single topic. Also, we need to help the learners identify and better understand how they learn and seek out learning opportunities appropriate to their individual styles.

4. Identify and teach essential terminology and concepts. Language is the foundation of learning because we use language to communicate ideas and experiences. The acquisition of specialized vocabulary is a fundamental step in the acquisition of new learning. For example, before someone can learn to do the work of the social worker, he or she must first master the terminology and basic concepts related to the profession's values, roles, principles, and practice theories. The teacher, however, should carefully plan the introduction of new concepts in order to avoid overloading the learner with too much new material at one time.

5. Help people learn by helping them develop skills and techniques that facilitate learning. These include reading, writing, verbal communication, listening, time management, problem solving, goal setting, decision making, and so on.

6. When planning a class or training session, begin with an analysis of learner characteristics (e.g., developmental stage, formal education, prior work experience, life experience, etc.) and the identification of the knowledge, values, and skills they are expecting (and expected) to learn. Then select or design the methods that are most likely to engage the learners and push and pull them toward the learning objectives.

7. Review and consider using existing curricula and teaching materials, but realize that such materials nearly always need to be modified and adapted. Materials and methods that worked well with one group of learners may not work for others.

8. To the extent possible, use teaching techniques that actively engage both the learner's mind and body (e.g., role-plays, simulation exercises, debates, discussions). Reduce to a minimum the time spent in formal presentations. Lectures are among the least effective methods. As humans, we are thinking, feeling, and behaving beings. In order to teach, we must attend to and activate the learner's thinking, feelings, and behavior.

9. When teaching a skill, utilize the model known as "watch one, do one, teach one." First, have the learners observe someone performing the skill activity, then have them do it, and, finally, have them teach it to someone else. Another model is to understand the skill, use the skill, find new uses for the skill, and, finally, teach the skill to someone.

10. Place emphasis on helping the learner immediately use the information, knowledge, or skill being taught. In the human services there is only one reason for learning and that is to do something with whatever has been learned. Thus, encourage the learner to ask: Why am I interested in this topic? What can I do with it? How can I apply it? How will it help me answer some other question or solve a problem?

11. Critically evaluate your teaching. There are four levels on which we can assess our effectiveness as teachers.

- *Level 1.* We may simply ask the learners if they liked it. This is the most commonly used method of evaluating teaching. The problem is that one can enjoy a class or a workshop, but learn little or nothing. Moreover, learning is not always an enjoyable experience.
- *Level 2.* We can determine if the learners actually learned something new. Did they leave the session with knowledge or skills that they did not have when they began? To assess training at this second level, some type of pre-session and postsession testing is necessary.
- *Level 3.* Assuming that new learning occurred, we can then ask if the new knowledge and skills were used after the session. To assess training at this level, we need a follow-up system for monitoring the learner's behavior subsequent to the training session.
- *Level 4.* Finally, we can determine whether the learners' application of the new knowledge and skills had a positive impact on their lives or work. Unless what is learned has a real and a positive impact, the session was of little value no matter how enjoyable or how much was learned.

SELECTED BIBLIOGRAPHY

Bercher, Harvey J. *Staff Development in Human Service Organizations.* Englewood Cliffs, N.J.: Prentice Hall, 1988.

Orlich, Donald C. *Staff Development: Enhancing Human Potential.* Boston, Allyn and Bacon, 1989.

14.49 Preparing a Budget

PURPOSE: To prepare an estimate of income and expenditures for a human services agency or a special project.

DISCUSSION: A budget is an important planning tool that lists an agency's anticipated income and its intended use during a designated period, usually one or two years. Typically, a budget will be revised several times during the period it is in use. For example, the *preliminary budget* will be used to estimate expenses and serve as the basis for planning to secure funding to carry out the programs included in that preliminary budget. That budget will be revised once various commitments have been made by the funding sources. This *operating budget,* when approved by a legislative body (in the case of a public agency) or by a board of directors (in the case of a private agency), becomes the authorization for the agency's executive director to spend the amounts listed for each budget category. However, in the course of the budget period, there may be a shortfall in one or more income categories, unanticipated costs in expenditure categories, or emergent reasons to shift funds for one category to another. In these situations, the budget revisions would need official approval from the agency's governing body.

Given the relative fluidity of a budget, agencies typically have some flexibility to make some changes in programming or staffing during budget periods. However, it is best to anticipate substantial changes far enough in advance to include the necessary funds in the preliminary budget. Social workers wanting to propose changes that have budget implications should anticipate the budget development time schedule and plan their advocacy efforts to coincide with that schedule.

A budget must be the most accurate estimate possible. As part of the process of building a budget, many questions must be asked and answered. For example:

- What agency goals and objectives are to be addressed during the budget period?
- How do any proposed programmatic changes affect the agency's income and expenses?
- What types and how many employees are needed to carry out the agency's programs? What salaries and benefits and needed to attract and retain them? What liability insurance is needed to protect the employees and the agency? What training will be required for staff and volunteers—and what is the cost of that training?
- What type of programs are needed to reach and serve the agency's consumers? How might changes in program activities affect budget items such as numbers of staff with various competencies, training expenses, travel, supplies and equipment, consultation, and so on?
- What central office space and outreach locations are needed? What is required to keep the space clean, well maintained, and protected? What will be the cost of rent, utilities, insurance, security, and so forth?
- What is required to develop and maintain community support for the agency such as printing and publications, postage, public relations materials, membership development activities, audits, and the like?
- What total income will be needed to carry out the anticipated programs during the budget period? What are the sources of this income (e.g., agency fund-raising efforts, United Way, government appropriations, fees for service, grants, contracts, bequests, etc.) and how reliable is each as a base of support?

In a stable organization, the budget should be built on past experience with allowance for anticipated changes in income or expenditures or to accommodate new programming. In an era of declining support for human services, funding for new programs must come through curtailment of some programs or more efficient use of existing resources. Since most human services agencies are highly labor intensive, the personnel aspects of the budget become the most critical to consider if any substantial change is anticipated. In addition, the constant tug between efficiency (cost per unit of service) and effectiveness (ability to achieve service objectives) should be addressed as part of the budgeting process.

Three types of budgeting are commonly found in human service agencies: (1) line-item budgeting, (2) incremental budgeting, and (3) program or functional budgeting. Each yields different information about the cost of doing business.

Line-Item Budgeting

This type of budget is the most commonly used in social agencies. It requires that the various income and spending categories be identified and that the amount of money anticipated in each category be stated (see Figure 14.4). The accounting system of the agency is usually organized around these categories, making it possible to obtain a historical picture of the income and expenditures that will serve as the basis for projecting the future. Since a preliminary budget is a planning device, it must be prepared in advance of the year it will be in effect. In other words, next year's budget

FIGURE 14.4   Sample Line-Item Budget

Categories	Last Actual Year	Year-to-Date	Current Budget	Proposed Budget
Income				
Beginning Balance	6,375	10,648	6,000	32
Contracts for Service	17,358	7,156	15,000	18,000
Contributions	5,392	938	5,000	5,000
Grants	5,000	2,500	5,000	–0–
Gifts and Bequests	14,321	7,106	10,000	10,000
Investment Income	4,987	2,386	5,000	5,000
Membership Dues	2,510	1,050	2,500	2,500
Program Service Fees	48,746	24,657	50,000	55,000
Sales	–0–	–0–	–0–	–0–
United Way Allocation	20,000	10,000	20,000	29,000
Total Income	124,689	66,443	118,500	124,532
Expense				
Salaries	67,518	35,447	70,894	74,439
Employee Benefits	4,756	2,557	5,114	5,265
Payroll Taxes	2,171	1,180	2,360	2,385
Consultation Fees	10,000	4,120	10,000	11,000
Professional Development	2,500	1,195	2,500	2,500
Total Personnel	86,945	44,499	90,868	95,589
Supplies and Equipment	8,938	6,053	9,000	9,500
Telephone	3,063	1,600	3,200	3,200
Printing and Photocopying	984	407	600	600
Occupancy	12,000	6,300	12,600	13,200
Travel	570	287	600	600
Membership Dues	1,000	1,000	1,000	1,000
Miscellaneous	541	295	600	600
Total Operating Expenses	27,096	15,942	27,600	28,700
Total Expenses	114,041	60,411	118,468	124,289
Ending Balance	10,648	6,020	32	243

must be based on incomplete information about how well this year's budget estimated income and expenses. Thus, a preliminary line-item budget will reflect educated guesses about how each budget line will play out during the remainder of the current year and how it will change during the subsequent year.

The line-item budget must then be backed up by an audit report verifying the last year's actual income and expenditures and listing the amounts of any other assets, endowment, or building fund reserves that are excluded from the operating budget.

Incremental Budgeting

Based on estimates of increases or decreases in revenue, a series of budget projections might be built on the basis of the current line-item budget. That is, using a "what if?" approach, a budget might be developed to reflect the impact of 5 and 10 percent budget reductions, no change in revenue, or 5 and 10 percent revenue increases. An incremental budget is particularly helpful in reflecting the impact of inflation and identifying the service implications of either increases and decreases. Such a budget is useful in assessing the cost of adjusting an organization's current program to provide new services. The availability of computer spreadsheet programs (see Item 9.4) has simplified the process of developing incremental budgets and thus examining the impact of various alternatives.

Program or Functional Budgeting

A final type of budget used by social agencies is the program or functional budget. Again, this is based on a line-item budget and adds the feature of attributing portions of the total cost in each income and expense category to the various components or functions of agency operation. This approach makes it possible to estimate income and expenditures related to any function of the agency, thus providing a picture of the cost-effectiveness of that function. Attributing the income or expenses to particular program areas calls for careful estimates (e.g., the amount of executive director's time devoted to fundraising) and an accurate identification of how income is generated (e.g., fees received for a particular service).

Preparing a program budget involves using the income and expense items from the "Proposed Budget" column (see Figure 14.4) of the line-item budget and projecting a distribution of those items according to both the operational support services (i.e., management, fund-raising) and each of the various service programs (e.g., adoption, foster care, family counseling) of the agency.

SELECTED BIBLIOGRAPHY

Hildreth, W. Bartley, and Rodger P. Hildreth. "Budgeting and Fiscal Management." In *Handbook of Human Services Administration*, edited by Jack Rabin and Marcia B. Steinhouer. New York: Marcel Dekker, 1988.

Kettner, Peter M., Robert M. Moroney, and Lawrence L. Martin. *Designing and Managing Programs: An Effectiveness-Based Approach.* Newbury Park, Calif.: Sage, 1990.

Miller, Lynn E, ed. *Managing Human Service Organizations.* New York: Quorum Books, 1989.

Weiner, Myron E. *Human Services Management: Analysis and Applications*, 2nd ed. Belmont, Calif.: Wadsworth, 1990.

14.50 The 5 Ps of Marketing Human Services

PURPOSE: To interest the public in participating in or supporting the work of a human services organization.

DISCUSSION: Increasingly, human services agencies draw on the marketing technology of modern business to attract needed resources. Most social workers are not accustomed to thinking about their agency's services as a product to be advertised, displayed, and sold. Doing so, however, helps workers better understand what actions are necessary to attract funding, the clients who need their services, competent board members and volunteers, and paraprofessional staff members such as foster parents.

Horejsi (1989) suggests that five concepts—the 5 Ps—should be considered when developing a human services marketing strategy. He also suggests that it helps to understand the dynamics of the marketing process if social workers think about all the factors that influence their own decisions when they consider buying an automobile or some other major item.

Product

Successful salespeople are enthusiastic about their product and they can explain its advantages, as compared to the other products, that might attract the potential customer's interest. Thus, social agency personnel must truly believe in the worth of their product (service). They must be able to explain its worth and advantages in simple language and, if possible, back up their beliefs with data drawn from independent evaluations.

If social workers and other agency personnel really believe in their services, their conviction will be communicated in their statements and nonverbal behavior. If, for some reason, the agency's "product" is not "selling" well (e.g., not attracting support or clients), it is time to figure out why and modify or improve the service so it becomes more attractive.

Potential Buyer (or Consumer)

In order to attract supporters and clients to a service program, it may be necessary to conduct some type of market survey. What are the characteristics of those who buy this product? What are its most attractive features? Who has used the service in the past? If other services have stronger community support, why are they now more attractive than yours? The answers to such questions help an agency better understand its potential supporters and consumers and help target marketing efforts toward those groups most likely to respond.

For purposes of marketing, it is important to remember that there is no such thing as a general public. There are, however, subgroups of people who share common interests and values. It is important to determine which subgroups are most likely to be interested in a particular program. Demographic factors such as age, religion, ethnic background, income, and education may have a bearing on which subgroups can be attracted to which agency. An agency should not waste time trying to attract those unlikely to ever develop interest in supporting or using its services.

For human services agencies there are several important subgroups or special publics that a marketing strategy might address, depending on what aspect of the agency or program is being promoted.

- *Agency family.* This includes the board, members of various committees, and the staff.
- *Volunteers.* People who have volunteered their time to assist an agency in providing services have a special commitment to that agency and are especially interested in its activities.
- *Clients, former clients, and their families.* Those who have benefited from the agency's efforts can become valuable advocates for an agency. One negative evaluation from this group can offset the public relations benefits from several satisfied clients.
- *Supporters.* Many agencies have a group of members or other interested supporters who provide various forms of assistance such as financial contributions, assistance with fund-raising efforts, and speakers' bureau participants.
- *Community influencers.* Each community has a few people who help to shape public opinion (e.g., the media, people who speak out on issues) or make important decisions that affect human services (e.g., elected officials, directors of other agencies, United Way board members). They must be informed about the services of an agency.
- *Special-interest groups.* Associated groups that have a particular interest in your agency's work might include such professional bodies or organizations as NASW, the AMA, the local bar association, related human services agencies, or influential groups such as the League of Women Voters, NAACP, and so on.

Place

Once the attention of the target audience has been attracted, the agency needs a place or location where the services can be provided and an identity for the program established. In the human services field, this place of business is typically the social agency. Whether or not the targets of the marketing approach decide to contribute or use an agency's services will depend, in part, on their first impressions of the agency's building and offices, its personnel, and its program. First impressions are exceedingly powerful. Consumers will appreciate an appropriate atmosphere when entering the agency and expect respect, courtesy, and fairness in their treatment from clerical and professional staff.

Price

In the marketplace, price is measured in terms of dollars (i.e., how much a customer has to pay to get the wanted product). In the human services, price is more appropriately viewed as what an agency supporter or consumer must give up (i.e., pay) in order to support or utilize the services. If contributors or volunteers give their money and time, they are not able to give those dollars or hours to some other worthy cause. Thus, they want to know that their gifts are appreciated and will make a real difference in someone's life. Or perhaps they want to make sure their association with the agency will yield some personal benefit, such as interesting training, job-related experience, or a feeling of being useful.

It is important to be completely honest about price. For example, in an effort to recruit foster parents, a child welfare agency needs to be accurate in describing the "price" to be paid by the foster parent in terms of time, frustration, worry, and probably some out-of-pocket expenses. If one is not honest, the buyer will later feel cheated and become justifiably angry with the agency.

Promotion

Working with the media (see Item 14.51) is an effective way to reach a large number of people with a message about an agency. Stories in newspapers and on TV can make people aware of a particular agency and its needs, but they are not usually effective in bringing people to the decision that they will support it with their time or money. The same can be said for presentations and public appearances at service clubs, schools, public meetings, and so on; they help, but it takes something more to get a real commitment. When it comes to making that final decision of whether to support an agency, face-to-face interaction with agency personnel is of critical importance.

As in business, a satisfied customer is the best advertisement an agency can have; on the other hand, a dissatisfied customer can do a lot of damage to an agency's image and reputation. As a general rule, presentations by satisfied customers (e.g., long-time financial supporters, enthusiastic volunteers, clients pleased with agency services, etc.) are more persuasive than presentations by agency staff.

SELECTED BIBLIOGRAPHY

Andreason, Allan R. *Strategic Marketing for Nonprofit Organizations*, 4th ed. Englewood Cliffs, N.J.: Prentice Hall, 1990.

Fink, Justin. "Adapting and Adopting a Marketing Perspective for the Community Service Agency." In *Managing Human Service Organizations,* edited by Lynn E. Miller. New York: Quorum Books, 1989.

Horejsi, Charles R. "Foster Home Recruitment: A Marketing Perspective." Missoula: Department of Social Work, University of Montana, 1989. (Unpublished document).

Lauffer, Armand, and E. Allen Brawley. "Should Marketing Techniques Replace Traditional Planning and Coordinating Methods in the Design and Development of Programs?" In *Controversial Issues in Communities and Organizations,* edited by Michael J. Austin and Jane Isaacs Lowe. Boston: Allyn and Bacon, 1994, pp. 236–250.

Wolf, Thomas. *Managing a Nonprofit Organization.* New York: Simon and Schuster, 1990.

14.51   Dealing with the Media

PURPOSE: To inform the public and generate support for the services offered by an agency.

DISCUSSION: The public has a right to know about the social programs and agencies supported by taxes or voluntary contributions. All too often, the public hears only negative information about these services and the people who use them. Social workers have a responsibility to help the public fully understand the impact of human services on the quality of life for all persons. Social workers can make a valuable contribution to their agencies, clients, and community by developing the skills to work with the media in providing this information.

General Advice
Keep the following points in mind when working with the media.

- *Be proactive.* Rather that hoping the media will come to you for information or a story, reach out to them. Work at creating opportunities to describe your agency and program in a positive way. Remember that human-interest stories are especially attractive to reporters.
- *Have the authority to speak for the agency.* Make sure you are authorized to represent the agency and, if more than one person from the agency is authorized to deal with the media, make sure the efforts are coordinated. Also, be clear if at any time you are speaking for yourself rather than for the agency.
- *Establish personal relationships with the media.* If the reporters and photographers know and trust you and are aware that you are willing to help them, it can mean the difference between your agency or program just getting covered and getting good coverage. Keep the media informed of what is going on in your agency, be sure the information is accurate, and avoid professional jargon.
- *Be available.* Make it easy for the media to contact you by providing all reporters who cover your agency with your home and office telephone numbers and the name and numbers of someone else to call if you are not available.
- *Observe deadlines.* Know the deadlines of news shows and do not expect reporters to attend to your interests when they have deadlines to meet. If necessary, be willing to reschedule so they can give your story full attention.
- *Be fair.* When you release a story, make sure that all media organizations get your news release or a phone call as close to the same time as you can manage.
- *Be understanding.* If your story does not run, there may be good reasons. It could have been thrown out at the last minute for something of more urgent news value. It is all right to ask if there was something wrong with the story— something that could be corrected in future stories.
- *Make corrections when necessary.* Handle errors in stories carefully. Unless a serious error has been made, no comment is usually necessary. When a comment is in order, go to the reporter who made the error and handle the correction in private. Explain the error and indicate any damage that may have been caused. Control your emotions and focus only on the facts.
- *Say thanks.* Express your appreciation every time you submit material, whether it is used or not. At least once a year, thank your media professional's boss for the interest and investment in your program.

The Press Kit
A useful tool for establishing and maintaining relationships with either the print or electronic media is to prepare a press kit for distribution to editors and reporters. A press kit is simply a 9½'' × 12 '' two-pocket folder that contains information that in-

terprets the agency and suggests stories for the media. The folder should be colorful or in some way attract the attention of the reporter. A cover letter should be included that draws attention to the contents of the press kit.

Meltsner (no date, 4) suggests the following materials as the minimum for inclusion in a press kit.

- *Agency information.* This may be a brochure, annual report, or a brief description of the agency's goals, programs, and clientele.
- *Calling card.* A business card should contain the agency contact person's name, address, and telephone number. This should be displayed prominently, perhaps by stapling it to the pocket of the folder.
- *Campaign or public relations effort information.* If you have a particular goal for this public relations effort, such as raising funds for a specific program or recruiting volunteers to work with troubled children, explain this with a brochure about the project or a short information sheet.
- *At least one backgrounder.* A backgrounder is a sheet that familiarizes the reader with concepts, terms, and data that might be useful in preparing a story about the agency—for example: What is mental health? What kind of problems are addressed in family counseling? What is the legal definition of child abuse? What is a developmental disability?
- *A fact sheet or news release.* Depending on what you want the media to cover, you may include a fact sheet that contains basic information (who, what, where, when, why and how) that allows the reporter to create his or her own story. A news release is a one- to three-page story that can be printed as is or reduced or expanded into the reporter's own story. If possible, include a black-and-white photograph with a caption to help the reporter visualize the situation you are addressing.
- *A public service announcement.* Prepare a draft of a 30-second radio spot describing your project.
- *At least one reprint.* To suggest ideas for a story, include previously published articles about the agency or the project.

The Newspaper Release

When preparing a newspaper release, you will improve the chances of it being used if the format is familiar to the reporter and the information requires a minimum of editing. For example, a newspaper may want a news release typed double or triple spaced and with wide margins so it can be easily edited or transmitted electronically. Contact each newspaper for specific instructions regarding their preferences.

Write in a clear, simple, and logical style. Use short sentences and paragraphs. Remember that reporters are interested in the *who, what, where, when, and why* of a story. Begin with the most important information and place the less critical information and supplemental details at the end. Keep in mind that editors often shorten a story by cutting from the end. Remember, too, that editors like direct quotations and that by providing one or two glossy print photographs it is possible to add human interest to the story.

Be sure to clearly identify your agency's name, address, and phone number and provide the name of the person to be contacted for further information. The newspaper will need to know if the item is for "immediate release" or if it should be held for release on a specific date.

Radio and Television News

Information presented on a television or radio news broadcast can reach a large segment of the public. The human-interest flavor of stories originating from social agencies is especially amenable to the images of television. The social worker attempting to utilize these forms of media should know how to prepare materials for broadcast and be well prepared if being interviewed for radio or television.

If you are hoping for television coverage, schedule the event to be covered when a camera crew is likely to be most available—usually between 10:00 A.M. and 2:00 P.M. Avoid evenings and weekends.

If you expect to be interviewed or be a guest on a talk show, be clear about what you want to say and then rehearse. Have in mind some case examples, but be sure to disguise them in a way that will protect confidentiality. Radio and television news stories are almost always concise, making it necessary to limit your message to 30 to 60 seconds. Also, avoid using words or giving examples that would be offensive or misunderstood by the public.

If necessary, consider videotaping the event or story yourself. Television stations sometimes are willing to consider using a good-quality tape if it is brief and newsworthy.

SELECTED BIBLIOGRAPHY

Brawley, Edward A. "Mass Media." In *Encyclopedia of Social Work,* 19th ed., vol.2, edited by Richard L. Edwards. Washington, D.C.: NASW Press, 1995, pp. 1675–1682.

Fox, James Alan, and Jack Leaven. *How to Work with the Media.* Newbury Park, Calif.: Sage, 1993.

Jones, Clarence. *How to Speak TV, Print and Radio: A Self-Defense Manual When You're the News,* 3rd ed. Tampa, Fla.: Video Consultants, 1990.

Meltsner, Susan. "Public Relations Tools for Human Service Providers: The Press Kit." (Unpublished materials, not dated).

Smith, Jeanette. *The New Publicity Kit.* New York: John Wiley & Sons, 1995.

14.52   Fund-Raising for a Human Services Agency

PURPOSE: To secure funds from the community to support a special project or the ongoing work of a social agency.

DISCUSSION: If a private, not-for-profit human services agency is to survive and develop its programs, it must have a secure and expanding funding base. In the final analysis, that depends on the willingness of numerous individuals to contribute their money to the agency rather than to another cause.

A key to agency survival is what some prefer to call *fund development*. This refers to the identification and nurturance of contributors who genuinely believe in the value of the agency and can be counted on to make a significant contribution, year after year.

Many local health and human services agencies are affiliated with large federated campaigns such as the United Way or the American Cancer Society. A small, independent agency must compete with these experienced and sophisticated fund-raising agencies for the interest, goodwill, and money of potential contributors.

For some agencies, a major fund-raising campaign is an occasional event in which funds to start a new program or build a facility are solicited. Inexperienced persons are seldom prepared for the demands and complexity of such a campaign. It takes time, energy, and know-how to successfully raise funds. It is estimated that it will take a minimum of three months to plan and raise funds from individuals and local businesses (e.g., through canvassing and direct mail); three to six months to raise funds from local foundations, service clubs, and unions; and at least six to eight months to raise funds from a national foundation, United Way, or financial institution (Community Resource Center, no date). Also, that investment of time and energy usually means that other responsibilities in the agency must be set aside in order to free time for fund-raising. Thus, it is important to assess the need and the chances of success before embarking on a fund-raising effort.

Guidelines for Fund-Raising

Several principles can assist the social workers in a fund-raising effort.

- Realize that even under the best of circumstances, raising money for human service agencies is a difficult and time-consuming activity.
- Fund-raising for the ongoing work of a social agency should employ methods that can be repeated each year.
- Perquisite to success in fund-raising is a sound marketing program that keeps the public well informed about the agency and its services (see Items 14.50 and 14.51).
- It is critical to plan ahead. Allow plenty of time (i.e., 12 to 18 months), remembering that the most difficult time to raise funds is when you urgently need them.
- Look for money at the local level first. Local people are the ones most likely to have a vested interest in seeing the program succeed.
- Fund-raising is a very personal activity. In reality, people give money to other people, not to an organization or cause. Build networks and get to know key people in the organizations you plan to solicit and have those individuals help you gain access to and establish credibility with others in that organization.
- It costs money to raise money. Make sure that the cost of fund-raising is built into the agency's budget.
- Get volunteers and the agency board of directors involved. They will have credibility in the community and their involvement increases their ownership of the program.

- It is important to research the priorities of potential funding sources and match their priorities with yours.
- Fund-raising involves asking people for their money. If you do not ask, you will not get it. (Some suggestions on how to ask are given later.)
- Get expert advice if you are unsure of how to proceed in a fund-raising campaign. You can damage future efforts if you attempt to carry out a poorly developed plan.

Elements of a Fund-Raising Campaign

Hundreds of decisions and actions make up a successful fund-raising campaign. Here are some of the major steps to follow.

1. *Formulate a goal.* After a careful examination of agency needs, establish a realistic goal as to how much money is to be raised and set a realistic time frame for reaching that goal.

2. *Consult those with expertise.* Draw together those who have worked on previous campaigns and determine what has and has not worked. Consider hiring a professional fund-raiser if you own prior efforts have not been successful, if you are unsure how to proceed, or if you need to raise more than $100,000.

3. *Develop a plan.* Select the strategy and methods most likely to be successful. Draw on the agency's former experience and use an approach that has worked in the past. Be cautious about attempting an approach with which you have no experience. Construct a budget while recognizing that it costs money to raise money. Factor in the amount of staff time needed and the cost of postage, supplies, public information materials, and travel.

4. *Select a chairperson.* This person should be a respected and trusted individual with good name recognition in the community. Most importantly, the chairperson must be someone who has the energy and time required and is committed to achieving the campaign goal. Recruit the chairperson during the planning stage so he or she can shape the overall strategy. This individual must be capable of recruiting many other volunteers.

5. *Build an organizational structure.* A successful campaign requires an organizational structure that ensures rapid communication, coordination, and careful monitoring of campaign activities and volunteers. Because many of the contributions will come from those working on the campaign, the effort should embrace and involve a great many individuals, community groups, and organizations. Many campaigns use some type of pyramid structure made up of several team captains, each responsible for overseeing the work of several campaign workers. A campaign might also have several divisions or special units that seek contributions from certain segments of the community (e.g., labor unions, small businesses).

6. *Recruit and train the campaign workers.* Workers must be asked to help—people seldom volunteer for fund-raising. The campaign chair, board members, and friends of the agency must actively recruit as volunteers persons who have the contacts and influence necessary to secure contributions. Some of the individuals willing to help may not be comfortable asking for money. They can help with other important tasks such as preparing informational packets, office work, and book-keeping.

7. *Prepare informational material.* Simply written brochures should explain the agency's program, what money is needed, and how it will be spent. This information may also need to be presented in the form of newspaper, television, and radio ads. Agency staff who best know the various programs the agency offers should play a key role in identifying appropriate content. Other materials—such as logos, letterhead, banners, slide shows, bumper stickers, press releases, speeches, and so on—are also needed. It is important that public relations experts provide guidance on the preparation of these items. Pursue contributions for these materials from wealthy individuals or very large corporations.

8. *Maintain proper records.* The campaign must maintain a complete and accurate record of contributions and expenses. Any hint of dishonesty, fraud, or incomplete bookkeeping will seriously damage the agency's ability to raise funds in the future.

9. *Provide recognition.* All those who contributed and all those who worked on the campaign should receive recognition and thanks. This creates a sense of pride and goodwill and increases the chances that these people and groups will assist in future campaigns.

10. *Evaluate the campaign.* After the campaign is complete, the agency board, campaign chairperson, and other key leaders should carefully evaluate what worked, what did not work, and how future campaigns could be improved. This evaluation should determine how much it cost (money, staff time, etc.) to raise the funds. If the campaign was not successful or if it was burdensome for the agency, outside consultation may be needed. Suggestions for persons who might serve as consultants might be obtained from religious, educational, or other human service agencies in your community. A national source is the American Association of Fund-Raising Counsel, Inc., 500 Fifth Avenue, New York, NY 10036.

Asking for Money

Many of us are hesitant to ask others for money, but that is what fund-raising is all about. Following are several suggestions to help reduce this problem.

- Those who ask others for money must have already given their fair share. Those doing the asking must be able to say, "I have given $500; I am asking that you give at least $250."
- It is critically important that the right person ask another for money and that the request be made in the right way, for the right reason, and at the right time. This is a further reminder that people do not give money to agencies or even causes; people give primarily because a specific person (e.g., someone they know and trust) has asked them to give.
- Small amounts of money can be raised from an individual by mail and telephone campaigns. Big money is raised through face-to-face contact with the donor.

- Ask for a specific amount of money and be sure to ask for enough (e.g., "We need $1,000 to send five children to camp").
- Assess the person's capability of giving before you ask. In other words, do some background research and determine what an individual or company is capable of giving. Ask for that amount.
- Be persistent. Keep asking until you get what you want or receive a firm "no."
- If an individual cannot make a cash donation, ask if an in-kind donation might be possible (e.g., time, used equipment, expertise).

SELECTED BIBLIOGRAPHY

Community Resource Center. "Some Principles of Philanthropy." Denver: Community Resource Center, not dated. (Unpublished materials).

Edles, L. Peter. *Fundraising.* New York: McGraw-Hill, 1993.

Lauffer, Armand. *Getting the Resources You Need.* Beverly Hills, Calif.: Sage, 1982.

Lord, James Gregory. *The Raising of Money.* Cleveland: Third Sector Press, 1987.

14.53   Developing Grant Applications

PURPOSE: To secure funding from a governmental agency or private foundation.

DISCUSSION: The resources available to a social agency are usually fully committed for operating existing programs. Any incremental increases in funds that might be obtained each year are often consumed by normal salary increases and inflation. The opportunity to demonstrate or test program innovations or conduct research on some aspect of the agency's program frequently cannot be done without the infusion of grant funds. A social worker who is knowledgeable about locating sources of grant funds and skilled at preparing applications for such funds is a valuable asset to his or her agency.

Before a social worker (or team of workers) can begin the grant-writing process, three prerequisites must be met. First, the idea or program innovation to be demonstrated or studied must be clearly identified and carefully thought out. Second, in addition to the persons developing the program or project, the agency's administrators and governing body must be committed to the idea. Finally, an assessment of the competence and capacity of both the individuals and the agency to carry out the activity must indicate that this work can be successfully completed. The worker should be prepared to invest considerable up-front time and effort into preparing a grant application, which frequently must be done in addition to ongoing work assignments. Yet, it is often the only way to improve services.

Sources of Grant Funding

A variety of funding sources might be considered. Sometimes a local or national business will underwrite a project that is of interest to them. A computer company, for example, might donate equipment to demonstrate the potential effectiveness of a computerized interagency referral network.

Also, a group of persons interested in a project might undertake a fund-raising effort (see Item 14.52) to help support this activity. However, the primary sources for a project are grants from government agencies or private foundations.

Government Grants.   The largest amount of money is available through agencies of the federal government, although states may also allocate such funds. Most government grants relate to areas that the sponsoring agency has defined in relation to its purpose and priorities. The public is notified of available funding through a *Request for Proposals* (RFP). Grant applications are reviewed by a panel of experts and awarded on a competitive basis. Some discretionary funds may also be available to staff at government agencies to allow for innovative program ideas that are not currently among the agency's established priorities. It is helpful to discuss your ideas with persons in the regional and national offices of the government agencies who administer the funds in your area of interest (e.g., aging, child welfare, AIDS) before investing much time and energy in developing a proposal. These staff members can help you assess the fit between your proposal and the agency's interest and provide such facts as the typical size of grants the odds of success.

Two published sources of information are particularly useful regarding grant possibilities from the federal government. The *Catalog of Federal Domestic Assistance* is an essential sourcebook published each year with a supplement that updates after six months. It contains a comprehensive listing and description of federal programs. Programs are cross-referenced by function (e.g., housing, health), by subject (e.g., drug abuse, economic development), and by the federal agency in which the program is administered. The description of each program includes information such as uses and restrictions on the funds, eligibility requirements, and the application and award process. A second source is the *Federal Register.* It is published every government working day and contains notices, rules and regulations, guidelines, and proposed rules and regulations for every federal grant-giving agency. Both the *Catalog of Federal Domestic Assistance* and the *Federal Register* are usually available through public libraries, university libraries, or the research and grant administration office of most universities. Copies can be obtained from the Superintendent of Documents, Government Printing Office, Washington, D.C. 20402 or on the Internet.

Private Foundations.   Another potential source of support for innovative program ideas is the private foundation. Small agencies and service demonstration projects are more likely to obtain support from these private sources than from government agencies. Most foundations develop specialized areas of interest, and some make resources available only for programs located in a specific geographic region. Perhaps the most helpful sources are directories developed by the Foundation Center that annually publishes *The Foundation Directory* (Feczko). Part 1 of that directory includes those foundations that give away more than $200,000 per year and Part 2 contains those that give smaller amounts. The Foundation Center also periodically publishes a series of specialized directories of grant sources that are focused on areas such as children, youth, and families; aging; the economically disadvantaged; health; and women and girls. Another directory, *The Directory of Corporate and Foundation Givers* (Jankowski 1993), provides background information about potential funding sources in the private sector. Once again, many local libraries and universities will have copies of these publications.

Computer Searches. Several databases are also available to aid in searching for funding sources—both governmental agencies and foundations. Searches by topic (key words), geographic region, funding agency, and academic discipline make it possible to narrow a vast amount of information to a small number of organizations or RFPs that are appropriate for the project. The Sponsored Programs Information Network (SPIN), for example, is an extensive on-line database of potential sources available in many research universities.

Guidelines for Developing a Proposal

The planning and preparation of a proposal is a labor-intensive process. Make sure you have the necessary time and motivation. A hastily written proposal, or the so-called all-purpose proposal, has little chance of success. If it is worth doing at all, it is worth doing well. Several guidelines are of critical importance.

1. *Do your homework.* Make a thorough study of the potential funding source (foundation or government agency) before deciding to submit a proposal. Pay special attention to official funding priorities, history of prior awards, eligibility, geographical limitation, type and size of grants available, funding cycle, process for selection, and so on. Secure the name, address, and phone number for the proper contact person.

2. *Make informal inquiries.* Save time for yourself and for the funding agency by informally inquiring about its possible interest in your ideas. However, assume that the recipient of your inquiry is busy, impatient, skeptical, not especially interested in your problems, and faced with many more requests than he or she can even read thoroughly, let alone fund. Be very businesslike in your approach. Be prepared to describe your proposal clearly and concisely in one or two pages or in five minutes on the phone. If you think you will be making an application, obtain an application packet and all relevant instructions.

3. *Write the proposal.* Study the instructions and follow them to the letter. Be prepared to answer each and every question. You should anticipate answering the following questions.

- What do you want to do, how much will it cost, and how much time will it take?
- How does the proposed project relate to the funding agency's area of interest and priorities?
- Are there other projects like the one you are proposing? How is yours similar or different?
- How do you plan to carry out the project? Does the proposed staff have the necessary training and experience? Why should you conduct this project, rather than someone else?
- Who stands to benefit from the proposed project? What impact will it have on your agency, clients, discipline, community, state, or nation? How will you measure, evaluate, and report the impact?

The written proposal must be very clear and well organized. Budgets must usually be prepared according to a specified outline. Often the proposal cannot exceed a certain number of pages. Proposals submitted after the closing date are not accepted.

4. *Be a good salesperson for your project.* Your written proposal and/or oral presentations should reflect knowledge, enthusiasm, and commitment. If those selecting proposals to be funded become convinced that the people associated with a particular proposal are especially capable and responsible, they may work extra hard on finding a way to fund the proposal.

5. *Be accountable.* If you receive the grant requested, be prepared to carry out the project according to your written plan and within the proposed budget. The acceptance of a grant carries with it the responsibility for proper money management, submitting regular progress reports, reporting project results, and giving appropriate credit to the funding source. Stewardship is very important.

Proposal Contents.   A formal grant proposal should carefully follow the outline required by the funding source. In general, the following components are expected.

1. *Cover page.* Include the project title, principal investigators, name of agency, dates for project activity, total budget request, and signatures of authorized agency personnel approving application.

2. *Abstract.* Prepare a short statement of the objectives and procedures to be used, methods of evaluation, and plan for disseminating results.

3. *Statement of problem and objectives.* Indicate the rationale for this project and prepare a clear statement of objectives in measurable terms.

4. *Methodology, procedures, and activities to be followed.* Describe the design and approach of the project, who will be served, the administrative structure for the project, and lay out a clear plan of action with phases and dates for activity detailed.

5. *Evaluation methods.* Describe how the results or outcomes of the activity will be assessed.

6. *Dissemination of results.* Indicate how the results of the project will be disseminated so that others can benefit from the knowledge gained from this activity.

7. *Personnel and facilities.* Describe the staff required to carry out the project, include resumés of key personnel who will be assigned to this activity, and indicate how new staff will be selected. Also, describe any special equipment required, and indicate how the agency will make space available to accommodate project activities.

8. *Budget.* Provide a detailed budget of the anticipated costs of the project. Indicate what will be required from the funding source and what will be contributed by the agency or other sources. Many funding sources require that matching funds from local sources be identified as a requirement for funding. In some instances, a cash match is required, but in others, in-kind contributions (e.g., staff time or office space) are acceptable. A budget will usually include personnel costs (including fringe benefits), outside consultants or evaluators for the project, consumable materials (supplies, printing, postage), equipment, travel, and indirect costs. The latter relates to the real costs to an agency such as the space, heat, light, and so on consumed by the project staff. Some federal agencies limit the indirect cost to 8 percent of the project expenses.

Reasons for Rejection. Finally, keep in mind the reasons that grant proposals are unsuccessful. Reviewers most commonly mark down proposals for the following reasons.

   1. The proposal is either too trivial or beyond the ability and experience of the investigator or agency.

   2. The need for the proposed project is not properly documented and/or the objectives are not clearly stated and relevant to the need.

   3. The reviewer is not convinced that the proposed plan would achieve the desired results due to the competence of the staff, quality of the plan, or the support of the requesting agency.

   4. There is not adequate commitment by the agency and/or community to continuing the service if the project proves successful and this grant is subsequently discontinued.

   5. The proposal is not realistic in estimates of the funds, personnel, or equipment required to successfully carry out the project.

   6. The evaluation procedure is inappropriate or unclear.

   7. The proposal is poorly written.

   8. The budget is not adequately developed, the required matching money is not evident, or the request is beyond the resources of the funding agency.

   9. The proposal fails to follow the guidelines or meet the deadline for submitting a proposal.

SELECTED BIBLIOGRAPHY

Catalog of Domestic Assistance. Washington, D.C.: U.S. Government Printing Office, most recent edition.

Feczko, Margaret Mary, ed. *The Foundation Directory.* New York: The Foundation Center, most recent edition.

Federal Register. Washington, D.C.: U.S. Government Printing Office, published daily.

Hall, Mary. *Getting Funded: A Complete Guide to Proposal Writing,* 3rd ed. Portland, Ore.: Portland State University, 1988.

Jankowski, Katherine E. *The Directory of Corporate and Foundation Givers: 1993.* Washington, D.C.: The Taft Group, 1993.

Locke, Lawrence F., Waneen Wyrick Spirduso, and Stephen J. Silverman. *Proposals that Work,* 3rd ed. Newbury Park, Calif.: Sage, 1993.

Ries, Joanne B., and Carl G. Leukefeld. *Applying for Research Funding: Getting Started and Getting Funded.* Newbury Park, Calif.: Sage, 1994.

14.54   Legislative Advocacy

PURPOSE: To create public policy by working proactively to introduce and support the passage of social legislation.

DISCUSSION: The social worker most often reacts to social policy proposals and seeks to influence the actions of policy makers. However, on occasion, the social worker should initiate efforts to have social legislation, written, considered and approved by legislative bodies. This involves identifying the factors that should be included in the legislation, writing or working with the appropriate legislative officer to draft a bill, seeking sponsors, giving testimony, and other activities required to get the proposal heard by the appropriate legislative body.

At one time or another, most social workers become involved in a proactive effort to initiate and pass a specific piece of legislation. Dear and Patti (1981, 289) have formulated seven principles or tactical guidelines for such an effort at the state level of government; these guidelines can be "used by part-time, single-issue advocates who make an occasional foray into the legislative arena to promote a bill of immediate interest to their agency or a client constituency."

1. Introduce the bill early in the session or ideally, before the session has begun.
2. It is advisable to have more than one legislator sponsor a bill.
3. The advocate of social legislation should seek to obtain the sponsorship of the majority party. . . . It is even more beneficial to obtain meaningful bi-partisan sponsorship with the primary sponsor a member of the . . . majority.
4. Whenever possible, the advocate should obtain the support of the Governor and the relevant state agencies.
5. The advocate should seek influential legislators as sponsors of proposed legislation, provided that they are willing to exercise their influence in promoting the bill.
6. The advocate should press for open committee hearings on the bill and, when such hearings are held, attempt to arrange for testimony in behalf of the bill by expert witnesses.
7. The advocate should use the amendatory process as a strategy for promoting a favorable outcome for the bill. (pp. 290–294)

SELECTED BIBLIOGRAPHY

Dear, Ronald, and Rino Patti. "Legislative Advocacy: Seven Specific Tactics." *Social Work* 26 (July 1981): 289–296.

Mahaffey, Maryann, and John Hanks, eds. *Practical Politics: Social Work and Political Responsibility.* Silver Spring, Md.: NASW Press, 1982.

Moore, Elliott Davis. "Influencing Legislation for the Human Services." In *Skills for Effective Human Services Management,* edited by Richard L. Edwards and John A. Yankey. Silver Spring, Md.: NASW Press, 1991.

Richan, Willard. *Lobbying for Social Change.* New York: Haworth, 1991.

Walls, David. *The Activist's Almanac: The Concerned Citizen's Guide to Leading Advocacy Organizations in America.* New York: Simon and Schuster, 1993.

14.55   Influencing Decision Makers

PURPOSE: To influence the actions of legislators and other community decision makers regarding human services issues.

DISCUSSION: Decisions that are made at the local, state, and national levels by elected representatives and other public officials have substantial impact on the quality of people's lives and, more specifically, on the human services. Because social work professionals are in a unique position to observe how public social policy helps or hinders the most vulnerable members of society, that perspective needs to be communicated to and considered by public officials. Armed with a careful analysis of the issue and the people making the decision (see Items 12.30 and 12.31), the social worker is prepared to influence the outcome of the decision-making process.

Persuasive Communication

Legislators and other decision makers do not usually seek out social workers to hear their opinions on legislation. Therefore, the social worker must be assertive and especially planful and tactful in the effort to persuade decision makers. To do that, the social worker should keep the following principles in mind.

- An individual is most likely to be persuaded by someone he or she perceives as having intelligence, self-confidence, competence, trustworthiness, and high status.
- An individual is most likely to be persuaded by someone he or she likes and perceives as being similar to himself or herself (e.g., a person who is authoritarian and dogmatic is most likely to be persuaded by someone with similar characteristics).
- An individual is most likely to be persuaded by someone he or she perceives as being powerful, whether that power is real of imagined.
- An individual is most likely to be persuaded by someone who can provide rewards or punishment, with whom future interaction is anticipated, and from whom social acceptance is desired.
- An individual who is confused, is uncertain, is insecure, needs approval, and has a strong desire for affiliation with others is more easily persuaded than a person not displaying these characteristics.

Social workers do not usually have the power or status to directly influence decision makers. Consequently, they must often work through others who are in a better position to be heard by legislators. However, their skills in assessing a decision maker's values and the arguments to which he or she responds can be a valuable contribution to the process, even if someone else will be representing the position supported by the social worker. At other times, however, it is possible for the social worker to cultivate personal relationships with decision makers and become quite effective in influencing decisions. The viewpoint of the social worker might be communicated through personal contact, in writing, or both.

Visiting with a Policymaker

Many legislators and other key decision makers spend their time in a somewhat restricted environment; they speak primarily with staff members, lobbyists, and colleagues. Hence, they often welcome the opportunity to hear the positions of members of their constituency. This communication might occur by attending a legislator's "open forum" or "town meeting" or by talking with the decision maker individually at city hall, the courthouse, or the state capitol—or by a visit when the legislative body is not in session.

The following guidelines can help to make visits with decision makers effective.

- *Use time efficiently.* The decision maker's time is valuable. If you are to get that person's full attention and have a favorable climate for communicating your information, you must be efficient. When planning an individual meeting, schedule an appointment in advance and ask that a specific amount of time be reserved for the meeting. Be on time, even though you may have to wait for the legislator to complete other responsibilities before meeting with you. Also, get to the point quickly. Have your presentation planned so that you can pack a lot of information into a short time period. In both "town meetings" and individual meetings, an indirect approach to the topic may prohibit you from getting to the substantive issues.
- *Be positive.* Begin on a friendly note. Find a reason to praise the decision maker for some action taken in relation to prior contacts (if appropriate) and thank him or her for being willing to take time to hear your position on this matter.
- *Express your conviction.* Let the legislator know that, as a social worker, you are in a unique position to recognize the implications of this decision. While it would be counterproductive to be abrasive or overbearing, leave no doubt in the legislator's mind that you believe in what you are proposing. Back up your view with facts and examples. If the information is at all detailed, prepare a handout that can be distributed to the decision maker and others who may be present.
- *Be specific.* Be very sure that the person knows what you want him or her to do. Are you simply offering information? Do you want him or her to propose an amendment to a piece of legislation? Do you want him or her to vote in a particular way?
- *Follow up in writing.* Send or leave a statement that reflects your position and provides the facts that you presented. The purpose of this document is to supply material that will be placed in the legislator's file on the topic and to remind him or her of your position when it is time to take action. Be sure that your name, address, and telephone number are on the materials so you can be contacted to clarify points or provide information on related matters.

Writing a Policymaker

Although face-to-face contact is probably the most effective way to influence a legislator or other decision maker, many times that is not possible because of constraints of time, distance, resources, or the availability of the decision maker. Letters, telegrams, fax messages, e-mail, and telephone calls, when properly timed, can also be effective in influencing decisions. The addresses and telephone numbers of public officials will usually be listed periodically in newspapers or available at the local library. Locating other officials may require more research.

The following guidelines should be observed when writing to a decision maker.

- *Be accurate.* Be sure that you use the correct spelling of the person's name, the proper title, and the accurate address. Be sure that the decision maker has correct information about you in case he or she wants to respond to your communication.
- *Be brief and to the point.* Limit your communication to one page. Focus only on one issue or piece of legislation in each communication. If you are interested in several matters, send separate correspondence so each can be filed with materials about those matters.
- *Clearly identify the issue or bill that concerns you.* Provide identifying details (e.g., the bill's number, name, dates) so there can be no misunderstanding of what you are writing about.
- *Write simply and clearly.* Remember that those who will read your material are very busy and may receive many pieces of correspondence each day. Make it easy for them to understand the points you wish to make. Clear and direct communication tells the reader you know what you are talking about.
- *Begin in a positive manner.* Address the legislator in a respectful manner and use titles appropriate to the office. If possible, praise or compliment the legislator for some previous action or statement and relate the preferred action on this matter to other positions he or she has supported.
- *Provide facts and figures that support your position.* Explain the impact of the decision and how many people will be affected. Short case examples are often effective in helping the reader understand how the issue affects individuals. If possible, describe how the action you support will save tax money in the future.
- *Clearly identify the action you desire.* Make sure the reader knows what you want to happen (e.g., vote for HR 254, oppose the filibuster of SB 1543).
- *Pay attention to timing.* Be sure to time communicating your opinion to just precede the debate on the topic. Typically, a legislator will make up his or her mind early in the hearing process and long before time for a final vote.
- *Follow up the action.* After the decision or vote is completed, write again thanking the legislator for considering your viewpoint if he or she took the action you requested. If not, express regret about that action. Such follow-up reminds the person that you are truly concerned about the issue and will continue to observe his or her actions on this matter.

SELECTED BIBLIOGRAPHY

Gaby, Patricia V., and Daniel M. Gaby. *Nonprofit Organizations Handbook: A Guide to Fundraising, Grants, Lobbying, Membership Building, Publicity, and Public Relations.* Englewood Cliffs, N.J.: Prentice-Hall, 1979.

House, Peter W., and Roger D. Shull. *Rush to Policy: Using Analytic Techniques in Public Sector Decision Making.* New Brunswick, N.J.: Transaction Books, 1988.

Moore, Elliott. "Influencing Legislation for the Human Services." In *Skills for Effective Human Services Management,* edited by Richard L. Edwards and John A. Yankey. Silver Spring, Md.: NASW, 1991, pp. 76–89.

Richan, Willard. *Lobbying for Social Change.* New York: Haworth, 1991.

Smith, Virginia W. "How Interest Groups Influence Legislators." *Social Work* 24 (May 1979): 234–239.

15 Evaluation and Termination

INTRODUCTION

The helping process ends with a final evaluation of the intervention effort and the careful termination of the professional relationship. This chapter focuses on those ending activities.

Broadly speaking, the evaluation process assesses whether the intervention was effective and efficient. *Effectiveness* refers to whether the objectives were reached; *efficiency* refers to the ratio between the resources applied and the outcome. Ideally, an intervention is both effective and efficient. However, an intervention may be effective but not efficient, as in a situation where much time and effort and many resources are necessary to achieve a desired goal. Needless to say, an intervention that does not achieve its objectives is neither effective nor efficient.

Social workers and social agencies must be concerned with both practice and program evaluation. *Practice evaluation* is concerned with assessing the worker's interventive efforts. Have they brought about the changes that were anticipated to the individuals, families, groups, organizations, or communities they serve? Practice evaluation can be either formative or summative. *Formative evaluation* relates to the assessment that takes place during the course of the helping process. It is intended to assist the worker in tracking progress and making changes in the intervention plan, if necessary. In this sense, it is the monitoring of practice (addressed in Chapter 14). However, when monitoring continues to the end of the process, it becomes a form of *summative evaluation* in which one can assess the final outcome and the factors that contributed to its relative success or failure.

The second form of evaluation used by social workers is *program evaluation,* which attempts to evaluate the effectiveness and efficiency of a program serving a large number of clients or perhaps even a whole community. Program evaluation, too, can be both formative and summative. It is formative when it is used as the basis for examining a program and changing aspects of its functioning to better serve the agency's clients or community. It is summative when, for example, it is used to report the results of a demonstration effort to a board of directors or a funding source.

The social worker should always begin an intervention with a clear description of the goals and objectives. Without a statement of its objectives, it is impossible to decide later whether an intervention was successful. Evaluation of a practice or a program requires the selection or the design of an instrument or measurement procedure that can detect whether change has occurred and the amount of that change. Some procedures may also help to identify the factors or variables in a situation that contributed to the change. When deciding what procedures to use, the social worker should consider are the following:

- *Validity.* Does the procedure actually measure what it is assumed or believed to measure?
- *Reliability.* Does the procedure yield similar results when the measurement is repeated under similar circumstances?
- *Ease of application.* Is the procedure sufficiently brief, easy to use, and understandable to the nonspecialist?
- *Useful.* Does the procedure yield information that is relevant to social work practice and likely to be used by workers and agencies?
- *Sensitive.* Is the measurement procedure able to detect relatively small levels of change and degrees of difference?
- *Nonreactive.* Can the procedure detect differences without modifying or influencing the phenomena being measured?

Full reporting of the factors that allow one to answer all of these questions is not usually attached to descriptions of existing measurement tools. However, it is important for the social worker to seek that information and, if it is not available, to recognize those possible limitations to the evaluation.

Related to evaluation is ***termination.*** A key element of effective practice is the ability to complete the helping process with a smooth and satisfying termination at the end of the change activity. All social work practice depends on a productive helping relationship (see Chapter 3) and the termination of that relationship must occur at the appropriate time and with a positive outcome. The social worker who is sensitive to issues surrounding termination helps the client leave the relationship with positive feelings and improved ability to sustain any gains made during the period of service.

S E C T I O N   A
TECHNIQUES AND GUIDELINES FOR DIRECT PRACTICE

Perhaps the most commonly used method of practice evaluation in the provision of direct services is the single-subject (or single-system) design. It should be part of the repertoire of every social worker. This tool is applicable when it is possible to establish a baseline of client functioning before the intervention begins and when intervention focuses on a discrete behavior or a planned change that is fairly easy to measure in terms of frequency, intensity, or duration. In some cases, other tools such as individualized rating scales or the repeated use of rapid assessment instruments are used to measure change over time.

Many social work interventions (e.g., referral, brokering, coordinating services, advocacy) do not lend themselves to the type of measurement and baselining required by the single-subject design. For those, other methods such as of goal attainment scaling, an outcome checklist, and task achievement scaling can be used to evaluate the effectiveness of direct practice.

15.1   Single-Subject Designs (SSD)

PURPOSE: To evaluate the impact of an intervention by using a baseline and subsequent measurements of change.

DISCUSSION: The case study or the study of an intervention with a single individual, a single group, or just one community for the purpose of advancing social work knowledge and evaluating practice is as old as social work itself. However, beginning in the mid 1970s, this method attracted additional attention when new methodologies for the study of a single case were developed and when increasing pressure was placed on human services agencies to demonstrate their effectiveness.

Bloom, Fischer, and Orme (1995) identify four purposes for using the single-subject design in practice evaluation.

1. To assess the case situation and to monitor changes in people and events over time
2. To evaluate whether positive or negative changes have occurred in targeted events
3. To evaluate whether the practitioner's interventions were causally linked with these changes . . .
4. To enable practitioners to compare effectiveness among interventions (p. 289)

Also known as single *N* or *N* = 1 research, single case-study design, time series research, single organism research, and single system research, single-subject designs are the most universally used evaluation tools in social work practice. There are more than a dozen variations of this design, but only the most basic elements of single-subject research will be addressed here.

The phrase *single-subject design* denotes a focus on a single practice situation—usually a single individual but possibly a family, small group, organization, or community. Also, the term *single-subject design* distinguishes this approach from the more traditional multiple-subject or experimental/group design. In the single-subject design, the client becomes his or her own control group. An individualized baseline—one relevant and meaningful in terms of the client's unique problem, situation, and goals—is used as the benchmark from which change is measured over the course of the intervention. The establishment of one or more baseline measures is essential, regardless of what version of the single-subject design is used.

The term *target behavior* refers to the behavior that the intervention intends to change. When selecting the target behavior, Polster and Lynch (1985) suggest that since it may not always be possible to measure all aspects of the desired change, the target behaviors selected must be representative of the changes which must occur to indicate successful accomplishment of the intervention goals. The target behavior must also be one which the worker, other cooperative persons (collaterals) in the environment, or the individual (subject) have opportunities to measure. Behaviors which are covert and leave no reliable evidence of having occurred, or which occur in places or at times when no one is available to record them, are not suitable as target behaviors. (p. 384)

A *baseline* is usually established by observing the frequency, intensity, or duration of the target behavior over a period of days or weeks. When time does not permit observation prior to intervention, it may be possible to retrospectively establish a baseline with information gathered from interviews with the client focusing on previous patterns of behavior; from interviews with the client's family or significant others; or from agency records, police reports, school reports, and the like.

The term *multiple baseline* refers to the use of more than one baseline. For example, in work with a child having trouble in school, one baseline might focus on frequency of school attendance, a second on grades received on weekly assignments, and a third on a teacher's weekly rating of the student's level of cooperation in the classroom. Unless the target problem is highly specific, multiple baselines are usually necessary in order to capture the impact of an intervention. In some cases, the client's score on a rating scale such as those in the WALMYR Assessment Scales (see Item 12.18) can be used as a baseline; changes in the client's score on repeated administrations suggest the impact of intervention.

The various versions of the single-subject design are identified by a set of initials. The letter *A* refers to the period in which baseline data are collected. The letter *B* refers to the intervention period. Thus, an *AB* single-subject design refers to the establishment of a baseline followed by intervention. The measured change from the baseline is attributed to the impact of intervention.

The *ABA* version removes the intervention (*B*) after a period of time and takes a second baseline measurement. If there is a return to the original (baseline) level of functioning, it is assumed that the change was caused by the intervention and not other factors in the client's life.

The *ABAB* design goes one step further, adding a fourth stage to the *ABA* by restarting the intervention. If there is again a change from the second baseline, the worker can be quite sure that the intervention is responsible for the change.

The *BAB* variation begins immediately with an intervention, eventually withdraws the intervention in order to establish a baseline, and then restarts the intervention. This particular design is used when it is not feasible to establish a baseline before beginning an intervention—for example, in an abusive situation.

Another useful version of the single-subject design is termed the multiple-element design or the *ABCD* design, which is used to evaluate the impact of a series of different interventions, one following the other. For example, after the establishment of the baseline (*A*), the first intervention (*B*) is tried for several weeks; then a second intervention (*C*) is implemented and subsequently, a third intervention (*D*). This design makes it possible to compare the relative effectiveness of several different interventions on a particular target behavior.

A simple graph can record the results of intervention. While statistical procedures are available to evaluate single-subject data, the visual inspection of a graph will be adequate in most cases. Figure 15.1 is a graph showing the baseline (*A*), the intervention (*B*), a removal of the intervention (*A*), and then a return to the intervention (*B*). In this *ABAB* design, the presenting problem was marital conflict expressing itself in frequent verbal arguments. The husband and wife sought professional assistance because they wanted to learn how to "talk more and argue less." Note that two weeks prior to the start of the first intervention period, the clients were asked to make daily records of the number of times they argued (shouting, name calling, etc.) and the number of times they talked calmly with each other for at least a three-minute period. Only the weekly totals are shown on the graph. The intervention, consisting of a weekly joint interview and a weekly small group discussion with three other couples, was aimed at increasing the amount of time they spent in amicable conversation. After five weeks of intervention, the couple was asked to take a three-week "vacation" from treatment. After that, the second five-week period of intervention began. A visual inspection of the graph shows that the first five-week intervention did reduce the frequency of arguments and increased the couple's talking together. When the intervention stopped, the couple talked less and argued more. The second period of intervention again moved the couple in the direction of positive change.

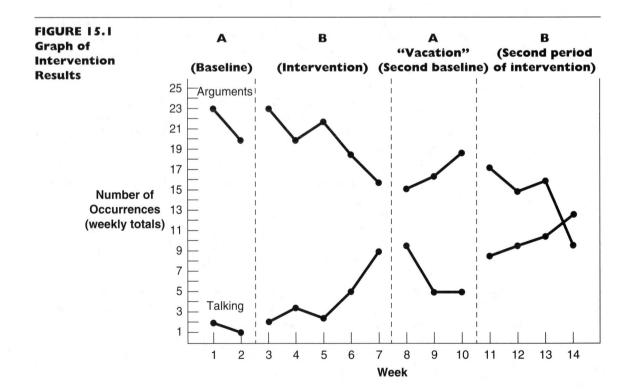

**FIGURE 15.1
Graph of
Intervention
Results**

SELECTED BIBLIOGRAPHY

Bloom, Martin, Joel Fischer, John G. Orme. *Evaluating Practice: Guidelines for the Accountable Professional,* 2nd ed. Boston: Allyn and Bacon, 1995.

Blythe, Betty, Tony Tripodi, and Scott Briar. *Direct Practice Research in Human Service Agencies.* New York: Columbia University Press, 1994.

Jordan, Cathleen, and Cynthia Franklin. *Clinical Assessment for Social Workers: Quantitative and Qualitative Methods.* Chicago: Lyceum Books, 1995.

Polster, Richard, and Mary Lynch. "Single-Subject Designs." In *Social Work Research and Evaluation,* 2nd ed., edited by Richard Grinnell. Itasca, Ill.: F. E. Peacock, 1985.

Tripodi, Tony. *A Primer on Single-Subject Design for Clinical Social Workers.* Washington, D.C.: NASW Press, 1994.

15.2 Rapid Assessment Instruments (RAI)

PURPOSE: To increase precision in assessment and evaluation by using instruments for clinical measurement.

DISCUSSION: Given the pressure by funding agencies and third-party payers such as insurance companies, Medicaid, and Medicare, social workers must constantly search for better ways of measuring the impact of their therapeutic services. The tools often called rapid assessment instruments (RAIs), when coupled with the single-subject design, provide a feasible method of evaluating clinical interventions for a wide variety of problems. In this application, the client's initial score on an RAI is used as a baseline and subsequent changes in the score are taken as indicators of change.

According to Fischer and Corcoran (1995, 9), RAIs are "standardized paper-and-pencil questionnaires that can be filled out by the client in a relatively short period of time, that can be easily administered and scored by the practitioner, and that give fairly accurate pictures of the client's condition at any point in time and/or over a period of many administrations." One widely used set of RAIs, the WALMYR Assessment Scales, was described in Item 12.18. There are, however, many others.

Every clinical social worker should have access to a variety of RAIs. An excellent source is the two-volume sourcebook by Fischer and Corcoran (1995) that describes over 320 rapid assessment instruments and explains how to select, administer, score, and interpret these measures. Included in this collection are RAIs for use with adults, couples, families, and children. Each instrument is classified by area of problem or concern.

These areas and the number of instruments listed under each area (i.e., the number shown in parentheses) are as follows: Abuse (5); Anger, hostility, and aggression (7); Anxiety and fear (24); Assertiveness (12); Beliefs—rational and irrational (12); Children's behaviors/problems (9); Death concerns (4); Depression and grief (20); Eating problems (12); Family functioning (18); Geriatric concerns (8); Guilt (1); Health issues (18); Identity (2); Interpersonal behavior (20); Locus of control (17); Loneliness (5); Love (5); Marital/couple relationship (25); Mood (3); Narcissism (1); Obsessive-compulsive (5); Parent-child relationship (12); Perfectionism (1); Phobias (10); Problem solving (3); Procrastination (2); Psychopathology and psychiatric symptoms (14); Rape (2); Satisfaction with life (2); Schizotypical symptoms (4); Self-concept and esteem (9); Self-control (3); Self-efficacy (3); Sexuality (9); Smoking (1); Social functioning (2); Social support (9); Stress (11); Substance abuse (11); Suicide (11); and Treatment satisfaction (4).

SELECTED BIBLIOGRAPHY

Fischer, Joel, and Kevin Corcoran. *Measures for Clinical Practice,* 2nd ed. (Two volumes) New York: Free Press, 1995.

15.3 Task Achievement Scaling (TAS)

PURPOSE: To determine the degree to which the client and/or worker completed agreed upon intervention tasks.

DISCUSSION: *Task Achievement Scaling (TAS)* is a simple and flexible evaluation tool. It is especially useful when the intervention does not lend itself to the use of baselining or single-subject designs. Examples include the referral of a client to an agency, obtaining information for a client, arranging transportation or day care, or securing housing for a client. Also, TAS can be used in brief service situations, such as when a client and worker meet only one or two times.

The TAS procedure was developed for use in task-centered practice and research. In task-centered practice, work toward the client's objectives is broken down into many separate actions or tasks. A task is usually something that is to be accomplished by the client or the worker in a matter of days or, at most, in a couple of weeks. The tasks are selected by mutual agreement. Each task must make sense to the client, be feasible, and be directly related to the client's problem or goal. Usually, not more than two or three tasks are worked on at any one time.

In task-centered work, a session typically begins with a review of what has been accomplished since the last session. The two or three tasks that the client and worker have previously selected for accomplishment are discussed in detail. Successful task achievement is reinforced by the worker. If there is little progress, the reasons are examined and modifications are made in task planning and implementation prior to the next session.

Task achievement scaling refers to rating the degree to which the agreed upon task has, in fact, been achieved. Ideally, the rating is done by both worker and client. But in many cases, only the worker will do the rating. Reid and Epstein (1972, 1977) have utilized the following four-point rating scale: (4) completely achieved; (3) substantially achieved, action is still necessary; (2) partially achieved, considerable work remains to be done; and (1) minimally achieved or not achieved. Where appropriate, a fifth rating—(No) for "No opportunity to work on task"—can be used.

Reid and Epstein (1977) describe the task achievement scale as follows:

(4) *Completely achieved.* . . . tasks that are fully accomplished, e.g., a job has been found, a homemaker secured, financial assistance obtained. It may also be used for tasks that

are fully accomplished "for all practical purposes:" if a couple's task was to reduce quarreling a rating of (4) could be given if they reached a point where hostile interchanges occurred infrequently, no longer presented a problem, and they saw no need for further work on the task.

(3) *Substantially achieved.* The task is largely accomplished though further action may need to be taken before full accomplishment is realized. Thus, if the task is to improve work performance, significant improvement would merit a rating of (3) even though further improvement would be possible and desirable.

(2) *Partially achieved.* Demonstrable progress has been made on the task but considerable work remains to be done. For example, if the task is to obtain a job, a rating of (2) could be given if the client has been actively looking for work and found a job he could take (and might) but was reluctant to. Or this rating would be appropriate for a couple who had made some headway on a shared task of finding things of mutual interest to do together even though they and the caseworker may be dissatisfied with their progress. Specific evidence of task accomplishment is required, however. . . .

(1) *Minimally achieved* (or not achieved). This rating is used for tasks on which no progress has been made or on which progress has been insignificant or uncertain. If a client's task were to locate and enter a suitable vocational training program, a rating of (1) would be given if the client were unable to locate a program, even though much effort had gone into searching for one.

(No) *No opportunity* to work on task. For example, client cannot carry out task in classroom because school is closed by teachers' strike. (p. 289)*

Note that only results are rated, not good intentions, effort, or motivation. The TAS is typically used to evaluate session-by-session progress. But a slight elaboration of the scale permits a summary of task ratings and the calculation of a percentage figure that can serve as a crude end-of-service outcome measure. To do this, use this five-point rating scale:

(4) Completely achieved
(3) Substantially achieved
(2) Partially achieved
(1) Minimally achieved
(0) No progress

By summing the final rating on each task and then dividing this sum by the highest sum possible, a percentage of success is determined. For example, if, over a series of six sessions, a total of seven separate tasks were agreed upon and targeted for accomplishment, the maximum score possible would be 28 (7 tasks × 4 = 28). A summary score of 28 would indicate that all seven tasks were completely achieved. If, however, the seven individual task ratings were actually 4, 4, 3, 3, 3, 2, and 1, the summed score would be only 20. As the final step, divide 20 by 28 and arrive at an end-of-service outcome of 71 percent. In other words, the client achieved 71 percent of all that was agreed upon, planned, and translated into tasks.

The appealing feature of TAS is its simplicity and the fact that it can be used when more rigorous procedures are not feasible because of insufficient time or data. Moreover, it does not intrude upon the helping process. Needless to say, it has limitations as an evaluation tool; but when no other tool can be utilized, the TAS does yield a crude measure of effectiveness. More importantly, it measures those activities that the client has identified as being important.

SELECTED BIBLIOGRAPHY

Alter, Catherine, and Wayne Evens. *Evaluating Your Practice: A Guide to Self-Assessment.* New York: Springer, 1990.

Berlin, Sharon B., and Jeanne C. Marsh. *Informing Practice Decisions.* New York: Macmillan, 1993.

Reid, William, and Laura Epstein, eds. *Task Centered Practice.* New York: Columbia University Press, 1977.

Reid, William, and Laura Epstein. *Task Centered Casework.* New York: Columbia University Press, 1972.

15.4   Goal Attainment Scaling (GAS)

PURPOSE: To measure the degree to which the client has reached individualized goals.

DISCUSSION: *Goal Attainment Scaling (GAS)** is a procedure that permits an evaluation of an intervention, even when the objectives and goals of the intervention are unique to a particular client. GAS has been utilized in mental health, drug abuse programs, probation and parole, and a number of other settings.

An application of GAS begins during the contracting and goal-setting phases. Goals are selected and written onto a form called a "Goal Attainment Follow-Up Guide." The format of the guide is the same for all clients, but the scale content is individualized. The guide consists of a succession of scales, each of which represents a series of possible client outcomes—both positive and negative—related to an agreed upon area of client functioning, such as interpersonal relations, employment, parenting, and so on. Each area becomes the focus of a separate scale.

Figure 15.2 presents a completed Goal Attainment Follow-Up Guide focusing on five individualized areas of a client's functioning (education, suicide, manipulation, drug abuse, and dependency on agency). For each of the five areas, a five-point outcome scale has been constructed. The possible outcomes range from the "most unfavorable" (–2) to "most favorable" or "best anticipated" (+2). There are three steps in constructing a goal attainment follow-up guide.

*Material on GAS was adapted from Hagedorn et al., National Institute on Mental Health, A Working Manual of Simple Program Evaluation Techniques for Community Mental Health Centers (Washington, D.C.: U.S. Government Printing Office, 1976), DHEW Pub. No. (ADM) 79–404, pp. 223–230.

1. *Identify the major areas of functioning in which intervention is expected to have an impact.* For example, typical goal areas in mental health settings include alcohol, depression, education, interpersonal relationships, and work performance. Usually, the number of areas should not exceed four or five.

2. *Assign a number to each goal area to indicate its importance in comparison with other goal areas.* The final score reflects the relative value of the results achieved. For example, if "drug abuse" is viewed as two times more important than "family relationship," drug abuse could be assigned a weight of 20 and the family area a weight of 10. Thus, when the summary Goal Attainment Score is computed for the client, the outcome in the drug abuse goal area would have twice as much influence on the final score as the outcome in the family relationship goal area.

3. *Specify five levels of possible outcome in relation to each goal area.* These outcomes should be progressive. The lowest is the "most unfavorable outcome thought likely"; next is "less than expected success." The third or middle level is "expected level of success." The top levels are "more than expected success" and "best anticipated success." Statements of potential outcome are tailored to the needs, capabilities, and aspirations of the client. The statements should be specific, observable (so there is little confusion as to the level of outcome that actually occurs), and realistic (so the scale is relevant to the client's situation). A check (✓) is placed in the cell that best describes the client at the time the follow-up guide was constructed (i.e., when intervention began). This serves as the baseline.

These three steps create the GAS Guide. Experience suggests that it takes a minimum of 20 to 30 minutes to complete the follow-up guide.

The evaluation of an intervention using the GAS Guide requires the use of a follow-up interview to determine the client's level of functioning on each scale. These interviews may occur at intervals during intervention (e.g., every six weeks) and at termination or shortly after. Follow-up interviews may be in person or by telephone. It takes approximately 40 minutes to conduct the follow-up interview and complete the scoring.

Scoring requires determining the level on each scale that best describes the client at the time of follow-up and placing an *X* in the appropriate cell. From a scored follow-up guide, it is possible to calculate two numerical measures of treatment efficacy: (1) a summary Goal Attainment Score and (2) a Goal Attainment Change Score. Calculating these measures is a problem for many users of GAS because it involves the use of a rather complex formula.

A summary Goal Attainment Score is generated by transforming the scores on the individual scales into a single numerical value. This value is a global index of the degree to which goals have been met. The recommended means of obtaining a Goal Attainment Score is a formula reported by Kiresuk and Sherman (1968). It produces a statistic that is essentially an average of attainment on all scales, corrected for the number of scales, the "weight" (relative importance) of the scales, and the intercorrelation of the scales.

FIGURE 15.2 Sample Five-Scale Goal Attainment Follow-Up Guide

Crisis Intervention Center (CIC)
Goal Attainment Follow-up Guide

Client: Jan Smith
Level at intake: ✓

Worker: Jim Green
Level at Follow-up: X

Guide developed: 9/23/93

Date of follow-up: 1/16/94

Scale Headings and Scale Weights

Check whether scale has been mutually negotiated between patient and CIC	Yes _X_ No ___	Yes ___ No _X_	Yes ___ No _X_	Yes _X_ No ___	Yes _X_ No ___
Scale Attainment Levels	Scale 1: Education ($w_1 = 20$)	Scale 2: Suicide ($w_2 = 30$)	Scale 3: Manipulation ($w_3 = 25$)	Scale 4: Drug Abuse ($w_4 = 30$)	Scale 5: Dependency on CIC ($w_5 = 10$)
a. (−2) Most unfavorable treatment outcome thought likely	Patient has made no attempt to enroll in high school.	Patient has committed suicide. ✓	Patient makes rounds of community service agencies demanding medication and refuses other forms of treatment. ✓	Patient reports addiction to "hard narcotics" (heroin, morphine).	Patient has contacted CIC by telephone or in person at least seven times since her first visit.
b. (−1) Less than expected success with treatment	Patient has enrolled in high school, but at time of follow-up has dropped out.	Patient has acted on at least one suicidal impulse since her first contact with the CIC but has not succeeded.	Patient no longer visits CIC with demands for medication but continues with other community agencies and still refuses other forms of treatment. ✓	Patient has used "hard narcotics" but is not addicted and/or uses hallucinogens (LSD, pot) more than four times a month. ✓	Patient has contacted CIC 5–6 times since intake.

	Goal 1 (School)	Goal 2 (Suicidal impulses)	Goal 3 (Treatment acceptance)	Goal 4 (Drug use)	Goal 5 (CIC contact)
c. (0) Expected level of treatment success	Patient has enrolled and is in school at follow-up, but is attending class sporadically (misses an average of more than a third of her classes during a week).	Patient reports she has had at least four suicidal impulses since her first contact with the CIC but has not acted on any of them.	Patient no longer attempts to manipulate for drugs at community service agencies but will not accept another form of treatment.	Patient has not used "hard narcotics" during follow-up period and uses hallucinogens between 1–4 times a month. **x**	Patient has contacted CIC 3–4 times since intake.
d. (+1) More than expected success with treatment	Patient is enrolled, is in school at follow-up, and is attending classes consistently but has no vocational goals. **x**	Patient reports she has had one or two small suicidal impulses since first contact but has not acted on them. **x**	Patient accepts non-medication treatment at some community agency. **x**	Patient uses hallucinogens less than once a month.	Patient has contacted CIC 1–2 times since intake.
e. (+2) Best anticipated success with treatment	Patient has enrolled, is in school at follow-up, is attending classes consistently, and has some vocational goals.	Patient reports she has had no suicidal impulses since her first contact with the CIC	Patient accepts non-medication treatment and by own report shows signs of improvement.	At time of follow-up, patient is not using any illegal drugs.	Patient has not contacted CIC since intake. **x**

Source: Hagedorn et al. 1976, p. 224.

A Goal Attainment Change Score indicates the difference in a client's status before and after intervention; it is determined by subtracting the summary Goal Attainment Score calculated at the time the follow-up guide was constructed from the score calculated at the time of follow-up. A negative score indicates deterioration; a score near zero indicates little or no change; a positive score indicates progress.

As a possible alternative to the calculation of one or both of these scores, the worker may prepare a statement of outcome by simply writing a few sentences that describe the client's change on the scales (e.g., Ms. Smith moved from –2 to +1 in the area of education on her GAS follow-up guide). However, the use of calculations is necessary in program evaluation where the data on many clients must be combined.

An evaluator can obtain valuable information about program results from a study of GAS follow-up guides, including the following:

1. The types of problems chosen as a target of intervention and their relative frequency
2. The types of problems on which particular workers or the agency as a whole make the most or least amount of progress
3. The types of problems worked on relative to particular client groups (e.g., most common targets of intervention among clients over age 65)

SELECTED BIBLIOGRAPHY

Alter, Catherine, and Wayne Evens. *Evaluating Your Practice: A Guide to Self-Assessment.* New York: Springer, 1990.

Bloom, Martin, Joel Fischer, and John G. Orme. *Evaluating Practice: Guidelines for the Accountable Professional.* Boston: Allyn and Bacon, 1995.

Gabor, Peter A., and Richard M. Grinnell, Jr. *Evaluation and Quality Improvement in the Human Services.* Boston: Allyn and Bacon, 1994.

Hagedorn, Homer, Kenneth Beck, Stephen Neubert, and Stanley Werlin (National Institute of Mental Health). *A Working Manual of Simple Program Evaluation Techniques for Community Mental Health Centers.* Washington, D.C.: Government Printing Office, 1976, DHEW Pub. No. (ADM) 79–404.

Kiresuk, Thomas J., and Robert E. Sherman. "Goal Attainment Scaling: A General Method for Evaluating Comprehensive Community Mental Health Programs." *Community Mental Health Journal* 4 (1968): 445–453.

15.5 Service Plan Outcome Checklist (SPOC)

PURPOSE: To record client progress on a menu of outcome goals typically addressed in an agency.

DISCUSSION: *The Service Plan Outcome Checklist (SPOC)* is a recording and monitoring tool intended for use in collecting data on progress made by clients from intake to termination. A SPOC is an example of an evaluation tool that makes use of a list or a menu of possible intervention outcomes (goals) from which the social worker and client select those that are relevant to their particular concerns. Its use is possible within a practice setting where the desired service outcomes are similar for many of the clients served by the agency.

A major advantage of the SPOC is that it is easy to use and demands less time to complete than either task achievement scaling (see Item 15.3) or goal achievement scaling (see Item 15.4). Its major disadvantages are that the possible outcomes contained in the menu must be stated in rather global terms and it does not establish a baseline of functioning.

The sample SPOC presented in Figure 15.3 was designed for use in a public child welfare agency (Horejsi, in press). It was modeled after a goal checklist developed by Fraser, Pecora, and Haapala (1988) and serves to illustrate the SPOC format and outcome statements. These outcome statements could be modified and expanded to reflect the practice goals common to other types of agencies. Figure 15.3 is drawn from the "parent section" of this SPOC; a "child section" (not included here) lists possible goals for work with children in this same child welfare setting.

The review of the items on the SPOC form by clients can assist them in identifying a range of issues that might become goals in the helping process. Seeing such a list helps clients recognize that their problems are not entirely unique and that the agency has experience in addressing many types of problems and issues. Clients can also see that each selected outcome will be evaluated at some point, implying that change is expected and possible.

The SPOC is also a useful tool for the worker and agency. Summary data for all cases can be quickly tabulated by computer or by hand. Thus, a worker can examine his or her practice with information about the types of problems addressed and the degree to which goals were achieved. The agency can use these same data to make decisions on how to strengthen its programs and services and set priorities for staff training.

SELECTED BIBLIOGRAPHY

Fraser, Mark, Peter Pecora, and David Haapala. *Families in Crisis: Findings from the Family-Based Intensive Treatment Project* (Vol. II). Salt Lake City: University of Utah Graduate Schoool of Social Work, 1988.

Horejsi, Charles. *Assessment and Case Planning in Child Protection and Foster Care Services.* Englewood, Colo.: American Humane Association, (in press).

15.6 Individualized Rating Scales (IRS)

PURPOSE: To create a measurement scale that is unique to a client and situation.

DISCUSSION: The term *individualized rating scale (IRS)* relates to scales that the social worker and client devise to measure some particular client problem or concern. According to Bloom, Fischer, and Orme (1995, 161), these easy-to-use scales "are tailor-made for each client and situation as the need arises, to measure whatever has been identified as important targets, along whatever dimensions seem most appropriate." The two

FIGURE 15.3   Service Plan Outcome Checklist*

Client/Family   Worker   Date

Instructions: Complete Steps 1–3 within one to two weeks of intake:

Step 1   In the far left column, select and check (✓) all outcomes that are targets for intervention. The outcomes selected should be tied directly to those behaviors or conditions that place the child at risk (including risks to the child in foster care).

If a desired outcome does not appear on the menu, describe the outcome(s) in spaces #26 and #27.

Step 2   Under the column headed "Person Who Defined Outcome and Date Began," record who selected the outcome (e.g., initials of worker, court, parent, child, etc.). Also, write in the date the work (intervention) toward that outcome began.

Step 3   In the far right column (i.e., titled "The Three High-Priority Outcomes"), record the social worker's and/or the client's selection of the three outcomes that are to be given highest priority in terms of time, resources, and attention.

Step 4   At the time work on each item is completed, record progress toward achieving the outcome in the column titled "Rating When Intervention Ended." Progress is rated on the scale ranging from 1 = "no progress" to 7 = "fully achieved." Ideally, this rating will be made jointly by the client and social worker.

Select and Check (✓) Desired Outcomes for Intervention	Person Who Defined Outcome and Date Began	Rating When Intervention Ended			Check (✓) the Three High-Priority Outcomes
		(Circle Rating)			
		No Progress	About Half Achieved	Fully Achieved	
__01 A working relationship between parent and worker/agency		1 2	3 4 5	6 7	
__02 Parent able to manage his or her anxiety or depression		1 2	3 4 5	6 7	
__03 Parent able to control his or her anger and tendency toward violence		1 2	3 4 5	6 7	
__04 Parent manages money and household budget		1 2	3 4 5	6 7	
__05 Parent secures needed housing for self and child		1 2	3 4 5	6 7	
__06 Parent establishes/maintains control over addictions and chemical dependency		1 2	3 4 5	6 7	

*The "Service Plan Outcome Checklist" is modeled after Mark. W. Fraser, Peter Pecora, and D. Haapala, *Families in Crisis: Findings from the Family-Based Intensive Treatment Project,* Vol. II. Salt Lake City: University of Utah Graduate School of Social Work, 1988; and the *Workbook for Supervisors: Case Planning,* Nashville: Tennessee Department of Human Services, 1988.

Select and Check (✓) Desired Outcomes for Intervention	Person Who Defined Outcome and Date Began	Rating When Intervention Ended			Check (✓) the Three High-Priority Outcomes
		(Circle Rating)			
		No Progress	About Half Achieved	Fully Achieved	
__07 Parent maintains a satisfactory and violence-free relationship with spouse/partner	_____ _____	1 2	3 4 5	6 7	
__08 Parent protects child from abuse by others	_____ _____	1 2	3 4 5	6 7	
__09 Parent takes proper physical care of self	_____ _____	1 2	3 4 5	6 7	
__10 Parent copes effectively with separation, loss, or grief	_____ _____	1 2	3 4 5	6 7	
__11 Parent secures needed medical/ dental care/treatment for child	_____ _____	1 2	3 4 5	6 7	
__12 Parent secures needed psycho- logical care/treatment for child	_____ _____	1 2	3 4 5	6 7	
__13 Parent effectively copes with own disability	_____ _____	1 2	3 4 5	6 7	
__14 Parent accepts and copes with child's disability	_____ _____	1 2	3 4 5	6 7	
__15 Parent accepts and respects self as worthwhile person	_____ _____	1 2	3 4 5	6 7	
__16 Parent establishes/maintains supportive and helpful relation- ships with friends, neighbors, or relatives	_____ _____	1 2	3 4 5	6 7	
__17 Parent establishes/maintains supportive and helpful recrea- tional and leisure-time activities for self	_____ _____	1 2	3 4 5	6 7	
__18 Parent maintains home that is clean and safe for children	_____ _____	1 2	3 4 5	6 7	
__19 Parent establishes/maintains clear and nonabusive communi- cation with child	_____ _____	1 2	3 4 5	6 7	
__20 Parent follows through on refer- ral and makes use of needed resources, agencies, and profes- sional assistance	_____ _____	1 2	3 4 5	6 7	

(continued)

FIGURE 15.3   Continued

Select and Check (✓) Desired Outcomes for Intervention	Person Who Defined Outcome and Date Began	Rating When Intervention Ended							Check (✓) the Three High-Priority Outcomes
		No Progress		About Half Achieved		Fully Achieved			
__21 Parent establishes/maintains behavior patterns free of criminal acts or association with deviant persons	_____ _____	1	2	3	4	5	6	7	
__22 Parent learns/practices non-abusive methods of discipline and child management	_____ _____	1	2	3	4	5	6	7	
__23 Parent visits child in foster care on regular basis	_____ _____	1	2	3	4	5	6	7	
__24 Parent works cooperatively with foster parent to prepare child for reunification	_____ _____	1	2	3	4	5	6	7	
__25 parent accepts instruction from foster parent on how to care for child	_____ _____	1	2	3	4	5	6	7	
__26 _____ _____	_____ _____	1	2	3	4	5	6	7	

main types of individualized rating scales are the self-anchored scale and the observer rating scale. The rating on a *self-anchored scale* is decided by the client; the rating on an *observer rating scale* is decided by a person who has observed the client. Fischer and Corcoran (1994, Vol. 1) explain the basic procedure for creating such scales.

> Once the problem area is defined, you present to the client a picture of a social or psychological thermometer, with one end being the most intense end of the problem and the other the least intense. Then you select the number of points for the scale. We usually recommend 0–10 or 1–9, although if the client has difficulty in discriminating among that many points, you can collapse the scale to 1–7 or 1–5 points. Make sure you are clear with the client that they are equal intervals, so that the difference between 1 and 2 on the scale is no greater than the difference between 5 and 6. Finally, you and the client attempt to anchor the scale points using as much concrete detail to define each point as possible. (p. 30)

The self-anchored scale is especially useful because it can be used to measure the intensity of feelings and inner conflicts. Who but the client can possibly measure the intensity of his or her own pain, guilt, or anxiety? Following is an example of a nine-point, self-anchored scale measuring the intensity of a mother's anger toward her child named Karen.

1 · · · · 2 · · · · 3 · · · · 4 · · · · 5 · · · · 6 · · · · 7 · · · · 8 · · · · 9

No awareness of anger.   Moderate feelings of anger.   Intense anger. Want to
Enjoy time with Karen.   Some bitterness and   strike out and hurt
    resentment.   Karen. Have feelings of
    hatred. Want her to die.

A rating scale, because it is completed by an observer, must be of a more behavioral nature. A seven-point rating scale measuring this mother's anger might look like this:

1 · · · · · · 2 · · · · · · 3 · · · · · · 4 · · · · · · 5 · · · · · · 6 · · · · · · 7

Mother smiles at Karen.   Mother speaks sharply.   Mother yells and
Holds her gently.   Handles Karen in rough   screams at Karen.
    manner. Mother frequently   Threatens or hits child.
    frowns or scowls.

SELECTED BIBLIOGRAPHY

Bloom, Martin, Joel Fischer, and John Orme. *Evaluating Practice: Guidelines for the Accountable Professional.* Boston: Allyn and Bacon, 1995.
Fischer, Joel, and Kevin Corcoran. *Measures for Clinical Practice*, 2nd ed. (two volumes). New York: Free Press, 1994.

15.7 Differential Impact Scoring (DIS)

PURPOSE: To obtain client's perceptions on changes that have occurred since intervention began and differentiate changes attributed to the intervention from those attributed to other factors.

DISCUSSION: When a client is receiving services from more than one professional and more than one agency, how does one determine which intervention has had an impact? And, how does one account for changes in the client's life circumstances that may cause either an improvement or a worsening of the situation but that have nothing to do with the interventions? A limitation in our usual attempts to secure a "before-and-after" measure is that the identified change, whether positive or negative, may have resulted from influences other than the worker's or the agency's intervention. In such cases, it would be inappropriate for an agency either to claim credit for positive change or to assume responsibility for negative changes. The *ABA* and *ABAB* single-subject designs (see Item 15.1) attempt to address this problem, but for practical and ethical reasons it is not always feasible to stop and then later restart an intervention as a way of determining which of several interventions might be having an impact.

The procedure called ***Differential Impact Scoring (DIS)*** is a method of separating out the impact of a specific intervention from other factors and interventions that also influence the client. A major limitation of DIS is that it depends on self-reported data. Perceptions voiced by a client may or may not be an accurate description of what really happened.

The example of DIS is drawn from a study (Horejsi 1972) of a lay volunteer program's impact on the functioning of youths on probation, as perceived by the parents of those youths; its basic format and scoring procedure can be adapted for use in other settings. During the months of contact with the volunteer, these adolescent clients also had regular contact with their probation officer, and many of the youths and their families were simultaneously receiving services from mental health, social service and health care agencies, school programs, and other professionals. To determine if the volunteers were having an impact, respondents (i.e., the parents) were asked 37 questions about whether they had observed changes in their child's school attendance, grades, money management, choice of friends, control of anger, communication with family, and so on. (Two sample questions are shown in Figure 15.4). If the respondent expressed the belief that a change (either "better" or "worse") had occurred, a follow-up question asked whether the respondent believed

---

**FIGURE 15.4
Sample
Questions
from
Interview
Schedule**

Item 16. What about the frequency with which you and (youth's name) have disagreements or arguments? Has this improved, remained the same, or gotten worse?

A _____ improved   B _____ remained the same   C _____ worse

(If either improved or worse) In your opinion, to what extent did the volunteer have something to do with (this improvement) (this change for the worse)?

1 _____ Volunteer had a great deal to do with the change.

2 _____ Volunteer had quite a bit to do with the change.

3 _____ Volunteer had only a little bit to do with the change.

4 _____ Volunteer had nothing to do with the change.

Item 24. Do you think things have improved, remained the same, or gotten worse in regard to how often (youth's name) gets into arguments or fights with other kids?

A _____ improved   B _____ remained the same   C _____ worse

(If either improved or worse) In your opinion, to what extent did the volunteer have something to do with (this improvement) (this change for the worse)?

1 _____ Volunteer had a great deal to do with the change.

2 _____ Volunteer had quite a bit to do with the change.

3 _____ Volunteer had only a little bit to do with the change.

4 _____ Volunteer had nothing to do with the change.

the volunteer had anything to do with the perceived change; possible responses were "great deal," "quite a bit," "only a little," and "nothing."

An *item score* ranging from +10 to –10 was obtained by a multiplication procedure. For example, an individual item score of zero would result if a parent stated that his or her child's school attendance had either "improved" (+2) or "gotten worse" (–2) and that the volunteer had "nothing" (0) to do with this change. An item score of plus six (+6), for example, would result if the parent stated that his or her child's school attendance had "improved" (+2) and that the volunteer had "quite a bit" (3) to do with the change (i.e., $2 \times 3 = 6$). All possible item scores are shown in Figure 15.5.

A *summary score* for each youth was obtained by summing all 37 item scores. A high positive summary score resulted when a parent reported many improvements and attributed most of them to the volunteer's intervention. A low positive score resulted when a parent perceived few improvements that could be attributed to the volunteer's influence. A negative summary score indicated that negative changes had occurred and the parents believed that the volunteer's intervention had caused the deterioration. Theoretically, summary scores could range from a high of 370 ($2 \times 5 \times 37$) to a low of –370 ($-2 \times 5 \times 37$).

The DIS is at best a crude measure, but it can prove useful when other approaches are not feasible. Magura and Moses (1986) use a similar approach in their *Parent Outcome Interview*, an instrument designed to obtain the client's perceptions of agency services in child welfare cases. In addition to asking respondents whether a change had occurred (i.e., better or worse), a series of open-ended follow-up questions probed for the reasons why the services were or were not effective and, if effective, how the improvement in functioning took place. Such an approach requires additional interview time with the respondents (i.e., the Parent Outcome Interview required two hours to administer) but yields a more detailed understanding of which interventions are effective and why.

FIGURE 15.5 Possible DIS Item Scores

Parent's Evaluation of Child's Functioning	Parent's Perception of Volunteer's Contribution to Change	Individual Item Score
Improved (+2)	"great deal" (5)	$2 \times 5 = 10$
Improved (+2)	"quite a bit" (3)	$2 \times 3 = 6$
Improved (+2)	"only a little" (1)	$2 \times 1 = 2$
Improved (+2)	"nothing" (0)	$2 \times 0 = 0$
Remained the same (0)		0
Worse (–2)	"nothing" (0)	$-2 \times 0 = 0$
Worse (–2)	"only a little" (1)	$-2 \times 1 = -2$
Worse (–2)	"quite a bit" (3)	$-2 \times 3 = -6$
Worse (–2)	"great deal" (5)	$-2 \times 5 = -10$

SELECTED BIBLIOGRAPHY

Horejsi, Charles. "Attitudes of Parents Toward Juvenile Court Volunteers." *Federal Probation* (June 1972): 13–18.

———. "Juvenile Probationers' Behavior and Attitudes Rating Scale." In *Tests and Measurements in Child Development: Handbook II*, edited by Orval Johnson. San Francisco: Jossey-Bass, 1976, pp. 1092–1093.

Magura, Stephen, and Beth Moses. *Outcome Measures for Child Welfare Services*. Washington, D.C.: Child Welfare League of America, 1986.

15.8   Termination of Service

PURPOSE: To terminate the professional relationship between social worker and client in a timely and responsible manner.

DISCUSSION: Closing a case, or terminating services to a client, should be viewed as a planned component of the helping process. When deciding if termination is appropriate, the following factors should be considered.

- Have the intervention objectives been reached?
- Has an agreed upon time limit to service provision been reached?
- Is the problem or situation that brought the client to the agency sufficiently resolved so the client can now function at an acceptable level and not be at risk of being harmed by self or others?
- Has the worker and/or agency made a reasonable investment of time, energy, and skill without measurable results?
- Has the client and/or worker reached a point where one or both do not anticipate benefit from future contacts?
- Has the client become inappropriately dependent on the worker or agency?
- Would the client be more appropriately served by another agency or professional?

In some situations, a transfer of the client to another worker within the agency is necessary. This, too, is a type of termination. An intraagency transfer is necessary:

- When the worker will no longer be available to serve the client (e.g., worker moving to another job, etc.)
- When the client will be better served by another agency staff member
- When a conflict between the worker and client cannot be resolved and is interfering with service provision or client progress
- When, for some reason, the worker simply does not like the client and cannot develop or demonstrate necessary empathy and warmth
- When there is a serious and insurmountable gap in mutual understanding and communication caused by difference in values, religious beliefs, language, or cultural background

Ideally, termination is a mutual decision by worker and client that occurs when the service objectives have been reached. Many situations are far from ideal, however. All too often, the client decides to end the relationship before reaching the objectives, and sometimes circumstances dictate that the worker decide unilaterally to terminate. Examples of the latter include times when:

■ The client is considered to be a physical danger to the worker or continually harasses the worker
■ The client files a lawsuit or an official complaint against the worker
■ The client violates, without good cause, a financial agreement regarding the payment of fees for service

In the case of an intraagency transfer and in the case of a termination by the worker, the client should be notified in writing, and, if possible, during a face-to-face meeting. The reasons and circumstances surrounding the transfer or termination should be clearly documented in the case record.

The social worker has an obligation to make a termination or transfer as positive an experience as possible. Several guidelines can aid in this process.

1. The worker should do everything possible to keep termination from being abrupt or unexpected. Termination should be discussed during the planning and contracting phase of the helping process. The client should be reminded from the beginning that intervention is goal oriented and time limited. The client will be gradually prepared for termination if the intervention includes, as it should, an ongoing monitoring of progress.

2. In a case where an adult client wants to terminate but the social worker thinks he or she should continue, the worker should explain to the client the possible consequences of terminating. If the client still wishes to terminate, his or her decision should be respected. Usually a child or adolescent client does not have the authority to decide the termination of services; in cases involving a minor, the minor's parent or guardian make the decision.

3. The termination of a service provided under court order requires special consideration. The Colorado Chapter of NASW (1989) offers the following guidance:

> The social worker must determine whether all terms of the order have been met before terminating service. There may be cases in which the client seeks termination against the recommendation of the social worker and in violation of the court orders. In these cases, the social worker is obligated to fully inform the client of the possible consequences of the action, to tell the client that termination will be reported to the court, and to advise the client to discuss the matter with his or her attorney. (p. 9)

4. Special attention must be given to any termination prompted by an administrative decision to cut back on the services provided, to restrict case transfers within the agency, or to modify a client service contract once the worker who has serviced the client leaves or changes positions within the agency. The social worker also faces an ethical dilemma when a third-party payer (e.g., an insurance company, Medicaid, etc.) decides to end financial reimbursement for the services needed by a client. For such situations, the Colorado Chapter of NASW (1989, 9) provides the following guidance: "The social worker should be directed in these and other dilemmas by his or her primary responsibility to the client. When the social worker judges that the client is jeopardized by agency policy or administrative decision, he or she should first advocate in behalf of the client within the agency. If the conflict cannot be resolved within the agency, assistance may be sought from NASW [and other potential advocates]."

5. The social worker must anticipate how the termination might affect other persons in the client's family and social network. In situations where a termination may place the client or others at risk of harm, it may be appropriate to notify others of the termination. This notification must, of course, be done in ways consistent with the law and ethics concerning confidentiality.

6. In some cases, termination can be difficult because of a social worker's own psychological needs. A worker with personal problems may want to be needed and appreciated so strongly that he or she maintains regular contact with a client even when there is no professional reason for doing so. This reflects a lack of self-awareness and is, of course, professionally irresponsible and unethical.

7. As termination approaches, it is desirable to gradually decrease the frequency of contact. If the client is quite dependent on the worker, this weaning process should be accompanied by efforts to connect the client with natural helpers and informal resources within his or her neighborhood or social network.

8. The feelings of loss and anger that often accompany the ending of any important relationship should be broached by the worker, even if not mentioned by the client. The scheduling of a follow-up interview or telephone contact several weeks after official termination may be reassuring to the client who fears separation. Also, the client should be informed that he or she can return to the agency if the need arises.

9. The ending of a meaningful professional relationship should utilize some type of ritual to mark this transition. Fortune (1995) notes that such markers include culturally appropriate good-byes such as hugging and shaking hands and, in the case of terminations within a support group or treatment group, they might involve the exchange of small gifts, potluck meals, and celebrations at which the participants recall highlights in the group's experience. Such ending rituals are especially important in work with children.

SELECTED BIBLIOGRAPHY

Colorado Chapter of NASW. "Practice Standard Guidelines: Termination of Services for Adult Clients." *The Integrator: Chapter Newsletter* (April/May 1989).

Fortune, Anne. "Termination in Direct Practice" In *Encyclopedia of Social Work*, 19th ed., Vol. 3, edited by Richard L. Edwards. Washington D.C.: NASW, 1995, pp 2398–2404.

Hepworth, Dean, and Jo Ann Larsen. *Direct Social Work Practice*, 4th ed. Pacific Grove, Calif.: Brooks/Cole, 1993.

SECTION B
TECHNIQUES AND GUIDELINES FOR INDIRECT PRACTICE

A number of techniques are available for evaluating indirect practice. Some are used in conjunction with the internal evaluation of worker performance. For instance, peer review and worker evaluation methods can help agencies determine if their employees are performing well and can also assist workers in improving their functioning.

Agencies must also step back periodically and assess the programs they offer. Formal program evaluation, including questionnaires that ask clients to give feedback on their experience with the agency, can assist administrators in making judgments as to how best to use the resources available to the agency.

Although the new social worker will not usually have responsibility for conducting major program or agency assessments, the outcome of such evaluations can affect the worker. Thus, even the new social worker should be generally familiar with these indirect practice evaluation tools.

15.9 Peer Review

PURPOSE: To evaluate the quality of a social worker's practice by comparing his or her activities against a set of principles and standards.

DISCUSSION: The process of *peer review* refers to a periodic examination of a social worker's performance by a fellow worker who understands the agency's clientele, policies, and procedures. Essentially, peer review is a form of quality control. Some settings, like hospitals, are required by accrediting organizations or regulatory agencies to establish peer review systems.

The first step in developing a peer review procedure is for the social workers to agree on a set of principles or criteria that reflect good practice in their particular setting. In order to keep the process relatively simple, the number of criteria should probably not exceed 10. Those participating also need to agree on the procedure for selecting cases to be reviewed. The random selection of cases from a worker's active case file is a common approach. Peer review sessions should be regularly scheduled (e.g., monthly); a single session should be limited to about one-half hour. A system of rotation ensures that each worker has a chance to conduct a peer review on all other workers in his or her unit or department. This can be a valuable learning opportunity. Results of the review should be recorded on a form. A recurring problem found in the performance of an individual worker may require remediation. And a recurring problem among all of the workers may signal a system problem and the need to examine existing policies and procedures.

Figure 15.6 presents an example of peer review process for a five-worker unit within a family agency. Many variations are possible.

FIGURE 15.6   Sample Peer Review Policy and Review Form

Policy: Each social worker will participate in an ongoing cycle of peer review and consultation. The supervisor will be responsible for developing the peer review schedule. Each month, each social worker will have two cases reviewed by a peer and will also reveiw two cases of another worker. The cases will be drawn at random from the worker's active caseload. The reviewer will complete the peer review form and submit it to the supervisor.

On a quarterly basis, the supervisor will analyze the peer review reports, identify common performance problems, and meet with staff to formulate a plan to address common performance problems.

Schedule

Reviewer	November	December	January	February
Greta	Mary	Larry	Ruth	Jim
Jim	Greta	Mary	Larry	Ruth
Ruth	Jim	Greta	Mary	Larry
Larry	Ruth	Jim	Greta	Mary
Mary	Larry	Ruth	Jim	Greta

Monthly Peer Review Form

Date _____   Social Worker _____   Reviewer _____

Case name and number _____

	Yes	No	NA
1. Client problem(s) clearly stated in record.	_____	_____	_____
2. Client/family members involved in treatment planning.	_____	_____	_____
3. Written treatment plan in record.	_____	_____	_____
4. Intervention methods are appropriate for clients' problems.	_____	_____	_____
5. Frequency and duration of client contact is appropriate for problem.	_____	_____	_____
6. Treatment planning, worker's action, and approach used reflect concern for permanency planning.	_____	_____	_____
7. Appropriate and effective use made of community resources.	_____	_____	_____
8. Progress toward goals is evident.	_____	_____	_____
9. Case recording is clear, concise, and descriptive.	_____	_____	_____
10. Required agency forms completed and included in record.	_____	_____	_____

Other comments: _____

_____

_____

_____

_____

_____

SELECTED BIBLIOGRAPHY

Carter, Reginald. *The Accountable Agency.* Beverly Hills: Sage, 1983.

Jackson, Josephine. "Clinical Social Work and Peer Review." *Social Work* 32 (May–June 1987): 213–220.

Munson, Carlton. *Clinical Social Work Supervision, 2nd ed.* New York: Haworth, 1994.

15.10   Worker Performance Evaluation

PURPOSE: To understand the purpose and procedures of performance evaluations in order to make such assessments productive for both workers and agencies.

DISCUSSION:

According to Pecora and Austin (1987, 56), "*Worker performance appraisal* is essentially concerned with systematically assessing how well agency staff members are performing their jobs over a specified period of time. Performance evaluations are designed to measure the extent to which the worker is achieving the requirements of his or her position." The regular appraisal of its employees is a fundamental part of an agency's obligation to be accountable to its clients, its community, and those who provide financial support. At the same time, such a comprehensive job performance review provides the social worker with an important opportunity for professional growth.

Matheson, Van Dyk, and Millar (1995, 1) suggest that, if properly conducted, the following positive outcomes can accrue from worker performance evaluations.

- Increase the person's motivation to perform effectively.
- Increase the self-esteem of the person being evaluated.
- Allow new insights for the person or persons doing the appraisal.
- Result in more clarification and better definition of the job of the person being evaluated.
- Facilitate valuable communication among the individuals taking part.
- Promote a better understanding among participants, of themselves, and of the kind of staff development activities that are of value.
- Clarify organizational goals and facilitate their acceptance.
- Allow the organization to engage in human resource planning, test validation, and develop training programs.

Certainly the outcome of a performance evaluation may have either positive or negative consequences for the worker. It may lead to decisions to promote, increase salary, or grant other rewards or it may lead to a negative decision such as placing the worker on probation or the termination of employment. The later has the potential to entice a worker to compromise openness and self-disclosure and, therefore, limit the usefulness of this evaluation process for the worker's professional development. To minimize this possibility, the process must be carefully conducted and the criteria for evaluation must be clear, specific, realistic, and measurable.

Following are the three elements critical to a useful and valid performance evaluation.

1. *People.* The supervisor or other person serving as evaluator must be competent. That person must know what constitutes good practice and be able to develop a trusting relationship with the worker. That trust must center on the desire to help the worker develop his or her potential as a social worker. The evaluator must be able to identify both worker competencies and deficiencies in performance and be able to articulate them in a way that builds on worker strengths in order to correct deficiencies. The evaluator must understand that new workers can be expected to have unevenness in their performances.

2. *Criteria.* The criteria on which the evaluation will be based must be made clear *before* the worker enters the time period to be covered by the evaluation. The lack of clear criteria can cause confusion and hard feelings. A typical direct-service worker's performance appraisal would focus on areas such as:

- Capacity to establish and maintain appropriate relationships with clients (e.g., attitudes, values, and ethics as manifested in behavior toward clients; self-awareness and self-discipline; ability to manage especially difficult relationships)
- Knowledge and skills in the helping process (e.g., engagement of clients, data collection and assessment, planning and intervention, interviewing and communication skills, documentation of work and recordkeeping)
- Knowledge of and adherence to agency policies, procedures, and objectives
- Use of supervision and learning opportunities
- Management of workload and job stress
- Intraagency relations (e.g., communication, and teamwork with other staff members)
- Interagency relations (e.g., creation and maintenance of working relationships with other agencies, programs, and resources)
- Productivity (e.g., numbers of clients served, new programs started, fees generated)

3. *Process.* The examination of performance must focus on worker behavior, not on explanations or rationalizations for the behavior. The written aspect of the evaluation may take the form of a narrative statement, rating scales, or a combination. Once prepared, these written materials should be reviewed, discussed, revised, if necessary, and signed by both the worker and supervisor, with notation regarding any disagreements, and then placed in the worker's permanent record. The documentation of disagreements could help the worker defend against arbitrary personnel actions. From discussion of the evaluation materials, the worker and supervisor can establish goals, adjust assignments, and plan activities that will strengthen the worker's performance prior to the next evaluation.

SELECTED BIBLIOGRAPHY

Brody, Ralph. *Effectively Managing Human Service Organizations.* Newbury Park, Calif.: Sage, 1993.

Matheson, Wayne, Cornelius Van Dyk, and Kenneth Millar. *Performance Evaluation in the Human Services.* New York: Haworth Press, 1995.

Miller, Kenneth I. "Performance Appraisal of Professional Social Workers." *Administration in Social Work* 14 (1990): 65–85.

Pecora, Peter, and Michael Austin. *Managing Human Services Personnel.* Newbury Park, Calif.: Sage, 1987.

Rapp, Charles A., and John Poertner. *Social Administration: A Client-Centered Approach.* New York: Longman, 1992.

15.11   Program Evaluation

PURPOSE: To determine how well a social program is meeting its objectives.

DISCUSSION: A social program is a planned sequence of activities designed to achieve desired individual or social change. Hence, ***program evaluation*** refers to the systematic examination of a program to determine whether and/or how it is achieving its goals and objectives. A program evaluation focuses on three dimensions.

- *Program effort.* Descriptions of the type and quantity of activities, number of people served, staffing patterns, and so on
- *Program effectiveness.* Determination of the degree to which program objectives are being attained
- *Program efficiency.* Assessment of the cost of achieving the objectives

The following guidelines are useful in assuring that a program evaluation will be useful.

1. *Identify the users of the evaluation data and report* (e.g., administrators, practitioners, program planners, legislators, fund-raisers, etc.). What do they really want and need from this evaluation? What type of information can they understand and use? Is it reasonable to believe that evaluation results will affect the continuation, modification, or termination of the program? Do not begin a program evaluation effort unless the results can make a real difference in terms of the program's operation and the services provided.

2. *Decide if an evaluation is feasible.* Do you have the necessary time, money, and skill available? Do you have access to experts in program evaluation? Are the data you need actually available? Are all key staff members committed to the idea of evaluation? Is the program stable enough to undergo scrutiny? Has the program been in operation long enough to make an evaluation worthwhile?

3. *State the goals and objectives of the program.* Securing clear statements of the program goals and objectives is at once the most difficult and most critical step in making an evaluation. You cannot evaluate a program until you know precisely what it is trying to accomplish.

4. *Describe the program's interventions that are to be evaluated.* Intervention activities must be logically connected to program goals and objectives and must focus on factors or forces over which it has control. Clearly describe the units of intervention or the services. For example, to describe when an intervention activity is happening, you might ask, When does it begin and end? Does the worker decide when an intervention has occurred or does the client or someone else? Can you distinguish an intervention from other client-staff interactions? Can you decide when a service has been used? For example, if a client attended only two of five scheduled sessions of a parenting class, has he or she received parent training?

5. *Select measurable indicators of change.* Once you are clear as to the specific attitudes, behaviors, or conditions your program is trying to change, and you are clear as to the interventions used to bring about those changes, you need to select indicators of change that can be detected and measured. Make sure these indicators are ones that can be reasonably attributed to your program's intervention. Also, decide if it is reasonable to believe that the desired effects of the intervention will occur within the time frame you are using. If you cannot wait to measure long-term benefits, you must choose indicators that reflect more immediate changes.

6. *Select appropriate and feasible data collection and measurement tools and/or instruments.* Developing a valid and reliable instrument is a complex, time-consuming, and expensive process, so try to use available instruments. Examine evaluations done on similar programs and use instruments that others have found useful.

7. *Plan how you will collect, tabulate, and analyze the data.* Do not collect more data than you can manage and use. Make sure the data you want are actually available. For example, if you plan to gather data from case files, are you sure all of them contain the information you need? If your data are stored in the computer system, can you get them out? Can the information you seek be obtained without a release from the client? If your evaluation design involves contacting former service consumers, will you be able to locate them?

8. *Interpret the results of your evaluation.* The final product of your effort is to report the results. Caution should be used in making this interpretation. Factors other than the nature of the intervention may account for a program's success or failure. For example, successful programs often have a deeply committed and motivated person in a leadership position. These individuals "make" the program work despite obstacles. Such leadership factors may have as much to do with a successful outcome as program design or intervention method. On the other extreme are factors like low staff morale that produce poor outcomes despite a well-conceived program.

SELECTED BIBLIOGRAPHY

Chambers, Donald E., Kenneth R. Wedel, and Mary K. Rodwell. *Evaluating Social Programs.* Boston: Allyn and Bacon, 1992.

Fischer, Joel, and Kevin Corcoran. *Measures for Clinical Practice*, 2nd ed. (two volumes). New York: Free Press, 1994.

Krause, Daniel. *Effective Program Evaluation: An Introduction.* Chicago: Nelson-Hall, 1996.

Royse, David. *Program Evaluation: An Introduction.* Chicago: Nelson-Hall, 1992.

Schalock, Robert L., and Craig V. C. Thornton. *Program Evaluation: A Field Guide for Administrators.* New York: Plenum Press, 1988.

15.12   Client Satisfaction Questionnaire (CSQ)

PURPOSE: To determine the client's satisfaction with the services he or she has received.

DISCUSSION:*   A *Client Satisfaction Questionnaire (CSQ)* is a method of soliciting a client's opinions about the services he or she has received. A major limitation of a CSQ is that it records only the client's perceptions of what happened as a result of intervention. Certainly, reality may differ from perception, and perception may change over time. Another limitation is the tendency of a CSQ to yield data biased in the direction of positive responses, particularly if administered by mail. Dissatisfied clients are less likely than satisfied ones to return the questionnaire.

A short CSQ has the advantage of being easy to complete. A lengthy, detailed questionnaire will, of course, collect more information but may result in lower rate of completion. A CSQ, coupled with in-depth interviewing (by phone or face to face), is needed to secure detailed information on specific service variables related to the client's satisfaction and dissatisfaction.

Most often, a CSQ is administered at the point of service termination or shortly thereafter. Some agencies administer a CSQ after three to five interviews (and periodically thereafter if the client receives services for a longer period), at the point of termination, and perhaps two months following termination.

A brief "generic" CSQ, presented in Figure 15.7. Figure 15.8, presents a portion of a more detailed CSQ used in a shelter for abused women; it illustrates an alternative arrangement of questions and asks the client to respond on a four-point scale, ranging from "strongly disagree" to "strongly agree." Such a numerical scale facilitates the tabulation of data and makes possible the calculation of averages. Follow these four steps in using a CSQ:

1. *Decide what population of clients to sample.* The sample could be representative of agency clientele in general, of clients who have received a particular type of service, or of clients who make up a particular demographic group (e.g., clients over age 60). A basic knowledge of sampling methods is required in order to draw a representative sample. Criteria for CSQ distribution should be determined by the evaluator and relate to the purpose of the evaluation, statistical requirements, and administrative convenience.

2. *Design the questionnaire.* Keep it as simple and brief as possible and avoid professional jargon. The agency may want to gather certain client and demographic information in order to determine if satisfaction with or complaints about services are related to factors such as the client's ethnicity, age, socioeconomic status, and the like. However, asking for such information tends to weaken assurances of anonymity.

---

*Material in this section was adapted, in part, from Hagedorn et al., National Institute on Mental Health, *A Working Manual on Simple Program Evaluation Techniques for Community Mental Health Centers* (Washington, D.C.: U.S. Government Printing Office, 1976), DHEW Pub. No. (ADM) 79–404, pp. 230–237.

FIGURE 15.7   Sample Client Satisfaction Questionnaire

Evaluating Your Experience at ABC Agency

Thank you for taking a few minutes to evaluate the service you have received at our agency. Your answers to this brief questionnaire will help us to improve our services. Feel free to offer comments.

Instructions: For each question below, check (✓) your answer.

1. How do you feel about the way you were treated by the receptionist?
    ___ very dissatisfied   ___ dissatisfied   ___ mostly satisfied   ___ very satisfied
    ___ no feelings one way or the other
    Comments _____

2. How do you feel about the length of time you had to wait before our agency dealt with your problem or situation?
    ___ unhappy or dissatisfied   ___ pleased or satisfied
    ___ no feelings one way or the other
    Comments _____

3. Did you accomplish what you expected to achieve when you came to this agency?
    ___ yes, completely   ___ mostly, yes   ___ no real progress   ___ worse off now than before
    ___ I changed my mind about what I expected (please explain)
    Comments _____

4. Do you feel your situation/problem(s) has changed since you became involved with this agency?
    ___ things are now much worse   ___ things are somewhat better
    ___ things are somewhat worse   ___ things are much better
    ___ no change, one way or the other
    Comments _____

5. Which of the following statement comes closest to your feeling about the impact of this agency's services on your situation or problem?
    ___ agency made things much worse   ___ agency made things somewhat better
    ___ agency made things somewhat worse   ___ agency made things much better
    ___ agency had no impact, one way or the other
    Comments _____

6. How do you feel about the social worker who dealt with your problem or situation?
    ___ very dissatisfied   ___ dissatisfied   ___ satisfied   ___ very satisfied
    ___ no feelings on way or another
    Comments _____

7. If a friend needed services from an agency like ours, would you recommend our agency?
    ___ never   ___ probably not   ___ probably yes   ___ definitely yes
    Comments _____

8. Overall, how do you feel about your experience with our agency?
    ___ very dissatisfied   ___ dissatisfied   ___ very satisfied   ___ satisfied
    Comments _____

9. It is helpful for us to know something about the person who completed this questionnaire. Please check:
    ___ male   ___ client
    ___ female   ___ parent of agency client
                              ___ spouse of agency client

FIGURE 15.8
Evaluation
of Shelter
Services

Your comments will help us improve future services to women and children. Your answers are confidential and will in no way affect future contact we may have with you. Thank you for your cooperation.

Please circle the number that best represents your opinion of services you received.

Basic Needs	Strongly Disagree	Mostly Disagree	Mostly Agree	Strongly Agree
1. I felt safe from my abuser while in the shelter.	1	2	3	4
2. My room assignment was adequate for my family.	1	2	3	4
3. The shelter was clean.	1	2	3	4
4. My family had enough food.	1	2	3	4
5. The meals were nutritious.	1	2	3	4
6. The food tasted good.	1	2	3	4
7. I had access to enough personal care items (diapers, shampoo, toothpaste, etc.)	1	2	3	4
8. I had access to adequate clothing.	1	2	3	4
9. I had access to necessary medical care.	1	2	3	4
10. Transportation was available when I needed it.	1	2	3	4

3. *Administer the questionnaire.* This step can often be carried out by clerical staff, volunteers, or social service aides; however, those administering the questionnaire must be trained in its use in order to increase reliability. The assurance of confidentiality to respondents is very important. A mailed CSQ can provide the client with anonymity but does presume that the client can read. If the target population consists of former clients, the questionnaire can be either mailed or administered by phone. If it includes clients who are still in regular contact with the agency, the questionnaire can usually be administered by a receptionist. The greatest amount of work in administering the questionnaire will probably be in following up on those clients who fail to return the questionnaire; these clients will have to be called or sent a letter to obtain a reasonable return rate. If the responses are to be anonymous, there will be problems in follow-up; therefore, a guarantee of confidentiality without the added assurance of anonymity may be preferable. Statistical techniques can determine whether there are significant differences between those who return the questionnaire immediately and those who require urging.

4. *Tabulate and analyze the questionnaire data.* Manual tabulation may be possible for short questionnaires. Computer processing is desirable for long questionnaires and when a large number must be tabulated.

SELECTED BIBLIOGRAPHY

Berlin, Sharon B., and Jeanne C. Marsh. *Informing Practice Decisions.* New York: Macmillan, 1993.

Hagedorn, Homer, Kenneth Beck, Stephen Neubert, and Stanley Werlin. *A Working Manual of Simple Program Evaluation Techniques for Community Mental Health Centers.* Washington, D.C.: Government Printing Office, 1976, DHEW Pub. No. (ADM) 79–404.

Rapp, Charles A., and John Poertner. *Social Administration: A Client-Centered Approach.* New York: Longman, 1993.

Royse, David. *Program Evaluation: An Introduction.* Chicago: Nelson-Hall, 1992.

15.13   Agency Evaluation

PURPOSE: To identify data that should be collected to assess the ongoing performance of a social agency.

DISCUSSION: Social agencies are expected to demonstrate that they are efficient and effective in the provision of services. Agency boards, legislative bodies, and other funding sources regularly demand that agencies review their functioning and report the results of that evaluation. Individual workers, too, are often interested in performance indicators that might stimulate organizational changes necessary to improve the quality of services provided. Thus, it is useful for social workers to be familiar with some of the indicators typically used in agency performance reviews.

Evaluation must be preceded by a clear statement of goals. Often the first task in agency evaluation is for the governing board or other policymakers to explicate the current goals and objectives for the organization. It is only with this information that appropriate performance indicators can be selected and methods of data collection identified. Chambers, Wedel, and Rodwell (1992, 119) describe this early phase as making an *evaluability assessment*—that is, determining if there is sufficient clarity to initiate a viable appraisal process.

An agency's evaluation should address the degree to which its programs respond to community need, the quality of services offered, the satisfaction of clients, efficiency in use of resources, and so on. The following are some of the areas that should be considered in specifying an agency's goals.

- *Responsiveness.* Does the agency and its programs respond to public and community needs and identified concerns?
- *Relevance.* Do sponsors, constituents, and consumers find the programs appropriate to the needs they seek to address and do they consider them supportive of community values?

- *Availability.* Are the amount and type of services provided sufficient to meet the needs of the community?
- *Accessibility.* Is the location, cost, and times services are offered appropriate for the clientele of the agency? Are there other potential constituent groups who do not receive services due to accessibility issues?
- *Quality.* Do the services meet expected standards of quality as judged by client satisfaction and expert opinion?
- *Awareness.* Is the general population, as well as other human services providers, sufficiently aware of the services offered to assure that persons who need the services know how to obtain them?
- *Productivity.* Does the program efficiently use its resources to accomplish the agency's goals?

With clarity about the questions to be answered when collecting data, it is then possible to select a set of *performance indicators* that will help to measure the agency's level of success and, when appropriate, lead to changes for improving its functioning. Selecting appropriate indicators and finding accurate data regarding them is a complex task. For example, one such study regarding public welfare agencies, the Human Services Indicator Project, identified 500 possible indicators. These were screened to 75 data sets that "represented significant organizational performance areas, were factors over which managers had some control, and included areas where the data were likely to be easily available" (Neves, Wolf, and Benton 1986, 135). The following sampling of indicators illustrates a few essential areas to include in measures of agency success.

- *Personnel-related factors.* Rate of turnover, absenteeism, staff vacancies, number of hours contributed by volunteers, frequency of in-service training, and so forth
- *The intake process.* Data on the number and sources of referrals, number of telephone contacts, number of people on the waiting list, average length of time between first contact and initiation of service, and so on
- *Service-related factors.* Number of new cases opened each month, average length of service per case, number of clients served, number and type of cases referred elsewhere, number of former clients returning for service, average cost per client, client satisfaction with services, and so on
- *Staff productivity.* Size and type of caseload per worker, number of counseling sessions provided each day, number of hours spent per case, amount of inter- and intraagency contacts per month, number of miles of work-related travel each week, and the like
- *Cost of providing services.* Average cost of staff time per case, number of clients paying a fee for service, average travel cost per case, average time spent in case recording, estimated value of volunteer hours per week, and so on

These data, once collected, must be carefully analyzed. Data collected over time will allow for the examination of trends within the agency and adjustments to improve the efficiency and effectiveness of the agency. Also, the data can be compared to data from similar agencies, making it possible to gain a relative picture of the agency's functioning.

SELECTED BIBLIOGRAPHY

Chambers, Donald E., Kenneth R. Wedel, and Mary K. Rodwell. *Evaluating Social Programs.* Boston: Allyn and Bacon, 1992.

Harrison, Michael I. *Diagnosing Organizations: Methods, Models, and Processes.* Beverly Hills: Sage, 1987.

Neves, Carole M. P., James F. Wolf, and Bill B. Benton. "The Uses of Management Indicators in Monitoring and Performance of Human Service Agencies." In *Performance and Credibility: Developing Excellence in Public and Nonprofit Organizations,* edited by Joseph S. Whorley, Mark A. Abramson, and Christopher Bellavita. Lexington, Mass.: Lexington Books, 1986.

Sorenson, James L., Roni Hammer, and Charles Windle. "The Four A's—Acceptability, Availability, Accessibility, Awareness." In *Evaluation in Practice,* edited by Gerald Lansberg, William D. Neigher, Roni J. Hammer, Charles Windle, and J. Richard Woy. Rockville, Md.: National Institute of Mental Health, 1979.

Using the Cross-Reference Guide

Location of Selected Techniques and Guidelines Related to Client System Served

The chapters in Part III of *Techniques and Guidelines* were organized around the basic skills required of a social worker, the tasks that must be performed to manage one's workload, and the activities related to the worker's own personal and professional development. In Part IV, the various techniques were placed in five chapters that reflect the phases of the planned change process (i.e., progressing from intake and engagement to evaluation and termination). Some of these techniques and guidelines are unique to a particular activity or client system being served, whereas others are appropriate for use with several client groups. To facilitate ready access to the most appropriate technique a social worker might consider when working with a specific client group at a given phase of the change process, the following cross-referencing guide has been included in this edition.

A Cross-Referencing of Selected Techniques and Guidelines to Client Systems and Special Situations

Chapter	The Individual as Client	The Family as Client	People Having Special Needs or Requiring Unique Responses
8 Basic Communication and Helping Skills	All of Chapter 8	All of Chapter 8	All of Chapter 8
9 Workload and Caseload Management	9.4 9.10 9.7 9.8 9.9	9.4 9.10 9.7 9.8 9.9	9.4
10 Personal and Professional Development	10.8 10.9 10.10 10.11	10.8 10.9 10.10 10.11	
11 Intake and Engagement	All of Chapter 11, Section A	11.1 11.5 11.2 11.6 11.3 11.4	11.2 11.9 11.6 11.10 11.7 11.11 11.8
12 Data Collection and Assessment	12.1 12.6 12.14 12.19 12.2 12.8 12.15 12.20 12.3 12.9 12.16 12.21 12.4 12.10 12.17 12.22 12.5 12.11 12.18 12.25	12.2 12.15 12.3 12.18 12.7 12.12 12.13	12.19 12.26 12.20 12.21 12.24 12.25
13 Planning and Contracting	13.1 13.5 13.2 13.6 13.3 13.7 13.4	13.1 13.7 13.3 13.4 13.5	13.7
14 Intervention and Monitoring	All of Chapter 14, Section A	14.10 14.13 14.14	14.30 14.34 14.31 14.35 14.32 14.36 14.33 14.37
15 Evaluation and Termination	15.1 15.5 15.2 15.6 15.3 15.7 15.4 15.8	15.1 15.5 15.2 15.3 15.4	

Therapeutic and Self-Help Groups	Committees and Task-Oriented Groups	Agency Administration and Operation	Organizations and Communities	Professional/ Career Enhancement
All of Chapter 8	All of Chapter 8	All of Chapter 8	All of Chapter 8	
9.4		All of Chapter 9		
10.9 10.11 10.12	10.9 10.11 10.12	10.1 10.9 10.15 10.3 10.12 10.6 10.13 10.8 10.14	10.6 10.15 10.12 10.13 10.14	All of Chapter 10
11.7 11.11 11.8 11.9 11.10	11.4	11.3 11.4	11.12 11.13 11.14 11.15	
	12.29	12.27 12.29	12.27 12.31 12.28 12.32 12.29 12.30	
13.8	13.13	13.9 13.12 13.10 13.13 13.11 13.14 13.12	13.9 13.10 13.13	
14.22 14.23 14.24	14.39 14.43 14.40 14.44 14.41 14.45 14.42 14.47	14.38 14.47 14.52 14.40 14.49 14.53 14.44 14.50 14.54 14.45 14.51	14.48 14.55 14.56	
	15.9	15.10 15.11	15.12 15.13	15.9

Using the Conversion Guide

Comparison of Fourth Edition with Third Edition

Many social work education programs have found *Techniques and Guidelines* to be a helpful text in several classes, often requiring it in an introductory practice course and referring students to it repeatedly throughout their coursework and field placements. New editions pose a problem. Although new and extensively edited material appears in each new edition, students should not be expected to purchase another edition of the same book. To facilitate students and instructors bridging between the third and fourth editions of this book, the following conversion guide has been developed. For each two-column set, the chapter or item number from this edition appears in the left column and the corresponding location of the similar content in the third edition is identified in the right column. Those marked with xxxxx are new additions or a completely new arrangement of content.

4th Edition	*3rd Edition*	*4th Edition*	*3rd Edition*
Chapter 1	Chapter 1	Chapter 9	
Chapter 2	xxxxxxxxx	Item 9.1	Item 8.1
Chapter 3	Chapter 3	9.2	8.2
		9.3	8.3
Chapter 4	Chapter 2	9.4	xxx
Chapter 5	Chapter 5	9.5	8.4
Chapter 6	Chapter 4	9.6	8.6
Chapter 7	Chapter 6	9.7	8.7
		9.8	8.8
Chapter 8		9.9	8.9
Item 8.1	Item xxx	9.10	8.10
8.2	7.1		
8.3	7.2	Chapter 10	
8.4	7.3	Item 10.1	Item 15.7
8.5	7.6	10.2	xxx
8.6	xxx	10.3	9.1
8.7	7.7	10.4	9.2
8.8	13.29	10.5	9.3

4th Edition	3rd Edition
10.6	9.5
10.7	9.6
10.8	xxx
10.9	9.7
10.10	9.8
10.11	9.9
10.12	9.10
10.13	9.11
10.14	xxxx
10.15	9.12
10.16	9.13
Chapter 11	
Item 11.1	Item 10.1
11.2	10.2
11.3	10.3
11.4	10.4
11.5	10.5
11.6	10.6
11.7	10.7
11.8	10.8
11.9	10.9
11.10	10.10
11.11	10.11
11.12	15.1
11.13	15.6
11.14	15.11
11.15	16.1
Chapter 12	
Item 12.1	Item 11.1
12.2	11.2
12.3	11.3
12.4	11.4
12.5	11.5
12.6	11.6
12.7	11.7
12.8	11.8
12.9	11.9
12.10	11.10
12.11	xxxxx
12.12	11.11
12.13	11.12
12.14	11.13
12.15	11.14

4th Edition	3rd Edition
Item 12.16	Item 11.15
12.17	11.16
12.18	11.17
12.19	11.20
12.20	11.21
12.21	11.22
12.22	xxxxx
12.23	11.23
12.24	11.24
12.24	11.25
12.26	11.26
12.27	15.15
12.28	15.12
12.29	xxxxx
12.30	16.14
12.31	16.12
12.32	16.13
Chapter 13	
Item 13.1	Item 12.1
13.2	12.2
13.3	12.3
13.4	12.4
13.5	12.5
13.6	12.6
13.7	12.7
13.8	12.8
13.9	xxxx
13.10	xxxx
13.11	15.13
13.12	xxxx
13.13	16.3
13.14	16.4
Chapter 14	
Item 14.1	Item 13.1
14.2	13.2
14.3	13.3
14.4	13.4
14.5	13.5
14.6	13.5
14.7	13.7
14.8	13.8
14.9	13.9
14.10	13.10

4th Edition	3rd Edition
Item 14.11	Item 13.11
14.12	13.12
14.13	13.13
14.14	13.14
14.15	13.15
14.16	13.16
14.17	13.17
14.18	13.18
14.19	13.19
14.20	13.21
14.21	13.22
14.22	13.23
14.23	13.24
14.24	13.25
14.25	13.26
14.26	13.33
14.27	13.27
14.28	13.28
14.29	xxxxx
14.30	13.30
14.31	13.31
14.32	13.32
14.33	13.34
14.34	13.35
14.35	xxxxx
14.36	xxxxx
14.37	13.36
14.38	15.4
14.39	15.9
14.40	16.2
14.41	16.5
14.42	16.9
14.43	16.8
14.44	16.6
14.45	16.7
14.46	16.10
14.47	13.20
14.48	16.11
14.49	15.10
14.50	15.14
14.51	15.15
14.52	xxxxx
14.53	15.16
14.54	15.20
14.55	16.18
14.56	xxxxx

4th Edition	3rd Edition
Chapter 15	
Item 15.1	Item 14.1
15.2	xxxx
15.3	14.2
15.4	14.3
15.5	14.4
15.6	14.5
15.7	14.6
15.8	14.9
15.9	14.8
15.10	15.21
15.11	15.22
15.12	14.9
15.13	15.23

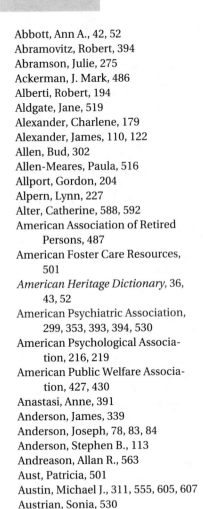

AUTHOR INDEX

SUBJECT INDEX